# The Die Cast Price Guide

## Post-War: 1946 to Present

## Douglas R. Kelly

ANTIQUE TRADER BOOKS

For Laura


To God Be The Glory


*Front cover models:* *In the foreground is Mebetoys A27 Ferrari P4. Both the front and rear hoods open on this model, and it originally came with number stickers. Behind the Ferrari is a Brooklin #6, the 1932 Packard Light 8 Coupe. This is the earlier Canadian version. Both models provided by the author.*

*Back cover model:* *Ertl's #7339 '55 Chevrolet Sidestep Pickup Truck. Like other current Ertl offerings, this model features opening doors, engine hood, and tailgate. Model provided by the author.*

Unless otherwise indicated, all photographs in this book are by the author.

ISBN:  0-930625-27-7

Library of Congress Catalog Card Number:  95-83769


Manufactured in the United States of America


Published by
**ANTIQUE TRADER BOOKS**
Dubuque, Iowa

# Contents

## PART ONE
### THE COMPLETE COLLECTOR

## PART TWO
### COMPANY HISTORIES AND LISTINGS (ALPHABETICAL BY MANUFACTURER)

# PART THREE
## ADDITIONAL RESOURCES

# Foreword

I was very flattered when Doug Kelly asked me to write the foreword for *The Die Cast Price Guide*. As a collector and manufacturer, I have seen many changes over the years. I have seen this hobby grow from the pursuit of a few "eccentric" collectors in the 1950s to the multi-million dollar industry that it is today.

I was a serious collector long before I started Brooklin Models Limited. I suppose it was a natural progression for me, influenced by the lack of "regular" American automobile models in those early years.

Since the end of World War II, hundreds of die cast manufacturers had entered the market. They were turning out Rolls-Royces, Cadillacs and Jaguars by the millions, and although some would not survive more than a couple of years, others did very well catering to that segment of the buying public. There obviously was a market for the more exotic models, but the great majority of Americans were driving Hudsons and Fords. Cars like these were seen on American roads in far greater numbers than Ferraris or Duesenbergs, and there were a lot of us collectors who wanted to buy them in miniature form.

I can remember contacting a very well-known mass producer of die cast models in the early 1960s and suggesting that they should consider producing "working man's" classics such as 1937 Chevrolets, 1949 Mercurys, etc. I was told, rather dismissively, that "this Company produced toys which were aimed at the child's market and that they would never consider anything else." Well, the times certainly have changed! I would suggest that at least 90% of all die cast production is now aimed at the collector market. I am also convinced that small specialist companies such as ourselves, along with enthusiastic collectors around the world, have had no small influence in this change of attitude.

The history of die cast toys and models is made up of legendary classics and obscure one-offs. As with any industry, manufacturers have experienced success, failure and everything in-between. This history makes for fascinating reading, particularly since it can be experienced via the toys and models that have survived the ravages of time.

These days the collector is faced with a multitude of choice in terms of manufacturer, vehicle, scale, quality and price. This huge variety can be confusing to sort out, and that is why *The Die Cast Price Guide* is an essential reference for both the experienced and the new collector.

Happy collecting.

*John Hall*
Managing Director
Brooklin Models Limited, Bath, England
March 1996

# Acknowledgments

**A** book—particularly one such as this—cannot come into being without the help and encouragement of interested "third parties." There were many third parties who contributed to *The Die Cast Price Guide,* to all of whom the author gratefully says thank you.

To my family—Laura, Paige and Caroline—for their love, support and patience during this project.

To Robert and Patricia Kelly, for a lifetime of love and encouragement.

To Manford Groves, for tirelessly tolerating marathon photo shoots during which his toy display room was well and truly trashed. Many of the photos in sections such as Corgi, Solido and Dinky came from his superb collection.

To Andrew Ralston, for the loan of photos and of archival material on many British and European manufacturers. And for his friendship.

To Harry Rinker, for approaching me with the idea for a book on die cast models and toys.

To Ferd Zegel, for allowing me to photograph some of his extensive collection of die cast toys and models. His Tekno and Vilmer collections, in particular, are among the finest in the world.

To John Bain, for his accommodation of a last-minute photo shoot during the height of the Christmas holidays. His collection of high-end die cast and white metal models has to be seen to be believed, and it provided a number of the photographs for those sections.

To Mark Storms, for the loan of many of the subjects pictured in the section on Hot Wheels.

To Jeff Bray of Diecast Miniatures, for help in locating obscure models.

To Len Mills of Lledo PLC, for his help and cooperation with a tour of the factory and for providing information on manufacturing processes.

To Gates Willard, for the loan of some early post-war Dinky Toys, and for his encouragement and friendship.

To Joyce French for instilling in me a love of the written word.

To Mike and Sue Richardson, for their pioneering work in the field of toy company research.

To John Gibson, for the loan of Tootsietoy photographs and for help with company history.

To Renny Schoonmaker, for tracking down a trio of elusive toys for photography purposes, and for steadfast friendship.

To Jerry Fralick and Ross Englehart of The Dinky Toy Club of America, for information on model identification, and for friendship and encouragement.

To Dr. Edward Force, for his ground-breaking work in the field of cataloging toy and model cars. His "Classic Miniature Vehicles" book series is indispensable for the serious miniature vehicle collector.

To Paolo Rampini, for his superb work in publishing photographs and details of model and toy cars.

To Alvin and Earl Herdklotz of Midgetoy, for their help in researching the Midgetoy story.

To Jay Olins of the Die Cast Car Collectors Club, for listings and information on Danbury Mint and Franklin Mint products.

To my editor, Allan Miller, for his patience and guiding hand on this project.

To Jaro Šebek, who skillfully designed this blend of words and pictures.

To Elizabeth Stephan, for her copyediting and proof reading expertise.

And to the lady who sold me that Matchbox Unimog (mint, no box) so many years ago at a small antiques show. See what you did?

# Introduction

There is a manufacturer of die cast cars on every street corner. Or so it might seem to the person who wants nothing more than to buy a toy that he or she had as a kid. Perhaps they want a miniature replica of that classic sitting out in the garage, but it is often simpler than that: they just like the way that little Buick or Austin looks, and can't imagine their mantlepiece without it.

Since the end of World War II, hundreds of companies have taken a shot at the die cast toy and model market. Legends like Dinky, Hubley and Solido have endured for decades, supplying the kids of the world with miniature duplicates of the cars they saw on the road everyday. Others, like Londontoy or Goodee, did their thing for a while and then sank beneath the waves. It wasn't that these shorter-lived manufacturers necessarily produced an inferior product; more often it was a combination of factors that led to their demise. A company could make a superbly detailed product, packaged in an attractive box and priced to sell at or below the cost of the competition. But if nobody out there in consumer-land knew about the product, it was doomed from the start.

It is this combination of well-known classic brands and obscure oddities that makes the die cast collecting hobby so fascinating. Although there have been no published surveys of collectors (we're not so organized a hobby as to have exit polls at toy and model shows), it is obvious even to the casual observer that die cast is an on-the-move hobby. Companies like Matchbox Collectibles and The Franklin Mint advertise their wares in national magazines like *Parade* and *TV Guide*. Major retailers such as The Sharper Image and F.A.O. Schwarz now carry Maisto BMW's and Hot Wheels Corvettes. And one trip down the die cast aisle of a Toys R Us or a Wal-Mart may leave you wondering if other kinds of toys are even *made* anymore.

Add to this the growth in recent years of collector interest in older toys and models. Shows around the country bring out old Corgis, Matchboxes and Tootsietoys by the truckload, and people are buying them. Collectors with home computers meet with other collectors in "cyberspace" and buy, sell and trade die cast toys and models every day. And each month, hobby magazines advertise all kinds of old and new die cast for sale.

Until now, there was no single source that brought all of these diverse elements of the die cast hobby together "under one roof." *The Die Cast Price Guide* is that source. In these pages, you will find a wealth of information about a hobby that attracts new collectors everyday. You can read about the history of the companies that laid the groundwork for today's manufacturers. You will find complete listings of products for all of the most popular makes, as well as for some lesser-known brands that until now occupied dimly-lit corners of the die cast world. And the "up-close" photography will enable you to enjoy what many consider to be miniature works of art.

This book is a celebration of die cast cars and trucks, old and new. Other die cast toys, such as aircraft and boats, will not be found between these covers. Those segments of the hobby are covered by other publications; for more information, see Books and Periodicals in Part Three.

*An 8-wheel Foden "Esso" Petrol Tanker, made by Morestone in the mid-1950s. This was number one of four different Foden trucks that Morestone made using a common cab. The British company's roots go back to the late 1940s; eventually they were connected with the Budgie line of die cast toys.*

*The Die Cast Price Guide* is just that, a *guide*. A "jumping-off point," if you will. The values listed here should not be thought of as set in stone, since there is not (nor could there be) an "official" value for any die cast toy. Perceptions of value differ greatly from one individual to another. A 1960s French die cast model may be the holiest of Holy Grails to one collector, while another collector wouldn't give a plug nickel for it. That said, it must be remembered that most items have an established **general** value that has developed over a period of time (sometimes decades). A price higher or lower than that general value is considered by most in the hobby to be over- or under-priced.

**The prices in *The Die Cast Price Guide* are current market values for near mint to mint condition examples, with the original packaging, where applicable.** For a model to meet this criteria, it must be in original condition—restored and/or repainted examples, no matter how professionally done, do not command anywhere near the price of an original. And, examples that are in lesser condition (whether with paint chipping, missing parts or what-have-you), will consequently be worth less than the original condition example. Some dealers and collectors use a number system to describe condition, such as "C10" for a perfect example, C8 for an excellent condition example, and so forth. The C10 designation is perhaps the only one that is indisputable, if one accepts it as describing a truly perfect specimen. Even then, there are those who will point out that a 100% perfect model never leaves the factory; there is almost always some small imperfection that can be found. Obviously, such a grading system is open to debate, given that assessing condition is more art than science.

It is an old saw, but one worth repeating: an object is worth only what a person is willing to pay for it at any given time. That price has to be agreed upon by buyer and seller, both of whom are hopefully making an informed decision. *The Die Cast Price Guide* provides the tools needed to make that happen.

For more information on this subject, please refer to Chapter Two, "Collecting Smart," beginning on page 17.

Prices in *The Die Cast Price Guide* have been arrived at using a variety of resources, including sales observed at toy and model shows; dealer and shop advertisements; countless conversations with collectors and dealers; prices paid at auctions; and from other publications on the subject. (Many of these books and magazines are listed in Part Three: Additional Resources, at the back of this book. The author recommends them highly as an excellent way to learn more about the hobby of die cast collecting.)

Inevitably, there will be those who feel that some prices in this book are too low, or that others are too high. That is the nature of this endeavor; no two people will have exactly the same experience at a show, at an auction or even by mail order. But when we come together and share information, the collector wins. Such information can be the stuff of future editions.

It is the author's hope that the information contained herein will serve not only to educate and inform, but also to entertain. These are toys, after all. Webster's defines a toy as ". . . any article to play with, especially a plaything for children . . . ."

Even the most seasoned collector will occasionally open the cabinet, take out a model car and roll it across the table when nobody is looking. You don't have to be a child to love toy cars.

# PART ONE

## The Complete Collector

# How They're Made

You know that prized die cast car sitting on your shelf? You know, the rare one with the original box that you got for next-to-nothing. The one that's going to put your kids through college. Have you ever wondered how it was made? Maybe you thought little elves did that kind of thing.

It's a bit more complicated than that. A number of industrial processes and machines are used, each of which requires the skilled hands of a trained professional. The process, though, follows a logical sequence of events, the final goal being a miniature car or truck that the buying public can't live without.

Although specific processes vary somewhat from company to company, the basic steps are the same. Lledo PLC is an excellent example. Founded in 1982 by Matchbox co-founder Jack Odell (Lledo is Odell spelled backward), this British company has become one of the leading manufacturers of lower-priced die cast models in the world. It now employs some 350 people, and is located in the town of Enfield, in North London, an area rich in die cast tradition. Lledo is the last of the mass production die cast firms that still manufactures it's products in England, companies like Corgi and Matchbox having transferred manufacturing to the Far East a number of years ago.

A peak inside the factory at Lledo serves to illustrate how a product goes from the "How about we make a fill-in-the-blank?" stage to the store shelf.

## Kicking It Around

When a subject for a die cast model is proposed, several questions must be answered up front. First and foremost is cost: can it be made cheaply enough to recover the production costs in a reasonable period of time? Tooling up to produce a die cast model is very expensive; a mistake at this early stage can result in a substantial loss to the company. "Will the public buy it?" is the next question. The item must sell in great enough quantity to not only recover costs, but make a profit as well.

And the issue of a model's "fit" with the company's product line must be addressed. This is particularly important for a company like Lledo, which has spent years building a "brand identity." This would preclude a 1967 Ford Mustang, for example, from fitting into the company's "Days Gone" series, since that line is generally made up of pre-World War II models. The "Vanguards" series of 1950s and '60s vehicles might seem a better choice, but it is made up of English and European vehicles.

A better choice would be a vehicle such as the Austin Seven "Mini" (a 1959 example having been introduced by Lledo in 1995, as part of the afore-mentioned Vanguards collection). The Mini has great world-wide appeal, and fits in well with the English theme of the Vanguards line.

Once a subject has been approved, a mock-up is made in plastic by a skilled model-maker. This allows the model to be carefully scrutinized for detail and

*Top: a resin "test" shell of Lledo's DG 73 1955 VW Transporter Van, ready for a final check before proceeding to the tooling stage. This shell is made from the resin female mold, the white pieces of which can be seen behind the shell.*
*Bottom: professional tool and die maker at Lledo using the tools of his trade.*

*Photo courtesy of Lledo.*

3

*Die casting machine in the Lledo factory. Note the castings being emptied into the container at the bottom.*

overall proportion. Changes and improvements are discussed and noted, and all of this data is then given to a draftsman, who produces drawings to exact specifications. These drawings include the details of the actual molds that will be used, as well as drawings for the wooden "pattern." The pattern is an over-sized version of the model (some three to four times the size of the final example), that allows for further examination of accuracy and detail.

From this pattern, a "female" mold is made of resin, which then serves to produce a final resin model of the vehicle. This over-sized version is the final opportunity to check that everything is correct, particularly the fit of the interior components such as windows and seats, etc.

It is an odd fact of model design (and of the human brain) that many models (whether die cast or plastic) are actually too wide compared to the real vehicle. The reason is that a model accurately scaled down to three or four inches in length will often appear too narrow. Some model and toy manufacturers, therefore, add some width to the finished product in order to make it appear correct.

*Castings are hung on racks in preparation for painting.*

## Heavy Metal

Now that the final resin model has been approved, the steel dies can be cut. These are the actual molds that will be used to produce the models, so they must be dead-on accurate. They are made by skilled tool makers, who are highly trained in such methods.

The steel dies consist of two main sections which are installed in a die casting machine. One section is bolted to the machine, the other to a moving part (sometimes called a "platen"). A metal alloy, generally made up of about 95% zinc, with the remainder made up of aluminum and copper, is heated to its melting point. The alloy is generally known as "Zamak" here in the United States, and "Mazak" in the United Kingdom. This molten metal is injected under high pressure into the space created by the two halves of the die. The mixture cools almost instantly, at which point the moving half die is moved out of the way to allow the resulting casting to be ejected into a bin.

The raw casting is then placed with others into a hexagonal section rotating drum. The drum tumbles the castings (and extra pieces such as the "gates" and "runners" used in the casting process) over and over. This tumbling action, known as "fettling," removes any unwanted "flashing" (extra metal bits) from the casting and results in a clean finish.

After fettling, the casting is placed onto a conveyor belt. This takes it through a machine that washes it in a weak acid solution, and then dries it. This serves to de-grease the surface in preparation for painting.

The casting is now put on a hanger which moves through an electrostatic painting chamber. Inside, a number of rotating discs, mounted on hydraulic cylinders, rotate up and down as the casting moves around them in a 360° arc. These discs spray the casting with enamel. From here the casting, still on the hanger, moves into a large oven which "bakes" the enamel at temperatures up to 200°F, not only drying it but hardening it as well.

Additional items such as the baseplate and radiator are cast in the same fashion, and are put through the same fettling, degreasing and painting regimen. Plastic parts, such as headlights or bumpers, are made using plastic molding machines.

*Photo courtesy of Lledo.*

*Defective castings, sprues and gates being loaded into a holding furnace, to be melted down for future use. The furnace reaches a temperature of over 800°F.*

## Logo Artwork and the Printing Process

If the model in question is to feature additional artwork (and many Lledos do, particularly the commercial vehicles), it is now placed into a pad printing machine. Pad printing is also known as "tampo" printing, and it is a process that allows an image to be printed on uneven, undulating surfaces. The pad printing machine moves the models, which are mounted on metal jigs, underneath a large rubber stamping assembly that applies the ink to the model, in much the same way that a roller works on a printing press. The artwork used in this process is created by Lledo's art department, which carefully researches and creates company logos, typefaces and other images for use on the models. Some models require four or more passes of the rubber stamp to apply the artwork, one for each color in the process. The result, if all has gone smoothly, is a die cast model with a precisely registered print job, ready for final assembly.

Plastic parts are attached to the body casting, including any interior fittings such as seats and dashboard. The baseplate is also tended to at this time, including the fitting of the axle/wheel assembly. (By the way, Lledo turns out some 150,000 individual wheels each day. They vary in size from 3/8 inch diameter to over half an inch, and come in a number of different colors and configurations, depending on the model on which they'll be used.) Despite the march of technology, much of this assembly work is still carried out by hand, there being no computer on earth that can assess quality of fit and finish as well as the human brain.

If you turn a Lledo over, you will see one or more flattened rivets in the baseplate. These project down from the inside of the body casting, and are flattened, or spread, with a special tool once the body and baseplate are put together during final assembly. This is

*Pad printing machine prints artwork on Lledo 1950 Bedford Vans. The blurred pink objects at the top are the pads moving at high speed as they contact the surface of the models.*

*Final assembly: a row of Lledo trucks receive their steering wheels, axles, wheels, tires and other assorted parts as needed. These procedures are done by hand.*

the most common (and cost-effective) method of adhering body to baseplate (the other method uses screws put into the baseplate from underneath).

The completed model is now carried along a conveyor belt past workers who insert the model into a plastic holder, assemble the cardboard box (printed with appropriate artwork) and then place the holder with model into the box. Viewed from the outside, the model is visible through a cellophane window. From there, our model is packed into shipping boxes with hundreds (or thousands) of its twin brothers, and shipped out of Enfield, North London to shops and dealers around the globe.

## Tradition versus the Cost of Doing Business

The Lledo factory complex represents the cutting edge of die cast model making. In an era when all of the other mass producers of die cast toys and models have moved production to China and Thailand, this company remains in the place where it all started. Skilled labor costs more in North London than in the Far East, but Lledo has developed a formula for making it all work. Most Lledo products are not of the same quality as models from Paul's Model Art or Brooklin, but they cost far less. And they can turn out many times the number of models that a smaller manufacturer can produce. This high volume production, combined with efficient manufacturing methods allows Jack Odell's company to do business in an increasingly competitive market.

*A finished Lledo: the Vanguards DG 73 1955 Volkswagen Transporter Van. This model is a left-hand drive export version. The VW emblem is cast into the front of the vehicle, and the printing on the side is made up of four colors (red, blue, gold and white). The pad printing machine was able to print the ink evenly across the indented door moldings.*

Walking through the production areas of the factory reminds one of a scaled-down General Motors. There are model cars and trucks in various stages of completion everywhere one looks, and the noise and the heat generated by the machinery can be intimidating.

But there is order in the hustle and bustle. Order that allows these draftsman and tool makers and artists to create miniature petrol tankers, fire engines and double-deck buses.

And there are no little elves on the payroll.

# Collecting Smart

There is a saying in the real estate game: "the three most important criteria for selling a home are location, location and location." That's a backhanded way of emphasizing the overwhelming role played by the address of the house.

In the world of die cast collecting, the three most important criteria for determining the demand for (and the price of) a toy or model are condition, condition and condition. The shape it's in is simply critical, and an otherwise rare and desirable piece will often sit for months on a dealer's table because of poor condition.

The majority of collectors want to acquire items that look the way they did when they left the factory. There is something almost surreal about a Hubley truck, for example, that is in the same condition as when it was shipped out of the Pitney Road plant in Lancaster, Pennsylvania, in late 1957. How could it have survived this long? Why didn't a child take it out back and run it around the sandbox and then leave it out in the rain when it was time to come in for supper? It still has all of its paint intact, and with the wonderful period graphics on the box it represents something of a "snapshot" of life in the United States at that time. Toy and model vehicles reflect the tastes and "texture" of a culture as few other toys do.

When you spend $50 or $500 or $5,000 on an old toy, you've probably got more on your mind than just putting it in the cabinet. Although some collectors are unconcerned with future value, most will admit that resale is a real possibility down the road. And, if the item in question increases in value with the passage of time, so much the better. A profit can be made when it comes time to say goodbye.

Unfortunately, it will be a long goodbye if the item isn't in at least very good or better condition. Near mint to mint condition sells fastest (although it's no guarantee of making a sale), and lesser-condition pieces tend to hang around for a while.

What constitutes "near mint" or "mint"? It is more art than science. There are those who contend that there is no such thing as a truly mint condition, since every piece that comes from a manufacturer can be found to have at least a tiny flaw. Strictly speaking, that may be so. But in the real world, items in superb original condition do turn up, and for all intents and purposes appear to be in perfect shape.

Near mint is self-explanatory: an item that has only the smallest of imperfections. It can be a tiny chip in the paint, or a slight scratch. But overall, the model looks very close to perfect. And it should be complete: no missing hubcaps or antennas, etc.

Generally, all of this applies to older pieces. New (or very recently made) products are naturally expected to be in at least near mint condition and complete, since the passage of time hasn't had the chance to do its dirty work. Also, many current die casts (particularly those that are considered scale models) are not "played with" the way Corgis and Tootsietoys were years ago. They are considered "collectibles" as soon as they roll off the assembly line, and collectors treat them as such.

Many of these modern products are of high quality, accurately depicting classic and contemporary vehicles. They can bring a lot of enjoyment to the buyer, as they allow

*Below Left: a slightly chipped Goodee Pickup Truck (three inch size), made by New Jersey-based Excel Products in the mid-1950s. The paint chipping would put this example into the Excellent category; not quite near mint. Note also the extra metal "flashing" along the bottom of the windshield frame.*

*Below Right: a heavily chipped model. Aside from the fact that this Dinky #254 Austin Taxi has had Corgi wheels and tires fitted, it is also missing one of its windshield pillars. These factors put it into the Poor condition category. It's a good candidate for restoration.*

him or her to study and appreciate the history of the automobile or truck. However, the collector can get burned when current products are thought of as investments. One of the reasons that older, or "obsolete," toys and models often make good investments, is due to **attrition.** Most of them simply didn't survive the ravages of time, and consequently, there are relatively few examples in existence. This alone doesn't guarantee demand, but it is a key factor.

Most current toys and models, no matter how "limited" the number made, will survive in far greater numbers than one made in 1946. Or 1956 or 1966. As a result, there will be many more to satisfy demand, and that situation likely will not change in the foreseeable future. These toys and models will be preserved as they are, and after the initial hype dies down, a collector can find himself or herself trying to sell in a saturated market. However, there are exceptions. Identifying them, though, takes hard work and (usually) some good luck.

## Chipping and "To Restore or Not to Restore?"

Chipping is the term for a condition that is fairly common with die cast models. Despite being "baked on" the surface of the model, paint often will chip off over time, unless the model is handled carefully. Sometimes it is easy to see, and one can assess the condition of the item accordingly (see photos on page 7).

But there is a type of chipping that is harder to spot. This is when the chipped area has been painted over in an attempt to spruce up the model (or sometimes to deliberately hide the flaws). It can take close examination of the model under good light to see it. The chipped area will be painted the same color as the area around it, of course, but the edges of the chipping will still be visible. It somewhat resembles wooden trim that has been painted over after a quick sanding.

There is nothing wrong with restoration of a distressed toy or model. Such work can bring a battered old classic back to life for people to enjoy. And if the work is done professionally, it can certainly increase the value of the piece (although it will still be a fraction of the value of a completely mint original). But when a restored or repaired piece is passed off as an original, someone gets ripped-off. "Buyer beware" is excellent advice to bear in mind when considering a purchase. Examining and handling as many original examples as possible will go a long way toward insuring a smart purchase.

## The Original Box and its Relation to Price

It is a fact of collecting that an item's original box (or blister pack) can significantly increase its value. Why this is so, nobody is certain. Prior to the 1980s, an original box was a nice bonus, one that could add, say, another 10% to the asking price. But in the past ten years, original packaging has been blown out of proportion, to the point where it will sometimes double or even triple the cost of a toy or model.

Considering that we're talking about cardboard with printing on it, this seems silly. But as time goes on, cardboard can and does deteriorate, and some boxes are so rare as to be essentially unobtainable. So collectors are willing to pay a premium for them.

*The Die Cast Price Guide* lists prices for toys and models in near mint to mint condition with the original packaging. Without the original packaging, the price can drop by 10%-50%.

### When It Comes Time to Sell

Collectors are often shocked when they go to sell their toys or models to a dealer: the dealer only offers them half what they're worth! Once the shock wears off, they realize why: a dealer is in business to make a profit. He or she can't do that if they buy a $100 model for $100. They generally offer from forty to sixty cents on the dollar, depending on condition, rarity, and so forth.

Add to this the fact that the dealer has overhead expenses such as rent, utility bills, inventory costs, etc., and it becomes obvious that they can't pay full retail value for your toy or model.

If you want to get the best price, you will need to sell to a collector. That can be done by taking a table at a show, or by putting your items up

*Budgie Miniature #60, the Rover 105 Squad Car, made in the mid-1960s. This blister card packaging was adopted by many manufacturers in the 1960s, including Matchbox and Hot Wheels. Budgie stapled these "bubble" assemblies to the cards, whereas some other manufacturers used glue to adhere them.*

for auction or by placing an ad in a hobby publication. Or you may already happen to know of someone who is an avid collector of what you have to sell.

## Finding the Toys and Models You Want

There are antique toy shows and model shows throughout the world that cater to the collector of older items, and they represent an excellent way to learn about the many different manufacturers. You'll find $1 junkers sharing space with rare and exotic pieces worth thousands of dollars. Negotiating over price is part of the fun at these events.

Auctions are also a good place to look for older die casts, but beware of getting involved in bidding wars, which can occur when two or more people want the same item. The result in this kind of situation is that the winning bidder pays an inflated price. If one keeps one's head, however, auctions can be a great way to acquire rare or unusual die casts. For a list of these events, see Shows and Auctions in Part Three.

For new products, retail stores are a good place to start. Wal-Mart, Toys R Us and even supermarkets carry die cast toys and models, and usually at reasonable prices.

Magazines and newsletters about toys and models are another good place to look. Most of them carry advertising, made up of both small dealers and large manufacturers. The publications vary in terms of quality, but the majority of them have something to offer. A listing is provided in Books and Periodicals in Part Three.

## The Insurance Question

Whether beginner or veteran, a collector sooner or later will wonder, "Should I insure my collection?" The short answer (and the right answer) is yes. It doesn't matter if your collection is made up of large 1/18 scale new models or small, rare old Tootsietoys. Fire doesn't care about the wonderful story behind that scarce piece on the top shelf. It will destroy your collection in the twinkling of an eye, and the same goes for flood, earthquake or your sister's kid (you know, the bull in the china shop).

Some insurance companies offer the option of a "rider" attached to your homeowner's or tenant's policy, and that may be sufficient. Or you might want to consider a "stand-alone" policy that will allow you to customize the coverage to your particular needs. The cost generally ranges from $2 to $15 (annually) per $1,000 of coverage. That's negligible when you compare it to the cost of replacing that collection that you worked for so long to create.

## Care and Feeding

Displaying a die cast collection is part of the fun of collecting. But there are some things to watch out for when choosing a home for your treasures. First and foremost is location. While it may seem a good idea to put them where everyone can enjoy them, high-traffic areas are a no-no. A shoulder accidentally brushing a shelf or cabinet can bring the whole kit and kaboodle down with a crash. Pick a quiet, out-of-the-way spot where the collection can be experienced in a relaxed manner.

Putting your die casts on an open-front bookcase may allow easy access, but it also allows easy dust. Be prepared to dust often to keep them in top condition. And be sure they are not in direct sunlight, even for short periods. The sun will fade them very quickly. Also, miniature vehicles aren't the same as other collectibles: these things **roll.** The last thing you want is for a prized acquisition to plunge to its death on a tile floor. Be sure that can't happen by putting something under potential rollers; a domino placed underneath (which can also preserve tires by lifting them slightly off the surface) does the trick for some items.

The ideal display environment is a glass cabinet enclosing the collection. While these can be expensive, they are an excellent investment, and will show your collection to best advantage.

*Original boxes can increase the value of a die cast toy or model by 10%-50% (sometimes more, depending upon rarity). On top of this pile is the box for Mercury #29 Alfa Romeo Giulia Canguro, from the mid-1960s; at left is a box for Louis Surber's current re-issue of the 1960s Quiralu Jaguar XK140; and on the right is a box for Milton #305 Chevrolet Impala State Patrol (early 1970s).*

*The box for the currently-available Best 1/43 scale #9039 Porsche 908. This type of window box has been used since the 1970s, and it consists of a plastic display box to which the model is attached, usually by a removable screw that goes into the baseplate of the model. This arrangement is preferred by most manufacturers since it protects the model while allowing the customer to examine it.*

# The Year Was 1946

*The history of the die cast toy is a rich one, starting as it did in the late 19th century in Chicago, Illinois. It was there that the Dowst Manufacturing Company began making small die cast novelties, such as flat irons, that they sold to the commercial laundry industry. Out of this modest beginning would grow the legendary "Tootsietoy" line of toy vehicles, followed in the 1930s by Frank Hornby's "Dinky" products. These two companies laid the foundation for a post-war boom in die cast toys and models.*

*Following World War II, a small company in the midwestern United States decided to enter the die cast toy market. The path that Midgetoy followed over the next four decades provides a fascinating picture of the development of the die cast toy industry.*

**Y**ou've no doubt seen these things around. They're the die cast toys with the covered wheel arches. They pop up on dealer's tables at shows across the country, and some of them are going for pretty healthy prices. When you get curious enough to pick one up for a more detailed examination, you might think you're looking at a Tootsietoy. After all, it does have a nice paint job, and the size is about right.

Guess again. It's a Midgetoy you've found, and if you were born after World War II, it'll probably bring back some memories. For thirty-five years, this midwestern firm supplied America's kids with inexpensive die cast toys. Midgetoys were sold in national stores like F.W. Woolworth, G.C. Murphy and J.C. Penney. They could also be found in variety shops in towns across America. And it all started with two brothers whose company needed something to take up the slack during the slow times.

## No More Defense Work

With the end of the war came a return to normal business for brothers Alvin and Earl Herdklotz, making dies for companies like General Motors. A & E Tool and Gage Co., the company they formed in 1943, had made precision tooling during the war, including gages that measured the shape and contours of airplane propellers. But now A & E was looking for a new market to expand into. They decided to enter the toy field with a line of die cast vehicles made in their own factory in Rockford, Illinois. Since Tootsietoys and Dinkys were well-established names in the die cast game, A & E decided to market toys that were more basic, in order to save on production costs. Without a baseplate, for instance, the toys could be cast as a single piece, and the savings could

*The first Midgetoy product: the 4-in-1 Truck Set. This toy was introduced in 1946, and its sales figures prompted the company to add to the Midgetoy line. It was made until 1949 or 1950. The three rear body shells could be placed on the rear bed to make different vehicles (the "4" in the title presumably includes the cab/chassis unit by itself). The set came in the yellow cardboard "sleeve."*

be passed on to the consumer. This lower price point would be critical to the success of Midgetoys. As Al said, "Our toys were for the kid on the other side of the tracks."

They were also durable. At the New York Toy Fair one year, they managed to convince a security guard, who weighed some 300 pounds, to stand on a Midgetoy. He did, and it didn't break. After that, the guard told anyone who would listen that they should go see the Midgetoy exhibit, since Midgetoys were tough as nails.

The first Midgetoy (pronounced Midget•oy, with three syllables) was introduced in 1946: the 4-in-1 Truck Set. Numbered 8000 in the company's literature, the set consisted of a basic cab unit, the back of which had two holes punched in it to accept one of three bodies: dump, stake or oil. In this way, a child could make up three different toys, although an early Midgetoy catalog said it was four: "The three bodies are interchangeable on the basic cab unit making four different toys. An eye-catching combination that will delight any youngster." The set came in a yellow cardboard sleeve, and it sold well enough in its first two years that the company decided to expand the line.

The next two Midgetoys were destined to become two of the most famous. In 1947, the "Buck Rogers"-type Spaceship Car was introduced. It had three wheels (two in front, one at the rear) and was shaped like a teardrop, reflecting the bulbous science fiction "style" of the day. It measured about 3 1/2 inches, and was painted a solid shade of either orange or blue. This toy was made for three or four years, then discontinued. This was standard procedure for Midgetoy through the years, as the company reacted to trends and market shifts.

The third entry into the market was the "Futuristic Auto," which may be the most recognizable of all Midgetoys. It was made starting in 1948, and it became one of the company's best-sellers. This toy, which also measured 3 1/2 inches in length, remained in production for the standard three to four years, then was discontinued. But according to Earl Herdklotz, so many people asked for it that it was brought back into production. This went on until the mid to late 1960s, which is why it can be readily found at old toy shows. It came in various colors, including red, blue and a light, milky green.

## Where the Rubber Meets the Road

Until the early 1950s, Midgetoys were made with rubber wheels, which were purchased from outside sources. These presented problems in the production process, however, due to there being variations in the thickness of the rubber. This caused the tires to "hang up" on the tighter metal surfaces of the production line, causing delays. The company eventually installed machinery that allowed them to make plastic wheels in their own factory. The plastic used was not brittle, but rather had a semi-soft feel, and the wheels were now of a uniform size.

At first, Midgetoys had open wheel arches (the 4-in-1 Truck Set being an example). In the late 1940s, though, the company chose to change that on a number of models: they enclosed the ends of the axles within the bodywork of the vehicle, so that only the lower one-third to one-half of the wheel showed. While some feel this detracts from the toy's appearance, Al and Earl Herdklotz say they went this route to protect small fingers from injury (some other manufacturers simply crimped the axle ends of their die cast vehicles, which could result in sharp edges). The closed arch "look" gave many Midgetoys a distinctive appearance. In fact, the method of crimping closed the slots to hold the axle end in the body was patented by A & E, and they enforced it vigorously.

*A "reject" casting of the truck from the 4-in-1 Truck Set. Note the break in the step under the door. There are also holes behind the cab. Traces of red paint on the casting indicate that it was painted, then stripped.*

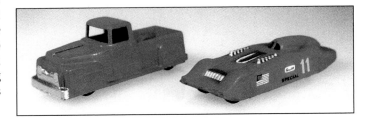

***Top:*** *the "Futuristic Auto," which made its debut in 1948. One of the most recognizable Midgetoys, it was in production until the late 1960s.*

***Bottom:*** *the 1949 Ford Pickup next to the Bonneville Racer, both part of the Junior line.*

*Where it all started: the original factory is still standing at 1202 Eddy Avenue in Rockford, Illinois. An old "A&E Tool and Gage Co." sign is still visible on the roof.*

The Buck Rogers Spaceship and the Futuristic Auto were the start of what would become the Junior series of Midgetoys, all measuring about 3½ inches in length. By the end of the 1940s, in fact, there were four separate "lines" of Midgetoy cars and trucks being offered: the Midget, Junior, King Size and Jumbo.

## The Midgets

From the late 1940s until the late 1960s, these were the smallest Midgetoys, measuring around 2½ to 2¾ inches in length. Early Midgets included a Hot Rod, a Fire Truck, an MG Sports Car, a Corvette Convertible, a four-seat Amphibious Vehicle (called the "Battle Bug") and even a Cannon. In addition, the IndyCar from the Junior series was sometimes sold with the Midgets, since it was smaller than the other Juniors. For true rarity in the Midget series, the Battle Bug Amphibian can't be beat. It rarely turns up for sale.

## The Juniors

This was the next largest size of Midgetoys, averaging 3½ inches in length. In addition to the Spaceship Car and the Futuristic Auto, this series included the Bonneville Racer (also called the "Flat Racer"), which was based on the long, high-powered land rockets that vied for the World Land Speed Record at the Bonneville Salt Flats.

Other Juniors included the IndyCar (mentioned in the Midgets section), a Cadillac Convertible, a Fire Truck, a Jeep and a Hot Rod. Also, the MG Sports Car from the Midget series was sometimes sold along with the Juniors, since it was of an "in-between" length. Pick-up Trucks would prove to be consistently good sellers in the Midgetoy line, and the first one, modeled after a 1949 Ford, was introduced into the Junior line in 1950. It was 3¼ inches in length. Two other pick-ups were added in later years: a Ford Ranchero (three inches) in 1970, and a 1971 Ford (3½ inches).

In the mid-1950s, a Greyhound Scenic Cruiser Bus was added to the Juniors. And in 1960, a Volkswagen Beetle joined the group, at 2⅞ inches in length.

In 1967, they began to package the Junior series in a new kind of blister pack. Matchbox had been putting their cars in blister packs, but with the car inside the box. Midgetoy went them one better by putting the car on top of its box in the blister pack, so the customer could see the toy. Also, Midgetoy charged just forty-nine cents to Matchbox's fifty-nine cents. The Matchbox was higher-quality (with windows, base-plate, etc.), but the Midgetoy was larger and cost less. According to Earl, this new packaging caught on: "We got an order for 18,000 dozen right off the bat, from J.C. Penney."

## The King Sizes

The King Size line included a Ford Pick-up, a Fire Truck, a Convertible, an Oil Truck, a Four Door Sedan and a Coupe. Also, there were two King Sizes that were the same cast-ing: one was a Station Wagon, with windows on the sides, and the other was an Ambulance, which did not have the windows punched out. The King Sizes averaged 4½ to 4¾ inches in length.

The King Sizes were also available in a Military version, with some of the same castings that were used for the standard King Sizes. But there were several castings done just for the Military versions, such as a Tank and a Personnel Carrier (Troop Truck). The popularity of all of the Military Midgetoys came and went over time, according to Earl Herdklotz. "We made them starting in the late 1940s, since there was quite a demand for Military toys then, and then again during the Korean War. After that, there wasn't much call for them."

*The "Midgetoy Oil Co." Truck, part of the Jumbo line. At an average length of six inches, the Jumbos were among the largest Midgetoys made (along with the Tractor Trailers).*

## The Jumbos

This was the largest of the four lines, each unit measuring around six inches in length. Included were an Oil Truck, a Convertible, a Bus, a Fire Truck, a Tank and a Pick-up Truck. At one time, the Pick-Up Truck was made with a red, yellow and black cardboard insert in the bed. It read, "TOWING SERVICE," and had artwork of a toolbox, spare tire and jack, along with the "Midgie" elf logo. Some Jumbos were also done in the military olive drab color.

## The Heavy Iron

In addition to the four main lines, Midgetoy also put out several larger vehicles. These included an Oil Tanker, a Moving Truck, a Fire Truck and a Car Transporter. All were articulated, and the Car Transporter came packaged with two Midgets.

Midgetoy also put out a line of die cast trains starting in the late 1940s. These included a Streamlined Diesel called the Santa Fe Super Chief, and an old western-style locomotive. Die cast toy airplanes were also part of the product line; a B-57 Bomber and a Navy Cutlass figured prominently in this group.

## Competitive Market

By the early 1950s, Midgetoy was firmly established behind Tootsietoy as the number two-selling American die cast toy. The 1950s and 1960s would be prosperous times for American die cast manufacturers, with new items being introduced as market conditions and public taste dictated.

But there were tough times coming. By the late 1960s, the Vietnam War had forced the price of zinc alloys through the roof. Add to this the increasing competition from plastic toy manufacturers, and just putting out their established product line finally became impossible for Midgetoy. So they ceased production of most of their established toys, and introduced the "Mini" line. These were simpler, smaller (about two inches long on average) die cast toys that used less metal and could therefore be sold at a lower price. These smallest Midgetoys included a Jaguar, a Jeep, a Chevrolet Corvette and a Dodge Charger.

Some of the other, smaller Midgetoys continued in production, but the 1970s saw the company concentrate on the Mini line and on the marketing of sets. These new sets came packaged on a blister card and were named, for example, "Go Camping." This set contained a Charger, Camper, Sailboat (plastic), gas pumps and a Jeep. Other sets were marketed, and can sometimes be found today in the original blister pack.

## Calling it Quits

In 1981, the brothers retired and sold the company to a group of investors who lost no time running the company into the ground. In the space of two years, this group took a going concern that employed some 100 people and turned it into five people working part-time. No new products were introduced, and when one of the principals suffered a fatal heart attack in 1983, the Herdklotz brothers bought back the business.

What they got, however, was a facility with machinery that had been allowed to fall into disrepair. Rather than re-starting production, they decided to sell off the remaining inventory.

Few toys represent the tastes and "texture" of a culture the way toy cars do. Midgetoys show us a little of what life was like for kids growing up in the United States in the 1940s, '50s and '60s.

*Page from a late 1940s Midgetoy catalog, depicting the Midget, Junior and King Size lines in their counter display boxes. These boxes rarely turn up for sale today, and when they do, they generally have a high price tag.*

# Market Report

Looked at as a whole, the die cast collecting hobby is experiencing growth and consolidation at the same time. How is this possible? The reason lies in the division between collectors of older pieces and collectors of new products.

Before the "boom" in new die cast that we've been witnessing over the last five years, most collectors were involved with searching out examples of older toys and models. Before the recession hit in the late 1980s, both shows and auctions were doing a pretty healthy business when it came to obsolete die cast. But as the downturn in the economy began, many collectors decided to sell. This, along with a continual influx of items onto the market (from attics, basements and estate sales) created a large supply of older pieces.

In terms of common pieces, this flooding of the market continues today. This is a wonderful market for the collector who wants these items, of course, but it also provides a stark contrast to the availability of the rarer pieces.

Most collectors, sooner or later, arrive at a point where only the truly rare and unusual interest them. Since, by definition, the rare items are in short supply, they tend to sell quickly and at high prices. Major auction houses like Christie's, Lloyd Ralston and Vectis (in England) hold regular die cast events, and as at shows, the common stuff goes begging. But original condition unusual items sell quite well, and often at twice to three times the price listed here in *The Die Cast Price Guide*. "Auction fever" has something to do with this, but so does the difficulty of finding these high-demand pieces in excellent or better original condition.

This consolidating of the market will continue, since the supply of the high-demand items can, at best, only remain the same.

## Older Die Cast

**Dinky:** Still the leader in this size (roughly 1/43), although Corgi is a close second. Near mint or better examples with original box will almost always find a buyer, but they have to be pre-1970. The market for 1970s Dinkys is significantly smaller than for 1940s, '50s and '60s examples. The exceptions are TV or character-related models, like the Thunderbirds and Star Trek items.

Over the years, Christie's South Kensington, the London-based auction house, has emerged as one of the leaders in offering high-end Dinkys. At a "Dinky Only" auction in June 1995, they achieved some shockingly high prices for several 39 series cars, including $1,980 for a tan and brown 39c Lincoln Zephyr. That was topped by the incredible $2,160 paid for a 39e Chrysler Royal in red and yellow. The 39 series American cars always attract heated bidding, but these must be records.

At the same auction, a #121 "Goodwood" Sports Cars Gift Set (with original box) went for $1,710, and a #514 Guy "Weetabix" Van brought $865.

At their September 1995 auction, Christie's offered a group of original Meccano factory drawings of Dinky Toys, covering the period from the late 1940s until the early 1960s. A drawing for the #260 Royal Mail Van, dated 1/26/54, sold for $163, and a drawing for the #919 Guy "Golden Shred" Van, dated 12/28/56, brought a whopping $1,458.

As rare and desirable as these were, though, they took a back seat to lot #235. It was an original wooden mock-up model of an unissued (i.e., never produced) Albion "Milk Marketing Board" Tanker Truck, with original factory drawings and a later (circa 1980) non-factory replica model, and it brought the high price of the sale: $4,010.

Outrageous prices? Perhaps. But for the Dinky collector, this was an opportunity to own a unique piece of toy history. These kinds of items will always have a market, and the author believes the drawings that sold for $150-$300 were **bargains**.

Expect the demand for high-quality Dinkys to continue. But beware of reproductions and fakes, because they're out there. There are several legitimate manufacturers of Dinky repros, and those are easily distinguished from the genuine article. But restored originals and out-and-out phonies have surfaced in recent years, so know what you're buying before you take out the checkbook.

By the way, the enduring popularity of Dinkys has resulted in the forming of the Dinky Toy Club of America, based in Maryland. This organization puts on a Dinky Show in the Fall; for more information, see Books, Periodicals and Clubs in Part Three.

## Corgi: Second only to Dinky, Corgis continue to represent a very popular category in the older market. Like Dinky, the most popular are the 1950s and '60s models, although the 1970s and '80s Corgis do have a following. One reason is that Corgi still produces die cast toys (models?), which have helped bring buyers of the new products into the secondary market. The re-release of the Chipperfield's Circus models in 1995 was eagerly received by American collectors, particularly those who can't afford to buy the originals put out years ago. And currently-made movie-related Corgis continue to sell well, including the James Bond cars and the Chitty Chitty Bang Bang replica model that the company started putting out several years ago.

Vintage Corgis in general are healthy, and should continue to be so.

## Tootsietoy: Unquestionably the most popular American brand among collectors of older pieces. The smaller (three and four inch) Tootsies, for the most part, can be found at most any toy show in decent quantity. The larger items (such as the tractor trailers and the six inch cars) are tougher to find, particularly in near mint condition with original packaging.

As with Dinky, the smart collector will examine and handle as many original Tootsietoys as possible. There are companies making replacement parts for post-war Tootsietoys, and some of the new parts are dead ringers for the originals. From a cosmetic standpoint, of course, this is good, but beware of a super-low price on a Tootsietoy that looks perfect.

## Matchbox: The 1-75 line is still very strong here in the United States, as evidenced by the number of Matchbox collectors clubs, books and newsletters devoted to the subject. Vintage 1-75 Matchboxes are easy to find at shows and even at general flea markets and antique shops. Most 1-75 collectors look for examples that have the original box. A high percentage of boxes have survived, thanks to the marketing of Lesney through the years, which encouraged kids to display their Matchbox "models" with the boxes.

An old 1-75 without its box will usually be very reasonably priced, and it is certainly collectible and enjoyable. But if resale is a concern, the collector would be well-advised to stick with boxed examples. Unboxed Matchboxes are hard to sell, unless the item is a rarity.

## Hot Wheels: Perhaps the fastest-growing segment of the vintage die cast market. These things continue to attract new collectors as the baby boomers who had them as kids now can afford to "recapture their youth" by buying early examples. Although the earliest (1968-early '70s) Hot Wheels are always in great demand, even the later 1970s and some of the 1980s cars draw a lot of interest at shows and auctions. This goes for "loose" examples (a car without its original packaging) and mint in the blister pack examples alike.

Hot Wheels have been getting a great deal of coverage in the mainstream media, as well as hobby publications. And the publication of another book, *The Complete Book of Hot Wheels*, by Bob Parker, has focused further attention on the Mattel cars. The growth of Hot Wheels collecting can be traced in part to an auction at Christie's in late 1994. This was the first time that a major auction house featured Hot Wheels, and the sale received a lot of attention. A few items did very well, including a 1970-vintage "three-pack" blister card consisting of an Oldsmobile 442, a Custom Fleetside and a '32 Vicky, which sold for $920. The one that got all the press, though, was the "Beach Bomb" with surfboards in the rear. Including the 15% buyer's premium, this rare VW Van shattered the estimate of $1,500-$2,000, reaching $4,025.

> *The Matchbox "Models of Yesteryear" series has been produced since 1956, and is a mixed bag in terms of value. Yesteryears have always had a large following in the United Kingdom and Europe, but less so in the United States. Most American Matchbox enthusiasts concentrate on the 1-75 line. Also, with Tyco's acquisition of Matchbox in 1992, Yesteryears are now sold almost exclusively through direct mail by Matchbox Collectibles. This has met with some resistance from collectors, many of whom want to be able to buy the models in a retail setting.*
>
> *Some of the Yesteryear models are very accurate and well made. From an investment point of view, the best bet are the early examples (those made up until about the late 1960s).*

Lost in the attention given the Beach Bomb, however, was that many of the Hot Wheels lots did not reach their minimum estimates. (Only two of the twenty-eight lots were unsold, though.) This overall weak auction performance only served to heat up collector demand for older Hot Wheels. The things still disappear from dealer's tables very quickly.

**Miscellaneous American:** After Tootsietoy and Hot Wheels, names like Hubley, Ralstoy, Midgetoy and Johnny Lightning are the most popular American makes among collectors. The resurgence in interest in old Johnny Lightning cars is a direct result of the activities of Playing Mantis (see the new die cast section) and of intense interest in the similar Hot Wheels cars.

*Although they were not made in this country, Cragstan or "Sabra" die cast models have been surfacing at shows over the last couple of years, and they represent a "sleeper" in terms of potential. They were made in the late 1960s-early '70s, and were accurate 1/43 scale models of contemporary American cars. They were made in Israel (a country not known for its toy industry) by Gamda Koor, and imported by Cragstan into the United States under the "Detroit Seniors" name. (They were also marketed in Israel and elsewhere under the Sabra name). With models like a Ford Mustang, a Buick Riviera and a Chevrolet Chevelle Station Wagon (the model most commonly found), they appeal to American collectors. Generally priced anywhere from $15-$30, they are under-priced compared to Dinkys and Corgis of the same vintage. (An original box would bring a little more.)*

Hubley has always been a very popular brand, and like Tootsietoy, the most in-demand are the larger pieces like the seven-inch to thirteen-inch cars and the seven-inch to nineteen-inch trucks. Hubleys are popular subjects for restoration and repair, so keep a sharp eye out for examples that look "too perfect." Also, original Hubley boxes command a premium, so original examples with good boxes often sell for well over the guide price.

**European Manufacturers:** Mercurys, Teknos, Solidos, Märklins, Polistils and C.I.J.s all have their own following among American collectors, but to a much lesser extent than Dinky or Tootsietoy. Overall, prices for these European classics are lower than in Europe and the United Kingdom, but availability here is also lower.

These companies gave Corgi and Dinky a run for their money in the past (some are still going strong) by putting out accurate, high-quality die cast models and toys. Many of them are very collectible, and with increased exposure through publications like *The Die Cast Price Guide*, more American collectors may find themselves looking for these pieces at shows and auctions.

**Japanese Manufacturers:** This is a growing category in older die cast. Tomica has been getting a lot of attention recently for their small (mostly 1/50 to 1/80 scale) die cast toys made in the 1970s and '80s. (They also made a larger line called "Dandy.") But Diapet models, made in the 1960s and '70s by Yonezawa (apparently the same company that put out large tinplate toy cars for many years) are also becoming collectible. They were mostly 1/43 scale (which is gaining popularity among American collectors) and many of them can be found for $20-$30 with the original box.

Two Japanese makes that rarely turn up in this country are Cherryca Phenix and Asahi, both produced in the 1960s. Most of the models in these series were of Japanese cars, and the lines were not exported to the United States in any numbers. The models from both companies were well made and accurate.

## New Die Cast

A walk down the die cast aisle of any major retail store will provide evidence of the explosion in the new die cast market. Long-time competitors like Bburago, Hot Wheels and Matchbox have been joined in the last couple of years by upstarts like Maisto and Racing Champions. These new companies are competing in all of the traditional markets: 1/64 to 1/72 scale low-end toys ($2-$5 range), 1/24 scale mid-range models ($8-$12) and 1/18 scale models ($15-$28). These three sizes represent the vast majority of sales through retail chains, and it's not just kids who are buying.

People who grew up in the 1950s, '60s and '70s are now financially able to "revisit their childhood." Buying a 1/18 scale Pontiac GTO is a whole lot easier on the wallet than the 1/1 version, and it's a lot easier to display, too.

While all of this is happening down at the mall, there is a subtle shift taking place with smaller retailers. Hobby and specialty shops are not carrying die cast models in the same numbers as a few years ago. One reason, of course, is that huge discount chain store that just opened across the street. Why should people be expected to pay $35 for a 1/18 model when they can get it for half of that at the mega store? As a result, the hobby and specialty shops tend to carry the less widely-available lines, and in a different scale: 1/43. This scale was popularized in Europe starting in the 1950s, and has been growing in popularity here in the United States. There are 1/43s being made in Germany and China that are every bit as well-detailed as the larger 1/18 models, and usually for about the same price.

In terms of investment potential, new products (including those made from about 1985 onward) are risky at best. It's simply supply and demand; a company that has invested $50,000-$100,000 in tooling and production for a new model is going to pump out as many units as it believes it can sell. And although a large number of those units may wind up trashed by energetic kids, many of them will survive intact. (In some cases, it's a safe bet that up to 80%-90% of the production of a model will wind up being stashed away.) This means that demand for the item will never catch up to supply (at least not in the foreseeable future).

Should there turn out to be great demand for the item, though, what is to stop the manufacturer from cranking up the equipment to turn out more? This can result in the market being flooded, and that's when the collector (or speculator) who bought three cases of the things gets burned.

There are occasional exceptions, but they are few and far between. The old saying applies here: collect what you like and leave the calculator in the drawer. If you're concerned with future value, stick to older (1970s and earlier) toys and models.

**Hot Wheels**: Always at or near the front of the die cast toy market since their introduction in 1968, Mattel's little $1 racers experienced a boom period in 1994 and 1995 that shows no signs of letting up. It is not unusual to see three or four adults (usually men, but not always) sorting through the Hot Wheels racks at major chain stores, looking for that latest hot item that they can't live without.

**Johnny Lightning:** If you were a kid in the 1960s or '70s, you probably had a few Johnny Lightnings to race along with your Hot Wheels. The JL name was resurrected in 1994 by Playing Mantis, a Michigan-based company, and they have made reproductions of eighteen of the original JL cars. These are not made with the original molds, but are instead re-creations of the originals.

They also released a Muscle Car series in 1995 that has been well-received by collectors. At around $2 apiece, JL's are slightly more expensive than Hot Wheels, but they have a real following now, complete with a collector's club and newsletter put out by Playing Mantis (see Additional Resources in Part Three).

**Racing Toys and Models:** One of the most competitive categories, and for good reason. The growing popularity of auto racing (especially NASCAR and IndyCar) is driving (no pun intended) this market. Racing Champions, Inc., the Illinois-based company, has been putting out their NASCAR and IndyCar toys (models?) in a variety of scales for several years, and in 1995 added their 1/64 NASCAR SuperTruck series. Going head to head with Hot Wheels and Johnny Lightning, these are priced in the $2-$4 range, and are bought by both kids and adults. A new company got into the act in 1995, Action Performance Companies, Inc., who released their own 1/64 SuperTruck series. These are of a little higher quality than the competition, and are priced at $5-$7, depending on where you find them. Action has already built a sizeable following for these products.

Long-time die cast players Ertl and Revell offer NASCAR die cast models as well, and even European companies like Quartzo are getting into the act. European companies, such as Onyx and Paul's Model Art, put out Formula One, IndyCar and Endurance Racing Cars in varying scales.

Add to all this the fact that racing die casts are sold at the actual race events, and racing collectors have a very broad choice.

*The biggest advantage of collecting new products (as opposed to the old stuff) is price. And many manufacturers have really upped their game in recent years, to the point where a new product had better have a minimum level of detail and faithfulness to the real car (or truck). Without this authenticity, the product will wind up in the half-off bin faster than day-old bread.*

**1/18 Scale:** A lot of companies have entered this market in the past couple of years, and it shows. In large retail stores, 1/18 scale models that started at $20-$25 can often be found for $10-$13. Much of the customer base for 1/18 scale models is made up of casual collectors and the non-collector who buys one on impulse. Bburago's Dodge Viper is a good example, having sold in huge numbers in all kinds of retail stores since its release in 1993.

Many 1/18s are extremely well-made and well-detailed, so you get a lot of bang for the buck. Whether any of them will ever increase in value is anyone's guess.

**1/43 Scale:** Another market that has seen rapid growth recently, with companies from all over the world entering the fray. Paul's Model Art, the German company, stood the 1/43 market on its ear a few years ago with its superbly well-made models that sell for around $25. Other manufacturers scrambled to catch up, and collectors benefit from this competition. Schabak and Siku in Germany, Vitesse and Onyx in Portugal, Brumm, Best and Bang in Italy, Corgi and Lledo in England...they all have their followings. The company that makes accurately detailed 1/43s for $25-$40 is the one that will survive. They will also be the one whose products may someday increase in value on the secondary market.

**White Metal:** These are handmade metal models that are technically cast in a die, although some people refer to them as molds. The leader in this field is the United Kingdom-based Brooklin Models, who have been producing 1/43 examples since the 1970s. Some of them have appreciated in value quite well, and Brooklins have a following in the United States. At around $65 retail, they represent good value, considering the high level of detail and the time involved in making them by hand.

Other white metal manufacturers like Durham Classics and Western Models also have a following here, although not as large as that of Brooklin.

## The Three R's: Re-Issues, Reproductions and Restoration

If you want instant fireworks, get a couple of toy or model collectors together and ask them about repros. Stand back, or you'll get singed by the passionately-expressed opinions that will start flying around.

Reproductions of old toys and models are here to stay, and some of them are great collectibles in their own right. But they do have an effect on the original, which usually is to drive the value of the original down. This tends to drive owners of originals nuts. After the repro has been out for awhile, though, the value of the original sometimes returns to normal. It depends upon collector interest in the original. (A reproduction, by the way, is an item that is essentially a re-creation of the original, using new tooling; a re-issue is an item made using the actual original tooling.)

Since this is a relatively recent development on the die cast scene, it is too early to tell whether any of these will increase in value. If the price is right, though, a repro can be a cost-effective way to enjoy old die casts.

Restoration is another hotly-debated topic among collectors. Certainly, a restoration or repair can never return a toy or model to its original state. It may look that way if the work is done professionally, but the fact is that the item in question has been altered.

The die cast market is seeing more and more of this work done to older pieces. (It's done with new products, as well, but the question of value is far less critical there.) Well-done work, of course, can bring a toy or model "back to life," for another generation to enjoy. And as long as the piece is not represented as being original, that's fine. The individual or individuals doing the work (and/or selling the piece) has a moral obligation to make the work known to any potential buyer, who then must make the purchasing decision.

# PART TWO
# Company Histories and Listings (Alphabetical)

## Using the Guide:

Please bear the following in mind when consulting this guide:

1- Prices listed are for **original, unrestored, near mint to mint condition original examples,** with **original packaging and all accessories** where appropriate. A toy or model that has been repaired or restored in any way is worth less than the values listed here, sometimes considerably so. For more information on this subject, see the "Collecting Smart" section in Part One.

2- CRP is an abbreviation for "Current Retail Price," and is used to indicate the value of a model or toy that is widely availabe in a retail or mail order setting.

3- The values in *The Die Cast Price Guide* are not set in stone. They reflect the prices that these items sell for at toy shows and auctions, in toy and hobby shops and through collector and dealer advertisements. Ultimately, the price to be paid for any item is up to the buyer and the seller.

4- New and previously unknown items still turn up on dealer's tables and auction blocks. Every effort has been made to provide as accurate and up-to-date a listing as possible for each manufacturer. Bear in mind, however, that a model or toy may have been produced even if it is not listed in *The Die Cast Price Guide.*

# Ahi

Ahi was a Japanese manufacturer of small die cast cars and trucks in the late 1950s and early 1960s.

Because of the relatively high percentage of American cars that were part of the range, it is logical to assume that they were exported to this country. With the cars being 1/80 to 1/90 scale, they were undoubtedly intended to compete with Matchbox products.

Along with the British sports cars and American sedans, Ahi included some unusual subjects, such as a Volvo Amazon and an Opel Kapitan. There was also a series of Military trucks that featured "loads" such as missiles or lumber. Compared to the competition at the time, the castings were crude, and the axles were very basic. They extended through the wheels too far, with the ends crimped to hold them in place. But Ahi's had a certain charm, and they are not easy to find today.

## Ahi toys were 1/90 scale, except where indicated

| Name | Price |
| --- | --- |
| Cadillac | $15 |
| Chrysler | 15 |
| Dodge | 15 |
| Imperial | 15 |
| Plymouth | 15 |
| Pontiac | 15 |
| Rambler | 15 |
| Buick | 15 |
| Chevrolet Impala | 15 |
| De Soto Diplomat | 15 |
| Ford | 15 |
| Oldsmobile | 15 |
| Volkswagen 1200 | 20 |
| Opel Kapitan | 15 |
| Porsche 356A | 25 |
| Alfa Romeo Giulietta Sprint | 15 |
| Ferrari 375 Coupe | 25 |
| Volvo Amazon 122 S | 15 |
| Austin A105 | 15 |
| Daimler | 15 |
| Jaguar XK150 Roadster | 15 |
| MGA 1600 | 15 |
| Citroën DS 19 | 15 |

| Name | Price |
| --- | --- |
| Mercedes-Benz 300SL Roadster | $15 |
| Rolls-Royce Silver Wraith | 20 |
| Jaguar Mk IX | 15 |
| Austin Healey | 15 |
| Renault Floride | 15 |
| MG TF Roadster | 15 |
| Midget Racer | 15 |
| Maserati Racer | 15 |
| Ferrari 500 Formula 2 | 25 |
| Mercedes-Benz W 25 Racer (1930s style) | 15 |
| Mercedes-Benz W 196 Racer | 15 |
| Mercedes-Benz RW 196 Racer | 15 |
| International Harvester | 15 |
| Fiat 1800 | 15 |
| Simca Aronde P 60 | 15 |
| Mercedes-Benz 220SE | 15 |
| Volvo PV 544 | 15 |

### "Antique" automobiles II (1/80 scale):

| Name | Price |
| --- | --- |
| 1902 Ali Coold Frankline | 10 |
| 1903 Cadillac | 10 |
| 1903 Rambler | 10 |
| 1904 Darracq | 10 |

| Name | Price |
| --- | --- |
| 1904 Oldsmobile | $10 |
| 1904 Oldsmobile Truck | 10 |
| 1907 Vauxhall | 10 |
| 1909 Stanley Steamer | 10 |
| 1911 Buick | 10 |
| 1914 Stutz Bearcat | 10 |
| 1915 Ford Model T | 10 |

### Military trucks (all based on a 1/120 scale Dodge flat-bed, painted olive green):

| Name | Price |
| --- | --- |
| Dodge Radar Truck | 10 |
| Dodge Searchlight Truck | 10 |
| Dodge Tank Carrier | 10 |
| Dodge Crane Truck | 10 |
| Dodge Covered Truck | 10 |
| Dodge Ambulance Truck | 10 |
| Dodge Cement Mixer Truck | 10 |
| Dodge Lumber Truck | 10 |
| Dodge Barrel Truck | 10 |
| Dodge Missile Carrier | 10 |
| Dodge Rocket Launcher Truck | 10 |
| Dodge Truck with machine gun | 10 |

# Arbur Products

A small English manufacturer of die cast toys, Arbur did business in the late 1940s to early 1950s and was known for making models based on the products of other manufacturers, such as the Dinky Fire Trucks and the Dinky #23p Gardner MG Record Car. The models listed here are 1/50 scale unless otherwise indicated.

| Name | Price |
| --- | --- |
| MG Record Car (1/43 scale) | $40 |
| Sunbeam Coupe (1/43 scale) | 50 |

| Name | Price |
| --- | --- |
| Fire Truck | $50 |
| Scammell Tractor Trailer | 35 |

| Name | Price |
| --- | --- |
| Tractor Trailer Truck (came as flat or open) | $35 |
| Tractor Trailer Van | 35 |

# Asahi

The Asahi Toy Co. (A.T.C. as it is also known) began making toy cars in tinplate during the late 1940s or early 1950s. These high quality toys have earned the company a loyal following among collectors of 1950s tin toys.

Around 1960, Asahi expanded into the die cast market with its "Model Pet" line, based on full-size Japanese cars like the Hino Contessa and Datsun Bluebird. (The only non-Japanese subjects were the Hillman Minx and the Austin A50.) With windows and suspension (some also had opening doors and hoods), the Asahis were high quality, comparing favorably with the Corgis and Dinkys of the era.

Asahi may have exported its models to the United Kingdom. But add their right-hand drive arrangement to the fact that they rarely surface in this country, and it becomes likely that they were not imported into the United States.

Production ended sometime in the early 1970s, after a number of motorcycle models had

been added to the series. In recent years, a Rolls-Royce die cast model has surfaced that is made by a company named Asahi. Whether this is the same company is unclear; a logo different from Asahi's original appears on the model and its window box. Date of production is unknown, although it appears to have been made during the 1980s. Whether there were other models made is also unknown. Orange is the most common color seen, with gray reported, as well.

*Asahi number 27
Toyota Corona, with original box. This
model had suspension and windows,
as well as an opening hood.*

## Asahi models were 1/43 scale, except where indicated

| # | Name | Price | # | Name | Price | # | Name | Price |
|---|------|-------|---|------|-------|---|------|-------|
| 1 | Toyota Crown | $120 | 20A | Toyota Crown (gold plated) | $120 | 41 | Toyota Crown Police Car (black and white) | $55 |
| 1A | Toyota Crown (gold plated) | 160 | 20B | Toyota Crown Police Car (black and white) | 150 | 43 | Honda RC 162 Motorcycle (1/35) | 30 |
| 2 | Toyota Masterline Station Wagon | 120 | 21 | Toyota Masterline Station Wagon | 100 | 44 | Suzuki 750 GT Motorcycle (1/35) | 30 |
| 2A | Toyota Masterline Ambulance (white) | 220 | 21A | Toyota Masterline Ambulance (white) | 150 | 45 | Nissan Skyline 2000 GT Coupe | 50 |
| 3 | Subaru 360 (1/40) | 130 | 22 | Prince Gloria | 100 | 46 | Yamaha 650 XS Motorcycle (1/35) | 30 |
| 4 | Toyota Land Cruiser (green) | 150 | 22A | Prince Gloria Taxi | 140 | 47 | Datsun Sunny Coupe 1400 | 50 |
| 5 | Datsun Bluebird | 130 | 23 | Toyota Land Cruiser with hood (green) | 150 | 48 | Honda 750 Motorcycle (1/35) | 30 |
| 6 | Prince Skyline | 130 | | | | 50 | Honda 750 Police Motorcycle (1/50) | 30 |
| 6A | Prince Skyline (gold plated) | 180 | 24 | Mitsubishi Colt 1000 | 80 | 51 | Toyota Corona Mk.II 2000 G SS | 50 |
| 7 | Toyota Corona | 100 | 25 | Datsun Bluebird | 80 | 52 | Datsun Bluebird UHT | 50 |
| 8 | Austin A50 Cambridge | 160 | 26 | Hino Contessa 1300 | 80 | 54 | Nissan Cedric 2600 GX | 50 |
| 9 | Hillman Minx | 150 | 27 | Toyota Corona | 100 | 55 | Toyota Crown Taxi (yellow) | 55 |
| 10 | Nissan Cedric | 120 | 29 | Hino Contessa 1300 Coupe | 70 | 56 | Toyota Crown Firecar (red) | 55 |
| 10A | Nissan Cedric Taxi | 160 | 30 | Mazda Familia | 70 | 57 | Toyota Crown Ambulance (white) | 55 |
| 11 | Toyota Corona Station Wagon | 100 | 31 | Toyota Sports 800 | 80 | 58 | Mitsubishi Galant GTO Rally | 50 |
| 12 | Toyota Crown | 120 | 32 | Nissan Silvia Coupe | 70 | 59 | Nissan Skyline 2000 GT Rally | 50 |
| 12A | Toyota Crown Police Car | 180 | 33 | Nissan Cedric | 70 | 60 | Yamaha Police Motorcycle with Sidecar (1/35) | 30 |
| 13 | Mazda R 360 Coupe | 120 | 34 | Honda S 800 Roadster | 90 | 61 | Yamaha Police Motorcycle (1/35) | 30 |
| 14 | Toyota Publica | 100 | 35 | Honda S 800 Coupe | 90 | 62 | Yamaha Motorcycle with Sidecar (1/35) | 30 |
| 15 | Prince Skyline Sports Convertible | 130 | 36 | Toyota 2000 GT Coupe | 80 | | | |
| 16 | Prince Skyline Sports Coupe | 130 | 37 | Honda N 360 | 80 | 101 | Toyota Toyoace Truck (1/48) | 140 |
| 17 | Datsun Bluebird | 100 | 38 | Toyota Crown Super | 50 | 102 | Toyota Toyoace Covered Truck (1/48) | 140 |
| 18 | Isuzu Bellett | 120 | 39 | Toyota Crown Coupe | 50 | 103 | Honda Motorcycle (1/40) | 70 |
| 19 | Toyota Coupe Sports | 100 | 40 | Mitsubishi Galant GTO | 50 | | | |
| 20 | Toyota Crown | 100 | | | | | | |

# Bang

When the Italian company known as Box went through a reorganization in 1991, it was split into at least two different companies. These were Bang and Best, now considered to be two separate lines of die cast models.

Bang concentrates on 1/43 scale vintage race car models, with Ferrari being the dominant marque. The company puts out multiple liveries for each casting, and releases new models each year. They are manufactured in Italy, and are generally of very good quality. The baseplates are plastic.

The following listing is for the current Bang product line; "CRP" denotes Current Retail Price, which is generally in the range of $20-$25.

*Bang #8004, Ferrari 348 GTB. This is a well-detailed model, as evidenced by the side mirrors and sharp body casting.*

## Bang models are 1/43 scale

| # | Name | Price | # | Name | Price | # | Name | Price |
|---|------|-------|---|------|-------|---|------|-------|
| 401 | Ferrari 250 GTO (red) | CRP | 1015 | Ferrari 250 GTO (red) | CRP | 7084 | Ferrari 250 GT SWB (red) | CRP |
| 402 | Ferrari 250 GTO (white) | CRP | 1016 | Ferrari 250 GT SWB (red) | CRP | 7085 | Ferrari 250 GT SWB (white) | CRP |
| 405 | Ferrari 250 GT (red) | CRP | 1017 | Ferrari 250 GT (red) | CRP | 7086 | Ferrari 250 GT SWB (silver) | CRP |
| 406 | Ferrari 250 GT (gray) | CRP | 1018 | Mercedes-Benz 300 SL (cream) | CRP | 7087 | Mercedes-Benz 300 SL (cream) | CRP |
| 407 | Ferrari 250 GT (red) | CRP | 1019 | Ferrari 330 P4 (red) | CRP | 7088 | Mercedes-Benz 300 SL (red) | CRP |
| 409 | Ferrari 250 GTO (red) | CRP | 1020 | Cobra | CRP | 7089 | Mercedes-Benz 300 SL (silver) | CRP |
| 410 | Cobra (red) | CRP | 7071 | Ford GT 40 (gold) | CRP | 7090 | Mercedes-Benz 300 SL (black) | CRP |
| 411 | Cobra (black) | CRP | 7072 | Ford GT 40 (blue) | CRP | 7091 | Ford Mark II (blue) | CRP |
| 412 | Cobra (white) | CRP | 7073 | Ford GT 40 (blue) | CRP | 7092 | Ford Mark II (gold) | CRP |
| 414 | Cobra (black) | CRP | 7074 | Ford GT 40 (blue) | CRP | 7093 | Ford Mark II (yellow) | CRP |
| 415 | Ferrari 250 GT (red) | CRP | 7075 | Ferrari 250 GT SWB (red) | CRP | 7094 | Ford Mark II Roadster (red) | CRP |
| 420 | Cobra (white) | CRP | 7076 | Ferrari 250 GT SWB (gray) | CRP | 7095 | Ferrari 250 GTO (red) | CRP |
| 421 | Cobra (white) | CRP | 7077 | Ferrari 250 GT SWB (yellow) | CRP | 7096 | Ferrari 250 TDF (blue) | CRP |
| 422 | Cobra (red) | CRP | 7078 | Ferrari 250 GT SWB (red) | CRP | 7097 | Ferrari 330 P4 (red) | CRP |
| 423 | Cobra (blue) | CRP | 7079 | Ford Mark II (black) | CRP | 7098 | Ferrari 330 P4 (red) | CRP |
| 424 | Ferrari 250 TDF (red) | CRP | 7080 | Ford Mark II (blue) | CRP | 7099 | Mercedes-Benz 300 SL (blue) | CRP |
| 425 | Ferrari 250 TDF (metallic blue) | CRP | 7081 | Ford Mark II (black) | CRP | 7100 | Mercedes-Benz 300 SL (red) | CRP |
| 426 | Ferrari 250 TDF (red) | CRP | 7082 | Ford Mark II (red) | CRP | 7101 | Mercedes-Benz 300 SL (silver) | CRP |
| 427 | Ferrari 250 TDF (white) | CRP | 7083 | Ferrari 250 GT SWB (black) | CRP | 7102 | Mercedes-Benz 300 SL (silver) | CRP |
| 431 | Ferrari 250 TDF (silver) | CRP | | | | | | |
| 432 | Ferrari 250 GTO (blue) | CRP | | | | | | |
| 433 | Ferrari 250 TDF (white) | CRP | | | | | | |
| 438 | Cobra (green) | CRP | | | | | | |
| 441 | Ferrari 250 TDF (blue) | CRP | | | | | | |
| 444 | Ferrari 250 GTO (yellow) | CRP | | | | | | |
| 453 | Ford GT 40 (white) | CRP | | | | | | |
| 454 | Ford GT 40 (yellow) | CRP | | | | | | |
| 455 | Ford GT 40 (red) | CRP | | | | | | |
| 456 | Ford GT 40 (white) | GRP | | | | | | |
| 458 | Ferrari 250 GTO (silver) | GRP | | | | | | |
| 464 | Ferrari 250 GTO (red) | GRP | | | | | | |
| 1007 | Ford GT 40 (blue) | CRP | | | | | | |
| 1008 | Ferrari 250 GT SWB (red) | CRP | | | | | | |
| 1009 | Ford GT40 (yellow) | CRP | | | | | | |
| 1010 | Ferrari 250 GT (red) | CRP | | | | | | |
| 1011 | Mercedes-Benz 300 SL (red) | CRP | | | | | | |
| 1012 | Ferrari 250 GT SWB (silver) | CRP | | | | | | |
| 1013 | Ferrari 250 GTO (silver) | CRP | | | | | | |
| 1014 | Ferrari 250 TDF (red) | CRP | | | | | | |

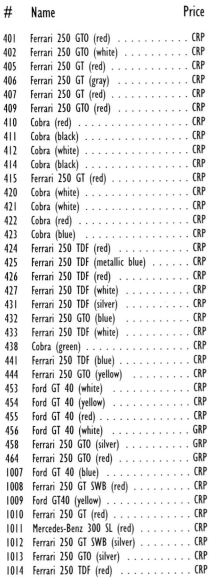

*Number 7107 in the Bang stable: the Ferrari 250 Testa Rossa 58. It was introduced in early 1995, and has fastening clips on both the front and rear hoods, in addition to aluminum wheels.*

| # | Name | Price |
|---|------|-------|
| 7103 | Ferrari 412P (yellow) | CRP |
| 7104 | Ferrari 412P (red) | CRP |
| 7105 | Ferrari 412P (white) | CRP |
| 7106 | Ferrari 412P (red) | CRP |
| 7107 | Ferrari 250 TR 58 (red) | CRP |
| 7108 | Ferrari 250 TR 58 (yellow) | CRP |
| 7109 | Ferrari 250 TR 58 (blue) | CRP |
| 7110 | Ferrari 250 TR 58 (white) | CRP |
| 7111 | Ferrari 250 GTO (red) | CRP |
| 7112 | Ferrari 250 GT (red) | CRP |
| 7113 | Ferrari 250 TDF (red) | CRP |
| 7114 | Ferrari 250 SWB (red) | CRP |
| 7115 | Cobra (red) | CRP |
| 7119 | Ferrari 330 P4 Spider (red) | CRP |
| 7120 | Ferrari 330 P4 Spider (red) | CRP |
| 7121 | Ferrari 330 P4 Spider | CRP |
| 7130 | Ferrari 250 TR 58 (yellow) | CRP |
| 8001 | Ferrari 348 GTS (red) | CRP |
| 8002 | Ferrari 348 GTS (yellow) | CRP |
| 8003 | Ferrari 348 GTS (black) | CRP |
| 8004 | Ferrari 348 GTB (blue) | CRP |
| 8005 | Ferrari 348 GTB (red) | CRP |

| # | Name | Price |
|---|------|-------|
| 8006 | Ferrari 348 GTB (white) | CRP |
| 8007 | Ferrari 348 TB (red) | CRP |
| 8008 | Ferrari 348 Spider (red) | CRP |
| 8009 | Ferrari 348 Spider (silver) | CRP |
| 8010 | Ferrari 348 Spider (gray) | CRP |
| 8011 | Ferrari 348 Spider (yellow) | CRP |
| 8012 | Ferrari 348 Spider (white) | CRP |
| 8013 | Ferrari 456 GT (red) | CRP |
| 8014 | Ferrari 456 GT (gray) | CRP |
| 8015 | Ferrari 456 GT (blue) | CRP |
| 8016 | Ferrari 456 GT (red) | CRP |
| 8017 | Ferrari 456 GT (black) | CRP |
| 8018 | Ferrari 348 tb ("MonteShell") | CRP |
| 8020 | Ferrari 348 GT | CRP |
| 8021 | Ferrari 348 GT | CRP |
| 8022 | Ferrari 348 GT | CRP |
| 8025 | Ferrari 355 GTB (red) | CRP |
| 8026 | Ferrari 355 GTB (yellow) | CRP |
| 8027 | Ferrari 355 GTB (red) | CRP |
| 9301 | Ferrari 348 tb (white) | CRP |
| 9302 | Ferrari 348 tb (white) | CRP |
| 9303 | Ferrari 348 tb (red) | CRP |

| # | Name | Price |
|---|------|-------|
| 9305 | Ferrari 348 tb (yellow) | CRP |
| 9306 | Ferrari 348 tb (red) | CRP |
| 9308 | Ferrari 348 tb (red) | CRP |
| 9312 | Ferrari 348 tb (yellow) | CRP |
| 9314 | Ferrari 348 tb (red, blue and yellow) | CRP |
| 9316 | Ferrari 348 tb (red) | CRP |
| 9318 | Ferrari 348 tb (white, blue and yellow) | CRP |
| 9323 | Ferrari 348 tb (red) | CRP |
| 9401 | Ferrari 348 | CRP |
| 9402 | Ferrari 348 | CRP |
| 9403 | Ferrari 348 | CRP |
| 9406 | Ferrari 348 | CRP |
| 9408 | Ferrari 348 | CRP |
| 9411 | Ferrari 348 | CRP |
| 9412 | Ferrari 348 | CRP |
| 9416 | Ferrari 348 | CRP |
| 9422 | Ferrari 348 | CRP |
| 9423 | Ferrari 348 | CRP |
| 9433 | Ferrari 348 | CRP |
| PR507 | Ford GT 40 (yellow) | CRP |

# Barclay

This northern New Jersey-based American manufacturer is better known for the die cast toy vehicles and toy soldiers that it made prior to World War II. But Barclay also made die casts after the war, in particular a series of two-inch to three-inch long cars and trucks with no baseplates. These were simple castings, designed no doubt to gain a share of the market dominated by Tootsietoy.

Barclay often did not put their name on the toy, which can make identification difficult. The two examples shown here are representative of the trucks, however, with their soft plastic black wheels.

Some of these items were packaged as the "Bottle Series," which was marketed during the 1960s. The Bottle vehicles were sold on a blister card, as were many (if not all) of the Barclays.

The values given below are for near mint or better examples by themselves; for a Barclay in the original blister packaging, add an additional 25%-50%.

*Typical Barclays from the 1960s. At left is the two-inch Dump Truck, the rear of which actually does dump. At right is the three-inch "U.S. MAIL" Tractor Trailer. Both trucks have a red cab and blue rear section, and both have the characteristic soft plastic wheels that the company used on so many of its toys.*

| Name | Price |
|------|-------|
| Two-door Sedan (1.5 inches) | $5 |
| Vintage Car | 10 |
| Volkswagen Beetle | 20 |
| Police Car | 15 |

| Name | Price |
|------|-------|
| Chief Police Car | $15 |
| Sports Racing Car | 15 |
| Open Wheel Racing Car | 15 |
| Convertible Sports Car (driver and passenger) | 20 |

| Name | Price |
|------|-------|
| "Pepsi Cola" Truck | $25 |
| "Hertz" Moving Van | 15 |
| Dump Truck | 15 |
| Side Dump Truck | 15 |

| Name | Price |
|---|---|
| Lumber Truck | $15 |
| Oil Truck | 20 |
| "U.S. Mail" Tractor Trailer (three inches) | 20 |
| "Woolworth" Tractor Trailer (three inches) | 20 |

**Miltary Trucks:**

| Name | Price |
|---|---|
| Open-back Army Truck | 15 |
| Closed-back Army Truck | 15 |
| Army Oil Truck | 15 |
| Military Ambulance (white "long nose" with red cross on cab roof) | 15 |

| Name | Price |
|---|---|
| Military Ambulance ("Cab over" with red cross on cab roof) | $15 |

**Sets:**

| Name | Price |
|---|---|
| Transport Set (#330) (Car carrier with two 1.5-inch cars) | 40 |
| Double Transport Set (#440) (Double deck car carrier with four 1.5-inch cars) | 65 |
| "Miniature Autos" set of seven of the 1.5-inch cars (blister card) | 50 |

| Name | Price |
|---|---|
| "Speedway Track" Game (two die cast race cars with a ten-foot plastic track) | $20 |

[Barclay also marketed "double" blister packs of two vehicles, such as the two dump trucks or the two sports cars. These were usually priced at twenty-nine cents, which appears at the top right of the card. If found together still intact in the blister, add $10-$20 to the value of the two items.]

# Bburago

This Italian company is a major player in today's new die cast model market, having begun manufacturing its products in the mid-1970s. For its first ten years, Bburago was probably best known for its line of Formula One race cars, made in several scales. The accuracy of these toys/models was acceptable at the time, and Bburago got a lot of mileage out of the castings, sometimes issuing two or three different liveries of the same basic body.

Alongside the Formula One line (newer models of which are still being produced in 1/24 scale), Bburago expanded their offerings during the 1980s to include vintage and contemporary models. As the product line grew, the accuracy of the models improved to today's high standard. The company concentrates on 1/18 and 1/24 scale products, many of which also come in kit form. (Although the #3020/7020/3520 1936 Mercedes-Benz 500K is 1/20 scale, and several of the cars in the 1/24 scale series are actually 1/25 scale.) There is also a 1/43 scale line, called the "Pocket" series, which is aimed more at the children's market.

In 1992, Bburago debuted what may be the best-selling die cast model in modern history, the 1/18 scale Dodge Viper RT/10. It comes in several different configurations (including ready-built and kit forms), and is a highly accurate model. Like the rest of the Bburago line, it is available in most major

chain stores such as Wal-Mart and Toys R Us, which has contributed to its high sales figures.

*Note:* Bburago often "re-uses" model numbers when a model is replaced by a new or updated model. So, for example, #6101 has been used for both the 1981-era Ferrari and for the 1990s-era car, as well.

Current Retail Price (CRP) for the 1/18 Bburagos is around $20; the 1/24 scale models sell in the $12-$15 range; and the 1/43 "Pocket" cars sell for anywhere from $2.50-$4.

*The Ferrari 126 C4 (1984 era), which was #6111 in the Bburago 1/24 Grand Prix line.*

| # | Name | Price |
|---|---|---|
| **1/14 Scale Formula One (mid-1970s - 1981):** | | |
| 2101 | Ferrari 312T2 (1976) | $50 |
| 2102 | Tyrell P34/2 (1976) | 40 |

| # | Name | Price |
|---|---|---|
| 2103 | Brabham BT46 (1978) | $40 |
| 2105 | Lotus 79/JPS MK4 (1978) | 40 |
| 2106 | Lotus Essex MK3 (1981) | 40 |

| # | Name | Price |
|---|---|---|
| 2107 | Tyrell 009 (1979) | $40 |
| 2108 | Ferrari 312T5 (1980) | 50 |
| 2109 | Renault RE20 (1980) | 40 |

*Bburago's 1983-84-era Alfa Romeo 179, numbered 6102 in the 1/24 Grand Prix series.*

| # | Name | Price |
|---|------|-------|
| 3721 | Porsche 356 B Coupe | CRP |
| 3724 | Chevrolet Corvette | CRP |
| 3725 | Dodge Viper RT/10 | CRP |
| 3731 | Porsche 356 B Cabriolet | CRP |
| 3732 | Ferrari F40 | CRP |
| 3735 | Bugatti EB 110 | CRP |
| 3737 | Lamborghini Countach | CRP |
| 3739 | Ferrari 348 TB | CRP |
| 3741 | Lamborghini Diablo | CRP |
| 3746 | Ferrari 456 GT | CRP |
| 3760 | Porsche 911 Carrera | CRP |
| 3765 | Dodge Viper RT/10 | CRP |

**1/24 Bijoux:**

| # | Name | Price |
|---|------|-------|
| 1501 | Citroën 15 CV TA | CRP |
| 1502 | Jaguar XK 120 Roadster | CRP |
| 1503 | Bugatti Atlantic | CRP |
| 1506 | Ferrari 250 LM "Monza" | CRP |
| 1507 | Ferrari 250 Testa Rossa | CRP |
| 1508 | Jaguar XK 120 Coupe | CRP |
| 1509 | Mercedes-Benz SSK | CRP |
| 1510 | Ferrari 250 GTO | CRP |
| 1511 | Ferrari 275 GTB 4 | CRP |
| 1524 | Chevrolet Corvette | CRP |
| 1532 | Ferrari F40 | CRP |
| 1535 | Bugatti EB 110 | CRP |
| 1536 | Ferrari 456 GT | CRP |
| 1539 | Ferrari 348 TB | CRP |

**1/24 Kit Bijoux:**

| # | Name | Price |
|---|------|-------|
| 5501 | Citroën 15 CV TA | CRP |
| 5502 | Jaguar XK 120 Roadster | CRP |
| 5504 | Ferrari Testa Rossa | CRP |
| 5506 | Ferrari 250 LM "Daytona" | CRP |
| 5507 | Ferrari Testa Rossa | CRP |
| 5509 | Mercedes-Benz SSK | CRP |
| 5510 | Ferrari 250 GTO | CRP |
| 5513 | Ford AC Cobra 427 | CRP |
| 5524 | Chevrolet Corvette | CRP |
| 5532 | Mercedes-Benz 300 SL | CRP |
| 5537 | Lamborghini Countach | CRP |
| 5539 | Ferrari 348 TB | CRP |
| 5540 | Ferrari F40 | CRP |

**1/24 VIP:**

| # | Name | Price |
|---|------|-------|
| 0503 | Bugatti Atlantic | CRP |
| 0504 | Ferrari Testa Rossa | CRP |
| 0506 | Ferrari 250 Le Mans | CRP |
| 0510 | Ferrari 250 GTO | CRP |
| 0511 | Ferrari 275 GTB 4 | CRP |
| 0513 | Ford AC Cobra 427 | CRP |
| 0522 | Mercedes-Benz 300 SL | CRP |
| 0524 | Chevrolet Corvette | CRP |
| 0532 | Ferrari F40 | CRP |
| 0535 | Bugatti EB 110 | CRP |
| 0537 | Lamborghini Countach | CRP |
| 0538 | Bugatti "Type 55" | CRP |
| 0541 | Lamborghini Diablo | CRP |
| 0542 | Ferrari F40 Evoluzione | CRP |
| 0563 | Porsche 959 Turbo | CRP |
| 0572 | Ferrari GTO | CRP |

**1/18 Diamonds:**

| # | Name | Price |
|---|------|-------|
| 3002 | Mercedes-Benz SSKL | CRP |
| 3004 | Ferrari Testa Rossa | CRP |
| 3005 | Bugatti "Type 59" | CRP |
| 3006 | Jaguar SS 100 | CRP |
| 3007 | Ferrari 250 Testa Rossa | CRP |
| 3008 | Alfa Romeo 2300 Spider | CRP |
| 3009 | Mercedes-Benz SSK | CRP |
| 3010 | Lancia Aurelia B24 S | CRP |
| 3011 | Ferrari 250 GTO | CRP |
| 3013 | Mercedes-Benz 300 SL | CRP |
| 3014 | Alfa Romeo 8C 2300 M | CRP |
| 3015 | Mercedes-Benz 300 SL | CRP |
| 3016 | Jaguar "E" Cabriolet | CRP |
| 3018 | Jaguar "E" Coupe | CRP |
| 3019 | Ferrari Testa Rossa | CRP |
| 3020 | Mercedes-Benz 500 K | CRP |
| 3021 | Porsche 356 B Coupe | CRP |
| 3022 | Ferrari F40 | CRP |
| 3024 | Chevrolet Corvette | CRP |
| 3025 | Dodge Viper RT/10 | CRP |
| 3026 | Jaguar "E" Cabriolet | CRP |
| 3027 | Ferrari GTO | CRP |
| 3028 | Lamborghini Diablo | CRP |
| 3029 | Ferrari 348 TB Evoluzione | CRP |
| 3031 | Porsche 356 B Cabriolet | CRP |
| 3032 | Ferrari F40 | CRP |
| 3034 | Chevrolet Corvette | CRP |
| 3035 | Bugatti EB 110 | CRP |
| 3036 | Ferrari 456 GT | CRP |
| 3037 | Lamborghini Countach | CRP |
| 3038 | Jaguar "E" Coupe | CRP |
| 3039 | Ferrari 348 TB | CRP |
| 3041 | Lamborghini Diablo | CRP |
| 3042 | Ferrari F40 Evoluzione | CRP |
| 3045 | Bugatti EB 110 | CRP |
| 3046 | Ferrari 456 GT | CRP |
| 3047 | Lamborghini Countach | CRP |
| 3050 | Porsche 911 Carrera | CRP |
| 3051 | Porsche 356 B Cabriolet | CRP |
| 3055 | Bugatti EB 110 | CRP |
| 3057 | Ferrari GTO Rally | CRP |
| 3060 | Porsche 911 Carrera | CRP |
| 3065 | Dodge Viper RT/10 | CRP |

**1/18 Kit Diamonds:**

| # | Name | Price |
|---|------|-------|
| 7002 | Mercedes-Benz SSKL M.M. | CRP |
| 7005 | Bugatti "Type 59" G.P. | CRP |
| 7006 | Jaguar SS 100 Targa F. | CRP |
| 7007 | Ferrari Testa Rossa L.M. | CRP |
| 7008 | Alfa Romeo 2300 Touring | CRP |
| 7009 | Mercedes-Benz SSK Mont. | CRP |
| 7010 | Lancia Aurelia B24 S | CRP |
| 7011 | Ferrari 250 GTO Nurb. | CRP |
| 7013 | Mercedes-Benz 300 SL | CRP |
| 7014 | Alfa Romeo 8C G.P. Monaco | CRP |
| 7016 | Jaguar "E" Cabriolet Tour de F | CRP |
| 7018 | Jaguar "E" Coupe | CRP |
| 7019 | Ferrari Testa Rossa | CRP |
| 7020 | Mercedes-Benz 500K R. | CRP |
| 7021 | Porsche 356 B Coupe | CRP |
| 7024 | Chevrolet Corvette | CRP |
| 7025 | Dodge Viper RT/10 | CRP |
| 7027 | Ferrari GTO | CRP |
| 7032 | Ferrari F40 | CRP |
| 7035 | Bugatti EB 110 | CRP |
| 7039 | Ferrari 348 TB | CRP |
| 7041 | Lamborghini Diablo | CRP |

**1/18 De Luxe:**

| # | Name | Price |
|---|------|-------|
| 3505 | Bugatti "Type 59" | CRP |
| 3507 | Ferrari 250 Testa Rossa | CRP |
| 3509 | Mercedes-Benz SSK | CRP |
| 3511 | Ferrari 250 GTO | CRP |
| 3513 | Mercedes-Benz 300 SL | CRP |
| 3514 | Alfa Romeo 8C 2300 M. | CRP |
| 3516 | Jaguar "E" Cabriolet | CRP |
| 3519 | Ferrari Testa Rossa | CRP |
| 3520 | Mercedes-Benz 500K R. | CRP |
| 3521 | Porsche 356 B Coupe | CRP |
| 3525 | Dodge Viper RT/10 | CRP |
| 3527 | Ferrari GTO | CRP |
| 3528 | Lamborghini Diablo | CRP |
| 3529 | Ferrari 348 TB Evoluzione | CRP |
| 3534 | Chevrolet Corvette | CRP |
| 3536 | Ferrari 456 GT | CRP |

**1/18 Executive:**

| # | Name | Price |
|---|------|-------|
| 3702 | Mercedes-Benz SSKL C | CRP |
| 3718 | Jaguar "E" Coupe | CRP |

| # | Name | Price |
|---|------|-------|

### 1/24 Super:

| # | Name | Price |
|---|------|-------|
| 0102 | Porsche 911 S | CRP |
| 0104 | Ferrari Testa Rossa | CRP |
| 0105 | Mercedes-Benz 190 E | CRP |
| 0111 | Mercedes-Benz 500 SEC | CRP |
| 0112 | Range Rover Safari | CRP |
| 0115 | Lancia Delta S4 | CRP |
| 0116 | Peugeot 205 Safari | CRP |
| 0119 | Alfa Romeo 75 Gr. A | CRP |
| 0121 | Porsche 959 | CRP |
| 0125 | Fiat Tipo | CRP |
| 0127 | Fiat Punto | CRP |
| 0129 | Ferrari 348 TB Evoluzione | CRP |
| 0130 | Mercedes-Benz 300 SL | CRP |
| 0131 | Peugeot 405 Raid | CRP |
| 0133 | Ferrari 512 BB | CRP |
| 0135 | Fiat Tipo Taxi | CRP |
| 0137 | Lamborghini Countach | CRP |
| 0148 | Ferrari 308 GTB | CRP |
| 0154 | Fiat Cinquecento Rally | CRP |
| 0188 | Alfa Romeo 75 Polizia | CRP |
| 0189 | Alfa Romeo 75 Carabin | CRP |
| 0190 | Alfa Romeo 75 G. di F. | CRP |
| 0192 | Ferrari GTO Rally | CRP |
| 0194 | Fiat Cinquecento | CRP |
| 0198 | Renegade Jeep CJ-7 | CRP |
| 0199 | Porsche 924 Turbo Gr. 2 | CRP |

### 1/24 Kit Super:

| # | Name | Price |
|---|------|-------|
| 5102 | Porsche 911 Armel | CRP |
| 5105 | Mercedes-Benz 190E | CRP |
| 5106 | Peugeot 205 Turbo 16 | CRP |
| 5115 | Lancia Delta S4 | CRP |
| 5119 | Alfa Romeo 75 | CRP |
| 5121 | Porsche 959 Raid | CRP |
| 5129 | Ferrari 348 TB Monteshell | CRP |
| 5131 | Peugeot 405 Raid | CRP |
| 5133 | Ferrari 512 BB Daytona | CRP |
| 5142 | Kremer Porsche 935 T. | CRP |
| 5148 | Ferrari 308 GTB | CRP |
| 5172 | Ferrari GTO Pioneer | CRP |
| 5173 | BMW 635 CSi | CRP |
| 5194 | Fiat Cinquecento Rally | CRP |
| 5199 | Porsche 924 Turbo | CRP |

### 1/24 Grand Prix:

| # | Name | Price |
|---|------|-------|
| 6101 | Ferrari 126 K Turbo | $20 |
| 6101 | Ferrari 641/2 (27) | CRP |
| 6102 | Alfa Romeo 179 | 20 |
| 6102 | Benetton B188 | 20 |
| 6102 | Benetton Ford | CRP |
| 6103 | Renault RE30 | 20 |
| 6103 | Grand Prix F1 | CRP |
| 6104 | Brabham BT52 | 20 |
| 6104 | Race Champion | CRP |
| 6105 | Williams FW08C | 20 |
| 6106 | McLaren MP4/2 | 20 |
| 6107 | Lotus 97T | 20 |
| 6108 | Williams FW14 | CRP |
| 6109 | Burago Racing | CRP |
| 6110 | Formula USA | CRP |
| 6111 | Ferrari 126 C4 | 20 |

| # | Name | Price |
|---|------|-------|
| 6112 | Detroit Cup | CRP |
| 6115 | Williams FW 16 | CRP |
| 6121 | Formula 3000 | CRP |
| 6122 | Indy Team | CRP |
| 6128 | Ferrari 641/2 (28) | CRP |
| 6132 | Monza Grand Prix | CRP |

### 1/43 Pocket:

| # | Name | Price |
|---|------|-------|
| 4102 | Mercedes-Benz 190E | CRP |
| 4103 | Porsche 924 Turbo | CRP |
| 4104 | Ferrari Testa Rossa | CRP |
| 4106 | Ferrari 512 BB Daytona | CRP |
| 4107 | Ferrari GTO Rally | CRP |
| 4108 | Ferrari F40 | CRP |
| 4109 | Mercedes-Benz 300 SL | CRP |
| 4110 | Porsche 928 Gr. A | CRP |
| 4112 | Suzuki Vitara Raid | CRP |
| 4114 | Porsche 911 | CRP |
| 4116 | Peugeot 205 Safari | CRP |
| 4117 | Ferrari 308 GTB | CRP |
| 4119 | Fiat Uno | CRP |
| 4122 | Renegade Jeep | CRP |
| 4127 | Lamborghini Countach | CRP |
| 4128 | Ferrari F40 | CRP |
| 4129 | Ferrari 348 TB Evoluzione | CRP |
| 4130 | Renault Clio RT | CRP |
| 4131 | Land Rover Aziza | CRP |
| 4133 | Ferrari 512 BB | CRP |
| 4134 | Fiat Tipo Rally | CRP |
| 4135 | Lancia Delta S4 | CRP |
| 4136 | Ferrari 456 GT | CRP |
| 4137 | Lamborghini Countach | CRP |
| 4138 | Fiat Cinquecento Rally | CRP |
| 4139 | Ferrari 348 TB | CRP |
| 4140 | MCA Centenaire | CRP |
| 4141 | Lamborghini Diablo | CRP |
| 4143 | Ford Sierra Gr. A | CRP |
| 4144 | Fiat Punto | CRP |
| 4146 | Ferrari 456 GT | CRP |
| 4148 | Ferrari 308 GTB Rally | CRP |
| 4150 | Peugeot 405 Raid | CRP |

| # | Name | Price |
|---|------|-------|
| 4151 | Lamborghini Diablo | CRP |
| 4152 | Chevrolet Corvette | CRP |
| 4153 | Porsche 911 Carrera Super Cup | CRP |
| 4155 | Citroën Xantia | CRP |
| 4157 | Ferrari Testa Rossa | CRP |
| 4158 | BMW 535i | CRP |
| 4160 | Renault Clio 16V | CRP |
| 4161 | Porsche 959 | CRP |
| 4165 | Citroën Xantia 16V | CRP |
| 4167 | BMW M3 G.T. Cup | CRP |
| 4168 | Ferrari F40 Evoluzione | CRP |
| 4170 | Mig Georgia Centenaire | CRP |
| 4171 | Land Rover Raid | CRP |
| 4175 | Ferrari GTO | CRP |
| 4176 | Ferrari 456 GT | CRP |
| 4178 | BMW 535i | CRP |
| 4179 | Fiat Tipo | CRP |
| 4181 | Mercedes-Benz 300 SL | CRP |
| 4183 | Ford Sierra Rally | CRP |
| 4185 | Porsche 911 Carrera '93 | CRP |
| 4189 | Ferrari 348 TB | CRP |
| 4190 | Peugeot 405 Safari | CRP |
| 4191 | Porsche 928 | CRP |
| 4192 | Chevrolet Corvette | CRP |
| 4193 | Fiat Cinquecento | CRP |
| 4194 | Suzuki Vitara | CRP |
| 4195 | Porsche 911 Carrera Cup | CRP |
| 4197 | BMW M3 DTM | CRP |
| 4200 | 2-piece. Gift Set | CRP |
| 4300/1 | 5-piece. Set | CRP |
| 4300F | 5-piece. Set | CRP |

### 1/87 Design:

| # | Name | Price |
|---|------|-------|
| 4713 | Mercedes-Benz 300 SL | CRP |
| 4719 | Ferrari Testa Rossa | CRP |
| 4732 | Ferrari F40 | CRP |
| 4735 | Bugatti EB 110 | CRP |
| 4736 | Ferrari 456 GT | CRP |
| 4739 | Ferrari 348 TB | CRP |
| 4763 | Porsche 959 | CRP |

*The best-selling die cast model of the modern era? It just may be: Bburago's #3025 Dodge Viper RT/10 in 1/18 scale.*

# Beaut

Beaut Manufacturing Co. was a northern New Jersey firm that put out a handful of die cast toys from 1946 until 1950. They were simple castings, with large black tires, and were generally styled on pre-war cars.

The group included a Sedan (pictured here); a Taxi; a Police Car; a Fire Chief Car; and a Van. They were each a little under four inches in length, and today generally sell in the $15-$30 range.

*The Beaut Sedan, which measures 3.75 inches in length. This example was painted a light green, and had the characteristic black wheels.*

# Benbros

Like so many manufacturers of die cast toys, Benbros had its beginnings in post-World War II London, where brothers Nathan and Jack Benenson started the company. At first going by the name "Benson Bros.," they changed the name to Benbros in 1951.

There were two basic lines of die cast toys offered. The first was the "TV Series" of 1/70 to 1/90 scale vehicles, launched in 1954. These came in a box made to look like a television set of the 1950s. In the late 1950s, the box was changed to reflect the new name of the line, "Mighty Midgets." This series was made until 1965.

The other, larger Benbros die casts were of roughly 1/38 to 1/50 scale, consisting of commercial, military and construction vehicles. These were produced during the latter half of the 1950s, and perhaps into the 1960s. They are listed at the end of the Benbros listing.

*The Benbros "Euclid" Dump Truck, which was first produced in 1957-1958. The dump bed tips back to allow the operator to dump the load. This example has some paint chipping, and so would be valued below the $50 near mint price listed here.*

| # | Name | Price | # | Name | Price | # | Name | Price |
|---|------|-------|---|------|-------|---|------|-------|
| 1 | Horse Drawn Hay Cart | $25 | 23 | AEC Box Van | $25 | 45 | Bedford Articulated Low Loader | $25 |
| 2 | Horse Drawn Log Cart | 25 | 24 | Field Gun | 10 | 46 | Bedford Articulated Petrol Tanker | 40 |
| 3 | AA Motorcycle and Side car | 30 | 25 | Spyker | 10 | 47* | Bedford Articulated Crane Lorry | 15 |
| 4 | Stage Coach with Four Horses | 25 | 26 | 1904 Vauxhall 5 hp | 10 | 48 | Bedford Articulated Flat Lorry with Chains | 25 |
| 5 | Horse Drawn Gipsy Caravan | 15 | 27 | 1906 Rolls-Royce | 10 | 49 | Karrier Bantam 'Coca-Cola' Bottle Lorry | 55 |
| 6 | Horse Drawn Milk Cart | 25 | 28 | Foden 8-wheel Flat Lorry with Chains | 25 | 50* | RAC Land Rover | 40 |
| 7 | Three-Wheeled Electric Milk Trolley | 25 | 29 | RAC Motorcycle and Sidecar | 40 | | (*Number not confirmed ) | |
| 8 | Foden Tractor and Log Trailer | 25 | 30 | AEC Army Box Van | 30 | | | |
| 9 | Dennis Fire Engine with Escape Ladder | 25 | 30 | Bedford Army Box Van | 25 | | | |
| 10 | Crawler Bulldozer | 15 | 31 | AEC Lorry with Tilt | 15 | | | |
| 11 | Crawler Tractor with Hay Rake | 15 | 31 | Bedford Lorry with Tilt | 25 | | | |
| 12 | Army Scout Car | 15 | 32 | AEC Compressor Lorry | 15 | | | |
| 13 | Austin Champ | 15 | 32 | Bedford Compressor Lorry | 25 | | | |
| 14 | Centurion Tank | 15 | 33 | AEC Crane Lorry | 15 | | | |
| 15 | Vespa Scooter with Rider | 25 | 33 | Bedford Crane Lorry | 25 | | | |
| 16 | Streamlined Express Locomotive (TV Series only) | 25 | 34 | AA Land Rover | 25 | | | |
| 16 | Chevrolet Nomad Station Wagon (Mighty Midget only) | 15 | 35 | Army Land Rover | 25 | | | |
| 17 | Crawler Tractor with Disc Harrow | 15 | 36 | Royal Mail Land Rover | 25 | | | |
| 18 | Hudson Tourer | 15 | 37 | Wolseley Six-Eighty Police Car | 15 | | | |
| 19 | Crawler Tractor and Trailer | 15 | 38 | Daimler Ambulance | 30 | | | |
| 20 | Foden 8-wheel Flat Lorry | 15 | 39 | Bedford Milk Float | 15 | | | |
| 21 | Foden 8-wheel Open Lorry | 15 | 40 | American Ford Convertible | 15 | | | |
| 22 | ERF Petrol Tanker | 25 | 41 | Army Hudson Tourer | 25 | | | |
| 23 | AEC Box Van | 15 | 42 | Army Motorcycle and Sidecar | 40 | | | |
| | | | 43 | Bedford Articulated Box Van | 25 | | | |
| | | | 44 | Bedford Articulated Lowside Lorry | 25 | | | |

**Larger scale (1/43 scale unless noted):**

| Name | Price |
|------|-------|
| Bulldozer | 40 |
| Ferguson Tractor | 65 |
| Ferguson Hydraulic Shovel | 45 |
| Excavator | 35 |
| Daimler Ambulance | 75 |
| Dodge Army Radar Truck (1/50) | 85 |
| AA Land Rover (1/38) | 80 |
| AEC Flat Truck with Chains (1/45) | 75 |
| AEC Truck (1/45) | 75 |
| AEC Covered Truck (1/45) | 75 |
| AEC Army Covered Truck (1/45) | 75 |
| AEC Excavator Truck (1/45) | 85 |
| AEC Lorry-Mounted Crane (1/45) | 85 |
| "Esso Motor Oil" Tanker (1/45) | 75 |
| "Petrol Goes a Long Way" Tanker (145) | 75 |
| "Euclid" Dump Truck (1/50) | 50 |

# Best

One of two lines of die casts (the other being Bang) launched when the company known as Box re-organized in 1991, Best 1/43 scale models are currently available in shops and at shows. They are made in Italy, so it is no surprise that Ferraris dominate the product line, with Porsche and Jaguar also being well-represented.

Like the Bang models, some Best models are simply Box models with new Best baseplates. They are sold in the standard plastic window box, held by a screw to a plastic display plinth. As Best models are current products, the following listing indicates their value as "CRP" (Current Retail Price), which is in the $20 range.

| # | Name | Price | # | Name | Price | # | Name | Price |
|---|------|-------|---|------|-------|---|------|-------|
| 9001 | Ferrari 275 GTB/4 | CRP | 9014 v4 | Jaguar "E" Coupe | CRP | 9027 m6 | Jaguar "E" Spyder | CRP |
| 9002 | Ferrari 275 GTB/4 | CRP | 9014 b5 | Jaguar "E" Coupe | CRP | 9027 n3 | Jaguar "E" Spyder | CRP |
| 9003 rl | Ferrari 275 GTB/4 | CRP | 9015 | Ferrari 275 GTB/4 | CRP | 9027 rl | Jaguar "E" Spyder | CRP |
| 9003 g2 | Ferrari 275 GTB/4 | CRP | 9016 | Jaguar "E" Coupe | CRP | 9028 a7 | Jaguar "E" Spyder | CRP |
| 9004 | Ferrari 275 GTB/4 | CRP | 9017 | Ferrari 250 LM | CRP | 9028 v4 | Jaguar "E" Spyder | CRP |
| 9005 | Ferrari 275 GTB/4 | CRP | 9018 | Ferrari 250 LM | CRP | 9029 | Jaguar "E" Spyder | CRP |
| 9006 | Ferrari 275 GTB/4 | CRP | 9019 | Ferrari 330 P2 | CRP | 9030 | Jaguar "E" Spyder | CRP |
| 9007 | Ferrari 275 GTB/4 | CRP | 9020 | Ferrari 330 P2 | CRP | 9031 | Porsche 908/3 | CRP |
| 9008 | Ferrari 250 LM | CRP | 9021 | Ferrari 365 P2 | CRP | 9032 | Porsche 908/3 | CRP |
| 9009 | Ferrari 250 LM | CRP | 9022 | Jaguar "E" Coupe | CRP | 9033 | Porsche 908/3 | CRP |
| 9010 | Ferrari 250 LM | CRP | 9023 | Ferrari 250 LM | CRP | 9034 | Porsche 908/3 | CRP |
| 9011 | Ferrari 250 LM | CRP | 9024 | Ferrari 275 GTB/4 | CRP | 9035 | Jaguar "E" Spyder | CRP |
| 9012 r2 | Jaguar "E" Coupe | CRP | 9025 | Ferrari 250 LM | CRP | 9036 | Jaguar "E" Spyder | CRP |
| 9012 n3 | Jaguar "E" Coupe | CRP | 9026 | Ferrari 365 P2 | CRP | 9037 | Jaguar "E" Spyder | CRP |

| # | Name | Price | # | Name | Price | # | Name | Price |
|---|------|-------|---|------|-------|---|------|-------|
| 9038 | Jaguar "E" Spyder | CRP | 9054 | Ferrari 250 LM | CRP | 9070 | Ferrari 290 MM | CRP |
| 9039 | Porsche 908/3 | CRP | 9055 | Ferrari 750 Monza | CRP | * | Ferrari 330 GTC | CRP |
| 9040 | Porsche 908/2 | CRP | 9056 | Ferrari 750 Monza | CRP | * | Alfa Romeo TZ 2 | CRP |
| 9041 | Porsche 908/2 | CRP | 9057 | Porsche 908/3 | CRP | SI01 | Ferrari GTB/4 Coupe | CRP |
| 9042 | Porsche 908/2 | CRP | 9058 | Ferrari 860 Monza | CRP | SI02 | Ferrari 275 GTB/4 Spyder | CRP |
| 9043 | Porsche 908/2 | CRP | 9059 | Alfa Romeo TZ I | CRP | SI03 | Jaguar "E" Spyder | CRP |
| 9044 | Ferrari 750 Monza | CRP | 9060 | Alfa Romeo TZ I | CRP | SI04 | Jaguar "E" Coupe | CRP |
| 9045 | Ferrari 750 Monza | CRP | 9061 | Alfa Romeo TZ I | CRP | 1001 | Ferrari 275 GTB/4 Coupe (silver) | CRP |
| 9046 | Ferrari 750 Monza | CRP | 9062 | Alfa Romeo TZ I | CRP | 1002 | Ferrari 275 GTB/4 Spyder (silver) | CRP |
| 9047 | Ferrari 750 Monza | CRP | 9063 | Ferrari 290 MM | CRP | 2001 | Ferrari 275 GTB/4 Coupe (gold) | CRP |
| 9048 | Ferrari 750 Monza | CRP | 9064 | Ferrari 290 MM | CRP | 2002 | Ferrari 275 GTB/4 Spyder (gold) | CRP |
| 9049 | Ferrari 750 Monza | CRP | 9065 | Porsche 908/2 | CRP | 1003 | Ferrari 330 P2 (silver) | CRP |
| 9050 | Porsche 908/3 | CRP | 9066 | Porsche 908/2 | CRP | 1004 | Ferrari 750 Monza (silver) | CRP |
| 9051 | Ferrari 860 Monza | CRP | 9067 | Alfa Romeo TZ I | CRP | 2003 | Ferrari 300 P2 (gold) | CRP |
| 9052 | Ferrari 860 Monza | CRP | 9068 | Alfa Romeo TZ I | CRP | 2004 | Ferrari 750 Monza (gold) | CRP |
| 9053 | Ferrari 860 Monza | CRP | 9069 | Ferrari 290 MM | CRP | | | |

*number unknown*

*Best #9039, the Porsche 908/3. This is based on the model that Brian Redman and Jo Siffert drove at the 1970 Targa Florio race; many of the Best models are of specific race liveries such as this.*

# Bestbox

This Holland-based company put out a series of small, Matchbox-style die cast models during the 1960s. They were mostly in the 1/55 to 1/70 scale range, except for the Daf trucks, which were around 1/100 scale.

| # | Name | Price | # | Name | Price | # | Name | Price |
|---|------|-------|---|------|-------|---|------|-------|
| 501 | Daf 600 Saloon | $25 | 2505 | Ford Model T Coupe | $20 | 2513 | Jaguar E Convertible | $20 |
| 502 | Daf 1400 Refuse Truck | 20 | 2506 | Ford Model T Sedan | 20 | 2514 | Mercedes-Benz 280 SL Convertible | 20 |
| 503 | Daf 1400 Fire Engine | 25 | 2507 | Ford Model T Advertisement | 20 | 2515 | Opel Rekord 1900 | 20 |
| 504 | Daf Torpedo Tipping Truck | 25 | 2507A | BMW 2000 CS | 25 | 2516 | Mercedes-Benz 250 SE Coupe | 20 |
| 505 | Daf Torpedo Open Truck | 20 | 2508 | Volkswagen 1600 TL | 30 | 2517 | 1966 Ferrari 312 Formula I | 20 |
| 506 | Daf Torpedo Closed Van | 20 | 2509 | Mercedes-Benz 220 SE Coupe | 20 | 2518 | Brabham Formula I | 15 |
| 2501 | Ford Model T Pickup | 20 | 2509A | B.R.M. Formula I | 20 | 2519 | Cooper-Maserati Formula I | 15 |
| 2502 | Ford Model T Tanker | 20 | 2510 | Citroën ID 19 Station Wagon | 20 | 2520 | Lotus Formula I | 15 |
| 2502A | Porsche 911S | 25 | 2511 | Ford Taunus 17 M Super | 20 | 2521 | Citroën Dyane | 20 |
| 2503 | Ford Model T Breakdown | 20 | 2512 | Opel Rekord | 20 | 2522 | Ford Transit Van | 20 |
| 2504 | Ford Model T Delivery Van | 20 | 2512A | Honda Formula I | 20 | | | |

# Box

**B**ox was an Italian manufacturer of 1/43 scale die cast models during the 1980s. The line featured numerous examples of Ferraris decorated in various liveries of famous races of the 1960s.

In 1991, Box was re-organized into at least two separate companies, Bang and Best. Many of the Box models were simply given new baseplates and released under one of the two new names.

Box models still generally sell at their original release price, which was $15-$20 (referred to as CRP). The models came packaged in a standard plastic display box, with the model held to the display base with a screw.

*Box #8435 Ferrari 250 LM, in 1964 Nurburgring livery as driven by Rindt and Maglioli.*

| # | Name | Price | # | Name | Price | # | Name | Price |
|---|------|-------|---|------|-------|---|------|-------|
| 8401 | Ferrari 250 GTO | CRP | 8422 | AC Cobra 289 | CRP | 8442 | Ferrari 275 GTB 4 | CRP |
| 8402 | Ferrari 250 GTO | CRP | 8423 | AC Cobra 289 | CRP | 8443 | Jaguar E | CRP |
| 8403 | Ferrari 250 GTO | CRP | 8424 | Ferrari 250 GT | CRP | 8445 | Ferrari 250 LM | CRP |
| 8404 | Ferrari 250 GTO | CRP | 8425 | Ferrari 250 GT | CRP | 8446 | Ferrari 250 LM | CRP |
| 8405 | Ferrari 250 GT | CRP | 8426 | Ferrari 250 GT | CRP | 8447 | Ferrari P2 | CRP |
| 8406 | Ferrari 250 GT | CRP | 8427 | Ferrari 250 TDF | CRP | 8448 | Ferrari P2 | CRP |
| 8407 | Ferrari 250 GT | CRP | 8428 | Ferrari 275 GTB 4 | CRP | 8449 | Ferrari P2 | CRP |
| 8408 | Ferrari 250 GTO | CRP | 8429 | Ferrari 275 GTB 4 | CRP | 8451 | Ferrari 250 LM | CRP |
| 8409 | Ferrari 250 GTO | CRP | 8430 | Ferrari 275 GTB 4 | CRP | 8452 | Ferrari 275 GTB | CRP |
| 8410 | AC Cobra 289 | CRP | 8431 | Ferrari 250 TDF | CRP | 8453 | Ford GT 40 | CRP |
| 8411 | AC Cobra 289 | CRP | 8432 | Ferrari 250 GTO | CRP | 8454 | Ford GT 40 | CRP |
| 8412 | AC Cobra 289 | CRP | 8433 | Ferrari 250 GTO | CRP | 8455 | Ford GT 40 | CRP |
| 8414 | AC Cobra 289 | CRP | 8434 | Ferrari 250 LM | CRP | 8456 | Ford GT 40 | CRP |
| 8415 | Ferrari 250 GT | CRP | 8435 | Ferrari 250 LM | CRP | 8457 | Ferrari 250 LM | CRP |
| 8416 | Ferrari 275 GTB 4 | CRP | 8436 | Ferrari 250 LM | CRP | 8458 | Ferrari 250 LM | CRP |
| 8417 | Ferrari 275 GTB 4 | CRP | 8437 | Ferrari 250 LM | CRP | 8460 | Jaguar E Spyder | CRP |
| 8418 | Ferrari 275 GTB 4 | CRP | 8438 | AC Shelby Cobra | CRP | 8461 | Jaguar E Spyder | CRP |
| 8419 | Ferrari 275 GTB 4 | CRP | 8439 | Jaguar E Spyder | CRP | 8462 | Jaguar E Spyder | CRP |
| 8420 | AC Cobra 289 | CRP | 8440 | Jaguar E Spyder | CRP | 8463 | Jaguar E Spyder | CRP |
| 8421 | AC Cobra 289 | CRP | 8441 | Ferrari 250 TDF | CRP | 8464 | Ferrari 250 GTO | CRP |

# Bradscars

This was a small series of toy cars, made during the early 1950s in Brighton, England. The manufacturer, Bradshaws Model Products, was run by George Bradshaw. The cars were intended for use with "00" gauge model train layouts, and were roughly 1/75 scale. They were priced higher than the comparable Matchbox cars of the period, which no doubt hastened the departure of Bradscars from the scene after just a couple of years.

They were simple, one-piece castings, with no interiors, and the paint jobs were rather crude. The group included an Austin A30 (the baseplate read Austin 7); a Morris 6; and a Riley 1.5. A fourth model, a Jaguar Mark VII, was injection-molded plastic with plastic wheels (as opposed to metal wheels on the others). A Morris Minor was apparently also planned, but is believed not to have been produced.

As for colors, the Austin has been found in three different colors: black, red and green. The Morris was done in black, red, tan, blue and light green, and the Riley has been seen in red, black, gray and green. (The plastic Jaguar came in gray, black and green.) Features like headlights, grilles and bumpers were highlighted in silver.

The Morris and the Riley had tinplate baseplates, while that of the Austin was cast lead. Some of the baseplates were blank, but the Morris and the Riley also came with baseplates that had the name of the model, as well as "Bradscar (Regd)," and "BMP, Bradshaw, Hove, England." The Austin baseplate read, "Bradscar, Hove, England, Austin 7."

The 1955-1956 Bradshaws catalog does not include the Bradscars, so it is logical to assume that they had gone out of production by this time.

Bradscars are quite rare today. Although there is no record of them having been originally sold in boxes, a near mint or better condition example will still run from $30-$75.

# Brimtoy

Although better-known for its tinplate toys, Brimtoy did include several die cast vehicles in its "Pocketoy" series of the late 1940s-early 1950s. The company, Wells-Brimtoy Distributors Ltd., had its roots in pre-World War I England, and by 1949 was turning out all kinds of toys.

The Pocketoy line was launched that year, and it included six die cast vehicles among the tin and plastic offerings. These included a Vauxhall Coupe; a Vauxhall Saloon; and a Wolseley Sedan (each of these were numbered 222). Number 502 was a Sunbeam Talbot, #505 was a Buick and #510 was a Bedford LWB Truck. The vehicles had key-wind clockwork motors, and if found today in excellent or better condition, generally sell for $40-$55, with the Buick commanding somewhat more ($65-$70). The Vauxhall Coupe has been seen in four different colors: blue, yellow, red and green. The Saloon came in red or blue; the Sunbeam in cream, green, or blue; and the Buick in blue, red, green or cream. Colors for the Wolseley and the Bedford Truck are unknown. At least some, if not all, of these toys, came in individual boxes.

A non-clockwork version of the Sunbeam Talbot (with no baseplate) was also made, but there is debate as to whether this was a Wells-Brimtoy product. The Vauxhall Coupe may also have been produced by another manufacturer, perhaps as a result of purchasing the original tooling from Wells-Brimtoy.

# Britains

One of the most revered of the British toy companies, Britains traces its history back to 1845, when William B. Britain established a small factory in North London. Mechanical toys were the firm's strength until 1893, when the first of the now legendary toy soldiers were produced.

After the Second World War, Britains' toy vehicle line focused mainly on military and farm vehicles, with a series of civilian motorcycles produced during the 1960s and '70s. It should be noted that some of the pre-World War II toys were produced after the War; however, these are outside the scope of this book (as are the countless military and civilian figures put out by the firm). Further information on these and other Britains products can be obtained from books specifically devoted to the brand.

In 1987, Britains Ltd. was purchased by Dobson Industries Group, and the name of the company was changed to Britains Petite. The following listing provides information on Britains products up until the 1970s, as well as a selection of the farm vehicles made in recent years (many of which are still produced, hence the "CRP" designation).

| # | Name | Price |
|---|------|-------|
| **1/72 scale:** | | |
| LB 536 | Civilian Motorcycle | $35 |
| LB 548 | Telegraph Motorcycle | 35 |
| LB 550 | Police Motorcycle | 35 |
| LV603 | Fordson WOT Articulated Truck | 35 |
| LV604 | Fordson Tractor (blue) | 35 |
| LV607 | Bedford Army Covered Truck (dark green) | 30 |
| LV608 | Bedford Truck (red/blue) | 30 |
| LV609 | Austin Champ (dark green) | 30 |
| LV610 | Centurion Tank (dark green) | 50 |
| LV611 | Sexton Self Propelled Gun (dark green) | 50 |
| LV612 | Ford Thames ET 6 Army Truck (dark green) | 35 |
| LV613 | Ford Thames ET 6 Army Covered Truck (dark green) | 35 |
| LV614 | Ford Thames ET 6 Articulated Truck | 35 |
| LV615 | Saracen Armoured Vehicle (dark green) | 30 |
| LV616 | Ford Thames ET 6 Farm Truck | 30 |
| LV617 | Ford Thames ET 6 Ambulance (white) | 30 |
| LV618 | Ford Thames ET 6 Army Ambulance (dark green) | 30 |
| LV619 | Ford Thames ET 6 Royal Mail Van (red) | 50 |
| LV620 | Bedford Open Army Truck (dark green) | 30 |
| **1/32-1/35 scale (unless otherwise noted):** | | |
| 59F | 4-wheel Farm Lorry | 200 |
| 127F | Fordson E 27 N Tractor (dark blue/orange) | 350 |
| 128F | Fordson E 27 N Tractor (dark blue/orange) | 350 |
| 129F | Timber Trailer (green) | 35 |
| 130F | Farm Trailer (green/orange) | 35 |
| 135F | Disc Harrow (green) | 35 |
| 136F | Roller (dark blue) | 35 |
| 138P | 4 Furrow Trailed Plough (green) | 35 |

| # | Name | Price |
|---|------|-------|
| 148P | Motorcycle | $50 |
| 149 | Motorcycle | 50 |
| 171F | Fordson Diesel Major Tractor (blue/orange) | 250 |
| 172F | Fordson Diesel Major Tractor (blue/orange) | 250 |
| 173F | 3 Furrow Mounted Plough (blue/orange) | 25 |
| 174F | Muledozer (orange/silver) | 25 |
| 175F | Cultivator (orange/gray) | 25 |
| 176F | Vicon-Lely Rake (orange/cream) | 25 |
| 1334 | 4-wheel Military Truck (dark green) | 150 |
| 1335 | 6-wheel Military Truck | 150 |
| 1433 | Army Truck Caterpillar Type (green or dark green) | 150 |
| 1448 | Austin Staff Car (dark green) | 190 |
| 1512 | Army Ambulance (green) | 170 |
| 1513 | Volunteers Corps Ambulance (blue) | 320 |
| 1793 | Army Motorcycle with Sidecar (dark green) | 100 |
| 1855 | Balloon Barrage Unit (1/70 scale) (green) | 320 |
| 1876 | Carden-Vickers Bren Gun Carrier (dark green) | 70 |
| 1877 | Troop Transport Truck (dark green) | 100 |
| 1879 | Army Truck & Trailer with Gas Cylinders (1/70 scale) (green) | 210 |
| 2024 | "BRITAINS" Van (light blue) | 380 |
| 2026 | (9705) Howitzer (green) | 15 |
| 2041 | Clockwork Trailer (green) | 60 |
| 2045 | Clockwork "BRITAINS" Van (light blue) | 450 |
| 2048 | Army Truck & Trailer (green) | 220 |
| 2057 | (9487) Union Gun (green) | 25 |
| 2058 | (9486) Antique Gun (black) | 25 |
| 2064 | (9745) 155mm Gun (green) | 30 |
| 2102 | (9760) Austin Champ closed or open (dark green) | 70 |
| 2106 | Heavy Howitzer (green) | 60 |

| # | Name | Price |
|---|------|-------|
| 2107 | (9740) Heavy Howitzer (green) | $60 |
| 2150 | (9770) Centurion Tank (green) | 300 |
| 2152 | (9499) Waterloo Gun (black) | 50 |
| 2154 | Centurion Tank Desert (beige) | 350 |
| 2173 | (9720) Anti Tank Gun (green) | 15 |
| 2174 | (9750) Anti Tank Gun (green) | 60 |
| 2175 | (9748) 155mm Gun mounted on Centurion Tank (green) | 250 |
| 2183 | Fort Henry Cannon (green) | 20 |
| 9153 | Motorcycle (4 pieces) | 150 |
| 9321 | Ford TW35 Powered Tractor (blue/white) | CRP |
| 9422 | Farm Tractor (green/yellow) | CRP |
| 9512 | Farm Land Rover (green/white) | CRP |
| 9514 | Massey Ferguson Tractor and Yardscraper (red/white) | CRP |
| 9515 | Valmet 805 Tractor (red/black) | CRP |
| 9517 | Massey Ferguson MF 2680 (red/white) | CRP |
| 9520 | Massey Ferguson 135 Tractor (red/white/black) | 50 |
| 9521 | Volvo BM 2654 Tractor (red) | 20 |
| 9522 | Massey Ferguson 595 Tractor (red/gray) | 40 |
| 9522 | Massey Ferguson 590 Tractor (red/gray) | 150 |
| 9524 | Ford 6600 Tractor (blue/gray) | 35 |
| 9525 | Fordson Super Major Tractor (blue/orange or blue/tan) | 110 |
| 9526 | Fordson Super Major Tractor (blue/orange) | 120 |
| 9526A | Deutz DX 110 Tractor (green/black) | 25 |
| 9527 | Ford Super Major 5000 (blue/gray) | 80 |
| 9527A | Ford 500 Tractor Square Cab (blue/gray) | 70 |
| 9527B | Ford Force 5000 Tractor (blue/gray) | 70 |
| 9527C | Ford Force 5000 Tractor with Cab (blue/gray) | 70 |
| 9527D | Fiat 880 DT Half-Track Tractor (dark red/gray) | 25 |
| 9528 | Fiat 880 DT Tractor (dark red/gray) | 25 |

| # | Name | Price |
|---|------|-------|
| 9528A | Hesston-Fiat 880 DT Tractor (dark red/gray) | $160 |
| 9529 | Massey Ferguson 135 Tractor (red/white/gray) | 50 |
| 9530 | 3 Furrow Mounted Plough (blue/yellow or orange/yellow) | 20 |
| 9533 | Roller (light blue) | 20 |
| 9534 | Disc Harrow (light blue) | 20 |
| 9535 | Mule Dozer (orange) | 20 |
| 9536 | Cultivator (red/yellow) | 20 |
| 9537 | Vicon Lely Rake (orange/gray) | 20 |
| 9538 | Vicon Spreader (maroon/yellow) | 20 |
| 9539 | Animal & Bale Transporter (brown) | 20 |
| 9540 | Massey Ferguson Manure Spreader (maroon/yellow or green/yellow) | 20 |
| 9542 | Forage Harvester (orange/green) | 20 |
| 9543 | Push Off Buckrake (maroon/yellow) | 20 |
| 9544 | Disc Mower (green/yellow) | 15 |
| 9546 | Plough Set (green) | 15 |
| 9548 | Crop Sprayer (maroon/gray/yellow) | 15 |
| 9549 | Heavy Roller (blue) | 15 |
| 9550 | Farm Trailer (green/orange) | 20 |
| 9551 | 4 Furrow Plough (green/red) | 25 |
| 9555 | Plough (blue) | 15 |
| 9556 | New Holland 376 Baler (red/gray) | 20 |
| 9556A | New Holland 377 Baler (red/gray) | 20 |
| 9557 | Bale Sledge (blue/yellow) | 15 |
| 9558 | 8 wheel Wagon (green/red) | 15 |
| 9559 | Timber Trailer (orange/gray) | 20 |
| 9560 | Timber Trailer (orange/gray) | 20 |
| 9561 | Bamford Heavy Cultivator (black/yellow) | 15 |
| 9563 | Bamford BL 58 Baler (blue/yellow) | 20 |
| 9566 | Forage Trailer (blue/orange/gray) | 20 |
| 9567 | Chafer Tank-Sprayer (yellow) | 15 |
| 9568 | Animal Transporter (red/gray/blue) | 15 |
| 9569 | Mercedes-Benz Unimog (green/yellow/black) | 15 |
| 9570 | Massey Ferguson 760 Combine Harvester (red) | 15 |
| 9571 | Land Rover Utility (blue/white) | 20 |
| 9572 | Massey Ferguson 125 Tractor & Loader (gray/yellow/red) | 30 |
| 9573 | Land Rover Set | 25 |
| 9574 | Front End Loader (gray/red/yellow) | 15 |
| 9575 | Land Rover & Horse Box Trailer (brown/blue) | 30 |

| # | Name | Price |
|---|------|-------|
| 9576 | Farm Land Rover (blue/white) | $20 |
| 9577 | Safari Land Rover (black/white) | 25 |
| 9580 | J.C.B. Excavator | 35 |
| 9580A | Animal Transporter (blue/white/red) | CRP |
| 9583 | Iveco Tipper Truck (red/gray) | CRP |
| 9594 | Safari Land Rover (black/white) | 25 |
| 9597 | Multi Set Ford | 40 |
| 9604 | Milk Transporter (blue/white) | CRP |
| 9610 | Police Land Rover (white/red) | 25 |
| 9629 | Dump Trailer (yellow) | 15 |
| 9630 | Fordson Super Major Industrial Tractor & Trailer (yellow) | 50 |
| 9630A | Ford Super Major 5000 Industrial Tractor (yellow) | 50 |
| 9670 | Dumper (red) | 20 |
| 9672 | Norton Military Motorcycle | 15 |
| 9674 | Chopper | 20 |
| 9675 | Chopper | 20 |
| 9676 | Civilian Land Rover (blue) | 25 |
| 9677 | Long Fork Chopper | 35 |
| 9678 | N.V. Agusta Motorcycle | 35 |
| 9679 | BMW Military Motorcycle | 25 |
| 9680 | Drag Chopper Motorcycle | 35 |
| 9681 | German Army Sidecar | 30 |
| 9682 | Harley-Davidson Military Motorcycle | 20 |
| 9683 | Drag Racing Motorcycle | 40 |
| 9684 | Speedway Motorcycle | 25 |
| 9685 | Lambretta Scooter | 75 |
| 9686 | Triumph Thunderbird Motorcycle | 40 |
| 9687 | Honda Motorcycle | 30 |
| 9688 | BMW 600 Motorcycle | 45 |
| 9689 | Harley-Davidson Motorcycle | 45 |
| 9690 | Triumph Thunderbird Motorcycle | 45 |
| 9691 | Greeves Challenger Motorcycle | 45 |
| 9692 | Harley-Davidson Motorcycle | 40 |
| 9693 | Honda Motorcycle | 40 |
| 9694 | BMW 600 Motorcycle | 45 |
| 9696 | Triumph Racing Motorcycle | 45 |
| 9697 | Triumph Police Motorcycle | 40 |
| 9698 | Triumph Military Motorcycle | 40 |
| 9699 | BMW Motorcycle with Sidecar | 55 |
| 9700 | Gun (dark green) | 20 |
| 9705 | Howitzer (dark green) | 15 |
| 9706 | A.A. Gun (dark green) | 15 |
| 9710 | Gun (dark green) | 25 |
| 9715 | Gun (dark green) | 20 |
| 9720 | Anti-Tank Gun (dark green) | 15 |

| # | Name | Price |
|---|------|-------|
| 9721 | Antique Gun (black) | $15 |
| 9724 | Howitzer (dark green) | 20 |
| 9725 | Howitzer (dark green) | 30 |
| 9726 | American Civil War Field Piece (brown) | 15 |
| 9730 | Naval Gun (dark green) | 50 |
| 9732 | German Field Gun PAK 38 (green) | 15 |
| 9735 | A.A. Gun (dark green) | 60 |
| 9736 | Naval Gun (brown/gold) | 15 |
| 9737 | Antique Gun (brown) | 15 |
| 9740 | Heavy Howitzer (dark green) | 50 |
| 9745 | U.S. 155 mm Gun (green) | 25 |
| 9748 | Gun Mounted on Centurion Tank (dark green) | 250 |
| 9750 | Anti-tank Gun (dark green) | 50 |
| 9760 | Austin Champ (dark green) | 70 |
| 9764 | Searchlight (dark green) | 50 |
| 9765 | Searchlight (dark green) | 80 |
| 9770 | Centurion Tank (dark green) | 280 |
| 9777 | Military Land Rover (dark green) | 30 |
| 9778 | Military LWB Land Rover (dark green) | 30 |
| 9781 | Scout Car (dark green) | 25 |
| 9782 | Military SWB Land Rover (dark green) | 35 |
| 9783 | Kubelwagen (dark green) | 25 |
| 9910 | Readymix Mercedes Truck Mixer (orange/black) | CRP |
| 9911 | Shell Petrol Tanker (Volvo) (yellow/white/red) | CRP |
| 9912 | Dynapac CA25 Road Roller (orange/black) | CRP |
| 9913 | J.C.B. Excavator (yellow/red) | CRP |
| 9914 | Redland Heavy Tipper (green/gray) | CRP |
| 9915 | Mercedes Breakdown Truck (white/red/black) | CRP |
| 9917 | Police Land Rover (white/black) | CRP |
| 9918 | J.C.B. Digger with man (yellow/red/black) | CRP |
| 9919 | Tipping Dump Truck (yellow) | CRP |
| 9940 | Atlas Copco Compressor with man (orange/black) | CRP |
| 9943 | Winget Cement Mixer (yellow/black) | CRP |
| 9944 | Pipe Transporter with pipes (yellow/black/white) | CRP |
| 9980 | Unimog and Pipe Transporter (orange/black/white) | CRP |
| 9981 | Land Rover and Safety Trailer (orange/white) | CRP |

# Brooklin

**B**rooklin Models Ltd. was started in the mid-1970s, in the village of Brooklin, in Ontario, Canada. John Hall, a long-time collector of toy and model cars, began hand-casting metal models for himself and fellow collectors. Within a few years he and his wife Jenny had built this part-time hobby into a full-time business. John's preference was (and is) for American cars, and the Brooklin line has always included both classics and rarities. In 1979 the Halls moved themselves and Brooklin Models Ltd. to Bath, England, where they have since built Brooklin into the leading hand-built white metal 1/43 scale model company in the world.

Brooklins are known for their high quality paint finish, smooth casting surfaces and weighty feel. They have become the de facto standard by which other white metal models are judged, and many of the early examples now command high prices on the collector market.

Over the years, some Brooklin models have been dropped from the line, while others have remained in production for many years. In addition, a number of the models have been produced in special colors and liveries for businesses or special events. This listing provides information on the basic models, with as much color and detail information as space will permit. *Note*: The first eight models were made in both Canada and the United Kingdom; Canadian examples generally cost anywhere from $100-$750. This listing is comprised of the United Kingdom-manufactured versions; it should be remembered that collectors often add "detailing" to Brooklin models, such as bare metal foil to highlight chrome features. While this type of work can enhance appearance, it does change the condition of the model from the original state. It is up to the individual as to whether he or she will pay more or less for the piece. For further information on Brooklin models, see Part Three, Additional Resources.

The "CRP" (Current Retail Price) for new Brooklins is $60-$70 in the United States; this is reflected in the values given for the models numbered from the high 20s until the end.

## Lansdowne and Robeddie

These two white metal 1/43 scale model series are also produced by Brooklin. Lansdowne is comprised of British automobiles and Robeddie is made up of Swedish marques. The two series are listed after the Brooklin listing.

*Brooklin #6, the 1932 Packard Light 8 Coupe. This is the earlier Canadian version.*

*1950s "space-age" design: Brooklin's 1957 Mercury Turnpike Cruiser. It's number 28 in the Brooklin series.*

| # | Name | Price |
|---|------|-------|
| BRK 1 | 1933 Pierce Arrow | |
| | silver . . . . . . . . . . . . . . . . | $300 |
| | light blue . . . . . . . . . . . . | 100 |
| BRK 2 | 1948 Tucker Torpedo | |
| | Maroon . . . . . . . . . . . . . . | 200 |
| | Gold . . . . . . . . . . . . . . | 60 |
| BRK 3 | 1930 Ford Victoria . . . . . . . . . . | 150 |
| BRK 4 | 1937 Chevrolet Coupe . . . . . . . . | 150 |
| BRK 5 | 1930 Ford Model A Coupe . . . . . . | 100 |
| BRK 6 | 1932 Packard Light 8 Coupe . . . . . | 150 |
| BRK 6A | 1932 Packard Light 8 Convertible . . | 60 |
| BRK 7 | 1934 Chrysler Airflow . . . . . . . . . | 75 |
| BRK 8 | 1941 Chrysler Newport Indianapolis | |
| | Pace Car white (Chrysler logo) . . . | 60 |
| BRK 9 | 1940 Ford Van | |
| | many liveries . . . . . . . . . . | 60-750 |
| BRK 10 | 1949 Buick Roadmaster . . . . . . . . | 75 |
| BRK 11 | 1956 Lincoln Continental Mark II | |
| | black . . . . . . . . . . . . . . . | 150 |
| | blue . . . . . . . . . . . . . . . | 60 |
| | convertible . . . . . . . . . . . . | 60 |
| BRK 11A | 1957 Lincoln Continental Mark II . . . . | 60 |
| BRK 12 | 1931 Hudson Greater 8 . . . . . . . . | 90 |
| BRK 13 | 1956 Ford Thunderbird | |
| | white . . . . . . . . . . . . . . | 100 |
| | red . . . . . . . . . . . . . . . | 60 |
| BRK 13A | 1956 Ford Thunderbird Convertible | |
| | green . . . . . . . . . . . . . . | 60 |
| BRK 14 | 1940 Cadillac V16 . . . . . . . . . . | 60 |
| BRK 15 | 1949 Mercury Coupe | |
| | cream . . . . . . . . . . . . . . | 200 |
| | blue or red . . . . . . . . . . . . | 115 |
| BRK 15A | 1949 Mercury Convertible . . . . . . . | 60 |
| BRK 16 | 1935 Dodge Van many liveries . . . | 60-500 |
| BRK 16A | 1935 Dodge Pick-up | |
| | many liveries . . . . . . . . . | 90-350 |
| BRK 17 | 1952 Studebaker Starlight Coupe . . . . | 85 |
| BRK 17A | 1952 Studebaker Starlight Convertible . . | 60 |
| BRK 18 | 1941 Packard Clipper red . . . . . . . | 60 |
| BRK 19 | 1955 Chrysler C300 . . . . . . . . . | 60 |
| BRK 20A | 1953 Buick Skylark . . . . . . . . . | 60 |
| BRK 21 | 1963 Corvette Stingray white . . . . . | 60 |

*Number 8 in Brooklin's Lansdowne series is the 1954 Triumph Renown.*

| # | Name | Price |
|---|------|-------|
| BRK 22A | 1958 Edsel Citation . . . . . . . . . . | $60 |
| BRK 23 | 1956 Ford Fairlane . . . . . . . . . | 60 |
| BRK 24A | 1968 Ford Mustang Fastback . . . . . | 60 |
| BRK 25A | 1958 Pontiac Bonneville . . . . . . . | 60 |
| BRK 26 | 1955 Chevrolet Nomad . . . . . . . | 60 |
| BRK 26A | 1955 Chevrolet Nomad Fire Car . . . | 90 |
| BRK 27 | 1957 Cadillac Eldorado . . . . . . . | 60 |
| BRK 28 | 1957 Mercury Turnpike Cruiser . . . . | 60 |
| BRK 29 | 1953 Kaiser Manhattan . . . . . . . | 40 |
| BRK 30A | 1954 Dodge Royal 500 Convertible | |
| | top up . . . . . . . . . . . . . | 60 |
| BRK 30A | 1954 Dodge Royal 500 Convertible | |
| | top down . . . . . . . . . . . . | 60 |
| BRK 31A | 1953 Pontiac van "Mobiloil" . . . . . | 60 |
| BRK 31B | 1953 Pontiac van "Sunoco" . . . . . | 60 |
| BRK 32 | 1953 Studebaker Starliner . . . . . | 60 |
| BRK 32A | 1953 Studebaker 2 Tone . . . . . . | 60 |
| BRK 33 | 1938 Phantom Corsair . . . . . . . | 60 |
| BRK 34 | 1954 Nash Ambassador maroon . . . | 60 |
| BRK 34A | 1954 Nash Ambassador 2 tone . . . | 60 |
| BRK 35 | 1957 Ford Skyliner . . . . . . . . . | 60 |
| BRK 36 | 1952 Hudson Hornet . . . . . . . . | 60 |

| # | Name | Price |
|---|------|-------|
| BRK 37 | 1960 Ford Sunliner . . . . . . . . . . | $60 |
| BRK 38 | 1939 Graham Sharknose . . . . . . . | 60 |
| BRK 39 | 1953 Oldsmobile Fiesta . . . . . . . | 60 |
| BRK 40 | 1948 Cadillac Sedanet . . . . . . . | 60 |
| BRK 41 | 1959 Chrysler 300E Convertible . . . . | 60 |
| BRK 42 | 1952 Ford F1 Ambulance . . . . . . | 60 |
| BRK 43 | 1948 Packard Station Sedan . . . . . | 60 |
| BRK 44 | 1961 Chevrolet Impala . . . . . . . | 60 |
| BRK 45 | 1948 Buick Roadmaster Convertible . . | 60 |
| BRK 46 | 1959 Chevrolet El Camino . . . . . . | 60 |
| BRK 47 | 1965 Ford Thunderbird . . . . . . . | 60 |
| BRK 48 | 1958 Chevrolet Impala . . . . . . . | 60 |
| BRK 49 | 1954 Hudson Italia . . . . . . . . . | 60 |
| BRK 50 | 1948 Chevrolet Aero Sedan . . . . . | 60 |
| BRK 51 | 1951 Ford Victoria . . . . . . . . . | 60 |
| BRK 52 | 1941 Hupmobile Skylark . . . . . . . | 60 |
| BRK 53 | 1955 Chevrolet Cameo Pick-up . . . . | 60 |
| BRK 54 | 1953 Airstream Wanderer . . . . . . | 60 |
| BRK 55 | 1951 Packard Mayfair . . . . . . . . | 60 |

**Lansdowne Models:**

| | | |
|---|------|---|
| LDM 1 | 1958 Austin Healey Sprite Mk 1 . . . | 60 |
| LDM 2 | 1957 Vauxhall Cresta . . . . . . . . | 60 |
| LDM 3 | 1956 MG Magnette 2A . . . . . . . | 60 |
| LDM 4 | 1962 Morris Mini Van "Lansdowne" . . | 60 |
| LDM 5 | 1957 Rover 90 P4 . . . . . . . . . | 60 |
| LDM 6 | 1961 Wolseley 6/110 . . . . . . . . | 60 |
| LDM 7 | 1951 Ford Zephyr Zodiac . . . . . . | 60 |
| LDM 8 | 1954 Triumph Renown . . . . . . . . | 60 |

**Robeddie Models:**

| | | |
|---|------|---|
| RE 1 | 1969 Volvo P1800S . . . . . . . . . . | 70 |
| RE 2 | 1973 Volvo 144GL . . . . . . . . . | 70 |
| RE 3 | 1969 Saab 99 . . . . . . . . . . | 70 |
| RE 4 | 1950 Volvo PV831 . . . . . . . . . | 70 |
| RE 5 | 1950 Volvo PV60 . . . . . . . . . | 70 |
| RE 6 | 1964 Volvo PV544 . . . . . . . . . | 70 |
| RE 7 | 1954 Volvo PV445 Duett . . . . . . . | 70 |
| RE 8 | 1953 Volvo PV544 Van . . . . . . . | 70 |
| RE 9 | 1957 Volvo Amazon 120 . . . . . . . | 70 |

*This is a Canadian version of number 4 in the Brooklin line, the 1937 Chevrolet Coupe.*

# Brumm

**B**rumm is an Italian firm that entered the 1/43 scale die cast model scene in 1972. Of the four lines of models they make, the "Revival" series is the largest and perhaps best-known. It is made up of Ferraris, Fiats and Lancias, naturally enough, with many of the models being vintage racing cars including examples from Grand Prix racing of the 1930s-1960s. The line also includes some obscure and interesting models of Fiat passenger cars.

The other three lines appear to be out of production now, but most of the models are still available on the secondary market at or near their original retail price. The "Old

Fire" series is comprised of early steam-powered vehicles of the 17th, 18th and 19th centuries; the "Brumm" series is a group of horse-drawn models; and the "Historical" series also is made up of horse-drawn vehicles.

Brumm also issues "Limited Edition" models from time to time. These are generally existing models done in a new color or race livery.

Most Brumm models have interiors and windows, and the tires are rubber. Accuracy and quality of these models are generally very good for the price ($15-$20, which is the CRP noted in the listings).

| # | Name | Price |
|---|------|-------|
| **Revival series:** | | |
| R1 | 1923 Morgan Sport Open | CRP |
| R2 | 1923 Morgan Sport Closed | CRP |
| R3 | 1929 Darmont Sport Open | CRP |
| R4 | 1929 Darmont Sport Closed | CRP |
| R5 | 1913 Bedelia Sport Open | CRP |
| R6 | 1913 Bedelia Sport Closed | CRP |
| R7 | 1922 Sanford Sport Open | CRP |
| R8 | 1922 Sanford Sport Closed | CRP |
| R9 | 1904 Fiat 75 HP Corsa | CRP |
| R10 | 1905 Fiat 110 HP Corsa | CRP |
| R11 | 1911 Fiat S74 Corsa | CRP |
| R12 | 1949 Fiat 500 C Open | CRP |
| R13 | 1949 Fiat 500 C Closed | CRP |
| R14 | 1923 Fiat Eldridge | CRP |
| R15 | 1902 Ford 999 Corsa | CRP |
| R16 | 1907 Fiat F2 Corsa Grand Prix | CRP |
| R17 | 1908 Fiat S61 Corsa | CRP |
| R18 | 1906 Renault G.P. 3B | CRP |
| R19 | 1909 Benz (Blitzen) | CRP |
| R20 | 1906 Locomobile "Old 16" Corsa | CRP |
| R21 | 1936 Fiat 500 Prima Serie | CRP |
| R22 | 1936 Fiat 500 Prima Serie | CRP |
| R23 | 1936 Fiat 500 Prima Serie | CRP |
| R24 | 1949-55 Fiat 500 Pompieri | CRP |
| R25 | 1905 Ford 999 Rekord | CRP |
| R26 | 1911 A.L.F.A. Corsa | CRP |
| R27 | 1903 Renault Parigi-Madrid | CRP |
| R28 | 1951-55 Fiat 500 C "Belvedere" | CRP |
| R29 | 1951-55 Fiat 500 C "Belvedere" | CRP |
| R30 | 1937-39 Fiat 1100 (508 C) | CRP |
| R31 | 1937-39 Fiat 1100 (508 C) | CRP |
| R32 | 1937-39 Fiat 1100 (508 C) | CRP |
| R33 | 1937-39 Fiat 1100 (508 C) | CRP |
| R34 | 1937-39 Fiat 1100 | CRP |
| R35 | 1952 Ferrari 500/F2 | CRP |
| R36 | 1950 Alfa Romeo 158 | CRP |
| R37 | 1939 Mercedes "W 154" M 163 K Gran Prix | CRP |
| R38 | 1936 Auto Union 12 Cilindri Mot. post. | CRP |
| R39 | 1921 Bugatti "Brescia" | CRP |
| R40 | 1921 Bugatti "Brescia" | CRP |
| R41 | 1933 Bugatti "Type 59" | CRP |
| R42 | Bugatti "Type 59" Biposto | CRP |
| R43 | 1951 Alfa Romeo 159 | CRP |
| R44 | 1952 Ferrari 500/F2 | CRP |
| R45 | 1946-49 Fiat 500 B | CRP |
| R46 | 1946-49 Fiat 500 B | CRP |
| R47 | 1937 Fiat 500 A | CRP |
| R48 | 1949 Fiat 500 C | CRP |
| R49 | Furgoncino Fiat 500 C | CRP |
| R50 | 1949 Fiat 500 C | CRP |
| R51 | Furgoncino Fiat 500 B | CRP |
| R52 | 1946-49 Fiat 500 B | CRP |
| R53 | Furgoncino Fiat 500 C | CRP |
| R54 | 1949-55 Fiat 500 C | CRP |
| R55 | Furgoncino Fiat 500 B | CRP |
| R56 | Furgoncino Fiat 500 B | CRP |
| R57 | Furgoncino Fiat 500 C | CRP |
| R58 | 1936-48 Lancia Aprilia | CRP |
| R59 | 1939-48 Lancia Aprilia | CRP |
| R60 | 1939-44 Lancia Aprilia | CRP |
| R61 | 1947 Lancia Aprilia | CRP |
| R62 | 1937-39 Fiat 1100 (508 C) | CRP |
| R63 | 1937-39 Fiat 1100 (508 C) | CRP |
| R64 | 1948-49 Fiat 1100 B | CRP |
| R65 | 1949-53 Fiat 1100 E | CRP |
| R66 | 1940 Ferrari 815 Sport | CRP |
| R67 | 1940 Ferrari 815 Sport | CRP |
| R68 | 1958 Ferrari D 246 | CRP |
| R69 | 1958 Ferrari D 246 | CRP |
| R70 | 1937 Mercedes W 125 | CRP |
| R71 | 1938 Mercedes W 125 | CRP |
| R72 | 1954-60 Mercedes W 196 | CRP |
| R73 | 1911 Blitzen Benz | CRP |
| R74 | 1948 Talbot Lago F/1 | CRP |
| R75 | 1939 Maserati 8 cil. | CRP |
| R76 | 1956 Ferrari-Lancia D 50 | CRP |
| R77 | 1931 Alfa Romeo 2300 8 cil. | CRP |
| R78 | 1932 Alfa Romeo 2300 8 cil. | CRP |
| R79 | 1949-55 Fiat 500 B | CRP |
| R80 | 1949-55 Fiat 500 C | CRP |
| R81 | 1911 Benz (Blitzen) | CRP |
| R82 | 1921 Bugatti Brescia | CRP |
| R83 | 1937-39 Fiat 1100 (508 C) | CRP |

*Brumm number R108, a model of Germany's 1937 Auto Union Rekordwagen Grand Prix car.*

| # | Name | Price |
|---|------|-------|
| R84 | Fiat 1100 (508 C) | CRP |
| R85 | Fiat 1100 (508 C) | CRP |
| R86 | Fiat 1100 (508 C) | CRP |
| R87 | Bugatti 57-S | CRP |
| R88 | Bugatti 57-S | CRP |
| R89 | Alfa Romeo 1900 | CRP |
| R90 | Alfa Romeo 1900 | CRP |
| R91 | Alfa Romeo 1900 | CRP |
| R92 | 1957 Maserati 250 F | CRP |
| R93 | Ferrari Testa Rossa | CRP |
| R94 | Ferrari Testa Rossa | CRP |
| R95 | 1951 Lancia Aurelia | CRP |
| R96 | Lancia Aurelia | CRP |
| R97 | Lancia Aurelia | CRP |
| R98 | Vanwall F.1 | CRP |
| R99 | 1930 Bentley | CRP |
| R100 | 1930 Bentley | CRP |
| R101 | 1948 Jaguar XK 120 Roadster | CRP |
| R102 | Jaguar XK 120 | CRP |
| R103 | Jaguar XK 120 | CRP |
| R104 | Jaguar XK 120 | CRP |
| R105 | Jaguar XK 120 | CRP |
| R106 | Jaguar XK 120 | CRP |
| R107 | 1935 Auto Union Rekordwagen | CRP |
| R108 | 1937 Auto Union | CRP |
| R109 | 1938 Auto Union Tipo D | CRP |
| R110 | 1936 Auto Union | CRP |
| R111 | 1940 Maserati 8 cil. | CRP |
| R112 | 1938 Maserati 8 cil. | CRP |
| R113 | 1951 Talbot Lago F1 | CRP |
| R114 | 1932 Bentley | CRP |
| R115 | 1905 Darracq V8 | CRP |
| R116 | 1905 Napier 6 | CRP |
| R117 | Porsche "Speedster" | CRP |
| R117 | Porsche "Speedster" | CRP |
| R118 | 1952 Porsche 356 | CRP |
| R119 | 1952 Porsche 356 | CRP |
| R120 | 1952 Porsche 356 | CRP |
| R121 | 1952 Porsche 356 | CRP |
| R122 | 1957 Ferrari 801 | CRP |
| R123 | 1961 Ferrari 156 | CRP |
| R124 | 1961 Ferrari 156 | CRP |
| R125 | 1951 Ferrari 375 F1 | CRP |
| R126 | 1952 Ferrari 375 | CRP |
| R127 | 1956 Lancia Ferrari D50 | CRP |
| R128 | 1956 Lancia Ferrari D50 | CRP |
| R129 | 1954 Jaguar D-Type | CRP |
| R130 | 1954 Jaguar D-Type | CRP |
| R131 | 1955 Lancia B 24 | CRP |
| R132 | 1955 Lancia B 24 | CRP |
| R133 | 1956 Lancia B 24 | CRP |
| R134 | 1956 Lancia B 24 | CRP |
| R135 | 1957 Maserati 250 F | CRP |
| R136 | 1957 Maserati 250 F | CRP |
| R137 | 1957 Maserati 250 F | CRP |
| R138 | 1931 Alfa Romeo 2300 8 cil. | CRP |
| R139 | 1938 Alfa Romeo 8C 2900 B | CRP |
| R140 | 1938 Alfa Romeo 8C 2900 B | CRP |
| R141 | 1938 Alfa Romeo 8C 2900 B | CRP |
| R142 | Ferrari 126C4 | CRP |
| R143 | Ferrari 126C4 | CRP |

| # | Name | Price |
|---|------|-------|
| R144 | 1952 Porsche 356 | CRP |
| R145 | 1954 Alfa Romeo 1900 | CRP |
| R146 | 1957 Jaguar D-Type | CRP |
| R147 | 1955 Jaguar D-Type | CRP |
| R148 | 1954 Jaguar D-Type | CRP |
| R149 | 1956 Jaguar D-Type | CRP |
| R150 | 1956 Jaguar D-Type | CRP |
| R151 | 1956 Jaguar D-Type | CRP |
| R152 | 1956 Jaguar D-Type | CRP |
| R153 | 1957 Jaguar D-Type | CRP |
| R154 | 1960 Jaguar D-Type | CRP |
| R155 | Ferrari Testa Rossa | CRP |
| R156 | Ferrari Testa Rossa | CRP |
| R157 | 1966 Ferrari 330 P3 | CRP |
| R158 | 1966 Ferrari 330 P3 | CRP |
| R159 | 1967 Ferrari 330 P4 | CRP |
| R160 | 1967 Ferrari 330 P4 | CRP |
| R161 | 1967 Ferrari 330 P4 | CRP |
| R162 | 1951 Lancia Aurelia B20 | CRP |
| R163 | 1953 Jaguar XK120 | CRP |
| R164 | 1953 Jaguar XK120 | CRP |
| R165 | 1956-58 Fiat 1400 B | CRP |
| R166 | 1956-58 Fiat 1400 B | CRP |
| R167 | 1953 Ferrari 500/F.2 | CRP |
| R168 | 1952 Ferrari 375 | CRP |
| R169 | 1936 Bugatti 57S | CRP |
| R170 | 1936 Bugatti 57S | CRP |
| R171 | 1968 Ferrari 312/F.1 | CRP |
| R172 | 1968 Ferrari 312/F.1 | CRP |
| R173 | 1933 Bugatti "Type 59" | CRP |
| R174 | 1933 Bugatti "Type 59" | CRP |
| R175 | 1947 Mercedes "W154" | CRP |
| R176 | 1956 Simca 5 | CRP |
| R177 | 1947-48 Fiat 1100E furgone | CRP |
| R178 | Fiat 1100E furgone | CRP |
| R179 | Fiat 1100E furgone | CRP |
| R180 | Fiat 1100E furgone | CRP |
| R181 | Fiat 1100E | CRP |
| R182 | 1947 Ferrari 125 | CRP |
| R183 | 1947 Ferrari 125 | CRP |
| R184 | 1928 Bentley speed six "Barnato" | CRP |
| R185 | 1928 Bentley speed six | CRP |
| R186 | 1955 Lancia B24 | CRP |
| R187 | 1955 Mercedes 300 SLR | CRP |
| R188 | Mercedes 300 SLR | CRP |
| R189 | Mercedes 300 SLR | CRP |
| R190 | Mercedes 300 SLR | CRP |
| R191 | 1951 Ferrari 375 | CRP |
| R192 | 1951 Ferrari 375 | CRP |
| R193 | 1956 Porsche 550 | CRP |
| R194 | 1955 Porsche 550 | CRP |
| R195 | 1954 Porsche 550 | CRP |
| R196 | 1955 Ferrari 555 F.1 | CRP |
| R197 | 1954 Ferrari 555 F.1 | CRP |
| R198 | 1952 Porsche 356 | CRP |
| R199 | Vanwall F.1 | CRP |
| R200 | 1970 Ferrari 512 S | CRP |
| R201 | 1970 Ferrari 512 S | CRP |
| R202 | 1970 Ferrari 512 S | CRP |
| R203 | 1971 Ferrari 512 S | CRP |
| R204 | 1954 Lancia D24 | CRP |

| # | Name | Price |
|---|------|-------|
| R205 | 1953 Lancia D24 | CRP |
| R206 | 1953 Porsche 356 | CRP |
| R207 | Porsche 356 | CRP |
| R208 | 1952 Porsche 356 | CRP |
| R209 | 1954 Lancia D24 | CRP |
| R210 | 1979 Ferrari 512 BB LM | CRP |
| R211 | 1981 Ferrari 512 BB LM | CRP |
| R212 | 1980 Ferrari 512 BB LM | CRP |
| R213 | 1981 Ferrari 512 BB LM | CRP |
| R214 | 1980 Ferrari 512 BB LM | CRP |
| R215 | 1949-53 Fiat 1100E | CRP |
| R216 | 1956-58 Fiat 1400B | CRP |
| R217 | Porsche 917 | CRP |
| R218 | Porsche 917 | CRP |
| R219 | Porsche 917 | CRP |
| R220 | Porsche 917 | CRP |
| R221 | Porsche 917 | CRP |
| R222 | Ferrari 156 | CRP |
| R223 | Maserati 250/12 cil. | CRP |
| R224 | Porsche 356C | CRP |
| R225 | Porsche 356C | CRP |
| R226 | Porsche 356C | CRP |
| R227 | Ferrari 512M | CRP |
| R228 | Ferrari 512M | CRP |
| R229 | Ferrari 512M | CRP |
| R230 | Ferrari 512M | CRP |
| R231 | Ferrari 512M | CRP |
| R232 | Porsche 550 RS | CRP |
| R233 | Porsche 550 RS | CRP |
| R234 | Porsche 550 RS | CRP |
| R235 | Porsche 550 RS | CRP |
| R236 | Porsche 550 RS | CRP |

**Old Fire series:**

| # | Name | Price |
|---|------|-------|
| X1 | Cugnot's Steam Wagon | CRP |
| X2 | Newton's Cart | CRP |
| X3 | Gurney's Carriage | CRP |
| X4 | Trevithick's Carriage | CRP |
| X5 | Bordino's Carriage | CRP |
| X6 | Verbiest's Turbine Vehicle | CRP |
| X7 | Pecquer's Truck | CRP |
| X8 | Evans's Amphibian | CRP |
| X9 | Fourness' Cart | CRP |
| X10 | Pagani's Locomotive | CRP |

**Brumm series:**

| # | Name | Price |
|---|------|-------|
| 1 | Closed Landaulet | CRP |
| 2 | Open Landaulet | CRP |
| 3 | Landaulet Coupe | CRP |
| 4 | Dormeuse Coupe | CRP |
| 5 | Closed Landau | CRP |
| 6 | Open Landau | CRP |
| 7 | Spyder (top up) | CRP |
| 8 | Spyder (top down) | CRP |
| 9 | Phaeton (top up) | CRP |
| 10 | Phaeton (top down) | CRP |
| 11 | Open Dog Cart | CRP |
| 12 | Vis-a-Vis (top up) | CRP |
| 13 | Vis-a-Vis (top down) | CRP |
| 14 | Milord (top up) | CRP |
| 15 | Milord (top down) | CRP |
| 16 | 9-Spring Coupe | CRP |

| # | Name | Price |
|---|------|-------|
| 17 | Mail Coach | CRP |
| 18 | 8-Spring Duc (top up) | CRP |
| 19 | Brumm di Milan | CRP |
| 20 | Papal Carriage | CRP |
| 21 | London Cab | CRP |
| 22 | Dress Chariot | CRP |
| 23 | Post Chaise | CRP |
| 24 | Royal Mail Coach | CRP |
| 25 | Tilbury | CRP |
| 26 | Napolean's Coach | CRP |

**Historical series:**

| # | Name | Price |
|---|------|-------|
| 0 | One Horse | CRP |

| # | Name | Price |
|---|------|-------|
| 01 | Two Horses | CRP |
| 02 | Four Horses | CRP |
| 03 | Brumm de Milan and one horse | CRP |
| 04 | Papal Carriage and four horses | CRP |
| 05 | Napolean III's Duc and four horses | CRP |
| 06 | Mail Coach and four horses | CRP |
| 07 | Cab Dell Atrice and one horse | CRP |
| 08 | Pauline Bonaparte's Dormeuse | CRP |
| 09 | Emile Loubet's Phaeton | CRP |
| 010 | Gran Gala Vis-a-Vis and four horses | CRP |
| 011 | Wilhelm II's Dog Cart and one horse | CRP |
| 012 | Botticella de Roma and one horse | CRP |

| # | Name | Price |
|---|------|-------|
| 013 | Earl of Caledonia's Dress Chariot and four horses | CRP |
| 014 | Empress Eugenie's Milord and one horse | CRP |
| 015 | George Sand's Spyder and one horse | CRP |
| 016 | English Mail Coach and one horse | CRP |
| 017 | Bavarian Landau and four horses | CRP |
| 018 | Royal Mail Coach and four horses | CRP |
| 019 | Tilbury and two horses | CRP |
| 020 | Portantina Sedan Chair and two horses | CRP |
| 021 | Napolean's Coach and four horses | CRP |

# Buby

Not exactly known as a hotbed of die cast manufacturing, Argentina has nevertheless produced its share of toy and model cars. Buby may be the best-known of these, having apparently started production of its 1/43 scale series around 1960. Included in this series were both American and European models.

The company also launched a line of 1/64 scale die casts around 1970. It is not known how long these were in production, although a number of them were still being produced in the late 1970s. Fit and finish of Bubys ranged from fair to good; certainly, the 1/43 scale models suffered in comparison to the Corgi and Dinky products of the day.

This listing includes the 1/43 and 1/64 models that are known to have been produced.

*This is Buby #1037, the Fiat 128 Rally car. Like many Bubys, it featured opening doors and hoods.*

**1/43 scale:**

| # | Name | Price |
|---|------|-------|
| 1000 | Buick Century Ambulance (white) | $100 |
| 1000A | Buick Century Army Ambulance (green) | 100 |
| 1001 | Buick Century Station Wagon (blue/white) | 100 |
| 1002 | Ford Fairlane 500 (blue/white) | 100 |
| 1002A | Ford Fairlane 500 Rally (red) | 100 |
| 1002B | Ford Fairlane 500 "El Corsaro" (red) | 100 |
| 1003 | Ford Fairlane 500 Policia (blue/white) | 100 |
| 1004 | Ford F 100 Pickup (red) | 60 |
| 1004A | Army Pickup (green) | 60 |
| 1004B | Covered Pickup (blue/black, green/black) | 60 |
| 1005 | Volkswagen 1200 (gray, red, black) | 110 |
| 1006 | Ford F 100 Wrecker (yellow) | 50 |
| 1007 | Willys Jeep Station Wagon (red, blue, brown) | 140 |
| 1008 | Mercedes-Benz 300 SL Roadster (silver, red, blue) | 60 |

| # | Name | Price |
|---|------|-------|
| 1008A | Mercedes-Benz 300 SL Roadster Rally (white, red) | $60 |
| 1009 | Chevrolet Impala (pink/white, blue/white) | 60 |
| 1010 | Chevrolet Bel Air (blue/white) | 60 |
| 1010A | Chevrolet Bel Air Taxi (yellow, yellow/black) | 75 |
| 1010B | Chevrolet Bel Air Policia (blue/white) | 50 |
| 1011 | Renault Dauphine (yellow, green, red, cream, blue) | 50 |
| 1011A | Renault Dauphine Rally (green, blue, yellow, red) | 50 |
| 1012 | Mercedes-Benz 220 SE (gray, blue, red) | 50 |
| 1012A | Mercedes-Benz 220 SE Rally (red) | 50 |
| 1013 | Mercedes-Benz 220 SE A.C.A. (red, blue, yellow, green) | 50 |
| 1014 | Fiat 1500 D (gray, red) | 50 |
| 1014A | Fiat 1500 D Rally (gold) | 50 |
| 1015 | Fiat 1500 D (blue, gray, red) | 50 |

| # | Name | Price |
|---|------|-------|
| 1015A | Fiat 1500 D Rally (gold, red) | $50 |
| 1016 | Pontiac GTO (red, beige, orange) | 80 |
| 1016A | Pontiac GTO Rally (red, beige, orange) | 80 |
| 1017 | Fiat 1500D Pickup (red, gray, blue) | 75 |
| 1018 | Mercedes-Benz L 114 Truck (yellow/gray, blue/gray, green/gray) | 60 |
| 1019 | Mercedes-Benz L 114 Tipping Truck (blue/orange, yellow/orange) | 60 |
| 1020 | Ford Falcon (red, blue, light blue, beige) | 50 |
| 1020A | Ford Falcon (blue, green, white) | 30 |
| 1021 | Ford Falcon Rally (beige, yellow/black) | 40 |
| 1021A | Ford Falcon Rally (blue, green) | 25 |
| 1021B | Ford Falcon Policia - early '60s (blue/white) | 50 |
| 1021C | Ford Falcon Policia - 1970 (blue/white) | 30 |
| 1021D | Ford Falcon TC Rally (blue, green, beige) | 25 |
| 1022 | IKA Renault Torino 380W (yellow, orange, blue) | 35 |

*The box for the #1037 Fiat Rally car.*

*Buby #1021A Ford Falcon Rally car, with "speed"-type wheels.*

| # | Name | Price |
|---|------|-------|
| 1022A | IKA Renault Torino 380W (red) | $30 |
| 1023 | IKA Renault Torino TC (blue, orange, silver, white) | 30 |
| 1025 | Fiat 125 (red, blue, white, silver, yellow) | 35 |
| 1025A | Fiat 125 Rally (white, red/black, orange/black) | 25 |
| 1028 | Fiat 1600 (blue, brown, gold, red, cream) | 40 |
| 1029 | Fiat 1600 Rally - 1968 (yellow, cream) | 40 |
| 1030 | Peugeot 504 (brown, green) | 40 |
| 1030A | Peugeot 504 (blue, white, green, gold) | 25 |
| 1031 | Peugeot 504 Rally - 1969 (yellow/black) | 40 |
| 1031A | Peugeot 504 Rally - 1973 (red, gray, green) | 25 |
| 1032 | Chevrolet Chevy Nova (red, blue, yellow, green) | 40 |
| 1033 | Chevrolet Chevy Nova Rally (orange, green, yellow/black) | 40 |
| 1034 | Renault 6 (green, red, cream) | 20 |
| 1035 | Renault 6 Rally Assistance (red) | 20 |
| 1035A | Renault 6 A.C.A. (yellow) | 20 |
| 1036 | Fiat 128 (red, blue, white, green, cream) | 25 |
| 1037 | Fiat 128 Rally (blue/black, orange/black, cream, white) | 25 |
| 1037A | Fiat 128 TV IAVA (cream) | 25 |
| 1038 | Fiat Concorde 700 S Tractor (orange/blue) | 75 |
| 1041 | Pontiac GTO Stock Car (blue, white, orange, green) | 60 |
| 1043 | IKA Renault Torino Policia (blue) | 25 |
| 1044 | IKA Renault Torino Policia (white) | 25 |
| 1045 | Ford Falcon Taxi - 1970 (yellow/black) | 30 |
| 1046 | Chevrolet Camaro TL (blue, red) | 35 |
| 1047 | Chevrolet Camaro TL Rally (white) | 35 |
| 1051 | Peugeot 504 Firecar (red) | 25 |
| 105 | Mercedes-Benz 190 SL Roadster (red) | 60 |
| 106 | Alfa Romeo Giulietta Roadster (light green) | 60 |
| 122 | Ferrari 156 Formula I (red) | 55 |
| 125 | Alfa Romeo 2600 Coupe Bertone (cream) | 55 |
| 151 | Porsche Carrera 6 (orange) | 50 |
| 157 | BMW 2000 CS (white) | 45 |
| 164 | Simca 1100 (blue) | 40 |

| # | Name | Price |
|---|------|-------|
| 165 | Ferrari 365 GTB4 (red) | $60 |
| 169 | Chaparral 2F (white) | 40 |
| 171 | Opel GT 1900 (blue) | 40 |
| 180 | Mercedes-Benz C 111 (orange) | 40 |
| 181 | Alpine Renault A 110 (SE/SU/WN) (white) | 45 |
| 197 | Ferrari 512 M (red) | 60 |
| 16 | Ferrari Daytona (orange) | 60 |
| 18 | Porsche 917/10 TC (orange) | 50 |
| 21 | Matra Simca Bagheera (blue) | 40 |
| 22 | Renault 12 Station Wagon (light green) | 25 |
| 22A | Renault 12 Station Wagon A.C.A. (yellow) | 25 |
| 26 | Ford Capri 2600 RV (orange) | 25 |
| 27 | Lancia Stratos (orange) | 25 |
| 42 | Renault 4 Van "A.C.A." (yellow/black) | 25 |
| 42A | Renault 4 Paris Fire Van (red) | 25 |
| 42B | Renault 4 Fire Van (red) | 25 |
| 44 | Ferrari BB (yellow/red) | 50 |
| 49 | Porsche 928 (yellow) | 35 |
| 50 | Peugeot 504 Rally (green) | 20 |
| 52 | Lancia Beta Coupe (orange) | 20 |
| 56 | Citroen 2 CV 6 (light green) | 20 |
| 57 | Alpine Renault A 442 Turbo (light green) | 20 |
| 58 | Renault 5 Alpine (white) | 20 |
| 63 | Porsche 911 Turbo (beige) | 20 |
| 66 | Land Rover 109 (blue) | 20 |
| 75 | BMW 3000 CSL (yellow/blue) | 20 |

**1/64 scale:**

| # | Name | Price |
|---|------|-------|
| 1 | Valiant Sedan (plastic) | 30 |
| 1A | Ford Falcon Policia - 1963 (blue) | 15 |
| 2 | Ford Falcon Argentine Type (red) | 15 |
| 3 | Fiat 600 E (red) | 15 |
| 4 | Fiat 1500 D (blue) | 15 |
| 5 | Peugeot 404 (red) | 15 |
| 6 | Citroen 3CV (pink) | 15 |
| 7 | IKA Renault Torino 380 W (green) | 15 |
| 8 | Chevrolet Nova (red) | 15 |
| 9 | Citroen Ami 8 Station Wagon (blue) | 15 |
| 10 | Mercedes-Benz L 114 Truck (yellow/gray) | 15 |
| 11 | Mc Laren-Ford (SE/SU) (red) | 15 |
| 12 | Fiat 128 Saloon (white) | 15 |
| 13 | Peugeot 504 (red, blue) | 15 |

| # | Name | Price |
|---|------|-------|
| 14 | Renault 12 (red) | $15 |
| 15 | Fiat 697N Covered Truck & Trailer (orange/gray/green) | 25 |
| 16 | Fiat 697N Cement Truck (blue/gray, yellow/gray) | 25 |
| 17 | Fiat 697N Crane Truck (orange/yellow) | 25 |
| 18 | Ford Falcon Competition (red) | 15 |
| 19 | Fiat 600 E Rally (red) | 15 |
| 20 | Fiat 1500 D Competition (yellow) | 15 |
| 21 | Peugeot 404 Competition (red) | 15 |
| 22 | Citroen 3 CV Rally (white/black) | 15 |
| 23 | IKA Renault Torino 380 W Rally (green) | 15 |
| 24 | Chevrolet Nova Rally - 1968 (red) | 15 |
| 25 | Fiat 128 Rally - 1973 (SE/SU/RN) (white) | 15 |
| 26 | Peugeot 504 Rally (blue) | 15 |
| 27 | Renault 12 Rally (red) | 15 |
| 28 | Peugeot 404 Taxi (yellow/black) | 15 |
| 29 | Peugeot 504 Firecar (red) | 15 |
| 30 | Maserati Indy (blue) | 15 |
| 31 | Maserati Indy "A Team" (white) | 15 |
|  | Centurion Tank (1/60) (dark green) | 75 |
| 1030 | Maserati INDY Coupe | 15 |
| 1030 | Maserati INDY Coupe | 15 |
| 1040 | Mercedes-Benz 350SL Coupe | 15 |
| 1040 | Mercedes-Benz 350SL Coupe | 15 |
| 1041 | Mercedes-Benz 350SL Coupe Rally | 15 |
| 1050 | Ford Mustang II | 15 |
| 1051 | Ford Mustang "Dukes of Hazzard" | 15 |
| 1052 | Ford Mustang II Cobra | 15 |
| 1060 | Citroën 3CV Sedan | 15 |
| 1070 | Ford Sierra | 15 |
| 1081 | Chevrolet Nova Sedan | 15 |
| 1090 | Maserati Bora Coupe | 15 |
| 1091 | Maserati Bora Rally | 15 |
| 1120 | Volkswagen Gacel Sedan | 15 |
| 1140 | Renault 12 Sedan | 15 |
| 1141 | Renault 12 Rally | 15 |
| 1160 | Renault 18 Sedan | 15 |
| 1161 | Renault 18 "Policia" | 15 |
| 1162 | Renault 18 "Marlboro" | 15 |
| 1170 | Renault 12 Wagon | 15 |
| 1171 | Renault 12 "Rescue" | 15 |
| 1180 | 1964 Opel Kapitan Ambulance | 15 |

| # | Name | Price | # | Name | Price | # | Name | Price |
|---|------|-------|---|------|-------|---|------|-------|
| 1190 | Ford F100 Tow Truck | $15 | 1240 | Renault Fuego Coupe | $15 | 2020 | Chevrolet C60 "Esso" Oil | $15 |
| 1212 | VW BUGGY "Dufour" | 15 | 1241 | Renault Fuego "Cazalis" | 15 | 2030 | Chevrolet C60 Fire Pumper | 15 |
| 1220 | Ford Bronco Pickup | 15 | 1250 | Ford Sierra XR4 Coupe | 15 | 2040 | Chevrolet Semi Refrigerator | 15 |
| 1221 | Ford Bronco-Roll Bar | 15 | 1251 | Ford Sierra XR4 Coupe "Bardahl" | 15 | 2050 | Chevrolet Semi Cattle | 15 |
| 1224 | Ford Bronco "NASA" | 15 | 1260 | Renault Kombi | 15 | 2060 | Fiat Cement Mixer | 15 |
| 1227 | Ford Bronco Wagon | 15 | 1261 | Renault "Aerolineas" | 15 | 3010 | Ford Van 4 X 4 "Thunder" | 15 |
| 1230 | Ford Van "Marlboro" | 15 | 1263 | Renault School Bus | 15 | 3020 | Ford Van 4 X 4 "Cracker" | 15 |
| 1231 | Ford Van "Coca Cola" | 15 | 1264 | Renault "World Tour" | 15 | 3030 | Jeep CJ5 4 X 4 "Madmex" | 15 |
| 1233 | Ford Van "John Player" | 15 | 1265 | Renault "Lufthansa" | 15 | 3040 | Jeep CJ5 4 X 4 "Vagabond" | 15 |
| 1234 | Ford Van "Las Lenas" | 15 | 1270 | Jeep CJ5 (open) | 15 | 3050 | Ford Bronco 4 X 4 "Old Iron" | 15 |
| 1235 | Ford Van "Peugeot" | 15 | 1270A | Jeep CJ5 "Lee" | 15 | 3060 | Ford Bronco 4 X 4 "Outlaw" | 15 |

# Budgie

The history of Budgie can be traced back to the late 1940s, when a British toy wholesaler, Morris & Stone, launched their "Morestone" series of die cast toys. Some of the toys were manufactured by outside vendors, including Modern Products, but Morris & Stone opened its own die casting facility in 1954.

In 1956, Morestone debuted its "Esso Petrol Pump Series," which was made up of 1/70 and 1/80 scale cars and trucks, sold in "Esso" gas pump-style boxes. The name of this series was changed in 1959 to "Budgie Miniatures," joined that year by the larger Budgie series of 1/43 to 1/60 scale cars and trucks. These were produced until 1966, when Budgie Models Ltd. went under along with its parent company, S. Guiterman & Co. Ltd., which had taken over Morris & Stone in 1961.

Budgie #238 Scammell Scarab Artic Van in the "British Railways" livery. This version was made during the early 1960s.

When Budgie and Guiterman went out of business, Modern Products bought the rights to the Budgie name, and continued the Miniatures series until 1969. Mattel's Hot Wheels cars were red-hot by 1969, and Modern Products felt the heat enough to shift gears, producing models for H. Seener Ltd., a toy and souvenir distributor. Several old Budgies (using what was left of the original tooling) were produced for Seener, including the #101 Taxi (now numbered 703) and the #236 Routemaster Bus (704, 705, 706). Modern Products was bought in 1983 by a company named Starcourt, which began re-issuing some of the original Budgies, including the Aveling Barford Road Roller. But Seener and Starcourt parted ways, and Seener joined forces with Corgi to produce the Taxi and the #102 Rolls-Royce

Silver Cloud (for which he apparently owned the tooling). These "Seerol" models came out in 1985 and can still be bought at or near the original retail price. Starcourt made Budgies until 1985, at which point they sold the business.

A word of caution: Some of the original tooling for the Modern Products toys and the Budgie toys was bought by the English company "Autocraft" several years ago. Autocraft is a reputable manufacturer of copies and reproductions of classic toys, and would no doubt do a very good job if they decide to re-issue any of these toys. But the wary collector will beware any of these modern examples being passed off as originals. If their track record is any indication, Autocraft will make it clear that these are re-issues (usually on the baseplate).

*At left a Budgie Miniature #60: The 105R Rover Squad Car in original "World Toy House" bubble pack (WTH was a U.S. distributor of Budgies). At right is the Modern Removal Truck, #58 in the Budgie Miniature series. It had a lowering tailgate.*

| # | Name | Price |
|---|------|-------|
| 100 | Horse Drawn Hansom Cab | $20 |
| 101 | Austin FX4 Taxi (see also #703) | 20 |
| 101 | Austin FX4 Taxi: 25th anniversary | 25 |
| 102 | Rolls-Royce Silver Cloud | 20 |
| 202 | International Refrigerator Lorry | 50 |
| 204 | Volkswagen Pick-Up | 50 |
| 206 | Leyland Hippo "Coal and Coke" Lorry | 60 |
| 208 | RAF Personnel Carrier | 50 |
| 210 | US Army Personnel Carrier | 50 |
| 212 | British Army Personnel Carrier | 50 |
| 214 | Thornycroft Mobile Crane | 65 |
| 216 | Renault Lorry | 45 |
| 218 | Seddon AA Mobile Traffic Control Unit | 110 |
| 220 | Leyland Hippo Cattle Transporter | 50 |
| 222 | International Tank Transporter with Tank | 65 |
| 224 | 0-6-0 Tank Locomotive | 25 |
| 226 | Foden Dumper | 45 |
| 228 | Karrier Bantam Bottle Lorry | 100 |
| 230 | Seddon Articulated Timber Transporter | 60 |
| 232 | Seddon Low Loader with Cable Drums | 50 |
| 234 | International Low Loader with Caterpillar Tractor | 50 |
| 236 | AEC Routemaster bus (see also #'s 704, 705, 706) | 25 |
| 238 | Scammell Scarab Artic. Van (see also #702) | |
| | British Railways | 90 |
| | Railfreight | 75 |
| | 1985 re-issues | 30 |
| 240 | Scammell Scarab Wagon | 80 |
| 242 | Euclid Dumper | 45 |
| 244 | Morris Breakdown Lorry | 60 |
| 246 | Wolseley Six-Eighty Police Car | 75 |
| 248 | Horse Drawn Stage Coach with four horses | 70 |
| 252 | Austin Articulated Container Lorry | 60 |
| 254 | AEC Merryweather Fire Escape | 55 |
| 256 | Foden Aircraft Refueling Tanker | 100 |
| 258 | Daimler Ambulance | 80 |
| 258 | Daimler Ambulance - reissued 1991 in kit form | 15 |
| 260 | Ruston-Bucyrus 10-RB Excavator | 65 |
| 262 | Racing Motorcycle | 75 |
| 264 | Racing Motorcycle Combination | 75 |

| # | Name | Price |
|---|------|-------|
| 266 | Motorcycle and Delivery Sidecar | $75 |
| 268 | AA Land Rover | 80 |
| 270 | Leyland Articulated Petrol Tanker | 65 |
| 272 | Supercar | 170 |
| 274 | Ford Thames Trader Refuse Lorry | 60 |
| 276 | Bedford Long Wheelbase Tipper Lorry | 60 |
| 278 | RAC Land Rover | 75 |
| 280 | AEC Super Fueller Tanker | 400 |
| 282 | Euclid Scraper | 45 |
| 288 | Leyland Bulk Flour Tanker | 65 |
| 290 | Bedford Ice Cream Van | 80 |
| 292 | Leyland Bulk Milk Tanker | 75 |
| 294 | Bedford TK Horse Box | 65 |
| 296 | Motorway Express Coach | 110 |
| 296 | Blue Line Sightseeing Coach | 320 |
| 298 | Alvis Salamander Crash Tender | 90 |
| 300 | Lewin Sweepmaster Road Sweeper | 65 |
| 302 | Commer Cabin Service Lift Truck | 65 |
| 304 | Bedford TK Glass Transporter | 60 |
| 306 | Fiat Tractor with Shovel | 60 |
| 308 | Seddon Pit Alligator Low Loader | 70 |
| 310 | Leyland Cement Mixer | 70 |
| 312 | Bedford Super Tipmaster | 45 |
| 314 | Fiat Tractor with Dozer Blade | 75 |
| 316 | Albion Overhead Maintenance Vehicle | 50 |
| 318 | Euclid Mammoth Articulated Dumper | 70 |
| 322 | Scammell Routeman Pneumajector Transporter | 75 |
| 324 | Commer Douglas Prospector Duomatic Tipper | 80 |
| 326 | Scammell Highwayman Gas Transporter | 95 |
| 452 | AA Motorcycle and Sidecar with Rider | 65 |
| 452 | AA Triumph Motorcycle and Sidecar with Rider | 65 |
| 454 | RAC Motorcycle and Sidecar with Rider | 65 |
| 454 | RAC Triumph Motorcycle and Sidecar with Rider | 65 |
| 456 | Solo Motorcycle with Rider | 50 |
| 456 | Solo Triumph Motorcycle with Rider | 50 |

**The following Budgies were re-issued during the 1980s:**

| # | Name | Price |
|---|------|-------|
| 701 | Aveling-Barford Diesel Road Roller | 20 |

| # | Name | Price |
|---|------|-------|
| 702 | Scammell Scarab Articulated Van | |
| | LMS | $30 |
| | GWR | 30 |
| | Royal Navy | 30 |
| 703 | Austin FX4 Taxi | 15 |
| 704 | AEC Routemaster bus: Shop Linker | 15 |
| 705 | AEC Routemaster bus: "25 Faithful Years" | 15 |
| 706 | AEC Routemaster bus: Watford FA Cup Final | 15 |

**Budgie Miniature series:**

| # | Name | Price |
|---|------|-------|
| 1 | AA Motorcycle and Sidecar | 35 |
| 2 | RAC Motorcycle and Sidecar | 35 |
| 3 | AA Bedford Van | 25 |
| 4 | AA Land Rover | 25 |
| 5 | Wolseley 6/80 Police Car | 20 |
| 6 | Cooper-Bristol Racing Car | 20 |
| 7 | Mercedes-Benz Racing Car | 20 |
| 8 | Volkswagen 1200 Saloon | 30 |
| 9 | Maudslay Horse Box | 30 |
| 10 | Karrier GPO Telephones Van | 30 |
| 11 | Morris Commercial Van | 20 |
| 12 | Volkswagen Microbus | 30 |
| 13 | Austin FX3 Taxi | 40 |
| 14 | Packard Convertible | 30 |
| 15 | Austin A95 Westminster Countryman | 20 |
| 16 | Austin-Healey 100 | 35 |
| 17 | Ford Thames 5 cwt. Van | 50 |
| 18 | Foden Dumper | 20 |
| 19 | Rover 105R | 20 |
| 20 | Plymouth Belvedere Convertible | 30 |
| 20 | Austin A95 Emergency Vehicle | 30 |
| 21 | Bedford TK Tipper Lorry | 20 |
| 21 | Oldsmobile Town Sedan | 35 |
| 22 | Bedford TK Crane Lorry | 20 |
| 22 | Cattle Transporter | 25 |
| 23 | Bedford TK Cement Mixer | 20 |
| 24 | Bedford TK Refuse Lorry | 20 |
| 25 | Bedford TK Cattle Lorry | 20 |
| 26 | Aveling-Barford Road Roller | 15 |
| 27 | Wolseley 6/80 Fire Chief Car | 20 |
| 50 | "BP Racing Service" Road Tanker | 20 |
| 51 | "Shell" Road Tanker | 20 |

| # | Name | Price |
|---|------|-------|
| 52 | "Shell BP" Road Tanker | $20 |
| 53 | "National" Road Tanker | 20 |
| 54 | "BP" Road Tanker | 20 |
| 55 | "Mobil" Road Tanker | 20 |
| 56 | GMC Box Van | 20 |
| 57 | International Parcels Van | 20 |
| 58 | "Modern Removals" Van | 20 |
| 59 | AEC Merryweather Fire Engine | 20 |
| 60 | Rover 105R Squad Car | 20 |
| 61 | Austin A95 Countryman "Q Car" | 20 |

**Budgie Gift Sets:**

| | | |
|---|------|-------|
| 4 | Gift Set #4 | 175 |
| 5 | Gift Set #5 | 200 |
| 8 | Gift Set #8 | 150 |
| 12 | Gift Set #12 | 175 |

**"Bubble-pack" Miniature 3-vehicle Sets:**

| | | |
|---|------|-------|
| 95 | Town Set | 75 |
| 96 | Road Construction Set | 75 |
| 96 | Service Set | 75 |
| 97 | Truck Set | 75 |
| 98 | Utility Vehicle Set | 75 |
| 99 | Traffic Set | 75 |

*This Budgie #224 0-6-0 Tank Locomotive with box is an example of the later version with "British Railways" decals (earlier versions had the words cast into the body).*

# Cam-Cast

**O**ther than the fact that it produced a couple of toy trucks during the 1950s, not much is known about this American company. Cam-Cast was apparently located in Edgerton, Ohio; the trucks were roughly 1/50 scale, and each was available in a number of different liveries.

In addition to "Western Auto," the Van shown here was available in liveries such as "North American Van Lines," "Pillsbury's Best" and "Evan Motor Freight," among others. The other casting was of an Oil Tanker, and it came in such liveries as "Gulf," "Marathon Oil" and "Sunoco." As can be seen in the photo, the style was very simple, with silver highlighted windows and headlight/grille; the flat sides of the Van obviously made for easy application of a company's logo.

Cam-Casts are scarce; excellent condition examples don't turn up often. A current value for either type of truck in excellent or better condition would be $40-$75. *Note:* it is not known whether these trucks came in individual boxes.

*The Cam-Cast Van in Western Auto livery.*

# Chad Valley

Chad Valley was a British company that had for many years been known for its tinplate toys when it launched a series of die cast toys in 1948 or 1949. They had a wind-up clockwork motor to power them, and they were very simple designs. During the early 1950s, the company produced a line of die cast cars for The Rootes Group (such as #236, #237 and #238), to be used as promotionals at the dealerships (as well as to be sold as toys). These were more accurate representations of the real vehicles.

Like many companies, Chad Valley got good mileage out of some of its tooling: the Commer truck cab and chassis appeared in numerous configurations and the "Razor Edge" Rolls-Royce body lent itself to three "different" toys. The company apparently made these die casts until 1956.

As might be expected, the Rootes Group models are among the most sought after of the Chad Valley die casts.

## Note: Chad Valleys were 1/50 scale unless otherwise indicated

| # | Name | Price |
|---|------|-------|
| 220 | Rolls-Royce Razor Edge Saloon (1/43) (red, blue, green, black) | $160 |
| 221 | Rolls-Royce Razor Edge Traffic Control Car (1/43) (black) | 160 |
| 222 | Rolls-Royce Razor Edge Police Car (1/143) (black) | 160 |
| 223 | Record Car (1/43) (red, light blue, pink) | 175 |
| 224 | Double Decker Bus (1/76) (red, green) | 250 |
| 225 | Commer Open Lorry | 140 |
| 226 | Commer Flat Truck | 140 |
| 227 | Commer Timber Wagon | 140 |
| 228 | Commer Cable Layer (red/green) | 160 |
| 229 | Commer Breakdown Lorry | 160 |
| 230 | Commer Milk Truck (with eight milk churns) | 175 |
| 231 | Commer Fire Engine (red) | 175 |
| 232 | Commer Tower Repair Wagon | 150 |

| # | Name | Price |
|---|------|-------|
| 233 | Commer Milk Tanker (blue/cream, green/cream) | $170 |
| 234 | Commer Petrol Tanker | 150 |
| 235 | Tractor (1/43) | 140 |
| 236 | Hillman Minx (1/43) (dark blue, gray, red) | 135 |
| 237 | Humber Super Snipe (1/43) (dark green, gray) | 130 |
| 238 | Sunbeam-Talbot (1/43) (green, light blue, brown) | 150 |
| 239 | Dust Cart | 150 |
| 240 | Commer Avenger Coach (1/76) (red, green, blue) | 220 |
| 241 | Karrier Public Health Vehicle | 140 |
| 242 | Commer Truck (red) | 185 |
| 243 | Bulldozer | 150 |
| 244 | Farm Trailer | 50 |

| # | Name | Price |
|---|------|-------|
| 245 | Manure Spreader | $80 |
| 247 | Stacutruc (light blue/yellow) | 190 |
| 500 | Guy Van | |
| | "Chad Valley" | 225 |
| | "Guy Motors" | 225 |
| 503 | Fordson Tractor (1/43) (red, yellow) | 175 |
| 504 | Guy Ice Cream Truck (1/43) | 240 |
| 507 | Humber Hawk (1/43) | 190 |
| 509 | Hay Rake | 70 |
| 550 | Saloon (1/70) | 40 |
| 551 | Single Decker Coach (1/70) | 40 |
| 552 | Van (1/70) (red) | 40 |
| 553 | Post Office Van (1/70) (red) | 40 |
| 554 | Ambulance (1/70) (white) | 40 |

# Charbens

Charbens was one of the many die cast toy manufacturers located in North London just after the end of World War II. The owners, Charles and Benjamin Reid, combined the first part of their names to form the company name, and the factory was located at 219 Hornsey Road, London. Although the firm had been founded in the late 1920s, it is for their "Old Crocks" series of vintage toy cars, launched in 1955, that they are best known.

That series is listed here, along with other Charbens products. The Old Crocks cars came in individual boxes printed to resemble a trunk (usually beige, but later examples were light blue). The series was re-named "Showcase Veterans" in 1960, and the cars now came in clear plastic display cases, the model held in place by a rubber band. In addition, the cars were packed in blister packs, and were called "Mini Cars."

Near mint to mint examples of the Charbens models are hard to find, since the lead used in the casting process reacts with the zinc, producing "metal fatigue." This results in damaged models.

While the Old Crocks were of approximately 1/90 scale, the other Charbens were generally in the 1/43 to 1/50 range.

| # | Name | Price |
|---|------|-------|

### Old Crocks Series (roughly 1/90 scale):

| # | Name | Price |
|---|------|-------|
| OC1 | 1904 Darracq Genevieve (red, orange, blue) | $15 |
| OC2 | 1904 Spyker (yellow/black) | 15 |
| OC3 | 1914 "Old Bill" Double Deck Bus (red, orange) | 15 |
| | cast in two halves | 15 |
| | single casting | 25 |
| OC4 | 1907 Ford Model T (blue) | 15 |
| | cast in two halves | 15 |
| | single casting | 15 |
| OC5 | 1907 Vauxhall (light green) | 15 |
| OC6 | 1906 De Dion Bouton (dark red/silver, light green/silver) | 15 |
| OC7 | 1898 Panhard (light green/silver, brown/silver) | 15 |
| OC8 | 1906 Rolls-Royce Silver Ghost (silver) | 15 |
| OC9 | 1903 Standard 6 hp (dark red/beige, brown/beige) | 15 |
| OC10 | 1902 Wolseley (light blue/black, light blue/silver) | 15 |
| OC11 | 1908 Packard Runabout (light green/silver) | 15 |
| OC12 | 1905 Vauxhall Hansom Cab (orange/beige/silver) | 15 |
| OC13 | 1900 Straker Steam Lorry (blue, light blue) | 15 |
| OC14 | Stephenson's Rocket Locomotive (yellow/black) | 15 |
| OC15 | Rocket Tender (yellow/red/black) | 15 |
| OC16 | 1909 Albion Pickup (dark blue, light blue) | 15 |

| # | Name | Price |
|---|------|-------|
| OC17 | 1912 Rover Roadster (orange/black) | $15 |
| OC18 | 1911 Mercedes-Benz (green/black) | 15 |
| M19 | Bedford Horse Transport (brown) | 25 |
| OC20 | 1910 Lanchester (blue/black) | 15 |
| OC21 | 1922 Morris Cowley Roadster (beige/black) | 15 |
| OC22 | 1900 Daimler (red/black) | 15 |
| OC23 | 1904 Autocar (dark blue/black) | 15 |
| OC24 | 1870 Grenville Steam Carriage (light green) | 15 |
| OC25 | 1905 Napier Record Car (violet, red) | 15 |
| OC26 | Fire Engine (red) | 25 |
| OC27 | Articulated Breakdown Truck (orange/light green, dark green/blue/orange) | 15 |
| OC28 | 1913 Mercer Runabout (yellow/black) | 15 |

### Military trailers (roughly 1/90 scale, and all painted green):

| # | Name | Price |
|---|------|-------|
| M30 | Mobile Searchlight | 15 |
| M31 | Mobile Twin Bofor Gun | 15 |
| M32 | Mobile Radar | 15 |
| M33 | Mobile Field Gun | 15 |
| M34 | Mobile Rocket Gun | 15 |
| M35 | Armoured Car | 30 |
| | Royal Mail Van (red) | 50 |
| | Police Van (blue) | 50 |
| | Van (blue, red) | 50 |
| | Ambulance (white) | 60 |
| | Tanker (red, blue, green) | 60 |
| | Scammell G.W.R. Mechanical Horse (brown/cream, blue/cream) | 60 |
| | Javelin Saloon (black) | 90 |
| | Morris "ESSO" Van (red, green) | 60 |

| # | Name | Price |
|---|------|-------|
| | Morris Fire Engine (red) | $80 |
| | Morris Station Wagon (blue, red) | 80 |
| | "DAIRY MILK" Pedestrian Electric Vehicle (dark blue) | 90 |
| | "HOVIS" Pedestrian Electric Vehicle (orange) | 90 |
| 6 | Farm Tractor (red) | 60 |
| 8 | Tipping Truck (green/black/yellow) | 50 |
| 9 | Motor Coach (red, blue, cream) | 80 |
| 10 | Royal Mail Van (red) | 60 |
| 11 | Ambulance (white) | 60 |
| 12 | "CARTER PATERSON" Van (red, dark green) | 60 |
| 13 | Police Van (blue, green) | 60 |
| 14 | Post Office Van (red) | 60 |
| 15 | Dennis Fire Engine (red) | 80 |
| 17 | Tractor & 3 Trailers (red) | 80 |
| 18 | Tractor & Grass Cutter (red/yellow) | 80 |
| 19 | Tractor & Harvester (red/green/yellow) | 80 |
| 20 | Mobile Crane (red/green/yellow) | 35 |
| 21 | Muir Hill Dumper (orange/green) | 50 |
| 26 | Armoured Car (green) | 50 |
| 28 | Steam Roller (red, orange) | 40 |
| 31 | Cable Lorry (light blue/yellow) | 60 |
| 32 | Alfa Romeo Racing Car (red) | 90 |
| 33 | Cooper-Bristol Racing Car (green) | 80 |
| 34 | Ferrari Racing Car (red) | 90 |
| 36 | Horse Transport Box (dark red) | 75 |
| 37 | Rocket Gun on Lorry and Trailer | 60 |

# Cherryca Phenix

Tin toys account for the vast majority of playthings produced by toy makers in Japan over the past 60 years. But there have been a few "rebels" who have produced superb examples of the die cast art.

One of these is Cherryca Phenix. Initially marketed in the early 1960s as the "Micropet" series by a company called Taiseiya Co. Ltd., the name Cherryca Phenix was added along the way, perhaps to make these 1/43 models more appealing to the European and British markets. (Taiseiya was eventually bought by Yonezawa,

*Cherryca Phenix #6, the Buick Electra. This is a left-hand drive, battery-powered example. The battery box hanging down below the body somewhat spoils the lines of the model.*

45

makers of the Diapet line of die casts.) Production of these models apparently stopped sometime in the mid-1960s.

Although comprised predominantly of Japanese makes, the series did have its share of European and American models, as well. In general, the models were quite accurate, and like their competitors Dinky and Corgi, they had window glazing, interiors and suspension. Some were also outfitted with electric lights, powered by a battery located in the baseplate. Each model came in an individual, two-piece box that featured artwork of the car contained inside.

These models rarely turn up in the United States, which could lead one to assume they were not imported here. However, the two examples pictured here are left-hand drive, so perhaps they did make it to these shores.

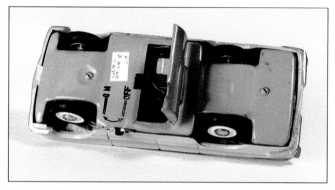

The opened battery box beneath the Cherryca Phenix Buick Electra (the sticker was added by the owner for identification purposes).

A left-hand drive version of the Cherryca Phenix #7 Ford Falcon.

| # | Name | Price |
|---|------|-------|
| 1 | Hino Contessa gray, red/cream | $250 |
| 2 | Nissan Cedric Station Wagon (beige/gray) | 250 |
| 3 | Mercedes-Benz 300 SL Roadster (red) | 280 |
| 4 | Datsun (chrome) | 100 |
| 5 | Chevrolet Impala (blue) | 280 |
| 6 | Buick Electra (white/green, tan) | 280 |
| 7 | Ford Falcon (green/cream, blue/cream) | 280 |
| 8 | Volkswagen 1200 (red, blue, green) | 280 |
| 9 | Volkswagen Karmann Ghia Roadster (cream, blue) | 320 |
| 10 | Dodge Polara (blue/gray) | 320 |
| 11 | Mercedes-Benz 300 SL Hardtop (white) | 280 |
| 12 | Datsun 1200 Station Wagon (light green) | 250 |
| 13 | Datsun 1200 Pickup (light green) | 250 |
| 14 | Isuzu Bellel 2000 De Luxe (orange/gray) | 270 |
| 15 | Ford Thunderbird (pink/gray) | 280 |
| 16 | Datsun Fairlady Roadster (light green, red) | 280 |
| 17 | Lincoln Continental (green, light gray) | 300 |
| 18 | Mercedes-Benz 220 SE (blue) | 280 |
| 19 | Citroën DS 19 Convertible (light green/red) | 320 |
| 20 | Cadillac 62 Special (light blue) | 300 |
| 21 | Chevrolet (chrome) | 120 |
| 22 | Datsun Bluebird (blue, cream) | 420 |
| 23 | Jaguar Type E Roadster (red, white) | 250 |
| 24 | Prince Gloria (blue, violet, black) | 260 |
| 25 | Nissan Cedric (brown, black) | 260 |
| 26 | Toyota Crown (red, blue) | 260 |
| 27 | Toyota Crown Station Wagon (gray) | 260 |
| 28 | Toyota Corona (light blue) | 240 |

| # | Name | Price |
|---|------|-------|
| 29 | Mercedes-Benz 300 SL Roadster (red) | $280 |
| 30 | Isuzu Bellet (light blue, cream) | 250 |
| 31 | Prince Skyline 1500 (blue, orange) | 250 |
| 32 | Datsun Bluebird (beige) | 220 |
| 33 | Mitsubishi Colt 1000 (blue) | 230 |
| 34 | Hino Contessa (light blue, red) | 230 |
| 35 | Nissan Cedric Taxi (yellow/blue) | 280 |
| 36 | Toyota Crown Police Car (black/white) | 280 |
| 37 | Toyota Crown Taxi (yellow/blue) | 280 |
| 38 | Honda S 600 Roadster (red/white) | 220 |
| 39 | Prince Sprint Coupe (blue, violet) | 230 |
| 40 | Toyota Corona Coupe (blue, violet) | 230 |
| 41 | Daihatsu Compagno (blue) | 210 |
| 42 | Mitsubishi Debonair (brown, black) | 210 |
| 43 | Nissan Cedric Police Car (black/white) | 260 |

| # | Name | Price |
|---|------|-------|
| 44 | Mazda Luce (beige, red) | $220 |
| 45 | Mitsubishi Colt 1000 Rally (red) | 240 |
| 46 | Datsun Bluebird Rally (orange) | 240 |
| 47 | Nissan Skyline Rally (blue, violet) | 240 |
| 48 | Prince Gloria Rally (blue) | 240 |
| 50 | Isuzu Bellet GT (yellow) | 250 |
| 001 | Fordson Major Tractor and Trailer | 220 |
| OT1 | 1892 Peugeot | 80 |
| OT2 | 1896 Peugeot | 80 |
| OT3 | 1898 Peugeot Victoria | 80 |
| OT4 | 1899 Peugeot Victoria | 80 |
| OT5 | 1901 Decauville Vis-a-Vis | 80 |
| OT6 | 1901 Delahaye Vis-a-Vis | 80 |
| FL-1 | Buick Electra | 280 |
| FL-2 | Ford Falcon | 280 |

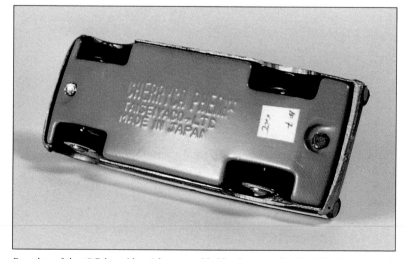

Baseplate of the #7 Falcon (the sticker was added by the owner for identification purposes).

# C.I.J.

The Compagnie Industrielle du Jouet was founded in 1930 by Marcel Gourdet and Fernand Migault in the French town of Briare. Gourdet had been making tinplate toys for some ten years prior to this, and the company continued in that vein during the 1930s. They made large tinplate clockwork-powered cars for Citroën and Renault, as well as the well-known Alfa Romeo P2 Racing Car that today commands big money when one turns up for sale.

After the war, tinplate production was re-started, but it was the debut of a die cast Renault 4CV in 1/43 scale in 1949 that changed the company's fortunes. The success of this toy led C.I.J. to launch a series of 1/43 to 1/50 scale die casts, comprised mainly of contemporary French vehicles (although there were a couple of American cars, and even a VW Beetle). The series did quite well during the first half of the 1950s, but by 1957 the company was feeling the pressure of intense competition from the likes of Solido and French Dinky. Marcel Gourdet left the company that year, and a slow decline began that even a name change (to C.I.J. Europarc) in 1960 couldn't halt.

During the early 1960s, C.I.J. added some models that had been originally put out by J.R.D., but by 1965 C.I.J. had gone under. The company left behind a legacy of well-made and accurate die cast toys (models) that are now very much sought after by collectors.

The J.R.D. connection meant that C.I.J. produced a number of "hybrid" models using parts from the old J.R.D. stock. In many cases, the ex-J.R.D. models were left with their original J.R.D. baseplate, although now packaged in a C.I.J. box. This, along with C.I.J.'s tendency to switch decals and paint jobs around to make "new" models, made for some unusual creations. Some of these, as they were made for only a short period, are now quite rare. This accounts for one version of a model being priced at, for example, $100, while another version of the same casting will be listed at $2,000.

The easiest to find C.I.J. is undoubtedly the #3/48 Renault 4CV, which was made from 1949/1950 right up until 1964. *Note:* C.I.J.'s came in individual boxes, many of which featured great period artwork of the vehicle.

*C.I.J. #3/16 Plymouth Belvedere with original box.*

Also, it should be noted that, although the author is not aware of original C.I.J.'s being re-issued, several J.R.D. re-issues (including the Citroën Traction Avant) appeared around 1985. These were made using the original tooling, and packaged in boxes using the original artwork. However, the perfect brightness of the box and the "85" on the bottom of the model serve to identify it as a re-issue.

*C.I.J. photos courtesy of Andrew Ralston.*

## C.I.J.'s were 1/43 to 1/50 scale, unless otherwise indicated

| # | Name | Price |
|---|------|-------|
| | **\* denotes an ex-J.R.D. model, added to the C.I.J. line in 1965** | |
| 3/1 | Renault De Rovin Sports | $100 |
| 3/2 | Renault Etoile Filante | 110 |
| 3/3 | Facel Vega Facellia | 100 |
| 3/4 | Citroën ID 19 Estate | 120 |
| 3/5 | Panhard Dyna Junior (open or closed) | 100 |
| 3/6 | Citroën Ami 6 | 100 |
| 3/7 | Simca 1000 | 80 |
| 3/8 | Simca 1000 Police Car | 120 |

| # | Name | Price |
|---|------|-------|
| 3/9 | Simca 1000 Coupe Bertone | $120 |
| 3/10 | Volkswagen 1200 | 110 |
| 3/10A* | Citroën Traction Avant | 120 |
| 3/12 | Mercedes-Benz 220 | 110 |
| 3/13* | Peugeot 404 | 100 |
| 3/15 | Chrysler Windsor | 135 |
| 3/16 | Plymouth Belvedere | 135 |
| 3/20 | Panhard "ENERGIC BP ENERGOL" Tanker (1/60) | 70 |
| 3/21 | Renault "SHELL" Tanker (1/60) | 80 |

| # | Name | Price |
|---|------|-------|
| 3/23 | Berliet GLC 19 "SHELL" Tanker | $140 |
| 3/25 | Renault Covered Truck (1/60) | 50 |
| 3/26 | Trailer (1/60) | 25 |
| 3/27 | Notin Caravan | 60 |
| 3/27A | Notin Caravan (transparent roof) | 60 |
| 3/28 | Cattle Trailer | 30 |
| 3/30 | Fire Engine | 100 |
| 3/31 | Sugar Beet Trailer (1/35) | 30 |
| 3/32 | Seed Trailer (1/35) | 30 |
| 3/33 | Renault E30 Tractor (1/35) | 110 |

| #     | Name                                    | Price |
|-------|-----------------------------------------|-------|
| 3/34  | Farm Trailer                            | $30   |
| 3/35  | Renault R 3040 Tractor (1/35)           | 100   |
| 3/35A | Water Tank Trailer (1/35)               | 30    |
| 3/36  | Timber Trailer with log (1/35)          | 30    |
| 3/37  | Gift Set: 3/33 with 3/34                | [no known price] |
| 3/38  | Gift Set: 3/33 with 3/35A               | [no known price] |
| 3/39  | Gift Set: 3/33 with 3/36                | [no known price] |
| 3/39A | Gift Set: 3/33 with 3/31                | [no known price] |
| 3/40  | Renault 120CV Coach (1/60)              | 75    |
| 3/41  | Citroën ID Estate Ambulance             | 135   |
| 3/42  | Renault Colorale Prairie                | 90    |
| 3/43  | Renault Colorale Savane                 | 90    |
| 3/44  | Renault Colorale Van                    | 110   |
| 3/45  | Renault Prairie Taxi                    | 120   |
| 3/46  | Peugeot 403 Estate                      | 80    |
| 3/46A | Peugeot 403 Estate (later model)        | 80    |
| 3/46E | Peugeot 403 Estate "Secours Routier"    | 150   |
| 3/46P | Peugeot 403 Estate "Police"             | 130   |
| 3/47  | Panhard Dyna 130                        | 100   |
| 3/48  | Renault 4 CV                            | 100   |
| 3/48A | Renault 4 CV (later model)              | 90    |
| 3/48B | Renault 4 CV "CINZANO"                  | 950   |
| 3/49  | Renault 4 CV Police                     | 110   |
| 3/50  | Renault 4CV Alpine Coupe                | 100   |
| 3/51  | Renault Fregate                         | 90    |
| 3/51A | Renault Fregate "Chocolat Kemmel"       | 1600  |
| 3/51B | Renault Fregate Amiral                  | 90    |
| 3/52  | Renault Fregate Grand Pavois            | 120   |
| 3/53  | Renault Manoir Break de Chasse          | 120   |
| 3/53A | Renault Manoir Ambulance                | 185   |
| 3/54  | Panhard Dyna Z                          | 80    |
| 3/54T | Panhard Dyna Z Taxi                     | 150   |
| 3/55  | Renault Colorale Ambulance              | 150   |
| 3/56  | Renault Dauphine                        | 80    |
| 3/56S | Renault Dauphine (with windows)         | 150   |
| 3/56T | Renault Dauphine Taxi                   | 150   |
| 3/57  | Renault Dauphine Police Car             | 110   |
| 3/58  | Renault Floride Hardtop                 | 85    |
| 3/60  | Renault 1000Kgs Van (plain gray)        | 80    |
| 3/60  | Renault 1000Kgs "PRIMISTERES"           | 950   |
| 3/60A | Renault 1000Kgs "ASTRA" Van             | 200   |

*The #3/10 Volkswagen Beetle 1200, with original box depicting the Bug driving alongside a lake.*

| #      | Name                                | Price |
|--------|-------------------------------------|-------|
| 3/60B  | Renault 1000Kgs "BOUCHERIE" Van     | $950  |
| 3/60P  | Renault 1000Kgs Mail Van (France)   | 180   |
| 3/60P  | Renault 1000Kgs Mail Van (Germany)  | 125   |
| 3/60PB | Renault 1000Kgs Mail Van (Belgium)  | 950   |
| 3/60S  | Renault 1000Kgs "SHELL" Van         | 175   |
| 3/60T  | Renault 1000Kgs PTT Van & Trailer   | 180   |
| 3/61   | Renault 1000Kgs Ambulance           | 150   |
| 3/61M  | Renault 1000Kgs Military Ambulance  | 220   |
| 3/62   | Renault 1000Kgs Bus                 | 130   |
| 3/62N  | Renault 1000Kgs "TEINTURERIE" Van   | 500   |
| 3/63   | Renault 1000Kgs Police Bus          | 165   |
| 3/63A  | Renault 1000Kgs "BONICEL" Van       | 2500  |
| 3/63B  | Renault 1000Kgs "CHOCOLAT COTE D'OR" Van | 2200 |
| 3/65   | Renault Colorale Pickup Chariot de Police | 150 |
| 3/66   | Renault 300Kg Dauphinoise Estate    | 75    |

| #      | Name                                        | Price |
|--------|---------------------------------------------|-------|
| 3/67   | Renault 300Kg Dauphinoise Van               | $75   |
| 3/68   | Renault 300Kg Dauphinoise Van "POSTES" (France) | 120 |
| 3/68PB | Renault 300Kg Dauphinoise Van "POSTES" (Belgium) | 530 |
| 3/69   | Renault 300Kg Dauphinoise "Gendarmerie"     | 120   |
| 3/70   | Renault 120CV Covered Artic. Wagon          | 100   |
| 3/70A  | Renault 120CV Covered Artic. Wagon "POTASSES D'ALSACE" | 1100 |
| 3/72   | Renault 120CV "SHELL" Tanker                | 135   |
| 3/73   | Renault 120CV Timber Truck                  | 90    |
| 3/75   | Renault 120CV Heat Exchange Transporter     | 165   |
| 3/76*  | Citroën 2CV Van (marked J.R.D.)             | 550   |
| 3/76A  | Boat and trailer                            | 35    |
| 3/77*  | Articulated Berliet "KRONENBOURG"           | 135   |

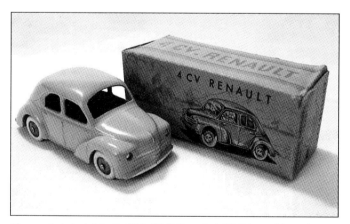

*The one that started it all: C.I.J. #3/48 Renault 4 CV. This model was in production for some 15 years, going through a number of updates during that time.*

*This Dyna Panhard (#3/47) also was made in a clockwork-powered version (#4/47).*

| # | Name | Price | | # | Name | Price | | # | Name | Price |
|---|------|-------|---|---|------|-------|---|---|------|-------|
| 3/77A | Saviem JM240 "KRONENBOURG" (trailer marked J.R.D.) | $920 | | 3/82 | Renault 120CV Digger | $80 | | 3/92 | Renault Estafette Bus | $140 |
| 3/78* | Unic Tractor and wagon "KRONENBOURG" | 225 | | 3/82A | Saviem JM240 Digger | 80 | | 3/93 | Renault Estafette "GENDARMERIE NATIONALE" Bus | 180 |
| 3/79 | Saviem 57 Bottle Truck "PREFONTAINES" | 850 | | 3/83 | Renault 120CV Breakdown "BOURGET ET MONTREUIL" | 110 | | 3/94 | Renault 2.5T "EVIAN" Truck | 260 |
| 3/80 | Renault 120CV Tipper | 60 | | 3/83A | Renault 120CV Breakdown | 110 | | 3/95 | Renault 2.5T Fire Engine | 260 |
| 3/80A* | Saviem Artic. "TRANSCONTINENTAL EXPRESS" (trailer marked J.R.D.) | 1450 | | 3/84 | Berliet Lorry Monuted Crane "SABLIERES DE LA LOIRE" | 195 | | 3/96 | Renault 2.5T Searchlight Truck and Trailer | 150 |
| 3/81 | Renault 120CV Crane Truck | 65 | | 3/89 | Citroën 1200Kg Van Police | 150 | | 3/97 | Saviem JM240 Missile Launcher (civilian) | 270 |
| 3/81A | Saviem JM240 Crane Truck | 75 | | 3/89B | Citroën 1200Kg Van "BRANDT" | 520 | | 3/97M | Saviem JM240 Missile Launcher (military) | 180 |
| | | | | 3/90 | Renault Estafette Van | 70 | | | | |
| | | | | 3/91 | Renault Estafette Police Van | 100 | | | | |

#3/2 Renault Etoile Filante: The only record racing car in the C.I.J. series.

The very rare #3/89B Citroën 1200Kg "Brandt" Promotional Van with original box. The basic casting for this model was originally a J.R.D., re-painted in the colors of the Belgian retailer Brandt, and re-packaged as part of the C.I.J. series around 1964. It was re-issued a few years ago, with several other J.R.D. models.

The #3/27 Notin Caravan with box.

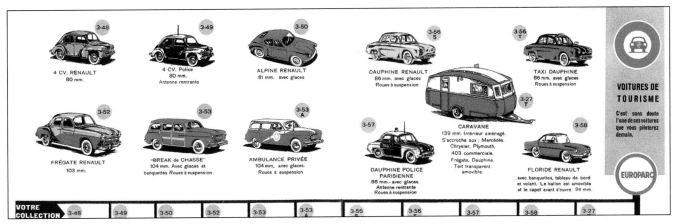

Spread from a circa 1960 C.I.J./Europarc catalog. Note the multiple versions produced of some of the basic bodies.

| # | Name | Price |
|---|------|-------|
| 3/98 | Renault 2.5T Radar Truck (military) | $150 |
| 3/99 | Renault 2.5T Mobile Cannon (military) | 150 |
| 4/20 | Clockwork version of 3/20 (1/60 scale) | 60 |
| 4/21 | Clockwork version of 3/21 (1/60 scale) | 70 |
| 4/30 | Clockwork version of 3/30 | 120 |
| 4/42 | Clockwork version of 3/42 | 100 |
| 4/43 | Clockwork version of 3/43 | 100 |
| 4/44 | Clockwork version of 3/44 | 120 |
| 4/45 | Clockwork version of 3/45 | 250 |
| 4/47 | Clockwork version of 3/47 | 110 |
| 4/48 | Clockwork version of 3/48 | 100 |
| 4/50 | Renault 2.5T Cattle Truck | 125 |
| 4/51 | Clockwork version of 3/51 | 80 |
| 4/67 | Saviem JM240 Semi Trailer | 450 |
| 4/68 | Saviem JM240 Military Tanker | 300 |
| 4/68A | Saviem JM240 Artic. Covered Truck | 300 |
| 4/69 | Saviem LRS Artic. "SHELL" Tanker | 140 |
| 4/70 | Saviem LRS Artic. "MOBIL" Tanker | 275 |
| 4/71 | Somua-Saviem "B.P." Artic. Tanker | 150 |
| 4/71A | Saviem LRS "B.P." Tanker | 150 |
| 4/71B | Saviem JM240 "B.P." Tanker | 220 |
| 4/72 | Saviem JM240 with electricity Transformer | 190 |
| 4/73 | Saviem JM240 with cement container | 180 |
| 4/74 | Saviem S7 Troop Transport | 150 |
| 4/75 | Saviem LRS Semi Cable Carrier | 170 |
| 4/75A | Saviem JM240 Semi Cable Carrier | 170 |
| 4/76 | Saviem S7 Covered Truck | 120 |
| 4/77 | 4/76 with trailer | 150 |
| 4/78 | Saviem JM 240 Dump Truck | 100 |
| 4/80 | Somua Dump Truck | 100 |
| 4/80A | Saviem LRS Dump Truck | 100 |
| 4/80B | Saviem JM240 Dump Truck | 110 |

| # | Name | Price |
|---|------|-------|
| 4/81* | Berliet GAK Refuse Wagon | $100 |
| 4/82 | Saviem JM 240 Shovel Truck | 150 |

**Micro-Miniatures (late 1950s-early 1960s):**

| # | Name | Price |
|---|------|-------|
| M1 | Renault Bus (1/120) | 60 |
| M2 | Peugeot 403 (1/80) | 40 |
| M3 | Renault 120 HP Box Van (1/120) | 30 |
| M4 | Renault 120 HP Dump Truck (1/120) | 30 |

| # | Name | Price |
|---|------|-------|
| M5 | Panhard 4 HL Tank Truck (1/120) | $30 |
| M6 | Renault 1000Kgs Ambulance (1/100) | 40 |
| M7 | Renault 1000Kgs Van (1/100) | 30 |
| M8 | Renault Dauphine (1/80) | 40 |
| M9 | Simca Ariane (1/80) | 40 |
| M10 | Renault 1000Kgs Army Ambulance (1/100) | 50 |

*A Renault bus, the #3/40 120CV Coach. The ladder at the rear is tinplate.*

# Conrad

This German company is known primarily for its line of 1/43 to 1/50 scale trucks and construction equipment. Conrad was an outgrowth of the Gescha company, which had begun producing die cast models during the 1960s. This product line was re-named Conrad in the early 1970s, and the firm has been turning out high quality die casts ever since.

The following listing is by no means exhaustive; it is intended as a "cross-section" of Conrad models that have been produced through the years. For more information on the company's products, see Part Three, Additional Resources. In particular, the author recommends Dr. Edward Forces's book *Classic Miniature Vehicles Made in Germany.*

| # | Name | Price |
|---|------|-------|
| | **Obsolete models (most, if not all of the following are out of production):** | |
| 250 | Demag Air Drill Truck | $120 |
| 265 | O&K MH6 Wheel Backhoe (red) | 150 |
| 266 | P&H Mobile Crane (yellow) | 120 |
| 275 | Vogele Asphalt Paver (green) | 65 |

| # | Name | Price |
|---|------|-------|
| 276 | Caterpillar 769 B Dump Truck (yellow) | $65 |
| 277 | O&K Track Shovel (red) | 50 |
| 278 | Liebherr 961 Shovel (yellow) | 150 |
| 278A | Liebherr 965 Shovel (yellow) | 100 |
| 279 | Liebherr 961 Backhoe (yellow) | 150 |
| 279A | Liebherr 965 Backhoe (yellow) | 100 |
| 280 | Liebherr 961 Track Shovel (yellow) | 150 |

| # | Name | Price |
|---|------|-------|
| 280A | Liebherr 731 Dozer-Ripper (yellow) | $100 |
| 281 | Liebherr 961 Backhoe (red, yellow) | 150 |
| 282 | Liebherr 921 Wheel Backhoe (yellow) | 120 |
| 283 | Liebherr Tower Crane (yellow) | 120 |
| 286 | Caterpillar 12F Grader (yellow) | 120 |
| 287 | Caterpillar D9 G Dozer (yellow) | 110 |
| 288 | Caterpilar 920 Loader (yellow) | 100 |

| # | Name | Price |
|---|------|-------|
| 2881 | Caterpillar 920 Log Loader (yellow) . . . | $80 |
| 2884 | Clark 125 B Wheel Loader (yellow) | 90 |
| 289 | Poclain SC 150 Track Backhoe (red) . . . | 80 |
| 290 | Atlas AB 1302 Wheel Backhoe (orange) | 125 |
| 2901 | Atlas Wheel Backhoe with Blade (orange) . . . . . . . . . . | 65 |
| 293 | Case Tractor Loader (yellow) . . . . . . . | 85 |
| 3010 | Mercedes-Benz Low Loader Semi (red/black/yellow) . . . . . . . . . . | 80 |
| 302 | Pokorny DW 95 Air Compressor (yellow) . . . . . . . . . . | 150 |
| 3020 | Mercedes-Benz Container Semi (blue/white) . . . . . . . . . . | 80 |
| 3030 | Mercedes-Benz Open Semi (yellow) . . . . | 70 |
| 3031 | Mercedes-Benz Covered Truck and Trailer (blue/gray) . . . . . . . . . . | 90 |
| 3032 | Mercedes-Benz Covered Truck (blue/gray) | 80 |
| 3040 | Mercedes-Benz Dump Truck (orange, yellow) . . . . . . . . . . | 70 |
| 3041 | Mercedes-Benz Garbage Truck (red/white, blue/white) . . . . . . . . . . | 80 |
| 3042 | Mercedes-Schorling Sweeper (orange) . . . | 70 |
| 3050 | Mercedes-Liebherr Cement Mixer (red/black/yellow) . . . . . . . . . . | 90 |
| 3061 | Mercedes-Benz Truck with Crane (orange) . . . . . . . . . . | 60 |
| 3070 | Krupp Crane Truck (yellow) . . . . . . . | 100 |
| 3071 | P & H Crane Truck (yellow) . . . . . . . | 100 |
| 3072 | Liebherr Crane Truck (yellow) . . . . . . | 120 |

**Following is a cross-section of Conrad models currently available at retail or recently discontinued:**

| # | Name | Price |
|---|------|-------|
| 1015 | Volkswagen Santana | CRP |
| 1020 | Audi Quattro Coupe . . . . . . . . . . | CRP |
| 1023 | American LaFrance Fire Truck . . . . . . | CRP |
| 1024 | American LaFrance Fire Truck . . . . . . | CRP |
| 1028 | 1947 Volvo LV 153 Stakebed . . . . . . | CRP |
| 1029 | Volvo LV 293 C2LF Stakebed . . . . . . | CRP |
| 1030 | 1928 Volvo Fire Engine . . . . . . . . . | CRP |
| 1031 | 1902 White Pie Wagon . . . . . . . . . | CRP |
| 1032 | Man KVB "M. Griesham" . . . . . . . . | CRP |
| 1033 | 1958 Magirus with Stetter Mixer . . . | CRP |
| 1034 | 1955 Mercedes Racer Transport . . | CRP |
| 1035 | Man 1920 Gas Tanker "M. Griesham" . . . | CRP |
| 1036 | 1950 Magirus Low Side Dump . . . . | CRP |
| 1037 | Volvo Titan L395 Flatbed/Sides . . . . | CRP |
| 1503 | Mercedes Wagon . . . . . . . . . | CRP |
| 1504 | Mercedes Coupe 300CE . . . . . . . . | CRP |
| 1608 | Mercedes Van Type 208 . . . . . . . . | CRP |
| 1620 | Mercedes-Benz 507D Van . . . . . . . . | CRP |
| 2011 | Potain Tower Crane . . . . . . . . | CRP |
| 2012 | Zeppelin ZBK100 Tower Crane . . . . | CRP |
| 2013 | BPR-Cadillon GT2210 Tower Crane . . | CRP |
| 2014 | Potain Fast Erecting Tower Crane . . | CRP |
| 2020 | Liebherr EC-H Tower Crane . . . . . . | CRP |
| 2022 | Liebherr HC-112-K Tower Crane . . . | CRP |
| 2023 | Liebherr 28K Mobile Tower Crane . . | CRP |
| 2081 | Demag AC435 Superlift Crane . . . | CRP |

| # | Name | Price |
|---|------|-------|
| 2083 | Liebherr LTM1025 Mobile Crane . . . . . . | CRP |
| 2084 | Faun 4-Axle Mobile Crane . . . . . . . . | CRP |
| 2085 | Liebherr 1090 Crane 5 Axle . . . . . . . | CRP |
| 2086 | Demag AC155 Crane . . . . . . . . . | CRP |
| 2421 | Furukawa 345 Wheel Loader . . . . . . | CRP |
| 2422 | O & K L55 Wheel Loader . . . . . . . . | CRP |
| 2425 | Hanomag 70E Wheel Loader . . . . . . | CRP |
| 2427 | Hanomag 15F Wheel Loader . . . . . . | CRP |
| 2428 | Hanomag CL310 Compactor/Bucket . . | CRP |
| 2502 | Grove AMZ66 Manlift . . . . . . . . | CRP |
| 2703 | Case Vibromax 1102 Roller . . . . . . | CRP |
| 2704 | Case Vibromax 854K Tire-Drum . . . | CRP |
| 2710 | Bomag BW 213 D Roller . . . . . . . . | CRP |
| 2711 | Bomag BW 120 AD-2 Roller . . . . . . | CRP |
| 2721 | Dresser 830E 200T Dump . . . . . . | CRP |
| 2722 | Dresser 210M 55 Ton Dump . . . . . | CRP |
| 2771 | O & K RH120 C Shovel . . . . . . . . | CRP |
| 2772 | Demag H135S Hydraulic Shovel . . . | CRP |
| 2803 | Liebherr 722 Dozer . . . . . . . . . | CRP |
| 2804 | Liebherr RL422 Pipelayer . . . . . . | CRP |
| 2815 | Zeppelin ZR28 Abi Pile Driver . . . . | CRP |
| 2817 | Zeppelin ZM 15 Wheel Excavator . . | CRP |
| 2818 | Furukawa W625E Wheel Backhoe . . | CRP |
| 2819 | Furukawa 625E Track Backhoe . . . . | CRP |
| 2827 | Liebherr 984 Shovel . . . . . . . . | CRP |
| 2828 | Liebherr 984 Backhoe . . . . . . . . | CRP |
| 2829 | Liebherr R912 Track Hoe . . . . . . | CRP |
| 2830 | Liebherr A912 Lit. Wheel Clam . . . | CRP |
| 2831 | Liebherr HS882 Track Lat Crane . . . | CRP |
| 2832 | Liebherr A932 Scrap Grapple . . . . | CRP |
| 2833 | Liebherr 310 Wheel Backhoe . . . . | CRP |
| 2834 | Liebherr 954 Backhoe . . . . . . . . | CRP |
| 2835 | Liebherr 932 Track Scrap Hand . . . | CRP |
| 2842 | Fuchs Excavator With Magnet . . . . | CRP |
| 2882 | Liebherr L522 Wheel Loader . . . . . | CRP |
| 2883 | Liebherr L507 Wheel Loader . . . . . | CRP |
| 2887 | Liebherr 531 Wheel Loader . . . . . | CRP |
| 2892 | Case-Poclain 1088 Maxi Backhoe . . | CRP |
| 2894 | Case 1288 Track Excavator . . . . . | CRP |
| 2903 | Atlas 1704 Track Backhoe . . . . . . | CRP |
| 2904 | LI Atlas 1304 Wheel Excavator/Cla . . | CRP |
| 2934 | Case 580 Super K with Serial # . . . | CRP |
| 2936 | Case 590X Tractor Backhoe Load . . | CRP |
| 2954 | Massey Ferguson 60HX Loader/Backhoe . . | CRP |
| 2981 | Linde R14 Forklift . . . . . . . . | CRP |
| 2982 | Linde R16 Forklift . . . . . . . . | CRP |
| 2983 | Fenwick T20 Forklift . . . . . . . . | CRP |
| 2984 | Jungheinrich Ece Forklift . . . . . . | CRP |
| 2985 | Linde E25 Forklift . . . . . . . . | CRP |
| 2994 | Jungheinrich Forklift . . . . . . . . | CRP |
| 2995 | Jungheinrich Forklift . . . . . . . . | CRP |
| 2997 | Jungheinrich EJC 12.5 Forklift . . . | CRP |
| 2998 | Yale Forklift . . . . . . . . . . | CRP |
| 2999 | Kalmar Forklift 40' Container . . . . | CRP |
| 3015 | Mercedes Semi Bulker "L" Hoist . . | CRP |
| 3027 | MB Semi Tanker Linde . . . . . . . | CRP |
| 3037 | Man Small Truck . . . . . . . . . | CRP |
| 3052 | MB Putzmeister Mixer/Pumper . . . | CRP |
| 3060 | MB Semi Suction Unit . . . . . . . | CRP |
| 3064 | (B) MB Mixer "Blank Betonova" . . . . | CRP |

| # | Name | Price |
|---|------|-------|
| 3064 | MB 4 Axle Concrete Mixer . . . . . . | CRP |
| 3066 | MB Suction Vehicle Vacuum TA . . . . | CRP |
| 3069 | MB Schorling P17 Snow Sweeper . . | CRP |
| 3079 | MB-Faun Drain Cleaner Vacuum . . | CRP |
| 3086 | MB Putzm 52/5 5 Axle Concrete Pump . . | CRP |
| 3088 | Liebherr LTF 1030 Crane . . . . . . | CRP |
| 3093 | MB Schwing 32xL Pump . . . . . . | CRP |
| 3095 | Putmeister Concrete Pump 3 Axle . . | CRP |
| 3264 | Iveco Stetter 4x Mixer . . . . . . . | CRP |
| 3274 | Iveco 4 Axle Dump . . . . . . . . | CRP |
| 3330 | Bedford Semi Flatbed . . . . . . . | CRP |
| 3464 | Steyer/Stetter 4x Mixer . . . . . . | CRP |
| 3520 | Freightliner T/T Container . . . . . . | CRP |
| 3523 | MB M Griesheim Bulk Gas Semi . . | CRP |
| 3744 | Volvo NL 12 Concrete Mixer . . . . | CRP |
| 3755 | Volvo NL 12 Atlas Gondola Truck . . | CRP |
| 3775 | Volvo NL 12 Conventional Dump . . | CRP |
| 3776 | Volvo Low Sideboard Truck . . . . . | CRP |
| 3777 | Volvo NL 10 Water Truck . . . . . . | CRP |
| 3812 | Freightliner Conv/Talbert . . . . . . | CRP |
| 3819 | Freightliner Conv Air Products . . . | CRP |
| 3826 | Freightliner Conv Dump Trailer . . . | CRP |
| 3928 | Volvo NL 12 Semi with Refrig. Trailer . . | CRP |
| 4111 | Man/Schmitz Heavy Haulage Trailer . . | CRP |
| 4127 | Man Semi Linde TVTS30 Tanker . . . | CRP |
| 4150 | Man Semi Concrete Mix Stetter . . . | CRP |
| 4165 | Man 4 Axle Mixer "Liebherr" . . . . | CRP |
| 4166 | Man Haller Suction Truck . . . . . . | CRP |
| 4167 | Man 4 Axle Roll-Off . . . . . . . . | CRP |
| 4196 | MB Silo Transporter . . . . . . . . | CRP |
| 4199 | Man Atlas 130.1 Crane Truck . . . . | CRP |
| 4236 | Iveco Euro Cargo Truck . . . . . . | CRP |
| 4298 | Iveco Eurotech Truck . . . . . . . | CRP |
| 4315 | Volvo F12 Semi Bulk Carrier . . . . | CRP |
| 4317 | Volvo F16 Logging Truck/Trailer . . | CRP |
| 4392 | Volvo F12 Air Crash Tender . . . . | CRP |
| 4564 | Volvo FL10 3x Concrete Mixer . . . | CRP |
| 4589 | Volvo FL6 Container Tailgate Lift . . | CRP |
| 4594 | Volvo Schwing KVM 52 Concrete Pump . . | CRP |
| 4608 | Volvo FH12 With Refrig. Trailer . . | CRP |
| 4609 | Volvo FH16 With 4 Axle Trailer . . | CRP |
| 4840 | Iveco Euro Trekker Dump . . . . . . | CRP |
| 4961 | Iveco Eurostar with Tank Trailer . . | CRP |
| 5017 | Mercedes 800 Tractor . . . . . . . | CRP |
| 5066 | Elgin Pelican Sweeper . . . . . . . | CRP |
| 5201 | Kassbohrer Pisten Bully Snow . . . | CRP |
| 5403 | Rosenbauer Fox Fire Pump . . . . . | CRP |
| 5404 | MB M Griesham Acetylene Cutter . . | CRP |
| 5405 | Putmeister Concrete Mix Trailer . . | CRP |
| 5406 | Demag SC40DS-2 Compressor . . . | CRP |
| 5422 | Mercedes Articulated Bus . . . . . | CRP |
| 5423 | Man Luxury Coach Bus . . . . . . . | CRP |
| 5505 | E-1 Hush 95' Ladder Fire Truck . . | CRP |
| 5506 | E-1 Hush 80' Ladder Fire Truck . . | CRP |
| 5510 | E-1 Hush Pumper Fire Truck . . . . | CRP |
| 6036 | Man Type L2000 Truck . . . . . . . | CRP |
| 6107 | Man F2000 Semi Container Truck . . | CRP |
| 6165 | Man F2000 Liebherr 904 Mixer . . . | CRP |

# Corgi Classics

Following a management buy-out in early 1984, Corgi began to focus its energies on its newly re-launched Corgi Classics line of die cast models. The success of the first new Classic, the Thornycroft Van (first produced in 1985), led the company to expand the line to include Public Service Vehicles (including buses, of course) and passenger cars.

Also in 1985, Corgi re-issued four of the original Classics cars from the 1960s. These are differentiated from the originals by the words "Special Edition" on the baseplates, and by boxes lacking a picture of the model.

In 1989, American toy giant Mattel acquired Corgi. And, in 1990, production of Corgi products was moved to the Far East. These two developments disappointed many in the United Kingdom, who had always considered Corgi to be a British company, first and foremost. Following a 1991 move from its long-time home in Swansea to Mattel's United Kingdom headquarters in Leicester, Corgi continued to produce the Classics lines along with a line of simpler Corgi toys aimed at the children's market. (These generally were made with the "speedwheel" style of wheel, and not being particularly collectible, are outside the scope of this book.)

The "American Classics" series was launched in 1994, comprised of American buses, Fire Service vehicles and Vintage trucks. The same year saw the debut of Corgi's "Original Omnibus Company," a line of 1/76 scale British buses.

And, in 1995, Corgi came full circle: a group of investors, led by Corgi Managing Director Chris Guest, bought the collecting arm of Corgi from Mattel, making Corgi an inde-

*A 1915 Ford Model T, one of the original Corgi Classics made during the mid-to late-1960s.*

pendent British company once again. (The toy side of the Corgi line has been kept by Mattel, which has folded the toys into its Hot Wheels line, with the name Corgi to no longer be used.)

Although most of the Classics models listed here are still in production, some have increased in value in just a few year's time; these are listed with their current higher value, while the others are listed as "CRP" (Current Retail Price). And certain castings (particularly the buses) are produced in more liveries than could possibly be listed here, so a sampling is given in these cases.

Values given are for mint condition original examples in original boxes.

| Name | Price |
|---|---|
| **Original "Classics" Car series:** | |
| 1927 Bentley 3 litre | |
|    mid-green, red | $75 |
|    red (Sold as an Avenger set with | |
|       Purdy's Lotus Elan) | 190 |
| 1915 Model T Ford | |
|    yellow, blue, black | 65 |
| 1910 Daimler 38hp | |
|    orange-red | 65 |
| 1910 Renault 12/16 | |
|    yellow, purple | 55 |
|    scarlet (Basil Brush) | 125 |
| 1912 Rolls-Royce Silver Ghost | |
|    silver | 65 |
|    scarlet, yellow (Hardy Boys) | 160 |
| **1980s re-issues of 1960s Classics models:** | |
| 1927 Bentley 3 litre | |
|    green, red, black | 10 |
|    pewter | 35 |

| Name | Price |
|---|---|
| 1915 Model T Ford | |
|    red, black, blue | $10 |
| 1910 Renault 12/16 | |
|    brown, blue, yellow | 10 |
| 1912 Rolls-Royce Silver Ghost | |
|    silver, black, red | 10 |
| **1/36th scale cars:** | |
| Bentley 'R' | |
|    white, two-tone blue | 30 |
|    black, cream | 20 |
| Chevrolet Bel-Air | |
|    various colors | 10 |
| Ford Thunderbird | |
|    various colors | 15 |
|    red/white (hood down) | 25 |
| Jaguar XK120 | |
|    various colors | 15 |
|    cream/black (414) | 40 |
|    red/black | 40 |

| Name | Price |
|---|---|
| MG TF | |
|    various colors | $25 |
| Mercedes-Benz 300SL Gullwing | |
|    red, silver | 10 |
| Mercedes-Benz 300S | |
|    various colors | 10 |
|    two-tone green (hood down) | 65 |
| Rolls-Royce Silver Dawn | |
|    red/black, silver/black | 15 |
|    beige/cream | 30 |
| **1/43rd scale cars:** | |
| Ford Lotus Cortina | |
|    various colors, liveries | 10 |
| Ford Popular | |
|    various colors | 10 |
| Ford Zephyr | |
|    various colors | 10 |
| Ford Zodiac | |
|    various colors | 10 |

| Name | Price |
|---|---|
| **Jaguar Mk II** | |
| various colors | $15 |
| maroon/black (Inspector Morse) | 45 |
| **Saab 96** | |
| various colors | 10 |
| **Mercedes-Benz 300 SL Roadster** | |
| various colors | 10 |
| **Morris Minor** | |
| various colors, liveries | 15 |
| black (British school of Motoring) | 25 |
| Police panda car | 25 |
| **Morris Minor Convertible** | |
| various colors, open and closed | 15 |
| **Morris Minor Traveller** | |
| dark green | 25 |
| black | 15 |
| **Mini Cooper** | |
| various colors | 10 |
| **Austin Healey 3000** | |
| various colors, hardtop and convertible | 10 |
| **Ferrari 250 GTO** | |
| red | 10 |
| **Jaguar E Type** | |
| various colors | 15 |
| **Jaguar XK120** | |
| various colors | 15 |
| **MGA** | |
| various colors | 10 |
| **Porsche 356B** | |
| various colors | 10 |
| **Triumph TR3A** | |
| hard top: red body, black top | 10 |
| **Mr Bean's Mini** | 25 |

**Gift Sets:**

| Name | Price |
|---|---|
| Racing Fords (Popular, Cortina and Zodiac) | 60 |
| Racing Zephyrs (three Zephyrs) | 40 |
| Rally (Jaguar Mk II, Ford Cortina, Austin Healey hard top and MGA soft top) | 40 |
| Police cars (Jaguar MK II, Morris Minor and Ford Zephyr | 60 |
| Jaguar E Type 30th Anniversary (open top version and soft top version) | 30 |
| Jaguar Through the Years (E Type, XK120 and Mark II) | 40 |
| Stirling's Choice (Jaguar XK120 and Austin Healey) | 25 |
| The Racing E Types (ivory soft top and red soft top) | 25 |
| Austin Healey Winner (red and white hard top, green soft top, blue open top) | 45 |
| The Jaguar Collection (red Mark II, green XK120 open top and red open top E Type) | 45 |
| Abingdon (red MGA hard top, white MGA and Morris J van) | 45 |
| Ferrari (blue, green and gray) | 35 |
| RAC Rally (three Jaguar XK120s: in cream, green and white) | 45 |
| Monte Carlo (three red Mini Coopers in red with numbers 37, 52 and 177) | 45 |
| Italian Job (three Mini Coopers) | 45 |

| Name | Price |
|---|---|
| First Time Out (three Jaguar XK120s: red, white and blue) | $35 |
| Tour de France (red Ferrari 250, white Jaguar Mk II and red Mini Cooper) | 35 |
| Alpine Rally (red Ford Cortina, red Austin Healey and red Mini Cooper) | 35 |

**Buses:**

| Name | Price |
|---|---|
| **AEC Regent** | |
| Eastbourne, Nottingham, Leicester City liveries | 45 |
| London Transport (Wisk Soap or Maples), Newcastle liveries | 30 |
| Other liveries such as Glasgow, Brighton and Hove and Liverpool | 20 |
| **Bristol K Utility** | |
| London Transport, Bristol | 35 |
| **Daimler CW Utility** | |
| West Bromwich, Derby, Sheffield | 35 |
| **Daimler Fleetline** | |
| Birmingham, Manchester | 40 |
| **Guy Arab** | |
| Southdown | 50 |
| Birmingham | 40 |
| Other liveries such as Yorkshire, Maidstone and District, Wolverhampton | 35 |
| **Leyland Atlantean** | |
| Ribble, Hull | 40 |
| **Thornycroft** | |
| Portsmouth | 45 |
| City | 35 |
| Thomas Tilling | 30 |
| Other liveries such as East Surrey, Douglas Corporation, South Wales | 25 |

**Coaches:**

| Name | Price |
|---|---|
| **AEC Regal** | |
| Various liveries such as Hanson, Western Welsh, Oxford, Timpson's, West Riding | $25 |
| **Bedford OB** | |
| Southdown | 250 |
| Norfolk | 115 |
| Royal Blue | 115 |
| Bluebird | 65 |
| MacBraynes | 55 |
| South Midlands, Premier | 50 |
| Crosville, Grey Cars, East Yorkshire, Hants and Sussex | 40 |
| Southern Vectis, Eastern, Wallace Arnold | 30 |
| Other liveries such as Southern National, Murgatroyd, Devon General, Edinburgh | 25 |
| **Burlingbam Seagull** | |
| Stratford Blue | 65 |
| Ribble, Yelloway | 35 |
| Other liveries such as King Alfred, Neath and Cardiff | 25 |
| **Daimler Duple coach** | |
| Swan, Blue Bus Services, Burwell and District | 25 |
| **Leyland Tiger** | |
| Liveries such as Ribble, Bartons, Red and White | 25 |
| **Trolleybuses** | |
| Karrier W Trolleybus | |
| Newcastle | 30 |
| Sunbeam Trolleybus | |
| Reading | 30 |

*One of the more popular of the current Corgi Classics is this Morris Minor Traveller, first released in 1994. Like many Corgi Classics models, it comes with separate side mirrors and front bumper over-riders (none of which are attached to this example).*

| Name | Price |
|---|---|

## Trams:

Double deck, closed top and open front
  Bradford . . . . . . . . . . . . . . . . . . . . . $45
  Birmingham . . . . . . . . . . . . . . . . 40
  Other liveries such as Southampton,
    Birkenhead, Leeds, London . . . . . . . . 25
Double deck, closed top and closed front
  Liveries such as Leicester, Newcastle,
    Portsmouth, Belfast . . . . . . . . . . 25
Double deck, open top and open front
  Liveries such as Bournemouth, Croydon,
    Bath Electric Tramways, South Shields . . . 25
Single deck
  Liveries such as Derby, Ashton-under-Lyne,
    Southampton . . . . . . . . . . . . . . . 25

## American Coaches:

Yellow Coach 743
  Greyhound Lines (includes New York
    World's Fair) . . . . . . . . . . . . . . . . 40
  Burlingham Trailways . . . . . . . . . . . . 40
  Champlain . . . . . . . . . . . . . . . . . 40
Motor Coach Industries MCI
  Demonstration bus, Peter Pan Trailways,
    Peter Pan Birthday . . . . . . . . . . . 40

## Gift Sets:

Transport of the early 1950s (Bedford OB coach,
  AEC Regent bus) . . . . . . . . . . . . . . 70
Barton's 1950s transport (Bedford OB coach,
  AEC Regent bus) . . . . . . . . . . . . . . 40
60 Years of Transport (closed top tram, Bedford
  OB coach, Thornycroft bus) . . . . . . . . 240
Island Transport Jersey (two Bedford OB
  coaches) . . . . . . . . . . . . . . . . . . 35
Yelloway (AEC Regal coach, Bedford OB coach) . . 45
Coventry bus set (Bedford OB coach and AEC
  Regent bus) . . . . . . . . . . . . . . . . 35
AEC bus set (AEC Regal coach, AEC Regent bus) . . 35
Gosport and Fareham bus set (AEC Regal coach,
  AEC Regent bus) . . . . . . . . . . . . . . 40
Silver Service bus set (AEC Regal coach, Bedford
  OB coach) . . . . . . . . . . . . . . . . . 45
Devon bus set (AEC Regal coach, AEC Regent
  bus) . . . . . . . . . . . . . . . . . . . . 40
East Rent set (AEC Regal coach, Bedford OB
  coach) . . . . . . . . . . . . . . . . . . . 40
South Wales bus set (AEC Regal coach, Bedford
  OB coach) . . . . . . . . . . . . . . . . . 40
East Lancashire bus set (Guy Arab bus, Leyland
  Tiger coach) . . . . . . . . . . . . . . . . 60
W. Alexander and Sons Ltd bus set (Guy Arab
  bus, Leyland Tiger coach) . . . . . . . . . 60
Regent Bus (two AEC Regents) . . . . . . . . 30
Whittie Buses (Burlingham Seagull, AEC Regal) . 45
From Corkhills to de Vanenburg (two Bedford
  OB coaches) . . . . . . . . . . . . . . . . 45
Premier Buses (Leyland Tiger, Bedford OB coach) 45
York Brothers (Burlingham Seagull, AEC Regal) . 45
Devon General (Guy Arab, Leyland Atlantean) . . 60

| Name | Price |
|---|---|

## Original Omnibus Company (1/76th scale):

AEC Reliance
  DevonGeneral, Oxford . . . . . . . . . . $25
Bristol K (lowbridge)
  Hants and Dorset, West Yorkshire, Western
    National . . . . . . . . . . . . . . . . . 25
Bristol L
  Merthyr Tydfil, United, Maidstone & District . . . 25
Leyland Leopard
  Midland Red, Ribble . . . . . . . . . . . 25

## O.O.C. Bus Sets:

Thames Valley (Bristol K, Bristol L) . . . . . . 40
Crosville (Bristol K, Bristol L) . . . . . . . . . 40

## Fire Vehicles:

American La France Aerial Rescue Truck
  Original (1968 model) (various types) . . . . 85
  re-issue, open cab . . . . . . . . . . . . 40
  Centerville, closed cab . . . . . . . . . . 40
  Denver, closed cab . . . . . . . . . . . . 40
American La France Pumper
  various liveries such as Chicago, Denver,
    Orlando . . . . . . . . . . . . . . . . . 35
Mack CF Pumper
  Chicago . . . . . . . . . . . . . . . . . . 35
Chevrolet Fire Chief Car
  Chicago . . . . . . . . . . . . . . . . . . 20
AEC Pumper
  Liveries such as Nottinghamshire, Hertfordshire,
    Cleveland . . . . . . . . . . . . . . . . 35
AEC Ladder
  Cardiff, Stoke, Bristol, Dublin . . . . . . . 40
Simon Snorkel Fire Engine
  West Glamorgan . . . . . . . . . . . . . . 40

## Gift Set:

La France set (Scottdale, South River) . . . . . 40

## Comic and Superhero models:

Morris 1000 van: The Rover . . . . . . . . . 15
Bedford CA van: Adventure . . . . . . . . . . 15
Morris J van: The Midland . . . . . . . . . . 15
Volkswagen van: The Skipper . . . . . . . . . 15
Ford Popular van: Hotspur . . . . . . . . . . 15
Ford Popular van: The Beezer . . . . . . . . . 15
Morris 1000 van: Tiger . . . . . . . . . . . . 15
Volkswagen van: Lion . . . . . . . . . . . . . 15
Morris J van: The Topper . . . . . . . . . . . 15

## Gift Sets:

Beano and Dandy (two Bedford CA vans) . . . . 75
Beano (AEC bus, Morris J van) . . . . . . . . 35
Dandy (Morris J van, Bedford CA van) . . . . . 35
Eagle (Bedford CA van, Volkswagen van) . . . . 35
Beano (Morris 1000 van, Morris J van) . . . . . 35
X-Men (Bedford CA van, Morris J van) . . . . . 35
Spiderman (Morris J van, Morris 1000 van) . . . 35
Captain America (Volkswagen van, Ford Popular
  van) . . . . . . . . . . . . . . . . . . . . 35

| Name | Price |
|---|---|

## Commercial Vehicles:

AEC Cabover van
  LMS Parcels (Puck Matches) . . . . . . . $115
  Royal Mail . . . . . . . . . . . . . . . . 40
  Other liveries such as His Master's Voice,
    Weetabix, Great Western Railway . . . . . 25
AEC Cabover Tanker
  Liveries such as Carles Capel, Somerlite
    Oil, Mobilgas . . . . . . . . . . . . . . 30
AEC Truck
  Pickfords . . . . . . . . . . . . . . . . . 25
AEC Truck with Trailer
  Billy Smart's Circus, S. Houseman, J. Ayers . . 45
AEC Flatbed Truck and Trailer
  British Road Services . . . . . . . . . . . 45
AEC Flatbed with chains
  Greenall Whitley . . . . . . . . . . . . . 45
Bedford 'O' Articulated
  London Brick Company Limited . . . . . . . 25
Bedford 'O' Box Van
  Carter Paterson
    green roof . . . . . . . . . . . . . . . . 35
    red roof . . . . . . . . . . . . . . . . . 65
  Other liveries such as Millers Baking Powder,
    Terry's of York, Cadburys, Post Office
    Telephones . . . . . . . . . . . . . . . 25
Bedford Pantechnicon
  Waring and Gillows . . . . . . . . . . . 120
  Pickfords . . . . . . . . . . . . . . . . . 65
  Frasers of Ipswich . . . . . . . . . . . . 75
  Going for Gold (gold plated) . . . . . . . 75
  Steinway and Sons . . . . . . . . . . . . 45
  Camp Hopson . . . . . . . . . . . . . . 45
  Bishops . . . . . . . . . . . . . . . . . . 40
  Wylie and Lochhead . . . . . . . . . . . 45
  Weetabix . . . . . . . . . . . . . . . . . 35
  Other liveries such as Michael Gerson,
    Howells & Son, Blackpool Circus . . . . . 25
ERF eight-wheel Flatbed
  Eddie Stobart . . . . . . . . . . . . . . . 75
ERF Tanker
  Blue Circle, Esso . . . . . . . . . . . . . 35
Foden Flatbed
  Pickfords . . . . . . . . . . . . . . . . . 35
Foden Flatbed with Chains
  Guinness . . . . . . . . . . . . . . . . . 35
Foden Tanker
  Guinness . . . . . . . . . . . . . . . . . 75
  Milk Marketing Board . . . . . . . . . . 35
  Hovis . . . . . . . . . . . . . . . . . . . 35
  Regent (elliptical) . . . . . . . . . . . . . 35
Bedford Truck with Trailer
  Billy Smart's Circus . . . . . . . . . . . . 45
Mack Van
  Buffalo Fire Department . . . . . . . . . . 20
  Greyhound Express Van Service . . . . . . 20
  Olther liveries such as Pepsi-Cola, Carnation,
    Stanley Tools . . . . . . . . . . . . . . 15

| Name | Price |
|---|---|
| Renault Van | |
| Royal Mail | $125 |
| Gervais Danone | 35 |
| Other liveries such as The Lipton, Courvoisier | 15 |
| Scammell Highwayman Tractor and Trailers | |
| R. Edwards and Sons Ltd | 50 |
| Scammell Scarab | |
| British Railways | 60 |
| Other liveries such as Royal Mail, British Road Services, Rail freight | 25 |
| Thornycroft van | |
| Lyons Swiss Rolls | 110 |
| Grattans | 105 |
| Jacobs | 65 |
| Allenburys Foods | 45 |
| Goodyear | 45 |
| Radio Steiner | 40 |
| Nurdin and Peacock | 40 |
| Arnotts Biscuits | 40 |
| Other liveries such as Eddershaws, Lincolnshire Police, Huntley and Palmers, McDougalls | 25 |
| Royalty series | |
| Liveries such as Buckingham Palace, Balmoral, Sandringham | 15 |
| Royalty series with open back or tilt | |
| Liveries such as LMS Express Parcels, Red Cross Field Ambulance, East Anglian Fruit Company | 35 |
| Thornycroft Beer Lorry | |
| Liveries such as Swan Brewery, St. Winifreds, Charles Wells | 15 |
| Chipperfield's Circus—new 1994-onwards series (all are at Current Retail Price) | |
| Scammell Highwayman and two trailers | |
| Bedford Articulated Truck | |
| Scammell with Crane | |
| ERF 8-wheel Rigid Truck | |
| AEC Pole Open Pole Truck | |
| Bedford CA Van (booking van) | |
| Bedford Pantechnicon-Bertie Smee Wardrobe | |
| Scammell Highwayman with Pole Trailer and Caravan | |
| AEC Regal Coach (living accornmodation) | |
| Bedford articulated cab and Horsebox | |
| Closed Pole Truck with Caravan | |
| AEC Truck and Cages Trailer | |
| Bedford CA Van | |
| Liveries such as Express Dairies, Manchester Evenings News, Corgi Collectors Club | 15 |
| Bedford Dormobile | |
| various colors | 15 |
| Ford Model T van | |
| Lyons Tea | |
| white roof | 15 |
| black roof | 150 |
| NAFFI | 60 |
| Other liveries such as John Menzies, Twinings Tea, Steiff, Royal Mail | 15 |

| Name | Price |
|---|---|
| Ford Model T tanker | |
| Liveries such as Rimers, Dominion, National Benzole | $15 |
| Ford Popular van | |
| Liveries such as Pearsons Carpets, Eastbourne Motors, Sheldon light haulage | 15 |
| Morris J Van | |
| Bovril | 35 |
| Family Assurance Friendly Society Ltd. | 35 |
| Post Offices Telephones | 25 |
| Royal Mail | 25 |
| Other liveries such as Wall's Ice Cream, Pickfords | 15 |
| Morris Minor van | |
| BATR | 60-80 |
| Royal Mail | 35 |
| Post Office Telephones | 35 |
| Corgi Collectors Club | 35 |
| MacFisheries | 25 |
| Guernsey Post Office | 25 |
| Other liveries such as Michelin, Bristol Water, Foyles for Books, Colmans Mustard | 15 |
| Morris Minor Pick-up | |
| Wimpey, London Brick Company Ltd. | 15 |
| Mini Van | |
| Liveries such as RAC Radio Service, Royal Mail, Police | 15 |
| Volkswagen van | |
| Blue (no livery) | 15 |
| Bosch Auto Electrical, Corgi Collectors Club (1992) | 15 |
| Volkswagen Camper | |
| Various colors | 15 |

**Classics Gift Sets:**

| Name | Price |
|---|---|
| Royal Mail (Bedford 'O' Box van, Morris Minor van) | 65 |
| GPO Telephones (AEC Cabover van, Morris Minor van) | 45 |
| Shell 1910-40 (AEC Cabover tanker, Thornycroft van) | 35 |
| Shell 1950-60 (Bedford 'O' Box van, Bedford Pantechnicon) | 40 |
| British Railways (Ford Popular van, Bedford CA van) | 35 |
| British Railways (Bedford 'O' Box van, Morris J van) | 35 |
| The Times (Thornycroft bus, Ford Model T van) | 25 |
| London Markets (three Ford Model T vans) | 30 |
| Police Morris Minor vans (two vans) | 35 |
| Battle of Britain 50th Anniversary (Bedford OB coach RAF, Morris Minor van RAF, Ford Zephyr RAF) | 40 |
| National Resources (Bedford CA van Gas, Ford Popular van NCB, Morris J van Electricity, Morris Minor van Water) | 45 |
| 225th Anniersary of York Fair (Bedford OB coach, Bedford Pantechnicon) | 45 |

| Name | Price |
|---|---|
| Northern Collection (Bedford OB coach, Bedford Pantechnicon) | $45 |
| United Dairies (AEC Cabover van, AEC Cabover tanker) | 30 |
| Ray's Delivery (Thornycroft van, Ford Model T van) | 55 |
| England's Glory (Thornycroft van, Ford Model T van) | 30 |
| Ford Model T set (two Model T vans, two Model T tankers) | 40 |
| Minor and Popular vans (two Minors, two Populars) | 50 |
| Pickfords (Bedford Pantechnicon, Morris Minor van, Ford Popular van) | 120 |
| Corgi 'We're on the move' (Bedford OB coach, Bedford Pantechnicon) | 35 |
| Military set (Thornycroft bus, Ford Model T van) | 35 |
| Ford Utility set (two Ford Model T vans) | 15 |
| Morris Minor van set (three vans) | 85 |
| The Times (Bedford CA van, Morris Minor van) | 25 |
| Ian Allen 50th Anniversary (AEC Regent bus, Bedford CA van) | 25 |
| Cumbrian set (Bedford 'O' Box van, Morris J van) | 40 |
| Terry's Chocolate (Thornycroft van, Ford Model T van) | 30 |
| Ford Popular vans | 40 |
| BRS Parcels Service (Bedford 'O' Box van, Morris J van) | 35 |
| Strathblair (Bedford OB coach, Morris J van) | 35 |
| Leicestershire and Rutland Police (Morris Minor van, Jaguar MkII) | 30 |
| Metropolitan Police (Morris Minor Panda, Bedford OB coach) | 30 |
| Toymasters (Bedford CA van, Morris J van) | 25 |
| LMS Railway (AEC Cabover van, Thornycroft van) | 20 |
| D-Day (Ford Popular, Morris J van, Bedford 'O' van, open top tram) | 70 |
| Yellowstone National Park Service (Ford T tanker, Ford T car) | 40 |
| Greene King Brewery (AEC Cabover tanker, Thornycroft beer lorry) | 30 |
| Charringtons (AEC Cabover tanker, Thornycroft beer lorry) | 30 |
| Whitbread Brewery (Bedford 'O' Box van, Ford Model T van) | 30 |
| John Smith's Brewery (AEC Cabover tanker, Thornycroft beer lorry) | 30 |
| Whitbread 250th Anniversary (AEC Cabover tanker, Thornycroft beer lorry) | 35 |
| Ruddles Brewery (Bedford 'O' Box van, Thornycroft beer lorry) | 35 |
| Bass Brewery set (Thornycroft open back with crates, Ford Model T van) | 35 |
| Websters Brewery (AEC Cabover tanker, Thornycroft beer lorry) | 35 |

# Corgi Toys

Corgi toys were launched in 1956 by Mettoy Co. Ltd., in Swansea, South Wales. Mettoy, founded by Philipp Ullmann and Arthur Katz, had been producing tinplate toys for some years. They had also been making a line of die cast cars and trucks known as "Castoys" since 1948, which came with a clockwork motor and windows, features which would serve the company well when the Corgi line was introduced. Castoys are now quite rare. (The Castoys are listed at the end of this section, after the Husky/Corgi Juniors.)

From the beginning, Corgis gave the established Dinky toys a run for their money. They offered the buyer features that hadn't been available until then, such as windows. In fact, Corgis were often called "the ones with windows" to differentiate them from the competition. A number of the early Corgis also were fitted with friction-powered motors, a feature which was discontinued in 1959.

In addition to producing models of nearly every type of vehicle in the world, the 1960s saw Corgi Toys enter one of its most lucrative markets: that of the television and movie related toy. Cars such as Chitty Chitty Bang Bang and the Batmobile proved to be best sellers (and are highly prized in original condition by today's collectors), but even they played second banana to a certain British sports car driven by a certain British spy. The James Bond Aston Martin hit the shelves in 1965 and proved to be a blockbuster that is still selling, re-issues of the car being currently available.

Over the years, Corgi produced two lines of smaller die cast toys. The "Husky" series was introduced in 1965, comprised of American, British and European models. In 1969, the Husky name was dropped, being replaced by "Corgi Juniors" in 1970. More and more of the Corgi Juniors were produced using "Whizzwheels," to compete against the hugely popular Hot Wheels cars. Corgi Juniors were phased out in the mid-1970s.

The other small Corgi line was called "Rockets," and these were made from 1970-72. They were also designed to gain a share of the market dominated by Hot Wheels. They featured Whizzwheels, and a number of accessories and race sets on which to run them were also available.

While the late 1970s proved to be the end of the road for Meccano's Dinky Toys, Mettoy continued producing Corgi Toys for markets all over the world. The 1980s, though, would present serious challenges for the company, and in 1984 a management buy-out occurred, with the "new" Corgi being launched on March 29. The following year, Corgi began to concentrate on its series of classic models, relaunching the "Corgi Classics" line to great success. Although there had been a few "Corgi Classics" models produced during the 1960s, the series now took off in a major

Corgi Toys #303S, the Mercedes-Benz 300SL Open Roadster with original box. This model made its debut in 1958 and was in production until 1960.

The #229 Chevrolet Corvair, made by Corgi starting in 1961.

way, and in fact is now the main focus of the company's efforts. See the Corgi Classics section for more infomation on these well-detailed models.

As for packaging, the standard Corgis always came in individual boxes. Gift sets came in larger boxes, of course, and the smaller Husky and Corgi Jr. cars came in blister packs. Originally, the boxes were light blue, with artwork of the car on the box. In 1959, though, the company began using a yellow and light blue box style, which lasted until 1967. A succession of styles followed this, leading in the late 1980s to the predominantly tan boxes of today's Corgi Classics. (The values given here are for near mint to mint examples in their original boxes.)

*Note on listings:* An "M" after the number indicates the model is friction-powered; the motor should be checked when considering a purchase.

## Gift Sets:

| # | Name | Price |
|---|------|------:|
| IA | Carrimore Car Transporter with four cars | $650 |
| IB | Ford 500 Tractor and beast carrying trailer | 135 |
| IC | Ford Sierra and Caravan | 25 |
| 2A | Land Rover and Horsebox | 110 |
| 2B | Unimog Dumper and Cub | 150 |
| 3A | RAF Land Rover and Bloodhound Missile | 175 |
| 3B | Batmobile and Bat Boat with Bat Hubs | 400 |
|    | Whizzwheels | 190 |
| 4A | RAF Land Rover and Bloodhound Missile Set | 400 |
| 4B | Country Farm Set with hay load | 50 |
| 5A | Racing Cars | 240 |
| 5B | Agricultural Set | 320 |
| 5C | Country Farm Set | 90 |
| 6A | Rocket Age Set | 1,050 |
| 6B | VW Transporter and Cooper Maserati | 160 |
| 7A | Massey Tractor and Trailer | 120 |
| 7B | Daktari Set | 110 |
| 8A | Combine Harvester, Tractor and Trailer | 400 |
| 8B | Lions of Longleat Regular or cast wheels | 160 |
|    | Whizzwheels | 120 |
| 9A | Corporal Missile and Launcher Set | 640 |
| 9B | Tractor with Shovel and Trailer | 200 |
| 10A | Rambler Marlin with Kayaks | 190 |
| 10B | Centurion Tank and Transporter | 80 |
| IIA | ERF Dropside Truck and Trailer | 190 |
| IIB | London Set (bus, taxi and 204 Mini) | 135 |
| 12A | Circus Crane and Cage | 280 |
| 12B | Grand Prix Set | 400 |
| 12C | Glider Set | 65 |
| 13A | Fordson Tractor with Plough | 120 |
| 13B | Renault 16 Tour De France | 120 |
| 13C | Peugeot Tour De France | 65 |
| 14A | Jeep Tower Wagon | 65 |
| 14B | Giant Daktari Set | 1,700 |
|    | Regular wheels | 480 |
|    | Whizzwheels | 350 |
| 15A | Silverstone Set | 1,600 |
| 15B | Land Rover and Horsebox | 75 |
| 16 | Ecurie Ecosse Set | 480 |
| 17A | Land Rover and Ferrari | 160 |
| 17B | Military Set | 70 |
| 18A | Fordson Tractor and Plough | 120 |
| 18B | Emergency Set | 65 |
| 19A | Circus Land Rover and Elephant Trailer | 220 |
| 19B | Flying Club Set | 50 |
| 19C | Emergency Set | 65 |
| 20A | Golden Guinea Set | 275 |
| 20B | Scammell Car Transporter Set | 800 |
| 20C | Emergency Set | 65 |
| 21A | ERF Milk Truck and Trailer | 320 |

| # | Name | Price |
|---|------|------:|
| 21B | Circus Crane and Menagerie Trailer | $1,600 |
| 21C | Superman Set | 200 |
| 22A | Agricultural Set | 950 |
| 22B | James Bond Set | 250 |
| 23A | Circus Set | 880 |
| 23B | Spiderman Set | 160 |
| 24A | Commer Construction Set | 130 |
| 24B | Mercedes and Caravan | 25 |
| 25A | Shell/BP Garage Set | 1,750 |
| 25B | VW Transporter and Cooper Maserati | 175 |
| 26A | Beach Buggy and Sailboat | 35 |
| 26B | Matra Rancho and Racing Car | 65 |
| 27 | Machinery Carrier and Cub Shovel | 160 |
| 28A | Car Transporter and four Cars | 800 |
| 28B | Mazda Pick-up and Dinghy | 40 |
| 29A | Massey Ferguson Tractor and Trailer | 145 |
| 29B | Ferrari Daytona and Race Car | 40 |
| 30A | Grand Prix Set | 235 |
| 30B | Circus Land Rover and Trailer | 45 |
| 31A | Buick Riviera Set | 200 |
| 31B | Safari Set (Land Rover and Trailer) | 65 |
| 32 | Tractor and Trailer | 160 |
| 33 | London Set | 185 |
| 35 | Chopper Squad | 45 |
| 36A | Oldsmobile Toronado and Speedboat | 240 |
| 36B | Tarzan Set | 200 |
| 37A | Lotus Racing Set | 400 |
| 37B | Fiat XI/9 and boat | 45 |
| 38A | Monte Carlo Set | 880 |
| 38B | Mini Camping Set | 70 |
| 38C | Jaguar XJ8 and Powerboat | 65 |
| 39A | State Landall | 95 |
| 40A | Avengers Set | |
|    | red Bentley | 640 |
|    | green Bentley | 800 |

| # | Name | Price |
|---|------|------:|
| 40B | Batman Triple Set | $235 |
| 41A | Ford H Transporter and six Cars | 760 |
| 41B | Silver Jubilee State Landau | 40 |
| 42A | Agricultural Set | 65 |
| 43A | Silo and Conveyor Belt | 65 |
| 44A | Police Land Rover and Horsebox | 50 |
| 45 | All Winners with 261 James Bond car | 720 |
| 46A | All Winners | 475 |
| 46B | Super Karts | 40 |
| 47A | Ford 5000 Tractor and Conveyor | 180 |
| 47B | Pony Club Set | 50 |
| 48A | Ford H Transporter and six Cars | 640 |
| 48B | Scammell Transporter | 800 |
| 48C | Jean Richard Circus | 200 |
| 49 | Flying Club Set | 35 |

## Single model Corgi Toys:

| # | Name | Price |
|---|------|------:|
| 50 | Massey Ferguson 65 Tractor | 90 |
| C50 | Massey Ferguson 50B Tractor | 40 |
| 51 | Massey Ferguson Tipper Trailer | 15 |
| 53 | Massey Ferguson Tractor with Shovel | 90 |
| 54 | Fordson Half-Track Tractor blue, brown, silver | 160 |
|    | with headlights in grille | 305 |
| 54 | Massey with shovel | 45 |
| 55 | Fordson Major Tractor | 80 |
| 55 | David Brown Tractor | 40 |
| 56 | Plough | 15 |
| 57 | Farm Tipper Trailer | 15 |
| 57 | Massey Ferguson Tractor with Fork | 100 |
| 58 | Beast Carrier | 25 |
| 60 | Fordson Power Major Tractor | 95 |
| 61 | Four-Furrow Plough | 15 |
| 62 | Ford Tipper Trailer | 15 |
| 64 | Conveyor on Jeep | 80 |
| 66 | Massey Ferguson 165 Tractor | 70 |

*This Chevrolet Corvette, #310 in the Corgi line, captured the lines of the full-size car quite well when it debuted in 1963 (it also came in silver and bronze color schemes). Corgi kept it in production until Chevy unveiled its new-for-1968 Corvette.*

| # | Name | Price |
|---|------|-------|
| 67 | Ford Super Major Tractor | $75 |
| 69 | Massey Ferguson 165 Tractor and shovel | 65 |
| 71 | Fordson Disc Harrow | 25 |
| 72 | Ford 5000 Tractor and Rear Trencher | 125 |
| 73 | Massey Ferguson Tractor and Saw | 95 |
| 74 | Ford 5000 Tractor and Scoop | 95 |
| 100 | Dropside Trailer | 20 |
| 101 | Platform Trailer | 20 |
| 102 | Rice's Pony Trailer | 25 |

| # | Name | Price |
|---|------|-------|
| C154 | John Player Special Lotus | $25 |
| C154 | Texaco Special Lotus | 25 |
| 155 | Lotus Climax Racing Car | 45 |
| C155 | Shadow Formula I Racing Car | 30 |
| 156 | Cooper Maserati Racing Car | 40 |
| C156 | Graham Hill's Shadow | 25 |
| 158 | Lotus Climax Racing Car | 40 |
| C158 | Elf Tyrell Ford Formula I | 35 |
| 159 | Cooper Maserati | 40 |
| C159 | Indianapolis Racing Car | 35 |
| C160 | Hesketh 308 Formula I | 35 |

| # | Name | Price |
|---|------|-------|
| 202 | Morris Cowley | $135 |
| 202M | Morris Cowley | 150 |
| 202 | Renault R16 | 25 |
| 203 | Vauxhall Velox | 120 |
| 203M | Vauxhall Velox | 175 |
| 203 | Mangusta de Tomaso | 25 |
| 204 | Rover 90 | 125 |
|  | white and red two-tone | 240 |
| 204M | Rover 90 | 160 |
| 204 | Morris Mini Minor | 90 |
| 205 | Riley Pathfinder | 100 |
| 205M | Riley Pathfinder | 140 |
| 206 | Hillman Husky Estate | 85 |
| 206M | Hillman Husky Estate | 130 |
| 207 | Standard Vanguard | 115 |
| 207M | Standard Vanguard | 175 |
| 208 | Jaguar 2.4 Saloon | 120 |
| 208M | Jaguar 2.4 Saloon | 150 |
| 209 | Riley Pathfinder Police Car | 90 |
| 210 | Citroën DS19 | 85 |
|  | yellow with black roof | 150 |
| 211 | Studebaker Golden Hawk | 80 |
| 211M | Studebaker Golden Hawk | 130 |
| 213 | Jaguar Fire Chief Car | 115 |
| 214 | Ford Thunderbird Hard Top | 100 |
| 214M | Ford Thunderbird Hard Top | 150 |
| 215 | Ford Thunderbird Open Sports | 90 |
| 216 | Austin A40 | 75 |
|  | red with black roof | 135 |
| 216M | Austin A40 Mechanical | 115 |
| 217 | Fiat 1800 | 75 |
| 218 | Aston Martin DB4 Saloon | 100 |
| 219 | Plymouth Sports Suburban | 65 |
| 220 | Chevrolet Impala | 80 |
| 221 | Chevrolet Yellow Cab | 70 |
| 222 | Renault Floride | 55 |
| 223 | Chevrolet Impala State Patrol | 50 |
| 224 | Bentley Continental | 80 |
| 225 | Austin Seven | 90 |
|  | yellow | 210 |
| 226 | Morris Mini-Minor | 85 |
|  | yellow | 200 |
| 227 | Mini Cooper Competition | 210 |
| 228 | Volvo P1800 | 75 |
| 229 | Chevrolet Corvair | 40 |
| 230 | Mercedes-Benz 220SE Coupe | 60 |
| 231 | Triumph Herald Coupe | 80 |
| 232 | Fiat 2100 | 50 |
| 233 | Heinkel Bubble Car | 80 |
| 234 | Ford Consul Classic 315 | 70 |
| 235 | Oldsmobile Super 88 | 75 |
| 236 | Austin A60 Driving School Car | 65 |
| 237 | Oldsmobile Sheriff Car | 75 |
| 238 | Jaguar Mk 10 Saloon | 90 |
| 239 | VW Karmann Ghia | 80 |
| 240 | Fiat Jolly | 70 |
| 241 | Ghia L64 | 75 |
| 242 | Ghia-Fiat 600 Jolly | 150 |
| 245 | Buick Riviera | 60 |
| 246 | Chrysler Imperial | 75 |
|  | metallic turquoise | 220 |

*The Holmes Wrecker, #1142 in the Corgi line from 1967 until 1974. The cab tilts forward to reveal the engine, and the two towing booms at the rear actually work. The two figures came with the truck.*

| 104 | Dolphin 20 Cabin Cruiser on Winchcon Trailer | 35 |
|---|---|---|
| 107 | Batboat | |
|  | tinplate boat fin | 135 |
|  | red plastic fin | 50 |
| 109 | "Pennyburn" Trailer (with three tools) | 45 |
| 112 | Rice Beaufort Double Horse Box | 35 |
| 150 | Vanwall Racing Car | 65 |
| 150 | Surtees TS9 Formula I | 35 |
| 151 | Lotus XI Racing Car | |
|  | blue-green | 65 |
|  | silver | 95 |
|  | red | 280 |
| 151A | Lotus XI | |
|  | blue | 85 |
|  | lemon | 320 |
| C151 | Yardley McLaren M19A | 25 |
| 152 | BRM Racing Green | 70 |
| C152 | Ferrari 312 B2 | 35 |
| 153 | Bluebird Record Car | 110 |
| 153 | Team Surtees TS 9B | 35 |
| 154 | Ferrari Formula I | 45 |

| 161 | Santa Pod "Commuter" | 35 |
|---|---|---|
| 161 | Elf Tyrell Project 34 | |
|  | blue, white | 35 |
|  | First National | 50 |
| 162 | "Quartermaster" Dragster | 35 |
| C163 | Santa Pod Dragster | 60 |
| 164 | Ison Bros "Wild Honey" Dragster | 40 |
| 165 | Adams Brothers 4-Engine Dragster | 35 |
| 166 | Ford Mustang | 40 |
| C167 | USA Racing Buggy | 25 |
| C169 | Starfighter Jet Dragster | 35 |
| C170 | John Woolfe's 208 Dragster | 30 |
| 190 | John Player Lotus | 60 |
| 191 | Texaco Marlboro McLaren | |
|  | white, red | 60 |
|  | with driver | 105 |
| 200 | Ford Consul | 120 |
| 200M | Ford Consul | 150 |
| C200 | BMC Mini 1000 | 25 |
| 201 | Austin Cambridge | 120 |
| 201M | Austin Cambridge | 160 |
| 201 | Saint's Volvo P1800 (Whizzwheels) | 115 |
| 201 | Mini 1000 "Team Corgi" | 20 |

| # | Name | Price |
|---|------|-------|
| 247 | Mercedes-Benz 600 Pullman | $50 |
| 248 | Chevrolet Impala | 55 |
| 249 | Mini Cooper De Luxe | 80 |
| 251 | Hillman Imp | 45 |
| 252 | Rover 2000 | 70 |
| 253 | Mercedes-Benz 220 SE | 65 |
| 255 | Austin A60 Driving School Car | 125 |
| 256 | Volkswagen 1200 East African Safari | 120 |
| 258 | The Saint's Volvo P1800 | 125 |
| 259 | Citroën Le Dandy | 110 |
| 259 | Penguinmobile | 40 |
| 260 | Renault R16 | 45 |
| 260 | City of Metropolis Police Car | 45 |
| 261 | James Bond Aston Martin DB5 | 180 |
| 261 | Spiderbuggy | 75 |
| 262 | Lincoln Continental Executive Limousine | 80 |
| 262 | Captain Marvel Porsche | 30 |
| 263 | Rambler Marlin Sports Fastback | 45 |
| 263 | Captain America Jetmobile | 30 |
| 264 | Oldsmobile Tornado | 50 |
| 264 | The Incredible Hulk | 40 |
| 265 | Supermobile | 35 |
| 266 | Chitty Chitty Bang Bang | 220 |
| 266 | Superbike | 30 |
| 267 | Batmobile | 280 |
| 268 | Black Beauty | 200 |
| 268 | Batbike | 50 |
| 269 | James Bond Lotus Esprit | 55 |
| 270 | James Bond Aston Martin (1/43rd scale) | 135 |
| 271 | Ghia Mangusta de Tomaso | 50 |
| 271 | James Bond Aston Martin (1/36th scale) | 75 |
| 272 | James Bond Citroën 2CV | 35 |
| 273 | Rolls-Royce Silver Shadow | 75 |
| 273 | Honda Ballade Driving School Car | 35 |
| 274 | Bentley T Series | 50 |
| 275 | Rover 2000 TC | 65 |
| 275 | Mini Metro | 10 |
| C275 | Royal Wedding Mini Metro | 10 |
| 276 | Oldsmobile Toronado | 65 |
| C276 | Triumph Acclaim | 10 |
| C277 | Triumph Acclaim Driving School | 20 |
| 277 | The Monkees Monkeemobile | 260 |
| C279 | Rolls-Royce Corniche | 25 |
| C280 | Rolls-Royce Silver Shadow | 35 |
| 281 | Rover 2000 TC | 110 |
| 281 | Datapost Metro | 15 |
| 282 | Mini Cooper Rally Car | 75 |
| 283 | "Daf" City Car | 35 |
| C284 | Citroën SM | 40 |
| 284 | "Notruf" Mercedes-Benz 240D | 35 |
| C285 | Mercedes-Benz 240D | 10 |
| C286 | Jaguar XJ12C | 20 |
| C287 | Citroën Dyane | 15 |
| C288 | Minissima | 15 |
| C289 | VW Polo | 10 |
| 290 | Kojak Buick | |
| | (Kojak with hat) | 50 |
| | (Kojak without hat) | 75 |

| # | Name | Price |
|---|------|-------|
| 291 | AMC Pacer | $15 |
| 291 | Mercedes-Benz 240 Rally Car | 20 |
| 292 | Starsky and Hutch Ford Torino | 50 |
| C293 | Renault 5TS | 10 |
| 2932 | Renault 5 SOS Medecins | 30 |
| C294 | Renault Alpine | 10 |
| 292 | Sapeurs Pompiers | 15 |
| 298 | Magnum PI Ferrari 308 GTS | 30 |
| C299 | Ford Sierra 2.3 Ghia | 10 |
| 300 | Austin Healey | 100 |
| | blue | 240 |
| 300 | Chevrolet Corvette | 70 |
| 300 | Ferrari Daytona | 15 |
| 301 | Triumph TR2 | 95 |
| 301 | Iso Grifo 7 Litre | 40 |
| 301 | Lotus Elite | 15 |
| 302 | MGA | 105 |
| 302 | Hillman Hunter London to Sydney Marathon Winner | 95 |
| 302 | VW Polo | 10 |
| 303 | Mercedes-Benz 300SL Open Roadster | 80 |
| 303 | Roger Clark's 3 Litre V6 Ford Capri | 70 |
| 303 | Porsche 924 | 15 |
| | yellow "Hella" promotional | 40 |
| 304 | Mercedes-Benz 300SL Hard Top | 110 |
| 304 | Chevrolet SS350 Camaro | 50 |
| 305 | Triumph TR3 | 110 |
| 305 | Mini Marcos GT850 | 45 |
| 306 | Morris Marina 1.8 Coupe | 40 |
| 306 | Fiat XI/9 | 15 |
| 307 | Jaguar E Type | 75 |
| 307 | Renault Turbo | 15 |
| 308 | Monte Carlo Mini | 70 |
| 308 | BMW M1 Racer | 20 |
| 309 | Aston Martin Competition Model | 80 |
| | with spoked wheels | 140 |
| 309 | VW Turbo | 15 |
| 310 | Chevrolet Corvette Sting Ray | 50 |
| | bronze | 150 |
| 310 | Porsche 924 Turbo | 15 |
| 311 | 3 Litre V6 Ford Capri | 90 |
| 312 | Jaguar E Type (plated) | 80 |
| 312 | Marcos Mantis | 30 |
| 312 | Ford Capri S | 30 |
| 313 | Ford Cortina GXL | 70 |
| | mustard yellow | 220 |
| 314 | Ferrari Berlinetta 250LE Le Mans | 60 |
| C314 | Supercat Jaguar XJS-HE | 25 |
| 315 | Simca Sports Car | 40 |
| | metallic dark blue | 160 |
| C315 | Lotus Elite | 15 |
| 316 | NSU Sport Prinz | 75 |
| 316 | Ford GT70 | 55 |
| 317 | Monte Carlo Mini Cooper S | 160 |
| 318 | Lotus Elan S2 | 80 |
| | copper | 225 |
| 318 | Jaguar XJS Motul | 20 |
| 319 | Lotus Elan Hard Top | 75 |
| 319 | Lamborghini P400 GT Miura | 35 |
| 319 | Jaguar XJS | 30 |
| 320 | Saint's Jaguar XJS | 50 |

| # | Name | Price |
|---|------|-------|
| 321 | Monte Carlo Mini Cooper S | |
| | red, white roof, No. 52 | $225 |
| | red, white roof, No. 2 autographed | 450 |
| 321 | Porsche 924 Saloon | 25 |
| 322 | Rover Monte Carlo Rally | |
| | metallic red, white roof | 100 |
| | white, black bonnet (No. 21) | 190 |
| 323 | Citroën DS 19 Monte Carlo | 160 |
| 323 | Ferrari Daytona 365 GTB/4 | 15 |
| 324 | Marcos Volvo 1800 GT | 60 |
| 324 | Ferrari Daytona | 25 |
| 325 | Ford Mustang Competition | 45 |
| 326 | Chevrolet Caprice Police Car | 40 |
| 327 | MGB GT | 100 |
| 327 | Chevrolet Caprice Taxi | 35 |
| 328 | Monte Carlo Hillman Imp | 90 |
| 329 | Ford Mustang Rally Car | 35 |
| 329 | Opel Senator | 35 |
| 330 | Porsche Carrera 6 | |
| | white, red (No. 1 or No. 60) | 35 |
| | white, blue | 75 |
| 331 | Rally Ford Capri | 65 |
| 332 | Lancia Fulvia Sport Zagato | |
| | metallic blue | 35 |
| | yellow, black | 100 |
| 332 | Opel Emergency Doctor's Car | 35 |
| 333 | RAC/Sun Rally Mini Cooper S | 240 |
| C334 | Ford Escort | 15 |
| 334 | Mini Magnifique | 75 |
| 335 | Jaguar 4.2 Litre E Type 2+2 | 85 |
| 336 | James Bond Toyota 2000 GT | 225 |
| 337 | Chevrolet Stingray Stock Car | 50 |
| 338 | Chevrolet SS350 Camaro | 60 |
| C338 | Rover 3500 | 30 |
| 339 | 1965 Monte Carlo Mini Cooper S | 225 |
| 339 | Rover 3500 Police Car | 35 |
| 340 | 1967 Monte Carlo Sunbeam Imp | 100 |
| 340 | Rover Triplex | 30 |
| 341 | Mini Marcos GT 850 | 40 |
| 341 | Chevrolet Caprice Racer | 15 |
| 342 | Lamborghini P400 GT Miura | 40 |
| 342 | The Professionals' Ford Capri 3.0S | 80 |
| 343 | Pontiac Firebird | 40 |
| 344 | Ferrari 206 Dino Sport | 40 |
| 345 | MGC GT Competition Model | |
| | yellow, black bonnet | 80 |
| | orange (from Gift Set 48) | 210 |
| C345 | Honda Prelude | 15 |
| C346 | Citroën 2CV | 15 |
| 347 | Chevrolet Astro I Experimental Car | 35 |
| 348 | Mustang "Pop Art" Stock Car | 100 |
| 348 | Vegas Ford Thunderbird | 70 |
| 349 | "Pop Art" Mini (Mini "Mostest") | 1,500 |
| 350 | Thunderbird Guided Missile | 60 |
| 351 | RAF Land Rover | 65 |
| 352 | RAF Vanguard Staff Car | 80 |
| 353 | Radar Scanner | 40 |
| 354 | Commer Military Ambulance | 80 |
| 355 | Commer Van Military Police | 95 |
| 356 | VW Personnel Carrier | 80 |

| # | Name | Price |
|---|------|-------|
| 357 | Land Rover Weapons Carrier | $150 |
| 358 | 1961 Oldsmobile Staff Car | 75 |
| 359 | Commer Army Field Kitchen | 150 |
| C370 | Ford Cobra Mustang | 15 |
| 371 | Porsche Carerra | 40 |
| 373 | Volkswagen 1200 Police Car | 60 |
| C373 | Peugeot 505 | 15 |
| C374 | Jaguar 4.2 Litre E Type 2+2 | 45 |
| C374 | Jaguar 5.3 Litre | 45 |
| 375 | Toyota 2000 GT | 45 |
| 376 | Chevrolet Stingray Stock Car | 35 |
| 377 | Marcos 3 Litre | 45 |
| | white, gray sunroof | 85 |
| 378 | MGC GT | 105 |
| C378 | Ferrari 308 GTS | 15 |
| 380 | Alfa Romeo Pininfarina P3 | 20 |
| 380 | BASF BMW MI | 15 |
| 380 | GP Beach Buggy | 25 |
| 381 | Facom Elf Renault Turbo | 15 |
| 382 | Porsche Targa 911S | 35 |
| C382 | Lotus Elite | 15 |
| 383 | Volkswagen 1200 | 60 |
| | yellow "ADAC" | 150 |
| 384 | Adam Bros Probe 15 | 15 |
| 384 | VW 1200 Rally | |
| | blue | 70 |
| | "Caledonian Autominologists" | 160 |
| 384 | Renault 11 GTL | 25 |
| 385 | Porsche 917 | 30 |
| 386 | Bertone Runabout Barchetta | 20 |
| 387 | Chevrolet Corvette Stingray Coupe | 65 |
| 388 | Mercedes-Benz CIII | 35 |
| 389 | Reliant Bond Bug 700ES | 75 |
| 391 | James Bond 007 Ford Mustang | 180 |
| 392 | Bertone Shake Buggy | 30 |
| C393 | Mercedes-Benz 350SL | 35 |
| | metallic green | 90 |
| 394 | Datsun 240Z East African Safari | 40 |
| 395 | Fire Bug | 35 |
| 396 | Datsun 240Z US Rally | 40 |
| 397 | Can Am Porsche Audi | 35 |
| C400 | VW Driving School Car | |
| | metallic blue | 45 |
| | metallic red | 105 |
| C401 | VW Motor School Car | 45 |
| 402 | Police Cortina GXL | 60 |
| | white with "Polizei" lettering | 115 |
| 403 | Bedford "Daily Express" | 160 |
| 403M | Bedford "KLG Plugs" | 185 |
| 403 | Thwaites "Tusker" Skip | 30 |
| 404 | Bedford Dormobile | 95 |
| | yellow body, two-tone blue roof | 185 |
| 404M | Bedford Dormobile | 135 |
| 405 | Bedford "Utilicon" AFS | 110 |
| | red "Fire Dept" | 210 |
| 405M | Bedford "Utilicon" Fire Dept | 165 |
| C405 | Chevrolet Superior Ambulance | 35 |
| C405 | Ford Transit Milk Float | 15 |
| 406 | Land Roner 109 WB | 85 |
| 406 | Mercedes-Benz Unimog | 40 |
| 407 | Mercedes Bonna Ambulance | 35 |

| # | Name | Price |
|---|------|-------|
| 407 | Karrier Mobile Grocery | $120 |
| 408 | Bedford AA Road Services Van | 130 |
| 409 | Forward Control Jeep FC-150 | 45 |
| 409 | Mercedes-Benz Unimog Rear Dumper | 35 |
| 409 | Allis Chalmers Fork-lift Truck | 25 |
| 411 | Karrier Bantam Lucozade Van | 150 |
| 411 | Mercedes-Benz 240D Taxi | 35 |
| | all orange | 60 |
| 412 | Bedford Ambulance | |
| | cream (split windscreen) | 90 |
| | one piece windscreen | 190 |
| C412 | Mercedes-Benz Police Car | 35 |
| 413 | Karrier "Bantam" Butcher's Shop | 150 |
| 413 | Mazda Motorway Maintenance Truck | 35 |
| 414 | Bedford Military Ambulance | 100 |
| 414 | Coastguard Jaguar XJ12C | 35 |
| 415 | Mazda Camper | 30 |
| 416 | RAC Radio Rescue Land Rover | |
| | bright blue | 110 |
| | dark yellow "Touring Secours" | |
| | (Belgium special) | 370 |
| 416 | Buick Police Car | 35 |
| 417 | Land Rover Breakdown Truck | 65 |
| 418 | Austin Taxi | 35 |
| 419 | Ford Zephyr Police Car | |
| | white or cream | 90 |
| | "Politie" | 310 |
| | Rijkspolitie | 345 |
| 419 | AMC CJ-5 Jeep | 25 |
| 420 | Ford Thames Airborne Caravan | 65 |
| 421 | Bedford "Evening Standard" Van | 150 |
| 422 | Bedford "Corgi Toys" Van | |
| | yellow, blue roof | 225 |
| | blue, yellow roof | 480 |
| 422 | Riot Police | 25 |
| 423 | Rough Rider Van | 25 |
| 424 | Ford Zephyr Estate Car | 75 |
| C424 | Security Van | 15 |
| 425 | London Taxi (1/36th scale) | 15 |
| 426 | Chipperfield Circus Booking Office | 305 |
| 426 | Circus Booking Office Van | 40 |
| 428 | Mister Softee Ice Cream Van | 150 |
| C428 | Renault 5 Police Car | 15 |
| C429 | Police Jaguar XJ12C | 35 |
| 430 | Bermuda Taxi | 70 |
| C430 | Porsche 924 Polizei (Police) | 15 |
| 431 | Volkswagen Pick-up | |
| | yellow, red hood | 95 |
| | metallic gold | 280 |
| 431 | "Vanatic" Van | 25 |
| 432 | "Vantastic" Van | 25 |
| 433 | Volkswagen Delivery Van | 95 |
| 434 | Volkswagen Kombi | 95 |
| 435 | Dairy Produce Van | 105 |
| 435 | Superman Van | 40 |
| 436 | Citroën ID19 Safari | 65 |
| 436 | Spidervan | 40 |
| 437 | Cadillac Ambulance | 80 |
| 437 | Coca Cola Van | 35 |
| 438 | Land Rover | 40 |
| | green with gray or tan "Lepra" | 360 |

| # | Name | Price |
|---|------|-------|
| 439 | Chevrolet Fire Chief Car | $85 |
| 440 | Ford Consul Cortina Estate Car | 160 |
| 440 | Mazda Custom Pick-up | 25 |
| 441 | Volkswagen Toblerone Van | 115 |
| 441 | Golden Eagle Jeep | 20 |
| 443 | Plymouth US Mail Van | 95 |
| 445 | Plymouth Sports Suburban | 95 |
| 447 | Walls Ice Cream Van | 190 |
| 447 | 4x4 Renegade Jeep | 15 |
| 448 | 4x4 Renegade Jeep with Hood | 15 |
| 448 | Police Mini Van with figures | 165 |
| 450 | Austin Mini Van | |
| | green | 100 |
| | with painted grille | 155 |
| | with Countryman grille | 155 |
| 450 | Peugeot Taxi | 15 |
| 452 | Commer 5 Ton Dropside Lorry | 105 |
| 453 | Commer "Walls" Refrigerator Van | 160 |
| 454 | Commer Platform Lorry | 105 |
| 455 | Karrier "Bantam" Two-Tonner | 90 |
| No # | Karrier "Bantam" Two-Tonner (Mettoy | |
| | pre-Corgi issue) red "CWS Soft | |
| | Drinks" | 150 |
| 456 | ERF Dropside Lorry | 95 |
| 457 | ERF 44G Platform Lorry | 95 |
| 457 | Talbot Matra Rancho | 25 |
| 458 | ERF Tipper 64G Dumper | 65 |
| 459 | ERF 44G "Moorhouse" Van | 280 |
| 459 | Raygo "Rascal" Road Roller | 15 |
| 460 | ERF Neville Cement Tipper | 75 |
| 461 | Police "Vigilant" Range Rover | |
| | white "Police" | 25 |
| | white, red "Politie" (Dutch issue) | 65 |
| 462 | Commer Van | 160 |
| 463 | Commer Ambulance | 95 |
| 464 | Commer Police Van | |
| | metallic blue "County Police" | 75 |
| | blue, engraved "Police" | 75 |
| | green, engraved "Police" (German | |
| | issue) | 800 |
| | blue "Rijks Politie" (Dutch issue) | 240 |
| | "City Police" | 240 |
| 465 | Commer Pick-up Truck | 45 |
| 466 | Commer Milk Float | |
| | white, blue | 65 |
| | "Co-op" | 150 |
| 467 | London Routemaster Bus | |
| | red Selfridges | 65 |
| | red Hamleys | 40 |
| 468 | London Transport Routemaster Bus | |
| | red "Corgi Toys" | 95 |
| | green, cream, brown "Corgi Toys" | |
| | (Australian issue) | 820 |
| | red "Outspan Oranges" | 50 |
| | red "Gamages" | 225 |
| | red "Church's Shoes" | 150 |
| | red "Madame Tussaud's" | 190 |
| | red "Design Centre" (with | |
| | Whizwheels) | 190 |
| 470 | Forward Control Jeep with Hood | 40 |
| 470 | Greenline Bus | 15 |

| # | Name | Price |
|---|------|-------|
| 471 | Karrier Bantam Snack Bar Van | |
| | Joe's Diner | $105 |
| | Patates Frites (Belgian issue) | 250 |
| 471 | Silver Jubilee London Routemaster | |
| | Bus | 15 |
| 471 | F.W. Woolworths Silver Jubilee | |
| | London Bus | 25 |
| 472 | Public Address Vehicle | 110 |
| 474 | Musical Walls Ice Cream Van | 225 |
| 475 | Citroën Ski Safari | 120 |
| 477 | Land Rover Breakdown Truck | 40 |
| 478 | Forward Control Jeep Tower Wagon | 40 |
| 479 | Commer Mobile Camera Van | 125 |
| 480 | Chevrolet Yellow Cab | 65 |
| 481 | Chevrolet Police Patrol Car | 65 |
| 482 | Chevrolet Fire Chief Car | 80 |
| 482 | Range Rover Ambulance | 35 |
| 483 | Dodge "Kew Fargo" Tipper Truck | 35 |
| 483 | Belgian Police Range Rover | 60 |
| 484 | Dodge "Kew Fargo" Livestock Transporter | |
| | with five pigs | 45 |
| C484 | AMC Pacer Rescue | 15 |
| | "Secours" (French issue) | 35 |
| 485 | Mini Countryman with Surfer | 140 |
| 486 | Chevrolet Kennel Service Wagon | 75 |
| 487 | Chipperfields Circus Parade Land | |
| | Rover | 150 |
| C489 | Volkswagen Police Car Polo | 25 |
| 4894 | Volkswagen Polo ADAC | 25 |
| 490 | Volkswagen Breakdown Truck | 80 |
| 490 | Caravan | 15 |
| 491 | Ford Cortina Estate Car | 75 |
| 492 | Volkswagen 1200 Police Car | |
| | green, white "Polizei" | 75 |
| | all white "Politie" (Dutch issue) | 280 |
| 493 | Mazda B1600 Pick-up | 20 |
| 494 | Bedford Tipper Truck | |
| | red, yellow tipper | 65 |
| | red, silver tipper | 170 |
| 494 | 4x4 Open Back Truck | 10 |
| 497 | The Man from UNCLE Oldsmobile | |
| | cream | 560 |
| | dark blue | 225 |
| 499 | Citroën 1968 Olympic Winter Sports | 160 |
| 500 | US Army Land Rover | 270 |
| 506 | Police Panda Sunbeam Imp | 80 |
| 508 | Holiday Camp Commer Mini-Bus | 75 |
| 509 | Porsche Targa 911S Police Car | |
| | red, white, black "Polizei" | 65 |
| | white, orange "Rijks Politie" (Dutch) | 110 |
| 510 | Citroën Tour de France Team Manager's | |
| | Car | 130 |
| 511 | Chipperfields Performing Poodles | |
| | Pick-up | 560 |
| 513 | Citroën Safari Alpine Rescue Car | 320 |
| C516-631 | Mercedes Vans, various | 10 |
| C521 | Routemaster Bus, 'Haig' | 15 |
| C523 | Routemaster Bus 'British Diecast' | |
| | white/black lettering | 15 |
| | gold/white lettering | 30 |
| C524 | Routemaster Bus, 'Stevensons' | 15 |

| # | Name | Price |
|---|------|-------|
| C527 | Routemaster Bus, 'Timbercraft' | $40 |
| C529 | Routemaster, '1985 Calender' | 15 |
| C530 | Routemaster Bus, 'Yorkshire' | 15 |
| C535 | Mercedes Van 'Athlon' | 10 |
| 539 | 'Group 4' Van | 10 |
| 541 | Ford Police Cars | 15 |
| 542 | Bonna Ambulance | 15 |
| 548 | 'Securitas' Van | 10 |
| C558 | Routemaster, 'Radio Victory' | 15 |
| C566 | Routemaster Bus, 'Gelco' | 25 |
| C567 | Routemaster Bus, 'London' | 15 |
| C567 | Range Rover | 15 |
| 568 | 'Goodrich' Van | 10 |

| # | Name | Price |
|---|------|-------|
| C599/2 | AEC Regent, 'Woodhams' | $60 |
| C599/3 | Regent, 'Huntley & Palmers' | 60 |
| C599/4 | AEC Regent, 'Glasgow' | 30 |
| C599/5 | AEC Regent, 'Rhondda' | 25 |
| C599/6 | AEC Regent, 'Morecambe' | 25 |
| D599/10 | Regent, 'Brighton & Hove' | 20 |
| Q599/13 | AEC Regent, 'Halifax' | 25 |
| 600 | Ford Escort | 15 |
| 601-605 | Corgi Kits, various | 20-50 |
| 606 | Kit (Lamp Standards) | 10 |
| 607-11 | Corgi Kits, various | 35 |
| 601 | Fiat N-9 | 15 |
| 602 | BL Mini 1000, number '8' | 30 |

*Corgi Gift Set #10 from the late '60s featured a Rambler Marlin, two plastic kayaks and a trailer.*

| # | Name | Price |
|---|------|-------|
| C570 | Routemaster, 'Bus Society' | 15 |
| C571 | Routemaster, 'The Times' | 15 |
| C572 | Routemaster 'The Times' | 25 |
| C574 | Routemaster 'Blackpool' | 15 |
| 576 | Mercedes 207r Vans, various | 10 |
| 576 | Mercedes 207D 'Pompiers' | 15 |
| C580 | Routemaster, 'Guide Dogs' | 15 |
| C583 | Routemaster, 'Manchester' | 15 |
| 588 | Mercedes Vans | 10 |
| C589 | Routemaster, 'Autospares' | 15 |
| C590 | Routemaster, 'Medic Alert' | 15 |
| C591 | Routemaster, 'Medic Alert' | 15 |
| C596 | Routemaster, 'Harrods' | 15 |
| 597 | Ford Police Car | 10 |
| 598 | Range Rover Police | 10 |
| C599 | AEC Regent Bus, 'TSB' | 45 |
| C599/1 | AEC Regent, 'Wisk' | 35 |
| D599/1 | AEC Regent, 'Western' | 15 |

| # | Name | Price |
|---|------|-------|
| 602 | BL Mini 1000, 'CITY' | 15 |
| 602 | BL Mini 1000, 'Mini 25th' | 110 |
| 603 | Volkswagen Polo | 15 |
| 604 | Renault 5 | 15 |
| 605 | Austin Mini Metro | 15 |
| 607 | Circus Elephant Cage | 30 |
| 611 | Ford Escort 'Datapost' | 25 |
| 619 | Land Rovers | 10 |
| C619 | Range Rover | 10 |
| 621 | Ford Escort Police Van | 10 |
| C625 | Routemaster, 'Cityrama' | 15 |
| C627 | Routemaster, 'Model Motoring' | 15 |
| C628 | Routemaster, 'Polco Plus' | 15 |
| 630 | 'Kays' Mercedes Van | 10 |
| 631 | 'Blue Arrow' Mercedes Van | 10 |
| C633 | Routemaster, 'Hospital Radio' | 25 |
| C634 | AEC Regent Bus, 'Maples' | 40 |
| C638 | Routemaster, 'Weetabix' | 15 |

| # | Name | Price |
|---|---|---|
| C643 | AEC Regent, 'Newcastle Ale' | $30 |
| 656 | Ford Transit Vans, various | 15 |
| C674 | Ford Transits, various | 10 |
| C675/1 | Metrobus, 'Timesaver' | 30 |
| C675/2 | Metrobus 'Reading Goldline' | 25 |
| C675/3 | Metrobus 'W.Midlands Travel' | 25 |
| C675/4-15 | Metrobus Mk.II, various | 15 |
| C675/14 | BMW 635 | 10 |
| C676/1-12 | Minibuses, various | 15 |
| C676/16 | Metrobus, 'Strathclyde' | 15 |

| # | Name | Price |
|---|---|---|
| 802 | 1954 Mercedes-Benz 300SL | $20 |
| 803 | The Beatles' Yellow Submarine | 450 |
| 803 | 1952 Jaguar XK120 | 15 |
| 804 | Noddy's Car | |
| | with Mr. Tubby | 200 |
| | with Noddy only | 150 |
| 804 | 1952 Jaguar XK120 "Rally des Alpes" | |
| | cream | 15 |
| | cream with "spats" | 40 |
| 805 | The Hardy Boys' Rolls-Royce | 280 |

| # | Name | Price |
|---|---|---|
| C908 | French AMX Recovery Tank | $50 |
| C909 | Quad Gun Tractor, Ammunition Trailer | 50 |
| C1001 | HCB Angus Firestreak | 65 |
| C1002 | Sonic BL Landtrain and Trailers | 40 |
| C1003 | Ford Torino Road Hog | 25 |
| C1004 | Beep Beep Bus | 25 |
| C1005 | Police Land Rover | 25 |
| C1006 | Roadshow | 30 |
| C1007 | Land Rover and Compressor | 40 |
| C1008 | Chevrolet Caprice Fire Chief | 25 |
| C1009 | Maestro MG 1600 | 50 |
| 1011 | Angus Firestreak (no figures or accessories) | 25 |
| 1100 | Carrimore Low Loader | |
| | yellow cab, blue loader | 200 |
| | red cab, blue loader | 110 |
| 1100 | Mack Truck with Trans-Continental Trailer | |
| | orange, pale metallic blue | 65 |
| | orange, metallic lime green | 120 |
| 1101 | Carrimore Car Transporter | |
| | red cab, blue transporter | 130 |
| | blue cab, yellow transporter | 240 |
| 1101 | Warner and Swasey 4418 Hydraulic Crane | 35 |
| 1102 | Euclid TC12 Tractor and Dozer Blade | 175 |
| 1102 | Crane Fruehauf Discharge Dumper | 40 |
| 1103 | Euclid Twin Crawler Tractor | 100 |
| 1103 | Pathfinder Airport Crash Truck | 65 |
| 1104 | Machinery Carrier | 115 |
| 1104 | Racehorse Transporter (Bedford) | 65 |
| 1105 | Car Transporter | 160 |
| 1105 | Racehorse Transporter "Berliet" | 50 |
| 1106 | Decca Mobile Airfield Radar Van | 135 |
| 1106 | Mack Container Truck | 55 |
| 1107 | Berliet Container Truck | 50 |
| 1107 | Euclid Tractor and Dozer (with driver figure) | |
| | orange | 240 |
| | red | 320 |
| | lime green | 145 |
| 1108 | Bristol Bloodhound Guided Missile | 120 |
| 1108 | Michelin Container Truck | 35 |
| 1109 | Bristol Bloodhound Missile on Loading Trolley | 120 |
| 1109 | Michelin Articulated Truck | 35 |
| 1110 | Mobilgas Tanker | |
| | red | 225 |
| | blue, white "Shell" (Dutch promotional) | 2,800 |
| 1110 | JCB Crawler Loader | 50 |
| 1111 | Massey Ferguson Combine Harvester | 145 |
| 1112 | Corporal Guided Missile on Launching Ramp | 135 |
| 1112 | David Brown Combine | 105 |
| 1113 | Corporal Erector Vehicle and Missile | 275 |
| 1113 | Hyster Stacatruck | |
| | yellow, black with gray and red container | 45 |
| | Sealink | 95 |

*One of Corgi's many TV-related toys: the #290 Kojak Buick with original box. This item came with the figures of Kojak and the bad guy shooting at one another.*

| | | |
|---|---|---|
| 700 | Motorway Service Ambulance | 15 |
| 701 | Inter-City Minibus | 15 |
| 703 | Breakdown Truck | 15 |
| 703 | Fire Engine | 15 |
| C769 | Plaxton, various | 15 |
| C769/1-5 | Plaxton, various | 15 |
| C769/6 | Plaxton, 'Pohjolan' | 40 |
| C769/7-8 | Plaxton, various | 15 |
| C770-1 | Plaxton, various | 15 |
| C773-7 | Plaxton, various | 15 |
| C791 | Plaxton 'Swiss PTT' | 25 |
| C792-3 | Plaxton various | 15 |
| 801 | Noddy's Car | |
| | with black face golly | 880 |
| | pink, gray or tan face | 480 |
| 801 | 1957 Ford Thunderbird | 25 |
| 802 | Popeye's Paddle Wagon | 475 |

| | | |
|---|---|---|
| 805 | 1956 Mercedes-Benz 300SC | 15 |
| 806 | Lunar Bug | 95 |
| 806 | 1956 Mercedes-Benz 300SC | 15 |
| 807 | Dougal's Car | 240 |
| 808 | Basil Brush's Car | 120 |
| 809 | Dick Dastardly Racing Car | 110 |
| 810 | 1957 Ford Thunderbird | 20 |
| 811 | James Bond Moon Buggy | 400 |
| 831 | 1954 Mercedes-Benz 300SL | 15 |
| C900 | German Tiger Mk I Tank | 35 |
| C901 | British Centurion Mk III Tank | 35 |
| C902 | American M60 AI Medium Tank | 35 |
| C903 | British Chieftain Medium Tank | 35 |
| C904 | King Tiger Tank | 35 |
| C905 | SU 100 Tank Destroyer | 35 |
| C906 | Saladin Armoured Car | 35 |
| C907 | German Semi-Track Rocket Launcher | 60 |

| # | Name | Price |
|---|------|------|
| 1115 | Bloodhound Guided Missile | $95 |
| 1116 | Bloodhound Missile Platform | 75 |
| 1116 | Shelvoke and Drewry Revopak Refuse Lorry | 25 |
| 1117 | Bloodhound Missile Trolley | 65 |
| 1117 | Faun Street Sweeper | 25 |
| 1118 | International 6x6 Army Truck | |
| | green | 120 |
| | Dutch Army, silver grille | 275 |
| | US Army | 200 |
| C1118 | Airport Emergency Tender | 45 |
| 1119 | HDL Hovercraft SR-N1 | 75 |
| 1120 | Midland Red Motor Express Coach | 225 |
| 1121 | Chipperfields Circus Crane Truck | 160 |
| 1121 | Ford Transit Tipper | 30 |
| 1123 | Chipperfields Circus Animal Cage | 80 |
| 1124 | Corporal Guided Missile Launching Ramp | 50 |
| 1126 | Ecurie Ecosse Racing Car Transporter | 200 |
| 1126 | Dennis Snorkel Fire Engine | 45 |
| 1127 | Bedford Simon Snorkel Fire Engine | 90 |
| 1128 | Priestman "Cub" Shovel | 40 |
| 1129 | Milk Tanker | 240 |
| 1129 | Mercedes Articulated Truck | 25 |
| 1130 | Chipperfields Circus Horse Transporter | 215 |
| 1130 | Mercedes Tanker | 15 |
| 1131 | Carrimore Detachable Axle Machinery Carrier | 135 |
| 1131 | Mercedes Refrigerated Van | 30 |
| 1132 | Carrimore Low Loader | 280 |
| 1132 | Scania Truck | 15 |
| 1133 | Scania Giant Tipper | 15 |
| 1133 | Troop Transporter | 240 |
| 1134 | Army Fuel Tanker | 320 |
| 1134 | Scania Silo Truck | 15 |
| 1135 | Heavy Equipment Transporter | 400 |
| 1137 | Ford Tilt Cab H Series with Detachable Trailer | 100 |
| 1138 | Carrimore Car Transporter with Ford Tilt Cab | 115 |
| 1139 | Chipperfields Circus Menagerie Transporter | 550 |
| 1140 | Bedford Mobilgas Tanker | 240 |
| 1140 | Ford Transit Wrecker | |
| | white, red "24hour" | 10 |
| | white, red "Relay" | 15 |
| | red, yellow "Abschleppdeenst" | 30 |
| 1141 | Bedford Milk Tanker | 240 |
| 1142 | "Holmes Wrecker" Recovery Vehicle | 110 |
| C1143 | American La France Aerial Rescue Truck | 105 |
| 1144 | Chipperfields Circus Crane Truck | 560 |
| 1144 | Berliet Wrecker Recovery Vehicle | 45 |
| 1145 | Mercedes-Benz Unimog 406 with Gooseneck Dumper | 40 |
| 1146 | Carrimore Mk V Tri-deck Car Transporter | 140 |
| 1147 | Ferrymasters Truck | 145 |
| 1148 | Carrimore Mk IV Car Transporter | 150 |
| 1150 | Mercedes-Benz Unimog 406 with Snow Plow | 45 |

| # | Name | Price |
|---|------|------|
| 1151 | Scammell Artic | |
| | white, light blue (Co-op labels) | $230 |
| | "Co-op" (sold as set with 462 and 466) | 400 |
| 1152 | Mack Truck with Gloster Saro Articulated Petrol Tanker | |
| | white, red "Esso" | 45 |
| | white, red "Exxon" | 110 |
| 1153 | Priestman Boom Crane with Grab | 75 |
| 1154 | Giant Tower Crane | 65 |
| 1154 | Mack Priestman Crane Truck | 75 |
| 1155 | Skyscraper Tower Crane | 50 |
| 1156 | Volvo BM Concrete Mixer | 45 |
| 1157 | Ford Esso Tanker | 40 |
| 1158 | Ford Exxon Tanker | 65 |
| 1159 | Ford Car Transporter | 50 |
| 1160 | Ford Gulf Tanker | 35 |
| 1161 | Ford Aral Tanker | 90 |
| C1163 | Circus Human Cannon Truck | 45 |
| C1164 | Dolphinarium | 80 |
| 1169 | Ford Guinness Tanker | 60 |
| 1170 | Ford Car Transporter | 55 |

## Husky/Corgi Juniors:

| # | Name | Price |
|---|------|------|
| 1a | Jaguar Mk 10 | |
| | metallic blue | 25 |
| | dark blue | 25 |
| 1b | Jaguar Mk 10 (larger version) | |
| | metallic blue | 25 |
| | dark blue | 25 |
| 1c | Reliant TW9 Pick-up | |
| | orange | 25 |
| | tan | 25 |
| 1d | Grand Prix Racer | |
| | metallic (green, white) | 15 |
| 2a | Citroën Safari with Boat | |
| | yellow car, brown boat | 15 |
| 2b | Citroën Safari with Boat (larger version) | |
| | metallic gold car, brown boat | 25 |
| | metallic gold car, blue boat | 25 |
| 2c | Citroën Safari with Boat (Corgi Junior) | |
| | blue | 25 |
| | yellow | 25 |
| | metallic purple | 25 |
| 3a | Mercedes 220 | |
| | pale blue | 15 |
| 3b | VW 1300 Police Car | |
| | white/black | 30 |
| | white/black (Corgi Junior) | 15 |
| 3c | VW 1300 Police Car | |
| | white | 15 |
| 4a | Jaguar Mk 10 red 'FIRE' | 25 |
| 4c | Zetor 5511 Tractor | |
| | orange/red | 15 |
| | metallic green | 10 |
| 5a | Lancia Flamina light blue | 15 |
| 5b | Willys Jeep | |
| | metallic green | 15 |
| | brown (Corgi Junior) | 10 |
| | orange (Corgi Junior) | 10 |
| 5c | NASA Space Shuttle white, black | 10 |

| # | Name | Price |
|---|------|------|
| 6a | Citroën Safari Ambulance white | $25 |
| 6b | Ferrari Berlinetta 250GT | |
| | red | 15 |
| | maroon | 15 |
| 6c | De Tomaso Mangusta | |
| | yellow | 15 |
| | purple | 15 |
| 6d | Daily Planet Helicopter red, white | 10 |
| 7a | Buick Electra orange | 15 |
| 7b | Duple Vista 25 Coach | |
| | green, white | 25 |
| | red, white | 25 |
| | yellow, white (Corgi Junior) | 15 |
| | purple, white (Corgi Junior) | 10 |
| | orange, white (Corgi Junior) | 10 |
| 8a | Ford Thunderbird Open Top pink, black | 15 |
| 8b | Ford Thunderbird Hard Top yellow, blue top | 15 |
| 8c | Farm Tipper Trailer yellow/red | 10 |
| 9a | Buick Police Car | |
| | light blue | 15 |
| | dark blue | 15 |
| 9b | Cadillac Eldorado | |
| | blue | 15 |
| | metallic green (Corgi Junior) | 15 |
| | white, black (Corgi Junior) | 15 |
| 10a | Guy Warrior Coal Truck | |
| | red | 15 |
| | orange | 15 |
| | red (casting change: no rear corner windows) | 15 |
| 10b | Ford GT-70 orange | 15 |
| 11a | Forward Control Land Rover | |
| | green brown | 15 |
| | metallic green, brown (casting change: no rear windows) | 15 |
| 11b | Austin Healey LM Sprite red | 40 |
| 12a | VW Pick-up Tower Wagon | |
| | yellow, red | 15 |
| | white, blue | 15 |
| 12b | Ford Tower Truck | |
| | yellow | 15 |
| | white | 15 |
| 12c | Reliant-Ogle Scimitar | |
| | white | 35 |
| | metallic blue | 35 |
| 13a | Guy Warrior Sand Truck | |
| | yellow, brown | 15 |
| | blue | 15 |
| | yellow, brown (casting change: no rear corner windows) | 15 |
| | blue, brown | 15 |
| 13c | Guy Warrior Sand Truck (Corgi Junior) | |
| | green, brown | 15 |
| | white, brown | 15 |
| 14a | Guy Warrior Petrol Tanker 'Shell' yellow, white 'Shell' | 15 |
| 14b | Guy Warrior Petrol Tanker 'Shell' yellow, white 'Shell' (casting change: no rear corner windows) | 15 |

| # | Name | Price |
|---|------|-------|
| 14c | Guy Warrior Petrol Tanker 'Esso' | |
| | white (no rear corner windows, larger | |
| | model) . . . . . . . . . . . . | $15 |
| | Dutch promotional NV labels . . . . . . | 30 |
| 14d | Guy Warrior Petrol Tanker 'Esso' | |
| | (Corgi Junior) white . . . . . . . . . | 15 |
| 15a | Volkswagen Pick-up | |
| | turquoise, brown canopy . . . . . . . . | 20 |
| 15b | Studebaker TV Car | |
| | yellow . . . . . . . . . . | 15 |
| | metallic blue . . . . . . . . . | 15 |
| 15b | Studebaker TV Car (Corgi Junior) | |
| | yellow . . . . . . . . . . | 15 |
| | green . . . . . . . . . . | 15 |
| 15c | Mercedes School Bus | |
| | metallic blue . . . . . . . . . | 15 |
| | yellow . . . . . . . . . . | 10 |
| 16a | Dump Truck | |
| | yellow . . . . . . . . . . | 15 |
| | red . . . . . . . . . . | 15 |
| 16b | Land Rover Pick-up | |
| | metallic green . . . . . . . . . | 15 |
| 17a | Guy Warrior 'Milk' Tanker (oval tank) | |
| | white . . . . . . . . . . | 15 |
| 17b | Guy Warrior 'Milk' Tanker (oval tank) | |
| | white (casting change: no rear corner | |
| | windows) . . . . . . . . . . | 15 |
| 17b | Guy Warrior 'Milk' Tanker (square tank) | |
| | white . . . . . . . . . . | 15 |
| | cream . . . . . . . . . . | 15 |
| 17c | VW 1300 Beetle | |
| | metallic green . . . . . . . . . | 25 |
| 18a | Jaguar MKX | |
| | gold plated . . . . . . . . . | 15 |
| | silver plated . . . . . . . . . | 15 |
| 18b | Jaguar MKX gold plated (different | |
| | shades) . . . . . . . . . . | 30 |
| 18c | Wigwam Camper Van | |
| | orange . . . . . . . . . . | 15 |
| | blue . . . . . . . . . . | 15 |
| 19a | Commer Walk-thru Van | |
| | green, red doors . . . . . . . . . | 15 |
| | red . . . . . . . . . . | 15 |
| 19b | Speedboat on Trailer red, cream 'Husky', | |
| | gold trailer . . . . . . . . . | 10 |
| 19b | Speedboat on Trailer (Corgi Junior) red, | |
| | cream (gold or blue trailer) . . . . . . | 10 |
| 20a | Ford Thames Van red . . . . . . . . . | 30 |
| 20b | VW 1300 blue . . . . . . . . . | 25 |
| 20b | VW 1300 (Corgi Junior) | |
| | brown . . . . . . . . . . | 25 |
| | red . . . . . . . . . . | 25 |
| 21a | Military Land Rover green . . . . . . . | 15 |
| 21b | Military Land Rover green (casting | |
| | change: no rear corner windows) . . . . | 15 |
| 21b | Jaguar E Type 2+2 metallic maroon . . . | 40 |
| 21c | Mini Cooper S 1300 metallic purple . . . | 55 |
| 22a | Citroën Military Ambulance green . . . . | 15 |
| 22b | Aston Martin DB6 | |
| | metallic gold . . . . . . . . . | 30 |
| | purple . . . . . . . . . . | 30 |

| # | Name | Price |
|---|------|-------|
| 22b | Aston Martin DB6 (Corgi Junior) metallic | |
| | green . . . . . . . . . . | $15 |
| 22c | Formula 1 Racer yellow . . . . . . . . | 15 |
| 23a | US Army Tanker green . . . . . . . . . | 15 |
| 23b | Loadmaster Shovel | |
| | orange . . . . . . . . . . | 10 |
| | yellow . . . . . . . . . . | 10 |
| 23b | Loadmaster Shovel (Corgi Junior) | |
| | yellow . . . . . . . . . . | 10 |
| 24a | Ford Zephyr Estate Car | |
| | blue . . . . . . . . . . | 25 |
| | metallic red . . . . . . . . . | 30 |
| 24b | Aston Martin DBS green . . . . . . . . | 35 |
| 25a | Shelvoke and Drewry Refuse Van | |
| | light blue . . . . . . . . . | 15 |
| | dark red . . . . . . . . . | 15 |
| 25a | Shelvoke and Drewry Refuse Van | |
| | (Corgi Junior) orange . . . . . . . . | 15 |
| 26a | Sunbeam Alpine Hard Top | |
| | metallic bronze, blue hard top . . . . | 30 |
| | red, blue hard top . . . . . . . | 40 |
| 27a | Bedford TK Lorry | |
| | dark red . . . . . . . . . | 15 |
| | orange . . . . . . . . . . | 15 |
| 27a | Bedford TK Lorry (Corgi Junior) | |
| | orange . . . . . . . . . . | 15 |
| 27b | Formula 5000 Racing Car black . . . . . | 15 |
| 28a | Ford Breakdown Truck blue . . . . . . . | 15 |
| 28a | Ford Breakdown Truck (Corgi Junior) | |
| | blue . . . . . . . . . . | 15 |
| | green . . . . . . . . . . | 15 |
| 29a | ERF Cement Lorry yellow, red . . . . . | 15 |
| 29b | ERF Fire Engine red (no windows) . . . . | 15 |
| 29c | ERF Fire Engine red (new casting: large | |
| | cab with windows) . . . . . . . . . | 15 |
| 30a | Studebaker Ambulance white . . . . . . | 15 |
| 30b | Studebaker Ambulance (Corgi Junior) | |
| | white . . . . . . . . . . | 15 |
| 31a | Oldsmobile Starfire Coupe | |
| | metallic blue . . . . . . . . . | 15 |
| | green . . . . . . . . . . | 15 |
| 31b | Land Rover Breakdown | |
| | purple . . . . . . . . . . | 15 |
| | blue . . . . . . . . . . | 15 |
| 32a | VW Luggage Elevator | |
| | white, yellow . . . . . . . . . | 15 |
| | red, blue . . . . . . . . . | 15 |
| 32b | Lotus Europa metallic green . . . . . . | 20 |
| 33a | Farm Trailer | |
| | olive . . . . . . . . . . | 10 |
| | turquoise . . . . . . . . . | 10 |
| 33a | Farm Trailer (Corgi Junior) orange . . . | 10 |
| 33b | Jaguar E Type 2+2 | |
| | yellow . . . . . . . . . . | 30 |
| | blue . . . . . . . . . . | 30 |
| 34a | BM Volvo 400 Tractor red, yellow . . . . | 10 |
| 34a | BM Volvo 400 Tractor (Corgi Junior) | |
| | red, yellow . . . . . . . . . | 10 |
| 35a | Ford Camper | |
| | metallic blue . . . . . . . . . | 30 |
| | yellow . . . . . . . . . . | 30 |

| # | Name | Price |
|---|------|-------|
| 35a | Ford Camper (Corgi Junior) | |
| | green . . . . . . . . . . | $30 |
| | red . . . . . . . . . . | 30 |
| 36a | Simon Snorkel Fire Engine | |
| | red . . . . . . . . . . | 15 |
| 37a | NSU Ro80 metallic blue . . . . . . . . | 25 |
| 37b | NSU Ro80 (Corgi Junior) | |
| | metallic blue . . . . . . . . . | 15 |
| | metallic purple . . . . . . . . . | 15 |
| | metallic orange . . . . . . . . . | 15 |
| | metallic pink . . . . . . . . . | 15 |
| 38a | Single Horse Box green, white pony . . . | 10 |
| 38b | Single Horse Box (Corgi Junior) | |
| | red . . . . . . . . . . | 10 |
| | bronze . . . . . . . . . . | 10 |
| 39a | Jaguar XJ6 yellow . . . . . . . . . | 25 |
| 39b | Jaguar X16 (Corgi Junior) | |
| | yellow . . . . . . . . . . | 25 |
| | silver (Whizzwheels) . . . . . . . . | 25 |
| | maroon (Whizzwheels) . . . . . . . . | 25 |
| 40a | Ford Transit Caravan | |
| | green, white . . . . . . . . . | .30 |
| | red, white . . . . . . . . . | 30 |
| 40b | Ford Transit Caravan (Corgi Junior) | |
| | yellow . . . . . . . . . . | 25 |
| | blue . . . . . . . . . . | 25 |
| | gray . . . . . . . . . . | 25 |
| 41a | Porsche Carrera (Corgi Junior) white . . | 25 |
| 42a | Euclid Dump Truck yellow, red . . . . . | 10 |
| 42b | Terex Rear Dump Truck | |
| | red, yellow . . . . . . . . . | 10 |
| | yellow, red . . . . . . . . . | 10 |
| | blue, beige . . . . . . . . . | 10 |
| 43a | Farm Tractor with Blade yellow . . . . | 10 |
| 44a | Road Roller blue, orange 'Raygo | |
| | Rascal' . . . . . . . . . . | 10 |
| 45a | Mercedes Benz 280SL | |
| | silver . . . . . . . . . . | 15 |
| | yellow (Whizzwheels) . . . . . . . . | 15 |
| | metallic blue (Whizzwheels) . . . . . | 15 |
| | red (Whizzwheels) . . . . . . . . | 15 |
| 46a | Jensen Interceptor | |
| | metallic maroon . . . . . . . . . | 25 |
| | metallic green . . . . . . . . . | 25 |
| | orange . . . . . . . . . . | 25 |
| 47a | Scammell Concrete Mixer blue, white, | |
| | red . . . . . . . . . . | 15 |
| 48a | ERF Tipper Truck | |
| | red, silver . . . . . . . . . | 15 |
| | blue, yellow . . . . . . . . . | 15 |
| 49a | Pininfarina Modulo yellow . . . . . . | 15 |
| 50a | Ferrari 512S | |
| | maroon, white . . . . . . . . . | 15 |
| | maroon, silver . . . . . . . . . | 15 |
| 51a | Porsche 917 gold, red . . . . . . . . | 15 |
| 52a | Addams Probe metallic purple . . . . . | 15 |
| 54a | Ford D1000 Container Truck | |
| | red, orange . . . . . . . . . | 15 |
| | red, yellow . . . . . . . . . | 15 |
| 55 | Double Decker Bus red 'Esso Uniflo' . . . | 10 |

| # | Name | Price |
|---|------|-------|
| 56 | Ford Capri Fire Chief's Car red, white | $25 |
| 57 | Cadillsc Eldorado 'Hot Rodder' pink | 15 |
| 58 | Beach Buggy | |
| | metallic red | 10 |
| | metallic copper | 10 |
| 59 | Futura orange | 10 |
| 60 | VW Beetle Hot Rod | |
| | orange | 25 |
| | purple | 15 |
| 61 | Mercury Cougar Sheriff's Car white, black | 15 |
| 62 | Volvo PI8000 | |
| | metallic blue | 30 |
| | red | 25 |
| 63 | Ford Escort Rally metallic blue | 70 |
| 64 | Morgan Plus 8 | |
| | yellow | 25 |
| | red | 25 |
| 65 | Bertone Carebo purple | 15 |
| 67 | Ford Capri Dragster yellow 'Hot Pants' | 25 |
| 70 | US Racing Buggy blue Stars and Stripes | 10 |
| 72 | Mercedes-Benz CIII red | 10 |
| 73 | Alfa Romeo P33 blue | 10 |
| 74 | Berton Barchetta orange | 10 |
| 75 | Super Stock Car silver, Union Jack | 15 |
| 76 | Military Jeep green | 15 |
| 77 | Ital Bizzarini Manta pink | 15 |
| 78 | Old MacDonald's Lorry red, silver bonnet | 45 |
| 80-1 | Porsche Carrera white '4' | 15 |
| 80b | Fiat X1/9 white body | 10 |
| 80c | Leyland Van Marvel Comics dark green, Marvel Comics labels | 10 |
| 81a | Daimler Fleetline Bus red body, various labels | 10 |
| 82a | Can-Am Racer metallic blue | 10 |
| 82b | Yogi Bear's Jeep yellow body | 10 |
| 83a | Commando Car olive drab | 5 |
| 83b | Goodyear Blimp chrome plated | 15 |
| 84a | Daimler Scout Car olive drab | 5 |
| 84b | Bugs Bunny Buggy orange and red | 10 |
| 85a | Skip Dumper | |
| | yellow/red | 10 |
| | green/yellow | 10 |
| 86a | Fiat X1/9 (as 80b) many variations | 10 |
| 87b | Leyland Delivery Van | |
| | red 'Coca-Cola' | 10 |
| | white 'Pepsi-Cola' | 10 |
| | yellow 'Weetabix' | 10 |
| | orange 'W.H. Smith' promotional | 15 |
| 88a | Mobile Crane red | 10 |
| 89c | Citroën Dyane | |
| | yellow | 5 |
| | gold | 5 |
| | purple | 5 |
| 90a | Chevy Custom Van black 'Fireball' | 5 |
| 91a | Chevy Van | |
| | orange 'Chevrolet Van' | 5 |
| | orange 'U.S. Van' | 5 |

| # | Name | Price |
|---|------|-------|
| 91b | Vantastic Chevy Van black | $5 |
| 92a | VW Polo metallic green | 5 |
| 93a | Tug Boat orange, yellow, green | 5 |
| 93b | Dodge Magnum yellow | 5 |
| 94a | Porsche 917 metallic silver | 10 |
| 94b | Chevrolet Van blue 'Adidas' | 10 |
| 95a | Leyland Van (as 87b) red 'Coca Cola' | 10 |
| 96a | Field Gun and Soldiers olive drab | 5 |
| 96b | Ford Thunderbird | |
| | red 'Vegas' | 15 |
| | cream | 10 |
| 97a | Guy Tanker white 'Exxon' | 15 |
| 97b | Petrol Tanker various labels and colors | 10 |
| 98a | Marcos XP Growler Type orange | 10 |
| 98b | Mercedes Mobile Shop blue | 5 |
| 98c | Police Helicopter white | 5 |
| 99a | Jokermobile white | 10 |
| 100a | Hulkcycle green, black | 15 |
| 101a | Leyland Van red 'Kasperl Theater' German promotional | 15 |
| 102a | Renault 5 Turbo yellow | 5 |
| 103a | Ford Transit Breakdown white | 10 |
| 104a | Ford Mustang Cobra orange | 5 |
| 105a | Ford Escort metallic green | 10 |
| 107a | Austin Metro blue | 5 |
| 108a | Railroad Loco red | 5 |
| 111a | Railroad Coach red, yellow | 5 |
| 112a | Railroad Wagon red, green | 5 |
| 113a | Paddle Steamer yellow, white | 5 |
| 114a | Stagecoach red, yellow | 5 |
| 115a | James Bond 2CV yellow | 15 |

| # | Name | Price |
|---|------|-------|
| 116a | Mercedes Bus red, 'Espana 82' labels football promotional | $5 |
| 117a | Chevrolet Van white, 'Espana 82' labels (as 116a) | 5 |
| 119a | Chubb Airport Crash Tender red 'Flughafen Feuewghr' labels | 15 |
| 122a | Covered Wagon green | 5 |
| 123a | Chubb Airport Tender red 'Airport Rescue' | 10 |
| 124a | Mercedes-Benz 500 SL red 'Airport Rescue' | 5 |
| 125a | Transit Dropside yellow 'Wimpey' | 10 |
| 126a | Transit Wrecker yellow, German labels | 15 |
| 127a | Ford Escort ADAC yellow, 'ADAC' labels German | 15 |
| 128a | Fred Flintstone's Flyer orange | 15 |
| 129a | Ford Sierra Ghia | |
| | yellow | 10 |
| | metallic silver | 10 |
| | blue | 10 |
| 131a | Magnum Ferrari red | 15 |
| 133a | Magnum Buick black, white | 10 |
| 134a | Barney's Buggy red | 15 |
| 135a | Austin Metro Datapost white, blue, Datapost labels | 5 |
| 136a | Ferrari 308 GTs | |
| | red | 10 |
| | black | 10 |
| 137a | VW Polo Turbo cream | 5 |
| 138a | Rover 3500 Triplex white, blue | 5 |
| 139a | Porsche Carrera Turbo black | 5 |

*The ubiquitous double decker bus was well-represented in the Corgi line. This is #468, the London Transport Routemaster, in "Outspan" livery with "Whizzwheels."*

| # | Name | Price |
|---|------|-------|
| 140a | Ford Mustang Cobra yellow | $5 |
| 141a | Ford Capri 3.0s white | 15 |
| 146a | Ford Transit (as 125a) | 5 |
| 148a | USS Enterprise white | 15 |
| 149a | Klingon Warship metallic blue | 15 |
| 150a | Simon & Simon Buick Regal black, white | 25 |
| 151a | Willma's Coupe yellow | 15 |
| 152a | Simon & Simon 1957 Chevy black, white | 15 |
| 156a | 1957 Chevrolet Convertible white | 15 |
| 157a | Army Jeep olive drab | 5 |
| 158a | Centurion Tank olive drab | 5 |
| 161a | Opel Corsa 1.3sr yellow | 5 |
| 170a | Vauxhall Novared | 5 |
| 174A | Quarry Truck yellow | 5 |
| 175a | Pipe Truck red | 5 |
| 177a | Chemico Tanker dark blue | 5 |
| 178a | Container Truck green | 5 |
| 180a | Pontiac Firebird black | 5 |
| 181a | Mercedes-Benz 300SL red | 5 |
| 184a | Range Rover red | 5 |
| 190a | Buick Regal Police Car white, black, Arabian labels | 15 |
| 192a | Mercedes Ambulance white, Arabian labels | 15 |
| 193a | Chubb Fire Tender red, Arabian labels | 15 |
| 194a | Mercedes-Benz 240D Taxi red, Arabian labels | 15 |
| 200a | Rover 3500 ASA Pencil Sharpener | 15 |
| 204a | Renault 5 Turbo blue | 5 |
| 205a | Porsche Carrera 911 | |
| | black | 5 |
| | green | 5 |
| | yellow | 5 |
| 206a | Buick Regal | |
| | green | 5 |

| # | Name | Price |
|---|------|-------|
| | red | $5 |
| | blue | 5 |
| 207a | Ford Sierra, Police white, green, 'Polizei', German | 15 |
| 208a | Ford Sierra, Doctor white, red 'Notaret', German | 15 |
| 210a | Matra Rancho brown, Safari Park labels, German | 15 |
| 211a | Ford Escort, Driving School green, 'Fahrschule' labels, German | 15 |
| 212a | VW Polo blue, 'Siemens Wartungsdienst', German | 15 |
| 220a | Ford Transit Truck (as 125a) | 10 |
| 225a | Chubb Fire Tender Swiss Issue | 15 |
| 250a | Simon Snorkel Fire Engine red, 'Brandbil', Danish issue | 15 |
| 251a | ERF Fire Tender red, 'Falck', Danish issue | 15 |
| 252a | Ford Transit Wrecker red, 'Falck', Danish issue | 15 |
| 253a | Mercedes-Benz Ambulance white, 'Falck', Danish issue | 15 |
| 254a | Mercedes-Benz 240D Emergency Car white body, 'Falck', Danish issue | 15 |

**Corgi Rockets:**

| # | Name | Price |
|---|------|-------|
| 901 | Aston-Martin DB6 | 35 |
| 902 | Jaguar XJ-6 | 35 |
| 903 | Mercedes-Benz 280 SL | 35 |
| 904 | Porsche Carrera 6 | 35 |
| 905 | 'The Saint' Volvo P1800 | 70 |
| 906 | Jensen Interceptor | 40 |
| 907 | Cadillac Eldorado | 35 |
| 908 | Chevrolet Astro | 35 |
| 909 | Mercedes-Benz C111 | 35 |
| 910 | Beach Buggy | 35 |
| 911 | Marcos XP | 35 |
| 913 | Aston-Martin DBS | 35 |
| 916 | Carabo Bertone | 35 |

| # | Name | Price |
|---|------|-------|
| 917 | Pininfarina Alfa-Romeo | $35 |
| 918 | Bitzzarini Manta | 35 |
| 919 | Todd Sweeney Stock Car | 40 |
| 920 | Derek Fiske Stock Car | 40 |
| 921 | Morgan Open Sports | 40 |
| 922 | Rally Ford Capri | 50 |
| 923 | James Bond Ford Escort | 240 |
| 924 | Mercury Cougar XR7 | 45 |
| | James Bond version | 215 |
| 925 | James Bond Ford Capri | 280 |
| 926 | Jaguar Control Car | 120 |
| 927 | Ford Escort Rally | 135 |
| 928 | Mercedes 280 'SPECTRE' | 215 |
| 930 | Bertone Barchetta | 30 |
| 931 | Old MacDonald's Truck | 80 |
| 933 | Holmes Wrecker | 80 |
| 975 | Super Stock Gift Set 1 | 200 |
| 976 | Ford Capri and Trailer | 200 |
| 977 | Super Stock Gift Set 3 | 240 |
| 978 | OHMSS Gift Set | 800 |

**CASTOYS (pre-Corgi models):**

| # | Name | Price |
|---|------|-------|
| 502 | Standard Vanguard | 75 |
| 505 | Rolls-Royce | 75 |
| 510 | Standard Vanguard Police Car | 75 |
| 511 | Standard Vanguard Taxi | 75 |
| 512 | Standard Vanguard Fire Chief | 75 |
| 602 | Standard Vanguard | 75 |
| 810 | Limousine | 75 |
| 820 | Streamline Bus | 400 |
| 830 | Racing Car | 225 |
| 840 | 8-Wheel Truck | 75 |
| 850 | Fire Truck | 75 |
| 860 | Tractor | 75 |
| 870 | Delivery Van | |
| | "Royal Mail" | 325 |
| | "BOAC" | 325 |
| | "Express Delivery" | 275 |
| | "Post Office Telephones" | 350 |

*A spread from a 1957 Corgi Toys catalog, showing several of the early British cars in the range.*

# Crescent Toys

The Crescent Toy Company Ltd. was founded in London in 1922, and originally manufactured toys such as lead soldiers. Following the end of the Second World War, the company marketed a line of die cast toys made by Die Casting Machine Tools Limited (D.C.M.T.), in addition to manufacturing its own toys. As a result, some Crescent toys can be found with or without "DCMT" cast into the baseplate.

Perhaps the finest products resulting from this business relationship were two sets put out in the late 1940s. The first, known as the Garage Set, consisted of the D.C.M.T./Crescent Jaguar Saloon (#800) that could be placed on the car lift included in the set. The lift could be raised via a lever on the side; the set also included a "FREE AIR" sign as well as an oil dispenser. The box for the set has "GARAGE CAR LIFT" on it.

The other set was called "DIAL 999," and it, too, came in a simple box with artwork of the toy on it. This set consisted of the #804 Jaguar Police Car along with cast figures of two policeman and two crooks. The policemen are chasing the crooks, and one of the crooks is being attacked by a police dog.

Both sets are quite scarce (particularly with the original box), and therefore rarely turn up for sale. When they do, an asking price of $150-$300 is not unusual.

During the late 1940s, Crescent built a manufacturing facility in Wales, and began manufacturing its own line of die cast toy vehicles. These included a series of road vehicles and a number of farm vehicles, but the company is perhaps best known for the series of Racing Cars it produced beginning in 1956. Actually, it included eight racing cars and two "sports" cars, and the series was in production dur-

Photo Courtesy of Andrew Ralston.

*The elusive "DIAL 999" set put out by Crescent in the late 1940s. The car is the D.C.M.T. #804 Jaguar Police Car.*

ing 1956 and 1957, and may have continued until as late as 1960. These cars were very accurate and well detailed for their time, and are now highly sought after by collectors (as are the early road vehicles). The relative scarcity of the racing cars may be due in part to their original price being somewhat higher than that of contemporary Dinky Toys, which may have resulted in lower sales numbers.

Crescent also made a line of Military models starting in the 1950s, as well as other die cast toys and models. (They also produced a number of toy ships and airplanes.) The company appears to have been in business until about 1980.

*Note:* Most Crescent products, including the Racing Cars, came in individual boxes, so the prices are for a near mint to mint boxed example. The early road vehicles, however, generally did not have individual boxes. Also, be aware that reproductions of the racing cars exist. When or where (or by whom) these were made is unknown at present.

| # | Name | Price |
|---|------|-------|
| **Late 1940s Vehicles (various colors):** | | |
| 223 | Race Car | $45 |
| 422 | Nash Roadster | 40 |
| 423 | Petrol Tanker | 25 |
| 424 | Flat Truck | 25 |
| 425 | La Salle Sedan | 40 |
| 800 | Jaguar | 40 |
| 804 | Jaguar Police Car | 35 |
| 1221 | Fire Engine with Extending Ladder | 65 |
| **Racing Cars (late 1950s):** | | |
| 1284 | Mercedes-Benz W196 (silver) | 90 |
| 1285 | B.R.M. MkII (green) | 90 |
| 1286 | Ferrari 625 (red) | 110 |
| 1287 | Connaught A Series (green) | 90 |
| 1288 | Cooper Bristol (light blue) | 90 |

| # | Name | Price |
|---|------|-------|
| 1289 | Gordini 2.5 Litre (blue) | $90 |
| 1290 | Maserati 250F (red) | 90 |
| 1291 | Aston Martin DB3S (white/light blue) | 80 |
| 1292 | Jaguar D-Type (green) | 85 |
| 1293 | Vanwall (green) | 150 |

(Numbers 1284 through 1289 also came as a set, number 6300, in a display box; number 1290 later replaced number 1284 in the set. These sets rarely turn up and are therefore impossible to accurately value.)

| # | Name | Price |
|---|------|-------|
| **Miscellaneous Models:** | | |
| 1268 | Mobile Space Rocket | 115 |
| 1269 | Mobile Crane | 65 |
| 1272 | Scammell Scarab Artic. Truck | 115 |
| 1274 | Scammell Scarab and Low Loader Trailer | 115 |

| # | Name | Price |
|---|------|-------|
| 1276 | Scammell Scarab and Oil Tanker (Shell or Esso) | $140 |
| 2700 | Western Stage Coach | 110 |
| 2705 | Scammell Scarab Set | 350 |
| **Military Models (painted in military colors):** | | |
| 155 | Artillery Gun | 30 |
| 235 | Cannon, operable | [no known price] |
| 650 | Military Set (two #696 British Tanks, #698 Scout Car, #699 Russian Tank | [no known price] |
| 695 | Howitzer, unpainted, with spring and plunger | 15 |
| 696 | British Tank | 50 |
| 698 | Scout Car | 40 |

| # | Name | Price |
|---|------|-------|
| 699 | Russian Tank | $50 |
| 1248 | Field Gun | 15 |
| 1249 | 18-pounder Gun | 15 |
| 1250 | 25-pounder Artillery Gun | 15 |
| 1251 | 5.5 inches Medium Heavy Howitzer | 15 |
| 1260 | Supply Truck | 30 |
| 1263 | Saladin Armoured Scout Car | 30 |
| 1264 | Scorpion Tank | 25 |
| 1265 | M109 Self-Propelled Gun | 20 |
| 1266 | Recovery Vehicle | 20 |
| 1267 | Corporal Rocket and Lorry | 75 |
| 1270 | Heavy Rescue Crane | 70 |
| 1271 | Long Range Mobile Gun | 40 |
| 1271 | Artillery Force | 25 |
| 2154 | Saladin Set | 40 |

| # | Name | Price |
|---|------|-------|
| **Farm Models:** | | |
| 1802 | Tractor and Hayrake | $90 |
| 1803 | Dexta Tractor and Trailer | 50 |
| 1804 | Tractor and Disc Harrow | 95 |
| 1805 | Tractor | 70 |
| 1806 | Hayrake | 15 |
| 1807 | Disc Harrow | 15 |
| 1808 | Platform Trailer | 15 |
| 1809 | Ricklift Trailer | 15 |
| 1809 | Dexta Tractor | 35 |
| 1810 | Box Trailer/Farm Trailer | 30 |
| 1811 | Animal Trailer/Cattle Trailer | 25 |
| 1811 | DextaTractor and Trailer. | 25 |
| 1813 | Timber Wagon (Horse Drawn) | 135 |
| 1814 | Plough Trailer | 25 |
| 1815 | Hayloader | 20 |

| # | Name | Price |
|---|------|-------|
| 1816 | Roller Harrow | $15 |
| 1817 | Timber Trailer | 15 |
| 1818 | Tipping Farm Wagon | 15 |
| 1819 | Large Farm Wagon | 35 |
| 1822 | Bulldozer | 30 |
| **1970s Trucks:** | | |
| 1350 | Container Truck | 30 |
| 1351 | Petrol Tanker | 30 |
| 1352 | Girder Truck | 30 |
| 1353 | Platform Truck | 30 |
| 1360 | Cement Mixer | 15 |
| 1361 | Covered Truck | 15 |
| 1362 | Tipper Truck | 15 |
| 1363 | Recovery Vehicle | 15 |
| 1364 | Super Karrier | 15 |

# Cursor

This German company began life in the 1960s by producing a series of plastic models of historic German vehicles. The first die cast model appears to have come out around 1969, and since then a varied mix of models has been produced. Cursor has concentrated on German makes, with Mercedes-Benz being the dominant name.

The scale of these models ranges from 1/36 for some of the automobiles, to 1/50 for many of the trucks and other commercial vehicles.

Note that Cursor's numbering system is often confusing. The company frequently assigned two numbers to the same item, particularly when the item was re-released after being out of production. For example, the #569 66C Loader was originally released during the mid-1970s. The 1980s version, however, was numbered 124, and may still be in production.

The value of #124, therefore, would be CRP (Current Retail Price), whereas the value of the #569 is $80. Where possible, the value given here is for the original, earlier model. (A number of the 100-series models may have started out with different numbers, but the author does not have hard data on them.)

| # | Name | Price |
|---|------|-------|
| [No #] | Mercedes-Benz 2.5 Tipper Truck | $50 |
| 106 | Magirus-Deutz Box Van | 30 |
| 109 | Setra Tour Bus (gray) | 35 |
| 110 | Magirus Covered Truck with Trailer | CRP |
| 111 | Magirus Dump Truck | CRP |
| 112 | Kramer Backhoe (yellow) | CRP |
| 122 | Fendt Dieselross Tractor (silver) | CRP |
| 123 | Holder A60 Cultitrac (green, orange) | CRP |
| 126 | Holder G500 Tractor (orange) | CRP |
| 127 | Fendt Favorit Tractor (green) | CRP |
| 128 | Iveco-Magirus 256D Army Truck | CRP |
| 129 | Iveco-Magirus 256D Truck | CRP |
| 130 | Setra-Kässbohrer 58 Tour Bus (red/white) | CRP |
| 131 | Steyr Bus (red/white) | CRP |
| 132 | Steyr Post Bus (yellow) | CRP |
| 175 | Magirus Deutz Truck (green) | 40 |
| 266 | Hanomag Matador Truck (blue) | 75 |
| 291 | Mercedes-Benz 600SEL Sedan | CRP |

| # | Name | Price |
|---|------|-------|
| 367 | Hanomag Henschel Truck (gray) | $90 |
| 378 | Magirus Deutz 320 M Covered Truck (blue/red/yellow) | 40 |
| 474 | Benz 1923 First Diesel Truck (green/Brown) | 20 |
| 475 | Mercedes-Benz L 508 D Van (orange) | 60 |
| 475A | Mercedes-Benz L 613 D Van (orange) | 20 |
| 569 | MF 66 C Loader (yellow) | 80 |
| 569A | Hanomag 66 C Loader (yellow) | 80 |
| 570 | Fendt F 250 GT (green) | 70 |
| 677 | Fendt Favorit LS Tractor (green/white) | 25 |
| 679 | Kässbohrer D17 Truck Trailer (blue) | CRP |
| 775 | Mercedes-Benz L 206 D Truck (orange) | 40 |
| 877 | Magirus Deutz 90 D Van (ivory) | 30 |
| 967 | Fendt S4 Tractor (green) | 85 |
| 970 | Hanomag-Henschel Bus (orange, red) | 95 |

| # | Name | Price |
|---|------|-------|
| 970A | Hanomag-Henschel Ambulance (white) | $110 |
| 970B | Mercedes-Benz L 206 D Bug (red, blue, green, yellow) | 55 |
| 970C | Mercedes-Benz L 206 D Van (blue, green, red) | 50 |
| 970D | Mercedes-Benz L 206 D "HERTZ" Bus (yellow) | 100 |
| 974 | Mercedes-Benz Unimog U 1500 (green/gray) | 15 |
| 974A | Army Mercedes-Benz Unimog U 1500 (olive) | 15 |
| 1001 | Mercedes-Benz 200-280E (olive) | 40 |
| 1003 | Mercedes-Benz 200 Taxi | 30 |
| 1004 | Mercedes-Benz 200 Police | 30 |
| 1005 | Mercedes-Benz 230G (white) | 30 |
| 1006 | Puch 1980 Geländewagen | 30 |
| 1007 | Mercedes-Benz 190 (white) | 35 |
| 1008 | Kässbohrer Pisten-Bully | CRP |

| # | Name | Price | # | Name | Price | # | Name | Price |
|---|------|-------|---|------|-------|---|------|-------|
| 1010 | Mercedes-Benz 200-300 Sedan (silver) | CRP | 1173 | O & K L 25 Loader (red) | $75 | 1267B | Mercedes-Benz L 407 D Truck (blue) | $110 |
| 1011 | BMW 323 Baur Cabriolet (red, white, silver, black) | CRP | 1180 | Mercedes-Benz W 196 Racing Car (silver) | 15 | 1269 | Hanomag D 600 Bulldozer (yellow) | 40 |
| 1076 | Holder Farm Tractor (green) | $40 | 1267 | Mercedes-Benz L 408 D Truck (orange, yellow) | 40 | 1269A | Hanomag D 600 D Bulldozer (yellow) | 40 |
| 1168 | BMW Formula 2 Racing Car (white) | 55 | 1267A | Mercedes-Benz L 408 D Truck "DINKELACKER" (yellow) | 40 | 1269B | Hanomag MF 600 C Bulldozer (yellow) | 40 |

# Dalia

**D**alia provides an excellent example of the "traveling dies" phenomenon. Located in Spain, this company was founded in the 1920s, and produced a number of well-made die cast toys before World War II. Starting in about 1957, Dalia began marketing a line of (roughly) 1/38 scale die cast Vespa and Lambretta motor scooters. These were apparently produced until sometime in the 1960s. In the latter part of that decade, they also produced a handful of smaller (1/66 scale) die cast sports cars.

But the company may be best known for its relationship with two other die cast giants. Along with their production of the scooter line, Dalia became the licensee for Solido in Spain. This likely occurred during the mid- to late-1950s, because by 1957 or '58 Dalia was producing a number of Solido 1/43 scale die cast models for the Spanish market. These included a number of the excellent Solido 100 series castings. They were generally of very good quality, and the relationship lasted at least until the early 1970s. *Note:* The baseplates for some of the Dalia Solidos say Solido, while others say Dalia.

*Dalia-Tekno #829 Lincoln Continental with original box.*

In the late 1960s, Dalia and Tekno joined forces to produce a group of Tekno 1/43 scale models, which included Tekno's #930 Monza GT (the dies for which were used by a number of manufacturers) and their #829 Lincoln Continental. The boxes for the Dalia-Tekno products say just that—Dalia-Tekno—and they also state that the models were made in Spain. The baseplates, however, say Tekno. (Understandable, as it is less costly to print boxes than to re-tool a base plate.)

| # | Name | Price | # | Name | Price | # | Name | Price |
|---|------|-------|---|------|-------|---|------|-------|
| **Motor Scooter line:** | | | 10 | Vespa Scooter with Sidecar Red Cross (white/gray) | $75 | 17 | Lambretta Motor Tricycle Water Delivery (silver/beige) | $75 |
| 1 | Vespa Scooter (green) | $75 | 11 | Lambretta A Scooter (orange/black) | 75 | 18 | Vespa S Scooter (white/green) | 75 |
| 2 | Lambretta A Scooter (blue/orange) | 75 | 12 | Lambretta A Scooter with Sidecar (orange/black) | 75 | 19 | Vespa S Scooter with Sidecar (green/yellow) | 75 |
| 3 | Lambretta B Scooter (gray/pink) | 75 | 13 | Lambretta Motor Tricycle with Buckets (orange/beige) | 75 | 20 | Lambretta A Army Scooter (olive) | 75 |
| 4 | Lambretta Motor Tricycle (beige/green) | 75 | 14 | Lambretta Motor Tricycle with Drums (orange/beige) | 75 | 21 | Lambretta A Army Scooter with Sidecar (olive) | 75 |
| 5 | Vespa Scooter with Sidecar (light blue) | 75 | 15 | Lambretta Motor Tricycle Milk Delivery (white/beige) | 75 | 22 | Vespa S Army Scooter (olive) | 75 |
| 6 | Lambretta A Scooter with Sidecar (silver) | 75 | 16 | Lambretta Motor Tricycle Wine Delivery (light blue/beige) | 75 | 23 | Vespa S Army Scooter with Sidecar (olive) | 75 |
| 7 | Lambretta B Scooter with Sidecar (orange/black) | 75 | | | | 24 | Vespa Scooter "POLICIA" (black) | 75 |
| 8 | Lambretta Motor Tricycle "BUTANO" (orange) | 75 | | | | | | |
| 9 | Vespa Scooter Red Cross (white/gray) | 75 | | | | | | |

| # | Name | Price |
|---|------|-------|
| 25 | Vespa Scooter "POLICIA" with sidecar (black) | $75 |
| 26 | Go-kart (red, blue) | 90 |
| 27 | Lambretta Army Motor Tricycle (olive) | 75 |
| 28 | Vespa Scooter "TELEGRAFOS" (beige) | 75 |
| 29 | Vespa Scooter with Sidecar "TELEGRAFOS" (beige) | 75 |
| 30 | Lambretta Motor Tricycle with Cases (white/beige) | 75 |
| 31 | Vespa Scooter "IBERIA" (silver) | 75 |
| 32 | Vespa Scooter with Sidecar "IBERIA" (silver) | 75 |
| 33 | Lambretta Motor Tricycle "COCA-COLA" (white/orange) | 75 |
| 34 | Vespa Scooter Rally (blue) | 75 |
| 35 | Vespa Scooter with Sidecar Rally (blue) | 75 |
| 36 | Lambretta Motor Tricycle Red Cross (gray/white) | 75 |
| 37 | Lambretta A Scooter "COCA-COLA" (white/orange) | 75 |
| 38 | Lambretta A Scooter with Sidecar "COCA-COLA" (white/orange) | 75 |
| 39 | Vespa Scooter "MOP" (yellow/beige) | 75 |
| 40 | Vespa Scooter with Sidecar "MOP" (yellow/beige) | 75 |
| 41 | Lambretta Scooter "BUTANO" (orange) | 75 |
| 42 | Lambretta Scooter with Sidecar "BUTANO" (orange) | 75 |

**1/66 scale Cars:**

| # | Name | Price |
|---|------|-------|
| 501 | Porsche Carrera 6 | 35 |
| 502 | Ford GT Le Mans | 35 |
| 503 | Chaparral 2 F | 35 |
| 504 | Seat 850 Coupe | 35 |
| 505 | De Tomaso Mangusta | 35 |
| 506 | Renault Alpine | 35 |

**Dalia-Solido models:**

| # | Name | Price |
|---|------|-------|
| 1 | Jaguar D Le Mans (red, green, blue) | 90 |
| 2 | Maserati 250 F.1 (red, yellow, green) | 90 |
| 3 | Vanwall Racing Car (light blue, green) | 90 |
| 4 | Ferrari Testa Rossa (red, white, cream) | 140 |
| 5 | Porsche 550/1500 RS (red/black, yellow/black, silver/green) | 125 |
| 6 | Cooper 1500 F.2 (tan, white/blue, yellow white) | 90 |
| 7 | Porsche F.2 (silver/red, yellow/black, orange/silver) | 125 |
| 8 | Seat 1400-C (black green, black silver, red, green/yellow) | 130 |
| 9 | Renault Floride Convertible (copper, red, blue) | 90 |
| 10 | Mercedes-Benz 190SL Roadster (copper, silver, white) | 100 |
| 11 | Lotus F.1 (yellow, black) | 75 |
| 12 | Lancia Flaminia Coupe Pinin Farina (red, silver, blue, green) | 90 |
| 13 | Fiat Abarth Record (orange, red, white) | 90 |
| 14 | Seat 1400-C Taxi Barcelona (black/yellow) | 150 |

| # | Name | Price |
|---|------|-------|
| 15 | Seat 1400-C Taxi Madrid (black/red) | $150 |
| 16 | Alfa Romeo Giulietta Roadster (red, orange, light blue, green) | 90 |
| 17 | Ferrari 250 GT 2+2 (red, green, yellow) | 125 |
| 18 | Aston Martin DB 4 (blue, yellow, red, silver, copper) | 90 |
| 19 | Citroën Ami 6 (white/green, white/blue) | 90 |
| 20 | Ferrari 156 F.1 (light blue, red) | 100 |
| 21 | Fiat Abarth 1000 (orange, silver, tan) | 90 |
| 22 | Mercedes-Benz 220 SE Coupe (blue, red) | 90 |
| | "POLICIA" (black) | 150 |
| | Red Cross (white) | 150 |
| | "PTT" (white) | 150 |
| | "FALCK" (white) | 150 |
| | "AUTOPISTAS" (orange) | 150 |
| 23 | Alfa Romeo 2600 Coupe Bertone (cream, dark red, blue, green, silver) | 90 |
| 24 | Seat 1400-C "POLICIA" (black) | 150 |
| 25 | Panhard DB Le Mans (blue, silver, white) | 75 |
| 26-1 | Aston Martin DB 5 Vantage (white, cream, blue, green, copper) | 90 |
| 26-2 | Aston Martin DB 5 Vantage "The Saint" (white) | 165 |
| 27 | Seat 1400-C "IBERIA" (silver) | 150 |
| 28 | NSU Prinz (red, blue, green, orange/black) | 70 |
| 29 | Porsche GT Le Mans (green, blue, silver) | 125 |
| 30 | Fiat 2300 S Ghia Convertible (green, red, blue, white) | 110 |
| | "AUTOPISTAS" (orange) | 150 |
| 31 | Ford Thunderbird (red, blue, tan, metallic green) | 90 |
| 32 | Ferrari 2.5 L (red) | 100 |
| 33 | Seat 1500 (white, green, metallic blue) | 130 |
| | Taxi Barcelona (black/yellow) | 150 |
| | Taxi Madrid (black/red) | 150 |
| | "POLICIA" (black) | 150 |
| 34 | Harvey Indianapolis (dark green, yellow) | 70 |
| 35 | Simca Oceare Convertible (green, metallic blue) | 90 |
| 36-1 | Maserati 3.5 L Mistral (copper, beige, yellow, metallic blue) | 90 |
| | "NASA" (orange) | 150 |
| 37 | Ford Mustang (red, white, metallic Light blue) | 90 |
| 38 | B.R.M. F.1 (yellow, metallic green) | 65 |
| 39 | Alpine F.3 (dark green) | 65 |
| 40 | Lola Climax V8 F.1 (tan/red) | 65 |
| 41 | Porsche Carrera 6 (yellow/red) | 85 |
| 42 | Ford GT 40 Le Mans (yellow/blue) | 65 |
| 43 | Ferrari 330 P3 (light blue) | 90 |
| 44 | Alfa Romeo Giulia TZ (blue, orange) | 90 |
| 45 | Oldsmobile Toronado (orange, green) | 60 |
| 46 | Panhard 24 BT (silver) | 65 |
| | "URGENCIAS" (white) | 125 |
| | Fire Car (red) | 125 |

| # | Name | Price |
|---|------|-------|
| 47 | Chaparral 2 D (red) | $60 |
| 48 | BMW 2000 CS (white) | 60 |
| 49 | Simca 1100 (yellow) | 70 |
| 50 | De Tomaso Mangusta (tan) | 60 |
| 51 | Chaparral 2F (blue/red, blue/black, white/red) | 60 |
| 52 | Citroën Ami 6 S.W. (blue, green) | 80 |
| | Ambulance (white) | 150 |
| | "FALCK" (white) | 140 |
| | "BUTANO" (orange) | 140 |
| 54 | Opel GT 1900 (metallic blue, metallic green) | 60 |
| 55 | Ford Thunderbird Taxi (black/yellow) | 125 |
| 56 | Ford Thunderbird "POLICIA" (black) | 140 |
| 57 | Ford Mustang Rally (red) | 75 |
| 58 | Ford Mustang "POLICIA" (black) | 125 |
| 59 | Ford Mustang Taxi Barcelona (black/yellow) | 125 |
| 60 | Ford Mustang Taxi Madrid (black/red) | 125 |
| 61 | Oldsmobile Toronado Rally (orange) | 70 |
| 62 | Simca 1100 Red Cross (white) | 140 |
| 63 | Simca 1100 Taxi (black/yellow) | 130 |
| 64 | Alfa Romeo 2600 Coupe "IBERIA" (silver) | 115 |
| 65 | Alfa Romeo Carabo Bertone (orange) | 75 |
| 66 | Alpine Renault (yellow) | 70 |
| 67 | Maserati 3.5 L Mistral Rally (yellow/black) | 70 |
| 68 | Lola T70 MK 3B (red) | 60 |
| 69 | McLaren M8 B Can Am (orange) | 60 |
| 70 | Matra 650 (blue) | 60 |
| 71 | Porsche 914/6 (yellow) | 60 |
| 72 | Ferrari 365 GTB4 (red) | 75 |
| 73 | Buggy Bertone (metallic green) | 50 |

**Dalia-Tekno:**

| # | Name | Price |
|---|------|-------|
| 415 | Ford Taunus Van | |
| | "IBERIA" (black) | 240 |
| | "BUTANO" | 240 |
| | Ambulance (white) | 240 |
| | "TELEGRAFOS" | 240 |
| | "TEKNO" | 240 |
| | "POLICIA" (black) | 240 |
| | "AUTOPISTAS (orange) | 240 |
| | "MOP PROJECTOS" (yellow/tan) | 240 |
| 829 | Lincoln Continental | 60 |
| 832 | M.G. 1100 | 50 |
| 833 | Ford Mustang Hardtop | 50 |
| 834 | Ford Mustang Convertible | 50 |
| 914 | Ford D 800 Truck | 40 |
| 915 | Ford D 800 Stake Truck | 40 |
| 928 | Mercedes-Benz 230SL Hardtop | 60 |
| 929 | Mercedes-Benz 230SL Roadster | 60 |
| 930 | Monza GT Coupe | 45 |
| 931 | Monza GT Roadster | 45 |
| 933 | Oldsmobile Toronado | 50 |

# Danbury Mint

This Connecticut-based company specializes in 1/24 scale die cast models of 1920s through 1960s American automobiles, with the occasional foreign make thrown into the mix. Since issuing its first models in 1989, the Danbury Mint has established itself as a major player in the highly-detailed, accuracy-oriented segment of the market.

The detail and accuracy come at a price, of course, which is usually in the $90-$125 range. Danbury markets its products not only to the collector market, but to the general public as well, with advertisements in mainstream magazines like *TV Guide* and *Parade*.

Since all but a couple of DM models are currently available, prices on the secondary market have not risen appreciably. The following listing reflects this, with "CRP" (Current Retail Price) being the norm.

There is one exception, and that is the 1/18 scale 1969 Mario Andretti Brawner-Hawk IndyCar. Originally manufactured by Ertl, it debuted in 1993 to great acclaim. Somewhere along the way, The Danbury Mint took over the distribution, but it is apparently no longer in production. Originally priced at around $120, it now commands anywhere from $225-$300 on the collector market.

*Danbury Mint's 1953 Buick Skylark.*

*The 1966 Ford Mustang. Starting in 1990, Danbury also produced a cream convertible version of this car; it is no longer in production.*

*1949 Mercury Club Coupe.*

| # Name | Price | # Name | Price | # Name | Price |
|--------|-------|--------|-------|--------|-------|
| **1/24 scale (alphabetical by marque):** | | 1925 Ford Model T "First" Pickup (black) | CRP | 1965 Pontiac GTO (purple) | CRP |
| 1953 Buick Skylark Convertible (blue) | CRP | 1927 Ford Coke Delivery Truck (red/Coke graphics) | CRP | 1934 Packard V12 LeBaron Speedster (red) | CRP |
| 1959 Cadillac Series 62 Convertible (red) | CRP | 1931 Ford Model A Deluxe Roadster (black/brown) | CRP | 1933 Pierce Silver Arrow with Operating Trunk (silver) | CRP |
| 1932 Cadillac V-16 Sport Phaeton (green) | CRP | 1935 Ford 50-830 Half Ton Pickup (blue/black) | CRP | 1933 Pierce Silver Arrow with Inoperative Trunk (silver) | CRP |
| 1957 Chevrolet Bel Air Convertible (blue) | CRP | 1940 Ford Deluxe Coupe (red) | CRP | 1938 Rolls-Royce Phantom III (red) | CRP |
| 1958 Chevrolet Impala Convertible with Operating Trunk (turquoise) | CRP | 1942 Ford Half Ton Pickup (green) | CRP | 1927 Stutz Custom Series Black Hawk (black) | CRP |
| 1958 Chevrolet Impala Convertible with Inoperative Trunk (turquoise) | CRP | 1955 Ford Fairlane Crown Victoria (cream/black) | CRP | **1/16 scale:** | |
| 1958 Chevrolet Apache Pickup (blue) | CRP | 1956 Ford F-100 Pickup (vermilion) | CRP | 1929 Cord L29 Special Coupe (blue) | CRP |
| 1953 Chevrolet 3100 Pickup (green) | CRP | 1956 Ford F-100 Pickup (black) | CRP | 1953 Cadillac Eldorado Convertible (white) | CRP |
| 1957 Chevrolet Cameo Carrier Pickup (red) | CRP | 1956 Ford Thunderbird (red) | CRP | 1955 Chevrolet Bel Air 2-door Hardtop (red/white) | CRP |
| 1969 Chevrolet SS/RS Camaro Convertible (blue) | CRP | 1966 Ford Mustang Convertible (cream) | CRP | World War II Jeep (olive drab) | CRP |
| 1969 Chevrolet SS/RS Camaro Convertible (orange/white) | CRP | 1966 Ford Mustang Hardtop (red/black) | CRP | World War II Jeep Rocket Launcher (olive drab) | CRP |
| 1955 Chevrolet Nomad Station Wagon (turquoise/ivory) | CRP | 1934 Hispano Suiza J-12 (blue) | CRP | **1/32 scale:** | |
| 1948 Chrysler Town & Country Convertible (red/wood) | CRP | 1949 Jaguar XK120 (tan/silver) | CRP | 1926 Mack AC Rotary Pumper (red) | CRP |
| 1935 Duesenberg SSJ Speedster (gray/red) | CRP | 1931 Mercedes-Benz SSKL (white) | CRP | **1/18 scale:** | |
| 1958 Ferrari 250 Testa Rossa (red) | CRP | 1949 Mercury Club Coupe (black) | CRP | 1969 Andretti Brawner-Hawk IndyCar | $250 |
| | | 1949 Mercury Club Coupe Fire Chief (red) | CRP | | |
| | | 1949 Mercury Club Coupe Police Car (red) | CRP | | |

# D.C.M.T.

The initials stand for Die Casting Machine Tools Ltd., and the story of this British firm is a fascinating one. Following the end of World War II, this company, located in North London, began manufacturing die cast toys as a means of showcasing the potential of the die casting machines in which they specialized. These early toys were marketed by the Crescent Toy Company Ltd., also based in London. They included items such as the "DIAL 999" and "GARAGE CAR LIFT" sets, as well as a Fire Engine that featured a fireman climbing the ladder mounted on the rear of the truck. (For more information on the D.C.M.T.-Crescent connection, see the Crescent section in this book.)

D.C.M.T. also made at least one other truck, a "low loader" flat-backed Tractor Trailer, in the early 1950s. Three others—a Timber Truck—a Military Truck and a Tanker have also been attributed to them, but it is not certain that they manufactured these. In any event, all four trucks were to roughly 1/50 scale, and are valued today in the $30-$50 range when they are found in excellent or better condition.

But the real controversy stems from the "River series" of six 1/43 scale cars made during the 1950s. These included an Austin A40 Somerset, a Buick Roadmaster, a Daimler Conquest, a Ford Prefect,

*The Buick from the "River" series, sometimes attributed to D.C.M.T. This example has a friction-powered motor.*

Photo courtesy of Andrew Ralston.

a Standard Vanguard Saloon and a Standard Vanguard Station Wagon. There are two schools of thought on these models. The first states that they were all part of the "River" series made and marketed by D.C.M.T. The other school of thought states that, since neither the cars nor the boxes have any reference to D.C.M.T. on them, they must have been made by some other manufacturer. (These models also often turn up sufferering from "metal fatigue," while other D.C.M.T. products do not.)

In terms of value, these six (somewhat scarce) items generally sell in the $50-$75 range, with the Buick commanding an additional $25 or so. If the original box is present, add an additional $25-$50 to these figures.

Four of these models were later re-issued by Gamda of Israel; a photo of one, the Buick, can be seen in the section on Gamda, providing a useful comparison with the original D.C.M.T./River series version shown here.

D.C.M.T. also used a name for its products that would eventually become very well-known. The name was "Lone Star," and it may have been used as early as 1950. It was certainly very much in evidence by the middle part of the decade, as in 1956 D.C.M.T. launched the Lone Star "Road-masters," a series which would "put the company on the map" of the toy world. For more information, see the section on Lone Star.

# Detail Cars

This line of 1/43 scale die cast models of luxury and sports cars made its debut in late 1992. They are the products of the Italian company C.D.C., and as the product name implies, they were well-detailed from the start. But it was in late 1994, when C.D.C. entered into an agreement with Corgi Toys to take over the marketing of the line, that Detail Cars really began to gain recognition.

The models are made in China, and with their excellent quality they compete well with brands like Paul's Model Art

(the "Minichamps" line). In early 1995, C.D.C. announced their 1/43 model of the Volkswagen Concept 1 car, based on the prototype of the car that has been touted as the "successor" to the Beetle. The model seems to have sold quite well, and has brought Detail Cars a good deal of attention.

All of the models in the line are currently available, and are therefore listed as selling at CRP (Current Retail Price), which is $22-$27.

| # | Name | Price |
|---|---|---|
| 110 | 1990 Lamborghini Diablo (yellow) | CRP |
| 111 | 1994 Lamborghini Diablo S (red) | CRP |
| 112 | 1992 Lamborghini Diablo Roadster (yellow) | CRP |
| 113 | 1990 Lamborghini Diablo Roadster (blue) | CRP |
| 114 | 1993 Lamborghini Diablo Coupe (black) | CRP |
| 131 | 1992 Jaguar XJS Convertible Top Down (blue) | CRP |
| 132 | 1992 Jaguar XJS Convertible Top Up (silver) | CRP |
| 133 | 1992 Jaguar XJS Coupe (red) | CRP |
| 140 | Ferrari 512 TR (red) | CRP |
| 142 | Ferrari 512 TR Open (yellow) | CRP |
| 150 | 1987 Ferrari F40 (red) | CRP |
| 151 | 1987 Ferrari F40 Le Mans (red) | CRP |
| 153 | 1991 Ferrari F40 "Comil" (red) | CRP |
| 154 | 1993 Ferrari F40 "MonteShell" (multi-color) | CRP |
| 155 | 1994 Ferrari F40 "Totip" (multi-color) | CRP |
| 160 | 1991 Nissan 300ZX Coupe (black) | CRP |
| 161 | 1991 Nissan 300ZX Convertible (red) | CRP |
| 162 | 1991 Nissan 300ZX Softtop (blue) | CRP |
| 163 | 1991 Nissan 300ZX Convertible (red) | CRP |

| # | Name | Price |
|---|---|---|
| 164 | 1991 Nissan 300ZX Coupe (silver) | CRP |
| 165 | 1991 Nissan 300ZX "Monza" (multi-color) | CRP |
| 170 | 1993 Jaguar XJ220 Coupe (silver) | CRP |
| 171 | 1993 Jaguar XJ220 Coupe (green) | CRP |
| 172 | 1993 Jaguar XJ220 GT "Le Mans" | CRP |
| 174 | 1993 Jaguar XJ220 GT "Martini" | CRP |
| 193 | 1993 Ferrari 456 GT Coupe (red) | CRP |

| # | Name | Price |
|---|---|---|
| 200 | 1958 Alfa Romeo Giulietta Spider (red) | CRP |
| 201 | 1958 Alfa Romeo Giulietta Spider (white) | CRP |
| 202 | 1958 Alfa Romeo Giulietta Spider (blue) | CRP |
| 203 | 1958 Alfa Romeo Giulietta Spider Hardtop (red) | CRP |

*Detail Cars #261 Volkswagen Concept 1 Coupe. Note the wheel hubs, which are very accurate and sharply molded.*

| # | Name | Price |
|---|------|-------|
| 204 | 1958 Alfa Romeo Giulietta Spider Hardtop (white) | CRP |
| 205 | 1958 Alfa Romeo Giulietta Spider Softtop (gray) | CRP |
| 206 | 1958 Alfa Romeo Giulietta Monoposto "Mille Miglia" (red) | CRP |
| 210 | 1993 Chevrolet Corvette ZR1 Coupe (white) | CRP |
| 211 | 1993 Chevrolet Corvette ZR1 Convertible Top Down (red) | CRP |
| 212 | 1993 Chevrolet Corvette ZR1 Convertible Softtop (yellow) | CRP |
| 214 | 1993 Chevrolet Corvette ZR1 Convertible Top Down (green) | CRP |
| 215 | 1993 Chevrolet Corvette ZR1 Coupe "40th Anniversary" (red) | CRP |
| 220 | 1959 Porsche 356A Coupe (red) | CRP |
| 221 | 1959 Porsche 356A Coupe (silver) | CRP |
| 222 | 1957 Porsche 356A Convertible Top Up (red) | CRP |
| 223 | 1959 Porsche 356A Convertible with Tonneau (silver) | CRP |
| 224 | 1959 Porsche 356A Convertible Top Up (blue) | CRP |
| 225 | 1959 Porsche 356A Convertible Top Down (yellow) | CRP |
| 226 | 1959 Porsche 356A Coupe "Mille Miglia" (silver) | CRP |
| 227 | 1953 Porsche 356A Coupe "Carrera Panamericana" #200 (white) | CRP |
| 228 | 1953 Porsche 356A Coupe "Carrera Panamericana" #153 (silver) | CRP |
| 229 | 1957 Porsche 356A Convertible with Tonneau (silver) | CRP |
| 230 | 1994 Mercedes-Benz 320 SL Convertible Top Down (silver) | CRP |
| 231 | 1994 Mercedes-Benz 320 SL Convertible Top Down (red) | CRP |
| 233 | 1994 Mercedes-Benz 320 SL Coupe (blue) | CRP |
| 234 | 1994 Mercedes-Benz 320 SL Convertible Top Down (red) | CRP |
| 235 | 1994 Mercedes-Benz 320 SL Coupe (gray) | CRP |
| 240 | 1952 BMW 502 Coupe (black) | CRP |
| 241 | 1952 BMW 502 Coupe (red) | CRP |
| 242 | 1952 BMW 502 Convertible Top Down (blue) | CRP |
| 243 | 1952 BMW 502 Convertible Top Up (silver) | CRP |
| 244 | 1952 BMW 502 Convertible Top Down (red) | CRP |
| 245 | 1952 BMW 502 Coupe (gray) | CRP |
| 246 | 1952 BMW 502 Convertible Top Down (cream) | CRP |
| 250 | 1959 BMW 503 Coupe (red) | CRP |
| 251 | 1959 BMW 503 Coupe (silver) | CRP |
| 252 | 1959 BMW 503 Coupe (black) | CRP |
| 253 | 1959 BMW 503 Convertible Top Down (red) | CRP |
| 254 | 1959 BMW 503 Convertible Top Down (yellow) | CRP |
| 255 | 1959 BMW 503 Convertible Top Down (blue) | CRP |
| 256 | 1959 BMW 503 Convertible Top Up (black) | CRP |
| 260 | 1994 Volkswagen Concept 1 Coupe (yellow) | CRP |
| 261 | 1994 Volkswagen Concept 1 Coupe (red) | CRP |
| 262 | 1994 Volkswagen Concept 1 Coupe (green) | CRP |
| 263 | 1994 Volkswagen Concept 1 Convertible Top Down (yellow) | CRP |
| 264 | 1994 Volkswagen Concept 1 Convertible Top Down (red) | CRP |
| 265 | 1994 Volkswagen Concept 1 Convertible Top Down (green) | CRP |
| 266 | 1994 Volkswagen Concept 1 Convertible Top Up (silver) | CRP |
| 270 | Volkswagen Golf (red) | CRP |
| 271 | Volkswagen Golf (silver) | CRP |
| 272 | Volkswagen Golf (white) | CRP |
| 273 | Volkswagen Golf Convertible (red) | CRP |
| 274 | Volkswagen Golf Convertible (silver) | CRP |
| 275 | Volkswagen Golf Convertible (yellow) | CRP |
| 277 | Volkswagen Golf "Silverstone" (multi-color) | CRP |
| 280 | 1994 Ford Mustang GT (red) | CRP |
| 281 | 1994 Ford Mustang GT (yellow) | CRP |
| 282 | 1994 Ford Mustang GT (blue) | CRP |
| 287 | 1994 Ford Mustang Indy 500 Pace Car (red) | CRP |
| 290 | Ferrari F355 Berlinetta Coupe (red) | CRP |
| 291 | Ferrari F355 Berlinetta Coupe (yellow) | CRP |
| 292 | Ferrari F355 Berlinetta Coupe (blue) | CRP |
| 293 | Ferrari F355 Berlinetta Convertible (red) | CRP |
| 294 | Ferrari F355 Berlinetta Convertible (yellow) | CRP |
| 295 | Ferrari F355 Berlinetta Convertible (blue) | CRP |
| 296 | Ferrari F355 Berlinetta TS Closed Top (gray) | CRP |

# Diapet

The Diapet line was originally owned by the Japanese company Yonezawa Toys, a name revered by collectors of tinplate toy cars manufactured during the 1950s. Yonezawa launched the Diapet line of 1/40 scale cars and 1/50 to 1/60 scale trucks in the mid-1960s; construction vehicles and a line of 1/35 scale motorcycles followed. It is these groups of 1960s and 1970s products that are listed here.

Diapet models are still made today, although whether Yonezawa still is the manufacturer is unknown. The majority of the current series is comprised of Japanese makes such as Nissan, Toyota and Mazda. These new models sell in the $20-$40 range.

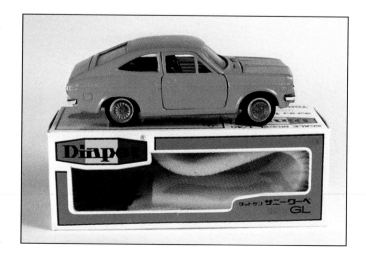

*Diapet's #212 Datsun Sunny Coupe with original box.*

| # | Name | Price |
|---|------|-------|
| A1 | Toyota Corona Mk II | $40 |
| A2 | Toyota Corona Mk II Police Car (white, black/white) | 45 |
| A3 | Datsun Fairlady Z | 40 |
| A5 | Toyota Crown Hardtop SL | 40 |
| A6 | Toyota Corona Mk II (chrome-plated) | 40 |
| A7 | Datsun Fairlady Z (chrome-plated) | 40 |
| A8 | Toyota Crown Hardtop Police Car (white/black) | 40 |
| A9 | Toyota Crown Hardtop | 40 |
| A10 | Toyota Corona Mk II Ambulance (white) | 50 |
| A11 | Mitsubishi Galant GTO | 40 |
| A12 | Toyota Celica 1600 GT | 40 |
| A13 | Toyota Corona Mk II "EAGLE MASK" | 45 |
| A14 | Toyota Corona Mk II | 45 |
| O11 | 61 Tank (chrome-plated) | 150 |
| O12 | M 40 Tank (chrome-plated) | 150 |
| K1 | Nissan Cedric Deluxe | 65 |
| K2 | Volkswagen 1300 | 65 |
| 113 | Datsun Fairlady Convertible | 100 |
| 119 | Prince Gloria | 80 |
| 120 | Nissan Cedric | 80 |
| 121 | Toyopet Crown | 80 |
| 123 | Mercedes-Benz 300 SL Roadster | 100 |
| 124 | Isuzu Bellett 1600 GT | 80 |
| 125 | Prince Skyline 1500 | 80 |
| 126 | Datsun Bluebird | 80 |
| 129 | Toyota Crown Police Car (white/black) | 85 |
| 131 | Honda S 600 Roadster | 85 |
| 133 | Mitsubishi Debonair | 80 |
| 134 | Nissan Cedric Police Car (white/black) | 90 |
| 137 | Nissan Silvia Coupe | 70 |
| 138 | Toyota Corona Coupe | 70 |
| 139 | Datsun Torpedo (chrome-plated) | 50 |
| 140 | Chevrolet Torpedo (chrome-plated) | 60 |
| 141 | Isuzu Truck (chrome-plated) | 100 |
| 142 | Isuzu Tipping Truck (chrome-plated) | 100 |
| 143 | Toyota Crown | 75 |
| 144 | Mitsubishi Colt 800 S.W. | 75 |
| 145 | Nissan Cedric | 70 |
| 146 | Toyota Corona | 70 |
| 147 | Hino Contessa Coupe | 65 |
| 148 | Subaru 1000 | 60 |
| 149 | Porsche 911 | 80 |
| 150 | Nissan President | 75 |
| 151 | Toyota Crown S.W. Ambulance (white) | 80 |
| 151A | Toyota Crown S.W. "TOSHIBA" (yellow/red) | 350 |
| 152 | Nissan Silvia Coupe Police Car (white/black) | 85 |
| 153 | Toyota Publica | 60 |
| 154 | Datsun Sunny 1000 | 70 |
| 157 | Volkswagen 1600 TL | 70 |
| 158 | Mazda Luce | 65 |
| 159 | Hato Bus (beige) | 90 |
| 160 | Toyota Corolla | 65 |
| 161 | Nissan Cedric Police Car (white/black) | 85 |
| 162 | Toyota 2000 GT Coupe | 75 |
| 163 | Nissan R 380 | 60 |

*An orange example of the full size car is just visible on the top edge of the original box for this #197 Datsun Fairlady Z.*

| # | Name | Price |
|---|------|-------|
| 164 | Nissan Gloria | $65 |
| 165 | Volkswagen 1300 | 75 |
| 166 | Mazda Cosmo Coupe | 65 |
| 167 | Mercedes-Benz 230-S | 95 |
| 168 | Honda N 360 | 65 |
| 169 | Honda S 800 Roadster | 70 |
| 170 | Toyota New Crown | 60 |
| 171 | Datsun New Bluebird | 65 |
| 172 | Suzuki 360 | 60 |
| 173 | Mazda Familia Coupe | 60 |
| 175 | Fiat 850 Roadster Bertone | 75 |
| 177 | Toyota Century | 70 |
| 178 | Isuzu Florian | 70 |
| 180 | Nissan Skyline 2000 GT | 65 |
| 181 | Honda S 800 Roadster | 70 |
| 182 | Sunny Coupe | 60 |
| 183 | Toyota Corona Coupe | 60 |
| 184 | Toyota Corona Coupe | 60 |
| 185 | Nissan Laurel | 60 |
| 186 | Nissan Cedric | 60 |
| 187 | Toyota Crown Police Car (white/black) | 75 |
| 188 | Toyota Crown Coupe | 60 |
| 189 | Toyota Publica | 60 |
| 191 | Subaru 1100 FF 1 | 65 |
| 192 | Mazda Cosmo Police Car (white/black) | 75 |
| 194 | Datsun Bluebird SSS Coupe | 60 |
| 195 | Subaru R2 | 60 |
| 196 | Mitsubishi Colt Galant | 60 |
| 197 | Datsun Fairlady Z 432 | 65 |
| 198 | Mazda Rotary Luce Coupe | 60 |
| 199 | Isuzu 117 Coupe | 60 |
| 200 | Toyota Corona II 1900 | 60 |
| 201 | Nissan Skyline 2000 GTR | 60 |
| 203 | Toyota Crown Ambulance (white) | 75 |
| 204 | Volkswagen 1300 | 70 |
| 205 | Nissan New Cedric | 60 |
| 206 | Toyota Corolla 1200 SL | 60 |
| 207 | Toyopet Crown | 50 |
| 208 | Nissan Cedric | 50 |
| 209 | Nissan Skyline 1800 | 60 |
| 210 | Nissan R 382 | 60 |
| 211 | Datsun Sunny 1200 GL | 55 |
| 212 | Datsun Sunny 1200 GL Coupe | 55 |
| 213 | Nissan Gloria | 55 |
| 214 | Toyota Sprinter Coupe | 55 |
| 215 | Toyota New Corona 1700 SL | 55 |
| 216 | Honda 1300 Coupe | 60 |
| 217 | Datsun Laurel 2000 GX Coupe | 55 |

| # | Name | Price |
|---|------|-------|
| 219 | Mazda Capella Rotary Coupe | $60 |
| 220 | Mazda Luce Rotary Coupe | 60 |
| 221 | Datsun Cherry X1 | 60 |
| 222 | Nissan Skyline HT 2000 GT Coupe | 60 |
| 223 | Datsun Coupe Sunny | 60 |
| 224 | Mazda Luce Rotary Coupe (chrome-plated) | 75 |
| 225 | Nissan Skyline 1300 | 55 |
| 226 | Nissan New Bluebird | 60 |
| 227 | Toyota Corolla Sprinter Coupe | 60 |
| 229 | Datsun Laurel 2000 GX Coupe | 60 |
| 230 | Nissan Skyline Police Car (white/black) | 75 |
| 231 | Mazda Luce Rotary Police Car (white/black) | 75 |
| 232 | Nissan Gloria Police Car (white/black) | 75 |
| 233 | Toyota Crown Taxi (orange/yellow) | 75 |
| 234 | Kawasaki 650 W-1 Motorcycle | 35 |
| 235 | Kawasaki 650 W-1 Police Motorcycle | 35 |
| 236 | Yamaha XS 650 Motorcycle | 35 |
| 237 | Yamaha XS 650 Police Motorcycle | 35 |
| 238 | Nissan Skyline Fire Chief (red) | 65 |
| 239 | Nissan Skyline Ambulance (white) | 65 |
| 240 | Datsun Bluebird Police Car (white/black) | 70 |
| 241 | Toyota Crown Police Car (white/black) | 70 |
| 242 | Datsun Sunny Police Car (white/black) | 70 |
| 243 | Nissan Gloria Taxi (orange/yellow) | 70 |
| 244 | Toyota Celica 1600 GT | 55 |
| 245 | Datsun Laurel Police Car (white/black) | 65 |
| 246 | Datsun Laurel Ambulance (white) | 65 |
| 247 | Toyota New Crown Coupe | 60 |
| 248 | Porsche 911S | 65 |
| 249 | Datsun Bluebird SSS Taxi (yellow/blue) | 75 |
| 250 | Toyota New Crown Station Wagon | 60 |
| 251 | Toyota Crown Wrecker (yellow/white) | 50 |
| 252 | Datsun Fairlady Z 240 Police Car (white/black) | 70 |
| 253 | Toyota New Corona Coupe | 55 |
| 254 | Nissan Laurel Coupe Radio Car (red white) | 80 |
| 255 | Porsche 911 S Police Car (white/black) | 80 |
| 256 | Mitsubishi Galant Coupe | 60 |
| 257 | Toyota Corolla Sprinter Coupe Rally | 60 |
| 258 | Datsun Laurel Coupe Rally | 60 |
| 259 | Mazda Cosmo Ambulance (white) | 75 |
| 260 | Isuzu 117 Coupe Rally | 55 |
| 261 | Nissan Cedric Coupe | 55 |
| 262 | Nissan Gloria Coupe | 55 |
| 263 | Toyota Crown Super | 55 |

| # | Name | Price |
|---|------|-------|
| 264 | Toyota Crown Super "Magic Motor" | $65 |
| 266 | Express Bus | 65 |
| 268 | Isuzu Bellet MX Coupe | 55 |
| 269 | Nissan New Cedric | 55 |
| 271 | Kawasaki 650 Motorcycle with Sidecar | 35 |
| 272 | Kawasaki 650 Police Motorcycle with Sidecar | 35 |
| 273 | Yamaha 650 Motorcycle with Sidecar | 35 |
| 274 | Yamaha 650 Police Motorcycle with Sidecar | 35 |
| 275 | Mazda Cosmo Coupe TV Car | 85 |
| 276 | Mitsubishi Galant Coupe | 60 |
| 277 | Toyota Crown Station Wagon Mail Car (red) | 80 |
| 278 | Bus | 90 |
| 279 | Hato Bus | 90 |
| 280 | Toyota New Crown Taxi (orange/yellow) | 60 |
| 281 | Isuzu 117 Coupe TV Car | 75 |
| 283 | Nissan Cedric Ambulance (white) | 75 |
| 286 | Suzuki Hustler Motorcycle | 25 |
| 289 | Toyota Dump Truck | 45 |
| 291 | Isuzu Fire Engine (red) | 50 |
| 292 | Mazda Savanna Coupe | 50 |
| 293 | Datsun Bluebird U Coupe | 50 |
| 294 | Yamaha 650 Racing Motorcycle | 25 |
| 296 | Toyota Crown Ambulance (white) | 60 |
| 297 | Go-kart (SE) | 45 |
| 298 | Suzuki Hustler 250 Motocross | 20 |
| 299 | Suzuki Hustler 250 Racing Motorcycle | 20 |
| 300 | Toyota Hiace Bus | 40 |
| 302 | Toyota Hiace Police Bus (white/black) | 50 |
| 306 | Yamaha 650 Motorcycle | 25 |
| 309 | Nissan Gloria Coupe | 50 |
| 312 | Toyota Crown Police Car (white/black) | 65 |
| 315 | Tanker | 35 |
| 316 | Cargo Truck | 35 |
| 317 | Crane Truck | 35 |
| 318 | Cement Mixer Truck | 35 |
| 322 | Honda Motorcycle | 20 |
| 324 | Toyota Crown (chrome-plated) | 50 |
| 325 | Nissan Gloria | 50 |
| 327 | Nissan Skyline | 50 |
| 328 | Nissan Gloria Fire Car (red) | 55 |
| 329 | Honda CB 750 Motorcycle | 25 |
| 330 | Toyota Crown "GAS SERVICE" | 45 |
| 332 | Animal Transporter | 45 |
| 501 | Lancia Fulvia Coupe | 70 |
| 502 | Fiat Dino Coupe Bertone | 70 |
| 503 | Nissan R 382 Racing Car | 60 |
| No # | Nissan Skyline GTR "PMC" | 375 |
| No # | Nissan Skyline GTR Hardtop "PMC" | 375 |
| No # | Prince Skyline 1500 (copper) | 275 |
| 0101 | Toyota Crown "JAL" (white/light blue) | 65 |
| 0102 | Mitsubishi Galant Hardtop | 45 |
| 0103 | Nissan Cedric Taxi (yellow/blue) | 65 |
| 0104 | Suzuki 500 Hustler Motocross | 20 |
| 0105 | Suzuki GT 750 Motorcycle | 20 |
| 0106 | Honda 750 Police Motorcycle | 25 |
| 0107 | Isuzu Tanker "SHELL" (red/yellow) | 40 |

| # | Name | Price |
|---|------|-------|
| 0108 | Toyota Crown Road Control Car | $55 |
| 0109 | Isuzu Concrete Mixer | 35 |
| 0110 | Bus (white/blue) | 45 |
| 0111 | Toyota Animal Transporter | 40 |
| 0112 | Fuso Bus "JNL" (white/blue) | 50 |
| 0113 | Fuso Dump Truck | 40 |
| 0114 | Toyota Mail Truck | 50 |
| 0115 | Isuzu Fire Engine (red/yellow) | 40 |
| 0116 | Datsun Skyline Coupe | 35 |
| 0117 | Honda 250 Motorcycle | 20 |
| 0118 | Yamaha DT 250 Motorcycle | 20 |
| 0119 | Kawasaki 250 Motorcycle | 20 |
| 0120 | Honda 750 Motorcycle with Sidecar | 30 |
| 0121 | Honda 750 Chopper | 20 |
| 0122 | Honda 750 Racing Motorcycle | 20 |
| 0123 | Mitsubishi Fuso Bus "JAL" (white/light green) | 40 |
| 0124 | Mazda Luce Custom | 35 |
| 0126 | Toyoace Truck | 35 |
| 0127 | Toyota Crown Station Wagon and Caravan | 55 |
| 0128 | Fuso Television Bus (white/blue/dark blue) | 50 |
| 0129 | Datsun Skyline Fire Car (red) | 35 |
| 0130 | Mitsubishi Galant Hardtop (pewter) | 40 |
| 0131 | Mitsubishi Galant Hardtop (chrome-plated) | 35 |
| 0132 | Fuso Bus (white/red, orange/yellow) | 40 |
| 0133 | Camping Bus | 35 |
| 0135 | Isuzu Truck | 40 |
| 0137 | Hato Bus (beige) | 65 |
| 0138 | Toyota 2000 GT Coupe | 45 |
| 0139 | Toyota Century | 40 |
| 0141 | Datsun Fairlady Z | 40 |
| 0143 | Isuzu 117 Coupe | 40 |
| 0144 | Toyopet Crown Ambulance (white) | 65 |
| 0145 | Nissan R 382 | 40 |
| 0146 | Honda Coupe 9 | 45 |
| 0148 | Datsun Cherry | 40 |
| 0153 | Kawasaki 650 Police Motorcycle | 25 |
| 0154 | Yamaha 650 Motorcycle | 25 |
| 0156 | Toyota Celica | 40 |
| 0158 | Porsche 911 | 50 |
| 0159 | Toyota New Crown Station Wagon | 40 |
| 0160 | Datsun Fairlady Police Car (white/black) | 60 |
| 0161 | Porsche 911 S Police Car (white/black) | 65 |
| 0162 | Datsun Cedric Hardtop | 40 |
| 0164 | Toyota New Crown Super | 40 |
| 0165 | Mitsubishi Fuso Bus (blue/white) | 50 |
| 0166 | Isuzu Bellet MX Coupe | 40 |
| 0168 | Kawasaki 650 Motorcycle with Sidecar | 25 |
| 0169 | Kawasaki 650 Police Motorcycle with Sidecar | 25 |
| 0170 | Yamaha Police Motorcycle with Sidecar | 25 |
| 0171 | Toyota New Crown Mail Car (red) | 45 |
| 0172 | Fuso Express Bus (white/red) | 50 |
| 0173 | Hato Bus (tan/red) | 55 |
| 0174 | Toyota New Crown Taxi (orange/yellow) | 60 |
| 0176 | Suzuki Hustler Motorcycle | 20 |
| 0177 | Toyota Dump Truck | 35 |

| # | Name | Price |
|---|------|-------|
| 0178 | Isuzu Fire Engine (red) | $45 |
| 0179 | Mazda Savanna Coupe | 40 |
| 0180 | Datsun Bluebird U Coupe | 40 |
| 0182 | Toyota New Crown Ambulance (white) | 60 |
| 0183 | Suzuki Racer Motorcycle | 25 |
| 0184 | Toyota Hi-Ace Bus | 45 |
| 0186 | Toyota Hi-Ace Police Bus (white/black) | 60 |
| 0189 | Toyota Crown Police Car (white/black) | 60 |
| 0192 | Fuso Crane Truck | 35 |
| 0193 | Toyota Hi-Ace Ambulance (white) | 55 |
| 0196 | Honda 750 Motorcycle | 20 |
| 0198 | Isuzu Diesel Bus (white/light blue) | 45 |
| 0199 | Isuzu Diesel Bus (yellow/green) | 45 |
| 0200 | Suzuki 750 Motorcycle | 20 |
| 0201 | Yamaha 650 Motorcycle with Sidecar | 20 |
| 0202 | Suzuki Motorcycle | 20 |
| 0203 | Elf Sanitary Truck | 30 |
| 0204 | Datsun Pickup | 35 |
| 0205 | Ace Wheel-Loader (yellow) | 30 |
| 0206 | Power Shovel | 30 |
| 0209 | Isuzu Dump Truck | 35 |
| 0210 | Nissan Cedric (chrome-plated) | 35 |
| 0211 | Nissan Gloria Police Car (white/black) | 50 |
| 0212 | School Bus (red/yellow) | 55 |
| 0213 | Fuso Lumber Truck | 35 |
| 0214 | Nippon Express Articulated Truck (yellow) | 45 |
| 0215 | Nissan Cedric Taxi (orange/yellow) | 45 |
| 0216 | Datsun New Skyline Station Wagon | 35 |
| 0220 | Suzuki 750 Motorcycle | 20 |
| 0221 | Datsun Skyline Fire Car (red) | 40 |
| 0222 | Dump Truck | 35 |
| 0223 | Fuso Articulated Truck | 30 |
| 0224 | Datsun Skyline Ambulance (white) | 50 |
| 0225 | Toyota Celica 2000 GT | 35 |
| 0226 | Power and Dozer Shovel (red/yellow) | 30 |
| 0227 | Shovel Dozer | 30 |
| 0228 | Porer Dozer | 30 |
| 0229 | Ichiko 375 Hydraulic Shovel | 35 |
| 0230 | Kindergarden Bus | 45 |
| 0231 | Nishi Nippon Bus (pink/green) | 45 |
| 0232 | Ambulance Bus (white) | 55 |
| 0233 | Elf Dump Truck | 30 |
| 0234 | Elf Fire Engine (red) | 35 |
| 0235 | Police Bus (black) | 55 |
| 0236 | Isuzu Covered Truck (yellow/blue) | 30 |
| 0237 | Isuzu Bus (yellow/blue/red) | 50 |
| 0238 | Fuso Bus Chuo (red/white) | 45 |
| 0239 | Fuso Bus (white/blue) | 45 |
| 0241 | Kawasaki 750 Motorcycle | 20 |
| 0242 | Nissan Skyline Station Wagon | 35 |
| 0243 | Fuso Bus "Automobile Library" | 50 |
| 0244 | Kindergarden Hiace Bus (red/white) | 40 |
| 0246 | Toyota Dump Truck | 35 |
| 0260 | Elf Power Shovel Truck | 220 |
| 0261 | Toyo Ace "NIPPON EXPRESS" | 40 |
| 0262 | Fuso Bus Tokai Bus | 50 |
| 0263 | Toyota Hiace "JAL" Bus (white/light blue) | 40 |

| # | Name | Price |
|---|------|-------|
| 0264 | Toyota Hiace Fire Bus (red) | $40 |
| 0265 | Prototype Racing Car | 30 |
| 0266 | Elf Lift Loader | 30 |
| 0267 | Toyoace Truck | 35 |
| 0268 | JNR Bus (blue/dark blue) | 45 |
| 0269 | Mitsubishi Fuso Bus (white/brown) | 45 |
| 0270 | Datsun Van (yellow) | 35 |
| 0271 | Datsun Mail Van (red) | 35 |
| 0272 | Datsun Breakdown Truck (white/blue/yellow) | 35 |
| 0273 | Toyota Fork-lift | 30 |
| 0274 | Bucket Lift Truck | 30 |
| 0275 | Ichiko K 1600 Mobile Crane | 30 |
| 0276 | Ichiko KK 400 | 30 |
| 0277 | Road Sweeper | 35 |
| 0278 | Honda 1300 Police Car (white/black) | 50 |
| 0279 | Toyota Fork-lift | 30 |
| 0281 | Toyota Crown Ambulance (white) | 50 |
| 0282 | Elf Crane | 25 |
| 0283 | Isuzu Fire Engine (red) | 35 |
| 0284 | Isuzu Crane Truck | 30 |
| 0285 | Isuzu Tanker | 275 |
| 0286 | Isuzu Concrete Mixer | 30 |
| 0288 | Fuso Bus Red Cross (white) | 45 |
| 0289 | Fuso Dump Truck | 30 |
| 0290 | Fuso Lift Van "NITTU" (yellow) | 35 |
| 0291 | Fuso Refuse Wagon | 35 |
| 0292 | Fuso Concrete Mixer | 35 |
| 0294 | Nissan Gloria Rally | 35 |
| 0295 | U.S. Army Jeep | 25 |
| 0296 | Suzuki Mini Police (white/black) | 40 |
| 0297 | Car Carrier | 50 |
| 0298 | Mazda Luce Taxi (orange/yellow) | 40 |
| 0299 | Mazda Luce Police Car (white/black) | 40 |
| 0300 | Datsun Skyline Ambulance (white) | 45 |
| 0301 | Datsun Sunny Coupe | 30 |
| 0302 | Fuso Car Transporter | 40 |
| 0303 | "JAF" Crown Van | 35 |
| 0304 | Elf Wrecker Truck "JAF" | 35 |
| 0305 | Toyota Truck | 275 |
| 0306 | N.H.K. Television Bus (white/blue) | 45 |
| 0308 | Datsun Prince Royal | 35 |
| 0310 | Diapet Truck | 30 |
| 0311 | Suzuki 750 Police Motorcycle | 20 |
| 0312 | Nissan Skyline "ALL NIPPON AIRWAYS" (white/blue) | 35 |
| 0313 | Nissan Skyline TV Car (white) | 35 |
| 0314 | Datsun Truck "ITO YOKADO" | 30 |
| 0315 | Datsun Bluebird U-73 | 30 |
| 0316 | Toyota Corona Station Wagon | 30 |
| 0317 | Komatsu Bulldozer (yellow) | 25 |
| 0318 | Kawasaki 85 Z Shovel Loader (yellow) | 25 |
| 0319 | Komatsu Bulldozer with Ripper (yellow) | 25 |
| 0320 | Willys Jeep Police (white/black) | 25 |
| 0321 | Nissan Bluebird Taxi (orange/yellow) | 35 |
| 0322 | Toyota Corona Station Wagon Police (white/black) | 35 |
| 0323 | Fuso Bus "ALL NIPPON AIRWAYS" (white/blue) | 40 |

| # | Name | Price |
|---|------|-------|
| 0324 | Ichiko Bucket Crane | $25 |
| 0325 | Ichiko Earth Screw | 25 |
| 0326 | Fuso Dump Truck | 25 |
| 0327 | Ichiko Oil Pressure Shovel | 25 |
| 0328 | Ichiko Bucket Crane | 25 |
| 0329 | Datsun Cherry F II Coupe | 30 |
| 0330 | Hato Bus (yellow) | 35 |
| 0331 | Kubota L 245 Tractor with Trailer (orange) | 40 |
| 0332 | Kubota L 245 Tractor with Disk (orange) | 40 |
| 0333 | Kubota L 245 Tractor with Roto-Tiller (orange) | 40 |
| 0334 | Toyota Hiace Police Bus (white/black) | 30 |
| 0335 | Toyota Hiace Ambulance (white) | 30 |
| 0336 | Kubota L 1500 Tractor (orange) | 40 |
| 0337 | Komatsu Loader | 25 |
| 0338 | Komatsu Ripper | 25 |
| 0339 | Caterpillar Shovel | 25 |
| 0340 | Caterpillar Bulldozer | 25 |
| 0342 | Ichiko Shovel | 25 |
| 0343 | Ichiko Oil Pressure Shovel | 175 |
| 0344 | Ichiko Crane | 25 |

*This is an example of a late '70s-early '80s Diapet, the 1/30 scale #T-2 Toyota Land Cruiser Jeep. The bazooka is plastic, and swivels 360 degrees.*

| # | Name | Price |
|---|------|-------|
| 0345 | Ichiko Pile Driver | 25 |
| 0346 | Honda Civic GF | 25 |
| 0347 | Toyota Crown Royal | 25 |
| 0348 | Fuso Bus "HOKURIKU" (white/red) | 35 |
| 0349 | Toyota Celica Rally | 25 |
| 0350 | Nissan Dump Truck | 25 |
| 0351 | Datsun Bottle Truck | 30 |
| 0352 | Fuso Container Truck (yellow/green) | 35 |
| 0353 | Toyota Crown Ambulance (white) | 50 |
| 0354 | U.S. Army Jeep with hood (olive) | 25 |
| 0355 | Toyota New Crown Station Wagon | 30 |
| 0356 | Fuso Concrete Mixer | 30 |
| 0357 | Mitsubishi Colt Galant Coupe | 35 |
| 0358 | Fuso Crane Truck | 30 |
| 0359 | Toyota New Crown Taxi (orange/yellow) | 45 |
| 0360 | Toyota Crown Police Car (white/black) | 45 |
| 0361 | Toyota Corolla Coupe | 30 |
| 0362 | Toyota Corolla 30 | 30 |
| 0363 | Datsun Fairlady Z | 30 |
| 0364 | Datsun Sunny Coupe with calendar on roof | 60 |

| # | Name | Price |
|---|------|-------|
| 0365 | Datsun Sunny Taxi with calendar on roof | $60 |
| 0366 | Fuso Ladder Fire Engine (red) | 35 |
| 0367 | M 41 Tank (olive) | 60 |
| 0368 | M 42 Tank (olive) | 60 |
| 0369 | Datsun Fairlady Z Rally | 35 |
| 0370 | Datsun Fairlady Z Police Car (white/black) | 45 |
| 0371 | Datsun President | 30 |
| 0372 | Toyota Crown Station Wagon Police Car (white/black) | 45 |
| 0373 | Toyota 2000 GT Rally | 30 |
| 0374 | Datsun Silvia 1800 LS Coupe | 30 |
| 0375 | Lancer Celeste 1600 Coupe | 30 |
| 0376 | Porsche 930 Turbo | 30 |
| 0377 | Toyota Corona Coupe Rally Montecarlo | 30 |
| 0378 | Toyota New Crown Ambulance (white) | 45 |
| 0380 | Fuso Snorkel Fire Engine (red) | 30 |
| 0381 | Fuso Car Carrier | 35 |
| 0382 | Komatsu Dump Truck | 25 |
| 0384 | Toyota Carina HT | 30 |
| 0385 | Nissan Cedric | 35 |
| 0386 | Kawasaki Road Roller | 25 |
| 0387 | Mitsubishi Fuso Bus (white/red) | 40 |
| 0389 | Toyota Crown Motor School Car | 40 |
| 0401 | Toyota Crown Hardtop | 15 |
| 0402 | Datsun Fairlady Z | 15 |
| 0403 | Toyota Celica 1600 GT | 15 |
| 0404 | Toyota Crown Police Car (white/black) | 20 |
| 0405 | Datsun Fairlady Z Police Car (white/black) | 20 |
| 0406 | Datsun 610 Coupe | 15 |
| 0407 | Toyota Corona Mark II SS | 15 |
| 0408 | Nissan Skyline 2000 GT | 15 |
| 0409 | Mitsubishi Colt Galant | 15 |
| 0410 | Toyota Century | 15 |
| 0411 | Toyota Crown Station Wagon | 15 |
| 0412 | Toyota Crown Station Wagon Ambulance (white) | 20 |
| 0413 | Nissan Cedric Hardtop GX | 15 |
| 0414 | Datsun Laurel Coupe | 15 |
| 0415 | Toyota Corona Mark II Red Cross (white) | 20 |
| 0416 | Nissan R 382 Racing Car | 15 |
| 0417 | Nissan Skyline 2000 GT | 15 |

| # | Name | Price | # | Name | Price | # | Name | Price |
|---|------|-------|---|------|-------|---|------|-------|
| 0418 | Toyota Crown Station Wagon Fire Chief (red) | $20 | 0469 | Subaru Van "FLOWER SHOP" (white/green) | $15 | 01392 | Fuso Fire Engine (red) | $25 |
| 0419 | Toyota Crown Taxi (yellow/orange) | 20 | 0601 | Nissan Cedric Hardtop 1973 | 35 | 01393 | Datsun Skyline | 25 |
| 0420 | Toyota Corona Mark II Police Car (white/black) | 20 | 0602 | Toyota Crown Hardtop | 35 | 01394 | Lotus Europa | 25 |
| 0421 | Nissan Cedric Taxi (yellow/orange) | 20 | 0603 | Datsun Fairlady Z Rally | 35 | 01395 | Datsun Bluebird Coupe | 25 |
| 0422 | Nissan Cedric Police Car (yellow/orange) | 20 | 0604 | Nissan Cedric Super Deluxe | 35 | 01396 | BMW 3.5 CSL | 25 |
| 0423 | Toyota Corona Private Police Car (black/white) | 20 | 0605 | Datsun Fairlady Z Police Car (white/black) | 35 | 01397 | Fuso "SHELL" Tanker (red/yellow) | 25 |
| 0424 | Toyota Celica Rally | 15 | 0606 | Toyota Crown Hardtop Police Car (white/black) | 35 | 01398 | Fuso Containers Truck | 25 |
| 0425 | Toyota Celica "JAL" (white/blue) | 15 | 0607 | Toyota Crown Hardtop Red Cross (white) | 35 | 01399 | JNR Bus (light blue/blue, white/blue) | 25 |
| 0426 | Subaru Leone | 30 | 0608 | Nissan Cedric Taxi (orange/yellow) | 35 | 01400 | Hato Bus (beige/brown) | 25 |
| 0427 | Honda Civic | 30 | 0609 | Nissan Cedric Police Car (white/black) | 35 | 01401 | Fuso Van | 25 |
| 0428 | Subaru Rex | 30 | 0610 | Toyota Crown Taxi (orange/yellow) | 35 | 01402 | Isuzu Dump Truck | 20 |
| 0429 | Honda Life | 30 | 0611 | Datsun Violet 1600 Hardtop | 35 | 01403 | Lamborghini Miura | 25 |
| 0430 | Mazda Chante | 30 | 0612 | Datsun Violet SSS Hardtop | 35 | 01404 | Lamborghini Miura Racing | 25 |
| 0431 | Mitsubishi Minica F 4 | 30 | 0613 | Toyota Crown Police Car (white/black) | 35 | 01407 | Fuso Truck "ITO YOKADO" | 25 |
| 0432 | Subaru Samber | 30 | 0614 | Toyota Celica LB | 35 | 01408 | Mitsubishi Fuso Bus (blue/white) | 25 |
| 0433 | Subaru Rex Police Car (white/black) | 30 | 0615 | Nissan Skyline 2000 GTR | 35 | 01409 | Fuso Tanker | 25 |
| 0436 | Daihatsu Electric Experimental Car | 40 | 0945 | Nissan Cedric Police Car (white/black) | 35 | 01410 | Ferrari 512 BB | 35 |
| 0437 | Suzuki Fronte | 30 | 0557 | Toyota M Saloon (1936) (pewter) | 25 | 01411 | Lamborghini Countach LP 500 S | 25 |
| 0438 | Subaru "PEPSI COLA" Truck (white) | 25 | 0958 | Datsun 17 (1935) (pewter) | 25 | 01412 | Toyota Corona Mk II Grande | 20 |
| 0439 | Datsun Violet Coupe | 15 | 0959 | Mitsubishi A (1915) (pewter) | 25 | 01413 | BMW 3.5 CSL Racing | 20 |
| 0446 | Dump Truck | 15 | 0971 | Datsun Torpedo (1932) (pewter) | 25 | 01414 | Komatsu Loader 510 | 20 |
| 0447 | Van "NITTU" (yellow) | 15 | 01379 | Mazda Cosmo AP Coupe | 25 | 01415 | Mitsubishi Galant Sapporo | 20 |
| 0448 | Mail Van (red) | 15 | 01381 | Fuso Car Carrier | 30 | 01416 | Alpine Renault A 310 | 20 |
| 0462 | Subaru Samber Mail Car (red) | 35 | 01385 | Nissan Cedric | 25 | 01417 | Rolls Royce Silver Shadow | 25 |
| 0464 | Toyota Crown Ambulance (white) | 15 | 01387 | Meitetu Bus | 25 | 01418 | Lotus Europa "JPS" | 20 |
| 0467 | Subaru Van "YAKULUTO" (white/blue) | 15 | 01390 | Honda Accord Coupe | 25 | 01419 | Chevrolet Corvette Coupe | 25 |
|  |  |  | 01391 | Porsche 930 Turbo Martini | 25 | 01420 | Nissan Auster Multi Coupe 1600 CS | 20 |
|  |  |  |  |  |  | 01421 | Maserati Bora | 20 |
|  |  |  |  |  |  | 01422 | Lancia Stratos | 20 |
|  |  |  |  |  |  | 01423 | Porsche 935 | 20 |

# The Dinky Collection

After Meccano Ltd. closed the doors of its Binns Road factory in November 1979, the Dinky name was mothballed for a number of years. In 1987, Matchbox Toys acquired the rights to the name, and in 1988 launched a new series entitled The Dinky Collection. Except for the 1/50 scale Mercedes-Benz Bus, the series has been 1/43 scale, and there were a total of thirty-two different models made.

In 1992, Matchbox Toys was acquired by Tyco, and in 1993 the last new Dinky Collection castings were released. Since that time, some of the models have been packaged together, as with the "Stars of the Silver Screen" tie-in set in 1994, and the "Golden Age of Sports Cars" set in 1995.

In early 1995, Matchbox Toys announced it would introduce three new models in the series: a 1957 Jaguar XK150, a 1957 Mercedes-Benz 300 Roadster and a 1968

*DY25, the 1958 Porsche 356A, with box.*

Volkswagen Karmann-Ghia. Although these models apparently did appear as part of the "Golden Age of Sports Cars" set, the author has not seen them as part of the Dinky Collection series in the United States.

Sold individually, the Dinky Collection models come in a plastic and cardboard display box, and with a few exceptions, most mint/boxed examples sell in the $15-$25 range.

*The DY11 1948 Tucker. This model caught the look of the ill-fated Tucker quite well, including the front "steerhorn" bumper.*

| # | Name | Price |
|---|---|---|
| DY1 | 1967 Jaguar E-Type Mk 1.5 dark green, yellow | $20 |
| DY2 | 1957 Chevrolet Bel Air red and white | 15 |
| DY3 | 1965 MGB GT dark blue, orange | 15 |
| DY4 | 1950 Ford E83W Van Heinz, Radio Times | 15 |
| DY5 | 1950 Ford V8 Pilot black, silver, saddlewood | 15 |
| DY6 | 1952 Volkswagen Beetle light blue, black, red | 20 |
| DY7 | 1959 Cadillac Coupe de Ville deep red and white, pink | 15 |
| DY8 | 1948 Commer 8cwt Van Sharp's Toffee, His Master's Voice | 15 |
| DY9 | 1949 Land Rover green, AA Road Service | 15 |
| DY10 | Mercedes-Benz Diesel Omnibus Type 0-3500 | 35 |
| DY11 | 1948 Tucker Torpedo red, metallic blue | 15 |

| # | Name | Price |
|---|---|---|
| DY12 | 1955 Mercedes-Benz 300SL Gull-Wing ivory, black | $15 |
| DY13 | 1955 Bentley 'R' Continental metallic blue, dark blue | 15 |
| DY14 | Delahaye 145 black, dark red | 15 |
| DY15 | 1953 Austin A40 van Brooke Bond Tea, Dinky Toys | 15 |
| DY16 | 1967 Ford Mustang Fastback metallic green, white | 15 |
| DY17 | 1939 Triumph Dolomite red | 40 |
| DY18 | 1957 Jaguar E-Type (open) red | 15 |
| DY19 | 1973 MGB GT V8 red | 15 |
| DY20 | 1955 Triumph TR4 white | 15 |
| DY21 | 1964 Austin Mini Cooper S white with black roof | 15 |
| DY22 | 1952 Citroën 15CV black, ivory | 15 |
| DY23 | 1956 Chevrolet Corvette hard-top red and white, copper and cream | 15 |
| DY24 | 1973 Ferrari 246 Dino GTS red | 15 |

| # | Name | Price |
|---|---|---|
| DY25 | 1958 Porsche 356A Coupe silver | $15 |
| DY26 | Studebaker Golden Hawk bronze and white | 30 |
| DY27 | 1957 Chevrolet Bel Air convertible blue with blue and white seats | 15 |
| | blue with blue and brown seats | 60 |
| DY28 | 1969 Triumph Stag white | 30 |
| DY29 | 1953 Buick Skylark light blue | 15 |
| DY30 | Austin-Healey 100 BN2 British racing green | 15 |
| DY31 | 1955 Ford Thunderbird red | 15 |
| DY32 | 1957 Citroën 2CV gray | 15 |

**Sports cars on display plinths:**

Set 1: Porsche 356A Coupe (red), Mercedes-Benz Gull Wing (silver) and Ferrari 246 Dino (metallic blue) . . . . . . . . . . . . . 45

Set 2: Triumph TR4 (red), Jaguar E-Type (open) (cream), Austin Healey (metallic blue) . . 45

# Dinky Toys

**I**f the title "Father of the Die Cast Toy" had to be given to one man, few would dispute Frank Hornby receiving the honor. He didn't invent the die casting process (one must look to the history of Tootsietoy for that), but he played an instrumental role in bringing that technology to children all over the world.

Born on May 15, 1863 in Liverpool, England, Hornby would have the course of his life forever changed on Christmas Eve 1899, when he was struck by an idea while traveling by train to visit relatives in Birmingham for the holidays. The idea—to produce a toy crane for children to build and play with—would result in Hornby's founding the

*Early post-war Dinky Toys. On the left is a #25d Tanker, next to a #30c Daimler. Although each has the white tires normally indicative of a pre-war specimen, these are examples of Meccano using up old tire stock that had been in storage since 1942 or 1943.*

Meccano company in 1900. During the next two decades he would build the business from a one-room workshop into one of the largest toy manufacturing concerns in the world. In 1920, "O" gauge Hornby Trains were added to the company's line of construction sets, and by the early 1930s it was decided to produce a line of figures and scale vehicles for use on the railway layouts.

## The First Dinky Toys

In 1932, the first "Modelled Miniatures" vehicles were released. These were small die cast "push-along" trains. In 1933, the legendary twenty-two series of road vehicles came out, a series made up of simple castings of sports cars and trucks. These were part of the "Modelled Miniatures" line, but in 1934 the brain-trust at Meccano realized that they needed a more marketable name for the small vehicles. The line was re-named "Dinky Toys," and by 1935 it included passenger cars, race cars, trucks, and even a travel trailer.

By the time of his death at the age of 73, in September 1936, Frank Hornby had seen the Dinky line of toys rise to world-wide prominence. The 1930s would be a "golden age" for die cast toys, and Dinky played a leading role. The company's success was helped in no small way by the monthly publication of *Meccano Magazine,* which featured articles and advertisements extolling the virtues of Meccano's products. Complete copies of *Meccano Magazine* are highly prized by collectors today.

When the Second World War put a stop to toy production, Meccano switched over to war work. As the war wound down in 1945, plans were being made to return to toy production. By the end of the year, Dinkys could be found in limited numbers, and it is believed that many if not all of these were "left-over" items that had sat in storage since 1942 or '43. This would explain why certain Dinkys thought to be post-war have pre-war features.

Along with resuming manufacture of some pre-war models, new models were introduced as time went on, and Dinky once again took its place as the world's leading die cast toy. Even the appearance of the new Matchbox toys in the early 1950s didn't throw Meccano off its game to any

great degree. The Matchboxes were, after all, of a smaller size and, therefore, in a different price category.

Dinky "Supertoys" were introduced in 1947. These included trucks like the Guys and Fodens, and Meccano marketed them as being bigger and better than the standard Dinkys. They were very well-detailed, but the higher price may account for the fact that a number of them were discontinued in the early 1950s. The relatively small number produced has made them very popular among collectors today, and prices are now quite high.

In 1953 and '54, Meccano re-numbered many of the Dinkys, in order to bring some semblance of order to what had become an extensive and complex product line. Also around this time, many of the models began to be packaged in individual boxes. Prior to this they were generally available in a box of six, from which the purchaser took his or her choice at the shop counter. These "six-pack" boxes, particularly if all six toys are present, command high prices on the collector circuit. Even empty boxes can go for anywhere from $30 to $300.

The events of 1956 would eventually shake Meccano to its core, and force the company to re-examine its product and position in the market. Mettoy's Corgi Toys made their debut that year, and after a year or two began to bite into

*#40g Morris Oxford.*

*#40b Triumph 1800 in drab green, which is an unusual color for this model.*

*#40f Hillman Minx.*

A box for the #254 Austin Taxi. Note the two-color paint job, which Meccano began using on some models in 1956. This box is typical for Dinkys of this period.

The #254 Austin Taxi proved to be one of the best-selling Dinkys of the 1950s.

Dinky's pie in a big way. Corgis had window glazing, opening doors and even friction motors. At first, Meccano responded merely be giving some existing models two-tone paint jobs, but it was inevitable that they would have to upgrade to compete. This they gradually did, adding features such as suspension, jewelled headlights, steering, etc., as the years went by.

In 1957, the Dinky Dublo toys were released as accessories to be used with Horby Dublo train sets. These were to a scale of OO, and they never caught on with the public. Although nicely turned out, they couldn't compete with Matchbox toys. Some Dublos were discontinued after a few years, while others remained in production until the mid-1960s.

## Increasing Competition

For Meccano, the 1960s would be a decade of great competition not only with Corgi, but also with Solido of France, Mercury of Italy, Tootsietoy of the United States and Tekno of Denmark. In 1963, Meccano was taken over by rival British toy manufacturer Lines Bros., maker (among other things) of the "Spot-On" line of die cast toys (models). The Spot-On line was gradually phased out as the company began to focus on the Dinky series. Now that they no longer had the die cast field to themselves (and especially after the "explosion" that rocked the toy world with the debut of Hot Wheels in 1968), Meccano began implementing cost-cutting measures such as putting stickers on their models instead of decals. They also began replacing the standard wheels with the "speedwheel" type in the late 1960s, a move duplicated by many other manufacturers.

Another cost-cutting move was to ship production of a line of six 1/42 American car models to Hong Kong during the mid-1960s. This proved to be unsuccessful, due to production problems and the low quality of the product that was turned out. It was tried again in the late 1970s with the #180 Rover 3500, again unsuccessfully. The Hong Kong models are listed after the Mini Dinky listing.

The Mini Dinky line made its debut in 1968, being to a stated scale of 1/65 (although the construction vehicles were about 1/130). Although several were very good models (with opening doors and hoods), many suffered from "metal fatigue" due to the poor quality of the metal alloy used. The models were made in Hong Kong and in Holland, and they came packaged in a clear plastic garage through which the model could be seen. A number of models were planned that never saw the light of day, and these are included in the Mini Dinky listing, which can be found at the end of the main Dinky listing. When Mini Dinky production ceased is unknown.

Also in 1968, Meccano shipped the tooling for a number of Dinkys to a firm called S. Kumar and Co. (also known as Atamco Private Ltd.), in India. This company manufactured the group of Dinkys as "Nicky Toys," and they were of generally inferior quality when compared to the British-made originals.

The Nicky Toys are listed after the Hong Kong Dinky listing.

Although Dinkys held onto their fair share of the market during the 1970s, the decade brought further turmoil to the company. Financial troubles rocked Meccano's parent company, Lines Bros., which went under in 1971. When the smoke cleared, Meccano was once again Meccano Ltd. But it was now owned by Airfix Industries, which did its best to "jump-start" the Dinky line with new products. A number of these were excellent products which sold moderately well, but by 1977 the handwriting was on the wall.

On November 30, 1979, the doors to the factory on Binns Road in Liverpool were closed for good. Thus ended a nearly fifty year tradition of die cast production. In 1988, Matchbox Toys, now the owners of the Dinky name, launched The Dinky Collection, which would become moderately successful in the ensuing years. But that line of models is currently "on the shelf," with no indication that it will ever be re-started. (For more information, see the section on The Dinky Collection.)

## French Dinky

In the mid-1930s, Meccano had established a Dinky Toys factory in Bobigny, in France. The Dinkys made there were similiar in style to the standard British product, but they were an entirely separate group of models.

After World War II, French Dinky production resumed with the twenty-four series of models, which were renumbered in 1959, some five or so years after renumbering had taken place in the British line. French Dinkys competed successfully with Solido and Norev in the French toy market until 1971, when most of the line was discontinued. Three new models appeared in 1972, but by 1974 production had been stopped altogether.

The French Dinkys are listed after the British models. The French listing is not intended to be exhaustive, but rather an introduction to the excellent items produced at the French factory.

In 1974, Meccano France arranged with Auto-Pilen of Spain to manufacture certain of the French Dinkys, to be marketed under the Dinky name. These were made from 1974-81, and are known to collectors as "Spanish Dinky."

In addition, the owner of Meccano, Airfix, made a deal with Solido to market a group of Solido models as Dinkys. These were made in 1980 and 1981 as part of Solido's "Cougar" series. They came in window boxes very much like the last English Dinky window boxes, and had plastic baseplates marked Dinky.

The Auto-Pilen and Solido Dinky models are listed at the end of the French Dinky listing.

## For More Information...

Fortunately for collectors, the Dinky story is well-documented. Three books in particular merit special mention. The first is *Dinky Toys & Modelled Miniatures* by Mike and Sue Richardson, first published by New Cavendish Books in 1981. This massive tome has since been revised and updated, and is filled with detailed information on dates, model variations, company history and so on.

*A History of British Dinky Toys* has been out of print for

many years, but is well worth the hunt. This pioneering work, first published in 1966 by Model Aeronautical Press, Ltd., and written by Cecil Gibson, is considered indispensable for the serious Dinky collector. It is also considered a collector's item in its own right.

And Dr. Edward Force's *Dinky Toys*, published by Schiffer Publishing, contains a price guide as well as a wealth of photos of Dinkys.

## Condition and Repair/Restoration

Given the world-wide popularity of Dinky Toys, it's no surprise that replacement parts are widely available for broken and incomplete specimens. While this can allow one to return a Dinky to its former glory, it also can cause problems for the potential buyer. Most people wouldn't knowingly pass off a repaired or restored Dinky as an original. But some work is so professionally done that even the experts can be fooled.

The phrase "caveat emptor" cannot be overstated: let the buyer beware. If a specimen looks too good to be true, it probably is. The would-be purchaser is advised to examine as many examples as possible, to acquire an eye for things such as original paint, original chrome pieces, original tires, etc.

## Pre-war vs. Post-war

As mentioned earlier, many pre-war models were also produced after the war. Early post-war examples can have pre-war features, such as the #30c Daimler and #25d Petrol Tanker pictured here. Although post-war, they both have white tires. In general, pre-war Dinkys came with white tires and post-war with black. But there undoubtedly were stocks of unused white tires in storage during the war (along with other parts), and it made good economic sense to use them up before turning out new ones.

Another way to distinguish pre- from post-war production is to examine the axles. In 1945, Meccano increased the diameter of the axles from .062 inches to .078 inches. This thicker unit was used on all Dinkys produced during the second half of the 1940s.

## Using This Listing

The listing provided here includes post-war examples only. Pre-wars generally have higher values, often two to three times that of a post-war example. And a rare or unusual color can push the price up to many times that of the same model in a more common color. The same applies to casting variations.

Aircraft and boats had been a part of the Dinky line of toys since before the war; however, these are outside the scope of this book and are therefore not listed here.

As always, the values given here are for near mint to mint original examples with the original box, where applicable.

Finally, bear in mind that this listing includes basic models and major variations only. To catalog every color and casting variation of every Dinky would, in itself, fill a book. For more information, please refer to the books mentioned earlier.

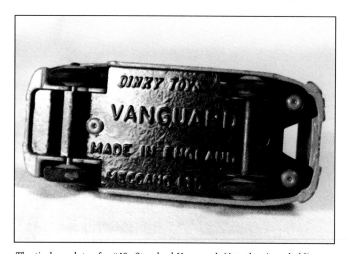

*The tin baseplate of a #40e Standard Vanguard. Note the rivets holding the baseplate to the body.*

| # | Name | Price |
|---|------|-------|

**"Dublo" Dinky models (OO scale):**

| # | Name | Price |
|---|------|-------|
| 061 | Ford Prefect fawn | $80 |
| 062 | Singer Roadster yellow | 80 |
| 063 | Commer Van blue | 65 |
| 064 | Austin Lorry green | 65 |
| 065 | Morris Pick-up red | 65 |
| 066 | Bedford Flat Truck gray | 65 |
| 067 | Austin Taxi blue/cream | 105 |
| 068 | Royal Mail Van red | 110 |
| 069 | Massey-Harrison Ferguson Tractor blue | 45 |
| 070 | AEC Mercury Tanker "Shell BP" red/green | 120 |
| 071 | Volkswagen Delivery Van "Hornby-Dublo" yellow | 95 |
| 072 | Bedford Articulated Flat Truck red/yellow | 95 |
| 073 | Land Rover, Trailer and Horse green/orange | 120 |
| 076 | Lansing-Bagnal Tractor and Trailer red | 95 |
| 078 | Lansing-Bagnal Trailer only red | 60 |

**Gift Sets:**

| 1 | Gift Set No. 1 Farm Equipment (#27a, 27b, 27c, 27g, 27h—this set was renumbered 398) | * |
| 1 | Gift Set No. 1 Military Vehicles (# 621, 641, 675, 676—this set was renumbered 699) | * |
| 2 | Gift Set No. 2: Commercial Vehicles (#25m, #27d, #30n, #30p, #30s) | * |
| 3 | Gift Set No. 3 Passenger Car Set (#27f, 30h, 40e, 40g, 40h, 140b) | * |
| 4 | Gift Set No. 4 Racing Cars (#23f, #23g, #23h, #23j, #23n—this set was renumbered 249) | * |

*These sets turn up for sale infrequently, and prices paid for them at auction vary dramatically. Assigning an accurate price to them is therefore impossible.*

**Single models:**

| 14a | BEV Electric Truck (renumbered 400) gray, blue | 50 |
| 14c | Coventry Climax Fork-lift Truck (renumbered 401) orange/green | 45 |
| 23a | Racing Car (re-issue of pre-war model; renumbered 220) red or blue with silver | 70 |
| 23b | Hotchkiss Racing Car (re-issue of pre-war model) silver, blue | 75 |
| 23c | Mercedes-Benz Racing Car (re-issue of pre-war model) silver, blue | 70 |
| 23d | Auto-Union Racing Car (re-issue of pre-war model) red, silver | 105 |
| 23e | "Speed of the Wind" Racing Car (re-issue of pre-war model; renumbered 221) red, silver | 65 |
| 23f | Alfa-Romeo Racing Car (renumbered 232; later #207 in "bubble pack") red | 145 |

| 23g | Cooper-Bristol Racing Car (renumbered 233; later #208 in "bubble pack") green | $130 |
| 23h | Ferrari Racing Car (renumbered 234; later #209 in "bubble pack") blue with yellow nose | 150 |
| 23j | HWM Racing Car (renumbered 235) green | 130 |
| 23k | Talbot-Lago Racing Car (renumbered 230; later #205 in "bubble pack") blue | 160 |
| 23m | "Thunderbolt" Speed Car silver with black detail, individually boxed | 255 |
| 23n | Maserati Racing Car (renumbered 231; later #206 in "bubble pack") red | 140 |
| 23p | Gardner's M.G. Record Car (re-issue of pre-war model) green with "M.G. Record Car" on base, individually boxed | 140 |
| 23s | Streamlined Racing Car (re-issue of pre-war model; renumbered 222) blue, green, silver | 85 |
| 25a | Wagon various colors | ** |

| 25b | Covered Wagon various colors | ** |
| 25c | Flat Truck various colors | ** |
| 25d | Petrol Tank Wagon various colors | ** |
| 25e | Tipping Wagon various colors | ** |
| 25f | Market Gardener's Van various colors | ** |

*** 25a through 25f were re-issues of pre-war models, and as such came with several different types of chassis, as well as in many different colors and liveries. The values for these trucks range from a low of around $90 for some late examples (such as a #25c Flat Truck or #25e Tipping Wagon), to a high of $500-$600 for certain early examples (such as an early #25b Covered Wagon or an early #25d Petrol Tank Wagon).*

| 25g | Trailer (renumbered 429) various colors | 40 |
| 25h | Streamlined Fire Engine (re-issue of pre-war model, renumbered 250) red | 110 |
| 25j | Jeep red, green, blue, brown | 145 |
| 25m | Bedford End Tipper (renumbered 410) various colors | 140 |
| 25p | Aveling-Barford Diesel Roller (renumbered 251) green with red rollers | 75 |
| 25r | Leyland Forward Control Lorry (renumbered 420) various colors | 120 |

| 25s | Six-wheeled Wagon (re-issue of pre-war model) green or blue with gray tilt | $130 |
| 25t | Flat Truck and Trailer (#25c and #25g, both items are the same color) | 210 |
| 25v | Bedford Refuse Wagon (renumbered 252) fawn with green shutters | 140 |
| | orange cab, gray rear, green shutters | 250 |
| 25w | Bedford Truck (renumbered 411) green | 165 |
| 25wm | Bedford Military Truck (renumbered 640) olive green | 330 |
| 25x | Commer Breakdown Lorry (renumbered 430) various colors | 150 |
| 25y | Jeep (renumbered 405) green, red | 80 |
| 27a | Massey-Harris Tractor (renumbered 300) red | 110 |
| 27ak | Farm Tractor and Hay Rake (#27a + #27k, renumbered 310) red/yellow | 210 |
| 27b | Halesowen Harvest Trailer (renumbered 320) tan/red, red/yellow | 45 |
| 27c | Massey-Harris Manure Spreader (renumbered 321) red | 45 |

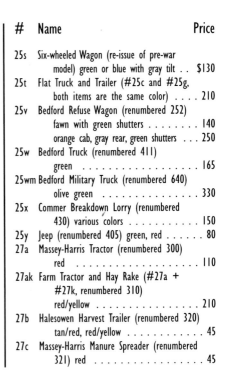

*#39c Lincoln Zephyr. The 39 series cars are very popular with collectors.*

| 27d | Land Rover (renumbered 340) orange, green, red | 115 |
| 27f | Estate Car (renumbered 344) green/brown | 125 |
| 27g | Moto-Cart (renumbered 342) green/brown | 75 |
| 27h | Disc Harrow (renumbered 322) red/yellow, white/red | 30 |
| 27j | Triple Gang Mower (renumbered 323) red/yellow/green | 40 |
| 27k | Hay Rake (renumbered 324) red/yellow | 40 |
| 27m | Land Rover Trailer (renumbered 341) orange, green, red | 30 |
| 27n | Field Marshall Farm Tractor (renumbered 301) orange | 130 |
| 29b | Streamline Bus (re-issue of pre-war model) two-tone blue or green with closed rear window | 105 |
| 29c | Double Deck Bus (re-issue of pre-war model; renumbered 290) red, green lower deck, gray or cream upper deck | 135 |
| 29e | Single Deck Bus green, blue, cream | 130 |
| 29f | Observation Coach (renumbered 280) gray, cream | 125 |

| # | Name | Price |
|---|------|-------|
| 29g | Luxury Coach (renumbered 281) blue, tan, red | $100 |
| 29h | Duple Roadmaster Coach (renumbered 282) red, blue | 130 |
| | yellow, green | 240 |
| 30a | Chrysler 'Airflow' Saloon (re-issue of pre-war model; renumbering of 32) green, blue, cream | 165 |
| 30b | Rolls-Royce Car (re-issue of pre-war model) tan, blue | 160 |
| 30c | Daimler (re-issue of pre-war model) tan, green | 160 |
| 30d | Vauxhall Car (re-issue of pre-war model) green, brown | 160 |
| 30e | Breakdown Car (re-issue of pre-war model) gray, green, red (closed rear window) | 80 |
| 30f | Ambulance (re-issue of pre-war model) gray/black, cream/black | 175 |
| 30h | Daimler Ambulance (renumbered 253) cream, white | 110 |
| 30hm | Daimler Military (renumbered 624) olive green | 220 |
| 30j | Austin Wagon (renumbered 412) blue, red | 125 |
| 30m | Rear Tipping Wagon (renumbered 414) orange/green, blue/gray | 125 |
| 30n | Farm Produce Wagon (renumbered 343) green/yellow, red/blue | 110 |
| 30p | Petrol Tanker green/"Petrol" | 110 |
| | red/"Petrol" | 110 |
| 30p | Petrol Tanker (renumbered 440) red/"Mobilgas" | 190 |
| 30pa | Petrol Tanker (renumbered 441) green/"Castrol" | 225 |
| 30pb | Petrol Tanker (renumbered 442) red/"Esso" | 190 |
| 30r | Fordson Thames Flat Truck (renumbered 422) red, green | 140 |
| 30s | Austin Covered Wagon (renumbered 413) blue/blue, blue/cream, red/cream | 210 |
| 30sm | Austin Covered Wagon (Military; renumbered 625) olive green | 400 |
| 30v | Electric Dairy Van cream/"NCB" (renumbered 491) | 135 |
| | cream/"Express Dairy" or gray/"Express Dairy" (renumbered 490) | 125 |
| | cream/"Job's Dairy" | 175 |
| 30w | Electric Articulated Lorry (renumbered 421) red/"British Railways" | 125 |
| 31a | Trojan 15cwt Van (renumbered 450) red/"Esso" | 200 |
| 31b | Trojan 15cwt Van (renumbered 451) red/"Dunlop" | 200 |
| 31c | Trojan 15cwt Van (renumbered 452) green/"Chivers" | 200 |
| 31d | Trojan 15cwt Van (renumbered 453) blue/"Oxo" | 325 |
| 33w | Mechanical Horse and Open Wagon (re-issue of two pre-war models; renumbered 415) various colors | 125 |

| # | Name | Price |
|---|------|-------|
| 34b | Royal Mail Van (re-issue of pre-war model) red/black or red roof, closed or open rear windows | $200 |
| 34c | Loud-speaker Van (renumbered 492) green, blue, tan, brown | 120 |
| 35a | Saloon Car (re-issue of pre-war model) gray, blue | 95 |
| 35b | Racer (re-issue of pre-war model) red, silver | 95 |
| 35c | MG Sports Car (re-issue of pre-war model) red, green | 110 |
| 35d | Austin 7 Car (re-issue of pre-war model) blue | 120 |
| 36 | Motor Cars Set with Drivers, Passengers, Footmen (includes cars 36a-36f; re-issue of pre-war set with post-war cars) Rare; accurate price data impossible | |
| 36a | Armstrong Siddeley (re-issue of pre-war model) blue, gray, red, green | 175 |
| 36b | Bentley (re-issue of pre-war model) green, blue, gray, tan | 175 |
| 36c | Humber Vogue (re-issue of pre-war model) brown, gray, blue, red | 160 |
| 36d | Rover (re-issue of pre-war model) green, blue | 150 |
| 36e | British Salmson Two-seater Sports (re-issue of pre-war model) red, blue, brown, green | 190 |
| 36f | British Salmson Four-seater Sports (re-issue of pre-war model) green, gray, tan, brown | 175 |
| 36g | Taxi with Driver (re-issue of pre-war model) green, red, brown, blue | 125 |
| 37a | Motor Cyclist-Civilian black cycle, green or gray rider | 50 |
| 37b | Motor Cyclist-Police black cycle/blue rider | 60 |
| 38a | Frazer-Nash BMW Sports Car (re-issue of pre-war model) gray, blue | 185 |
| 38b | Sunbeam-Talbot Sports Car (re-issue of pre-war model) various colors | 200 |
| 38c | Lagonda Tourer maroon, green, gray | 170 |
| 38d | Alvis Sports Tourer (re-issue of pre-war model) green, red | 160 |
| 38e | Armstrong Siddeley Coupe gray, green | 170 |
| 38f | Jaguar Sports Car various colors | 195 |
| 39a | Packard Super 8 Touring Sedan Car (re-issue of pre-war model) brown, green, olive | 165 |
| 39b | Oldsmobile 6 Sedan (re-issue of pre-war model) gray, cream, blue | 175 |
| 39bu | Oldsmobile 6 Sedan (U.S. issue) cream/blue, two-tone blue | 800 |
| | (price varies widely) | |
| 39c | Lincoln Zephyr Coupe (re-issue of pre-war model) brown, gray, red | 140 |
| 39cu | Lincoln Zephyr Coupe (U.S. issue) two-tonered, two-tone brown | 900 |
| | (price varies widely) | |
| 39d | Buick Viceroy Saloon Car (re-issue of pre-war model) Pre-war various colors | 160 |

| # | Name | Price |
|---|------|-------|
| 39e | Chrysler Royal Sedan (re-issue of pre-war model) various colors | $185 |
| 39eu | Chrysler Royal Sedan (U.S. issue) yellow/red, two-tone green | 900 |
| | (price varies widely) | |
| 39f | Studebaker State Commander Coupe blue, gray, green, yellow | 175 |
| 40a | Riley Saloon (renumbered 158) various colors | 110 |
| 40b | Triumph 1800 Saloon (renumbered 151) gray, blue, tan | 135 |
| | black | 600 |
| 40d | Austin Devon Saloon (renumbered 152) various colors | 160 |
| | green and pink (152 only) | 285 |
| | blue and yellow (152 only) | 285 |
| 40e | Standard Vanguard Saloon (renumbered 153) tan with open wheel arches | 160 |
| | tan with closed wheel arches | 140 |
| | light blue, cream | 160 |
| | dark blue | 400 |
| | red | 800 |
| | (price varies widely) | |
| 40f | Hillman Minx Saloon (renumbered 154) tan, green | 170 |
| | green and cream or blue and pink (154 only) | 385 |
| 40g | Morris Oxford Saloon (renumbered 159) green, gray | 135 |
| | tan | 270 |
| | dark green | 200 |
| | green and cream or red and cream (159 only) | 280 |
| 40h | Austin Taxi (renumbered 254) yellow, blue, black | 145 |
| | green and yellow (254 only) | 170 |
| 40j | Austin Somerset Saloon (renumbered 161) red, light blue | 165 |
| | red-blue | 280 |
| | black and cream or red and yellow (161 only) | 290 |
| 42a | Police Box (renumbered 751) Post-war | 45 |
| 42b | Motor Cycle Patrol dark blue and green | 110 |
| 43b | R.A.C. Motor Cycle Patrol black with blue sidecar and rider | 110 |
| 44b | AA Motorcycle Patrol (renumbered 270) black and yellow with tan rider | 110 |
| | with gray plastic wheels (270 only) | 70 |
| 46 | Pavement Set (cardboard) | 190 |
| 47 | Road Signs Set (re-issue of pre-war set; export #770) contains 12 signs (47e-47t) | 120 |
| 47a-47t | Individual road signs, such as "Steep Hill," "No Entry," etc. (all re-issues of pre-war signs, except for 47b and 47c, which were not issued post-war) | 15 |
| 49 | Petrol Pumps Set (#49a-49e; re-issue of pre-war set) | 175 |
| 49a | Bowser Petrol pump (green) | 40 |

| # | Name | Price |
|---|------|-------|
| 49b | Wayne Petrol Pump (blue) | $40 |
| 49c | Theo Petrol Pump (brown) | 40 |
| 49d | Shell Petrol Pump (red) | 40 |
| 49e | Oil Bin yellow | 40 |
| 100 | Lady Penelope's FAB 1 pink | 225 |
| 101 | Sunbeam Alpine (Touring Finish) blue, red | 170 |
| 101 | Thunderbirds II and IV (redesigned as #106) green | 240 |
| | metallic dark green | 360 |
| 102 | Joe's Car green | 160 |
| 102 | MG Midget (Touring Finish) green, yellow | 270 |
| 103 | Austin Healey 100 (Touring Finish) cream, red | 185 |
| 103 | Spectrum Patrol Car metallic red | 170 |
| 104 | Aston Martin DB3S (Touring Finish) blue, pink | 255 |
| 104 | Spectrum Pursuit Vehicle metallic blue | 165 |
| 105a | Garden Roller (renumbered 381) | 25 |
| 105b | Wheelbarrow (renumbered 382) | 25 |
| 105c | Four-Wheel Hand Truck (renumbered 383) | 25 |
| 105e | Grass Cutter (renumbered 384) | 25 |
| 105 | Triumph TR2 (Touring Finish) yellow, gray | 240 |
| 105 | Maximum Security Vehicle white | 175 |
| 106 | Austin Atlantic (renumbering of 140a) black, blue | 210 |
| | pink | 320 |
| 106 | "Prisoner" Mini Moke white with red and white striped canopy | 280 |
| 106 | Thunderbirds II and IV (redesign of #101) metallic blue | 145 |
| 107a | Sack Truck (renumbered 385) | 25 |
| 107 | Stripey the Magic Mini (with plastic figures) white with blue, red and yellow stripes | 320 |
| 107 | Sunbeam Alpine (Competition Finish) pale blue, red | 135 |
| 108 | MG Midget (Competition Finish) red, white | 190 |
| 108 | Sam's Car silver | 125 |
| | gold | 125 |
| | red | 175 |
| | blue | 175 |
| 109 | Austin-Healey 100 (Competition Finish) cream, yellow | 150 |
| 109 | Gabriel Model T Ford yellow/black | 120 |
| 110 | Aston Martin DB3S (Competition Finish) gray, green | 150 |
| 110 | Aston Martin DB5 red | 105 |
| 111 | Cinderella's Coach pink/gold | 25 |
| 111 | Triumph TR2 turquoise, pink | 150 |
| 112 | Austin-Healey Sprite Mark II red | 135 |
| 112 | Purdey's Triumph TR7 yellow | 70 |
| 113 | MGB cream | 105 |
| 114 | Triumph Spitfire gray, gold, red | 135 |
| | purple | 175 |
| 115 | Plymouth Fury Sports white | 125 |

| # | Name | Price |
|---|------|-------|
| 115 | U.B. Taxi yellow, blue and black | $80 |
| 116 | Volvo 1800 S red | 105 |
| 117 | Four-Berth Caravan with Transparent Roof blue and cream, yellow and cream | 65 |
| 118 | Tow-Away Glider Set (#135 Triumph 2000 with trailer and glider) car cream with blue roof | 320 |
| 120 | Happy Taxi white, yellow and blue | 65 |
| 120 | Jaguar 'E' Type red; came with interchangeable black roof and cream folded roof | 105 |
| 121 | Goodwood Racing Gift Set (#'s 112, 113, 120, 183, and nine plastic figures | 1,500 |
| | (price varies widely) | |
| 122 | Touring Gffl Set (#'s 188, 193, 195, 270, 295, 796) | 1,500 |
| | (price varies widely) | |
| 122 | Volvo 265 DL Estate Car blue/white | 45 |
| 123 | Mayfair Gift Set (#'s 142, 150, 186,194, 198, 199 and four plastic figures | 2,500 |
| | (price varies widely) | |

| # | Name | Price |
|---|------|-------|
| 123 | Princess 2200 HL Saloon bronze/blue, white/blue, white | 40 |
| 124 | Holiday Gift Set (#'s 137, 142, 796, 952) | 800 |
| | (price varies widely) | |
| 124 | Rolls-Royce Phantom V Limousine blue | 70 |
| 125 | Fun A'Hoy Set (#'s 130 and 796 with drivers) | 225 |
| 126 | Motor Show Set (#'s 127, 133, 151,171; or 127, 151, 159, 171 in later set) | 1,600 |
| | (price varies widely) | |
| 127 | Rolls-Royce Silver Cloud III green, gold | 165 |
| 128 | Mercedes-Benz 600 red, blue | 95 |
| 129 | MG Midget (#108 without driver or numbers; for US market) white, red | 475 |
| 129 | Volkswagen 1200 Sedan blue | 65 |
| 130 | Ford Consul Corsair red, blue | 90 |
| 131 | Cadillac Eldorado pink, yellow | 160 |
| 131 | Jaguar "E" Type 2+2 white, red, bronze, purple | 160 |

| # | Name | Price |
|---|------|-------|
| 132 | Ford 40-RV silver, blue, orange-red | $65 |
| 132 | Packard Convertible green, tan | 170 |
| 133 | Cunningham C-5R white with blue stripes | 125 |
| 133 | Ford Cortina 1965 gold with white roof, yellow | 110 |
| 134 | Triumph Vitesse green | 105 |
| 135 | Triumph 2000 green with white roof, white with blue roof | 105 |
| 136 | Vauxhall Viva white, blue | 95 |
| 137 | Plymouth Fury Convertible gray, green, blue, pink | 130 |
| 138 | Hillman Imp green, red | 95 |
| 139a | Ford Fordor Sedan (renumbered 170) yellow, red, green, tan | 175 |
| | cream and red, pink and blue (170 only) | 300 |
| 139am | U.S. Army Staff Car (Ford Fordor; renumbered 170m) olive green with white stars | 325 |
| 139b | Hudson Commodore Sedan (renumbered 171) blue/tan, cream/maroon, blue/gray | 190 |
| | red/blue, blue/gray, (171 only) | 325 |

*#621 3-Ton Army Wagon with original box.*

| # | Name | Price |
|---|------|-------|
| 139 | Fort Cortina blue | 120 |
| 140a | Austin Atlantic Convertible (see #106) | |
| 140b | Rover 75 Saloon (see #156) | |
| 140 | Morris 1100 blue | 65 |
| 141 | Vauxhall Victor Estate Car yellow | 70 |
| 142 | Jaguar Mark 10 blue | 90 |
| 143 | Ford Capri green/white | 120 |
| 144 | Volkswagen 1500 cream | 65 |
| | gold | 100 |
| 145 | Singer Vogue green | 110 |
| 146 | Daimler V8 2.5 Litre green | 95 |
| 147 | Cadillac 62 green | 120 |
| 148 | Ford Fairline pale green | 120 |
| | metallic green | 215 |
| 149 | Citroën Dyane bronze/black | 45 |
| 149 | Sports Cars Gift Set (#'s 107, 108, 109, 110, 111) | 2,000 |
| | (price varies widely) | |
| 150 | Rolls-Royce Silver Wraith two-tone gray | 110 |
| 151a | Medium Tank (U.S. export only) green | 225 |

| # | Name | Price |
|---|------|-------|
| 151b | Six-Wheeled Covered Transport Wagon (renumbered 620 for export) various shades of green and brown | $205 |
| 151 | Triumph 1800 Saloon (see #40b) | |
| 151 | Vaushalt Victor 101 yellow, red | 105 |
| 152a | Light Tank (renumbered 650 for export) green, brown | 215 |
| 152b | Reconnaissance Car (renumbered 671 for export) | |
| | gloss green | 210 |
| | matt green, brown | 160 |
| 152 | Austin Devon Saloon (renumbering of 40d) | |
| 152 | Rolls-Royce Phantom V Limousine blue, with driver and two passengers | 70 |
| | driver only | 50 |
| 153a | Jeep (renumbered 672 for export) green | 175 |
| 153 | Aston Martin DB6 blue, green | 100 |
| 153 | Standard Vanguard Saloon (renumbering of 40e) | |
| 154 | Ford Taunus 17M yellow/white | 70 |

*One of the Hong Kong Dinkys: the #006 Rambler Classic Station Wagon.*

| # | Name | Price |
|---|------|-------|
| 154 | Hillman Minx (renumbering of 40f) | |
| 155 | Ford Anglia turquoise | 135 |
| 156 | Rover 75 (renumbering of 140b) | |
| | cream, red | 135 |
| | two-tone green, blue/cream (156 Only) | 190 |
| 156 | Saab 96 metallic red | 110 |
| 157 | BMW 2000 Tilux blue/white | 95 |
| 157 | Jaguar XK 120 | |
| | yellow, red | 140 |
| | white, gray, turquoise and pink, yellow and gray | 325 |
| 158 | Riley (renumbering of 40a) | |
| 158 | Rolls-Royce Silver Shadow red, blue | 80 |
| 159 | Ford Cortina Mk II white | 105 |
| 159 | Morris Oxford Saloon (renumbering of 40g) | |
| 160 | Austin A30 turquoise, tan | 140 |
| 160 | Mercedes-Benz 250SE blue | 75 |
| 161b | Anti-Aircraft Gun on Trailer (re-issue of pre-war model; renumbered 690) | |
| | gloss green | 175 |
| | matt green, brown | 145 |
| 161 | Austin Somerset Saloon (renumbering of 40j) | |
| 161 | Ford Mustang Fastback 2+2 | |
| | white, yellow | 75 |

| # | Name | Price |
|---|------|-------|
| 162 | 18-Pounder Quick-Firing Field Gun Unit (re-issue of pre-war model; renumbered 691) contains 162a-c | $255 |
| 162a | Light Dragon Motor Tractor (re-issue of pre-war model) green | 150 |
| 162b | Trailer (re-issue of pre-war model) green | 40 |
| 162c | 18-Pounder Gun (re-issue of pre-war model) green | 45 |
| 162 | Ford Zephyr Saloon cream/green, two-tone blue | 165 |
| 162 | Triumph 1300 blue | 90 |
| 163 | Bristol 450 Coupe green | 105 |
| 163 | Volkswagen 1600 TL Fastback | |
| | red | 65 |
| | blue | 120 |
| 164 | Ford Zodiac Mk IV | |
| | silver | 95 |
| | bronze | 175 |
| 164 | Vauxhall Cresta gray/green, red/cream | 165 |
| 165 | Ford Capri green, purple | 85 |
| 165 | Humber Hawk green/black, red/cream | 165 |
| 166 | Renault R16 blue | 65 |
| 166 | Sunbeam Rapier cream/orange, two-tone blue | 140 |
| 167 | AC Aceca | |
| | cream | 270 |
| | cream/brown, cream/red, gray/red | 160 |
| 168 | Ford Escort | |
| | light blue | 75 |
| | red | 125 |
| | metallic blue | 125 |
| 168 | Singer Cazelle cream/brown, gray/green | 165 |
| 169 | Ford Corsair 2000E silver/black | 105 |
| 169 | Studebaker Golden Hawk green/cream, tan/red | 170 |
| 170 | Ford Fordor (renumbering of 139a) | |
| 170m | Ford Fordor US Army Staff Car (renumbering of 139am; renumbered 675) | |
| 170 | Lincoln Continental orange/white, blue/white | 170 |
| 171 | Austin 1800 blue | 85 |
| 171 | Hudson Commodore (renumbering of 139b) | |
| 172 | Fiat 2300 Station Wagon two-tone blue | 75 |

| # | Name | Price |
|---|------|-------|
| 172 | Studebaker Land Cruiser | |
| | green/blue | $175 |
| | red/cream, tan/cream | 280 |
| 173 | Nash Rambler green/red, pink/blue | 105 |
| 173 | Pontiac Parisienne red | 75 |
| 174 | Hudson Hornet red/cream, yellow/gray | 160 |
| 174 | Mercury Cougar blue | 65 |
| 175 | Cadillac Eldorado blue/black, purple/black | 75 |
| 175 | Hillman Minx blue/gray, green/tan | 165 |
| 176 | Austin A105 cream/blue, gray/red | 190 |
| 176 | NSU Ro80 | |
| | red | 70 |
| | blue | 185 |
| 177 | Opel Kapitan blue | 105 |
| 178 | Mini Clubman bronze, red | 65 |
| 178 | Plymouth Plaza pink/green, two-tone blue | 165 |
| 179 | Opel Commodore blue/black | 60 |
| 179 | Studebaker President yellow/blue, light blue/blue | 170 |
| 180 | Packard Clipper tan/red, orange/gray | 170 |
| 180 | Rover 3500 Saloon white | 30 |
| 181 | Volkswagen various colors | 105 |
| 182 | Porsche 356A Coupe | |
| | cream, red, blue | 170 |
| | pink/red | 325 |
| 183 | Fiat 600 green, red | 105 |
| 183 | Morris Mini Minor (Automatic) red/black, blue | 125 |
| 184 | Volvo 122S | |
| | red | 125 |
| | white | 360 |
| 185 | Alfa Romeo 1900 Super Sprint yellow, red | 125 |
| 186 | Mercedes-Benz 220 SE light blue, gray-blue | 65 |
| 187 | Volkswagen Karmann-Ghia Coupe red/black, green/cream | 125 |
| 187 | De Tomaso Mangusta 5000 red/white | 65 |
| 188 | Four-Berth Caravan green/cream, blue/cream | 65 |
| 188 | Jensen FF yellow | 90 |
| 189 | Lamborghini Marzal green/white, yellow/white, blue and white | 60 |
| 189 | Triumph Herald green/white, blue/white | 125 |
| 190 | Caravan orange/cream, blue/cream | 65 |
| 190 | Monteverdi 375L red | 65 |
| 191 | Dodge Royal Sedan | |
| | cream/brown, green/black | 170 |
| | cream/blue | 285 |
| 192 | De Soto Fireflite gray/red, green/tan | 190 |
| 192 | Range Rover bronze, yellow | 40 |
| 193 | Rambler Cross-Country Station Wagon yellow/white | 140 |
| 194 | Bentley S Series Coupe gray, bronze | 165 |
| 195 | Jaguar 3.4 Litre Mark II red, gray, cream | 140 |
| 195 | Range Rover Fire Chief red | 65 |

| # | Name | Price |
|---|------|-------|
| 196 | Holten Special Sedan | |
| | bronze/white | $95 |
| | turquoise/white | 125 |
| 197 | Morris Mini-Traveller | |
| | white/brown, green/brown | 120 |
| | green | 255 |
| | dark green/brown | 360 |
| 198 | Rolls-Royce Phantom V green/cream, | |
| | two-tone gray | 125 |
| 199 | Austin 7 Countryman | |
| | blue/brown | 120 |
| | orange | 335 |
| 200 | Matra 630 blue | 45 |
| 200 | Midget Racer silver | 55 |
| 201 | Plymouth Stock Car blue | 75 |
| 201 | Racing Car Set (#'s 240, 241, 242, | |
| | 243) | 480 |
| 202 | Customised Land Rover yellow | 35 |
| 202 | Fiat Abarth 2000 orange/white | 35 |
| 203 | Customised Range Rover black | 35 |
| 204 | Ferrari 312P red/white | 35 |
| 205 | Lotus Cortina rally white/red | 125 |
| 205 | Talbot Lago (Bubble Pack) blue | 325 |
| 206 | Customised Corvette Stingray red | 40 |
| 206 | Maserati (Bubble Pack) red/white | 325 |
| 207 | Alfa Romeo (Bubble Pack) red | 325 |
| 207 | Triumph TR7 Rally Car white/blue/red | 40 |
| 208 | Cooper-Bristol (Bubble Pack) green | 325 |
| 208 | VW Porsche 914 yellow, blue/black | 40 |
| 209 | Ferrari (Bubble Pack) blue with yellow | |
| | triangle on nose | 325 |
| 210 | Vanwall ("bubble pack"; renumbering of | |
| | #239) green | 85 |
| 210 | Alfa Romeo 33 red with black doors | 40 |
| 211 | Triumph TR7 Sports Car | |
| | blue-green | 75 |
| | white (British Leyland promotional) | 75 |
| | red | 65 |
| 212 | Ford Cortina Rally white/black | 125 |
| 213 | Ford Capri Rally red, bronze | 70 |
| 214 | Hillman Imp Rally blue | 95 |
| 215 | Ford GT Racing Car | |
| | white | 55 |
| | green | 65 |
| 216 | Dino Ferrari red, blue | 45 |
| 217 | Alfa Romeo Scarabeo OSI orange | 40 |
| 218 | Lotus Europa | |
| | yellow/blue | 65 |
| | yellow/black | 45 |
| 219 | Jaguar XJS Coupe white with "cat" | |
| | decals | 65 |
| 220 | Ferrari P5 red | 40 |
| 220 | Small Open Racing Car (renumbering | |
| | of #23a) | |
| 221 | Corvette Stingray gold, white | 45 |
| 221 | "Speed of the Wind" Racing Car | |
| | (renumbering of #23e) | |
| 222 | Hesketh Racing Car 308E | |
| | dark blue | 35 |
| | Olympus Special | 95 |

| # | Name | Price |
|---|------|-------|
| 222 | Streamlined Racing Car (renumbering | |
| | of #23s) | |
| 223 | McLaren M8A Can Am white/blue, | |
| | green | $35 |
| 224 | Mercedes-Benz CIII red | 35 |
| 225 | Lotus Formula 1 Racing Car red/blue | 35 |
| 226 | Ferrari 312/B2 red, bronze | 35 |
| 227 | Beach Buggy yellow with white hood | 35 |
| 228 | Super Sprinter blue/orange | 30 |
| 230 | Talbot-Lago Racing Car (renumbering of 23k) | |
| 231 | Maserati Racmg Car (renumbering of 23n) | |
| 232 | Alfa Romeo Racing Car (renumbering of 23f) | |
| 233 | Cooper-Bristol Racing Car (renumbering | |
| | of 23g) | |
| 234 | Ferrari Racing Car (renumbering of 23h) | |
| 235 | HWM Racing Car (renumbering of 23j) | |
| 236 | Connaught Racing Car green | 125 |
| 237 | Mercedes-Benz Racing Car white, | |
| | cream | 135 |
| 238 | Jaguar Type D Racing Car turquoise | 125 |
| 239 | Vanwall Racing Car (renumbered 210 in | |
| | "bubble pack") green | 85 |
| 240 | Cooper Racing Car white/blue | 25-35 |
| 240 | Dinky Way Gift Set (#'s 211, 255, 382, | |
| | 412 plus roadways and road signs) | 95 |
| 241 | Lotus Racing Car green | 45 |
| 241 | Silver Jubilee Taxi silver | 30 |
| 242 | Ferrari Racing Car red | 40 |
| 243 | BRM Racing Car green | 40 |
| 243 | Volvo Police Car white | 35 |
| 244 | Plymouth Police Car blue/white | 35 |
| 245 | Superfast Gift Set | |
| | (#'s 131, 153, 188) | 110-160 |
| 246 | International GT Gift Set | |
| | (#'s 187, 215, 216) | 175 |
| 249 | Racing Cars Gift Set | |
| | (renumbering of Gift Set No 4, with | |
| | #'s 231, 232, 233, 234, 235 | 1,500 |
| | (price varies widely) | |
| 249 | World Famous Racing Cars (bubble pack, | |
| | with #'s 230, 231, 232, 233, 234, | |
| | 239 | 1,700 |
| | (price varies widely) | |
| 250 | Fire Engine (renumbering of 25h) | |
| 250 | Mini Cooper S Police Car white | 75 |
| 251 | Aveling-Barford Diesel Roller (renumbering | |
| | of 25p) | |
| 251 | USA Police Car white/black | 75 |
| 252 | Bedford Refuse Wagon (renumbering of 25v) | |
| 252 | RCMP Car blue with white doors | 75 |
| 253 | Daimler Ambulance (renumbering of 30h) | 60 |
| 254 | Austin Taxi (renumbering of 40h) | |
| 254 | Police Range Rover white/red | 45 |
| 255 | Ford Zodiac Police Car white | 90 |
| 255 | Mersey Tunnel Police Van red | 90 |
| 255 | Police Mini Clubman blue with white | |
| | doors | 45 |
| 256 | Police Car (Humber Hawk) black | 160 |
| 257 | Canadian Fire Chief's Car (Nash Rambler) | |
| | red | 105 |

| # | Name | Price |
|---|------|-------|
| 258 | USA Police Car black with white front door | |
| | 1-DeSoto | $150 |
| | 2-Dodge | 150 |
| | 3-Ford Fairline | 150 |
| | 4-Cadillac | 150 |
| 259 | Fire Engine (Bedford) red | 125 |
| 260 | Royal Mail Van (Morris J) red with black | |
| | roof | 160 |
| 260 | Volkswagen "Deutsche Buntespost" | |
| | (export model; casting #129) | |
| | yellow | 190 |
| 261 | Fort Taunus 17M "Polizei" (export model; | |
| | casting #154) | |
| | white/green | 270 |
| 261 | Telephone Service Van green/black | 160 |
| 262 | Volkswagen Swiss Post PTT Car | |
| | yellow/black | |
| | casting #181 | 400 |
| | casting #129 | 95 |
| 263 | Airport Fire Rescue Tender (ERF) yellow | 70 |
| 263 | Superior Criterion Ambulance (without | |
| | flashing light) white | 90 |
| 264 | RCMP Patrol Car dark blue with white doors | |
| | Ford Fairline | 125 |
| | Cadillac | 140 |
| 265 | Plymouth Taxi yellow/red | 165 |
| 266 | Plymouth Taxi | |
| | "Metro Cab" on doors | |
| | yellow/red | 185 |
| 266 | ERF Fire Tender red with white escape | 80 |
| 266 | ERF Fire Tender "Falck" (export model) | |
| | red with white escape | 105 |
| 267 | Paramedic Truck red | 40 |
| 267 | Superior Cadillac Ambulance (with flashing | |
| | light) cream/red | 80 |
| 268 | Range Rover Ambulance white | 35 |
| 268 | Renault Dauphine Mini-Cab red | 135 |
| 269 | Jaguar Motorway Police Car white | 160 |
| 269 | Police Accident Unit white with red | |
| | stripe | 50 |
| 270 | AA Motor Cycle Patrol (reissue of 44b) | |
| 270 | Ford Panda Police Car blue with white | |
| | doors | 70 |
| 271 | TS Motor Cycle Patrol (export model) | |
| | yellow | 165 |
| 271 | Ford Transit Fire Appliance "Falck" | |
| | (export market) red | 125 |
| 271 | Ford Transit Fire Appliance red | 95 |
| 272 | ANWB Motor Cycle Patrol (export market) | |
| | yellow | 325 |
| 272 | Police Accident Unit white | 55 |
| 273 | RAC Patrol Mini Van blue/white | 240 |
| 274 | AA Patrol Mini Van | |
| | yellow | 205 |
| | yellow with white roof | 240 |
| 274 | Ford Transit Ambulance white | 45 |
| 274 | Mini Van "Joseph Mason Paints" (promotional) | |
| | red | 800 |
| | (price varies widely) | |

| # | Name | Price |
|---|------|-------|
| 275 | Brink's Arrmoured Car no gold; gray with white roof and Brinks stickers | $85 |
| 275 | Brink's Armoured Car with gold bullion; gray with Brinks decal | 190 |
| 275 | Armoured Car "Luis R. Picaso Manriquez" gray (price varies widely) | 1,000 |
| 276 | Airport Fire Tender red | 85 |
| 276 | Ford Transit Ambulance white | 45 |
| 277 | Police Land Rover blue/white | 40 |
| 277 | Superior Criterion Ambulance with flashing light blue/white | 100 |
| 278 | Plymouth Yellow Cab yellow | 35 |
| 278 | Vauxhall Victor Ambulance white | 105 |
| 279 | Aveling Barford Diesel Roller orange/yellow | 75 |
| 280 | Midland Mobile Bank white/silver/blue | 140 |
| 280 | Observation Coach (renumbering of 29f) | |
| 281 | Fiat 2300 Pathe News Camera Car black | 165 |
| 281 | Luxury Coach (renumbering of 29g) | |
| 281 | Military Hovercraft olive green | 40 |
| 282 | Duple Roadmaster Coach (renumbering of 29h) | |
| 282 | Austin 1800 Taxi blue/white | 85 |
| 282 | Land Rover Fire Appliance red | 45 |
| 282 | Land Rover Fire Appliance "Falck" export model red | 75 |
| 283 | BOAC Coach blue/white | 140 |
| 283 | Single Decker Bus red | 65 |
| 284 | London Austin Taxi black, dark blue | 50 |
| 285 | Merryweather Marquis Fire Engine red | 85 |
| 285 | Merryweather Marquis Fire Engine "Falck" export model red | 125 |
| 286 | Ford Transit Fire Appliance "Falck" export model red | 135 |
| 286 | Ford Transit Fire Appliance red | 105 |
| 287 | Police Accident Unit orange/cream, white/red | 105 |
| 288 | Superior Cadillac Ambulance "Falck" export model, without flashing light white/red, black/white | 140 |
| 288 | Superior Cadillac Ambulance (without flashing light) white/red | 65 |
| 289 | Routemaster Bus | |
| | red "Tern Shirts" | 160 |
| | red "Schweppes" | 160 |
| | red "Esso Safety Grip Tyres" | 125 |
| | red "Festival of London Stores" (promotional) | 190 |
| | red "Madame Tussaud's" (promotional) | 135 |
| | silver "Silver Jubilee" | 40 |
| 290 | Double Decker Bus (renumbering of 29c) | |
| 290 | SRN-6 Hovercraft red | 40 |
| 291 | Atlantean City Bus orange "Kenning" | 75 |
| 291 | Double Decker Bus Exide red | 190 |
| 292 | Atlantean Bus red/white Ribble or Corporation Transport | 165 |
| 293 | Atlantean Bus green/white Corporation Transport | 170 |
| 293 | Swiss Postal Bus yellow/white | 40 |

| # | Name | Price |
|---|------|-------|
| 294 | Police Vehicle Gift Set (#'s 250, 254, 287) | $200 |
| 295 | Atlantean Bus "Yellow Pages" yellow | 75 |
| 295 | Atlas Kenebrake Bus blue/gray | 75 |
| | blue | 125 |
| 296 | Duple Viceroy 37 Luxury Coach blue | 35 |
| 297 | Police Vehicles Gift Set (#'s 250, 255, 287) | 255 |
| 297 | Silver Jubilee Bus silver | 25 |
| 297 | SilverJubilee Bus "Woolworth's" (promotional) silver | 40 |
| 298 | Emergency Services Gift Set (#'s 258 Ford Fairlane, 263, 276, 277, 007, 008) (price varies widely) | 1,500 |
| 299 | Gift Set Crash Squad (#'s 244, 732) | 75 |
| 299 | Motorway Senrices Gift Set (#'s 257, 263, 269, 276 and 434) (price varies widely) | 1,600 |
| 299 | Post Office Services Gift Set (#'s 001, 012, 260, 261 and 750) | 640 |
| 300 | London Scene Gift Set (#'s 289 Esso, 184) | 105 |
| 300 | Massey-Harris Tractor (renumbering of 27a) (Massey-Ferguson from 1966 on) | |
| 301 | Field-Marshall Tractor (renumbering of 27n) | |
| 302 | Emergency Squad Gift Set (#'s 267, 288) | 105 |
| 303 | Gift Set Commando Squad (#'s 687, 667, 732, all olive drab) | 125 |
| 304 | Gift Set Fire Rescue (#'s 195, 282, 384) | 125 |
| 305 | David Brown Tractor red/yellow | 105 |
| | white | 95 |
| 308 | Leyland 384 Tractor red | 55 |
| | blue | 105 |
| 309 | Star Trek Gift Set (#'s 357, 358) | 125 |
| 310 | Farm Tractor and Hay Rake (renumbering 27ak) | |
| 319 | Week's Tipping Farm Trailer red/yellow | 40 |
| 320 | Halesowen Harvest Trailer (renumbering of 27b) | |
| 321 | Massey-Harris Manure Spreader (renumbering of 27c) | |
| 322 | Disc Harrow (renumbering of 27h) | |
| 323 | Triple Gang Mower (renumbering of 27j) | |
| 324 | Hay Rake (renumbering of 27k) | |
| 325 | David Brown Tractor and Disc Harrow white/red | 125 |
| 340 | Land Rover (renumbering of 27d) | |
| 341 | Land Rover Trailer (renumbering of 27m) | |
| 342 | Austin Mini-Moke green | 65 |
| 342 | Moto-Cart (renumbering of 27g) | |
| 343 | Farm Produce Wagon (renumbering of 30n) | |
| 344 | Estate Car (renumbering of 27f) | |
| 344 | Land Rover blue, red | 30 |
| 350 | Tiny's Mini Moke red with white and yellow-striped canopy | 160 |
| 351 | UFO Interceptor green | 85 |

| # | Name | Price |
|---|------|-------|
| 352 | Ed Straker's Car red | $85 |
| | gold-plated | 115 |
| | yellow | 135 |
| 353 | Shado 2 Mobile green | 70 |
| | blue | 95 |
| 354 | Pink Panther pink, with or without gyrowheel | 30 |
| 370 | Dragster Set with Launcher yellow/red dragster | 65 |
| 380 | "Convoy" Skip Truck yellow/orange | 25 |
| 381 | "Convoy" Farm Truck yellow/brown | 25 |
| 381 | Garden Roller (renumbering of 105a) | |
| 382 | "Convoy" Dumper Truck red and gray | 25 |
| 382 | Wheelbarrow (renumbering of 105b) | |
| 383 | "Convoy" NCL Truck (National Carriers Ltd.) yellow | 45 |
| 383 | Four-Wheeled Hand Truck (renumbering of 105c) | |
| 384 | "Convoy" Fire Rescue Truck red | 25 |
| 384 | Grass Cutter (renumbering of 105e) | |
| 385 | "Convoy" Royal Mail Truck red | 40 |
| 385 | Sack Truck (renumbering of 107a) | |
| 386 | Lawn Mower (renumbering of 751) | |
| 390 | Customised Transit Van blue | 45 |
| 398 | Farm Equipment Gift Set (renumbering of Gift Set No. I) | |
| 399 | "Convoy" Gift Set (#'s 380, 381, 382) | 65 |
| 399 | Farm Tractor and Trailer Set (#'s 300, 428) | 175 |
| 400 | BEV Electric Truck (renumbering of 14a) | |
| 401 | Coventry-Climax Fork Lift Truck (renumbering of 14c) | |
| 402 | Bedford Coca Cola Lorry red/white | 255 |
| 404 | Conveyancer Fork Lift Truck red/yellow, orange/yellow | 45 |
| 405 | Universal Jeep (renumbering of 25y) | |
| 406 | Commer Articulated Truck yellow/gray | 200 |
| 407 | Ford Transit blue/white "Kenwood" | 125 |
| | yellow "Hertz" Truck Rental (promotional) | 125 |
| 408 | Big Bedford Lorry (renumbering of 922) | |
| 409 | Bedford Articulated Lorry (renumbering of 921) | |
| 410 | Bedford End Tipper (renumbering of 25m) | |
| 410 | Bedford Van | |
| | Royal Mail | 40 |
| | John Menzies promotional | 45 |
| | Belaco promotional | 90 |
| | Marley Tiles promotional | 75 |
| | M. J. Hire Service promotional | 65 |
| | Danish Post (export market) | 120 |
| | Simpsons promotional | 125 |
| 411 | Bedford Truck (renumbering of 25w) | |
| 412 | Austin Wagon (renumbering of 30j) | |
| 412 | Bedford Van A yellow | 40 |
| 413 | Austin Covered Wagon (renumbering of 30s) | |
| 414 | Dodge Rear Tipping Wagon (renumbering of 30m) | |
| 415 | Mechanical Horse and Open Wagon (renumbering of 33w) | |

| # | Name | Price |
|---|------|-------|
| 416 | Ford Transit Van Motorway Services yellow | $65 |
| No # | Ford Transit Van "1,000,000 Transits" promotional yellow | 225 |
| 417 | Ford Transit Van Motorway Services yellow | 65 |
| 417 | Leyland Comet Lorry (renumbering of 931) | |
| 418 | Leyland Comet Lorry with hinged tailboard (renumbering of 932) | |
| 419 | Leyland Cement Wagon (renumbering of 933) | |
| 420 | Leyland Forward Control Lorry (renumbering of 25r) | |
| 421 | Hindle-Smart Electric Articulated Lorry (renumbering of 30w) | |
| 422 | Thames Flat Truck (renumbering of 30r) | |
| 424 | Commer Convertible Articulated Truck yellow/gray/white with blue tarp | 285 |
| 425 | Bedford TK Coal Wagon red | 225 |
| 428 | Large Trailer (renumbering of 951) | |
| 429 | Trailer (renurnbering of 25g) | |
| 430 | Commer Breakdown Lorry (renumbering of 25x) | |
| 430 | Johnson 2-ton Dumper orange/red | 40 |
| 431 | Guy 4-ton Lorry (renumbering of 911) | |
| 431 | Guy Warrior 4-ton Lorry tan/green, with or without windows | 640 |
| 432 | Foden Tipping Lorry white/yellow/red | 65 |
| 432 | Guy Flat Truck (renumbering of 912) | |
| 432 | Guy Warrior Flat Truck green/red, with or without windows | 525 |
| 433 | Guy Flat Truck with Tailboard (renumbering of 913) | |
| 434 | Bedford TK Crash Truck white/green "Top Rank" | 135 |
| | red/black/gray | 135 |
| 435 | Bedford TK Tipper gray/blue/red, yellow, yellow/black | 120 |
| | white/silver/blue | 280 |
| 436 | Atlas Copco Compressor Lorry yellow | 105 |
| 437 | Muir Hill 2WL Loader red, yellow | 35 |
| 438 | Ford D800 Tipper Truck (opening doors) red/yellow | 65 |
| 439 | Ford D800 Snow Plough and Tipper Truck blue/red, blue/pale blue | 90 |
| 440 | Ford D800 Tipper Truck (no opening doors) red, red/yellow | 65 |
| 440 | Petrol Tanker "Mobilgas" (renumbering of 30p) | |
| 441 | Petrol Tanker "Castrol" (renumbering of 30pa) | |
| 442 | Land Rover Breakdown Crane white/red | 40 |
| 442 | Land Rover Breakdown Crane "Falck" (export model) red, white/red | 65 |
| 442 | Petrol Tanker "Esso" (renumbering of 30pb) | |
| 443 | Petrol Tanker "National Benzole" yellow | 175 |
| 448 | Chevrolet El Camino Pick-up with Trailers green/white with two red trailers | 390 |
| 449 | Chevrolet El Camino Pick-up green/white | 135 |
| 449 | Johnston Road Sweeper (no opening doors) yellow, green | 75 |

| # | Name | Price |
|---|------|-------|
| 450 | Bedford TK Box Van "Castrol" green/white | $225 |
| 450 | Trojan Van "Esso" (renumbering of 3la) | |
| 451 | Johnston Road Sweeper (opening doors) green/orange | 75 |
| 451 | Trojan Van "Dunlop" (renumbering of 31b) | |
| 452 | Trojan Van "Chivers" (renumbering of 31c) | |
| 453 | Trojan Van "Oxo" (renumbering of 31d) | |
| 454 | Trojan Van "Cydrax" green | 200 |

*Original box for a Hong Kong-manufactured #004 Oldsmobile 88.*

| # | Name | Price |
|---|------|-------|
| 455 | Trojan Van "Brooke Bond Tea" red | 205 |
| 465 | Morris Van "Capstan" two-tone blue | 295 |
| 470 | Austin Van "Shell-BP" green/red | 185 |
| 471 | Austin Van "Nestle's" red | 185 |
| 472 | Austin Van "Raleigh Cycles" green | 210 |
| 475 | Ford Model T 1908 blue/red, blue/brown, blue/black | 85 |
| 476 | Morris Oxford "Bull-Nosed" 1913 yellow/blue/tan | 105 |
| 477 | Parsley's Car green | 165 |
| 480 | Bedford Van "Kodak" yellow | 170 |
| 481 | Bedford Van "Ovaltine" blue | 170 |
| 482 | Bedford Van "Dinky Toys" cream/orange | 175 |
| 485 | Ford Model T with Santa Claus red/white | 150 |
| 486 | Dinky Beats Morris Oxford (Bull-nosed) pink/green | 170 |
| 490 | Electric Dairy Van "Express Dairy" (renumbering of 30v) | |
| 491 | Electric Dairy Van "NCB" (renumbering of 30v) | |
| 492 | Election Mini-Van white with orange speakers | 360 |
| 492 | Loud-Speaker Van (renumbering of 34c) | |
| 501 | Foden Diesel 8-Wheel Wagon (renumbered 901) gray, brown, dark blue, red/tan, or two-tone blue | *** |
| 502 | Foden Flat Truck (renumbered 902) green, light blue, orange/green, blue/red, yellow/green | *** |
| 503 | Foden Flat Truck and Tailboard (renumbered 903) gray, red, blue/orange, two-tone green, blue/yellow | *** |
| 504 | Foden 14-ton Tanker (renumbered 941) red/tan, two-tone blue | *** |
| | red with "Mobilgas" decals | *** |

| # | Name | Price |
|---|------|-------|
| 505 | Foden Flat Truck with Chains (renumbered 905) green, maroon, red/gray | *** |
| 511 | Guy 4-ton Lorry (renumbered 911, then 431) green, brown, two-tone blue, red/tan | *** |
| 512 | Guy Flat Truck (renumbered 912, then 432) yellow, maroon, brown, gray, blue/red | *** |
| 513 | Guy Flat Truck with Tailboard (renumbered 913, then 433) yellow, gray, green, two-tone green, blue/orange | *** |
| 514 | Guy Van "Lyons" dark blue | *** |
| 514 | Guy Van "Slumberland" red | *** |
| 514 | Guy Van "Spratt's" (renumbered 917) red/cream | *** |
| 514 | Guy Van "Weetabix" yellow | *** |

*** All of the Foden and Guy trucks are highly sought after by collectors. Prices paid (usually at auction) therefore are often very high, and vary widely. A #502 Foden Flat Truck in blue/red, for example, might sell for $400, while the yellow/green version of the same truck can bring $1,700. These factors make an established value impossible.

| # | Name | Price |
|---|------|-------|
| 521 | Bedford Articulated Lorry (renumbered 921, then 409) with or without windows red, yellow | 225 |
| 522 | Big Bedford Lorry (renumbered 922, then 408) red/tan | 175 |
| | blue/yellow | 280 |
| 531 | Leyland Comet Lorry (renumbered 931, then 417) blue/brown, blue/yellow | 360 |
| | red/brown | 275 |
| | red/yellow | 200 |
| 532 | Leyland Comet Lorry with Hinged Tailboard (renumbered 932) green/red, green/orange, two-tone blue | 200 |
| 533 | Leyland Cement Wagon (renumbered 933, then 419) yellow "Ferrocrete" | 230 |
| 551 | Trailer (renumbered 951, then 428) green, gray, red | 55 |

| # | Name | Price |
|---|------|-------|
| 555 | Fire Engine with Extending Ladder (renumbered 955) with or without windows red with brown or silver ladder | $125 |
| 561 | Blaw-Knox Bulldozer (renumbered 961) | |
| | red, yellow | 125 |
| | plastic | 400 |
| 562 | Muir-Hill Dump Truck (renumbered 962) | |
| | yellow | 75 |
| 563 | Blaw-Knox Heavy Tractor (renumbered 963) | |
| | red, orange | 75 |
| 564 | Elevator Loader (renumbered 964) | |
| | yellow/blue | 130 |
| 571 | Coles Mobile Crane (renumbered 971) | |
| | yellow/black | 125 |
| 581 | Horse Box (renumbered 980 and 981) | |
| | red with "Express Horse Van Hire Service" on sides (U.S. model) | 650 |
| | red with "Express Horse Box Hire Service" on sides, "British Railways" on sides and cab roof | 200 |
| 582 | Pullmore Car Transporter (renumbered 982) with or without windows | |
| | blue with tan tracks | 165 |
| | all blue | 165 |
| 591 | AEC Tanker "Shell Chemicals" (renumbered 991) | |
| | red/yellow "Shell Chemicals" or "Shell Chemicals Ltd" | 240 |
| 601 | Austin Para Moke green/tan | 65 |
| 602 | Armoured Command Car green, blue-green | 55 |
| 604 | Land Rover Bomb Disposal Unit olive/orange | 90 |
| 609 | 105mm Howitzer with gun crew green | 45 |
| 612 | Commando Jeep green | 45 |
| 615 | US Jeep with 105mm Howitzer green | 65 |
| 616 | AEC Articulated Transporter with Chieftain Tank green | 95 |
| 617 | Volkswagen KDF with PAK anti-Tank Gun gray | 95 |
| 618 | AEC Articulated Transporter with Helicopter green | 100 |
| 619 | Bren Gun Carrier and Anti-Tank Gun green | 60 |
| 620 | Berliet Missile Launcher green | 160 |
| 620 | Transport Wagon with Driver (renumbering of 151b) | |
| 621 | 3-Ton Army Wagon green, with or without windows | 105 |

| # | Name | Price |
|---|------|-------|
| 622 | 10-Ton Army Truck green | $125 |
| 622 | Bren Gun Carrier green | 40 |
| 623 | Army Covered Wagon green | 85 |
| 624 | Daimler Military Ambulance (renumbering of 30hm) | |
| 625 | 6-Pounder Anti-Tank Gun green | 30 |
| 625 | Austin Covered Wagon (renumbering of 30sm) | |
| 626 | Military Ambulance green, with or without windows | 85 |
| 640 | Bedford Truck (renumbering of 25wm) | |
| 641 | Army 1-Ton Cargo Truck green, with or without windows | 75 |
| 642 | RAF Pressure Refueller gray | 160 |
| 643 | Army Water Carrier green, with or without windows | 125 |
| 650 | Light Tank (renumbering of 152a) | |
| 651 | Centurion Tank green | 100 |
| 654 | Mobile Gun green | 40 |
| 656 | 88mm Gun gray | 30 |
| 660 | Tank Transporter green | 160 |
| 661 | Recovery Tractor green, with or without windows | 170 |
| 662 | Static 88mm Gun with crew gray | 35 |
| 665 | "Honest John" Missile Erector green | 175 |
| 666 | Missile Erector Vehicle with Corporal Missile and Launching Platform green | 300 |
| 667 | Missile Servicing Platform Vehicle green | 215 |
| 667 | Armoured Patrol Car green | 40 |
| 668 | Foden Army Truck green | 45 |
| 669 | US Army Jeep green | 400 |
| 670 | Armoured Car green | 40 |
| 671 | Reconnaissance Car (renumbering of 152b) | |
| 672 | US Army Jeep (renumbering of 153a) | |
| 673 | Scout Car green | 40 |
| 674 | Austin Champ | |
| | green | 75 |
| | white (U.N. version) | 550 |
| 675 | US Army Staff Car (renumbering of 170m) | |
| 676 | Armoured Personnel Carrier green | 75 |
| 676 | Daimler Armoured Car (with Speedwheels) green | 35 |
| 677 | Armoured Command Vehicle green | 95 |
| 677 | Task Force Set (#'s 680, 681, 682) | 65 |
| 680 | Ferret Armoured Car green/tan | 20 |
| 681 | D.U.K.W. green | 20 |
| 682 | Stalwart Load Carrier green | 20 |
| 683 | Chieftain Tank green | 40 |
| 686 | 25-Pounder Field Gun green | 20 |

| # | Name | Price |
|---|------|-------|
| 687 | Convoy Army Truck green | $25 |
| 687 | Trailer for 25-Pounder Field Gun green | 25 |
| 688 | Field Artillery Tractor green | 60 |
| 689 | Medium Artillery Tractor green | 135 |
| 690 | Mobile Anti-Aircraft Gun (renumbering of 161b) | |
| 690 | Scorpion Tank green | 35 |
| 691 | Field Gun Unit (renumbering of 162) | |
| 691 | "Striker" Anti-Tank Vehicle green | 60 |
| 692 | 5.5 inches Medium Gun green | 60 |
| 692 | Leopard Tank green | 60 |
| 693 | 7.2 inches Howitzer green | 60 |
| 694 | Hanomag Tank Destroyer gray | 60 |
| 695 | Howitzer and Tractor (#'s 689, 693) | 210 |
| 696 | Leopard Anti-Aircraft Tank gray | 60 |
| 697 | 25-Pounder Field Gun Set (#'s 686, 687, 688) | 135 |
| 698 | Tank Transporter and Tank (#'s 651, 660) | 230 |
| 699 | Leopard Recovery Tank gray-green | 60 |
| 699 | Military Vehicles Gift Set (#'s 621, 641, 674, 676; renumbering of Gift Set No. 1) | |
| 751 | Lawn Mower (renumbered 386) | 135 |
| 752 | Goods Yard Crane (renumbered 973) yellow/blue | 65 |
| 753 | Police Controlled Crossing (plastic) | 135 |
| 754 | Pavement Set (card) | 75 |
| 755 | Lamp Standard Single Arm | 30 |
| 756 | Lamp Standard Double Arm | 45 |
| 760 | Pillar Box, "E II R" | 40 |
| 763 | Posters for Road Hoardings (paper) | 40 |
| 764 | Posters for Road Hoardings (paper) | 40 |
| 765 | Road Hoardings (plastic) | 100 |
| 766 | British Road Signs Country Set A contains: Narrow Bridge; Bend (left); Crossing No Gates; Cattle; Cross Roads; Road Narrows | 75 |
| 767 | British Road Signs Country Set B contains: Bend (right); Level Crossing; Hill 1 in 7; Hump Bridge; Bends for 1/4 miles; Low Bridge Headroom | 75 |
| 768 | British Road Signs Town Set A contains: No Entry (2); No Right Turn; Children; Round-about; Slow—Major Road Ahead | 75 |
| 769 | British Road Signs Town Set B contains: Halt at Major Road Ahead—No Waiting, Road Junction; School; 30/Derestriction (2) | 75 |
| 770 | Road Signs (12) (renumbering of 47) | |
| 771 | International Road Signs (12) | 170 |
| 772 | British Road Signs (24) (#'s 766, 767, 768, 769) | 400 |
| 773 | Traffic Signal 4-Face | 25 |
| 777 | Belisha Beacon | 15 |
| 778 | Road Repair Warning Boards (plastic) | 25 |
| 781 | Petrol Pump Station "Esso" | 95 |
| 782 | Petrol Pump Station "Shell" | 95 |
| 783 | Petrol Pump Station "BP" | 95 |
| 784 | Dinky Goods Train Set blue/red/yellow | 45 |
| 785 | Service Station (plastic) | 240 |
| 786 | Tyre Rack with Tyres "Dunlop" | 90 |

*Later production: at left is a #110 Aston Martin DB5 made in the late 1960s, next to a #189 Lamborghini Marzal, (produced from 1969 until 1977) in original plastic display box.*

| # | Name | Price |
|---|------|-------|
| 787 | Lighting Kit for Buildings | $30 |
| 788 | Marrell Bucket for #966 | 15 |
| 790 | Imitation Granite Chippings (plastic) | 25 |
| 791 | Imitation Coal (plastic) | 25 |
| 792 | Packing Cases (3) (plastic) | 25 |
| 793 | Pallets (plastic) | 25 |
| 794 | Loading Ramp (for 582/982) (renumbered 994) | 20 |
| 796 | Healey Sports Boat on Trailer green/white on orange trailer | 40 |
| 900 | Building Site Gift Set (#'s 437, 960, 961, 962, 965) (price varies widely) | 1,500 |
| 901 | Foden Diesel 8-Wheel Wagon (renumbering of 501) | |
| 902 | Foden Flat Truck (renumbering of 502) | |
| 903 | Foden Flat Truck with Tailboard (renumbering of 503) | |
| 905 | Foden Flat Truck with Chains (renumbering of 505) | |
| 908 | Mighty Antar with Transformer yellow/gray (price varies widely) | 950 |
| 911 | Guy 4-Ton Lorry (renumbering of 511; renumbered 431) | |
| 912 | Guy Flat Truck (renumbering of 512; renumbered 432) | |
| 913 | Guy Flat Truck with Tailboard (renumbering of 513; renumbered 433) | |
| 914 | A.E.C. Articulated Lorry, BRS red/gray/green | 235 |
| 915 | A.E.C. with Flat Trailer orange/white | 125 |
| 917 | Guy Van "Spratt's" (renumbering of 514) | |
| 917 | Mercedes-Benz Truck and Trailer blue/yellow/white | 125 |
| | green German beer version | 280 |
| 918 | Guy Van "EverReady" blue | 350 |
| 919 | Guy Van "Golden Shred" red (price varies widely) | 1,300 |
| 920 | Guy Warrior Van "Heinz" red/yellow (price varies widely) | 2,500 |
| 921 | Bedford Articulated Lorry (renumbering of 521; renumbered 409) | |
| 922 | Big Bedford Lorry (renumbering of 522; renumbered 408) | |
| 923 | Big Bedford Van "Heinz" with baked bean can | 475 |
| | with ketchup bottle | 2,000 |
| | (prices vary widely for both) | |
| 924 | Aveling-Barford Centaur Dump Truck red/yellow | 75 |
| 925 | Leyland Dump Truck (with tilt cab) white/red | 215 |
| 930 | Bedford Pallet-Jekta Van "Dinky Toys" orange/cream | 385 |
| 931 | Leyland Comet Lorry (renumbering of 531; renumbered 417) | |
| 932 | Leyland Comet Wagon and Hinged Tailboard (renumbering of 532; renumbered 418) | |
| 933 | Leyland Cement Wagon (renumbering of 533; renumbered 419) | |

| # | Name | Price |
|---|------|-------|
| 934 | Leyland Octopus Wagon yellow/green | $325 |
| | blue/yellow | 2,300 |
| | (price varies widely) | |
| 935 | Leyland Octopus Flat Truck with Chains green/gray | 2,000 |
| | blue/gray | 2,800 |
| | (prices vary widely for both) | |
| 936 | Leyland Eight-Wheeled Test Chassis red/silver | 160 |
| 940 | Mercedes-Benz Truck white/red/gray | 50 |
| 941 | Foden Tanker "Mobilgas" (renumbering of 504) | |
| 942 | Foden Tanker "Regent" blue/red | 550 |
| 943 | Leyland Octopus Tanker "Esso" red | 400 |
| 944 | "Shell-BP" Fuel Tanker (plastic tank) yellow/white | 325 |
| 945 | AEC Fuel Tanker 'Esso' white | 110 |
| 945 | Lucas Oil Tanker (promotional) green | 240 |
| 948 | Tractor-Trailer "McLean" red/gray | 235 |
| 949 | Wayne School Bus orange | 275 |
| 950 | Foden S20 Fuel Tanker red/white "Burmah" | 110 |
| | red/white "Shell" | 110 |
| 951 | Trailer (renumbering of 551; renumbered 428) | |
| 952 | Vega Major Luxury Coach (with electric lights) gray/maroon | 125 |
| 953 | Continental Touring Coach turquoise/white | 415 |
| 954 | Fire Station (plastic) | 325 |
| 954 | Vega Major Luxury Coach (no electric lights) | 125 |
| 955 | Fire Engine with Extending Ladder (renumbering of 555) | |
| 956 | Turntable Fire Escape (Bedford cab) red, with or without windows | 165 |
| 956 | Turntable Fire Escape (Berliet cab) red | 240 |
| 957 | Fire Services Gift Set (#'s 257, 955, 956) | 625 |
| 958 | Snow Plough yellow/black | 265 |
| 959 | Foden Dump Truck with Bulldozer Blade red/silver | 135 |
| 960 | Albion Lorry-Mounted Concrete Mixer orange/yellow/blue | 110 |
| 961 | Blaw-Knox Bulldozer (renumbering of 561) | |
| 961 | Vega Major Luxury Coach PTT (overseas model) yellow/white | 240 |
| 962 | Muir-Hill Dumper (renumbering of 562) | |
| 963 | (Blaw-Knox) Heavy Tractor (renumbering of 563) | |
| 963 | Road Grader orange/yellow | 45 |
| 964 | Elevator Loader (renumbering of 564) | |
| 965 | Euclid Rear Dump Truck yellow, with or without windows | 85 |
| 965 | Terex Dump Truck yellow | 270 |
| 966 | Marrel Multi-Bucket Unit yellow/gray | 175 |
| 967 | BBC TV Mobile Control Room green | 205 |
| 967 | Muir Hill Loader and Trencher yellow/orange | 45 |
| 968 | BBC TV Roving Eye Vehicle green | 210 |
| 969 | BBC TV Extending Mast Vehicle green | 215 |
| 970 | Jones Fleetmaster/Cantilever Crane red, yellow | 110 |

| # | Name | Price |
|---|------|-------|
| 971 | Coles Mobile Crane (renumbering of 571) | |
| 972 | Coles 20-ton Lorry Mounted Crane yellow/orange | $135 |
| 973 | Eaton Yale Articulated Tractor Shovel yellow/orange | 45 |
| 973 | Goods Yard Crane (renumbering of 752) | |
| 974 | AEC Hoyner Car Transporter blue/yellow/red | 110 |
| 975 | Ruston-Bucyrus Excavator (plastic body) red/yellow/gray | 360 |
| 976 | Michigan 180 III Tractor Dozer yellow/red | 45 |
| 977 | Servicing Platform Vehicle (Commercial) red/cream | 250 |
| 977 | Shovel Dozer yellow/red | 45 |
| 978 | Refuse Wagon green, metallic green, lime green, yellow | 90 |
| 979 | Racehorse Transport with two horses gray | 475 |
| 980 | Coles Hydra Truck 150T | 65 |
| 980 | Express Horsebox (U.S. model; renumbering of 581) | |
| 981 | British Railways Horsebox (renumbering of 581) | |
| 982 | Pullmore Car Transporter (renumbering of 582) | |
| 983 | Car Carrier and Trailer #'s 984 and 985 | 380 |
| 984 | Atlas Digger yellow/red/black | 65 |
| 984 | Car Carrier red/gray | 225 |
| 985 | Trailer for Car Carrier red/gray | 80 |
| 986 | Mighty Antar Low Loader and Propeller red/gray with brown propeller, with or without windows | 385 |
| 987 | ABC TV Control Room light blue/gray | 285 |
| 988 | ABC TV Transmitter Van light blue/gray | 325 |
| 989 | Car Carrier "Autotransporters" yellow/gray/blue (price varies widely) | 1,920 |
| 990 | Pullmore Car Transporter (#'s 154, 156, 161, 162 and 982) (price varies widely) | 2,200 |
| 991 | AEC Tanker (renumbering of 591) | |
| 994 | Loading Ramp for 582/982 (renumbering of 794) | |

**Mini Dinky line:**

| # | Name | Price |
|---|------|-------|
| 10 | Ford Corsair | 40 |
| 11 | Jaguar E-type | 40 |
| 12 | Corvette Stingray | 50 |
| 13 | Ferrari 250LM | 50 |
| 14 | Chevrolet Chevy II | 40 |
| 15 | Rolls-Royce Silver Shadow | not made |
| 16 | Ford Mustang | 50 |
| 17 | Aston Martin DB6 | not made |
| 18 | Mercedes-Benz 230 SL | 40 |
| 19 | MGB | 40 |
| 20 | Cadillac Coupe de Ville | 40 |
| 21 | Fiat 2300 Station Wagon | 40 |
| 22 | Oldsmobile Toronado | not made |
| 23 | Rover 2000 | not made |

| # | Name | Price |
|---|------|-------|
| 24 | Ferrari Superfast | not made |
| 25 | Ford Zephyr 6 | not made |
| 26 | Mercedes 250 SE | not made |
| 27 | Buick Riviera | not made |
| 28 | Ferrari F.I | not made |
| 29 | Ford F.I | not made |
| 30 | Volvo P.1800 | not made |
| 31 | Volkswagen 1600 TL Fast Back | not made |
| 32 | Vauxhall Cresta | not made |
| 33 | Jaguar Mk X | not made |
| 60 | Cooper F.I | not made |
| 61 | Lotus F.I | not made |
| 94 | International Bulldozer | $35 |
| 95 | International Skid Shovel | 35 |
| 96 | Payloader Shovel | 35 |
| 97 | Euclid R-40 | 35 |
| 98 | Michigan Scraper | 35 |
| 99 | Caterpillar Grader | 35 |

### Dinkys made in Hong Kong 1965-1967:

| # | Name | Price |
|---|------|-------|
| 001 | Buick Riviera blue with white roof | 100 |
| 002 | Chevrolet Corvair Monza red with black roof | 100 |
| 003 | Chevrolet Impala yellow with white roof | 100 |
| | solid yellow | 100 |
| 004 | Dodge Polara white/blue | † |
| 004 | Oldsmobile 88 white with blue roof | 100 |
| 005 | Ford Thunderbird blue with white roof | 130 |
| 006 | Rambler Classic Station Wagon green with silver trim | 100 |
| 180 | Rover 3500 white | 25 |
| 264 | Rover 3500 Police Car white | 25 |

† May not have been manufactured as part of the Hong Kong production.

### Nicky Toys (made in India 1968-early 1970s):

| # | Name | Price |
|---|------|-------|
| 113 | MGB Roadster | 40 |
| 115 | Plymouth Fury Convertible | 55 |
| 120 | Jaguar E-type | 40 |
| 134 | Triumph Vitesse | 40 |
| | (Nicky called this "Standard Herald") | |
| 142 | Jaguar Mk X | 50 |
| 144 | Volkswagen 1500 | 55 |
| | (Also produced in blue and white "Police" version) | |
| 146 | Daimler V8 (Actually a #195 Jaguar; also made in a red and white "Police" version) | 50 |
| 170 | Lincoln Continental | 50 |
| 186 | Mercedes-Benz 220 SE | 40 |
| | (Also made in a Taxi version) | 45 |
| 194 | Bentley S Coupe | 40 |
| 238 | Jaguar D-type | 40 |
| 239 | Vanwall | 40 |
| 295 | Standard 20 Mini Bus | 50 |
| 405 | Universal Jeep | 45 |
| 626 | Military Ambulance | 50 |
| 660/908 | Mighty Antar Tank Transporter | 70 |
| 693 | Howitzer | 40 |

| # | Name | Price |
|---|------|-------|
| 949 | Wayne School Bus | $90 |
| 962 | Dumper Truck | 50 |
| | (also made in a Military version) | 50 |

### French Dinky cars (number in parentheses is the new number assigned in 1959):

| # | Name | Price |
|---|------|-------|
| 22A | (505) Maserati 2000 sport | 75 |
| 23B | Hotchkiss/Renault racing car | 175 |
| 23C | Mercedes-Benz racing car (ex-U.K.) | 115 |
| 23D | Auto-Union racing car (ex-U.K.) | 100 |
| 23H | (510/1) Talbot-Lago racing car | 85 |
| 23J | (511/1) Ferrari racing car | 115 |
| 24A | (520/1) Chrysler New Yorker convertible | 100 |
| 24B | (521) Peugeot 403 saloon | 80 |
| 24C | (522) Citroën DS19 saloon | 100 |
| 24D | (523/1) Plymouth Belvedere | 100 |
| 24E | (524/1) Renault Dauphine | 75 |
| 24F | (525/1) Peugeot 403 Familiale estate car | 80 |
| 24H | (526) Mercedes-Benz 190SL coupe | 100 |
| 24J | (527) Alfa Romeo 1900 Super Sprint coupe | 90 |
| 24K/1 | Peugeot 402 saloon | 300 |
| 24K/2 | (528/1) Simca Chambord | 75 |
| 24L/1 | Peugeot 402 taxi | 300 |
| 24L/2 | (529) Vespa 400 | 75 |
| 24M/1 | Jeep, U.S. Army or civilian | 200 |
| 24M/2 | (530/1) Volkswagen Karmann-Ghia coupe | 100 |
| 24N/1 | Citroën I IBL (with spare wheel or boot) | 200 |
| 24N/2 | (531) Fiat 1200 Grande Vue not made as 24N/2 | |
| 240 | Studebaker coupe (ex-U.K.) | 300 |
| 24P | Packard sedan (ex-U.K.) | 300 |
| | (price varies widely) | |
| 24Q | Ford Vedette | 150 |
| 24R | (533/1) Peugeot 203 saloon | 110 |
| 24S | (534/1) Simca Huit Sport | 100 |
| 24T | (535) Citroën 2CV saloon | 100 |
| 24U | (536/1) Simca Aronde/Aronde Elysee saloon | 90 |
| 24UT | (537/1) Simca Aronde Elysee taxi | 80 |
| 24V | 538/1) Buick Roadmaster | 125 |
| 24X | Ford Vedette 1954 mode I | 75 |
| 24XT | (539/1) Ford Vedette taxi | 75 |
| 24Y | (540/1) Studebaker Commander coupe | unknown |
| 24Z | (541/1) Simca Versailles saloon | 75 |
| 24ZT | (542/1) Simca Ariane taxi | 100 |
| 35A/1 | Simca Cinq | 275 |
| 506/1 | Aston Martin DB3S | 80 |
| 531 | Fiat 1200 Grande Vue | 90 |
| 532 | Ford Lincoln Premiere | 100 |
| 543 | Renault Floride | 65 |
| 544 | Simca Aronde P.60 saloon | 65 |
| 545 | De Soto Diplomat sedan | 100 |
| 546/1 | Austin-Healey 100 | 65 |
| 546/2 | Opel Rekord taxi | 175 |
| 547 | Panhard PL17 saloon | 65 |
| 548 | Fiat 1800 estate car | 75 |
| 549 | Borgward Isabella coupe | 95 |
| 550 | Chrysler Saratoga hard top | 85 |
| 551/1 | Rolls-Royce Silver Wraith | 75 |
| 551/2 | Ford Taunus 17M "Polizei" | 155 |
| 552 | Chevrolet Corvair sedan | 65 |

| # | Name | Price |
|---|------|-------|
| 553 | Peugeot 404 saloon | $60 |
| 554 | Opel Rekord four-door saloon | 70 |
| 555 | Ford Thunderbird convertible | 80 |
| 556 | Citroën IDI9 ambulance | 85 |
| 557 | Citroën AMI 6 (3CV) saloon | 70 |
| 558 | Citroën 2CV saloon | 70 |
| 559 | Ford Taunus 17M two-door saloon | 80 |
| 500/2 | Citroën 2CV saloon | 70 |
| 501/2 | Citroën DS19 Police car | 150 |
| 503/2 | Porsche Carrera 6 racing car | 70 |
| 506/2 | Ferrari 275 GTB coupe | 100 |
| 507 | Simca 1500 break (estate car) | 70 |
| 508 | DAF 850 saloon | 70 |
| 509 | Fiat 850 saloon | 80 |
| 510/2 | Peugeot 204 saloon | 70 |
| 511/2 | Peugeot 204 cabriolet | 110 |
| 512 | Lesko Midjet go-kart | 40 |
| 513 | Opel Admiral saloon | 70 |
| 514 | Alfa Romeo Giulia 1600TI saloon | 80 |
| 515 | Ferrari 250 GT coupe | 80 |
| 516 | Mercedes-Benz 230 SL hard top | 75 |
| 517 | Renault R8 saloon | 60 |
| 518 | Renault R4L saloon | 60 |
| 518A | Renault R4L "Autoroutes" | 125 |
| 519 | Simca 1000 saloon | 60 |
| 520/2 | Fiat 600D saloon | 75 |
| 523/2 | Simca 1500 saloon | 60 |
| 524/2 | Panhard 24CT coupe | 75 |
| 525/2 | Peugeot 404 estate car | 70 |
| 528/2 | Peugeot 404 cabriolet | 125 |
| 530/2 | Citroën DS19 saloon | 100 |
| 533/2 | Mercedes-Benz 300 SE coupe | 80 |
| 534/2 | BMW 1500 saloon | 75 |
| 536/2 | Peugeot 404 saloon and trailer | 125 |
| 537/2 | Renault 16 saloon | 60 |
| 538/2 | Ford Taunus 12M two-door saloon | 75 |
| 539/2 | Citroën ID19 break (estate car) | 90 |
| 540/2 | Opel Kadett saloon | 60 |
| 541/2 | Mercedes-Benz coach | 100 |
| 542/2 | Opel Rekord two-door saloon | 75 |
| 1400 | Peugeot 404 taxi | 150 |
| 1401 | Alfa Romeo Giulia 1600 TI rally | 100 |
| 1402 | Ford Galaxie 500 saloon | 75 |
| 1403 | Matra M530 sports coupe | 75 |
| 1404 | Citroën ID 19 TV camera car RTL | 350 |
| | (price varies widely) | |
| 1405 | Opel Rekord 1900 coupe | 75 |
| 1406 | Renault R4 Sinpar Michel Tanguy | 125 |
| 1407 | Simca 1100 saloon | 60 |
| 1408 | Honda S800 coupe | 75 |
| 1409 | Chrysler 180 saloon | 60 |
| 1410 | Moskvitch 408 saloon | 75 |
| 1411 | Alpine Renault A310 coupe | 60 |
| 1412 | Jeep breakdown truck | 60 |
| 1413 | Citroën Dyane saloon | 60 |
| 1414 | Renault R8 Gordini saloon | 125 |
| 1414 | Renault R8S (special model) | 500 |
| | (price varies widely) | |
| 1415 | Peugeot 504 saloon | 50 |
| 1416 | Renault 6 saloon | 50 |
| 1417 | Matra Grand Prix racing car | 40 |
| 1419 | Ford Thunderbird coupe | 100 |

| # | Name | Price |
|---|---|---|
| 1420 | Opel Commodore coupe | $75 |
| 1421 | Opel GT 1900 coupe | 75 |
| 1422 | Ferrari Grand Prix racing car | 75 |
| 1423 | Peugeot 504 cabriolet | 120 |
| 1424 | Renault 12 saloon | 50 |
| 1424G | Renault 12 Gordini saloon | 90 |
| 1425 | Matra 630 Le Mans racing car | 50 |
| 1426 | Bertone Carabo Alfa Romeo P33 prototype | 60 |
| 1427 | Simca 1500 estate Police car | not issued |
| 1428 | Peugeot 304 saloon | 60 |
| 1429 | Peugeot 404 estate Police car | 100 |
| 1430 | Fiat Abarth 2000 Pininfarina prototype | 50 |
| 1431 | Porsche 917 Le Mans racing car | not issued |
| 1432 | Ferrari 312P Le Mans racing car | 50 |
| 1433 | Surtees TS.5 Grand Prix racing car | 40 |
| 1435 | Citroën Presidentielle | 300 |
| | (price varies widely) | |

### French Dinky Trucks and Commercial Vehicles:

| # | Name | Price |
|---|---|---|
| 25A | Ford Stake Truck | 125 |
| 25B | Peugeot D3A Van | 150 |
| 25BV | Peugeot D3A "POSTES" Van | 100 |
| 25C | Citroën H TUB Van | 100 |
| 25D | Tanker (re-issue of pre-war model) various liveries | 250 |
| 25D | Citroën Fire Van | 75 |
| 25G | Trailer (re-issue of pre-war model) | 25 |
| 25H | Ford Beverage Truck | 250 |
| 25I | Ford Wagon | 140 |
| 25J | Ford Covered Wagon | 125 |
| 25JB | Ford "SNCF" Covered Truck | 250 |
| 25JJ | Ford "CALBERSON" Covered Truck | 350 |
| | (price varies widely) | |
| 25JV | Ford "GRANDS MOULINS DE PARIS" Covered Truck | 350 |
| | (price varies widely) | |
| 25K | Studebaker Stake Truck | 200 |
| 25L | Studebaker Covered Truck | 200 |
| 25M | Studebaker Tipping Truck | 100 |
| 25M | Ford Tipping Truck | 100 |
| 250 | Studebaker Milk Truck | 325 |
| 250 | Ford Milk Truck | 275 |
| 25P | Studebaker Pick-up | 100 |
| 25Q | Studebaker Covered Pick-up | 100 |
| 25R | Studebaker Breakdown | 125 |
| 25R | Ford Breakdown | 125 |
| 25S | Two-Wheel Trailer | 35 |
| 25T | Two-Wheel Covered Trailer | 35 |
| 25U | Ford "Esso" Tanker | 125 |
| 25V | Ford Refuse Wagon | 100 |
| 29D | Renault TN4H Bus | 200 |
| 29D | Somua OP5 Bus | 135 |
| 29E | Isobloc Bus | 200 |
| 29F | Chausson Bus | 100 |
| 32AB | Panhard Articulated Truck | 200 |
| 32C | Panhard Articulated "Esso" Tanker | 110 |
| 32D | Delahaye Fire Truck | 135 |
| 32E | Berliet Fire Engine | 150 |
| 33A | Simca Cargo Van | 85 |

| # | Name | Price |
|---|---|---|
| 33AN | Simca Cargo Van "BAILLY" | $125 |
| 33B | Simca Cargo Tipping Truck | 75 |
| 33C | Simca Cargo Glass Truck | 100 |
| 34A | Berliet GML 10 Quarry Truck | 75 |
| 34B | Berliet Container | 85 |
| 35A | Citroën U23 Wrecker | 90 |
| 36A | Willeme Log Carrier | 100 |
| 36B | Willeme Covered Semi | 135 |
| 38A | Unic Multi-Bucket Marrel | 110 |
| 39A | Unic Boilot Car Transporter | 120 |
| 39B | Unic Pipe Line Transporter pierced trailer | 110 |
| 50 | Salev Mobile Crane | 60 |
| 70 | Covered Trailer | 40 |
| 80A | Panhard EBR75 FL11 Armoured Car | 60 |
| 80B | Hotchkiss Jeep | 65 |
| 80BP | Hotchkiss Jeep | 65 |
| 80C | A.M.X. 13 Tank | 60 |
| 80D | Berliet 6x6 Military Truck | 85 |
| 80E | ABS 155 Field Gun | 35 |
| 80F | Renault Goelette Military Ambulance | 80 |
| 90A | Richier Diesel Roller | 55 |
| 560 | Peugeot D3A "POSTES" Van | 100 |
| 560 | Citroën 2 CV Mail Van | 125 |
| 561 | Citroën H TUB "GLACES GERVAIS" Van | 165 |
| 561 | Renault 4 D PTT | 150 |
| 562H | Citroën 2 CV "WAGENNACHT" Van | 375 |
| 563 | Renault Estafette Covered Pickup | 65 |
| 564 | Renault Estafette Glass Truck | 85 |
| 564 | Armagnac 220 Caravan | 50 |
| 565 | Renault Estafette Camper | 90 |
| 566 | Citroën H TUB Police Van | 125 |
| 567 | Mercedes-Benz Unimog Snow-Plough | 100 |
| 568 | Berliet GAK Ladder Truck | 225 |
| 569 | Berliet Stradair Dump Truck | 150 |
| 570 | Peugeot J7 Van | 325 |
| 570P | Peugeot J7 Fire Van marked Meccano-France | 375 |
| 571 | Saviem Goelette Horse Box with Sulky | 450 |
| 572 | Berliet GBO Dump Truck | 275 |
| 575 | Panhard "SNCF" Articulated Truck | 125 |
| 577 | Berliet GAK Cattle Truck | 100 |
| 579 | Simca Cargo Glass Truck | 150 |
| 582 | Citroën Wrecker PL hook | 125 |

| # | Name | Price |
|---|---|---|
| 584 | Berliet GAK Covered Truck | $110 |
| 585 | Berliet GAK Dump Truck | 110 |
| 586 | Citroën P 55 Milk Truck | 300 |
| 587 | Citroën H TUB "PHILIPS" Van | 275 |
| 588 | Berliet GAK Beverage Truck | 125 |
| 588 | Berliet GAK "KRONENBOURG" Beverage Truck | 1,500 |
| | (price varies widely) | |
| 589 | Berliet GAK Breakdown | 150 |
| 589 | Berliet GAK "AUTOROUTES" Breakdown | 200 |
| 595 | Salev Mobile Crane | 60 |
| 596 | LMV Road Sweeper | 75 |
| 597 | Coventry Climax Fork Lift Truck | 75 |
| 676 | Daimler Armoured Car (marked England) | 50 |
| 800 | Renault 4 Sinpar 4x4 | 125 |
| 801 | A.M.X. Tank | 60 |
| 802 | ABS Field Gun | 35 |
| 803 | Unic "SNCF/PAM-PAM" Articulated Truck | 275 |
| 804 | Mercedes-Benz Unimog | 75 |
| 805 | Unic Multibucket Set | 350 |
| 806 | Berliet 6x6 Wrecker | 100 |
| 807 | Renault Goelette Military Ambulance | 75 |
| 808 | G.M.C. Wrecker Sahara | 225 |
| 808 | G.M.C. Wrecker | 225 |
| 809 | G.M.C. 6x6 Covered Truck | 225 |
| 810 | Dodge WC 56 Command Car 4x4 | 125 |
| 811 | Caravan | 50 |
| 812 | Small Trailer | 25 |
| 813 | AMX 155 Self-propelled Gun (with wire brace) | 60 |
| 813 | AMX 155 Self-propelled Gun (without wire brace) | 60 |
| 814 | Panhard AML Armoured Car | 60 |
| 815 | Renault 4 Sinpar 4x4 Gendarmerie | 125 |
| 816 | Hotchkiss Jeep with hook and driver | 60 |
| 816 | Berliet Missile Launcher | 150 |
| 817 | AMX 15T Tank | 60 |
| 818 | Berliet 6x6 Military Covered Truck | 75 |
| 820 | Renault Goelette Military Ambulance | 90 |
| 821 | Mercedes-Benz Unimog Military Covered Truck | 75 |
| 822 | White M3 Half-Track | 60 |
| 822 | White M3 Half-Track with machine-gun | 60 |

*Original box for a #128 Mercedes-Benz 600. This was the final box style used for Dinky Toys during the late 1970s.*

| # | Name | Price |
|---|------|-------|
| 823 | Field Kitchen Trailer | $40 |
| 823 | G.M.C. Military Tanker | 225 |
| 824 | Berliet Gazelle 6x6 Military Truck | 75 |
| 825 | D.U.K.W. Amphibian | 50 |
| 825 | D.U.K.W. Amphibian with driver | 50 |
| 826 | Berliet Wrecker | 100 |
| 827 | Panhard EBR FL-10 Armoured Car | 50 |
| 828 | Jeep Rocket Launcher | 40 |
| 829 | Jeep with Removable Gun | 40 |
| 881 | G.M.C. Pinder Truck and Trailer | 750 |
| | (price varies widely) | |
| 882 | Peugeot 404 and Pinder Caravan | 725 |
| | (price varies widely) | |
| 883 | AMX Bridge Layer BP marked "13t AMX" | 60 |
| 884 | Brockway Bridge Layer | 175 |
| 885 | Blaw-Knox Bulldozer | 90 |
| 885 | Saviem Girder Truck | 200 |
| 886 | Richier Road Grader | 60 |
| 887 | Muir Hill Dumper | 75 |
| 887 | Unic "AIR-BP" Tanker | 150 |
| 888 | Berliet GBO Saharien | 150 |
| 888 | Berliet GBO Saharien "LA LANGUEDOCIENNE" | 900 |
| | (price varies widely) | |

| # | Name | Price |
|---|------|-------|
| 889 | Coles Crane Truck marked 972 | $85 |
| 889 | Berliet Bus | 225 |
| 890 | Berliet Tank Transporter | 100 |
| 893 | Unic Pipe Line Transporter | 100 |
| 895 | Unic Multibucket | 100 |
| 896 | Willeme Covered Semi (trailer with 4 wheels) | 125 |
| 896 | Willeme Covered Semi (trailer with 2 wheels) | 125 |
| 897 | Willeme Log Carrier | 100 |
| 898 | Berliet T6 Transformer Carrier | 175 |

**French Dinkys made by Auto-Pilen of Spain:**

| # | Name | Price |
|---|------|-------|
| 500 | Citroën 2CV saloon | 50 |
| 510 | Peugeot 204 saloon | 40 |
| 518 | Renault R4 saloon | 40 |
| 520 | Simca 1000 Rally | 40 |
| 530 | Citroën DS23 saloon | 45 |
| 537 | Renault R16 saloon | 40 |
| 538 | Renault R16TX saloon | 50 |
| 1407 | Simca 1100 saloon | 40 |
| 1413 | Citroën Dyane saloon | 40 |
| 1415 | Peugeot 504 saloon | 50 |
| 1416 | Renault 6 saloon | 40 |

| # | Name | Price |
|---|------|-------|
| 1424 | Renault 12 saloon | $40 |
| 1424G | Renault 12 Gordini saloon | 75 |
| 1428 | Peugeot 304 saloon | 50 |
| 1450 | Simca 1100 saloon Police car | 40 |
| 1452 | Peugeot 504 saloon | 40 |
| 1453 | Renault 6 saloon | 45 |

**Auto-Pilen models made under Dinky name:**

| # | Name | Price |
|---|------|-------|
| 1451 | Renault 17TS coupe | 40 |
| 1454 | Simca Matra Bagheera coupe | 40 |
| 1455 | Citroën CX Pallas saloon | 45 |
| 1539 | VW Scirocco coupe | 40 |
| 1540 | Renault 14 saloon | 30 |
| 1541 | Ford Fiesta saloon | 30 |
| 1542 | Chrysler 1308GT (Alpine) saloon | 30 |
| 1543 | Opel Ascona two-door saloon | 30 |

**Solido-Cougar models made under Dinky name:**

| # | Name | Price |
|---|------|-------|
| 1401/500 | Citroën 2CV saloon | 25 |
| 1402/504 | Citroën Visa saloon | 25 |
| 1403/501 | Fiat Strada (Ritmo) two-door saloon | 25 |
| 1404/502 | BMW 530 saloon | 30 |
| 1405/503 | Alfa Romeo Alfetta GTV coupe | 30 |
| 1406/505 | Peugeot 504 saloon | 25 |

# Doepke

Although they made a line of rugged pressed-steel construction and earth-moving toys, Doepke is best-known in the die cast world for two die cast cars that they made in the early to mid-1950s. The company's full name was Charles William Doepke Manufacturing Company, Inc., and it was located in Rossmoyne, Ohio.

The two toys were also called "Model Toys," an apt description given their high degree of accuracy (for the era). The "MT Sports Car Kit" was released first, probably around 1951, and was quite obviously based on the MG TD. Why Doepke chose to call it the "MT" is unknown—perhaps getting permission from the British sports car maker proved difficult? Even the logo on the front of the radiator is octagonal in shape, but with the MT instead of MG.

The model was roughly to 1/10 scale, being around fifteen inches in length, and came unassembled in a large box. It had a die cast body with a pressed steel chassis, and at first the body came only with a coat of primer, ready to be painted by the purchaser (paint not included). Later, the model came painted (usually red).

The second model kit was released in 1954: a Jaguar XK120. This, too, came unassembled in a large box, and at nearly eighteen inches in length, also comes out to about 1/10 scale. It was always supplied fully painted, usually in a light blue.

As both models were convertible versions, the interiors can be clearly seen. Both cars had working steering, along with fairly accurate decals representing the dashboards. They also had working rear suspension.

The Jaguar is quite a bit rarer than the MG, apparently due to the Doepke factory burning down in the mid-1950s, putting an end to the product line. Most examples found today have had repair and/or restoration work done to them, or are in need of such. Interestingly, at the time these were on the market, there were "Factory Authorized Service Stations" located around the United States.

These were generally hardware stores or appliance stores that carried replacement parts for the models. Replacement parts are still made for things like the steering wheels and the tonneau cover on the MG.

Due to their "take-apart" nature, and the availability or reproduction parts, values vary widely on the Doepke cars. A built MG in very good to excellent condition may set you back only $250-$300, but an original condition example, unbuilt in the original box can easily run twice that. As for the Jaguar, a very good original can sell for $400 or more; an original, unbuilt and complete in the box (or built with the box), will find ready buyers in the $600-$800 range. Restored examples will cost less than this, but even they generally sell quickly.

# Dugu

**D**ugu s.a.s. produced two lines of die cast models starting in either 1962 or 1963. The company was located in Varallo Sesia, in Italy, and the first series was known as "Miniautotoys." It included models of actual antique cars housed in a museum called "Museo dell 'Automobile Biscaretti di Ruffia—Torino," as did the second series, known as the "Museo" series, launched in 1964.

The models in both series were quite accurate for their time, although they did tend to have an abundance of fragile plastic parts. Some unusual vehicles were modeled, such as the #9 Bernardi in the Miniautotoys series. This model

was reportedly a special model given only to those who joined a Dugu collector's club. This undoubtedly accounts for its relative scarcity.

Dugus came in individual cardboard window boxes; a sticker indicated the model contained inside (see photo).

Although production of both series ceased in 1972, some Dugus re-surfaced as "Sispla" models in the mid-1970s. They also apparently popped up again as "Oldcars" models; the casting for the Dugu/Sispla #4 Fiat Dump Trucks is identical to that of the #4 Fiat truck made by Oldcars starting around 1980 (see section entitled Oldcars).

*Number 3 in Dugu's "Miniautotoys" series, the 1911 Fiat 4 Tourer with box. The green body on this example may be a repaint, as red is the only original color thus far recorded for this model.*

| # | Name | Price |
|---|------|-------|
| 1 | Fiat 4 Closed Tourer 1911 (green/black) . . | $45 |
| 2 | Lancia Lambda 1925 (red/black, tan/black, green/black) . . . . . . . . . . | 45 |
| 3 | Fiat 4 Tourer 1911 (dark red/black) . . . . | 45 |
| 4 | Fiat Grand Prix 1907 (red) . . . . . . . . | 50 |
| 5 | Lancia Lambda Torpedo 1925 (green/black, tan/black, red/black) . . . . . . . . | 45 |
| 6 | Itala Palombella 1907 (green) . . . . | 45 |
| 7 | Itala 25/35 HP Closed Tourer 1912 (red) . . . . . . . . . . . . | 45 |
| 8 | Itala 25/35 HP Open Tourer 1912 (red) . . | 45 |
| 9 | Bernardi 3.5 HP (closed) 1896 (red) . . | 60 |
| 10 | Bernardi 3.5 HP (open) 1896 (red) . . . . | 60 |
| 11 | Fiat 3.5 HP (open) 1899 (blue/yellow) . . | 45 |
| 12 | Fiat 3.5 HP (closed) 1899 (blue/yellow) . . | 45 |
| 13 | Duesenberg SJ Town Car 1931 (green/black, yellow/brown) . . . . . . . | 60 |
| 14 | Fiat 509 2-Door 1925 (dark red/black) . . | 45 |
| 15 | Fiat 509 Tourer (open) 1925 (red/black) . . | 45 |
| 16 | Itala 35/45 HP Limousine 1909 (red/black) . . . . . . . . . . | 45 |
| 17 | Fiat Balilla Coppa d'Oro 1937 (red) . . . . | 50 |

| # | Name | Price |
|---|------|-------|
| 18 | Cord Phaeton (closed) 1936 (orange, yellow, light green) . . . . . . . . . . . . . . | $75 |
| 19 | Duesenberg SJ (open) 1931 (red) . . . . . | 60 |
| 20 | Cord Phaeton (open) 1936 (orange, light green) . . . . . . . . . . . . . . . . . | 75 |
| 21 | Rolls-Royce Silver Ghost 1933 (green, yellow/black) . . . . . . . . . . . . | 75 |
| 22 | Rolls-Royce Silver Ghost (open) 1933 (yellow/black) . . . . . . . . . . . . | 75 |
| 23 | Fiat-Eldridge Grand Prix 1923 (red) . . . . | 75 |
| 24 | Fiat S-76 Record Car 1911 (red) . . . . . . | 75 |

**"Museo" series:**

| # | Name | Price |
|---|------|-------|
| M1 | Benz Victoria 1893 (green/black) . . . . . . | 35 |
| M2 | Peugeot 2-1/2 HP 1894 (red/black) . . . . | 35 |
| M3 | Benz Estate Car 1899 (green/white) . . . . | 35 |
| M4 | Darracq 9-1/2 HP Tourer 1902 (red/white) . . . . . . . . . . . . . . | 35 |
| M5 | De Dion Bouton 1903 (cream) . . . . . . . | 35 |
| M6 | Legnano 6/6 HP Spider (closed) 1908 (red) . . . . . . . . . . . . . . . . | 35 |
| M7 | Legnano 6/6 HP Spider (open) 1908 (red) . . . . . . . . . . . . . . . . | 35 |

| # | Name | Price |
|---|------|-------|
| M8 | Fiat 500A 1936 (tan/black, red/black, green/black, blue/black) . . . . . . . | $35 |
| M9 | Brixia Züst Phaeton 1908 (red/black) . . . | 35 |
| M10 | Cisitalia 202 Coupe 1948 (red) . . . . . . | 50 |
| M11 | Lancia Theta 1914 (red/black) . . . . . . | 35 |
| M12 | Ansaldo 4C Open Tourer 1923 (yellow/black) . . . . . . . . . . . . | 35 |
| M13 | Fiat 500A Convertible 1936 (red/black, tan/black) . . . . . . . . . . . . | 45 |
| M14 | Fiat 519S Tourer 1923 (red/black) . . . . | 50 |

**"Sispla" models:**

| # | Name | Price |
|---|------|-------|
| 1 | Same Centauro Farm Tractor (orange) . . | 150 |
| 2 | Fiat 56 550 HP Farm Tractor (orange) . . | 125 |
| 2 | Fiat 600 Tractor (orange) . . . . . . . . | 100 |
| 2 | Fiat 640 Tractor (orange) . . . . . . . . | 100 |
| 2 | Someca 640 Tractor (orange) . . . . . . . | 100 |
| 3 | Fiat 697N Dump Truck (blue/gray, red/gray, green/gray) . . . . . . . . . . | 60 |
| 4 | Fiat 90NC Dump Truck (olive) . . . . . . | 60 |
| 4 | O. M. 100 Dump Truck (blue) . . . . . . | 60 |
| 5 | Fiat 90 NC Tanker "OLIO FIAT" (gray) . . | 60 |

# Durham Classics

**D**urham Classics is a manufacturer of hand-built, highly-detailed 1/43 white metal models. Located in Oshawa, Ontario, in Canada, the company is owned by founders Julian and Margaret Stewart. Julian Stewart worked closely with John Hall of Brooklin Models in the late 1970s, when Brooklin was still in Canada. Among other things, Stewart made the master models for Brooklin number 6 (1932 Packard Light 8) and number 7 (1934 Chrysler Airflow four-door).

In October 1980, the first Durham model was released: the two-door coupe version of the 1934 Chrysler Airflow. The operation grew and moved from the basement of the Stewart home into new facilities in 1986, the year that the second and third Durham Classics models came out.

There have been nearly twenty basic Durham models (castings), each of which has been released in a number of liveries and versions. These are generally limited in quantity to 200 or 300, so competition for certain versions can be intense. Although new models usually retail in the $95-

*The 1941 Chevrolet Suburban Carryall, Durham #17.*

$120 range, the price can go higher if there's great demand for the item.

This listing outlines the basic casting for each number, and the value for each currently available model is listed as CRP (Current Retail Price).

| # | Name | Price |
|---|------|-------|
| DC-1 | 1934 Chrysler Airflow nine liveries; two current (maroon, black/white "Highway Patrol") | CRP |
| DC-2 | 1953 Ford F-100 Pick-up Truck nine liveries; four current (dark blue, light blue "Bickells Farms," black "Midas," red "Wurlitzer" with jukebox) | CRP |
| DC-3 | 1939 Ford Panel Delivery Van 15 liveries; all discontinued | CRP |
| DC-4 | 1938 Lincoln Zephyr two-door coupe five liveries; two current (black, cream) | CRP |
| DC-5 | 1941 Chevrolet two-door coupe three current (brown, black "Michigan State Police," black "Idaho State Police," white "Ontario Police") | CRP |
| DC-6 | 1953 Ford F-100 Utility Truck four liveries; one current (yellow "Toronto Transportation") | CRP |
| DC-7 | 1954 Ford Courier Wagon seven liveries; two current (blue "Prairie Airways") | CRP |
| DC-8 | 1938 Lincoln Zephyr two-door convertible (top up) two liveries; both discontinued | CRP |
| DC-9 | 1938 Lincoln Zephyr two-door convertible (top down) two current (yellow, red) | CRP |
| DC-10 | 1941 Chevrolet Convertible (top up) one current livery (cream with black top) | CRP |
| DC-10 | 1941 Chevrolet Convertible (top down) one current livery (blue with tan tonneau) | CRP |
| DC-11 | 1941 Chevrolet Utility Pick-up three liveries, one current (green) | CRP |

| # | Name | Price |
|---|------|-------|
| DC-12 | 1941 Chevrolet Panel Delivery Van nine liveries, two current (gray, cream "North American Van Lines") | CRP |
| DC-13 | 1939 Ford Panel Van Extended Body four liveries; one current (cream "Sacramento Bee") | CRP |
| DC-14 | 1951 Ford Monarch two-door coupe two liveries; one current (blue) | CRP |

| # | Name | Price |
|---|------|-------|
| DC-15 | 1941 Ford Coupe two liveries; one current (beige) | CRP |
| DC-16 | 1953 Chevrolet 3/4 Ton Pick-up three liveries; two current (green, burgundy) | CRP |
| DC-17 | 1941 Chevrolet Suburban Carryall three liveries; one current (green "Niagara Tour") | CRP |

*Durham Classics #5, the 1941 Chevrolet in Michigan State Police livery. This model was first released in 1992.*

# Edil

This Italian company put out a series of 1/43 scale models of Italian cars starting in the mid-1960s. Except for the number 11 Mercedes-Benz, all were models of Italian cars. The last new model was issued in 1969 or 1970, after which production stopped.

Several of the Edils (such as the Mercedes-Benz and the number 9 Ferrari 275 GTB) were re-released in the early 1970s by the Turkish Meboto company, and they were of inferior quality compared to the original Edils. The Meboto baseplates still have the Edil logo.

| # | Name | Price |
|---|------|-------|
| 1 | Alfa Romeo Giulia GT (red, silver, blue) | $160 |
| 2 | Fiat 850 (blue, red) | 220 |
| 3 | Lancia Flavia Coupe (red, gray) | 130 |
| 4 | Alfa Romeo Giulia TI (gray, blue) | 150 |
| 5 | Alfa Romeo Giulia Police Car (green) | 170 |

| # | Name | Price |
|---|------|-------|
| 6 | Fiat 1500 (gray, light blue) | $150 |
| 7 | Fiat 124 (blue, red, gray) | 130 |
| 8 | Fiat 850 (blue, red) | 200 |
| 9 | Ferrari 275 GTB (red, silver, yellow) | 250 |
| 10 | Lamborghini Miura (red, orange) | 200 |

| # | Name | Price |
|---|------|-------|
| 11 | Mercedes-Benz 250SE (green) | $350 |
| 12 | Iso Grifo (blue, silver) | 130 |
| 13 | Lamborghini Marzal (orange, silver) | 160 |
| 14(?) | Opel Commodore | not issued |

# EFE (Exclusive First Editions)

EFE, as Exclusive First Editions is known in the hobby, entered the market in June 1989 with a die cast model of the well-known double-decker RT bus, the AEC Regent. Since then the company, located in Milton Keynes, England, has produced a variety of public transport and commercial vehicles, all to a consistent scale of 1/76 (OO). They have even modelled several passenger cars.

EFE's have a large following in England, where the vehicles modeled were seen in daily use for many years. The models are well-detailed and accurate, particularly considering their relatively small size. (EFE's are manufactured in the Far East.)

Since the market for EFE models is much smaller in the United States, accurate price data is scarce. In the United Kingdom, certain models that are no longer made command higher prices than the "Current Retail Price" listed here. For example, although the #10114 Bradford version of the AEC Bus sells for about $10, the same casting in the Devon

General version brings $200 or more when offered for sale. This kind of price variance is far more common in the United Kingdom than in the United States.

The following listing highlights the first few years of EFE production, detailing the many versions and liveries of models such as the AEC Mammoth Major Truck. The value of each model is listed as "CRP," which is around $7-$10 for most of the individual models. (This price, of course, assumes a mint condition, original model in the original cardboard and plastic window display box.) Some EFE models have been discontinued, and may therefore command a higher price than the CRP.

Note: EFE occasionally releases a "DL" (deluxe) version of a model, which generally is the standard model with an additional feature, such as a "load" for the back of a truck. In addition, there are accessories and "detailing" parts sold separately for EFE models, such as loads for the trucks, fleet numbers for the buses, etc.

| # | Name | Price |
|---|------|-------|
| **Automobiles:** | | |
| 401 | Triumph Roadster | CRP |
| 403 | Triumph Roadster | CRP |
| 501 | MGB | CRP |
| 503 | MGB | CRP |
| 601 | Triumph Vitesse | CRP |
| 603 | Triumph Vitesse | CRP |
| 701 | Austin-Healey Sprite | CRP |
| 703 | Austin-Healey Sprite | CRP |

| # | Name | Price |
|---|------|-------|
| **Commercial/Service Vehicles:** | | |
| 10101 | AEC RT London Transport Bus "Duracell" | CRP |
| 10102 | AEC RT Greenline Bus "Buxted" | CRP |
| 10103 | AEC RT London Country Bus "Birds Eye" | CRP |
| 10104 | AEC RT London Transport Bus "Schweppes" | CRP |
| 10107 | AEC RT London Transport Bus "Dulux" | CRP |

| # | Name | Price |
|---|------|-------|
| 10109 | AEC RT London Transport Bus "Bird's Custard" | CRP |
| 10111 | AEC RT London Transport Bus "Barclays" | CRP |
| 10112 | AEC RT London Transport Bus "Vernons" | CRP |
| 10113 | AEC RT Dundee Bus "Courier" | CRP |
| 10114 | AEC RT Bradford Bus | CRP |
| 10201 | AEC RT Open Top Bus "Beachy Head" | CRP |

| # | Name | Price |
|---|------|-------|
| 10202 | AEC RT Open Top Bus "Colemans" | CRP |
| 10203 | AEC RT Open Top Bus "Coronation" | CRP |
| 10204 | AEC RT Open Top Bus "Typhoo Tea" | CRP |
| 10301 | AEC Mammoth Major 6 Wheel Dropside "Fenland" | CRP |
| 10302 | AEC Mammoth Major 6 Wheel Dropside "Cyril Ridgeon & Son" | CRP |
| 10303 | AEC Mammoth Major 6 Wheel Dropside "J.D. Lown" | CRP |
| 10401 | AEC Mammoth Major 8 Wheel Flatbed "Bath & Portland" | CRP |
| 10402 | AEC Mammoth Major 8 Wheel Flatbed "London Brick" | CRP |
| 10501 | AEC Mammoth Major Box Van "London Carriers" | CRP |
| 10502 | AEC Mammoth Major Box Van "Startrite" | CRP |
| 10503 | AEC Mammoth Major Box Van "BRS" | CRP |
| 10504 | AEC Mammoth Major Box Van "PEK" | CRP |
| 10505 | AEC Mammoth Major Box Van "Oxydol" | CRP |
| 10601 | AEC Mammoth Major 8 Wheel Tanker "Century Oils" | CRP |
| 10602 | AEC Mammoth Major 8 Wheel Tanker "J. & H. Bunn" | CRP |
| 10604 | AEC Mammoth Major 8 Wheel Tanker "Mobilgas" | CRP |
| 10605 | AEC Mammoth Major 8 Wheel Tanker "Regent" | CRP |
| 10701 | AEC Mammoth Major 6 Wheel Flatbed "Furlong Bros." | CRP |
| 10702 | AEC Mammoth Major 6 Wheel Flatbed "Blue Circle" | CRP |

| # | Name | Price |
|---|------|-------|
| 10703 | AEC Mammoth Major 6 Wheel Flatbed "Wimpey" | CRP |
| 10703R | AEC Mammoth Major 6 Wheel Flatbed "Wimpey" | CRP |
| 10801 | AEC Mammoth Major 8 Wheel Dropside "British Steel" | CRP |
| 10802 | AEC Mammoth Major 8 Wheel Dropside "Whitbread" | CRP |
| 10803 | AEC Mammoth Major 8 Wheel Dropside "Marley" | CRP |
| 10804 | AEC Mammoth Major 8 Wheel Dropside "Macready's" | CRP |
| 10901 | AEC Mammoth Major 6 Wheel Tanker "Haygates" | CRP |
| 10902 | AEC Mammoth Major 6 Wheel Tanker "Lord Rayleighs Farms" | CRP |
| 10903 | AEC Mammoth Major 6 Wheel Tanker "LPG Transport" | CRP |
| 10908 | AEC Mammoth Major 6 Wheel Tanker "Welch's" | CRP |
| 11001 | AEC Mammoth Major Box Van "Croft" | CRP |
| 11002 | AEC Mammoth Major Box Van "Pickfords" | CRP |
| 11005 | AEC Mammoth Major Box Van "Lacons" | CRP |
| 11106 | AEC Mammoth Major Box Van "Rose's" | CRP |
| 11104 | RTL Double Decker Bus "Lockey's" | CRP |
| 11105 | RTL Double Decker Bus "Brylcreem" | CRP |
| 11901 | Harrington Cavalier Coach | CRP |
| 11903 | Harrington Cavalier Coach "Grey Green" | CRP |
| 12001 | AEC Mammoth Major 8 Wheel Tipper "Wimpey" | CRP |

| # | Name | Price |
|---|------|-------|
| 12002 | AEC Mammoth Major 8 Wheel Tipper "Tarmac" | CRP |
| 12101 | Harrington Cavalier Coach | CRP |
| 12102 | Harrington Cavalier Coach "East Yorkshire" | CRP |
| 12103 | Harrington Cavalier Coach "Hebble" | CRP |
| 12201 | Harrington Grenadier Coach | CRP |
| 12202 | Harrington Grenadier Coach "Premier Travel" | CRP |
| 12301 | Harrington Grenadier Coach | CRP |
| 12302 | Harrington Grenadier Coach "Grey Cars" | CRP |
| 12501 | Atkinson 6 Wheel Box Van "Wells" | CRP |
| 12601 | Atkinson 6 Wheel Dropside "McNicholas" | CRP |
| 12701 | Atkinson 8 Wheel Tanker "Charringtons" | CRP |
| 12801 | Atkinson 8 Wheel Flatbed "McPhees" | CRP |
| 12901 | Atkinson 8 Wheel Box Van "Fyffes" | CRP |
| 13001 | Atkinson Car Transporter | CRP |
| 13002 | Atkinson Car Transporter "Swift's" | CRP |
| 13303 | Atkinson Car Transporter "Midlands" | CRP |
| 13301 | Atkinson 8 Wheel Tipper "St. Albans" | CRP |
| 13402 | Leeds Horsefield Tramcar "CWS/Tizer" | CRP |
| 13403 | Leeds Horsefield Tramcar "Jacob's" | CRP |
| 19901 | Tate & Lyle 3 piece Gift Set | CRP |
| 19902 | Rank Hovis 3 piece Gift Set | CRP |
| 19904 | Taylor Woodrow Gift Set | CRP |
| 19003 | RTL 3 piece Gift Set | CRP |
| 19006 | Fisherman's Friend 3 piece Gift Set | CRP |
| 99903 | De-luxe Road Transport Set | CRP |

# Efsi

**E**fsi is one of those elusive names that turns up now and again on dealer tables. It is known that this Dutch company produced a line of roughly 1/70 scale die cast toys/models starting in the early 1970s. This is the series listed here.

The company may have continued making die cast toys and models through the 1980s until the present. For example, Efsi released a DAF 95 Truck in 1990 in fixed, trailer and articulated versions. In 1991, they released a Jonckheere Bermuda Bus in 1/87 scale. Both of these models sold for less than $10. Efsi models have made a re-appearance in the past year, apparently under the name "Efsi-OTO," or perhaps simply "OTO." DAF models figure prominently in the line. The models seen so far have been priced at $20 or less.

*Efsi #4050 Opel Rekord. Lots of "play value" for the small size (1/70 scale), with window glazing, suspension and opening doors.*

| # | Name | Price |
|------|------|------|
| 1010 | Ford Model T Truck | $10 |
| 1020 | Ford Model T Tanker | 10 |
| 1030 | Ford Model T Crane Truck | 10 |
| 1040 | Ford Model T Van | 10 |
| 1050 | Ford Model T Two Seater | 10 |
| 1060 | Ford Model T Sedan | 10 |
| 1070 | Ford Model T Ambulance | 10 |
| 1100 | Ford Model T Fire Van | 10 |
| 2010 | B.R.M. Formula I | 10 |
| 2020 | Honda Formula I | 10 |
| 2030 | Ferrari Formula I | 15 |
| 2040 | Brabham Formula I | 10 |
| 2050 | McLaren Formula I | 10 |
| 2060 | Lotus 49 C Formula I | 10 |
| 3020 | Commer Van | 15 |
| 3021 | Commer Ambulance | 15 |
| 3022 | Commer Service Van | 15 |
| 3023 | Commer Fire Van | 15 |
| 3024 | Commer Army Ambulance | 15 |
| 3025 | Commer U.S.A. Army Van | 15 |
| 3030 | Mercedes-Benz Open Truck | 10 |
| 3040 | Mercedes-Benz Covered Truck | 10 |
| 3041 | Mercedes-Benz Red Cross Truck | 10 |

| # | Name | Price |
|------|------|------|
| 3042 | Mercedes-Benz Army Truck | $10 |
| 3050 | Mercedes-Benz Dump Truck | 10 |
| 3051 | Mercedes-Benz Army Dump Truck | 10 |
| 3060 | Trailer | 10 |
| 3061 | Red Cross Trailer | 10 |
| 3062 | Army Trailer | 10 |
| 3080 | Mercedes-Benz Fire Engine | 10 |
| 3090 | Mercedes-Benz Tanker "SHELL" | 15 |
| 3091 | Mercedes-Benz Tanker "ELF" | 15 |
| 3092 | Mercedes-Benz Tanker "ARAL" | 15 |
| 3093 | Mercedes-Benz Army Tanker | 15 |
| 4010 | Ford Taunus 17 M | 15 |
| 4011 | Ford Taunus Stock Car | 15 |
| 4020 | Porsche 911 S | 15 |
| 4021 | Porsche 911 S Dutch Police Car | 15 |
| 4022 | Porsche 911 S Rally | 15 |
| 4030 | Jaguar E Type | 15 |
| 4040 | Mercedes-Benz 280SL | 15 |
| 4050 | Opel Rekord 1900 | 15 |
| 4060 | Mercedes-Benz 250 SE Coupe | 15 |
| 4061 | Mercedes-Benz 250 SE Coupe Rally | 15 |
| 4070 | BMW 2000 CS | 15 |
| 4071 | BMW 2000 CS Rally | 15 |

| # | Name | Price |
|------|------|------|
| 4080 | Volkswagen 1600 TL | $20 |
| 4090 | Citroën ID 19 | 15 |
| 4091 | Citroën ID 19 Ambulance | 15 |
| 4100 | Citroën Dyane 6 | 15 |
| 4110 | Ford Transit Van | 15 |
| 4111 | Ford Transit Ambulance | 15 |
| 4112 | Ford Transit Police Van | 15 |

*The #1050 Ford Model T by Efsi, a very basic toy car.*

# Eligor

This French line of die cast and plastic models traces its roots back to a pioneer of the die cast collecting hobby. In 1976, Jacques Greilsamer, author of the now-famous book *Catalogue of Model Cars of the World,* started the Eligor line, using old Norev tooling. However, many of the Eligors were die cast whereas the original Norevs had been plastic.

In 1986, Greilsamer sold the line to Louis Surber, the company that had been doing the actual production of the Eligor product. Since that time, many Eligors have been made of plastic. Whether die cast or plastic, though, Eligors generally are quite accurate and well-detailed for the price. Surber gets as much mileage as possible out of the basic castings, sometimes issuing a single model in ten or more liveries.

This listing is comprised of the early die cast Eligors made between 1976 and the early 1980s.

| # | Name | Price |
|------|------|------|
| 1001 | 1938 Citroën Traction Avant Convertible | $25 |
| 1002 | 1938 Citroën Traction Avant Convertible (closed) | 25 |
| 1003 | 1932 Delage D 8 S Convertible | 25 |
| 1004 | 1932 Delage D 8 S Convertible (closed) | 25 |
| 1005 | 1933 Citroën Rosalie | 25 |
| 1006 | 1937 Panhard Dynamic | 25 |
| 1007 | 1934 Citroën 500 Kg Van "DUBONNET" | 25 |
| 1008 | 1934 Citroën 500 Kg Van "ESSOLUBE" | 25 |
| 1009 | 1934 Citroën 500 Kg Van "LA VACHE QUI RIT" | 25 |
| 1010 | 1934 Citroën 500 Kg Van "NICOLAS" | 25 |
| 1011 | 1934 Citroën 500 Kg Van "GOODRICH" | 25 |
| 1012 | 1934 Citroën 500 Kg Van "CINZANO" | 25 |
| 1013 | 1934 Citroën 500 Kg Van "LEFEVRE UTILE" | 25 |

*This #1079 Eligor 1934 Ford V8 Camionette Van features colorful graphics for Sir Alan Cobham's Air Display.*

| # | Name | Price | # | Name | Price | # | Name | Price |
|---|------|-------|---|------|-------|---|------|-------|
| 1014 | 1938 Renault Juvaquatre | $25 | 1031 | Citroën Traction Avant | $25 | 1049 | Renault NN 2 Fire Car | $25 |
| 1015 | 1939 Hotchkiss Saloon | 35 | 1032 | Citroën Traction Avant Army (Germany) | 25 | 1050 | Citroën 500 Kg Van "MICHELIN" | 25 |
| 1016 | 1931 Peugeot 201 | 25 | 1032 | Citroën Traction Avant Army (France) | 25 | 1051 | Rolls-Royce Taxi Hotel | 25 |
| 1017 | 1923 Citroën 5 CV | 25 | 1033 | Peugeot 402 Darl'Mat | 35 | 1052 | Talbot Taxi Hotel | 25 |
| 1018 | Citroën 5 HP Van "BEBE CADUM" | 25 | 1034 | Citroën 500 Kg Van "BENEDICTINE" | 25 | 1505 | Citroën 500 Kg Van "REXOR AUTOTINT" | 40 |
| 1019 | Citroën 500 Kg Van "ST. RAPHAEL" | 25 | 1035 | Citroën Rosalie Taxi | 25 | 1505 | Citroën 500 Kg Van "ANDRE CITROEN" | 40 |
| 1020 | Citroën 500 Kg Fire Van | 25 | 1036 | Talbot Pacific Limousine - 1930 | 25 | 1505 | Citroën 500 Kg Van "FRANZ CARL WEBER" | 40 |
| 1021 | Citroën 500 Kg Ambulance | 25 | 1037 | Citroën 5 HP (closed) | 25 | 3001 | Magirus Deutz Fire Engine - 1925 | 35 |
| 1022 | Citroën 500 Kg Van "WATERMAN" | 25 | 1038 | Delage D 8 Chapron (open) | 25 | 3002 | Magirus Deutz Swiss Mail Bus - 1919 | 35 |
| 1023 | Citroën 500 Kg Van "LUSTUCRU" | 25 | 1039 | Delage D 8 Chapron (closed) | 25 | 3002 | Magirus Deutz Mail Bus - 1919 | 35 |
| 1024 | Citroën 500 Kg Van "RIVOIRE & CARRET" | 25 | 1040 | Renault NN 2 Torpedo | 25 | 3003 | International Harvester 844 Tractor | 35 |
| 1025 | 1928 Bugatti 35B Racing Car | 25 | 1041 | Renault NN 2 Landaulet | 25 | 3004 | Camion Unic 110 NC Truck | 35 |
| 1026 | Bugatti Atlantic Convertible | 40 | 1042 | Renault NN 2 Landaulet Taxi | 25 | 3005 | Liebherr 981 HD Excavator | 35 |
| 1027 | Bugatti Atlantic Convertible (closed) | 40 | 1043 | Mercedes-Benz Nurburg - 1929 | 25 | 3006 | International 953 Combine Harvester | 35 |
| 1029 | Citroën 500 Kg Van "BYRRH" | 25 | 1044 | Mercedes-Benz Nurburg Taxi Hotel | 25 | 3007 | Unic 110 NC "SNCF-SERNAM" Van | 35 |
| 1030 | Rolls-Royce Limousine - 1928 | 25 | 1047 | Rolls-Royce Silver Shadow | 25 | | | |
| | | | 1048 | Bentley T | 25 | | | |

# Eria

Eria was a French company that produced a series of roughly 1/43 models starting in 1957. (Actually, Eria may have been simply the name of the models.) Although simple products (only the last two had window glazing and probably none had suspension), they were quite accurate castings of full-size French automobiles of the period. Only one, the #36 Jaguar, was a non-French subject.

Production appears to have ceased in the early 1960s, most likely due to the company being unable to compete with the more-established French manufacturers like Solido and French Dinky.

Erias came with spun aluminum wheel hubs, and they appear to have had white tires. Whether they came packaged individually is unknown.

| # | Name | Price | # | Name | Price | # | Name | Price |
|---|------|-------|---|------|-------|---|------|-------|
| 30 | Citroën DS 19 (orange/cream, yellow/gray, purple/white) | $450 | 33 | Simca Aronde P60 (gray/cream, gray/red, green/gray) | $150 | 36 | Jaguar D LeMans (orange, yellow, blue) | $150 |
| 31 | Peugeot 403 (green, beige, gray) | 150 | 34 | Panhard PL 17 (yellow, pink, orange) | 150 | 37 | Peugeot 404 (blue) | 275 |
| 32 | Renault Dauphine (white, blue, green, gray) | 150 | 35 | Renault Estafette Van (gray, orange, blue, cream) | 150 | 38 | Citroën ID 19 Ambulance (white) | 400 |
| | | | | | | 39 | Citroën ID 19 Station Wagon (blue/white, orange/white) | 400 |

# Ertl

The Ertl Co., Inc. has been the king of the farm toy industry for five decades. The company was started in the mid-1940s by Fred Ertl Sr., who assembled toy tractors at his kitchen table. Out of this humble beginning grew a toy and model manufacturing giant, located in Dyersville, Iowa.

In addition to manufacturing a huge variety of tractors,

hay rakes and manure spreaders (all in numerous sizes), Ertl also produces dolls, farm play sets, model horses and a line of Thomas the Tank Engine toys. They also produce die cast banks, which constitute a collecting category by themselves. The banks are models of older vehicles, such as a 1923 Chevrolet Delivery Truck, and they have the requisite coin

*An Ertl International Paystar 5000 Gravel Trailer Truck of late 1970 to early-1980s vintage. This type of Ertl truck is valued at about $25.*

*The #7339 '55 Chevrolet Stepside Pickup Truck. Like other current Ertl offerings, this model features opening doors, engine hood and tailgate.*

deposit hole, usually cut into the roof. These banks have been made in countless versions and liveries over the years. For more information, see Part Three, Additional Resources.

Ertl currently manufactures several lines of die cast models, and it is these that comprise the following listing. The scale of the item is given where known, and the "CRP" value indicates that the item is still available at retail.

*Note:* In late 1993, Ertl released a 1/18 scale die cast model of the 1969 Brawner-Hawk IndyCar, as driven to victory by Mario Andretti in that year's Indianapolis 500. At a price of around $120, it represented Ertl's first entry into the high-end die cast model market dominated by names like Franklin Mint, Danbury Mint, etc. The model was superb in every respect, but Ertl made it for just a short while before apparently turning over the rights to Danbury Mint. To date, no other similiar models have been produced.

The Andretti model is considered scarce, and occasionally turns up for sale in the $300 range.

| # | Name | Price |
|---|------|-------|
| **Classic Vehicles 1/43 scale series:** | | |
| 2154 | '55 Chevy Cameo Pick-up with Crates and Barrels | CRP |
| 2155 | '55 Chevy Cameo Pick-up with Cover | CRP |
| 2159 | '55 Chevy Cameo Wrecker | CRP |
| 2503 | 1930 Chevy Truck | CRP |
| 2504 | 1932 Ford Panel Delivery Truck | CRP |
| 2517 | 1940 Woody Wagon | CRP |
| 2540 | 1957 Chevy | CRP |
| 2541 | 1952 Cadillac | CRP |
| 2586 | 1964-1/2 Mustang | CRP |
| 2587 | Checker Cab | CRP |
| 2588 | 1960 Corvette | CRP |
| 2589 | 1968 GTO | CRP |
| 2802 | 1957 Ford T-Bird | CRP |
| 2824 | 1938 Chevy Panel Truck | CRP |
| 2825 | 1950 Chevy Panel Truck | CRP |
| 2826 | 1951 GMC Panel Truck | CRP |

| # | Name | Price |
|---|------|-------|
| **American Muscle 1/18 scale series:** | | |
| 7158 | '57 Chevy Bel Air hardtop | CRP |
| 7190 | 1970 Chevelle SS 454 | CRP |
| 7301 | '73 Pontiac Trans Am | CRP |
| 7321 | '63 Corvette Stingray | CRP |
| 7323 | '70 Chevelle SS 454 | CRP |
| 7325 | '70 Mustang Boss 302 | CRP |
| 7326 | '70 Mustang Boss 302 | CRP |
| 7328 | '69 Pontiac GTO Judge | CRP |
| 7330 | '57 Chevy Bel Air hardtop | CRP |
| 7331 | '57 Chevy Bel Air hardtop | CRP |
| 7333 | '95 Dodge RAM Truck | CRP |
| 7339 | '55 Chevy Stepside Truck | CRP |
| 7340 | '55 Chevy Cameo Carrier Truck | CRP |
| 7350 | '69 Shelby GT-500 | CRP |
| 7351 | '69 Shelby GT-500 | CRP |
| 7365 | '63 Corvette Stingray | CRP |
| 7366 | '69 Camaro Z/28 | CRP |

| # | Name | Price |
|---|------|-------|
| 7367 | '69 Camaro SS 396 | CRP |
| 7368 | '69 Hemi Roadrunner | CRP |
| 7369 | Shelby Cobra 427 S/C | CRP |
| 7375 | '70 Plymouth Hemi 'Cuda | CRP |
| 7379 | '70 Plymouth AAR 'Cuda | CRP |
| 7383 | '78 Dodge Warlock | CRP |
| 7384 | '69 Hemi Roadrunner | CRP |
| 7385 | '78 Dodge Lil Red Truck | CRP |
| 7386 | Shelby Cobra 427 S/C | CRP |
| 7389 | '69 Charger Daytona | CRP |
| 7390 | '69 Charger Daytona | CRP |
| 7394 | Plymouth Prowler | CRP |
| 7467 | '69 Pontiac GTO Judge | CRP |
| 7603 | '70 Buick GSX | CRP |
| 7604 | '70 Buick GSX | CRP |
| **American Muscle 1/18 scale Stock Cars series:** | | |
| 7217 | Budweiser Monte Carlo | CRP |
| 7218 | Goodwrench Monte Carlo | CRP |
| 7219 | Kellogg's Monte Carlo | CRP |
| 7220 | McDonald's Thunderbird | CRP |
| 7221 | Raybestos Thunderbird | CRP |
| 7222 | Valvoline Thunderbird | CRP |
| **American Muscle 1/12 series:** | | |
| 7308 | '64 Pontiac GTO | CRP |
| 8776 | '64-1/2 Mustang | CRP |
| **Miscellaneous Vehicles:** | | |
| 4323 | Big Farm Pickup (1/32) | CRP |
| 4457 | Big Farm Pickup and Horse Trailer (1/32) | CRP |
| 4324 | Pickup with Ammonia Tank | ERTL |
| 4386 | GMC Dually Stretch Cab Pickup | CRP |

*An Ertl #1358 International Transtar II Truck in original box. This toy was made in the mid-1970s, and now sells in the $40-$50 range.*

# First Gear

This Iowa-based American company launched a series of 1/34 scale die cast truck models in 1992. The models are well-detailed, including features such as headlights, hood releases, and so forth. The models are manufactured in China.

Unlike other companies, First Gear does not market its products directly to retailers, or through a standard distribution system. Generally, a company or public service organization (such as a fire department) orders a set number of models from First Gear to be finished in the livery of the organization. An announcement of the model is then sent to mail order businesses and stores, which agree to purchase a minimum number of the model. These businesses then notify their customers, who usually pre-pay for the model.

First Gear models do turn up on the secondary market, at toy and model shows, and in advertisements in magazines. With few exceptions, prices for the First Gear trucks have not risen appreciably, so the models can generally be found for a price at or near the original release price. That is around $35-$40 for the various versions of the 1951 Ford F-6 and the 1952 GMC Cab-over truck. The larger 1960 Mack B-61 Tractor Trailer sells in various liveries for anywhere from $60-$80.

*First Gear's 1957 International Harvester R-200 Twin-Boom Wrecker in International Harvester livery.*

Since a truck can be produced for any company (or individual) willing to pay the price for a minimum number of units, there have been countless liveries produced over the years. To list them all is beyond the scope of this book, if indeed all of them are even known.

Following is a listing of the first two years of production, outlining the various body styles produced on the main cab/chassis models.

## Name

**1952 GMC Cab-over Engine Truck:**
Heavy Duty Wrecker
Insulated Dairy Van
Dry Goods Van
First Tanker
Full Rack Stakeside
One-half Rack Stakeside
Bottler's Body
Grain Box

**1951 Ford F-6 Truck:**
Dry Goods Van
First Tanker
Full Rack Stakeside
One-half Rack Stakeside
Bottler's Body
Grain Box

## Name

**1957 International Harvester R-190 Truck:**
Fire Truck
New Tanker
Dry Goods Van

## Name

**1957 International Harvester R-200 Truck:**
Furniture Van
Twin-Boom Wrecker

**1960 Mack B-61 Tractor Trailer:**
One body style, numerous liveries

*A 1951 Ford F-6 truck, in "Great Lakes Hybrids" livery. The tarp on top of this "grain box" type of body is metal.*

# Formaplast

This Italian company produced a number of 1/43 scale die cast commercial and farm vehicle models during the mid- to late-1970s, and then changed it's name to "Yaxon" in 1978. Many of the models apprently were made under the Yaxon banner for some time. The models were mostly of Italian makes; in fact, Formaplast must have been one of the few manufacturers that made models of Lamborghini tractors.

Formaplasts likely came in individual boxes.

| # | Name | Price |
|---|------|-------|
| 055 | Fiat 780 Tractor (orange) | $30 |
| 056 | Fiat 880DT Tractor (orange) | 30 |
| 070 | Scalvenzi Two-wheel Trailer | 15 |
| 071 | Manure Spreader | 15 |
| 072 | Tank Trailer | 15 |
| 073 | Fiat Tractor and Trailer (orange) | 30 |
| 074 | Fiat Tractor and Manure Spreader (orange) | 30 |
| 075 | Fiat Tractor and Tank Trailer (orange) | 30 |
| 081 | Omas Four-wheel Trailer (orange) | 15 |
| 082 | Scalvenzi Hay Loader | 15 |
| 085 | Same Buffalo 130 Tractor (red) | 30 |
| 086 | Lamborghini R 1056 Tractor (white) | 30 |
| 091 | Same Tractor and Trailer | 30 |
| 092 | Same Tractor and Manure Spreader | 30 |

| # | Name | Price |
|---|------|-------|
| 093 | Same Tractor and Trailer | $30 |
| 094 | Same Tractor and Tank Trailer | 30 |
| 095 | Same Tractor and Trailer | 30 |
| 096 | Lamborghini Tractor and Trailer | 30 |
| 097 | Lamborghini Tractor and Manure Spreader | 30 |
| 098 | Lamborghini Tractor and Trailer | 30 |
| 099 | Lamborghini Tractor and Tank Trailer | 30 |
| 0100 | Lamborghini Tractor and Trailer | 30 |
| 0300 | Fiat 170 Van "GOOD YEAR" | 30 |
| 0300 | Fiat 170 Van "FERRARI" | 30 |
| 0300 | Fiat 170 Van "FIAT" | 30 |
| 0300 | Fiat 170 Van "FORMATOYS" | 30 |
| 0301 | Fiat 170 Cella Tridimensional | 30 |
| 0302 | Fiat 170 Bergomi Refuse Wagon | 30 |

| # | Name | Price |
|---|------|-------|
| 0303 | Fiat 170 Log Semi-Trailer Truck | $30 |
| 0304 | Fiat 170 Truck | 30 |
| 0305 | Fiat 170 Covered Truck | 30 |
| 0306 | Fiat 170 Container Semi-Truck "GOFFREDO RUFFONI" | 30 |
| 0306 | Fiat 170 Container Semi-Truck "KUHNE & NAGEL" | 30 |
| 0311 | Mercedes Truck | 30 |
| 0312 | Mercedes Truck and Trailer | 30 |
| 0317 | Mercedes Container Truck "KUHNE & NAGEL" | 30 |
| 0317 | Mercedes Container Truck "GOTTARDI RUFFONI" | 30 |

# France Jouets

Located in Marseille, France, the firm of France Jouets began producing die cast models in 1959 or 1960. The models had lots of "play value," with features like moving buckets on the construction vehicles and large loads on the beds of the large tractor trailers.

FJ's can be found with either black or white tires, and a number of the models also came in a military olive green color in addition to a "civilian" version. Some models also came with window glazing. Although they don't often turn up in the United States, FJ's are generally priced reasonably given the quality and size of the models.

*Note:* After France Jouets ceased production in the late 1960s, the company played "musical molds," like many European manufacturers. Much of the tooling for these models was acquired by Safir, another French model maker, who re-issued a number of the France Jouets models during the mid-1970s.

| # | Name | Price |
|---|------|-------|
| 101 | Berliet GAK Road Tanker (red/yellow/black) | $40 |
| 102 | Berliet GAK Lumber Truck (red/yellow/black) | 40 |
| 103 | Berliet GAK Covered Truck (red/yellow/black) | 40 |
| 103 | Berliet GAK Covered Truck "SAVON ARMA" (red/yellow/black) | 90 |
| 104 | Berliet GAK Dump Truck (gray/yellow/black) | 40 |

| # | Name | Price |
|---|------|-------|
| 105 | Berliet GAK Grocery Truck (red/white/black) | $40 |
| 106 | Berliet GAK Street Sweeper (gray/green/black) | 40 |
| 107 | Berliet GAK Cement Mixer (red/yellow/black) | 40 |
| 108 | Berliet GAK Crane Truck (yellow/gray/black) | 40 |
| 109 | Berliet GAK Refuse Wagon (gray/silver/black) | 40 |

| # | Name | Price |
|---|------|-------|
| 110 | Berliet GAK E.D.F. Truck (yellow/gray/black) | $40 |
| 111 | Berliet GAK Stake Truck (yellow/green/black) | 40 |
| 112 | Berliet GAK Pipe Truck (yellow/green/black) | 40 |
| 113 | Berliet GAK Glass Truck (green/gray/black) | 40 |
| 114 | Berliet GAK Crane Truck (yellow/green/black) | 40 |

| # | Name | Price |
|---|------|-------|
| 115 | Berliet GAK Breakdown Truck (green/yellow/black) | $40 |
| 116 | Berliet GAK Bucket Truck (yellow/green/black) | 40 |
| 201 | Pacific Crane Truck (red/gray) | 60 |
| 201 | Pacific Army Crane Truck (olive) | 60 |
| 202 | Pacific Pipe Carrier Truck (red) | 70 |
| 202 | Pacific Pipe Carrier Truck (yellow) | 60 |
| 203 | Pacific Rocket Carrier (blue) | 80 |
| 203 | Pacific Army Rocket Carrier (olive) | 60 |
| 204 | Pacific Transformer Carrier (yellow) | 60 |
| 205 | Pacific Cement Carrier (yellow) | 40 |
| 206 | Pacific Atomic Gun Truck with guns (olive) | 60 |
| 207 | Naval Gun (olive) | 30 |
| 208 | Pacific Atomic Gun Truck with Searchlight (olive) | 60 |
| 301 | GMC Ambulance (white) | 40 |
| 302 | GMC Closed Army Truck (olive, beige) | 40 |
| 303 | GMC Truck with Machine-Gun (olive, beige) | 40 |
| 304 | GMC Rocket Launcher (olive, beige) | 40 |
| 305 | GMC Missile Transport (olive, white) | 40 |
| 306 | GMC Truck with Shovel (gray/yellow) | 40 |
| 307 | Trailer with Searchlight (olive, beige) | 15 |
| 308 | Trailer with Machine Gun (olive, beige) | 15 |
| 309 | Trailer with Radar (olive, beige) | 15 |
| 310 | Tank Trailer (olive, beige) | 15 |
| 311 | GMC Troop Carrier (olive, beige) | 40 |
| 312 | GMC Quarry Dumper (red/yellow, green/yellow) | 40 |

| # | Name | Price |
|---|------|-------|
| 313 | GMC Radar Truck (olive, beige) | $40 |
| 314 | GMC Street Sweeper (green/yellow) | 40 |
| 315 | GMC Van (red/yellow) | 40 |
| 316 | GMC Dump Truck (green/yellow) | 40 |
| 317 | GMC Meat Truck (red/white) | 40 |
| 318 | GMC Crane Truck (red/yellow) | 40 |
| 319 | GMC Covered Truck (green/yellow) | 40 |
| 320 | GMC Tanker (green/yellow) | 50 |
| 320 | GMC Tanker "ENERGOL" (green/yellow) | 50 |
| 321 | GMC Fire Engine (red) | 50 |
| 322 | GMC Searchlight Truck (olive, beige) | 40 |
| 323 | GMC Lumber Carrier (red/yellow) | 40 |
| 324 | Lumber Trailer (red/yellow) | 15 |
| 325 | Trailer (green/yellow) | 15 |
| 401 | Dodge Open Army Truck (olive) | 40 |
| 402 | Dodge Army Troop Carrier (olive) | 40 |
| 403 | Dodge Covered Army Truck (olive) | 40 |
| 404 | Dodge Anti-Aircraft Truck (olive) | 40 |
| 405 | Dodge Radar Truck (olive, white) | 40 |
| 406 | Dodge Searchlight Truck (olive, white) | 40 |
| 407 | Dodge Fire Truck (red) | 50 |
| 408 | Dodge Lance Rocket Truck (olive) | 40 |
| 409 | Dodge Ambulance Truck (white) | 40 |
| 410 | Dodge Rocket Carrier (olive, white) | 40 |
| 501 | Willys Open Army Jeep (olive) | 30 |
| 502 | Willys Covered Army Jeep (olive) | 30 |
| 503 | A.A. Gun Willys Jeep (olive) | 30 |
| 504 | Lance Rocket Willys Jeep (olive) | 30 |
| 505 | Army Radar Willys Jeep (olive) | 30 |
| 506 | Army Searchlight Willys Jeep (olive) | 30 |
| 507 | Fire Jeep (red) | 40 |

| # | Name | Price |
|---|------|-------|
| 508 | Police Jeep (blue) | $50 |
| 601 | Army Jeep and Gun (olive) | 40 |
| 602 | Army Jeep and Generator Trailer (olive) | 40 |
| 603 | Army Jeep and Trailer (olive) | 40 |
| 605 | Anti-tank Gun (olive) | 15 |
| 701 | Berliet Stradair Dump Truck (red/yellow, gray/yellow) | 40 |
| 702 | Berliet Stradair Grocery Truck (red/white) | 40 |
| 703 | Berliet Stradair Breakdown Truck (green/yellow) | 40 |
| 704 | Berliet Stradair Glass Truck (green/gray) | 40 |
| 705 | Berliet Stradair Crane Truck (red/yellow) | 40 |
| 706 | Berliet Stradair Sweeper-Flusher (gray/green) | 40 |
| 707 | Berliet Stradair Refuse Wagon (green/gray) | 40 |
| 708 | Berliet Stradair "COCA-COLA" Truck (yellow) | 60 |
| 708 | Berliet Stradair "KRONENBOURG" Truck (red) | 90 |
| 708 | Berliet Stradair "PIERVAL" Truck (white/black) | 90 |

# Franklin Mint

The Franklin Mint, in Franklin Center, Pennsylvania, is a producer of a variety of different collectible items. Among these are highly detailed die cast models. They are produced in several different scales, although 1/24 predominates.

The models are purchased via direct mail, usually in installment payments. Franklin markets its products not only to collectors, but to the general public as well. These models occasionally turn up for sale at collector's shows, and in ads in model and hobby magazines. Information on new Franklin Mint releases, as well as news and "for sale" ads, can be obtained from the Die Cast Car Collectors Club. For more information, see Part Three, Additional Resources.

In general, prices for Franklin Mint models have not increased on the secondary market. However, if a model is discontinued, its value may rise as a result of it no longer being obtainable direct from Franklin. "CRP" (current retail price) for Franklin models ranges from $90 to $130, depending on the model.

The 1948 Tucker Torpedo in 1/24 scale. This model is one of just a handful of models made of Preston Tucker's revolutionary car.

| Name | Price |
|------|------:|

### 1/8 scale (alphabetical by marque):
| | |
|---|---:|
| 1886 Benz Patent Motorwagen | CRP |
| 1957 Corvette Cutaway Engine | CRP |
| 1885 Daimler Single Track | CRP |

### 1/10 scale (alphabetical by marque):
| | |
|---|---:|
| 1985 Harley-Davidson Heritage Softail | CRP |
| 1957 Harley-Davidson XL Sportster | CRP |
| 1976 Harley-Davidson Electraglide | CRP |
| 1976 Harley-Davidson Electraglide Revised | CRP |
| 1976 Harley-Davidson Police Cycle | CRP |
| 1942 Indian 442 Motorcycle | CRP |

### 1/16 scale (alphabetical by marque):
| | |
|---|---:|
| 1931 Bugatti Royale | CRP |
| 1903 Ford Model A | CRP |
| 1913 Ford Model T | CRP |
| 1916 Ford Model T Fire Engine | CRP |
| 1899 Packard Model A1 | CRP |
| 1905 Rolls-Royce 10 HP | CRP |
| 1911 Stanley Steamer 62 Runabout | CRP |

### 1/24 scale (alphabetical by marque):
| | |
|---|---:|
| 1967 Airstream Trailer | CRP |
| 1938 Alvis Speedster | CRP |
| 1954 American LaFrance Fire Truck | CRP |
| 1935 Auburn 851 Speedster | CRP |
| 1929 Bentley Blower 8 | CRP |
| 1936 Bugatti Atalante 57SC | CRP |
| 1930 Bugatti Royale | CRP |
| 1929 Bugatti Royale Esders | CRP |
| 1949 Buick Riviera | CRP |
| 1949 Buick Roadmaster | CRP |
| 1953 Cadillac Eldorado | CRP |
| 1959 Cadillac Eldorado | CRP |
| 1957 Cadillac Eldorado Brougham | CRP |
| 1910 Cadillac Model Thirty | CRP |
| 1932 Cadillac V-16 | CRP |
| 1955 Chevrolet Bel Air Convertible | CRP |
| 1957 Chevrolet Bel Air Convertible (red) | CRP |
| 1956 Chevrolet Bel Air Convertible | CRP |
| 1957 Chevrolet Bel Air Convertible (black) | CRP |
| 1955 Chevrolet Bel Air Fire Chief | CRP |
| 1957 Chevrolet Bel Air Hardtop | CRP |
| 1955 Chevrolet Bel Air Hardtop (blue/white) | CRP |
| 1955 Chevrolet Bel Air Hardtop (red/white) | CRP |
| 1957 Chevrolet Bel Air Hot Rod | CRP |
| 1955 Chevrolet Bel Air Police | CRP |
| 1960 Chevrolet Impala (white) | CRP |
| 1960 Chevrolet Impala (red) | CRP |
| 1912 Christie Front Drive Steam | CRP |
| 1948 Chrysler Town & Country | CRP |
| 1937 Cord 812 Phaeton Coupe | CRP |
| 1956 Corvette | CRP |
| 1986 Corvette | CRP |
| 1957 Corvette | CRP |
| 1958 Corvette | CRP |
| 1955 Corvette | CRP |
| 1988 Corvette | CRP |
| 1959 Corvette | CRP |
| 1984 Corvette | CRP |

| | |
|---|---:|
| 1969 Corvette 427 Stingray | CRP |
| 1953 Corvette Convertible | CRP |
| 1968 Corvette L88 Stingray | CRP |
| 1978 Corvette Silver Anniversary | CRP |
| 1963 Corvette Stingray | CRP |
| 1967 Corvette Stingray | CRP |
| 1993 Corvette ZR-1 40th Anniversary | CRP |
| 1940 Duesenberg J | CRP |
| 1935 Duesenberg J | CRP |
| 1930 Duesenberg J Derham | CRP |
| 1930 Duesenberg J Derham Tourster | CRP |
| 1933 Duesenberg J Victoria | CRP |
| 1933 Duesenberg SJ Twenty Grand | CRP |
| 1958 Edsel Citation | CRP |
| 1989 Ferrari F40 | CRP |
| 1955 Ford Crown Victoria | CRP |
| 1932 Ford Deuce Coupe Hot Rod | CRP |
| 1932 Ford Deuce Coupe | CRP |
| 1960 Ford Falcon | CRP |
| 1964 Ford Mustang Convertible | CRP |
| 1940 Ford Pickup | CRP |
| 1940 Ford Pickup Sales and Service | CRP |
| 1957 Ford Skyliner | CRP |
| 1996 Ford F-150 Pickup 4WD | CRP |
| 1956 Ford Thunderbird (aqua/white) | CRP |
| 1956 Ford Thunderbird (red) | CRP |
| 1949 Ford Woody Wagon | CRP |
| 1924 Hispano-Suiza | CRP |
| 1925 Hispano-Suiza Kellner | CRP |
| 1938 Jaguar SS100 | CRP |
| 1961 Jaguar XKE | CRP |
| 1985 Lamborghini Countach | CRP |
| 1985 Lamborghini Police | CRP |
| 1941 Lincoln Continental | CRP |
| 1939 Maybach Zeppelin | CRP |
| 1957 Mercedes-Benz 300SC | CRP |
| 1957 Mercedes-Benz 300SC Roadster | CRP |
| 1954 Mercedes-Benz 300SL Gullwing (red) | CRP |

| | |
|---|---:|
| 1954 Mercedes-Benz 300SL Gullwing (silver) | CRP |
| 1935 Mercedes-Benz 500K Roadster | CRP |
| 1935 Mercedes-Benz 770K Pullman | CRP |
| 1926 Mercedes-Benz Model K | CRP |
| 1954 Mercedes-Benz Race Car W196 | CRP |
| 1904 Mercedes-Benz Simplex | CRP |
| 1948 MG-TC Roadster | CRP |
| 1956 Nash Metropolitan | CRP |
| 1912 Packard Victoria | CRP |
| 1988 Porsche 911 Carrera Targa (black) | CRP |
| 1988 Porsche 911 Carrera Targa (red) | CRP |
| 1977 Richard Petty Stock Car | CRP |
| 1970 Richard Petty Superbird | CRP |
| 1992 Rolls-Royce Corniche IV (white) | CRP |
| 1992 Rolls-Royce Corniche IV (blue) | CRP |
| 1929 Rolls-Royce Phantom I | CRP |
| 1955 Rolls-Royce Silver Cloud | CRP |
| 1907 Rolls-Royce Silver Ghost | CRP |
| 1925 Rolls-Royce Silver Ghost Tourer | CRP |
| 1911 Rolls-Royce Tourer | CRP |
| 1915 Stutz Bearcat | CRP |
| 1928 Stutz Black Hawk | CRP |
| 1948 Tucker | CRP |
| 1967 Volkswagen Beetle (yellow) | CRP |
| 1967 Volkswagen Beetle (white) | CRP |
| 1967 Volkswagen Cabriolet | CRP |
| 1962 Volkswagen Microbus | CRP |

### 1/32 scale (alphabetical by marque):
| | |
|---|---:|
| 1922 Ahrens-Fox R-K-4 | CRP |
| 1993 Mack Elite CL 613 Cab | CRP |
| 1993 Mack Elite CL 613 | CRP |
| 1993 Mack Refrigerated Trailer | CRP |
| 1939 Peterbilt-First Truck | CRP |
| 1987 Peterbilt 379 (red) | CRP |
| 1987 Peterbilt 379 (black) | CRP |
| 1987 Refrigerated Trailer for Peterbilt 379 | CRP |

*The Franklin Mint's 1948 Chrysler Town & Country Convertible in 1/24 scale. This model made its debut in late 1993.*

# Gaiety Toy

Gaiety Toys were made by Castle Art Products Ltd., of Birmingham, England, in the late 1940s. Castle Art was started in 1946, manufacturing precision die cast casters and sinkers. They branched out into toy production in the late 1940s with a line of die cast cars.

The new Line, called Gaiety Toy, included a three-wheel Morgan Sports Car (4.75 inches in length), which had a separately mounted steering wheel, but no driver figure. There were also three different Race Cars. The largest measured about five inches in length, and had a single driver. The slightly smaller "medium" length unit had two figures; and the smallest, at around 3.25 inches, had a single driver.

Castle Art also supposedly made a (roughly) 1/43 scale Fire Engine as part of the Gaiety line, but the author has yet to see evidence of its existence.

In addition to standard painted colors such as blue or red, Gaiety Toy cars also came in a chromed finish. This finish generally stands up well over time. The cars also came with or without a clockwork motor (although there is disagreement among collectors as to whether the smallest Race

Car ever came with the motor). The Morgan apparently was made for a time with rubber wheels on the front and a metal wheel at the rear. It has also been seen with metal fronts and a plastic rear. The Race Cars came with metal wheels, although some also had plastic tires on the metal wheels.

It is believed that the Gaiety Toy line was discontinued by 1950, which accounts at least in part for their scarcity today.

At least some, if not all, of the Gaiety cars came in individual boxes, which are now quite rare. One of the boxes for the Race Cars depicts a wonderful period racing scene. The key for the clockwork motor also rarely turns up with these toys.

A near mint to mint example of any of the Gaiety cars, in the original box and with the original key, could easily sell for $100-$200. An excellent to near mint unboxed example with no key would sell for $40-$75.

Castle Art Products continues in business in Birmingham today, manufacturing cabinet hardware such as drawer knobs, as well as metal hardware and unusual items such as plaques for coffins.

# Gama

Gama is short for Georg Adam Mangold, a German company located in Fürth, which is near Nuremberg. Mangold founded the company in 1882, and Gama produced clockwork-powered tinplate toys for many years.

In 1959, the company expanded into the die cast toy (model) business, releasing a line of 1/43 scale cars and 1/50 to 1/60 scale trucks and construction models. (Larger scales, such as 1/32 to 1/35, would occasionally be used for certain models.) Gama models were well detailed, and often offered lots of "play value," with features like opening doors and working cranes being the norm.

As might be expected, the names Mercedes-Benz, Opel and Volkswagen have always figured prominently in the product line, as has Faun with its numerous categories of trucks. The 1/50 scale #917 Faun Street Sweeper, made during the 1970s, is one of the few die cast models of street sweepers in existence.

## Name Changes and Number Switches

Production of Gama die cast models has continued to the present day, with a mix of contemporary and older subjects. The 1990s have seen new 1/43 models such as the Opel

Astra, Opel Corsa, the BMW 525i and an excellent Messerschmitt "bubble" car in convertible and hardtop form, which debuted in 1993. Even 1/24 scale hasn't been ignored, with a BMW M3 being offered in that scale beginning in 1993.

In 1994, Gama apparently decided to begin putting out its Gama models under the "Schuco" banner. Gama purchased the Schuco name, along with some of the original tooling for Schuco products, in 1980. Gama has marketed re-issues of some original Schuco tin toys for a number of years, and the 1994 name switch for the die cast series may have been caused by the success of the tinplate items. The Schuco name is very well known in the United States, and in Europe, and the company no doubt wanted to take advantage of that name recognition.

Gama-Schucos released in the last few years are evidence of Gama having upped their game in terms of quality: the models are now very well detailed and generally quite accurate. The current 1/43 models generally sell in the $20-$25 range.

Although many of the older Gama models had numbers starting with 8 or 9, the company instituted a new numbering system in the early 1980s that still confuses collectors today. Many of the 8- and 9-series of models, for example, appeared with new numbers in the 1100 series; these are noted as "renumberings" in the listing. Some models also popped up in the larger scale 2000 series, which are not listed here.

For more information on the numbering system, consult Dr. Edward Force's excellent book *Classic Miniature Vehicles Made in Germany,* which also contains details on the 2000 series.

Gama also occasionally repackaged the models of other manufacturers, resulting in, for example, a Conrad model being found in a Gama box (French Norev models were also sometimes used)—perfectly fine for business (especially when a company can purchase a bulk of models for a low price, then resell for a profit), but confusing for collectors.

The following listing is comprised of the original 1960s through 1980s line of Gama models. "CRP" refers to Current Retail Price, which is usually around $20-$25 for the 1/43 scale models.

*At left, Gama #9231, the Faun Power Shovel Truck, with original box. The crank at the rear operates the crane assembly.*

*At right, #924 Faun Dump Truck. Gama produced this 1/50 scale model for nearly 20 years, until the late 1970s. It also came in other color combinations.*

| # | Name | Price |
|---|------|-------|
| 420 | Deutz Intrac 2005 Tractor | $25 |
| 421 | Deutz Intrac 2005 Tractor with Sprayer Tank | 30 |
| 423 | Claas Dominator 100 Combine Harvester | 40 |
| 423 | Claas Dominator Combine Harvester | 30 |
| 424 | Deutz Tractor | 25 |
| 425 | Service Tractor | 25 |
| 427 | Mercedes-Benz Unimog U 120/425 | 25 |
| 428 | Claas Jaguar Combine Harvester | 40 |
| 430 | Hanomag Excavator | 25 |
| 4301 | Excavator with crane | 25 |
| 431 | Excavator | 25 |
| 446 | Volkswagen Transporter | 20 |
| 4464 | Volkswagen Transporter Ambulance | 20 |
| 4465 | Volkswagen Transporter Mail Van | 20 |
| 447 | Volkswagen Caravelle School Bus | 20 |
| 714 | Leopard Tank | 30 |
| 716 | Armored Vehicle | 30 |
| 717 | U.N. Armored Vehicle | 30 |
| 808 | Volkswagen 1302 "ADAC" | 30 |
| 815 | Volkswagen 1302 Mail Car | 30 |
| 816 | Volkswagen 1302 Fire Chief | 30 |
| 833 | Volkswagen 1302 "POLIZEI" | 40 |
| 8337 | Volkswagen Army Staff Car | 25 |
| 8338 | Volkswagen THW Car | 35 |
| 890 | Opel Kadett | 25 |
| 8901 | Opel Kadett "ADAC" | 20 |
| 891 | BMW M1 | 25 |
| 8914 | BMW M1 Rally | 25 |
| 8915 | BMW M1 Kit | 25 |
| 892 | Porsche 924 | 20 |
| 893 | Opel Rekord | 20 |
| 8931 | Opel Rekord "POLICE" | 20 |
| 8932 | Opel Rekord Doctor's car | 20 |
| 894 | BMW 733 | 20 |
| 8943 | BMW 733 Taxi | 25 |
| 895 | Volkswagen Golf | 20 |
| 8951 | Volkswagen Golf PTT Mail Car | 25 |

| # | Name | Price |
|---|------|-------|
| 8952 | Volkswagen Golf AVD Service Car | $25 |
| 898 | Volkswagen 1302 | 20 |
| 8981 | Volkswagen 1302 with paddleboats | 35 |
| 899 | Volkswagen 1200 | 60 |
| 900 | Volkswagen 1200 | 80 |
| 901 | Ford Taunus 17M | 80 |
| 902 | Opel Rekord | 80 |
| 903 | Jeep | 25 |
| 9031 | Safari Jeep | 20 |
| 9034 | Police Jeep | 25 |
| 90347 | Army Jeep | 15 |
| 9035 | Safari Jeep and Trailer | 25 |
| 9037 | Army Jeep | 20 |
| 9038 | Jeep and Trailer | 30 |
| 90387 | Army Jeep and Trailer | 25 |
| 90397 | Army Jeep and Field Kitchen Trailer | 30 |
| 90398 | THW Jeep and Field Kitchen Trailer | 20 |
| 904 | Army Jeep with Top | 20 |
| 9047 | Medical Corps Jeep | 20 |
| 9049 | Jeep and Trailer | 25 |
| 905 | Army Jeep with Machine Guns | 25 |
| 9051 | BMW R 75/S Motorcycle | 15 |
| 9052 | BMW R 75/S Racing Motorcycle | 15 |
| 9053 | BMW R 75/S Police Motorcycle | 15 |
| 90537 | BMW R 75/S Army Motorcycle | 15 |
| 9057 | Army Jeep with Machine Guns | 20 |
| 906 | Army Jeep with Searchlight | 25 |
| 9067 | Army Jeep with Searchlight | 20 |
| 907 | BMW 600 | 90 |
| 908 | Army Jeep with Radar | 60 |
| 908 | Volkswagen 1200 "ADAC" | 90 |
| 909 | Trailer | 10 |
| 910 | Army Jeep with Lance Rockets | 25 |
| 910 | Mercedes-Benz Tipping Truck | 90 |
| 9107 | Army Jeep with Lance Rockets | 25 |
| 911 | Mercedes-Benz Wrecker | 45 |
| 912 | Mercedes-Benz Fire Engine | 50 |
| 912 | Faun Fire Engine | 25 |
| 9121 | Faun Fire Engine | 25 |

| # | Name | Price |
|---|------|-------|
| 9122 | Faun Fire Engine | $20 |
| 9123 | Faun Fire Engine | 20 |
| 913 | Buick Invicta Coupe | 100 |
| 9130 | Buick Invicta Coupe | 80 |
| 914 | Fiat 25 R Tractor | 35 |
| 9141 | Ford 4000 Tractor | 25 |
| 915 | Volkswagen 1200 Mail Car | 90 |
| 916 | Volkswagen 1200 Fire Chief | 90 |
| 917 | Fiat 1800 Sedan | 60 |
| 9170 | Fiat 1800 Sedan | 50 |
| 917 | Faun Street Sweeper | 25 |
| 918 | Volkswagen Van "ARAL" | 75 |
| 9181 | Volkswagen Van "CONTINENTAL" | 75 |
| 9182 | Volkswagen Bus "GAMA" | 60 |
| 9183 | Volkswagen Bus with Roof Rack | 40 |
| 9184 | Volkswagen Safari Bus | 40 |
| 919 | Faun Cement Truck | 50 |
| 9191 | Faun Cement Trailer | 40 |
| 9192 | Faun Cement Truck | 40 |
| 9195 | Faun Cement Mixer Truck | 35 |
| 920 | Builder's Crane | 25 |
| 9201 | Builder's Crane | 20 |
| 9202 | Builder's Crane and Equipment | 60 |
| 9205 | Linde Fork Lift | 15 |
| 921 | Mercedes-Benz Covered Truck | 40 |
| 922 | Faun Excavator Truck | 45 |
| 9221 | Faun Excavator Truck | 25 |
| 923 | Faun Power Shovel Truck | 45 |
| 9231 | Faun Power Shovel Truck | 25 |
| 924 | Faun Dump Truck | 50 |
| 925 | O. & K. Excavator | 25 |
| 9251 | Demag Excavator | 20 |
| 9260 | O. & K. Power Shovel | 20 |
| 9261 | Demag Power Shovel | 20 |
| 9262 | JCB Hydraulic Shovel | 20 |
| 927 | Faun Dump Truck | 35 |
| 9271 | Faun Dump Truck | 25 |
| 9272 | Faun Covered Semi-Trailer | 35 |
| 92721 | Faun Cage Semi-Trailer | 20 |

| # | Name | Price |
|---|------|-------|
| 9274 | Faun Container Semi-Trailer | $35 |
| 9277 | Faun Army Dump Truck | 35 |
| 928 | Volkswagen "COCA-COLA" Truck | 120 |
| 9280 | Mercedes-Benz Dump Truck | 20 |
| 9281 | Mercedes-Benz Power Shovel | 20 |
| 92812 | Mercedes-Benz Ladder Truck | 30 |
| 92813 | Mercedes-Benz Searchlight Truck | 35 |
| 92817 | Mercedes-Benz Army Excavator | 30 |
| 92818 | Mercedes-Benz THW Excavator | 40 |
| 9282 | Mercedes-Benz Container Semi | 25 |
| 92821 | Mercedes-Benz Cage Semi | 30 |
| 92832 | Mercedes-Benz Tanker | 30 |
| 9284 | Mercedes-Benz Covered Semi | 25 |
| 9287 | Volkswagen "COCA-COLA" Truck | 95 |
| 9288 | Mercedes-Benz Wrecker | 25 |
| 929 | Faun Dump Truck | 50 |
| 9291 | Faun Tiltcab Dump Truck | 30 |
| 92927 | Faun Covered Army Semi-Trailer | 25 |
| 9294 | Faun Container Semi-Trailer | 25 |
| 92957 | Faun Army Semi-Trailer | 25 |
| 9296 | Faun Covered Truck | 25 |
| 92967 | Faun Covered Army Truck | 25 |
| 92968 | Faun Covered THW Truck | 20 |
| 9297 | Faun Covered Truck and Trailer | 20 |
| 9298 | Faun Crane Truck | 20 |
| 92987 | Faun Army Crane Truck | 20 |
| 9299 | Faun Tower Truck | 20 |
| 930 | Fiat Tractor and Covered Trailer | 45 |
| 9301 | Hay Trailer | 10 |
| 931 | Mercedes-Benz Truck and Trailer | 50 |
| 932 | Mercedes-Benz "SHELL" Tank Truck | 50 |
| 9321 | Faun "ESSO" Tank Truck | 30 |
| 93217 | Faun Army Tank Truck | 65 |
| 933 | Volkswagen 1200 "POLIZEI" | 70 |
| 933 | Volkswagen 1200 Police Car | 70 |
| 934 | Fiat 25 R Tractor with Plow | 45 |
| 9341 | Ford 4000 Tractor with Plow | 25 |
| 935 | Mercedes-Benz 220 S | 70 |
| 9350 | Mercedes-Benz 230 S | 60 |
| 9353 | Mercedes-Benz 230 S "POLIZEI" | 75 |
| 9354 | Mercedes-Benz 230 S "POLIZEI" | 75 |
| 9355 | Mercedes-Benz 230 S Taxi | 75 |
| 936 | Opel Rekord | 65 |
| 9360 | Opel Rekord | 65 |
| 937 | D.K.W. Munga | 65 |
| 9371 | D.K.W. Munga | 35 |
| 9377 | D.K.W. Army Munga | 35 |
| 9378 | D.K.W. THW Munga | 35 |

| # | Name | Price |
|---|------|-------|
| 938 | BMW 700 Coupe | $75 |
| 9380 | BMW 700 Coupe | 75 |
| 939 | Renault Floride | 55 |
| 9390 | Renault Floride | 55 |
| 940 | Fiat 25 R Tractor with Shovel | 45 |
| 9401 | Ford 4000 Tractor with Shovel | 25 |
| 9401 | Deutz Shovel Loader | 25 |
| 9402 | Krupp Crane Truck | 20 |
| 94021 | Krupp Crane Truck | 20 |
| 94027 | Krupp Army Crane Truck | 25 |
| 94028 | Krupp THW Crane Truck | 25 |
| 94031 | Krupp Bucket Truck | 25 |
| 94041 | Krupp Dump Truck | 20 |
| 94047 | Krupp Army Dump Truck | 20 |
| 94048 | Krupp THW Dump Truck | 25 |
| 9405 | Krupp Low Loader | 20 |
| 94051 | Krupp Low Loader with House | 30 |
| 94057 | Krupp Army Low Loader | 25 |
| 9406 | Krupp Fire Truck | 25 |
| 94067 | Krupp Army Radar Truck | 25 |
| 94068 | Krupp THW Truck | 25 |
| 9407 | Krupp Livestock Truck | 25 |
| 9408 | Faun Dump Truck | 20 |
| 94081 | Faun Pipe Transporter | 30 |
| 94087 | Faun Army Dump Truck | 20 |
| 94090 | Faun Cement Mixer | 20 |
| 94091 | Faun Garbage Truck | 20 |
| 94092 | Faun Car Carrier | 30 |
| 94093 | Faun Farm Truck | 20 |
| 94094 | Flat Trailer | 10 |
| 94095 | Faun Street Sweeper | 30 |
| 941 | Ford Taunus 12 M Coupe | 60 |
| 94111 | Deutz Shovel Loader with Trailer | 30 |
| 9412 | Deutz Shovel Loader | 20 |
| 94127 | Deutz Army Shovel Loader | 20 |
| 94128 | Deutz THW Shovel Loader | 20 |
| 942 | D.K.W. F-102 | 65 |
| 9420 | Clark Loader | 25 |
| 943 | Ford Taunus 20M Hardtop | 55 |
| 944 | Mercedes-Benz 250 | 65 |
| 9440 | Ahlmann Loader | 25 |
| 945 | Volkswagen 1600 Fastback | 60 |
| 946 | BMW 2000 CS Coupe | 50 |
| 947 | BMW 1800 Sedan | 50 |
| 9470 | BMW 1800 Sedan | 50 |
| 948 | Volkswagen Fire Bus | 60 |
| 9487 | Volkswagen Fire Bus | 50 |
| 949 | Volkswagen 1500 | 55 |

| # | Name | Price |
|---|------|-------|
| 9490 | Volkswagen 1500 | $55 |
| 9491 | Volkswagen 411 LE | 50 |
| 9492 | Audi 100 | 30 |
| 950 | Volkswagen Van "SHELL" | 75 |
| 950 | Faun Low Loader | 25 |
| 9501 | Faun Crane Truck | 25 |
| 9502 | Faun Excavator Truck | 25 |
| 9503 | Faun Telescopic Crane | 25 |
| 9507 | Faun Tank Transporter | 30 |
| 951 | Volkswagen Van | 50 |
| 9517 | Volkswagen Van "GAMA" | 50 |
| 9518 | Volkswagen Van "ESSO" | 50 |
| 952 | Volkswagen Mail Van | 50 |
| 9521 | Volkswagen Mail Van | 40 |
| 9527 | Volkswagen Mail Van | 40 |
| 9530 | Volkswagen Bus | 30 |
| 9531 | Volkswagen Bus "POLICE" | 30 |
| 9532 | Volkswagen Ambulance | 30 |
| 954 | Volkswagen Ambulance Bus | 60 |
| 9541 | Volkswagen Ambulance Van | 60 |
| 9542 | Volkswagen Fire Truck | 60 |
| 9547 | Volkswagen Ambulance Bus | 45 |
| 95477 | Volkswagen Army Ambulance | 25 |
| 95478 | Volkswagen THW Ambulance | 20 |
| 955 | Volkswagen Bus | 60 |
| 9550 | Linde Fork Lift | 20 |
| 956 | Volkswagen Pickup Truck | 50 |
| 9560 | Self-Propelled Excavator | 25 |
| 9561 | Volkswagen Pickup Truck | 35 |
| 957 | Volkswagen Cherry Picker | 60 |
| 9571 | Volkswagen "ADAC" Wrecker | 65 |
| 9572 | Volkswagen Cherry Picker | 30 |
| 9572 | Volkswagen Fire Truck | 35 |
| 9574 | Volkswagen Wrecker | 30 |
| 9575 | Volkswagen Fire Truck | 30 |
| 958 | Volkswagen Ladder Truck | 60 |
| 9581 | Volkswagen Ladder Truck | 30 |
| 959 | Volkswagen "POLICE" Bus | 60 |
| 959 | Volkswagen "POLIZEI" Bus | 60 |
| 9591 | Volkswagen "POLICE" Van | 60 |
| 9591 | Volkswagen "POLIZEI" Van | 60 |
| 9597 | Volkswagen "POLIZEI" Bus | 50 |
| 9600 | Fiat Abarth Record Car | 55 |
| 9601 | Porsche Carrera 6 | 35 |
| 9603 | Lotus-Ford 40 | 30 |
| 9604 | Chaparral 2F | 30 |
| 9605 | Porsche 917 | 30 |
| 9606 | Abarth 2000 Pinin Farina | 30 |
| 9610 | Ferrari Testa Rossa | 60 |
| 9620 | Opel Rekord | 45 |
| 9630 | N.S.U. Prinz 4 | 45 |
| 964 | Army Tank | 20 |
| 965 | Opel Kadett | 40 |
| 9650 | Opel Kadett | 40 |
| 9651 | Opel Kadett Rally | 40 |
| 9660 | Opel Rekord | 40 |
| 9670 | N.S.U. RO 80 | 35 |
| 9680 | Mercedes-Benz 350 SE | 30 |
| 96807 | Mercedes-Benz 350 SE Staff Car | 30 |
| 9681 | Mercedes-Benz 450 SE "POLIZEI" | 35 |
| 96882 | Mercedes-Benz 450 SE and Caravan | 30 |
| 96883 | Mercedes-Benz 450 SE and Boat Trailer | 30 |
| 9690 | Fiat 850 Coupe | 50 |

*Two Gama cars. At the left is a #902 Opel Rekord; at right is a #901 Ford Taunus 17M. Both cars are fitted with the later-style plastic wheels; earlier versions had turned-metal wheels. Both the Rekord and the Taunus were made from the beginning of Gama production (1959) until about 1965.*

| # | Name | Price |
|---|------|-------|
| 96983 | Camper and Boat Trailer ........ | $25 |
| 970 | Mercedes-Benz 230 SL ......... | 40 |
| 971 | Opel Admiral ................ | 30 |
| 9713 | Opel Admiral "POLIZEI" ........ | 60 |
| 9714 | Opel Admiral "POLIZEI" ........ | 40 |
| 9715 | Opel Admiral mechanical ....... | 60 |
| 972 | Mercedes-Benz 600 .......... | 45 |
| 9721 | Mercedes-Benz 600 gift set ..... | 50 |
| 973 | Porsche 911 ............... | 30 |
| 9734 | Porsche 911 "POLIZEI" ........ | 30 |
| 9735 | Porsche 911 "POLIZEI" ........ | 40 |
| 9735 | Porsche 911 Rally ........... | 30 |
| 9736 | Porsche 911 "POLIZEI" ........ | 30 |
| 974 | 1893 Benz Vis-a-vis .......... | 15 |
| 975 | 1893 Benz Victoria .......... | 15 |
| 976 | 1925 Opel Roadster .......... | 15 |
| 977 | 1925 Opel Limousine ......... | 15 |
| 978 | 1901 Mercedes-Benz Simplex .... | 15 |
| 979 | 1910 Three-Wheel Mail Coach .... | 35 |
| 980 | Caravan ................. | 30 |
| 981 | Luggage Trailer ............ | 10 |
| 9810 | Mercedes-Benz C 111 ........ | 25 |
| 9812 | Flat Trailer ............... | 10 |
| 982 | Tabbert Camping Trailer ....... | 15 |
| 9820 | VW-Porsche 914 ........... | 20 |
| 9821 | VW-Porsche 914 "POLIZEI" ..... | 25 |
| 9830 | Opel GT 1900 ............. | 20 |
| 9840 | Maserati Indy ............. | 25 |
| 985 | 1903 Opel Darracq .......... | 20 |
| 986 | 1909 Opel Doktorwagen ....... | 20 |
| 987 | 1928 Mercedes-Benz SSK ...... | 15 |
| 988 | 1892 Peugeot Vis-a-vis ....... | 20 |
| 989 | 1896 Peugeot Vis-a-vis ....... | 20 |
| 990 | 1901 Peugeot Decauville ...... | 20 |
| 991 | 1911 Fiat 4 Phaeton ......... | 25 |
| 992 | 1912 Fiat 4 Open Torpedo ..... | 25 |
| 995 | Ford Taunus .............. | 30 |
| 996 | Ford Consul .............. | 30 |
| 9961 | Ford Consul with Canoes ...... | 35 |
| 997 | Ford Granada ............. | 30 |
| 997 | "Old-timer" Book (three cars) .... | 50 |
| 998 | Traffic Control Gift Set ....... | 60 |
| 999 | Building Machines Gift Set ...... | 60 |

**Minette series:**

| # | Name | Price |
|---|------|-------|
| 1 | Porsche Carrera 6 ........... | 30 |
| 2 | Lotus-Ford 40 ............. | 25 |
| 3 | Cooper-Maserati Formula 1 ..... | 20 |
| 4 | Ferrari 312 Formula 1 ........ | 30 |
| 5 | N.S.U. RO 80 ............. | 25 |
| 6 | Ferrari 312 Formula 1 ........ | 30 |
| 7 | Lola Climax G.P. ........... | 20 |
| 9 | Ferrari 330 P 4 ............ | 35 |
| 10 | Matra Sport .............. | 20 |
| 11 | Lola Chevrolet ............ | 25 |
| 12 | McLaren-Ford G.P. .......... | 25 |
| 13 | Volkswagen 1302 ........... | 35 |
| 30 | Henschel Dump Truck ........ | 40 |
| 31 | Henschel Wrecker .......... | 40 |
| 32 | Henschel Box Truck ......... | 40 |
| 33 | Henschel Quarry Dumper ...... | 40 |

**Models released beginning in the early 1980s with new numbers:**

| # | Name | Price |
|---|------|-------|
| 1102 | BMW 528i Servicemobil ....... | CRP |

| # | Name | Price |
|---|------|-------|
| 1103 | BMW M1 Rally ............. | CRP |
| 1104 | Volkswagen 1302 (renumbering of 898) ..... | CRP |
| 1105 | Opel Kadett (renumbering of 890) ... | CRP |
| 1106 | Opel Kadett "ADAC" (renumbering of 8901) ...... | CRP |
| 1107 | BMW 735i ............... | CRP |
| 1108 | BMW M1 (renumbering of 891) ... | CRP |
| 1109 | BMW M1 Rally (renumbering of 8914) ............ | CRP |
| 1110 | BMW M1 Kit (renumbering of 8915) .. | CRP |
| 1110 | BMW 325i Convertible ....... | CRP |
| 1111 | Porsche 924 (renumbering of 892) .. | CRP |
| 1112 | Opel Rekord (renumbering of 893) .. | CRP |
| 1112 | Opel Kadett Caravan ......... | CRP |
| 1113 | Opel Rekord 2.0 "Polizei" (renumbering of 8931) ...... | CRP |
| 1113 | Mercedes-Benz 190E Danish Taxi .... | CRP |
| 1114 | Opel Rekord 2.0 Doctor Car (renumbering of 8932) ...... | CRP |
| 1114 | Mercedes-Benz 190E Rijkspolitie .. | CRP |
| 1115 | BMW 733i (renumbering of 894) .. | CRP |
| 1116 | BMW 733i Taxi (renumbering of 8943) ...... | CRP |
| 1116 | BMW 528i Taxi ............ | CRP |
| 1117 | Volkswagen Golf (renumbering of 895) ... | CRP |
| 1117 | Mercedes-Benz 190E Taxi ...... | CRP |
| 1118 | Volkswagen Golf AvD Car (renumbering of 8952) ...... | CRP |
| 1118 | Opel Kadett AvD Car ......... | CRP |
| 1119 | Porsche 911 Rally (renumbering of 9735) ...... | CRP |
| 1119 | Porsche 911 Coupe (renumbering of 973) ....... | CRP |
| 1120 | Opel Kadett GSi ........... | CRP |
| 1121 | BMW 325i ............... | CRP |
| 1122 | Opel Kadett GSi ........... | CRP |
| 1123 | Mercedes-Benz 450SE (renumbering of 9680) ...... | CRP |
| 1123 | Mercedes-Benz 190E "Polizei" ... | CRP |
| 1124 | Mercedes-Benz 450SE Camper (renumbering of 96882) ........ | CRP |
| 1124 | Opel Kadett Caravan ......... | CRP |
| 1125 | Mercedes-Benz 450SE Boat Trailer (renumbering of 96883) ...... | CRP |
| 1125 | Volkswagen 411 (renumbering of 9491) ...... | CRP |
| 1126 | Hymermobil Boat Trailer (renumbering of 96983) ...... | CRP |
| 1126 | Opel Rekord Taxi ........... | CRP |
| 1127 | Mercedes-Benz C111 (renumbering of 9810) ...... | CRP |
| 1127 | NSU RO-80 (renumbering of 9670) .. | CRP |
| 1128 | Volkswagen-Porsche 914 (renumbering of 9820) ...... | CRP |
| 1129 | Opel GT (renumbering of 9830) .. | CRP |
| 1130 | Citroën-Maserati (renumbering of 9840).. | CRP |
| 1130 | Opel Omega .............. | CRP |
| 1131 | BMW R75-5 Motorcycle (renumbering of 9052) ...... | CRP |
| 1131 | Opel Omega 3000 .......... | CRP |
| 1133 | Lotus-Ford 40 (renumbering of 9603) .. | CRP |
| 1133 | Opel Senator ............. | CRP |
| 1134 | Chaparral (renumbering of 9604) .... | CRP |

| # | Name | Price |
|---|------|-------|
| 1134 | Opel Senator 7 Race Car Trailer .... | CRP |
| 1135 | Porsche 917 (renumbering of 9605) .. | CRP |
| 1135 | Opel Kadett GSi Convertible ...... | CRP |
| 1136 | Abarth Pinin Farina 2000 (renumbering of 9606) ...... | CRP |
| 1136 | Volkswagen Corrado ......... | CRP |
| 1137 | Jeep and Trailer (renumbering of 9035) ...... | CRP |
| 1137 | Mercedes-Benz SL .......... | CRP |
| 1140 | Opel Ascona ............. | CRP |
| 1141 | Opel Ascona ............. | CRP |
| 1142 | BMW 633 CSi ............. | CRP |
| 1143 | Citroën 2CV6 ............. | CRP |
| 1144 | Citroën CX .............. | CRP |
| 1145 | Porsche 911 Carrera ........ | CRP |
| 1145 | Audi 80 "Polizei" .......... | CRP |
| 1146 | Audi 80 Taxi ............. | CRP |
| 1148 | Audi GT 5S .............. | CRP |
| 1149 | BMW 528i .............. | CRP |
| 1150 | Mercedes-Benz 230G ........ | CRP |
| 1151 | Mercedes-Benz 230G Boat Trailer .... | CRP |
| 1152 | Opel Kadett Race Car ........ | CRP |
| 1153 | Volkswagen Passat GLS ....... | CRP |
| 1153 | BMW M3 ............... | CRP |
| 1154 | Volkswagen Passat Variant ..... | CRP |
| 1154 | BMW M3 Race Car .......... | CRP |
| 1155 | BMW 528i "Polizei" ......... | CRP |
| 1156 | BMW 528i Doctor Car ........ | CRP |
| 1157 | Volkswagen Scirocco ........ | CRP |
| 1157 | BMW 528i "Politi" .......... | CRP |
| 1158 | Opel Corsa .............. | CRP |
| 1159 | Opel Corsa .............. | CRP |
| 1161 | Opel Vectra ............. | CRP |
| 1162 | Opel Vectra ............. | CRP |
| 1163 | Opel Kadett GSi Rally ........ | CRP |
| 1164 | Opel Lotus .............. | CRP |
| 1165 | BMW 528 Fire Chief Car ...... | CRP |
| 1166 | BMW 323i ............... | CRP |
| 1167 | Mercedes-Benz 190 ......... | CRP |
| 1168 | Volkswagen Polo ........... | CRP |
| 1168 | Mercedes-Benz 300CE ....... | CRP |
| 1169 | Volkswagen Santana ........ | CRP |
| 1169 | BMW 325i ............... | CRP |
| 1170 | Opel Ascona "Polizei" ....... | CRP |
| 1171 | Opel Ascona Doctor Car ...... | CRP |
| 1172 | Opel Ascona Fire Chief Car .... | CRP |
| 1173 | Audi Quattro Rally ......... | CRP |
| 1173 | Audi 80 Quattro ........... | CRP |
| 1174 | BMW 528i Camping Trailer ..... | CRP |
| 1175 | Hymer Wohnmobil .......... | CRP |
| 1176 | Opel Rekord 2.0E .......... | CRP |
| 1177 | Volkswagen Polo Coupe ...... | CRP |
| 1177 | Volkswagen Passat Sedan ..... | CRP |
| 1178 | Volkswagen Passat Variant ..... | CRP |
| 1179 | Mercedes-Benz 230SL (renumbering of 970) ........ | CRP |
| 1180 | Mercedes-Benz 600 (renumbering of 972) ........ | CRP |
| 1181 | 1893 Benz Vis-a-vis (renumbering of 974) ........ | CRP |
| 1182 | 1893 Benz Victoria (renumbering of 975) ........ | CRP |
| 1183 | 1925 Opel Roadster (renumbering of 976) ............. | CRP |

| # | Name | Price | # | Name | Price | # | Name | Price |
|---|------|-------|---|------|-------|---|------|-------|
| 1184 | 1901 Mercedes-Benz Simplex (renumbering of 978) | CRP | 1196 | Opel Kadett GSI | CRP | 1236 | Mercedes-Benz Container Semi (renumbering of 9282) | $20 |
| 1185 | 1903 Opel Darracq (renumbering of 985) | CRP | 1197 | Vauxhall Astra | CRP | 1236 | Mercedes-Benz Covered Semi | 20 |
| 1186 | 1909 Opel Doktorwagen (renumbering of 986) | CRP | 1198 | Opel Kadett GLS | CRP | 1401 | Faun Street Sweeper (renumbering of 917) | 20 |
| 1187 | 1928 Mercedes-Benz SSK (renumbering of 987) | CRP | 1199 | Opel Kadett GL Caravan | CRP | 1402 | Linde Fork Lift (renumbering of 9205) | 20 |
| 1188 | 1892 Peugeot Vis-a-vis (renumbering of 988) | CRP | 1201 | Volkswagen Bulli Bus (renumbering of 9530) | $20 | 1405 | Mercedes-Benz 230 Wrecker | 20 |
| 1189 | 1896 Peugeot Vis-a-vis (renumbering of 989) | CRP | 1201 | Volkswagen Kombi | 20 | 1406 | Linde H40 Fork Lift | 15 |
| 1190 | 1901 Peugeot Decauville (renumbering of 990) | CRP | 1202 | Volkswagen Bulli "Polizei" (renumbering of 9530) | 20 | 1502 | Hydraulic Shovel (renumbering of 9262) | 20 |
| 1191 | 1911 Fiat 4 Phaeton (renumbering of 991) | CRP | 1203 | Volkswagen Bulli Ambulance (renumbering of 9530) | 20 | 1503 | Mercedes-Benz Excavator (renumbering of 9281) | 20 |
| 1192 | 1912 Fiat 4 Open Torpedo (renumbering of 992) | CRP | 1205 | Volkswagen Transporter | 20 | 1504 | Builder's Crane (renumbering of 9202) | 20 |
| 1193 | Audi 100 | CRP | 1207 | Volkswagen Transporter (renumbering of 9517) | 20 | 1602 | Volkswagen Cherry Picker (renumbering of 9572) | 20 |
| 1193 | 1925 Opel Limousine (renumbering of 977) | CRP | 1207 | Volkswagen Transporter (no logo) | 20 | 1604 | Mercedes-Benz Wrecker (renumbering of 9288) | 20 |
| 1194 | 1910 Three-wheel Mail Coach (renumbering of 979) | CRP | 1208 | Volkswagen Pickup (renumbering of 9561) | 20 | 1605 | Mercedes-Benz Ladder Truck (renumbering of 92812) | 20 |
| 1195 | Opel Kadett GLS | CRP | 1231 | Mercedes-Benz Open Truck (renumbering of 9280) | 20 | 1606 | Mercedes-Benz Searchlight Truck (renumbering of 92813) | 20 |
|  |  |  | 1233 | Mercedes-Benz Covered Semi | 20 |  |  |  |
|  |  |  | 1234 | Mercedes-Benz Cage Semi (renumbering of 92821) | 20 |  |  |  |
|  |  |  | 1234 | Mercedes-Benz Covered Semi | 20 |  |  |  |

# Gamda

Start a discussion about the countries that have been major players in the die cast toy industry, and Israel is not likely to be part of the dialog. England, of course; Germany, Italy, France, yes; the United States and Japan, certainly. But Israel?

It turns out that Israel did indeed make a contribution to the field, and an important one. Habonim, a company located in Kibbutz Kfar Hanassi in northern Israel, purchased some old tooling from a Major Denfield. The tooling had been used by a British manufacturer (some historians believe it was D.C.M.T.) to produce a series of 1/43 scale die cast models during the late 1950s. In 1962, Habonim used the tooling to begin manufacture of a new line of die cast models, which it called "Gamda," and which included four of the ex-D.C.M.T. models. Habonim upgraded the models somewhat, adding window glazing and more attractive paint jobs. The Gamda cars were generally about 1/43 scale, while most of the trucks were 1/50 scale.

As time went on, new Gamdas were added, eventually bringing the total number of models in the series to more than thirty. As can be seen in the photos, the models were generally simple and rather crude in appearance, but this is part of their charm to collectors today.

Certain Gamdas, however, were very accurate representations of full-size vehicles, including the rare Bedford Driving School truck pictured here. This model is the same casting as the #621 3-ton Army Wagon made by Dinky from

1954-1963. Meccano, the manufacturer of Dinky Toys, apparently passed the tooling onto Habonim. Another accurate (and very sought after) Gamda was the Leyland "Egged" Bus, which came with metal interior seats and suspension. For that matter, even the ex-D.C.M.T. Buick Roadmaster was recognizable as a 1953-era Buick (particularly from the front, with its distinctive "smiling" Buick grille), although it was a bit too long and angular.

Since Gamdas were manufactured primarily for the home market in Israel, the series featured a number of military and United Nations vehicles. With the unpredictable political situation that existed, children could see these vehicles on the nation's streets every day.

*The Articulated Timber Truck. The log was made of real wood.*

Habonim got their money's worth from this one: Many of the Gamda trucks were variations of this basic cab/chassis unit. This is the Military Truck; note the plastic wheel hubs.

The Gamda Buick Roadmaster, which Habonim re-issued as a Gamda from tooling originally used by another manufacturer. The original box has one side in English, the other in Hebrew.

The rare Gamda Bedford "Driving School" Truck. This was a re-issue of the Dinky Toys #621, 3-ton Army Wagon.

Gamdas sold well enough to remain in production until 1965, at which point the line was discontinued. They were not exported out of Israel, which accounts for the difficulty in finding them today.

At some point during the late 1960s, Habonim entered into an agreement with another Israeli company, Koor, to launch a new series of 1/43 scale die cast models. This new line, designated "Sabra," would be imported into the United States by Cragstan as "Detroit Seniors." For more information, see the section entitled Sabra.

Gamdas came with rubber tires, and the earliest examples had spun metal hubs. Later, other types of wheel were used including a concave aluminum unit, and then a concave plastic wheel. Gamda baseplates were die cast, and were generally smooth, non-detailed affairs, with "MADE IN ISRAEL" and "GAMDA" (in either English and Hebrew or just Hebrew) in raised lettering.

The boxes for these models were quite colorful, with the Gamda logo (a traffic light) and product name in English on one side, and the same information in Hebrew on the opposite side. The remaining two sides had three circles—red, yellow and green (like a traffic light)—on a black background. One of the end flaps featured a drawing of the model inside.

The following listing comprises all of the Gamda models known to the author at present. In addition to these models, there apparently was also a set of military vehicles produced at some point. How many vehicles were included in the set is unknown, so it is not possible to assign a current value for such a set if found today.

The values in this listing are for near mint to mint examples in the original box.

| Name | Price |
| --- | --- |
| Ford Prefect (cream, green) | $60 |
| Buick Roadmaster Coupe (white/red) | 85 |
| Daimler Conquest Saloon (gray) | 100 |
| Leyland "Egged" Bus (blue/gray) | 150 |
| Bedford "Driving School" Truck | 85 |
| Covered Dairy Truck "TNUVA" (blue/cream) | 70 |
| Covered Truck "AMCOR" | 55 |
| Covered Mail Truck | 75 |
| Tipping Truck | 60 |
| Truck | 60 |
| Dump Truck | 50 |
| Mobile Canteen Truck | 75 |
| Articulated Tanker "DELEK" | 100 |
| Articulated Tanker "PAZ" | 100 |

| Name | Price |
| --- | --- |
| Articulated Tanker "SONOL" | $100 |
| Articulated Tanker "TNUVA" | 100 |
| Articulated Tanker U.N. (white) | 100 |
| Articulated Flat Truck (blue/red) | 70 |
| Articulated Timber Truck (blue/red) | 70 |
| Massey Ferguson Tractor (red) | 65 |
| Quicklime Spreader | 35 |
| Willys Jeep (white, red) | 50 |
| Willys Jeep U.N. (white) | 50 |
| Willys Military Jeep (tan) | 50 |
| Willys Military Police Jeep (green) | 50 |
| Willys Military Ambulance (tan) | 60 |
| Willys Station Wagon Van (orange) | 90 |
| Willys Station Wagon Army Van (tan) | 90 |

| Name | Price |
| --- | --- |
| Willys Station Wagon Police Van (green) | $90 |
| Willys Station Wagon Ambulance (white) | 100 |
| 25-pounder Gun (tan) | 25 |
| Military Truck (tan) | 55 |
| Centurion tank-1/45 (tan) | 60 |
| Centurion tank-1/90 (tan) | 40 |
| Centurion tank-1/120 (tan) | 30 |
| Armored Car (tan) | 55 |
| Tank Transporter (tan) | 80 |
| Military Covered Truck (tan) | 70 |
| Truck with Gas Cylinders | 75 |
| Vanguard Ambulance (white) | 85 |
| Vanguard Military Ambulance (tan) | 70 |

# Gasqui

Gasqui toys were made in Belgium, beginning around 1947. Like full-size cars of the immediate post-war period, some of the Gasqui's were based on pre-war designs; the Buick Coupe and Plymouth Sedan, based on 1942 and 1939 models respectively, are good examples.

This Belgian brand also included a Tatra, the Czechoslovakian car that had gained a reputation in the 1930s for being fast but unstable, and therefore lethal. The Gasqui model is one of the few ever produced of the Tatra.

Gasquis were simple castings, with no window glazing. But they were of acceptable accuracy when compared with the Dinky Toys of the same period, and at least two of the models came with clockwork motors. And, like the competition, Gasqui made their cars 1/43 scale, with the trucks being about 1/50 scale.

Gasquis appear to have gone out of production in the early 1950s. Whether the models came in individual boxes is unknown.

| Name | Price |
|---|---|
| Maserati Race Car (green, red, cream) | $80 |
| Plymouth Sedan (red, brown, green, gray, chrome-plated) | 125 |
| Buick Coupe (green, blue, red) | 125 |
| Buick Coupe with clockwork motor (red) | 185 |
| Tatra (blue, red, brown, green, gray) | 450 |
| Studebaker Champion (blue, brown, gray, green) | 450 |
| Ford Tudor (blue, gray, red, green) | 320 |
| Chevrolet Sedan (red, blue, gray) | 320 |

| Name | Price |
|---|---|
| Willys Jeep (red) | $100 |
| Willys Army Jeep (green) | 80 |
| Willys Red Cross Jeep (white) | 80 |
| Willys Jeep Station Wagon (red/yellow) | 320 |
| FN Breakdown Truck (gray, green) | 100 |
| FN Stake Truck (red, green) | 100 |
| FN Open Truck (green, red, gray) | 100 |
| FN Tanker (green/red, gray/green, gray/red, gray/yellow) | 100 |
| FN Covered Military Truck (green) | 100 |

| Name | Price |
|---|---|
| Mercury Ambulance (white, cream/red) | $150 |
| Mercury Van (red) | 150 |
| Mercury Army Ambulance (green) | 125 |
| Mercury Mail Van (yellow) | 220 |
| Bus (red, yellow, green, gray) | 150 |
| FN Military Breakdown Truck (green) | 100 |
| Mercury Van with clockwork motor (red) | 150 |
| Plymouth Staff Car (green) | 200 |
| Army Bus (green) | 150 |

# Goodee-Toys

This line of die cast toy cars and trucks is an excellent example of free market competition. Goodee-Toys (as they were referred to in company literature) were manufactured by the Excel Products Company, Inc., which was located in New Brunswick, New Jersey. The company doubtlessly entered the die cast toy market to compete with the likes of Tootsietoy and Hubley, but wound up producing the Goodee line for a relatively short period of time.

Part of the problem may have been the quality of the castings themselves. The author has a couple of Goodees in his collection that suffer from holes in the surface of the vehicle. Although Goodee-Toys don't suffer the devastating effects of metal fatigue, having holes in the hoods and doors of the cars can't help but hurt sales.

Whatever the reason, Goodee-Toys were only in production for a few years during the mid-1950s; they may have been made until as late as 1958. They came with rubber wheels mounted on simple metal axles; the axles were held in place in much the same way as the axles on Midgetoy vehicles. Goodee-Toys came in two sizes, three inch and six inch. The smaller toys were apparently

always painted a single color (like the toys pictured here), whereas the larger units were sometimes done in two colors, and with silver paint highlighting grilles, bumpers, etc. (Excel also made a line of Goodee-Toys airplanes.)

Non-motorized Goodee-Toys were one-piece castings with no baseplates. The motorized units (equipped with a friction motor) may have had a baseplate to house (and hide) the motor.

*Goodee-Toys Ford Police Car, three-inch version. This example is painted blue. With only the roof-mounted siren to go by, one might assume that a red example could be a Fire Chief car.*

Goodee-Toys were also sold in sets. The #100 Set, for example, consisted of nine cars and trucks contained in a counter-type display box. And the #5912 Assortment consisted of a counter display box that held twelve motorized Goodee-Toys in individual boxes.

Since they almost never turn up, these sets and assortment boxes have no established values. One could, of course, simply multiply the number of vehicles in the set or box by the value for one vehicle, then add something on for the box. As always, the selling price will come down to what the buyer is willing to pay and what the seller is willing to take.

| Name | Price |
| --- | --- |
| **Six-inch series:** | |
| 1954 DeSoto Station Wagon | $40 |
| 1953 GMC Pickup Truck | 30 |
| 1953 Ford Police Car | 30 |
| 1955 Ford Oil Tanker | 30 |
| American LaFrance Fire Truck | 25 |
| Military Jeep | 25 |

| Name | Price |
| --- | --- |
| **Three-inch series:** | |
| 1954 DeSoto Station Wagon | $25 |
| 1953 GMC Pickup Truck | 20 |
| 1953 Ford Police Car | 20 |
| 1955 Ford Oil Tanker | 20 |
| American LaFrance Fire Truck | 20 |
| Military Jeep | 20 |

| Name | Price |
| --- | --- |
| 1953 Studebaker Champion | $25 |
| 1953 Lincoln Capri | 25 |
| 1953 Cadillac Convertible | 25 |
| Moving Van | 20 |
| Step Van | 20 |
| Land Speed Racer | 25 |
| Land Speed Racer (with "bubble" type fenders) | 25 |

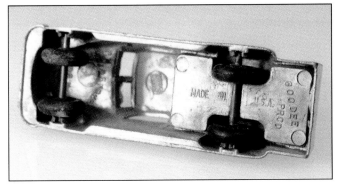

The underside of the three-inch GMC Pickup, showing the manufacturer information including the Goodee-Toys logo cast into the cab roof.

The three-inch GMC Pickup Truck in the Goodee-Toys line.

# Guisval

Guisval is the name of a line of Spanish die cast models that made its debut in 1967. The series was made up of predominantly European marques.

Guisvals were not widely imported into the United States, which partially accounts for their being relatively unknown here. They were of acceptable quality and accuracy, however. The following listing is comprised of those models issued during the 1960s and '70s. New Guisval models still occasionally surface (such as a 1990 Ferrari Testa Rossa in 1/24 and 1/43 scales, or a 1991 Toyota Celica Race Car in 1/43 scale), so the name appears to have survived to the present day.

Whether the original manufacturer is still producing them is unknown at present.

| # | Name | Price |
| --- | --- | --- |
| **1/37 scale models:** | | |
| 101 | Chevrolet Astro | $15 |
| 102 | Ferrari Can-Am | 15 |
| 103 | Ford Capri | 15 |
| 104 | Citroën SM Ambulance (white) | 20 |
| 105 | Ford Capri Ski Club | 15 |
| 106 | Citroën SM Tour de France | 15 |
| 107 | Ford Capri Rally | 15 |
| 108 | Citroën SM Safari | 15 |
| 109 | Ford Capri Policia | 20 |
| 110 | Fiat 130 Coupe | 20 |

| # | Name | Price |
| --- | --- | --- |
| **1/50 and 1/43 scale models:** | | |
| 151 | Scammell Artic. Truck with 2 Tractors | $15 |
| 152 | Scammell Artic. Truck with 2 Cars | 15 |
| 153 | Scammell Artic. Truck with 2 Trucks | 15 |
| 156 | Scammell Artic. Truck with 2 Racers | 15 |
| 157 | Scammell Artic. Truck with 2 Trucks | 15 |
| 171 | Scammell Breakdown Truck | 20 |
| 172 | Scammell Fire Engine | 20 |
| 173 | Scammell Stake Truck | 20 |
| 174 | Scammell Dump Truck | 20 |
| 175 | Scammell Cement Mixer | 20 |

| # | Name | Price |
| --- | --- | --- |
| 450 | Mercedes Covered Truck | $40 |
| 451 | Mercedes Crane Truck | 40 |
| 452 | Mercedes Bottle Truck | 40 |
| 453 | Mercedes Log Carrier | 40 |
| 454 | Mercedes Animal Transporter | 40 |
| 501 | 1907 Adler | 25 |
| 502 | Fiat Zero Roadster (closed) | 25 |
| 503 | 1924 Isotta Fraschini 8A Town Car | 25 |
| 504 | 1924 Isotta Fraschini 8A Convertible | 25 |
| 505 | 1907 Adler Town Car | 25 |
| 506 | Fiat Zero Roadster (open) | 25 |

| # | Name | Price | # | Name | Price | # | Name | Price |
|---|------|-------|---|------|-------|---|------|-------|
| | **1/66 scale models:** | | 24 | Go Bug Fire | $15 | 38 | Lotus 49 B Racing Car | $15 |
| 1 | Chaparral | $15 | 25 | Chevrolet Corvair Monza | 15 | 39 | Ferrari Dino Pinin Farina | 15 |
| 5 | Lotus-Ford 40 | 15 | 26 | MG 1100 | 15 | 40 | Porsche 917 | 15 |
| 8 | Ferrari 330 P 2 | 15 | 27 | Seat 124 | 15 | 41 | Lamborghini Marzal | 15 |
| 13 | Mini with Skis | 15 | 28 | Morris 1100 | 15 | 42 | Hatra Shovel (1/80 scale) | 15 |
| 14 | Land Rover with Missile | 15 | 29 | Seat 124 Policia | 15 | 43 | Chevrolet Corvair Monza (chrome-plated) | 15 |
| 15 | Hot Rod | 15 | 30 | Seat 850 Coupe | 15 | 44 | Alfa Romeo Osi Scarabeo | 15 |
| 16 | Mini Cooper | 15 | 31 | Renault 16 | 15 | 45 | Panther Bertone | 15 |
| 17 | Refuse Wagon (1/80 scale) | 15 | 32 | Seat 850 Coupe Rally | 15 | 46 | Ford 4000 Tractor | 15 |
| 18 | Ferrari P 4 | 15 | 33 | Lotus Ford STP | 15 | 47 | Case Bulldozer (1/80 scale) | 15 |
| 19 | Land Rover Circus | 15 | 34 | Lotus 63/2 | 15 | 48 | Taylor Crane (1/80 scale) | 15 |
| 20 | Horse Box (1/80 scale) | 15 | 35 | Ford Mustang - 1971 | 15 | 49 | Hatra Dumper (1/80 scale) | 15 |
| 21 | Dune Buggy | 15 | 36 | Lotus-Ford V 8 Racing Car | 15 | 50 | Hatra Cement Mixer (1/80 scale) | 15 |
| 23 | Go Bug | 15 | 37 | Ford Mustang Circus - 1971 | 15 | | | |

# Hartoy

**T**his Florida-based company was purchased by Phil Schaffer in 1988, and for several years was the United States distributor for Lledo. When that relationship ended in 1991, Hartoy developed and launched their own series of 1/64 scale trucks. Their first offering was a Mack truck in "Winn-Dixie" livery, and they have since expanded the product line dramatically.

The main series is called "American Highway Legends," and these are 1930s- and 1940s-era trucks. Great American manufacturers like Mack, Ford, GMC and Peterbilt are well-represented in this series, with both "fixed back" units and tractor trailers being offered. The company logos and graphics that appear on the rear of the trucks are sharply rendered, and the trucks are generally accurate.

The "Precision Engineered Models" series, or "PEM," as the company refers to it, is made up of modern tractor trailer trucks, such as a Kenworth T600 and a Mack CH600. Like the vehicles in the American Highway Legends series, these are offered in various liveries.

Hartoy also offers a Coca-Cola "Vintage & Modern" series, made up of castings used in the AHL and PEM series, with Coca-Cola graphics; a similar line is also made with Hershey's graphics.

All Hartoy trucks have rubber wheels, and although most of each vehicle is die cast, plastic is used for things such as rear bed covers, stakes on the stake trucks, etc. And of course, the window glazing is plastic.

As for Current Retail Price, which is the value given in the following listing, the smaller trucks such as the Mack and Peterbilt "fixed backs" usually sell at retail for $8-$14. The non-PEM tractor trailers range from $15-$25. The PEM trucks sell in the range of $35-$50.

| # | Name | Price | # | Name | Price | # | Name | Price |
|---|------|-------|---|------|-------|---|------|-------|
| | **American Highway Legends:** | | L02033 | Fram Canvas Back | CRP | L04015 | Indian Motorcycles Box Van | CRP |
| L01014 | Evinrude Box Van | CRP | L02042 | Royal Oak Drop Side | CRP | L04022 | GMC Parts Stake Body | CRP |
| L01015 | Central Truck Lines Box Van | CRP | L02044 | Timken-Detroit Drop Side | CRP | L04023 | Hartz Mountain Stake Body | CRP |
| L01016 | Breyers Box Van | CRP | L03012 | Gem Box Van | CRP | L04032 | Lipton Canvas Back | CRP |
| L01017 | Coles Express Box Van | CRP | L03013 | Wheaties Box Van | CRP | L04052 | Firestone Panel Stake | CRP |
| L01022 | Stanley Stake Body | CRP | L03015 | A&P Box Van | CRP | L04062 | Mobil Tanker | CRP |
| L01024 | New York Central Stake Body | CRP | L03016 | Montgomery Ward Box Van | CRP | L05013 | Ford Parts Box Van | CRP |
| L01032 | Mack Parts Canvas Back | CRP | L03022 | Rayovac Stake Body | CRP | L05062 | Flying A Tanker | CRP |
| L01043 | Peabody Drop Side | CRP | L03032 | Georgia-Pacific Canvas Back | CRP | L05082 | Dunkin Donuts Van Body | CRP |
| L01062 | Gulf Gasoline Tanker | CRP | L03033 | Weyerhauser Canvas Back | CRP | L05083 | Spalding Van Body | CRP |
| L01072 | Asplundh Stake Bed | CRP | L03052 | Mobil Panel Stake | CRP | L06012 | Jack Frost Box Van | CRP |
| L02012 | Wrigley's Box Van | CRP | L03053 | Exide Panel Stake | CRP | L51102 | Wrigley's 22' Bullnose Trailer | CRP |
| L02013 | Almond Joy Box Van | CRP | L03062 | Pennzoil Tanker | CRP | L51104 | Stroh's 22' Bullnose Trailer | CRP |
| L02014 | Friendly Box Van | CRP | L03063 | Quaker State Tanker | CRP | L51105 | Carolina 22' Bullnose Trailer | CRP |
| L02023 | Beech-Nut Stake Body | CRP | L04012 | Shakespeare Box Van | CRP | L51106 | Preston 22' Bullnose Trailer | CRP |
| L02024 | U.S. Gypsum Stake Body | CRP | L04013 | Birds Eye Box Van | CRP | L51109 | Indian Motorcycles 22' Bullnose Trailer | CRP |
| L02032 | Gold Medal Canvas Back | CRP | L04014 | Kelly Springfield Box Van | CRP | | | |

| # | Name | Price |
|---|------|-------|
| L51110 | Railway Express Agency Tractor Trailer | CRP |
| L51203 | Dutch Boy Tandem 22' Trailers | CRP |
| L52100 | Reese's 22' Bullnose Trailer | CRP |
| L52102 | Mayflower 22' Bullnose Trailer | CRP |
| L52103 | Entemann's 22' Bullnose Trailer | CRP |
| L52104 | Bekins 22' Bullnose Trailer | CRP |
| L52105 | Gillette 22' Bullnose Trailer | CRP |
| L52107 | Purina 22' Bullnose Trailer | CRP |
| L53103 | Peterbuilt 22' Bullnose Trailer | CRP |
| L53105 | Autolite 22' Bullnose Trailer | CRP |
| L53107 | Atlas Van Lines 22' Bullnose Trailer | CRP |
| L51202 | Wonder Bread Tandem 22' Trailers | CRP |
| L52202 | Scott Paper Tandem 22' Trailers | CRP |
| L52203 | Southern Pacific Tandem Tractor Trailer | CRP |
| L53203 | Dole Tandem 22' Trailers | CRP |
| L51302 | Leaman Transportation 32' Tank Trailer | CRP |
| L51303 | Shell 32' Tank Trailer | CRP |
| L53302 | Chevron 32' Tank Trailer | CRP |
| L53303 | Sunoco 32' Tank Trailer | CRP |
| L51402 | Roadway 32' Van Trailer | CRP |
| L52402 | Burma-Shave 32' Van Trailer | CRP |
| L52403 | White Rock 32' Van Trailer | CRP |
| L53402 | Overnite 32' Van Trailer | CRP |
| L53403 | Sherwin-Williams 32' Van Trailer | CRP |
| L55103 | Maxwell House 22' Bullnose Trailer | CRP |
| L55104 | Pennsylvania Railroad 22' Bullnose Trailer | CRP |
| L55402 | Ford Parts 32' Van Trailer | CRP |
| L55403 | Eckerd Drugs 32' Van Trailer | CRP |
| L56402 | Atlas Van Lines Tractor Trailer | CRP |

**Precision Engineered Models series:**

| # | Name | Price |
|---|------|-------|
| H70500 | Hershey's | CRP |
| M70502 | Albertsons | CRP |
| M70503 | Rayovac | CRP |
| M70504 | Kelly-Springfield | CRP |

| # | Name | Price |
|---|------|-------|
| M70505 | Stanley | CRP |
| M70506 | Wiley Sanders | CRP |
| M70507 | Stevens Transport | CRP |
| M70508 | Smucker's | CRP |
| M70509 | Atlas Van Lines | CRP |
| M71501 | Coca-Cola | CRP |
| M71502 | Southeastern | CRP |
| M71503 | Reynolds | CRP |
| M71504 | Bulldog National | CRP |
| M71505 | Friendly's | CRP |
| M71507 | Georgia-Pacific | CRP |
| M71508 | Pitt-Ohio | CRP |
| M71509 | Sweeney Transportation | CRP |
| M71510 | Teal's Express | CRP |

**Coca-Cola Vintage & Modern series:**

| # | Name | Price |
|---|------|-------|
| C01011 | Coca-Cola Box Van | CRP |
| C01031 | Coca-Cola Canvas Back | CRP |
| C01071 | Coca-Cola Stake Bed | CRP |
| C02011 | Coca-Cola City Delivery | CRP |
| C02021 | Coca-Cola Stake Body | CRP |

| # | Name | Price |
|---|------|-------|
| C02041 | Coca-Cola Drop Side | CRP |
| C03011 | Coca-Cola Box Van | CRP |
| C03041 | Coca-Cola Drop Side | CRP |
| C04031 | Coca-Cola Canvas Back | CRP |
| C04051 | Coca-Cola Panel Stake | CRP |
| C05081 | Coca-Cola Van Body | CRP |
| C52101 | Coca-Cola Tractor Trailer | CRP |
| C54401 | Coca-Cola 32' Van Trailer | CRP |
| C70501 | Coca-Cola Tractor Trailer | CRP |
| C71501 | Coca-Cola Tractor Trailer | CRP |

**Hershey's Vintage & Modern series:**

| # | Name | Price |
|---|------|-------|
| H03010 | M.S. Hershey Box Van | CRP |
| H03050 | Sweet Chocolate Panel Stake | CRP |
| H03060 | Hershey's Syrup Tanker | CRP |
| H04020 | Cake Kids Stake Body | CRP |
| H04030 | Hershey's Canvas Back | CRP |
| H04060 | Milk Chocolate Tanker | CRP |
| H51100 | Hershey's 22' Bullnose Trailer | CRP |
| H52100 | Reese's 22' Bullnose Trailer | CRP |

*Although released as part of a "limited edition" series entitled "The Great American Brewery Collection" in 1994, this Schaefer Beer truck is typical of Hartoy's American Highway Legends trucks. It's the Mack BM with die cast body, plastic rear cover and rubber tires.*

# Herpa

**T**his German manufacturer is best-known for its extensive line of 1/87 (HO) scale plastic models, which are highly detailed and accurate. But for the past several years, Herpa has also offered a line of 1/43 scale die cast models that are well-detailed and accurate. Mercedes-Benz and BMW figure prominently in the series, as would be expected from a German manufacturer.

The company expanded into die cast further in 1993 and 1994, debuting its line of 1/66 scale models called "Herpa Junior." These are models (toys) aimed at the children's market, but they are actually very accurate models as well, right down to the wheels. The series includes police cars, taxis, fire cars, etc., and is apparently marketed only in Europe (and perhaps the United Kingdom), so Juniors are not well known in the United States.

Herpa also offers a line of 1/500 scale die cast metal passenger airliners.

Current Retail Price for the standard 1/43 scale models ranges from $22-$30, which is comparable to other European 1/43 scale prices. Certain Herpa 1/43 models are of a higher quality (with opening parts and other detailed features), and are therefore priced higher (generally $40-$50). The Ferrari Testa Rossa models are examples of this higher price point.

| Name | Price | Name | Price | Name | Price |
|------|-------|------|-------|------|-------|
| BMW M3 GTR | CRP | Ferrari 348 tb | CRP | Mercedes-Benz E320 "Notarzt" | CRP |
| BMW 740i | CRP | Ferrari 348 ts | CRP | Mercedes-Benz E320 "Feuerwehr" | CRP |
| Ferrari F40 | CRP | AMG Mercedes-Benz C220 | CRP | Mercedes-Benz 600 SEL | CRP |
| Ferrari Testa Rossa | CRP | Mercedes-Benz E320 Limousine | CRP | Volkswagen Polo | CRP |
| Ferrari Testa Rossa ts | CRP | Mercedes-Benz E320 "Polizei" | CRP | | |
| Ferrari Testa Rossa Spider | CRP | Mercedes-Benz E320 "Taxi" | CRP | | |

# Hot Wheels

It's a safe bet that there isn't a single American man or woman between the ages of 18 and 40 who doesn't at least remember Hot Wheels. More likely, he or she owned at least a few (if not dozens) of the radical-looking die cast racers, and enjoyed racing them down that unforgettable orange track.

When Mattel unveiled Hot Wheels cars in 1968, no one was prepared for the tidal wave of popularity that these things would enjoy. Perhaps most shocked were the powers-that-be at companies like Lesney (Matchbox), who had gone along for years doing their thing on a level playing field. That field now tilted in favor of Mattel.

Automotive designer Harry Bradley and Mattel designer Howard Newman worked with Mattel Chairman Elliot Handler and R&D chief Jack Ryan to develop a new line of fast die cast cars for children. The project got underway in 1966, and the "Original Sixteen" Hot Wheels cars made their debut in 1968. They were unlike anything then available on toy store shelves. Painted in bright metallic colors and sporting exhaust headers, exposed engines and "mag" wheels, they immediately attracted kids' attention.

These were cars intended to be raced, and Mattel made sure that young drivers had what they needed. Track sets, starting gates, jumping ramps, lap counters and "speedometers" all were sold along with the cars.

As time went on, more and more models were introduced into the product line. There were also Hot Wheels comic books, lunch boxes, even a Saturday morning television show. Kids never had a chance: they and their parents bought Hot Wheels products in droves.

Through the 1970s, Hot Wheels remained a strong seller for Mattel. It would be in the 1980s that Mattel would expand

the exposure of Hot Wheels to include tie-in promotions with companies like McDonald's and Kellogg's. By the end of the decade, adults who once had Hot Wheels as kids began to enter the picture, collecting the older cars for nostalgic (and financial) reasons.

*Tinplate collectors buttons like this one came in every Hot Wheels blisterpack until 1972.*

*One of the "Original Sixteen": Hot Wheels #6212, the Custom Firebird. This model was in production during 1968 and 1969.*

*The Red Baron is one of the most-remembered of the early Hot Wheels. This example is one of the 1973 "enamels" that are now so prized by collectors. It's #6964, and is very similar to the #6400 Red Baron, first released in 1970.*

Mattel responded to this collector activity in 1993 by marketing replicas of eight of the "Original Sixteen" Hot Wheels, and these proved to be very popular with the collecting community.

Today, most Hot Wheels sold in retail outlets like Toys R Us or Wal-Mart cost about a dollar. On the secondary market, it's a different story. Older examples, of course, command higher prices, as indicated in the following listing. But even new issues can suddenly shoot up in price virtually overnight due to real or perceived "scarcity."

The popularity of Hot Wheels has led to the formation of collector's clubs and periodicals dedicated to the subject. See Part Three, Additional Resources, for more information.

## Packaging and Market Value

The following listing is a general overview of Hot Wheels produced from 1968 until the early 1990s. **A special note on packaging:** since Hot Wheels have always come on "blistercards," removing a car from its package damages the blistercard. For many years, of course, most people just tossed the opened blistercards in the trash. Therefore, a Hot Wheels car unopened in its original blistercard commands a higher price than a "loose" specimen by itself. In fact, for 1960s and 1970s cars, the value for certain unopened Hot Wheels cars can be double or triple (sometimes more) that of the same car with no packaging. With 1980s and 1990s examples, the value difference is usually much smaller, as

*The #6404 Classic Nomad, released in 1970 and 1971. This photo clearly shows the red stripe or "redline" wheels characteristic of the first few years of Hot Wheels production.*

*This #6451 Ambulance is from the "Heavyweights" line introduced in 1970.*

many more unopened examples have survived from these periods. **This listing provides the market value for single, "loose" Hot Wheels with no packaging.**

The values listed here are generally for the most commonly found color of each car. For example, the yellow version of a car might sell in the $40-$50 range, but the same car in green may command $200, due to relative scarcity or some other factor. In addition, many Hot Wheels cars were produced for a number of years before being phased out of production. This listing provides values for the car in its first year (or sometimes two) of existence; a later version of the car may sell for

significantly less or more than the original, first year example.

For these reasons, the reader is advised to consult one of the currently available books on Hot Wheels, such as Michael Strauss's excellent *Tomart's Price Guide to Hot Wheels*. This comprehensive work is well-illustrated and provides a wealth of information on Hot Wheels. More information on this and other books on the subject can be found in Part Three, Additional Resources.

*At left is a #6973 Ferrari 312P; this example came as part of the "Flying Colors" series in 1974. On the right is a #5880 Double Header, which was issued only in 1973, and is therefore quite scarce today.*

| #    | Name                  | Price |
|------|-----------------------|-------|
| **The 1968 "original sixteen":** | | |
| 6217 | Beatnik Bandit        | $15   |
| 6211 | Custom Barracuda      | 55    |
| 6208 | Custom Camaro         | 55    |
| 6215 | Custom Corvette       | 55    |
| 6205 | Custom Cougar         | 50    |
| 6218 | Custom Eldorado       | 45    |
| 6212 | Custom Firebird       | 40    |
| 6213 | Custom Fleetside      | 45    |
| 6206 | Custom Mustang        | 65    |
| 6207 | Custom T-Bird         | 55    |
| 6220 | Custom Volkswagen     | 15    |
| 6210 | Deora                 | 50    |
| 6214 | Ford J-Car            | 15    |
| 6219 | Hot Heap              | 15    |
| 6216 | Python                | 20    |
| 6209 | Silhouette            | 15    |
| **1969 models:** | | |
| 6264 | Brabham-Repco F1      | 15    |
| 6256 | Chapparal 2G          | 20    |
| 6251 | Classic '31 Ford Woody| 20    |
| 6250 | Classic '32 Ford Vicky| 25    |
| 6253 | Classic '36 Ford Coupe| 20    |
| 6252 | Classic '57 T-Bird    | 25    |
| 6267 | Custom AMX            | 40    |
| 6268 | Custom Charger        | 60    |
| 6266 | Custom Continental Mark III | 25 |
| 6269 | Custom Police Cruiser | 60    |
| 6257 | Ford Mark IV          | 15    |
| 6263 | Indy Eagle            | 15    |
| 6254 | Lola GT70             | 15    |

| #    | Name                  | Price |
|------|-----------------------|-------|
| 6262 | Lotus Turbine         | $15   |
| 6277 | Maserati Mistral      | 50    |
| 6255 | McLaren M6A           | 15    |
| 6275 | Mercedes-Benz 280SL   | 20    |
| 6276 | Rolls-Royce Silver Shadow | 50 |
| 6265 | Shelby Turbine        | 20    |
| 6261 | Splittin' Image       | 15    |
| 6260 | Torero                | 15    |
| 6259 | Turbofire             | 15    |
| 6258 | TwinMill              | 20    |
| 6274 | Volkswagen Beach Bomb (with surfboards in side slots) | 40 |
| 6274 | Volkswagen Beach Bomb—very rare variation (may have been a prototype) with surfboards in rear of vehicle. A very good example sold at auction for $4,025 in 1994 | |
| **1970 models:** | | |
| 6451 | Ambulance             | 45    |
| 6499 | Boss Hoss (came only as part of Hot Wheels "Club Kit"—see #6407 for value of individual car) | |
| 6420 | Carabo                | 25    |
| 6452 | Cement Mixer          | 30    |
| 6404 | Classic Nomad         | 45    |
| 6401 | The Demon             | 20    |
| 6453 | Dump Truck            | 20    |
| 6417 | Ferrari 312P          | 20    |
| 6469 | Fire Chief Cruiser    | 15    |
| 6454 | Fire Engine           | 45    |
| 6408 | Heavy Chevy           | 40    |

| #    | Name                  | Price |
|------|-----------------------|-------|
| 6189 | Heavy Chevy (came only as part of Hot Wheels "Club Kit"—see #6408 for value of individual car) | |
| 6421 | Jack "Rabbit" Special | $20   |
| 6411 | King 'Kuda            | 40    |
| 6190 | King 'Kuda (came only as part of Hot Wheels "Club Kit"—see #6411 for value of individual car) | |
| 6412 | Light My Firebird     | 20    |
| 6423 | Mantis                | 20    |
| 6417 | Mighty Maverick       | 40    |
| 6456 | Mod Quad              | 25    |
| 6410 | Mongoose              | 60    |
| 6455 | Moving Van            | 40    |
| 6405 | Nitty Gritty Kitty    | 45    |
| 6402 | Paddy Wagon           | 15    |
| 6419 | Peepin' Bomb          | 15    |
| 6416 | Porsche 917           | 20    |
| 6459 | Power Pad             | 40    |
| 6400 | Red Baron             | 25    |
| 6403 | Sand Crab             | 15    |
| 6413 | Seasider              | 60    |
| 6436 | "Sky Show" Deora (available only in the Sky Show set) . . . . price varies widely | |
| 6436 | Sky Show Fleetside (available only in the Sky Show or "Flying Circus" sets) . . . . . . . . . price varies widely | |
| 6409 | Snake                 | 75    |
| 6422 | Swingin' Wing         | 30    |
| 6407 | TNT-Bird              | 35    |
| 6450 | Tow Truck             | 30    |

| # | Name | Price |
|---|------|-------|
| 6424 | Tri Baby | $20 |
| 6457 | Whip creamer | 25 |

**1971 models:**

| # | Name | Price |
|---|------|-------|
| 6460 | AMX/2 | 35 |
| 6407 | Boss Hoss | 55 |
| 5178 | Bugeye | 40 |
| 6187 | Bye-Focal | 70 |
| 6472 | Classic Cord | 125 |
| 6466 | Cockney Cab | 40 |
| 6471 | Evil Weevil | 40 |
| 6018 | Fuel Tanker | 75 |
| 6461 | Grass Hopper | 30 |
| 6458 | Hairy Hauler | 35 |
| 6175 | The Hood | 40 |
| 6184 | Ice "T" | 50 |
| 6179 | Jet Threat | 50 |
| 5954 | Mongoose 2 | 100 |
| 5952 | Mongoose Rail Dragster (only available packaged with #5951 Snake Rail Dragster) | 75 |
| 6185 | Mutt Mobile | 60 |
| 6000 | Noodle Head | 60 |
| 6467 | Olds 442 | 175 |
| 6183 | Pit Crew Car | 75 |
| 6194 | Racer Rig | 75 |
| 6186 | Rocket-Bye-Baby | 60 |
| 6468 | S'Cool Bus | 125 |
| 6193 | Scooper | 75 |
| 6176 | Short Order | 40 |
| 6003 | Six Shooter | 60 |
| 5953 | Snake 2 | 65 |
| 5951 | Snake Rail Dragster (only available packaged with #5952 Mongoose Rail Dragster) | 70 |
| 6020 | Snorkel | 60 |
| 6006 | Special Delivery | 60 |
| 6188 | Strip Teaser | 65 |
| 6418 | Sugar Caddy | 40 |
| 6177 | T-4-2 | 50 |
| 6019 | Team Trailer | 75 |
| 6192 | Waste Wagon | 85 |
| 6192 | What-4 | 75 |

**1972 models:**

| # | Name | Price |
|---|------|-------|
| 6021 | Ferrari 512S | 90 |
| 6005 | Funny Money | 60 |
| 6169 | Mercedes-Benz C-III | 90 |
| 5881 | Open Fire | 85 |
| 5699 | Rear Engine Mongoose | 100 |
| 5856 | Rear Engine Snake | 100 |
| 6022 | Side Kick | 85 |

**1973 models:**

| # | Name | Price |
|---|------|-------|
| 6968 | Alive '55 | 80 |
| 6976 | Buzz Off | 90 |
| 5880 | Double Header | 75 |
| 6975 | Double Vision | 80 |
| 6967 | Dune Daddy | 75 |
| 6973 | Ferrari 312P | 125 |
| 6979 | Hiway Robber | 75 |
| 6980 | Ice "T" | 100 |
| 6962 | Mercedes-Benz 280SL | 100 |

| # | Name | Price |
|---|------|-------|
| 6978 | Mercedes-Benz C-III | $175 |
| 6970 | Mongoose (without plastic windows) (price varies widely) | 750 |
| 6981 | Odd Job | 90 |
| 6966 | Paddy Wagon | 25 |
| 6963 | Police Cruiser | 75 |
| 6972 | Porsche 917 | 150 |
| 6965 | Prowler | 175 |
| 6964 | Red Baron | 30 |
| 6974 | Sand Witch | 95 |
| 6982 | Show-Off | 90 |
| 6969 | Snake (without plastic windows) (price varies widely) | 750 |
| 6971 | Street Snorter | 100 |
| 6004 | Superfine Turbine | 200 |
| 6007 | Sweet "16" | 100 |
| 6977 | Xploder | 95 |

**1974 models:**

| # | Name | Price |
|---|------|-------|
| 8258 | Baja Bruiser | 50 |
| 8263 | Breakaway Bucket | 75 |
| 7617 | Carabo | 40 |
| 8273 | El Rey Special | 50 |
| 7621 | Funny Money | 40 |
| 7622 | Grass Hopper | 75 |
| 7619 | Heavy Chevy | 60 |
| 7616 | Rash I | 50 |

| # | Name | Price |
|---|------|-------|
| 7615 | Road King Truck (price varies widely) | $600 |
| 8259 | Rodger Dodger | 50 |
| 8261 | Sir Rodney Roadster | 45 |
| 8260 | Steam Roller | 40 |
| 7630 | Top Eliminator | 40 |
| 7620 | Volkswagen | 50 |
| 7618 | Winnipeg | 100 |

**1975 models:**

| # | Name | Price |
|---|------|-------|
| 7662 | American Victory | 20 |
| 7670 | Backwoods Bomb | 50 |
| 7671 | Chevy Monza 2+2 | 40 |
| 7665 | Chief's Special | 40 |
| 7650 | Emergency Squad | 20 |
| 7652 | Gremlin Grinder | 35 |
| 7664 | Gun Slinger | 40 |
| 8272 | Large Charge | 35 |
| 7653 | Mighty Maverick | 45 |
| 7660 | Monte Carlo Stocker | 40 |
| 7668 | Motocross I | 90 |
| 7644 | Mustang Stocker | 75 |
| 7648 | P-911 | 45 |
| 7661 | Paramedic | 40 |
| 7659 | Ramblin' Wrecker | 40 |
| 7666 | Ranger Rig | 40 |
| 7651 | Sand Drifter | 40 |

*The #6421 Jack Rabbit Special in the original blisterpack. This model was issued in 1970 and '71; the familiar orange and red blistercard was used until the mid-1970s.*

| # | Name | Price |
|---|------|-------|
| 7669 | Street Eater | $60 |
| 7649 | Super Van | 40 |
| 7647 | Torino Stocker | 50 |
| 7655 | Tough Customer | 20 |
| 7658 | Vega Bomb | 50 |
| 7654 | Warpath | 50 |

**1976 models:**

| # | Name | Price |
|---|------|-------|
| 9118 | American Hauler | 30 |
| 9089 | American Tipper | 25 |
| 9243 | Aw Shoot | 30 |
| 9120 | Cool One | 45 |
| 9241 | Corvette Stingray | 60 |
| 9119 | Formula 5000 | 30 |
| 9037 | Formula P.A.C.K. | 30 |
| 9090 | Gun Bucket | 20 |
| 9186 | Inferno | 45 |
| 8235 | Jet Threat II | 30 |

| # | Name | Price |
|---|------|-------|
| 9643 | Letter Getter | $15 |
| 9642 | Odd Rod | 25 |
| 9644 | Second Wind | 25 |
| 9646 | Show Hoss II | 45 |
| 9641 | Spoiler Sport | 20 |
| 9793 | Thrill Drivers Torino (only sold in "Thrill Drivers Corkscrew" set) | 80 |
| 9648 | T-Totaller | 15 |
| 9639 | Z Whiz | 25 |

**1978 models:**

| # | Name | Price |
|---|------|-------|
| 2013 | '57 T-Bird | 20 |
| 2016 | A-Ok | 15 |
| 2023 | Army Funny Car | 25 |
| 2022 | Baja Breaker | 15 |
| 2019 | Highway Patrol | 25 |
| 2014 | Hot Bird | 15 |
| 2012 | Jaguar XJS | 15 |

| # | Name | Price |
|---|------|-------|
| 2878 | The Incredible Hulk | $20 |
| 2850 | The Incredible Hulk | 30 |
| 2510 | Inside Story | 10 |
| 2853 | Motocross Team | 35 |
| 2501 | Royal Flash | 10 |
| 2503 | Spacer Racer | 15 |
| 2855 | Space Van | 45 |
| 2877 | Spider-man | 15 |
| 2852 | Spider-man | 35 |
| 2854 | S.W.A.T. Van | 35 |
| 2882 | The Thing | 20 |
| 2880 | Thor | 15 |
| 2500 | Upfront 924 | 10 |
| 2508 | Vetty Funny | 20 |

**1980 models:**

| # | Name | Price |
|---|------|-------|
| 1132 | 3-Window '34 | 15 |
| 1131 | '40s Woodie | 15 |
| 1172 | CAT Bulldozer | 10 |
| 1171 | CAT Dump Truck | 10 |
| 1168 | CAT Forklift | 15 |
| 1173 | CAT Wheel Loader | 10 |
| 1153 | Dodge D-50 | 10 |
| 1127 | Greyhound MC-8 | 20 |
| no # | Hammer Down (only sold in "The Great American Truck Race" set) | 75 |
| 1174 | Hiway Hauler | 20 |
| no # | Movin' On | 75 |
| 1169 | Peterbilt Cement Mixer | 10 |
| 1136 | Split Window '63 | 10 |
| 1126 | Stutz Blackhawk | 10 |
| 1129 | Super Scraper | 10 |
| 1130 | Tricar X8 | 10 |
| 1125 | Turbo Mustang | 10 |
| 1134 | Turbo Wedge | 10 |
| 1135 | 'Vette Van | 10 |

**1981 models:**

| # | Name | Price |
|---|------|-------|
| 1696 | '37 Bugatti | 10 |
| 1699 | Airport Rescue | 10 |
| 1690 | Bronco 4-Wheeler | 10 |
| 1691 | Cannonade | 10 |
| 1693 | Chevy Citation | 10 |
| 3303 | Circus Cats (Ringling Brothers graphics) | 50 |
| 3364 | Dixie Challenger | 10 |
| 3301 | Iron Man | 20 |
| 1697 | Minitrek | 10 |
| 1700 | Mirada Stocker | 10 |
| 1695 | Old Number 5 | 15 |
| 1692 | Omni 024 | 10 |
| 1689 | Peterbilt Tank Truck | 10 |
| 3305 | Racing Team | 50 |
| 3304 | Rescue Squad | 75 |
| 3300 | Silver Surfer | 20 |
| 1694 | Turismo | 10 |

**1982 models:**

| # | Name | Price |
|---|------|-------|
| 3252 | '35 Classic Caddy | 10 |
| 5179 | '55 Chevy | 10 |
| 3258 | Aries Wagon | 10 |
| 1698 | Cadillac Seville | 10 |
| 5282 | Camaro Z-28 | 10 |
| 3254 | Construction Crane | 10 |

*An example of late 1970s Hot Wheels: the #2014 Hot Bird. This gold example is from the "Golden Machines 6-pack."*

| # | Name | Price |
|---|------|-------|
| 9183 | Khaki Kooler | 25 |
| 9185 | Lowdown | 45 |
| 9184 | Maxi Taxi | 40 |
| 9244 | Neet Streeter | 35 |
| 9240 | Poison Pinto | 30 |
| 9088 | Rock Buster | 30 |
| 9521 | Staff Car (sold only in the "Military 6-pack") (price varies widely) | 500 |
| 9242 | Street Rodder | 40 |
| 8240 | TwinMill II | 30 |

**1977 models:**

| # | Name | Price |
|---|------|-------|
| 9649 | '31 Doozie | 30 |
| 9647 | '56 Hi-Tail Hauler | 35 |
| 9638 | '57 Chevy | 30 |
| 9640 | Fire Eater | 15 |
| 9645 | GMC Motor Home | 15 |

| # | Name | Price |
|---|------|-------|
| 2017 | Lickety Six | 20 |
| 2015 | Packin' Pacer | 15 |
| 2021 | Race Bait 308 | 15 |
| 2018 | Science Friction | 15 |
| 2020 | Stagefright | 15 |

**1979 models:**

| # | Name | Price |
|---|------|-------|
| 2505 | Auburn 852 | 10 |
| 2511 | Bubble Gunner | 15 |
| 2509 | Bywayman | 15 |
| 2879 | Captain America | 20 |
| 2851 | Captain America Van | 30 |
| 2507 | Dumpin' A | 10 |
| 2639 | Fire Chaser | 10 |
| 2506 | Flat Out 442 | 10 |
| 2502 | Greased Gremlin | 20 |
| 2504 | Hare Splitter | 10 |
| 2881 | Human Torch | 20 |

| # | Name | Price |
|---|------|-------|
| 3255 | Datsun 200SX | $10 |
| 3250 | Firebird Funny Car | 10 |
| 3253 | Ford Dump Truck | 10 |
| 3257 | Front Runnin' Fairmont | 10 |
| 3259 | Jeep CJ-7 | 10 |
| 3260 | Land Lord | 10 |
| 9037 | Malibu Grand Prix | 10 |
| 3261 | Mercedes-Benz 300 SEL | 10 |
| 3911 | Mercedes 540K | 10 |
| 5180 | P-928 | 10 |
| 2023 | Pepsi Challenger | 15 |
| 3281 | Peugeot 505 | 10 |
| 3256 | Rapid Transit | 10 |
| 2019 | Sheriff Patrol | 5 |
| 3251 | Sunagon | 10 |
| 5181 | Taxi | 10 |
| 3912 | Trash Truck | 10 |

### 1983 models:

| # | Name | Price |
|---|------|-------|
| 3919 | '40s Ford 2-Door | 10 |
| 3913 | '67 Camaro | 15 |
| 3928 | '80s Corvette | 15 |
| 3918 | '80s Firebird | 10 |
| 3925 | '82 Supra | 5 |
| no # | Airport Food Service (made in France) | 60 |
| no # | Airport Security (made in France) | 30 |
| 4708 | Airport Transportation (made in France) | 60 |
| 4368 | Beach Patrol | 10 |
| 3289 | BMW M1 | 15 |
| 4703 | Cargo Lift (made in France) | 50 |
| 3923 | Classic Cobra | 15 |
| 3920 | Classic Packard | 10 |
| 3291 | Double Decker Bus (made in France) | 75 |
| 3287 | Fiat Ritmo (made in France) | 25 |
| no # | Fireball Torino (made in Mexico) | 45 |
| 3288 | Ford Escort | 10 |
| 4018 | Ford Stake Bed Truck | 10 |
| 3915 | Formula Fever | 10 |
| 3768 | Long Shot | 10 |
| 3927 | NASCAR Stocker (says NASCAR Stocker on base) | 100 |
| 3927 | NASCAR Stocker (says Racing Stocker on base) | 30 |
| 4017 | Peterbilt Dump Truck | 10 |
| 3917 | Pontiac J-2000 | 10 |
| 3292 | Renault LeCar | 20 |
| 3916 | Rig Wrecker | 5 |
| 3924 | Thunder Roller | 10 |
| 3914 | Turbo Streak | 10 |

### 1984 models:

| # | Name | Price |
|---|------|-------|
| 5908 | '65 Mustang Convertible | 15 |
| 5907 | Baja Bug | 10 |
| 4920 | Battle Tank | 5 |
| 5910 | Blazer 4x4 | 10 |
| 5901 | Blown Camaro Z-28 | 10 |
| 9643 | Delivery Van "Frito Lay" | 75 |
| 5903 | Dodge Rampage | 15 |
| 5909 | Dream Van XGW | 15 |
| 7293 | Flame Runner | 10 |
| 5904 | Good Humor Truck | 10 |

| # | Name | Price |
|---|------|-------|
| 4372 | Lightning Gold | $15 |
| 5905 | Oshkosh Snowplow | 15 |
| 5906 | Phone Truck | 10 |
| 7292 | Predator | 10 |
| 7295 | Quik Trik | 10 |
| 3290 | Rolls-Royce Phantom II | 10 |
| 5902 | Sol-Aire CX4 | 10 |
| 2855 | Space Vehicle | 25 |
| 7299 | Speed Seeker | 10 |
| 5900 | Thunderbird Stocker | 35 |
| 4921 | Troop Convoy | 10 |
| 5911 | Turbo Heater | 10 |
| 7296 | Wind Splitter | 10 |

### 1985 models:

| # | Name | Price |
|---|------|-------|
| 9372 | Big Bertha | 5 |
| 9544 | Black Lightning | 15 |
| 9371 | Command Tank | 10 |

| # | Name | Price |
|---|------|-------|
| 9374 | Tank Gunner | $10 |
| 9545 | Thunderstreak | 15 |
| 9533 | Torino Tornado | 15 |
| 7531 | XT-3 | 10 |

### 1986 models:

| # | Name | Price |
|---|------|-------|
| 2544 | Back Burner | 5 |
| 2058 | Cargoyle | 10 |
| 2519 | Combat Medic | 5 |
| 2057 | Double Demon | 10 |
| 2062 | Eevil Weevil | 10 |
| 2059 | Fangster | 10 |
| 2524 | Highway Heat | 25 |
| 2534 | Path Beater | 15 |
| 2528 | Poppa 'Vette | 25 |
| 2538 | Power Plower | 15 |
| 2520 | Race Ace | 25 |
| 2537 | Rescue Ranger | 10 |

*The #3923 Classic Cobra with rubber tires, issued in 1983, originally came as one of the cars in the "Real Riders" line. This series is very popular with collectors today.*

| # | Name | Price |
|---|------|-------|
| 9523 | Fat Fendered '40 | 15 |
| 7527 | Fiero 2M4 | 5 |
| 9541 | Good Ol' Pick-Um-Up | 25 |
| 7532 | Gulch Stepper | 5 |
| 7528 | Jet Sweep X5 | 10 |
| 9531 | Mustang S.V.O. | 10 |
| 9537 | Nightstreaker | 10 |
| 7529 | Nissan 300ZX | 10 |
| 9542 | Pavement Pounder | 10 |
| 9534 | Redliner | 5 |
| 9375 | Roll Patrol Jeep CJ-7 | 5 |
| 9521 | Screamin' | 15 |
| 9535 | Silver Bullet | 10 |
| 1691 | Snake Busters Car (not issued on blistercard) | 15 |
| 9538 | Street Beast | 5 |
| 9536 | Street Scorcher | 15 |
| 9373 | Super Cannon | 10 |
| 7530 | Tall Ryder | 10 |

| # | Name | Price |
|---|------|-------|
| 2518 | Shell Shocker | 5 |
| 2522 | Stock Rocket | 25 |
| 2061 | Turboa | 10 |
| 2060 | Vampyra | 10 |

### 1987 models:

| # | Name | Price |
|---|------|-------|
| 3338 | Assault Crawler | 10 |
| 3715 | CAT Earth Mover | 10 |
| 3853 | CAT Road Roller | 25 |
| 1897 | Ferrari Testa Rossa | 10 |
| 3716 | Monster 'Vette | 10 |
| 3851 | Phantomachine | 5 |
| 1500 | Road Torch | 10 |
| 3286 | Sharkruiser | 5 |
| 3209 | Suzuki QuadRacer | 10 |
| 4059 | Tail GunnerT | 10 |
| 1456 | Thunderburner | 10 |
| 3852 | Zombot | 5 |

| # | Name | Price |
|---|------|-------|
| **1988 models:** | | |
| 5026 | Alien | $10 |
| 5027 | Flame Stopper | 5 |
| 4384 | Lamborghini Countach | 5 |
| 4392 | Nissan Hardbody | 10 |
| 4631 | Porsche 959 | 5 |
| 5022 | Radar Ranger | 10 |
| 5028 | Ratmobile | 5 |
| 9380 | Rocketank | 5 |
| 4389 | Rodzilla | 5 |
| 4699 | Shadow Jet | 5 |
| 5025 | Sting Rod | 10 |
| 4741 | Talbot Lago | 10 |
| **1989 models:** | | |
| 7672 | '32 Ford Delivery | 3 |
| 1792 | Ambulance | 3 |
| 1790 | Big Rig | 3 |
| 1791 | Chevy Stocker | 5 |
| 7670 | Custom Corvette | 5 |
| 2808 | Delivery Truck | 5 |
| 1468 | Ferrari F40 | 5 |
| 1789 | GT Racer | 3 |
| 1469 | Peugeot 205 Rallye | 10 |
| 1796 | Pontiac Banshee | 5 |
| 1795 | School Bus | 5 |
| 1470 | Street Roader | 5 |
| 7673 | T-Bucket | 10 |
| 7671 | VW Bug | 5 |
| **1990 models:** | | |
| 9726 | BMW 323 | 5 |
| 2102 | Corvette Funny Car | 5 |
| 2104 | Firebird | 5 |
| 4005 | Fire Chief | 5 |
| 2099 | Minitruck | 5 |
| 7609 | Nissan 300ZX | 5 |
| 7608 | Probe Funny Car | 5 |
| 9112 | Propper Chopper | 5 |
| 2173 | Purple Passion | 5 |
| 9738 | Range Rover | 3 |
| 9113 | Simpson's Family Camper | 3 |
| 9114 | Simpson's Nuclear Waste Van | 3 |
| **1991 models:** | | |
| 2098 | '55 Nomad | 10 |
| 2097 | '59 Caddy | 15 |
| 5667 | BMW 850i | 5 |
| 9258 | Buick Stocker | 5 |
| 5665 | Ferrari 250 | 4 |
| 5666 | Ferrari 348 | 3 |
| 4695 | Ford Aerostar | 3 |
| 9713 | Holden Commodore | 5 |
| 5672 | Lamborghini Diablo | 3 |
| 5638 | Limozeen | 5 |
| 2920 | Mazda MX-5 Miata | 3 |
| 9770 | Mercedes-Benz SL | 10 |
| 5673 | Mercedes-Benz Unimog | 3 |
| 5670 | Peugeot 405 | 3 |
| 7607 | Porsche 930 | 5 |
| 5343 | Ramp Truck | 5 |
| 9749 | Renault 5 Turbo | 3 |
| 5640 | Speed Shark | 10 |

| # | Name | Price |
|---|------|-------|
| 5637 | Street Beast | $3 |
| 5348 | Surf Patrol | 3 |
| 5669 | Toyota MR2 Rally | 8 |
| 5636 | Trailbuster | 7 |
| 9557 | VW Golf | 5 |
| 5674 | Zender Fact 4 | 5 |
| **1992 models:** | | |
| 2029 | '56 Flashsider | 3 |
| 1781 | Aeroflash | 3 |
| 3765 | Bulldozer | 3 |
| 5675 | Chevy Lumina | 3 |
| 3156 | Flashfire | 3 |
| 1384 | Goodyear Blimp | 5 |
| 3782 | Hiway Hauler | 3 |
| 0773 | Hummer | 3 |
| 2074 | Oshkosh Cement Mixer | 3 |
| 2073 | Recycling Truck | 3 |
| 3164 | Shock Factor | 3 |
| 2076 | Tank Truck | 3 |
| 2075 | Tractor | 4 |
| 2565 | #6 Valvoline | 3 |
| 2568 | #21 Citgo | 3 |
| 2115 | #25 Hot Wheels | 3 |
| 2698 | #26 Quaker State Indy Car | 3 |
| 2738 | #33 Duracell | 3 |
| 2628 | #42 Mello Yello | 3 |
| 2623 | #43 STP | 3 |
| 2743 | Castrol GTX Funny Car | 4 |
| 2841 | King Kenny Funny Car | 4 |
| **1993 models:** | | |
| 2638 | #1 Texaco | 4 |
| 2630 | #2 Pontiac Excitement | 4 |
| 2677 | #2 Texaco | 4 |
| 2739 | #3 Cytomax | 4 |
| 2690 | #3 Valvoline | 4 |

| # | Name | Price |
|---|------|-------|
| 2692 | #4 Penske | $4 |
| 2694 | #5 Penske | 4 |
| 2567 | #26 Quaker State Stock Car | 4 |
| 3021 | '93 Camaro | 5 |
| 3527 | Ammo | 4 |
| 5260 | Audi | 3 |
| 5414 | Beatnik Bandit | 3 |
| 3502 | Bus Boys | 4 |
| 5743 | Classic Nomad | 3 |
| 3092 | Corvette Split Window | 4 |
| 5730 | The Demon | 3 |
| 5265 | Dodge Viper | 3 |
| 3438 | Dragon Wagon | 4 |
| 3493 | Eye-Gor | 4 |
| 1691 | Gleamer Patrol | 3 |
| 3494 | Hot Wheels | 4 |
| 3026 | Jaguar XJ220 | 3 |
| 3510 | Lightning Storm | 4 |
| 5263 | Lexus SC 400 | 3 |
| 7609 | Nissan Custom Z | 3 |
| 3490 | Open Wide | 4 |
| 3029 | Oscar Mayer Wienermobile | 3 |
| 5707 | Paddy Wagon | 3 |
| 3036 | Pipe Jammer | 3 |
| 5700 | Red Baron | 3 |
| 3489 | Road Pirate | 4 |
| 5715 | Silhoutte | 3 |
| 3492 | Skull Rider | 4 |
| 3479 | Spiderider | 4 |
| 5708 | Splittin' Image | 3 |
| 3491 | Street Beast (3rd version) | 4 |
| 3501 | Street Dog | 4 |
| 3035 | Treadator | 3 |
| 5709 | TwinMill | 3 |
| 3050 | Vector "Avtech" WX-3 | 3 |

*Two recent releases. At left is the Purple Passion in the standard Hot Wheels packaging. This model was first released in 1990. At right is the same car in a different color, entitled "Gold Passion," one of the "Treasure Hunt" cars issued by Mattel in 1995.*

# Hubley

The Hubley Manufacturing Company was founded by John E. Hubley in 1893. Located in Lancaster, Pennsylvania, the firm produced a line of cast iron and steel toys until the onset of World War II, at which time the factory was switched over to making hand grenades and fuses for artillery shells.

Although Hubley himself had died in 1900, the owners of the business, Joseph T. Breneman and John Howard Hartman, carried on and, in 1936, expanded the toy line to include a series of die cast toys. The name of the new line was "Kiddie Toys." After the war ended, production of the Kiddie Toys resumed, with some of the pre-war designs being pressed back into service. As time went on, however, more and more new die cast toys were introduced.

Although a new, larger factory was built on Pitney Road in 1956, the die casting operations were still carried out in the old facility on Elizabeth Avenue (there was also a plastic molding factory in Lampeter, Pennsylvania). The toys made during the late 1940s and 1950s are considered by collectors to be among the company's best, particularly the line of Bell Telephone trucks. Many Hubleys produced during this time are very accurate representations of full-size vehicles; the #455 Jaguar and the #509 Chevrolet Corvette are excellent examples.

In 1960, Hubley launched a new line of 1/60 scale die cast models, named "Real Toys." These models were undoubtedly designed to compete with the models being offered by Dinky Toys and Corgi Toys. Although they were very accurate, well-made models, they did not have a significant impact on the market at the time. They were made for just a few years (until 1964) and this may account for their relative scarcity (and popularity) today. (The Real Toys were also manufactured in Canada during the same period, under the label "Real Types." The line consisted of the same models as the American line.)

Hubley competed successfully with Tootsietoy, Midgetoy and other American lines throughout the 1950s and '60s. In 1966, Gabriel Industries bought Hubley; many of the Hubley toys were kept in production, however. In 1969, Gabriel launched a new series of larger die cast trucks entitled "Steerables." The Hubley name was retained on the Steerable toys into the 1970s, but by 1976 the

*The Hubley "Real Toys" #551 Ford Panel Truck was simply the Country Squire Station Wagon with the rear windows cast in. This model came with decals for "Long Lee's Chinese Laundry," which could be applied over the rear side windows and along the sides of the body.*

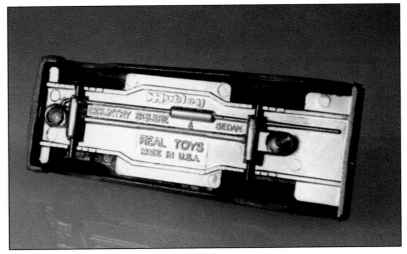

*The baseplate of the Real Toys Ford Panel Truck says "Country Squire & Sedan," indicating it could be used on more than one model.*

name was gone. The Columbia Broadcasting System bought the Hubley Toy Division from Gabriel in 1978, and there the Hubley saga ends.

## Wheels and Packaging

Like other manufacturers, Hubley used black rubber tires on its wheeled toys from 1946 until the later 1960s; plastic tires were then used more and more as the 1960s became the 1970s. Almost none of the rubber (or plastic) tires say "Hubley" on them.

Many Hubley toys came in individual boxes, often with colorful artwork of the toy inside. Finding a Hubley with its original box can be tricky, although many of the medium size (seven to eleven inches in length) truck boxes seem to have survived better than others.

An excellent source of information on Hubleys is a book entitled *Hubley Die-Cast Toys, 1936-1976,* written (and self-published) by Charles A. Jones. More information on this book can be found in Part Three, Additional Resources.

The following listing provides Hubley's original catalog number for each toy. Two numbers are often assigned to the same toy (i.e., #404A and #1404 for the 1934 Ford Coupe);

this is due to the toy being re-numbered by Hubley at some point during the production run. (It can also mean that the toy was changed or otherwise updated at some point, with the name being essentially unchanged.) Also provided in the listing is the overall length of each toy, since Hubley toys were often made in more than one size, and consistent scales were not a priority.

Hubley also made numerous boxed sets through the years. These are not listed here, but detailed information on them may be found in Charles A. Jones' book on Hubley.

*A Hubley #431A Ford Dump Truck. The black rubber tires are typical of Hubleys of the 1950s and '60s. In this chipped condition, this truck's value would be lowered to $25-$30.*

| # | Name | Price |
|---|------|-------|
| **"Real Toys" series (1/60 scale):** | | |
| 420 | Chevrolet Corvette | $50 |
| 421 | Ford Thunderbird | 40 |
| 422 | Studebaker Hawk | 40 |
| 423 | Chrysler Imperial | 40 |
| 424 | Chevrolet Pickup | 30 |
| 425A | Ford Falcon | 30 |
| 426A | Chevrolet Corvair | 40 |
| 427A | Ford Country Squire | 40 |
| 428A | Buick | 40 |
| 550 | GM Fire Bird III | 50 |
| 551 | Ford Panel Truck | 35 |
| 552 | Chevrolet Ambulance | 40 |
| 553 | Chevrolet Fire Chief | 40 |
| 554 | Ford Taxi | 50 |
| 555 | Ford State Police | 40 |
| 575 | Delivery Truck | 35 |
| 752 | Soft Drink Truck | 45 |
| 754 | Dump Truck | 35 |
| 755 | Tow Truck | 35 |
| 756 | School Bus | 35 |
| **General Hubley toys:** | | |
| 401A | Lincoln Continental Sedan (6") | 40 |
| 1401 | Lincoln Continental Sedan (6") | 40 |
| 402A | Fire Engine (6") | 30 |
| 1402 | Fire Engine (6") | 30 |
| 403A | Falcon Pickup Truck (6") | 30 |

| # | Name | Price |
|---|------|-------|
| 1403 | Falcon Pickup Truck (6") | $30 |
| 404A | 1934 Ford Coupe (6") | 40 |
| 1404 | 1934 Ford Coupe (6") | 40 |
| 405A | Corvair Station Wagon (6") | 40 |
| 1405 | Corvair Station Wagon (6") | 40 |
| 406 | Gas Truck (6") | 35 |
| 1406 | Gas Truck (6") | 35 |
| 429A | Log Truck (1952 Ford) (5³/₄") | 60 |
| 431A | Dump Truck (1952 Ford) (5⁵/₈") | 60 |
| 432A | Sports Car (MG) (5⁷/₈") | 55 |
| 451 | Tractor (5¹/₂") | 40 |
| 452A | Cadillac Sedan (7") | 90 |
| 452B | Stake Truck (1953 Truck) (7") | 75 |
| 453A | Tow Truck (1953 Ford) (7") | 75 |
| 454A | Log Truck (1953 Ford) (7¹/₂") | 70 |
| 455A | Sports Car (Jaguar) (7¹/₂") | 225 |
| 456 | Racer (post-war version) (7¹/₂") | 75 |
| 456A | Tractor (5¹/₂") | 40 |
| 457 | Racer (7") | 90 |
| 458 | Convertible (Buick) (7") | 100 |
| 458A | Dump Truck (Studebaker) (7¹⁵/₁₆") | 85 |
| 459 | Taxi-Cab (7") | 90 |
| 459A | Log Truck (Studebaker) (7⁵/₈") | 85 |
| 460 | Stake Truck (1947 Ford) (7") | 90 |
| 460A | Stake Truck (Studebaker) (7³/₈") | 75 |
| 461 | Pickup Truck (1947 Ford) (7") | 75 |
| 462 | Tow Truck (1947 Ford) (7") | 75 |
| 463 | Hook & Ladder (Dodge) (7¹/₂") | 80 |

| # | Name | Price |
|---|------|-------|
| 464 | Fire Engine (Dodge) (7¹/₂") | $65 |
| 465 | Convertible (Buick) (7") | 120 |
| 465A | Hook & Ladder (Dodge) (8¹/₂") | 100 |
| 466 | Air Compressor (1953 Ford) (6³/₄") | 70 |
| 468 | Hook & Ladder (1952 Ford) (11¹/₂") | 125 |
| 469 | Log Truck (1952 Ford) (10") | 125 |
| 469A | Log Truck (1957 Ford) (10³/₄") | 100 |
| 1469 | Log Truck (1957 Ford) (10³/₄") | 100 |
| 470A | Stake Truck (1947 Ford) (9¹/₂") | 140 |
| 470B | Dump Truck (1957 Ford) (9¹/₄") | 100 |
| 1470 | Dump Truck (1957 Ford) (9¹/₄") | 90 |
| 471 | Lumber Truck (1947 Ford) (9¹/₂") | 110 |
| 471A | Dump Truck (1952 Ford) (9¹/₂") | 90 |
| 471B | Hook & Ladder (1952 Ford) (11¹/₄") | 95 |
| 1471 | Hook & Ladder (1952 Ford) (11¹/₄") | 85 |
| 1471A | Farm Tractor & Trailer (10") | 60 |
| 472A | Hook & Ladder (10¹/₄") | 100 |
| 472B | Tractor (7") | 40 |
| 1472 | Tractor (7") | 30 |
| 1540 | Tractor (7") | 30 |
| 473 | Hook & Ladder (10") | 115 |
| 473A | Tractor (7¹/₄") | 40 |
| 474 | Tow Truck (1947 Ford) (9³/₄") | 150 |
| 474A | Farm Tractor & Wagon (10¹/₄") | 65 |
| 1474 | Farm Tractor & Wagon (10¹/₄") | 65 |
| 1541 | Farm Tractor & Wagon (10¹/₄") | 65 |
| 475 | Tractor (6³/₄") | 50 |
| 475A | Dump Truck (G.M.C.) (8¹/₂") | 65 |

| #     | Name                                      | Price |
|-------|-------------------------------------------|-------|
| 475B  | Thunderbird (1955) (9¼")                  | $200  |
| 476   | Dump Truck (1947 Ford) (9½")              | 75    |
| 476A  | Station Wagon (Studebaker) (8⅞")          | 135   |
| 477   | Cement Mixer (1947 Ford) (10")            | 100   |
| 477A  | Stake Truck (1952 Ford) (9½")             | 90    |
| 478   | Bell Telephone Truck (1947 Ford) (10½")   | 200   |
| 478A  | Dump Truck (1956 G.M.C.) (10")            | 85    |
| 479   | Log Truck (1956 G.M.C.) (11")             | 90    |
| 479A  | Motorcycle (8½")                          | 650   |
| 480   | Road Roller (10¼")                        | 75    |
| 481   | Road Scraper (10¾")                       | 75    |
| 482   | Bell Telephone Truck (G.M.C.) (8½")       | 160   |
| 482A  | Tow Truck (1956 G.M.C.) (9¾")             | 100   |
| 483   | Cement Mixer (1952 Ford) (10")            | 100   |
| 484   | Telephone Truck (1952 Ford) (10½")        | 200   |
| 484A  | Motorcycle (8½")                          | 500   |
| 485   | Deluxe Sports Car (M.G.) (9¼")            | 225   |
| 485A  | Pipe Truck (1956 G.M.C.) (11")            | 90    |
| 486   | Deluxe Sports Car (Thunderbird) (9¼")     | 175   |
| 487   | Cement Mixer (1956 G.M.C.) (10⅜")         | 100   |
| 488   | Power Shovel (8")                         | 85    |
| 489   | Grain Truck (1956 G.M.C.) (10")           | 115   |
| 490   | Tractor (9½")                             | 85    |
| 491   | Shovel Truck (1952 Ford) (13¼")           | 190   |
| 491A  | Station Wagon & Boat (16")                | 160   |
| 492   | Auto Transport (14")                      | 175   |
| 1492  | Auto Transport (14")                      | 175   |
| 493   | Lumber Truck (13¾")                       | 140   |
| 493A  | School Bus (9")                           | 45    |
| 1820  | School Bus (9")                           | 35    |
| 1821  | School Bus (9")                           | 30    |
| 494   | Bell Telephone Truck (1957 Ford) (9½")    | 300   |
| 494A  | Shovel Truck (1956 G.M.C.) (13")          | 200   |
| 496   | Tractor (9¼")                             | 100   |
| 1496  | Tractor (9¼")                             | 100   |
| 497   | Poultry Truck (1956 G.M.C.) (10")         | 200   |
| 497A  | Poultry Truck (1957 Ford) (10")           | 200   |
| 498   | Fish Hatchery (1957 Ford) (10")           | 225   |
| 499   | Road Roller (10½")                        | 95    |
| 500   | Tractor Trailer Set (1949 G.M.C.) (17½")  | 250   |
| 501   | Auto Transport (1949 G.M.C.) (18")        | 275   |
| 501A  | Tractor Loader (12¾")                     | 110   |
| 501B  | Tractor Loader (12¾")                     | 110   |
| 1501  | Tractor Loader (12¾")                     | 110   |
| 1952  | Tractor Loader (12¾")                     | 110   |
| 502   | Lumber Truck (1949 G.M.C.) (17½")         | 225   |
| 502A  | Tractor with Cultivator (9¼")             | 120   |
| 503   | Stake Truck (1949 G.M.C.) (17½")          | 200   |
| 503A  | Road Grader (12¾")                        | 85    |
| 1503  | Road Grader (12¾")                        | 85    |
| 1951  | Road Grader (12¾")                        | 85    |
| 504   | Bell Telephone Truck (1949 G.M.C.) (12½") | 200   |
| 504A  | Bell Telephone Truck (1952 Ford) (12½")   | 225   |
| 505   | Log Truck (1949 G.M.C.) (18")             | 130   |

| #     | Name                                      | Price |
|-------|-------------------------------------------|-------|
| 505A  | Log Truck (1952 Ford) (18")               | $130  |
| 505B  | Cat Loader (Crawler) (11")                | 95    |
| 1505  | Cat Loader (Crawler) (7¾")                | 95    |
| 1952  | Cat Loader (Crawler) (7¾")                | 95    |
| 506   | Carry All Set (1952 Ford) (19½")          | 225   |
| 507   | Motor Express (1952 Ford) (18")           | 185   |
| 507A  | Ford Tractor (10½")                       | 160   |
| 508   | Dump Truck (1952 Ford) (17")              | 175   |
| 508A  | Ford Tractor (11")                        | 175   |
| 1508  | Ford Tractor (11")                        | 175   |
| 509   | Custom Sports Car (12¾")                  | 475   |
| 509A  | Ford Tractor (12")                        | 175   |
| 1509  | Ford Tractor (12")                        | 175   |
| 1570  | Ford Tractor (12")                        | 175   |
| 510   | Log Truck (20½")                          | 175   |
| 511   | Carry All Set (20½")                      | 200   |
| 512   | Dump Truck (18")                          | 175   |
| 513   | Fire Pumper (14¼")                        | 175   |
| 514   | Cat Log Truck (22½")                      | 95    |
| 520   | Fire Truck (19")                          | 250   |
| 521   | Auto Transport (19½")                     | 250   |
| 522   | Air Force Bomber Transport (21¾")         | 150   |
| 525   | Tractor (Ford) (12")                      | 135   |
| 757   | Post Hole Digger-tractor accessory (1½")  | 60    |
| 758   | Scraper Blade-tractor accessory (3½")     | 60    |
| 801   | Dump Truck (Dodge) (10")                  | 60    |
| 1801  | Dump Truck (Dodge) (10")                  | 45    |
| 1805  | Dump Truck (Dodge) (10")                  | 35    |
| 802   | Truck with Tractor (Dodge) (10¼")         | 80    |
| 803   | Pipe Truck (Dodge) (11")                  | 90    |
| 851   | Stock Yard Truck (10")                    | 155   |
| 882   | Pickup Truck (12")                        | 50    |
| 1851  | Pickup Truck (12")                        | 40    |
| 901   | Power Shovel (15")                        | 80    |
| 1901  | Power Shovel (15")                        | 80    |
| 1953  | Power Shovel (15")                        | 80    |
| 902   | Dump Truck (11")                          | 60    |
| 1902  | Dump Truck (11")                          | 50    |
| 1852  | Dump Truck (11")                          | 45    |
| 903   | Bulldozer (8¾")                           | 75    |
| 1903  | Bulldozer (8¾")                           | 75    |
| 1950  | Bulldozer (8¾")                           | 75    |
| 926   | Tow Truck (12")                           | 55    |
| 1926  | Tow Truck (12")                           | 55    |
| 1853  | Tow Truck (12")                           | 55    |
| 927   | Stake Truck with Trailer (20½")           | 60    |
| 1927  | Stake Truck with Trailer (20½")           | 60    |
| 1860  | Stake Truck with Trailer (20½")           | 60    |
| 952   | Mr. Magoo Car (8½")                       | 80    |
| 953   | Tractor with Trailer Dump (24")           | 60    |
| 1953  | Tractor with Trailer Dump (24")           | 60    |
| 966   | Flat Bed with Shovel (20")                | 130   |
| 1966  | Flat Bed with Shovel (20")                | 130   |
| 1091  | Large Farm Set (Ford 6000)                | 220   |
| 1458  | Dump Truck (6½")                          | 35    |
| 1459  | Log Truck (8¾")                           | 40    |
| 1460  | Motor Express (8¾")                       | 40    |
| 1461  | Gas Truck (9")                            | 40    |
| 1480  | Beetlebug (VW) (7½")                      | 25    |
| 1481  | Beetlebug (VW) (7½")                      | 25    |

| #     | Name                                      | Price |
|-------|-------------------------------------------|-------|
| 1490  | Dump Truck (1958 Ford) (7½")              | $45   |
| 1491  | Log Truck (1958 Ford) (8")                | 45    |
| 493   | Rescue Truck (1958 Ford) (8¼")            | 50    |
| 1502  | Tractor Loader (12¼")                     | 95    |
| 1504  | Tractor with Stake Trailer (18½")         | 110   |
| 1506  | Tractor (11")                             | 135   |
| 1511  | Auto Transport (1958 Ford) (13")          | 90    |
| 1513  | Cattle Truck (1958 Ford) (11½")           | 85    |
| 1514  | Tanker Truck (1958 Ford) (12")            | 80    |
| 1515  | Lumber Truck (1958 Ford) (12")            | 80    |
| 1516  | Dump Truck with Bulldozer (1958 Ford) (14") | 105 |
| 1517  | Jeep with Speed Boat (15")                | 50    |
| 1518  | Rancher Jeep with Trailer (15")           | 75    |
| 1519  | Rancher Jeep with Trailer (15")           | 75    |
| 1520  | Tractor (9¼")                             | 60    |
| 1521  | Fire Jeep & Trailer (14")                 | 75    |
| 1524  | Fire Jeep & Trailer (14")                 | 75    |
| 1522  | Jeep with Howitzer (14")                  | 75    |
| 1523  | Custom Roadster with Cycle (15")          | 55    |
| 1550  | Hubley Tractor (9")                       | 70    |
| 1551  | Hubley Tractor Loader (12")               | 90    |
| 1708  | Scorcher Roadster (6")                    | 40    |
| 1709  | Lotus Racer (7⅞")                         | 25    |
| 1710  | Civilian Jeep (7")                        | 40    |
| 1711  | Jeep Wrecker (7")                         | 55    |
| 1712  | Jeep Surfer (7")                          | 45    |
| 1713  | All Purpose Jeep (7")                     | 40    |
| 1714  | G.I. Jeep (7")                            | 40    |
| 1769  | Army Bulldozer (5")                       | 50    |
| 1772  | Bulldozer (5")                            | 50    |
| 1803  | Front End Loader (7")                     | 50    |
| 1813  | Front End Loader (7")                     | 50    |
| 1804  | Bulldozer (6½")                           | 50    |
| 1814  | Bulldozer (6½")                           | 50    |
| 1805  | Road Grader (11")                         | 40    |
| 1815  | Road Grader (11")                         | 40    |
| 1806  | Power Boom (9")                           | 55    |
| 1816  | Power Boom (9")                           | 55    |
| 1807  | Earth Hauler (14")                        | 60    |
| 1817  | Earth Hauler (14")                        | 60    |
| 1862  | Dump Truck & Bulldozer (20")              | 80    |
| 1890  | U.S. Army Carry All (12")                 | 85    |
| 1910  | Steerable Pickup (7½")                    | 35    |
| 1911  | Steerable Log Truck (7¾")                 | 35    |
| 1912  | Steerable Hyside Dump (7¾")               | 35    |
| 1913  | Steerable Tow Truck (7¾")                 | 40    |
| 1914  | Steerable Snorkel Pumper (9½")            | 40    |
| 1915  | Steerable Cement Truck (7¾")              | 50    |
| 1916  | Steerable Sanitation Truck (8½")          | 60    |
| 1917  | Steerable Auto Transport (12")            | 75    |
| 1918  | Steerable Dump-N-Dozer (13½")             | 50    |
| 1928  | Pile Driver Truck (13")                   | 85    |
| 1929  | Carpenter's Truck (12")                   | 70    |
| 25131 | Steerable Dump Truck (8")                 | 35    |
| 25133 | Steerable Tow Truck (8")                  | 40    |
| 25135 | Steerable Cement Truck (7½")              | 45    |
| 25139 | Steerable "Gabriel Toys" (7⅞")            | 45    |
| 26143 | Smokey Bear with Jeep (7")                | 85    |
| 26167 | Mobile Field Force (9¾")                  | 50    |

# Joal

This company got its start in the late 1940s in Spain. In the late 1960s, Joal debuted a series of 1/43 scale model cars and a series of 1/50 scale trucks and construction vehicles. They were of decent quality, with window glazing and (on the car models) suspension.

At least one of the Joal models was not original to the company, that being the #108 Chevrolet Monza GT. This model was originally produced by Tekno starting about 1967. In 1970, the tooling was used by Kirk, Tenko's "parent" company, to put out the model under the Kirk banner. After Kirk went under in 1970 or '71, the molds found their way to Spain and into the Joal line, and that is the version shown here. It is possible that other Joal models are re-

issues of models originally made by other manufacturers.

Through the years new Joal models of construction vehicles have occasionally appeared on the market, although they were not easy to locate in the United States. However, Irwin Toy Limited of Canada now markets a line of Joal models. This series consists of original Joal 1/43 scale models made during the late '60s and early '70s. Included are the #109 Mercedes-Benz 230SL, the #114 Ferrari 250LM, and so on. The castings appear to be identical to those of the originals, which would make these models re-issues.

The following listing outlines the original Joal models made during the 1960s and 1970s.

*This #108 Chevrolet Monza by Joal was actually a third-generation model, having been originally produced by Tekno and then Kirk (see Joal company history). Joal released this version starting around 1970.*

| # | Name | Price |
|---|------|-------|
| 100 | Jaguar E Type Roadster | $20 |
| 101 | Simca 1000 | 20 |
| 102 | Renault R 8 | 20 |
| 103 | Seat 850 Coupe | 20 |
| 104 | Renault R 10 | 20 |
| 105 | Alfa Romeo Giulia TZ1 Canguro | 20 |
| 106 | Seat 124 | 20 |
| 107 | Mercedes-Benz 300SL | 20 |
| 108 | Chevrolet Monza | 20 |
| 109 | Mercedes-Benz 230SL Hardtop | 20 |
| 110 | Mercedes-Benz 230SL Roadster | 20 |
| 111 | Porsche Carrera 6 | 20 |
| 112 | Alfa Romeo Giulia SS | 20 |
| 113 | Chaparral 2 F | 20 |
| 114 | Ferrari 250 Le Mans | 25 |
| 115 | Iso Rivolta | 20 |
| 116 | Ferrari 612 Can-Am | 25 |
| 117 | Mercedes Benz C-111 | 20 |
| 118 | Adams Probe 16 | 20 |
| 119 | Ferrari 512S | 25 |

| # | Name | Price |
|---|------|-------|
| 120 | Twin Mill | $20 |
| 121 | Porsche 917K | 20 |
| 122 | McLaren M 80 | 20 |
| 123 | Seat 132 | 20 |
| 124 | Mercedes-Benz 350SL | 20 |
| 125 | Lamborghini Miura | 20 |
| 126 | Citroën SM | 20 |
| 127 | Citroën CX Pallas | 20 |
| 128 | Chrysler 150 | 20 |
| 129 | Ford Fiesta | 20 |
| 150 | Iso Rivolta and Caravan | 30 |
| 151 | Mercedes-Benz 230SL and Trailer | 30 |
| 152 | Citroën CX Pallas and Trailer | 30 |
| 153 | Citroën SM, Ford Fiesta and Trailer | 30 |
| 154 | Wrecker and Ford Fiesta | 20 |
| 155 | Chrysler 150, Ferrari Formula 1 and Trailer | 30 |
| 200 | Leyland Dumper | 20 |
| 200 | Leyland Dumper "Construccion" | 20 |
| 201 | Taylor Crane Truck | 20 |

| # | Name | Price |
|---|------|-------|
| 201 | Taylor Crane Truck "Autopistas" | $20 |
| 202 | Barreiros Cement Truck | 20 |
| 202 | Barreiros Cement Truck "Construccion" | 20 |
| 203 | Massey Ferguson Tractor | 25 |
| 204 | Farm Trailer | 10 |
| 205 | Farm Pulverisator | 10 |
| 206 | Massey Ferguson Tractor with Mechanical Shovel | 25 |
| 207 | Pegaso Truck with Boat Motor | 25 |
| 208 | Pegaso Tanker "BUTANO" | 30 |
| 209 | Pegaso Tanker "CAMPSA" | 30 |
| 210 | Bulldozer | 20 |
| 211 | Pegaso Multibucket | 20 |
| 212 | Pegaso Articulated Truck | 25 |
| 213 | Caterpillar 935 Traxcavator | 20 |
| 214 | Caterpillar Tractor | 20 |
| 215 | Caterpillar Fork Lift | 20 |
| 216 | Caterpillar 225 Excavator | 20 |
| 217 | Caterpillar 12 G Leveller | 20 |
| 218 | Caterpillar 825 B | 20 |

# Johnny Lightning

**I**t is said that imitation is the sincerest form of flattery. If that is true, then Topper was a very sincere company.

Henry Orenstein, the owner of Topper, looked at the success of Mattel's Hot Wheels line in 1968 and decided he could do that, too. He came out with his own line of ultra-fast die cast cars in 1969, and the battle was joined. Johnny Lightning never reached the sales levels of Hot Wheels, but for a time they did give the California-based Mattel a run for its money.

Using low-friction wheels and axles, Topper claimed their Johnny Lightning cars were faster than Hot Wheels. Kids across the country bought Johnny Lightnings and put them up against the best that Hot Wheels had to offer. Cars like the Custom XKE, the Nucleon and the Double Trouble pushed Johnny Lightning into the national spotlight, and an Indianapolis 500 win by Al Unser, Sr. in 1970 didn't hurt: he was driving the Johnny Lightning-sponsored car.

It all came to an end for Topper in late 1971, when the company went out of business. Collectors today prize those original Johnny Lightnings, along with the track and race sets that Topper marketed for use with the cars.

*An original Johnny Lightning, the Custom Mako Shark. This example is of the non-opening door variety. Note also the Hot Wheels-like "redline" wheels that Topper used on the Johnny Lightnings in 1969 and 1970.*

## From the Ashes
In 1992, the Michigan-based Playing Mantis company acquired the rights to the Johnny Lightning name, and eventually released a line of new Johnny Lightning cars. They were all reproductions of original Johnny Lightning cars, since the original tooling is reportedly long gone.

The first repro series was the Commemoratives, released in early 1994. It included cars such as the Movin' Van, the El Camino Surfer, etc. Selling for $2 to $3 in stores like Wal-Mart, Toys R Us, etc., the line proved successful enough that Playing Mantis has released two more lines, "Muscle Cars U.S.A.," and "Dragsters U.S.A." In addition, there have been four "Special Edition" cars, and a "Sky Show" set that featured a special El Camino.

Playing Mantis has successfully capitalized on a name that brings back good memories for a lot of people. The attention being focused on the new Johnny Lightnings has increased collector awareness of the old, original cars. Playing Mantis puts out a Johnny Lightning newsletter, sent to members of the Johnny Lightning Club. Members also get a crack at the "Special Edition" cars. For more information, see Part Three, Additional Resources.

The following listing provides values for both the original line and for the new cars put out by Playing Mantis. **For the section on the original cars, the values are for near mint to mint condition cars by themselves,** or "loose," as collectors would say. Since Johnny Lightnings came in blisterpacks, few have survived with the original packaging, which was most often discarded. For a car still in the original blisterpack, a value of one-and-a-half to two times the value given here is a good rule of thumb; this is an indicator of how highly the original packaging is valued by collectors.

The Current Retail Price (CRP) indicated for the new cars is for a mint condition example still in the blisterpack.

| Name | Price |
|------|-------|

## ORIGINAL TOPPER CARS

### 1969 models:

| | |
|------|-------|
| Custom GTO | $150 |
| Custom El Camino | 150 |
| Custom XKE (with opening doors) | 100 |
| Custom XKE (with sealed doors) | 45 |
| Custom Toronado | 100 |
| Custom T Bird | 100 |
| Custom Turbine (with painted interior) | 50 |
| Custom Turbine (with unpainted interior) | 25 |
| Custom '32 Ford | 30 |
| Custom Dragster | 30 |
| Custom Ferrari (with opening doors) | 125 |
| Custom Ferrari (with sealed doors) | 60 |
| Custom Eldorado | 100 |
| Custom Mako Shark (with opening doors) | 100 |
| Custom Mako Shark (with sealed doors) | 45 |

### 1970 models:

| | |
|------|-------|
| A.J. Foyt Indy Special | 40 |
| (also came in Parnelli Jones and Al Unser versions) | |
| Frantic Ferrari | 25 |
| Nucleon | 45 |
| Vulture | 55 |
| Jumpin Jag | 25 |

| Name | Price |
|------|-------|
| Sand Stormer | $25 |
| Sling Shot | 35 |
| Flame Out | 45 |
| Vicious Vette | 40 |
| T.N.T. | 35 |
| Leapin Limo | 45 |
| Parnelli Jones | 50 |
| Double Trouble | 45 |
| Triple Threat | 35 |
| Bug Bomb | 40 |
| Condor | 100 |
| Movin Van | 30 |
| Al Unser | 50 |
| Wasp | 50 |
| The Whistler | 65 |
| Mad Maverick | 35 |
| Baja | 50 |
| Custom Spoiler | 30 |
| Smuggler | 35 |
| Stiletto | 25 |
| Flying Needle* | 35 |
| Wedge* | 35 |
| Screamer* | 30 |
| Glasser* | 35 |
| Monster* | 25 |
| Bubble* | 30 |

| Name | Price |
|------|-------|

### 1971 models:

| | |
|------|-------|
| Wild Winner** | $55 |
| Pipe Dream** | 55 |
| Twin Blaster** | 55 |
| Hairy Hauler** | 55 |
| Big Rig** | 55 |

\* "Jet Powered" car
\*\* "Custom Car" that came in a special blisterpack with "snap-on" parts; these are difficult to find complete

## NEW PLAYING MANTIS CARS

### The Commemoratives:

| | | |
|---|------|-----|
| 101 | Custom El Camino Surfer | CRP |
| 102 | Custom Pontiac GTO | CRP |
| 103 | Custom XKE Sports Car | CRP |
| 104 | Custom '32 Roadster | CRP |
| 105 | Bug Bomb | CRP |
| 106 | Movin' Van | CRP |
| 107 | Vicious Vette | CRP |
| 108 | The Wasp | CRP |
| 109 | Custom Continental | CRP |
| 110 | Custom Toronado | CRP |
| 111 | Custom Thunderbird | CRP |
| 112 | Custom Mustang | CRP |
| 113 | Custom Spoiler | CRP |
| 114 | Custom Mako Shark | CRP |
| 115 | Custom Turbine | CRP |
| 116 | Triple Threat | CRP |
| 117 | Nucleon | CRP |
| 118 | T.N.T. | CRP |

### Muscle Cars U.S.A. series:

| | | |
|---|------|-----|
| 201 | '70 Superbird | CRP |
| 202 | '71 Hemi Cuda | CRP |
| 203 | '70 Boss 302 | CRP |
| 204 | '70 Super Bee | CRP |
| 205 | '69 GTO Judge | CRP |
| 206 | '70 Chevelle SS | CRP |
| 207 | '69 Cougar Eliminator | CRP |
| 208 | '69 Olds 442 | CRP |
| 209 | '65 GTO Ragtop | CRP |
| 210 | '72 Nova SS | CRP |

### Dragsters U.S.A. series:

| | |
|------|-----|
| The Hawaiian | CRP |
| Blue Max | CRP |
| Motown Shaker | CRP |
| Chi-Town Hustler | CRP |
| Drag-On Lady | CRP |
| Color Me Gone | CRP |
| Revellution | CRP |
| L.A.P.D. | CRP |
| Sox and Martin | CRP |
| '58 Christine | CRP |
| '55 Jukebox | CRP |

*Playing Mantis' Custom Mako Shark reproduction. The plastic collector's button shows the "serial" number of the individual car.*

# Jolly Roger

The "line" of Jolly Roger toys can only be called such if two models make up a line. In 1946 or '47, Tremo Mouldings of Cardiff, Wales, put out a model of Plymouth and a model of a Maserati Grand Prix race car. Many enthusiasts believe the Plymouth to be based on the 1939 model year.

Both models are a bit smaller than 1/43, each measuring about four inches in length. They appear to be rather clumsy copies of two models in the Belgian "Septoy" line, which came out at about the same time. But the Maserati bears such a close resemblance to the Maserati in another line—that of the British "Timpo Toys"—that it was almost certainly made from the same tooling. The Timpo version may have been made as early as 1946.

In any event, the two models can't have been made for very long. British model authority Mike Richardson has advanced the theory that the company did indeed "pirate" the designs of the models, and was therefore asked to cease and desist from producing any more.

Known colors on the Plymouth are green, brown and blue, while the Maserati has been found in red, blue and green. Both models came in individual boxes on which were printed the words "Jolly Roger," a pirate logo and information about the model. Each box also had artwork of the car.

These two models don't turn up very often, particularly in the United States. As for values, expect to pay anywhere from $50 to $100 for a boxed, near mint example of either one.

# J.R.D.

The history of J.R.D. is closely associated with that of yet another French die cast manufacturer, Companie Industrielle du Jouets, or C.I.J. When C.I.J. ended its relationship with the French car maker Citroën in 1935, the tooling for the Citroën toys that C.I.J. had been manufacturing was returned to the Citroën factory. A Monsieur Rabier, then employed by Citroën, secured some capital, dusted off the tooling, and formed a new company to continue the manufacture of Citroën promotional toys. That company was J.R.D.

Many tinplate and "plaster-and-flour" toys were made by J.R.D. during the 1930s. After the war, tinplate toy vehicles were again the order of the day. It wasn't until 1958 (or 1956, depending on who you talk to) that J.R.D. entered the die cast market. Naturally, French marques such as Citroën and Berliet dominated the line, although there was a very nice model of a Mercedes thrown in for good measure.

In general, J.R.D. models were well-made and very accurate, and are today very popular with collectors, particularly in Europe and the United Kingdom. The bodies were usu-

*J.R.D. #114 Citroën P55 Covered Truck with original box. The black tires indicate this example is from later in the production, perhaps 1961 or '62.*

ally a one-piece die cast unit attached to a tinplate base. The baseplate showed the name of the model, in addition to the legend "Made in France." Some form of the words "Miniatures J.R.D." also appeared on the baseplate. The wheels were die cast for quite a while, but spun-aluminum units showed up on some later models. White tires were used for most models, but later production models sometimes had black tires fitted. The early cars (#110 and #112 Citroëns) had no windows or interior fittings, but the later cars (numbers in the 150s) did. The later cars also had suspension. The Citroën vans (2CV and 1200 Kg) and the Berliet trucks came in a number of very sharp liveries, although most of the trucks and vans did not have windows, interior fittings or suspension.

The boxes used for many J.R.D. models featured artwork of the model on them (see photos); the exception was the boxes for most of the Vans, which had a label stuck onto has the end flaps to indicate the model.

Despite their excellent quality, production of J.R.D. models ceased in 1962 or 1963. In a sense, history now came full-circle as the remaining inventory of models was bought by C.I.J. J.R.D.'s old rival gave these remaining models numbers in the C.I.J. catalog, and sold them as C.I.J. models. These can be identified by typewritten paper labels that C.I.J. applied to the end flaps of the boxes; they also sometimes placed labels on the baseplates.

## Watch for Those Re-issues

In 1985, several of the original J.R.D. models were re-issued using the original tooling. The re-issue operation was reportedly quite casual until it was taken on by a company called "Mini-Racing," located in Nogent-sur-Marne, France. Six castings have been re-issued: the #112 Citroën 11 CV; #116 Citroën DS 19; #152 Citroën DS 19 Convertible; #110 Citroën 2CV; Citroën 2 CV Van; and Citroën 1200 Kg Van.

(The Vans, incidentally, come in a number of liveries that never appeared on the original J.R.D. Vans.)

Identifying one of these re-issues is simple, since the baseplates have an "85" on them. Also, the boxes are brighter and are made of a stiffer cardboard than the originals.

The following listing provides information and values for the full, original line of J.R.D.'s. Per the standard format, all values are for a near mint to mint condition example with the original box.

*A #155 Simca 1000 with original box. Like the other cars in the "150 series," this model had window glazing, interior fittings and suspension. This was the last of the J.R.D. models, issued in 1962.*

| # | Name | Price |
|---|---|---|
| 106 | Citroën H 1200 Kg Police Van (white/black) | $100 |
| 107 | Citroën H 1200 Kg Ambulance (white) | 110 |
| 108 | Citroën 2 CV Van "EDF" (gray) | 125 |
| 109 | Citroën 2 CV Fire Van (red) | 125 |
| 110 | Citroën 2 CV (ivory, gray, blue, green, orange) | 100 |
| 111 | Citroën 2 CV Van (gray) | 90 |
| 111A | Citroën 2 CV Van "COMAP" (blue) | 800 |
| 111B | Citroën 2 CV Van "RENFORT NYLON" (yellow) | 700 |
| 111C | Citroën 2 CV Van "SUDO" (blue) | 700 |
| 111D | Citroën 2 CV Van "YACCO" (dark gray) | 700 |
| 111E | Citroën 2 CV Van (blue) | 110 |
| 112 | Citroën 11 CV Normale (black, gray, light gray, beige) | 105 |
| 113 | Citroën H 1200 Kg Van (silver) | 90 |
| 113A | Citroën H 1200 Kg Van "ESSO" (silver) | 130 |
| 113B | Citroën H 1200 Kg Van "BONBEL/LA VACHE QUI RIT" (cream) | 950 |
| 113C | Citroën H 1200 Kg Van "COMAP" (blue) | 950 |
| 113D | Citroën H 1200 Kg Van "BRANDT" (yellow/blue) | 400 |
| 114 | Citroën P 55 Covered Truck (cream green, orange/green, yellow/green, red/green) | 120 |

| # | Name | Price |
|---|---|---|
| 115 | Citroën P 55 Army Truck and Tanker Trailer (olive) | $140 |
| 116 | Citroën DS 19 (green/gray, green/yellow, beige/orange, cream/blue, silver/blue) | 100 |
| 117 | Citroën 2 CV Van "TOURING CLUB" (white) | 125 |
| 117A | Citroën 2 CV Van "MONTBLANC" (white) | 1450 |
| 118 | Citroën 2 CV Van "AIR FRANCE" (white/blue) | 160 |
| 119 | Citroën 2 CV Van "CAISSE NATIONALE D'EPARGNE" (yellow) | 475 |
| 120 | Articulated Berliet TLR "KRONENBOURG" (cream/red) | 150 |
| 121 | Articulated Berliet TLR Tanker "TOTAL" (red/blue/white) | 175 |
| 122 | Unic Tanker "ANTAR" (red) | 150 |
| 123 | Unic Izoard "KRONENBOURG" (beige/red/white) | 225 |
| 123A | Unic Izoard "KRONENBOURG" (red/blue/white—promotional) | 1100 |
| 124 | Unic Izoard Circus Train (cream/red/green) | 225 |
| 125 | Berliet CACL Mobile Crane (orange, metallic blue) | 125 |
| 126 | Unic Lautaret Van "HAFA" (blue/pink) | 210 |
| 127 | Unic Lautaret Van and Trailer "TRANSPORTS INTERNATIONAUX" (orange green, orange blue, red/white) | 240 |

| # | Name | Price |
|---|---|---|
| 128 | Unic Milk Truck (blue/white, red/white) | $150 |
| 129 | Fruehauf Truck Trailer (orange/green, orange/blue, red/white) | 100 |
| 130 | Unic Izoard Road Tanker (silver/red) | 175 |
| 131 | Berliet GAK Refuse Wagon "GENEVE-VORAX" (silver, metallic blue) | 125 |
| 131A | Berliet GAK Refuse Wagon (silver, metallic blue) | 110 |
| 132 | Berliet GAK Road Tanker "ANTARGAZ" (red/black, blue black, silver black) | 225 |
| 133 | Berliet GAK Fire Truck (red/black, red/cream) | 225 |
| 134 | Berliet GAK "PREFONTAINES" (green/black) | 225 |
| 151 | Peugeot 404 (red, blue, metallic blue, white, light yellow) | 80 |
| 152 | Citroën DS 19 Convertible (orange, blue, metallic blue, green) | 100 |
| 153 | Mercedes-Benz 220 S (metallic blue, dark pink, ivory/beige) | 90 |
| 154 | Citroën Ami 6 (white/blue, white/orange) | 80 |
| 155 | Simca 1000 (blue, light blue, ivory, orange) | 80 |
| 156 | Jaguar E Coupe | never made |
| 157 | Fiat 2300 Station Wagon | never made |

# Kazan

This series of heavy trucks was named for the town in which they were made: Kazan in the former Soviet Union. Kazan is located some 500 miles east of Moscow, and it was there that these models of the then-new "Kamaz" truck were made.

The Kamaz was introduced in 1978, and the first Kazan model of it made its debut in late 1979. It was the #5320 "Dropside" version, in 1/43 scale. This was followed by a "tilt" version, a longer wheelbase version, a tanker, an articulated version, etc. These were made throughout the 1980s, and were of excellent quality for the time period. Plastic was used for certain parts such as the large box that covers the rear bed of many of the trucks (see photo), as well as for

mirrors and mudflaps. But the die cast cabs and chassis gave the models a hefty feel. The #53212 Tanker, in particular, is an imposing model, with the main section of the tank being composed of two cast sections.

Rubber tires were apparently used on the Kazan models in the early days, the manufacturer then switching to plastic along the way. The boxes that the models were packaged in were either of the standard cardboard and plastic window variety, or the two-piece all-plastic display type.

Although there were some new models planned for release during the early 1990s (such as the #55105 Dump Truck and the #43105 Military Truck), it is unclear whether any are still being produced.

*This Kazan model is the #5320 Dropside Truck with Tilt. The tilt mechanism allows the cab to tilt forward at about 45°, exposing the engine.*

| # | Name | Price |
|---|------|-------|
| 5320 | Dropside Truck | $20 |
| 5320 | Dropside Truck "1945-1985" | 20 |
| 5320 | Dropside Truck "1917-1987" | 20 |
| 5320 | Dropside Truck with Tilt | 20 |
| 5320 | Dropside Truck with Tilt "Lada Spares" | 20 |
| 5325 | 4x2 Dropside Truck | 20 |
| 5325 | 4x2 Dropside Truck with Tilt "Sovtransavto" | 20 |

| # | Name | Price |
|---|------|-------|
| 53212 | Long Wheelbase Truck | $25 |
| 53212 | Long Wheelbase Truck with tilt | 25 |
| 53212 | Long Wheelbase Truck with tilt "Sovtransavto" | 25 |
| 53212 | Tanker "Moloko" | 25 |
| 5410 | Tractor Unit | 10 |
| 5410 | Tractor Unit and Trailer | 25 |
| 5410 | Tractor Unit, Trailer and Tilt | 30 |

| # | Name | Price |
|---|------|-------|
| 5511 | Dump Truck | $20 |
| 5511 | Dump Truck "Moscow 1980" | 20 |
| 5511 | Dump Truck "Mocctpon" | 20 |
| 55105 | Dump Truck | 20 |
| 43105 | Military Truck 6x6 | 20 |

# Kemlows

**K**emlows Diecasting Products Ltd. was a contract manufacturer of die cast toys, located in the Wood Green section of London during the 1950s. As a "job shop," they made products for other companies, and the name Kemlows rarely appeared on the toys that they made. "Made in England" usually did appear on them, however.

The Tractor and Farm Cart set shown here was made by Kemlows as part of the "Master Model" series during the 1950s. The box also states that it is "A WARDIE PRODUCT," which presumably is a reference to the distributor of the series, B.J. Ward Ltd. The box end flap says "K 47," which may be a Kemlows product number. "BRITISH MADE" is cast into the underside of both the Tractor and the Cart.

Kemlows toys are quite charming, and are fairly scarce in the United States. The following listing represents toys that are known to have been made by Kemlows from the late 1940s until the mid-1950s. *Note:* The Ford Zephyr Mark I car and the Caravan were sold as a set by an unknown company; a near mint set with the original box would likely sell for $175-$200. The Zephyr and the Caravan may also have been sold individually.

*One of the toys in the "Master Model" line, manufactured by Kemlows and distributed by B.J. Ward Ltd., the Tractor and Farm Cart was presumably joined by other entries in the "Wee World" series.*

| Name | Price | Name | Price | Name | Price |
|---|---|---|---|---|---|
| Armored Car (1/60 scale) | $50 | Ford Zephyr Mark I (1/43 scale) | $90 | Articulated Lumber Truck (1/50 scale) | $50 |
| Field Gun (1/60 scale) | 20 | Caravan (1/43 scale) | 40 | Tractor & Farm Cart (roughly 1/87 scale; "Wee | |
| Flat Truck (1/50 scale) | 50 | Thornycroft Mighty Antar (1/60 scale) | 60 | World" series) | 30 |
| Thornycroft Mighty Antar (1/43 scale) | 75 | Removal Van "Pickford's" (1/60 scale) | 90 | | |

# Kirk

**A**lthough the name Kirk was part of the die cast scene for more than ten years, it doesn't turn up very often on the cars that it helped to make famous. In fact, it only appeared on models for about a year, but what a year it was.

Around 1960, the Kirk company purchased another Danish company known as H. Lange, which had been manufacturing die cast cars and trucks for Tekno since the late 1940s. Lange's marketing agreement with Tekno continued throughout the 1960s, during which time Tekno put out some of the finest die cast toys (models) in the world.

After the Lange/Tekno agreement ended in 1969, Kirk decided to produce the Tekno 900 sports car series and the Tekno Ford D800 trucks under its own name. (The #837 Saab was apparently also put out as a Kirk.) The baseplates

*A Kirk #933 Oldsmobile Toronado. Note the open headlights, activated by pressing down on the hood.*

were altered to say "Kirk" instead of "Tekno" (except the Mercedes-Benz 300SL which retained the Tekno baseplate), and the models were marketed under the name "Model Products." The models, which came in cardboard and plastic window boxes, were of the same high Tekno quality, but the arrangement didn't last long. In 1970 or '71, Kirk went out of business, and the Lange/Tekno side of the firm was taken over by Algrema. This is unfortunate, since Kirk had announced plans to introduce five new sports cars to the 900 series, only two of which made it into production: the #934 Toyota 2000GT and the #935 Porsche 911S. The other three planned models were a Chevrolet Corvette, a Dune Buggy and a Pontiac Firebird.

The Kirk name also was applied to kit versions of some of the 900 series cars, which were marketed in the United States by Model Products Corporation (MPC).

Since they were made for a relatively short time, the Kirk models are today a bit scarcer than their Tekno counterparts, but they also tend to be priced a bit lower, too. The following listing is for models in near mint to mint condition with their original boxes.

*You couldn't miss this one coming down the street. The #918T Ford D 800 Brewery Truck in "Tuborg's" livery came with 32 plastic bottle crates on the rear bed.*

| # | Name | Price | # | Name | Price | # | Name | Price |
|---|------|-------|---|------|-------|---|------|-------|
| 837 | Saab 99 | $60 | 920 | Ford D 800 Breakdown Truck Falck Zonen | $40 | 932A | Mercedes-Benz 280 SL Politi | $45 |
| 914 | Ford D 800 Tipping Truck | 50 | 926 | Jaguar E Type Roadster | 60 | 932B | Mercedes-Benz 280 SL Polizei | 45 |
| 915 | Ford D 800 Truck | 50 | 927 | Jaguar E Type Hardtop | 60 | 932C | Mercedes-Benz 280 SL Polis | 45 |
| 916 | Ford D 800 Covered Truck | 50 | 928 | Mercedes-Benz 280 SL Roadster | 60 | 933 | Oldsmobile Toronado | 60 |
| 917 | Ford D 800 Lumber Carrier | 50 | 929 | Mercedes-Benz 280 SL Hardtop | 60 | 934 | Toyota 2000 GT | 60 |
| 918 | Ford D 800 Brewery Truck | 50 | 930 | Chevrolet Monza GT | 50 | 935 | Porsche 911S | 50 |
| 918T | Ford D 800 Brewery Truck "TUBORGS" | 70 | 931 | Chevrolet Monza Spyder | 50 | 950 | Mercedes-Benz 0302 Bus | 60 |
| 919 | Ford D 800 "IRMA KAFEE" | 150 | 932 | Mercedes-Benz 280 SL Police | 45 | 950A | Mercedes-Benz 0302 PTT Bus | 80 |

# Lincoln Industries

Lincoln Industries Ltd. was located in Auckland, New Zealand, during the 1950s (and perhaps later). Around 1957, Lincoln acquired the tooling for a group of 1/43 scale die cast toys. The models are thought by some to have been originally produced by the British firm D.C.M.T. during the mid-1950s.

The group included the Buick Roadmaster, the Austin A40 Somerset and the Ford Prefect. (Lincoln may also have issued the Daimler Conquest and the two Standard Vanguards, but evidence of such has not turned up.) Lincoln issued these three models for an undetermined period, after which the tooling made its way to Israel, where Habonim's "Gamda" line featured three of the models. See the Gamda section, earlier in this book.

Lincoln also offered a series of approximately 1/87 scale die cast cars and trucks during the late 1950s. How long these were in production is unknown, but they are scarce in the United States (as are all of the Lincoln models).

| # | Name | Price | # | Name | Price | # | Name | Price |
|---|------|-------|---|------|-------|---|------|-------|
| 4050 | Austin A40 Somerset | $60 | 4301 | Fire Engine | $25 | 4307 | Wrecker | $25 |
| 4051 | Buick Roadmaster | 90 | 4302 | Truck | 25 | 4308 | Jaguar XK 120 Roadster | 30 |
| 4052 | Ford Prefect | 70 | 4303 | Land Rover | 25 | 4309 | Racing Car | 25 |
| | | | 4304 | Massey Feguson Tractor | 25 | 4310 | Pickup Truck | 25 |
| **1/87 scale series:** | | | 4305 | Dumper | 25 | 4311 | Van | 25 |
| 4300 | Tanker | 25 | 4306 | Bus | 25 | | | |

# Lion Cars

This Dutch manufacturer of die cast vehicles doesn't get the press that its better-known rival, Tekno, does. But Lion Cars have been around for 40 years, and they have produced some interesting models.

The company reportedly was founded in Holland, just after the end of World War II. To the author's knowledge, the company name was Lion Toys, even at that time. The nature of its business during its first ten years is unknown, but around 1956, Lion Toys released the first of a line of 1/43 scale die cast cars. They were fairly accurate examples, and were of good quality although they did not include features such as interior fittings or window glazing (two of these early models, the #13 DKW and the #14 Renault Dauphine were later fitted with windows).

Such features were added to new releases during the late 1950s and through the '60s and '70s. The vast majority of Lion Car models were of vehicles made by DAF, the large Dutch truck and car maker. Lion Toys specialized in supplying DAF and various other companies with "promotional" models, with the result that a single casting would appear in multiple liveries. The #59 DAF 2800 Eurotrailer is an excellent example, with more than fifty different liveries having been produced.

*A Lion Cars #55 Commer Van in "POSTERIJEN" livery, with original box. Produced during the early 1970s, this Van also came "plain," with no livery.*

The other make represented was that of Commer, with the first example appearing in the early 1960s (the #28 Van).

The following listing includes models produced from the start in 1956 until the mid- to late-1970s. The company reportedly has continued production, but since Lion Cars are not imported into the United States in any real numbers, data is scarce. It is known that Lion Toys released several new 1/50 scale DAF truck models in the early 1990s, as well as a Mercedes-Benz "Powerliner" tractor trailer.

| # | Name | Price |
|---|---|---|
| 10 | Volkswagen 1200 | $125 |
| 11 | Renault 4 CV | 125 |
| 12 | Opel Rekord | 90 |
| 13 | D.K.W. 3/6 | 100 |
| 14 | Renault Dauphine | 80 |
| 20 | DAF 1300 Chassis and Cabin | 100 |
| 21 | DAF 1300 Flat Truck | 60 |
| 22 | DAF 1300 Truck—various liveries | 110 |
| 22 | DAF 1400 Truck | 45 |
| 23 | DAF 1400 Truck with tilt—various liveries | 70 |
| 23 | DAF 1400 Army Truck with tilt | 50 |
| 24 | Trailer | 10 |
| 25 | Trailer with tilt—various liveries | 20 |
| 26 | DAF 1300 Breakdown Lorry | 90 |
| 26 | DAF 1400 Breakdown Lorry | 60 |
| 27 | Renault Goelette Van—various liveries | 130 |
| 28 | Commer Van—various liveries | 75 |
| 29 | DAF 600 | 110 |
| 30 | DAF Daffodil | 125 |
| 30 | DAF Daffodil (gold-plated) | 300 |
| 31 | DAF 750 Pickup | 75 |
| 31 | DAF 750 Pickup with tilt | 75 |
| 32 | DAF Torpedo Truck—various liveries | 75 |
| 33 | DAF 33 | 110 |

| # | Name | Price |
|---|---|---|
| 33/34 | DAF Torpedo Semi-Trailer | $80 |
| 33/35 | DAF 1400 Semi-Trailer | 30 |
| 33/35 | DAF 1400 Semi-Trailer Army (olive) | 30 |
| 36 | DAF 2600 Eurotrailer—various liveries | 40 |
| 37 | DAF 2600 Tank Trailer—various liveries | 40 |
| 38 | DAF SB 200 Bus—various liveries | 50 |
| 39 | DAF 33 Van | 55 |
| 39 | DAF 33 Van "REMIA" or "GROENPOL" liveries | 120 |
| 40 | DAF 55 Coupe | 75 |
| 40 | DAF 55 Coupe "CAMEL DAF RACING TEAM" | 150 |
| 40 | DAF 55 Coupe "LYONS INTERNATIONAL" | 150 |
| 40 | DAF 66 SL Coupe | 45 |
| 41 | DAF 44 Station Wagon | 50 |
| 42 | DAF Pony Semi Trailer | 60 |
| 42 | DAF 55 Coupe (with DAF emblem) | 85 |
| 43 | DAF 2000/2200 Covered Truck—various liveries | 45 |
| 43 | DAF 2000/2200 Military Covered Truck (olive) | 45 |
| 44 | DAF 44 | 75 |
| 44 | DAF 44 "GVB AMSTERDAM" or "MARATHON" | 175 |
| 45 | DAF Pony Truck | 60 |

| # | Name | Price |
|---|---|---|
| 46 | DAF 750 Pickup with hood | $60 |
| 46 | DAF 46 | 60 |
| 47 | DAF 2000/2200 Bulk Carrier—various liveries | 40 |
| 48 | DAF 2000/2200 Truck & Trailer—various liveries | 40 |
| 49 | Commer Van "TECHNISCHE UNIE" | 80 |
| 50 | DAF 2600 Car Carrier | 75 |
| 54 | Commer Van "VAN GEND & LOOS" | 35 |
| 55 | Commer Van "POSTERIJEN" | 35 |
| 55 | Commer Van | 30 |
| 56 | DAF 2000/2200 Tipping Truck | 40 |
| 57 | DAF 2600 Container Trailer | 55 |
| 58 | DAF 2800 Covered Truck | 25 |
| 59 | DAF 2800 Eurotrailer—various liveries | 40 |
| 60 | DAF 2800 Car Transporter | 45 |
| 61 | DAF 2800 Container Trailer | 35 |
| 62 | DAF 2800 Tank Trailer | 30 |
| 63 | DAF 2800 Truck and Trailer | 30 |
| 64 | DAF 2800 6-W. Truck and Trailer | 30 |
| 66 | DAF 2800 6-W. Covered Truck | 25 |
| 67 | DAF 2800 6-W. Tanker | 30 |
| 68 | DAF 2300 Covered Truck | 30 |
| 68 | DAF 2300 Military Covered Truck (olive) | 30 |

# Lledo

To say that Lledo is a British company is an understatement. The people who put out the "Models of Days Gone" and "Vanguards" die cast lines are fiercely proud of the fact that their products are designed and manufactured in Great Britain. None of this going to the Far East to save on production costs for them.

The founder, Jack Odell, had for many years been a partner in the Lesney Products company, makers of the famous Matchbox die cast toys. In 1982, Odell was looking for a way to help keep former Matchbox toolroom personnel employed, production for the Matchbox line having recently been moved to the Far East by Universal, the new owners of Matchbox. He solved the problem by creating a group of six models that were introduced in the spring of 1983. He named the company Lledo, which is Odell spelled backward, and he located the operation in Enfield in northern London, working with some of the former Matchbox people. Lledo is still located in Enfield today.

Five of those first six models were horse-drawn vehicles, which proved to be less than a rousing success. The sixth, however, would go on to become perhaps Lledo's best-known model: DG6, the 1920 Ford Model T Van. This model would lead the way in Lledo's successful marketing of its "promotional" models, which were models produced in small quantities for businesses willing to pay for them. This was good business, of course, and it helped Lledo's cash flow in those early days. However, it made collectors crazy, since acquiring some of these promotional models was virtually impossible.

Lledo eventually differentiated the standard models from the promotionals by marking the baseplate either "Days

*Undoubtedly the most famous Lledo of all, the DG6 1920 Ford Model T Van. This model has been produced in countless liveries through the years; this Kodak version was made in 1984.*

Gone" or "Promotional Model," and the Days Gone name was born. It is still used today.

Throughout the 1980s, Lledo added new models to the line and developed a loyal following in both Great Britain and the United States. Each new model was given a number with the "DG" prefix. Lledo also introduced new sub-series within the larger Days Gone series, such as the "Premier Collection," in 1991, and the "Vanguards" line in 1993. The Vanguards series introduced models of the 1950s and '60s to Lledo's product line.

*Lledo DG20, the 1936 Ford Stake Truck with original box. This "Goodrich Tires" version came out in 1986.*

*DG65, the Morris Minor Traveller. This is the original Vanguards version which was produced starting in 1994. The Traveller was upgraded in 1996, and produced as part of the "revamped" Vanguards series.*

Two other Lledo series bear mention here. In 1985, Lledo produced a series called "Fantastic Set-O-Wheels," which was designed for the United States market. These items were packaged in blisterpacks, were distributed here by Hartoy, and most of the models had "Made in England by Lledo (London) Ltd" on the baseplates. How long the series was produced is unknown; models in their original blisterpacks generally sell for around $20.

The other series of note was the "Marathons," a group of modern commercial vehicles (buses, tankers, etc.) marketed by Lledo in 1987 and 1988. The series evidently did not sell well and was discontinued. Marathons can be found today for $4 to $5 each.

## Gift Sets

Lledo has always released gift sets made up of its standard models, which are often especially painted or otherwise decorated for the gift set. Some sets, like the Commonwealth Games Set from 1986, still sell for a relatively low price (in this case, about $20) on the secondary market. On the other hand, the set entitled "Golden Days of Film," released in 1989, now sells for $75 or more.

More information on the gift sets can be found in Dr. Edward Force's book, *Matchbox and Lledo Toys;* and in John Ramsay's *British Diecast Model Toys.* See Part Three, Additional Resources.

## A New Direction

In late 1995, Lledo announced a major change for 1996. All of the models currently in production (with four exceptions) would be designated as Days Gone models. This would include models previously part of the Vanguards and Premier lines. The Days Gone series will continue to be made up of non-scale, lower-priced ($6-$8) models.

A new, more detailed series has been introduced, entitled "Vanguards." The models in this series come packaged in high quality, lift-off lid boxes, and the models are accurate representations of the full-size vehicles. The cars and "Light Commercials" are to a consistent scale of 1/43, while the "Heavy Commercials" are 1/64 scale. The price point is somewhat higher, at around $20 per model in the United States. The four exceptions mentioned earlier are now part of this new Vanguards series: the DG65 Morris Minor Traveller, the DG69 Morris Minor Van, the DG72 VW Beetle, the DG74 Austin 7.

## Using the Listing

The following listing is comprised of two parts. The first section includes all of the basic Days Gone models, including those that are no longer in production. For these models (such as the DG1, DG2, DG3, etc.), the current value on the secondary market is provided; this value is for the most commonly found livery of each model. Bear in mind that a model may be priced at, for example, $8 for the most common version, but another hard to find livery on the same model may sell for $100.

For the Days Gone models currently in production, CRP (Current Retail Price) is indicated; this is generally around $7 in the United States. *Note:* Most of the Days Gone models have been released in many different liveries. Certain models also have undergone casting and wheel changes over the years, producing countless variations. To list them all is outside the scope of this book. For more information on various liveries and variations, please turn to Part Three, Additional Resources.

The second section of the listing is comprised of the models in the new Vanguards series. The value given is CRP, which is about $15 in most places.

*Lledo's D-Day Set from 1994. It was made up of U.S. Army versions of (left to right) DG29, DG57 and DG30.*

| # | Name | Price | # | Name | Price | # | Name | Price |
|---|------|-------|---|------|-------|---|------|-------|

**Models of Days Gone:**

| # | Name | Price |
|---|------|-------|
| DG1 | Horse-Drawn Tram | $5 |
| DG2 | Horse-Drawn Milk Float | 8 |
| DG3 | Horse-Drawn Delivery Van | 8 |
| DG4 | Horse-Drawn Omnibus | CRP |
| DG5 | Shand Mason Horse-Drawn Fire Engine | 8 |
| DG6 | 1920 Ford Model T Van | CRP |
| DG7 | 1934 Ford Model 'A' Woody Wagon | 8 |
| DG8 | 1920 Ford Model T Tanker | 8 |
| DG9 | 1934 Ford Model 'A' Car | 8 |
| DG10 | 1935 Dennis Single-Deck Coach | 8 |
| DG11 | Horse-Drawn Removal Van | CRP |
| DG12 | 1934 Dennis Fire Engine | CRP |
| DG13 | 1934 Ford Model 'A' Van | CRP |
| DG14 | 1934 Ford Model 'A' Car with Hood | 8 |
| DG15 | 1932 AEC Regent Double-Deck Bus | CRP |
| DG16 | 1934 Dennis Parcels Van | CRP |
| DG17 | 1932 AEC Regal Single-Deck Bus | CRP |
| DG18 | 1936 Packard Van | CRP |
| DG19 | 1931 Rolls-Royce Phantom II Brewster | 8 |
| DG20 | 1936 Ford Stake Truck | CRP |
| DG21 | 1934 Chevrolet Van | CRP |
| DG22 | 1933 Packard Town Van | 8 |
| DG23 | 1954 Scenicruiser | 15 |
| DG24 | 1934 Rolls-Royce Playboy Brewster | 10 |
| DG25 | 1925 Rolls-Royce Silver Ghost Barker | 8 |
| DG26 | 1934 Chevrolet Bottle Delivery | CRP |
| DG27 | 1934 Mack Breakdown Truck | 8 |
| DG28 | 1934 Mack Canvas-Back Truck | CRP |
| DG29 | 1942 Dodge 4x4 | CRP |
| DG30 | 1939 Chevrolet Panel Van | CRP |
| DG31 | Horse-Drawn Brewers Dray | CRP |

| # | Name | Price |
|---|------|-------|
| DG32 | 1907 Rolls-Royce Silver Ghost | CRP |
| DG33 | 1920 Ford Model T Car | CRP |
| DG34 | 1932 Dennis Delivery Van | 8 |
| DG35 | 1932 Dennis Limousine | 8 |
| DG36 | 1939 Chevrolet Pick-up | CRP |
| DG37 | 1932 Ford Model A Panel Van | 8 |
| DG38 | 1925 Rolls-Royce Silver Ghost Saloon | 8 |
| DG39 | 1934 Mack Truck | 8 |
| DG40 | 1934 Mack Crane Truck | 5 |
| DG41 | 1928 Karrier E6 Trolley Bus | CRP |
| DG42 | 1934 Mack Tanker | CRP |
| DG43 | 1931 Morris Van | CRP |
| DG44 | 1937 Scammell 6-Wheeler | CRP |
| DG45 | 1908 Rolls-Royce Silver Ghost Coupe | 6 |
| DG46 | 1930 Bentley 4.5 Litre | CRP |
| DG47 | 1933 Austin Taxi | CRP |
| DG48 | 1939 Chevrolet Car | CRP |
| DG49 | 1931 AEC Renown Double Deck Bus | CRP |
| DG50 | 1926 Bull-nose Morris Van | CRP |
| DG51 | 1934 Chevrolet Box Van | CRP |
| DG52 | 1935 Morris Parcels Van | CRP |
| DG53 | 1926 Rolls-Royce Landaulet | 20 |
| DG54 | 1929 Rolls-Royce Saloon | CRP |
| DG56* | 1934 Model A Ford Van with high roof | 10 |
| DG57 | 1939 Ford Tanker | CRP |
| DG58 | 1950 Morris Z Van | CRP |
| DG59 | 1950 Bedford 30cwt Truck | CRP |
| DG60 | 1955 Dennis F8 Fire Engine | CRP |
| DG61 | 1953 Pontiac Delivery Van | CRP |
| DG62 | 1935 Ford Articulated Tanker | CRP |
| DG63 | 1950 Bedford 13cwt Delivery Van | CRP |
| DG64 | 1950 Bedford Ambulance | CRP |

| # | Name | Price |
|---|------|-------|
| DG65 | 1960 Morris Minor Traveller | CRP |
| DG66 | 1926 Dennis Delivery Van | CRP |
| DG67 | 1935 Ford Articulated Truck | CRP |
| DG68 | 1932 AEC Regent Open-top Bus | CRP |
| DG69 | 1960 Morris Minor Van | CRP |
| DG70 | 1939 Ford Canvas-Back Truck | CRP |
| DG71 | 1959 Morris LD150 Van | CRP |
| DG72 | 1952 VW Beetle | CRP |
| DG73 | 1955 VW Kombi Van | CRP |
| DG74 | 1959 Austin 7 Mini | CRP |
| DG75 | 1957 Bristol LD6G Lodekka Double Deck Bus | CRP |

*\* Not issued as a standard Days Gone model, only as a promotional*

**Vanguards series:**

| # | Name | Price |
|---|------|-------|
| VA1 | Ford Anglia | CRP |
| VA2 | VW Cabriolet | CRP |
| VA3 | Austin A40 Van | CRP |
| VA4 | Ford Anglia Van | CRP |
| VA5 | Triumph Herald | CRP |
| VA6 | Ford Thames Trader Van | CRP |
| VA7 | Bedford S Type Tanker | CRP |
| VA8 | Bedford S Type Van | CRP |
| VA9 | Ford Thames Trader Tanker | CRP |
| VA10 | Morris Minor Traveller | CRP |
| VA11 | Morris Minor Van | CRP |
| VA12 | VW Split-Screen Beetle | CRP |
| VA13 | Austin 7 Mini | CRP |

*The 1935 Bluebird land speed record car of Sir Malcolm Campbell, from Lledo's "Land Speed Legends" set. Four land speed record cars (the others were John Cobb's 1947 Railton Special, Craig Breedlove's Spirit of America and Richard Noble's Thrust 2) were sold in the set. It was offered by Kellogg's Corn Flakes in Great Britain in 1993, and originally cost £7.99 (about $13). It now sells for $50-$75 on the secondary market.*

# Londontoy

One could be forgiven for assuming that Londontoys are of British origin. The London, however, is London, Ontario, Canada, and it was there that Webster Brothers, Ltd. set up shop in 1930.

The company made die cast toys prior to World War II, presumably under the Londontoy label; in 1945 or '46, the Londontoy line was re-started. Londontoys came in two sizes, four inches long and six inches long, and they included pick-up trucks, fire trucks, tanker trucks and even passenger cars.

Londontoys were made both in Canada and the United States through an agreement made between the owner of the Webster Brothers equipment, M.A. Henry, and the Leslie Henry Co. of Mount Vernon, New York. It seems the Webster Brothers company had gone out of business in 1949, after which M.A. Henry exchanged the tooling for the Londontoy toys for cap pistol tooling from the Leslie Henry Co.

Londontoys can therefore be found both with and without the legend "Made in Canada" on the underside of the toy.

The four-inch vehicles had enclosed "fender skirts" that hid most of the wheels from view. The six-inch vehicles, however, featured open wheel arches. A number of different materials were used for the wheels on

these toys. Prior to the war, metal wheels were the norm. Wood and even cardboard wheels were then tried before they settled, after the war, on the rubber wheels most commonly found today.

In addition to the standard "free-rolling" vehicles, several (if not all) of the six-inch toys also were available with a friction or a wind-up motor. And the American versions of several of the six-inch toys sometimes sported an extra baseplate that makes the toy longer and heavier. These baseplates had a fairly detailed drivetrain on them.

Exactly when production of Londontoys ceased is not known. The style of the toys would seem to indicate that they would have appeared a bit outdated by the early 1950s.

Whether Londontoys came in individual boxes is unknown. It's quite possible they were marketed in a counter display type of box, from which the buyer could choose which toy he or she wanted. The following listing is for excellent or better condition examples without any original packaging.

*The #54 Master Deluxe Coupe was based on a 1941 or '42 Chevrolet. This example is the "POLICE" version, and it has the black rubber wheels that Londontoys began using after the war.*

| #  | Name | Price |
|----|------|-------|
| **Four-inch toys:** | | |
| 12 | Pickup Truck | $20 |
| 13 | Tanker (came plain or with gasoline company decals on sides) | 20 |
| 14 | Master Deluxe Coupe (Chevrolet) | 30 |
| 15 | Beverage Truck (plain or with soda decals) | 35 |
| 16 | Fire Truck | 20 |

| #  | Name | Price |
|----|------|-------|
| 17 | Bus | $20 |
| 31 | Six Window Sedan (Ford) | 30 |
| 32 | Sedan Delivery (plain or as an Army Ambulance) | 25 |
| 35 | Thunderbolt Racer | 30 |
| 42 | Tanker "IMPERIAL" | 20 |
| **Six-inch toys:** | | |
| 52 | Pickup Truck | 30 |

| #  | Name | Price |
|----|------|-------|
| 53 | Tanker | $30 |
| 54 | Master Deluxe Coupe (Chevrolet—plain and in FIRE CHIEF and POLICE versions) | 40 |
| 55 | Beverage Truck (plain or with soda decals) | 50 |
| 56 | Fire Truck | 30 |
| 57 | Bus | 30 |

# Lone Star

Lone Star was the name used by Die Casting Machine Tools Limited (D.C.M.T.) for several different series of die cast toys starting in the early 1950s. Located in North London, England, D.C.M.T. was founded in 1940 by a couple of engineers, Sidney Ambridge and Aubrey Mills. D.C.M.T. manufactured die casting machinery that was used by a number of British toy makers, including Lesney (makers of Matchbox) and Kemlows. D.C.M.T.'s earliest toys, made just after World War II, were marketed by the Crescent Toy Company Ltd. Crescent was also based in London.

By 1951, D.C.M.T. was using the name Lone Star for their western toys, such as cap pistols and cowboy outfits. But it would be their die cast toy and model cars that would grab the attention of the toy-buying public.

## Road-master vs. Roadmaster

In 1956, D.C.M.T. launched their Lone Star "Road-master" series, the earliest examples of which varied in scale from 1/35 to 1/40. Some of them came with plastic driver and passenger figures. These first-generation models were rather crude in appearance, and they came in yellow and red individual boxes that had the D.C.M.T. and Lone Star names. The line did not achieve a realistic look until around 1960, when D.C.M.T. struck a deal with Tootsietoys to manufacture a line of 1/50 scale American cars. This series, entitled the "Classic Series," was undoubtedly intended to compete with the highly successful Corgi and Dinky product lines of the day. The "Classic Series" was reportedly marketed in Europe and Canada, as well as in the United States.

In the United Kingdom these models were available starting in 1962, and they were now called "Roadmasters"

(no hyphen). They were a distinct improvement over the earlier Road-masters in terms of accuracy and quality. They came with suspension and windows, and also with rubber tires and chromed wheels. Some came in red and gray boxes that featured artwork of the car contained inside.

Later Roadmasters can be identified by white or black plastic tires with gray plastic wheels. Also, later models all came in the same red and yellow box depicting a Rolls-Royce, with the specific model name printed inside the end flap. Later products also had an interior and steering wheel.

Although it is believed that the Roadmaster series went out of production around 1966, the models apparently made a "last gasp" reappearance in 1970. These can be identified by a yellow box with a window panel, with the model name and number rubber-stamped on the end flap. Later that year, the Roadmaster line was dropped for good.

Around 1969, Lone Star released their "Roadmaster Major" series, which was comprised of 1/43 scale trucks. These were simple castings, often lacking windows and baseplates. Included in the series were a Tractor (called the "Farm King"), a Breakdown Truck (#1283) and a Tractor Trailer (#1289), among others.

A near mint condition Roadmaster Major in the original box today sells for $40-$50.

## The Impys and the Flyers

The Roadmaster name was retained for the "Impy" series of smaller die cast cars that was produced from 1966 until 1968. The Impys averaged three inches in length, a size that put them between the smaller Matchbox and larger Dinky and Corgi lines. The full name of the series was

*Roadmaster #1475: the Dodge Dart Phoenix sitting on a later "see-through" window box for a #1476 Rolls-Royce. The black plastic tires and gray plastic wheel hubs indicate that the Dodge is of the later type.*

*This #1472 Cadillac 62 Sedan from the Lone Star Roadmasters series is typical of the early Roadmasters: black rubber tires with chromed hubs. The box is the early red and gray type.*

"Roadmaster Impy Super Cars." Most of the Impys had opening doors, engine hood and rear trunk. These features were touted as giving the consumer extra value, but the opening doors and hoods often did not fit properly, and tended to spoil the look of the cars.

In 1968, the tidal wave of sales enjoyed by Mattel's Hot Wheels cars prompted D.C.M.T./Lone Star to "revamp" the Impy line of cars. They were now fitted with low-friction axles and "speed wheels," and most were given new metallic paint jobs. They also received a new name: Flyers.

The Impy trucks and other heavy vehicles were given the new name "Lone Star Commercials," and they, too, were eventually fitted with the speed wheels.

One of the most accurate of the Flyers was the number 7 Vauxhall Firenza. This model was introduced at the same time as the actual car, and initially came packaged in a blisterpack. Vauxhall used the model to promote the real car. Unlike many of the other Flyers, the opening features do not detract from the overall excellent appearance of the model. Interestingly, the Firenza also came in a left-hand drive version, with the Vauxhall name deleted from the baseplate and body. This model may have been marketed in the United States.

The Flyers were made until the mid-1970s. Later examples can be identified by their lack of opening doors and generally crude appearance.

Strangely, the Flyers were replaced in 1976 by a cheap series of toys called "Impys." They were quite different from the original Impy series, though, with no opening parts and dark windows (so an interior would not have to be fitted). This new line was produced until around 1983.

## Tuf-Tots

This line of low-cost, simple die cast cars and trucks was produced from 1969 until 1979, and was made up mostly of 1/118 scale trucks, with a few 1/86 scale sports cars added to the mix. Originally, the trucks had paper stickers which later were deleted; and the cars originally had number stickers and plastic drivers, both of which also vanished as time went on. Later Tuf-Tots cars also had a plastic roof.

Tuf-Tots initially came in separate boxes, but blisterpacks were introduced at some point. And, like many manufacturers, Lone Star offered some products in sets. Tuf-Tots could therefore be found in three car sets as well as in playsets that contained four cars and an accessory item, such as a bridge in the "Bridge Playset."

#1293 "Roadmaster Major" Farm King Tractor with Trailer, with original box.

This advertisement from the December 1966 issue of Meccano Magazine announced the addition of the #19 Volvo P1800S to the Impy line.

## Miscellaneous Products

Lone Star also issued a number of die casts that were not part of a specific series. Worthy of mention is a set of very tiny (just over one inch in length) die cast vehicles: a Land Rover, a School Bus, a Fire Truck, a Citroën DS and an Austin Truck. The set was called "Gulliver County," and the vehicles were quite accurate for their size. A mint condition boxed set was seen by the author in 1995 with an asking price of $125.

Lone Star also produced a die cast model of the London Routemaster Double Decker Bus, which became a popular souvenir item in the United Kingdom. It was produced in red "London Transport" livery, and was also used to commemorate special events such as Queen Elizabeth's Silver Jubilee in 1977, when it was released in silver with Silver Jubilee markings. The red version sells for about $10, while the silver example will fetch $20-$25.

D.C.M.T./Lone Star went out of business in 1983, although the toy division was kept in operation until the late 1980s. The western toys are reportedly still made in the Far East— all that remains of the Lone Star name.

The following listing is for near mint to mint condition models with the original packaging. *Note:* In some cases, a model is noted as

not having been produced. This is due to D.C.M.T.'s habit of announcing new models well before their actual introduction; they often went so far as to show the planned item on the boxes of existing products. Occasionally, whether for economic or legal reasons, a planned model was shelved before it reached the production stage.

*One of the first eight "Impy" models, the #17 Mercedes-Benz 220SE, with original window box. Opening parts, such as the door on this car, often gave the Impy models a somewhat clumsy appearance.*

| # | Name | Price |
|---|------|-------|
| **Road-masters series (1956 debut):** | | |
| | Daimler Conquest Roadster (1/40 scale) | $75 |
| | Ford Thunderbird (1/40 scale) | 75 |
| | MG TF (1/35 scale) | 75 |
| | 1904 Daimler | 40 |
| | 1904 Darracq Genevieve | 40 |
| | 1912 Ford Model T | 50 |
| | 1912 Morris Bullnose | 40 |
| **Roadmasters series (1962 debut):** | | |
| 1470 | Chevrolet Corvair | 50 |
| 1471 | Rambler Station Wagon | 50 |
| 1471 | Rambler Army Station Wagon | 60 |
| 1472 | Cadillac 62 Sedan | 75 |
| 1473 | Ford Sunliner Convertible | 75 |
| 1474 | Chevrolet El Camino Pick-up | 60 |
| 1475 | Dodge Dart Phoenix | 60 |
| 1476 | Rolls-Royce Silver Cloud | 75 |
| 1477 | Dodge Dart Phoenix "Police" | 50 |
| 1477 | Dodge Dart Phoenix "Polizei" | 65 |
| 1478 | Rambler Ambulance | 50 |
| 1479 | Chevrolet Corvair Fire Car | 50 |
| 1479 | Chevrolet Corvair "Feuerwehr" | 60 |
| 1480 | Chevrolet Corvair Staff Car | 50 |
| 1481 | Rambler Army Ambulance | 50 |
| 1482 | Citroën DS 19 | 60 |

| # | Name | Price |
|---|------|-------|
| **Impy Roadmasters:** | | |
| 10 | Jaguar Mark 10 | $25 |
| 11 | Gran Turismo Coupe (Chevrolet Corvette) | 35 |
| 12 | Chrysler Imperial | 30 |
| 13 | Ford Thunderbird—not produced | |
| 14 | Ford Zodiac Estate Car | 25 |
| 15 | Volkswagen Microbus | 35 |
| 16 | Ford Zodiac Estate Police Car | 25 |
| 16M | Mercedes-Benz 220SE Police Car | 25 |
| 17 | Mercedes-Benz 220SE | 25 |
| 18 | Ford Corsair | 25 |
| 19 | Volvo P1800S | 25 |
| 20 | Volkswagen Microbus Ambulance | 30 |
| 21 | Fiat 2300S Coupe | 20 |
| 22 | Rolls-Royce Silver Cloud Convertible | 20 |
| 23 | Alfa Romeo 1600 Giulia Spider | 25 |
| 24 | Foden Tipper | 25 |
| 25 | International Harvester Tractor with Shovel | 20 |
| 26 | Foden Fuel Tanker "MOBIL" | 30 |
| 27 | Ford Taunus 12M | 25 |
| 28 | Peugeot 404 | 20 |
| 29 | Foden Truck "Express Freight" or "Lucas Batteries" | 20 |
| 29 | Cement Mixer—not produced | |

| # | Name | Price |
|---|------|-------|
| 30 | Merryweather Turntable Fire Engine | $25 |
| 31 | Ford Transit Breakdown Truck | 25 |
| 32 | Ford Corsair Fire Chief Car | 25 |
| 33 | Austin Western Mobile Crane | 25 |
| 34 | Euclid 82-80 Crawler Tractor | 20 |
| 35 | Articulated Flat Truck—not produced | |
| 401 | Garage Ramp | 35 |
| 402 | Lock-up Garage | 25 |
| 404 | Mobil Petrol Pumps and Sign | 25 |
| **IMPY FLYERS:** | | |
| **Modified Impy models:** | | |
| 10 | Jaguar Mark 10 | 20 |
| 11 | Gran Turismo Coupe (Chevrolet Corvette) | 25 |
| 12 | Chrysler Imperial | 20 |
| 14 | Ford Zodiac Estate Car | 20 |
| 15 | Volkswagen Microbus | 25 |
| 16 | Ford Zodiac Estate Police Car | 15 |
| 16M | Mercedes-Benz 220SE Police Car | 15 |
| 17 | Mercedes-Benz 220SE | 20 |
| 18 | Ford Corsair | 20 |
| 19 | Volvo P1800S | 20 |
| 20 | Volkswagen Microbus Ambulance | 25 |
| 21 | Fiat 2300S Coupe | 15 |
| 22 | Rolls Royce Silver Cloud Convertible | 15 |

| # | Name | Price |
|---|------|-------|
| 23 | Alfa Romeo 1600 Giulia Spyder | $15 |
| 27 | Ford Taunus 12M | 20 |
| 28 | Peugeot 404 | 15 |

**New Flyers:**

| # | Name | Price |
|---|------|-------|
| 7 | Vauxhall Firenza Coupe | 20 |
| 9 | Maserati Mistral | 25 |
| 13 | Toyota 2000GT | 25 |
| 36 | Lotus Europa | 20 |
| 37 | Ford GT40—not produced | |
| 38 | Chevrolet Corvette | 20 |
| 39 | Ford Mustang Fastback | 25 |
| 40 | Cadillac Eldorado | 25 |

## LONE STAR COMMERCIALS:

**Modified Impy models:**

| # | Name | Price |
|---|------|-------|
| 24 | Foden Tipper | 15 |
| 26 | Foden Fuel Tanker "MOBIL" | 20 |
| 29 | Foden Truck "Express Freight" or "Lucas Batteries" | 15 |
| 30 | Merryweather Turntable Fire Engine | 15 |
| 31 | Ford Transit Breakdown | 20 |

**New Commercials:**

| # | Name | Price |
|---|------|-------|
| 41 | Builder's Supply Truck | 15 |
| 42 | Foden Half-cab Tipper | 15 |
| 44 | Marine Transport Truck (with plastic boat) | 20 |
| 46 | Leyland Drop-Side Lorry | 20 |
| 47 | Leyland High-Side Lorry | 20 |
| 47 | Foden Half-cab High-Side Lorry | 20 |
| 48 | Leyland Hopper Lorry | 20 |
| 48 | Foden Half-cab Hopper Lorry | 20 |
| 49 | Foden Half-cab Tipper | 20 |

**"New" Impy series (1976 onward):**

| # | Name | Price |
|---|------|-------|
| 50 | Six-wheel Tipper | $8 |
| 51 | Six-wheel Bulk Carrier | 8 |
| 52 | Six-wheel Crane Truck | 8 |
| 53 | Six-wheel Marine Transporter | 8 |
| 54 | Six-wheel Cement Mixer | 8 |
| 55 | Six-wheel Express Freight Truck | 8 |
| 56 | Six-wheel Low Sided Truck | 8 |
| 57 | Six-wheel Water Tank Truck | 8 |
| 58 | Six-wheel Sand Truck | 8 |
| 59 | Six-wheel Water Pipe Truck | 8 |
| 60 | Six-wheel Timber Truck | 8 |
| 61 | Six-wheel Petrol Tanker | 8 |
| 71 | Range Rover | 10 |
| 72 | Cadillac | 15 |
| 73 | Toyota Coupe | 10 |
| 74 | Corvette Stingray Fast Back | 10 |
| 75 | Range Rover Police Car | 8 |
| 76 | Corvette GT Rally | 10 |
| 77 | Jaguar | 10 |
| 78 | Maserati Mistral | 15 |
| 79 | Ford Mustang | 15 |
| 80 | Lotus Europa | 10 |
| 81 | Volvo 264 Coupe | 10 |
| 82 | Mercedes-Benz | 8 |
| 181 | Crane Truck | 8 |
| 182 | "Esso" Fuel Tanker | 10 |
| 183 | Low Loader (with Tuf-Tots car) | 15 |
| 184 | Articulated Transporter (with pipes and water tank) | 10 |
| 185 | Range Rover with speedboat on trailer | 10 |
| 185 | Cadillac with speedboat on trailer | 15 |
| 185 | Jaguar with cabin cruiser on trailer | 15 |
| 186 | Breakdown with Lotus Europa | 15 |

| # | Name | Price |
|---|------|-------|
| 188 | Boat Transporter | $15 |
| 189 | Timber Truck | 10 |
| 190 | Petrol Tanker and Trailer | 15 |
| 191 | Bulk Carrier and Trailer | 10 |
| 192 | Cement Mixer and Trailer | 10 |

**Tuf-Tots:**

| # | Name | Price |
|---|------|-------|
| 601 | Esso Tanker | 15 |
| 602 | Citroën DS Sports | 10 |
| 603 | Stingray Sports | 10 |
| 604 | Dodge Dart Sport | 10 |
| 605 | Mercedes Sport | 10 |
| 606 | Tow Truck | 10 |
| 607 | "Big L" Dump Truck | 5 |
| 608 | "Herts Farms" Jeep and Trailer | 10 |
| 609 | "M Autos" Truck with Petrol Pumps | 10 |
| 610 | "L.S. Construction" Tipper Truck | 5 |
| 611 | "Express Freight" Truck | 5 |
| 612 | Low Loader | 10 |
| 613 | Speedboat and Trailer | 10 |
| 614 | "City Refuse" truck | 5 |
| 615 | Cement Mixer Truck | 5 |
| 616 | Milk Delivery truck | 10 |
| 617 | Horse Box | 10 |
| 618 | Waste Disposal Truck | 5 |
| 619 | Citroën Coupe | 10 |
| 620 | Stingray Coupe | 15 |
| 621 | Dodge Dart Coupe | 10 |
| 622 | Mercedes Coupe | 15 |
| 623 | London Bus | 10 |
| 624 | Fire Engine | 5 |
| 625 | Caravan | 15 |
| 626 | Circus Cage Truck | 5 |
| 627 | Earth Mover | 5 |

*Impy Flyer #14 Ford Zodiac Estate Car, with speed wheels typical of the Flyer series.*

*Tuf-Tots #615 Cement Mixer. D.C.M.T./Lone Star made these simple, tiny (1/118 scale, or two inches long, on average) cars and trucks from 1969 until 1979.*

# Maisto

It is a fact of die cast collecting that models made in the Far East are among the finest in the world, in terms of fit and finish. It is also true that unraveling the maze of manufacturers and distributors to find out who made what is difficult at best. This is due to the fact that many manufacturers in China and Thailand act essentially as "job shops," producing die cast models in vast quantity for their customers. The customer takes delivery, and then has the models or toys packaged and shipped to wholesalers. An alternative exists for large orders, whereby the manufacturer can supply the product already packaged and decorated with the customer's artwork, if the order is large enough.

And then there is Maisto. Maisto is actually owned by Thailand-based Master Toy Company Limited. Master Toy apparently operates two factories: one in Canton, China, the other in Amphur Bangpakong, Thailand. May Cheong, a Hong Kong company that got its start in the late 1960s, is a division of Master Toy. It was May Cheong that began marketing low-cost die cast toys under the name "M C Toy" during the mid-1980s. In 1992, the company opened an office in the United States—Maisto International Inc.—in Fontana, California. Since that time, they have marketed a number of lines under the Maisto name.

Maisto calls their collector models "Special Edition," and this encompasses three different scales. The 1/18 scale series is the best-known among adult collectors; it includes Porsches and BMW's, as well as an early '50s VW Beetle and a Citroën of the same vintage. The 1/18 models are available at stores like Wal-Mart and Toys R Us, and the Current Retail Price is around $20.

The second series is made up of 1/12 scale models. Through 1995, it included two models. As might be expected, the 1/12's are quite large and heavy, and their Current Retail Price is anywhere from $75 to $100.

The 1/24 scale models make up the other collector's series, and their Current Retail Price is around $10.

Another series, named "Trophy," made its debut a few years back, and proved very popular with collectors. This is due to their being fairly accurate models of the real cars. Each car in the series is the same 4 1/2 inches in length (so they can all fit in the same size box), which varies the scale from around 1/38 to 1/40, depending on the car. The Trophy

*Maisto's 1/18 scale Porsche Boxster, released in 1994. Maisto was very accurate with this version of the German concept car (now called the 986 by Porsche).*

models come in individual boxes, and the Current Retail Price is around $4.

The same models in the Trophy series also come as "Power Racers," which merely have a pull-back motor added. These come in blisterpacks, and the Current Retail Price is $2-$3. Some of the Power Racers are also available from a Los Angeles-based company called Mega Toys; they package them under the name "Mega Masters." The Maisto name appears on the baseplate.

The models in these series are generally quite accurate, and they are priced to compete with the likes of Bburago and Ertl. Other toys marketed by Maisto, such as the "Slickers" and the "Mega Moto-Bot" lines, are aimed at the children's market and are outside the scope of this book.

*Other than the cheap headlights that make it look as though it's wearing goggles, this "Power Racers" Dodge Viper is very accurate, particularly for a $2 toy.*

| # | Name | Price |
|---|------|-------|
| **1/12 scale Special Edition:** | | |
| 33201 | Jaguar XJ220 | CRP |
| 33202 | 1959 Cadillac Eldorado | CRP |
| **1/18 scale Special Edition:** | | |
| 31801 | Mercedes-Benz 500SL | CRP |
| 31802 | Porsche 911 Speedster | CRP |
| 31803 | Lamborghini Diablo | CRP |
| 31804 | Ferrari 348ts | CRP |
| 31805 | BMW 850i | CRP |
| 31806 | 1955 Mercedes-Benz 300S | CRP |
| 31807 | Jaguar XJ220 | CRP |
| 31808 | Bugatti EB110 | CRP |
| 31809 | Corvette ZR-1 | CRP |
| 31810 | McLaren F1 | CRP |
| 31811 | 1966 Mercedes-Benz 280SE | CRP |
| 31812 | BMW 325i Convertible | CRP |
| 31813 | 1959 Cadillac Eldorado | CRP |
| 31814 | Porsche Boxster | CRP |
| 31815 | Mustang Mach III | CRP |
| 31816 | BMW 325i Convertible (working roof) | CRP |
| 31817 | 1955 BMW 502 | CRP |
| 31818 | Porsche 911 Carrera Cabriolet | CRP |
| 31819 | Lamborghini Diablo SE | CRP |
| 31820 | 1951 Volkswagen Export Sedan | CRP |
| 31821 | 1952 Citroën CV15 | CRP |
| **1/24 scale Special Edition:** | | |
| 31901 | Mercedes-Benz 500SL | CRP |
| 31902 | Porsche 911 Speedster | CRP |
| 31903 | Lamborghini Diablo | CRP |
| 31904 | Ferrari 348ts | CRP |
| 31905 | '94 Mustang GT | CRP |
| 31906 | 1992 Ford Explorer | CRP |
| 31907 | Jaguar XJ220 | CRP |
| 31908 | Bugatti EB110 | CRP |

| # | Name | Price |
|---|------|-------|
| 31909 | '95 Ford Explorer | CRP |
| 31910 | McLaren F1 | CRP |
| 31911 | Ford F-150 Pickup | CRP |
| 31912 | Dodge RAM Pickup | CRP |
| 31913 | '96 Dodge Caravan | CRP |
| 31919 | Lamborghini Diablo SE | CRP |
| **Trophy series (4.5 inches in length):** | | |
| | Mercedes-Benz 500SL Soft-top | CRP |
| | Porsche 911 SC | CRP |
| | BMW 325i Cabriolet | CRP |
| | Ferrari F40 | CRP |
| | VW Cabriolet | CRP |
| | Jaguar XJS V12 | CRP |
| | Aston Martin DB7 | CRP |
| | Porsche 959 | CRP |
| | Aston Martin Virage | CRP |
| | '63 Corvette | CRP |
| | Ferrari 348ts | CRP |
| | Mercedes-Benz 500SL Convertible | CRP |
| | Lotus Elan | CRP |
| | Ferrari Testarossa | CRP |
| | Corvette ZR-1 | CRP |
| | Jaguar E | CRP |
| | '57 Corvette | CRP |
| | Porsche 911 Speedster | CRP |
| | BMW Z1 | CRP |
| | Jaguar XJ220 | CRP |
| | Lamborghini Diablo | CRP |
| | BMW 850i | CRP |
| | Bugatti EB110 | CRP |
| | MG RV8 | CRP |
| | Porsche 911 Flatnose Turbo | CRP |
| | Ferrari GTO | CRP |
| | Lotus Esprit | CRP |
| | Ferrari 512TR | CRP |

| Name | Price |
|------|-------|
| Dodge Viper | CRP |
| Ferrari 456GT | CRP |
| **Power Racers (Trophy cars with motors):** | |
| Mercedes-Benz 500SL Soft-top | CRP |
| Porsche 911 SC | CRP |
| BMW 325i Cabriolet | CRP |
| Ferrari F40 | CRP |
| VW Cabriolet | CRP |
| Jaguar XJS V12 | CRP |
| Aston Martin DB7 | CRP |
| Porsche 959 | CRP |
| Aston Martin Virage | CRP |
| '63 Corvette | CRP |
| Ferrari 348ts | CRP |
| Mercedes-Benz 500SL Convertible | CRP |
| Lotus Elan | CRP |
| Ferrari Testarossa | CRP |
| Corvette ZR-1 | CRP |
| Jaguar E | CRP |
| '57 Corvette | CRP |
| Porsche 911 Speedster | CRP |
| BMW Z1 | CRP |
| Jaguar XJ220 | CRP |
| Lamborghini Diablo | CRP |
| BMW 850i | CRP |
| Bugatti EB110 | CRP |
| MG RV8 | CRP |
| Porsche 911 Flatnose Turbo | CRP |
| Ferrari GTO | CRP |
| Lotus Esprit | CRP |
| Ferrari 512TR | CRP |
| Dodge Viper | CRP |
| Ferrari 456GT | CRP |

# Majorette

This French manufacturer commenced operations in 1961 in Villeurbanne, an industrial suburb of Lyon. The founder, Emile Veron, was related to Joseph Veron, the founder of the Norev line of models; both the Norev and Majorette factories were located in Villeurbanne. (Joseph Veron, incidentally, reversed the letters of his last name to come up with the Norev name.)

The cars and trucks that Majorette produced during the 1960s and '70s were based on French, German and Italian makes such as Peugeot, Mercedes-Benz and Ferrari. The scale varied from 1/50 to about 1/90, depending on the subject, and window glazing was standard on most of the toys. Interior fittings were added later.

In 1980, Majorette bought the legendary Solido. This move made good business sense, since Solido's predominantly 1/43 scale products complemented Majorette's smaller toys well. In May 1993, Majorette, along with Solido, was purchased by another French company, the Ideal Loisirs Group. Today, Majorette produces a number of different lines of toys and models. The 100, 200, 300, 600, 2600, 3000, 3200 and 4500 series are aimed primarily at the children's market, with bright colors and "speed"-type wheels characterizing many of these toys. The 1/18 and 1/24 scale series are comprised of more accurate, high-quality models aimed primarily at the adult collector market.

These lines are included in the following listing along with the original Majorettes of the 1960s and '70s. *Note:* like many manufacturers, Majorette deletes and replaces its products on a regular basis, often using an existing number for a new toy or model. The #245 Saviem Oil Tanker shown here illustrates this: it's a 1970s (or early 1980s) example, and has been replaced at least a couple of times. The #245 currently produced is still a tanker, but it is a completely different casting (Citerne). In other cases, Majorette replaces a model with a totally different type of vehicle.

Majorette also produces a number of other toy lines, such as "scented" cars, cars and trucks with sounds and lights, and playsets. As these are aimed at the children's market, they are outside the scope of this book.

CRP (Current Retail Price) for new Majorettes are as follows: The 200 and 300 series toys sell for $1-$2. The 600 series items sell for around $5, while the 3000 series toys can be as low as $5 or as high as $15 or $20, depending on the size and complexity of the toy.

The 1/24 scale models sell for $10-$14, while the larger 1/18 scale models generally run from $16-$24. As with any new product, the price you will pay depends on whether you buy it from the bargain bin at a large chain store or in a small, specialist hobby shop.

*The "speed"-type wheels and plastic display box of this #245 Saviem Esso Tanker are typical of Majorette toys of the 1970s and '80s.*

| # | Name | Price |
|---|------|-------|
| **1960s AND 1970s PRODUCTION** | | |
| 1 | B.R.M. Formula 1 | $15 |
| 2 | Porsche Formula 1 | 15 |
| 3 | Citroën Metalmobil "AU PETIT POUCET" | 15 |
| 3 | Citroën Metalmobil "AU BON PATE" | 15 |
| 3 | Citroën Metalmobil "FRUITS DE PROVENCE" | 15 |
| 4 | Bernard Fire Truck | 15 |
| 4 | Bernard Fire Truck "VILLE DE MEGEVE" | 15 |
| 5 | Bernard Quarry Dumper | 15 |
| 5 | Bernard Quarry Dumper "VILLE DE MEGEVE" | 15 |
| 6 | Bernard Open Truck | 15 |
| 6 | Bernard Open Truck "GALLIACOLOR" | 15 |
| 6 | Bernard Flat Truck with Chains | 15 |
| 6 | Bernard Flat Truck with Chains "GALLIACOLOR" | 15 |
| 7 | Jeep and Trailer | 20 |
| 7 | Fire Jeep | 15 |
| 8 | Bernard Snow Plow | 15 |
| 8 | Bernard Snow Plow "VILLE DE MEGEVE" | 15 |
| 9 | Ferrari 250 LM | 25 |
| 10 | Ferrari 158 Formula 1 | 25 |
| 11 | Jeep and Horse Box | 15 |
| 12 | Bernard Circus Truck | 15 |
| 12 | Bernard Circus Truck "GALLIACOLOR" | 15 |
| 13 | Citroën DS 21 | 25 |
| 13 | Citroën DS 21 Driving School | 25 |
| 14 | Citroën DS 21 and Trailer with Boat | 35 |
| 15 | Citroën DS 21 and Caravan | 35 |
| 116 | Peugeot 404 S.W. Ambulance | 20 |
| 201 | Citroën GS | 20 |
| 201 | Caravan | 10 |

| # | Name | Price |
|---|------|-------|
| 202 | Volkswagen | $20 |
| 203 | Fiat 127 | 15 |
| 204 | Bernard Ladder Truck | 20 |
| 205 | Bernard Dump Truck | 20 |
| 205 | Scania Dump Truck | 10 |
| 206 | Peugeot 404 Ambulance | 20 |
| 206 | Citroën DS 21 Ambulance | 20 |
| 207 | Jaguar E Coupe | 15 |
| 208 | Bernard Snow Plow | 15 |
| 208 | Chrysler 180 | 10 |
| 209 | Pickup Camper | 10 |
| 210 | Volkswagen K 70 | 10 |
| 211 | Farm Tractor | 10 |
| 212 | Wrecker | 10 |
| 213 | Citroën DS 21 | 30 |
| 213 | Mercedes Benz 450SL Coupe | 15 |
| 214 | Citroën DS 21 and Trailer with Boat | 30 |
| 214 | Saviem Van "MAJORETTE" | 10 |
| 215 | Citroën DS 21 and Caravan | 30 |
| 215 | Unimog Tower Truck | 10 |
| 216 | Peugeot 404 S.W. Police | 20 |
| 217 | Peugeot 404 S.W. Police and Alpine on Trailer | 25 |
| 217 | BMW Turbo | 10 |
| 218 | Bernard Refuse Truck | 15 |
| 218 | Mercedes Benz Refuse Truck | 10 |
| 219 | Bernard Stake Truck | 20 |
| 219 | Matra Bagheera | 10 |
| 220 | Volvo 245 DL Station Wagon | 15 |
| 221 | Renault R 16 | 15 |
| 221 | Citroën Camargue | 10 |
| 222 | Scania Multi-Bucket Truck | 10 |
| 223 | Saviem Mobile Office | 10 |
| 225 | Safari Pickup Truck | 10 |
| 226 | Brabham Repco Formula 1 | 20 |
| 227 | Lotus Formula 1 | 20 |

| # | Name | Price |
|---|------|-------|
| 228 | B.R.M. Formula 1 | $20 |
| 229 | Ferrari 312 Formula 1 | 25 |
| 230 | Peugeot 204 Roadster | 20 |
| 230 | Renault 4L Telephone Van | 10 |
| 232 | Porsche 907 Le Mans | 15 |
| 232 | Porsche 907 "POP" | 15 |
| 233 | Panther Bertone | 10 |
| 233 | Panther Bertone "POP" | 10 |
| 234 | Simca 1100 | 15 |
| 235 | BMW 3.0 CSI | 15 |
| 236 | Saviem Flat Truck with Site Hut | 10 |
| 237 | Mercedes-Benz 280 SE | 15 |
| 237 | Mini Maharajah | 10 |
| 239 | Peugeot 504 | 15 |
| 239 | Matra Simca 670 | 10 |
| 241 | Daf Covered Truck | 15 |
| 242 | Snow Plow | 10 |
| 244 | Volkswagen Ambulance | 15 |
| 244 | Volkswagen U.S. Army Van | 15 |
| 245 | Daf Tanker | 15 |
| 245 | Saviem Tanker "Shell" | 15 |
| 246 | Daf Tower Truck | 10 |
| 247 | Daf Crane Truck | 10 |
| 248 | Beach Buggy Covered Type | 10 |
| 249 | Bobsleigh | 10 |
| 250 | Citroën SM | 15 |
| 253 | Ford 5000 Tractor | 10 |
| 255 | Hanomag Bulldozer | 10 |
| 256 | Amphibious Car | 10 |
| 257 | Renault R 5 | 15 |
| 258 | Dune Buggy | 10 |
| 259 | Caravan | 10 |
| 260 | Renault 17 | 10 |
| 313 | Wrecker Set | 10 |
| 314 | Volkswagen and Boat on Trailer | 15 |
| 315 | Volkswagen K 70 and Caravan | 15 |

| # | Name | Price |
|---|------|-------|
| 316 | Ford Tractor and Trailer | $15 |
| 317 | Renault R 16 and Trailer | 15 |
| 320 | Scania Lumber Semi Trailer | 15 |
| 322 | Scania Crane Truck | 15 |
| 323 | Scania Flat Truck | 10 |
| 324 | Scania Articulated Truck | 15 |
| 331 | Volkswagen and Canoe on Trailer | 15 |
| 338 | Chrysler 180 and Trailer | 15 |
| 340 | Chrysler 180 and Caravan | 15 |
| 343 | Safari Set | 15 |
| 351 | Citroën SM and Road Signs | 20 |
| 352 | Bob Sleigh and Trailer | 10 |
| 354 | Ford Tractor and Trailer | 15 |
| 361 | Bernard Artic. Truck | 10 |
| 362 | Fire Van and Trailer | 10 |
| 363 | BMW 3.0 CSI and Trailer | 15 |
| 364 | Bernard Artic. Tanker "Esso" | 15 |
| 365 | Scania Artic. Truck with Boat | 10 |
| 366 | Saviem Truck and Trailer | 10 |
| 367 | Bernard Artic. Van "Majorette" | 10 |
| 368 | Simca 1100 and Caravan | 10 |

## 1995 PRODUCTION

### Club 1/18 scale 4400 series:

| # | Name | Price |
|---|------|-------|
| 4401 | Peugeot 605 | CRP |
| 4402 | Mini Cooper 1964 | CRP |
| 4403 | Ferrari 365 GTS | CRP |
| 4404 | Ford Pick Up 1936 | CRP |
| 4405 | Cadillac Eldorado 1955 | CRP |
| 4406 | VW Coccinelle | CRP |
| 4407 | Citroën ZX Rallye | CRP |
| 4414 | Jeep Grand Cherokee Laredo | CRP |
| 4415 | Jeep Grand Cherokee Limited | CRP |
| 4418 | Mercedes 600S coupe | CRP |

### Platinum 1/18 scale 4400 series:

| # | Name | Price |
|---|------|-------|
| 4408 | BMW 850i | CRP |
| 4409 | Lexus LS 400 | CRP |
| 4410 | Mercedes 500SL | CRP |
| 4411 | AC Cobra 427 | CRP |
| 4412 | Chevrolet Corvette 58 | CRP |
| 4413 | Ford Thunderbird | CRP |
| 4416 | Chevy Nomad 57 | CRP |
| 4417 | Toyota Land Cruiser | CRP |

### Club 1/24 scale 4000 series:

| # | Name | Price |
|---|------|-------|
| 4102 | Jaguar type E | CRP |
| 4103 | Ferrari 365 GTB 4 Daytona | CRP |
| 4104 | AC Cobra 427 Roadster | CRP |
| 4106 | Mustang hard top | CRP |
| 4107 | Chevrolet Silverado | CRP |
| 4108 | Jeep Grand Cherokee Limited | CRP |
| 4109 | Jeep Grand Cherokee Laredo | CRP |
| 4201 | Porsche 944 Turbo | CRP |
| 4202 | Chevrolet Corvette Coupe | CRP |
| 4203 | Lamborghini Countach | CRP |
| 4204 | Chevrolet Corvette Roadster | CRP |
| 4208 | Porsche 944 S2 Cabriolet | CRP |
| 4210 | Mercedes 500 SL Roadster | CRP |
| 4211 | Lamborghini Diablo | CRP |
| 4212 | AC Cobra 427 | CRP |
| 4213 | Mercedes 500 SL Coupe | CRP |
| 4214 | Ford GT 40 | CRP |

*This McLaren Formula One race car was #289, and was available during the mid- to late-1980s.*

| # | Name | Price |
|---|------|-------|
| 4214 | Ford GT 40 "Le Mans" | CRP |
| 4215 | Porsche 911 | CRP |
| 4217 | Mustang cabriolet | CRP |

### 100 series ("Novacar"):

| # | Name | Price |
|---|------|-------|
| 101 | Ferrari 348 | CRP |
| 102 | Nissan 300 ZX | CRP |
| 103 | Chevrolet Corvette | CRP |
| 104 | Ferrari Testarossa | CRP |
| 105 | Mercedes 500SL | CRP |
| 106 | Peugeot 605 | CRP |
| 107 | Nissan Terrano | CRP |
| 108 | Kenworth | CRP |
| 109 | Impala Police | CRP |
| 110 | Renault Espace | CRP |
| 110 | Renault Espace Ambulance | CRP |
| 11 | Sport proto | CRP |
| 112 | F1 noire | CRP |
| 112 | F1 jaune | CRP |
| 113 | Combi VW caravelle | CRP |
| 114 | Ford Escort GT | CRP |
| 117 | Honda NSX | CRP |
| 119 | Jeep | CRP |
| 120 | Ferrari F40 | CRP |
| 121 | Van | CRP |

### 200 series:

| # | Name | Price |
|---|------|-------|
| 201 | Van Ford model A | CRP |
| 202 | Peugeot 405 T16 | CRP |
| 203 | VW Coccinelle | CRP |
| 205 | Jaguar Police | CRP |
| 206 | Twingo | CRP |
| 207 | Fire Engine | CRP |
| 208 | Tractor | CRP |
| 209 | Porsche 911 Turbo | CRP |
| 212 | Pontiac Firebird | CRP |
| 213 | Formula 1 | CRP |
| 214 | Nissan 300ZX | CRP |
| 215 | Chevrolet Corvette | CRP |
| 217 | Ford Thunderbird | CRP |
| 218 | Peugeot 405 MI 16 | CRP |
| 219 | Lamborghini Diablo | CRP |

| # | Name | Price |
|---|------|-------|
| 220 | Mustang SVO | CRP |
| 221 | Renault Safrane | CRP |
| 223 | Chevy Hot Rod | CRP |
| 224 | Jeep Cherokee | CRP |
| 225 | Renault 19 Cabriolet | CRP |
| 226 | Roller | CRP |
| 228 | 4 x 4 Towing Truck | CRP |
| 229 | Aston Martin DB7 | CRP |
| 230 | Custom Tow Truck | CRP |
| 231 | Mercedes 190E | CRP |
| 232 | Buggy | CRP |
| 233 | Renault mini van | CRP |
| 236 | 4 x 4 | CRP |
| 237 | Lamborghini Countach | CRP |
| 238 | F1 Racing | CRP |
| 239 | Chevrolet Blazer | CRP |
| 240 | Impala Police | CRP |
| 241 | Covered truck | CRP |
| 242 | Shovel engine | CRP |
| 243 | Ford mini van | CRP |
| 244 | Jeep CJ | CRP |
| 245 | Oil Tanker | CRP |
| 246 | Rescue Team | CRP |
| 247 | Garbage truck | CRP |
| 249 | GMC Jimmy | CRP |
| 250 | Mercedes 300TE | CRP |
| 254 | Citroën XM | CRP |
| 255 | Ambulance | CRP |
| 256 | Towing truck | CRP |
| 257 | BMW 325i | CRP |
| 258 | Pro Stock Firebird | CRP |
| 259 | British bus | CRP |
| 260 | Mercedes 500 SL Roadster | CRP |
| 261 | Explorer | CRP |
| 262 | Airport bus | CRP |
| 263 | Front end loader | CRP |
| 264 | Golf | CRP |
| 265 | Container | CRP |
| 267 | Crazy car | CRP |
| 268 | Pontiac Trans Sport | CRP |
| 274 | Super Dump truck | CRP |

| # | Name | Price |
|---|---|---|
| 275 | Ford Escort GT | CRP |
| 276 | 4 x 4 Toyota Runner | CRP |
| 278 | Mobile home | CRP |
| 280 | Ferrari F40 | CRP |
| 281 | Peugeot 205 GTI | CRP |
| 282 | F1 Ferrari | CRP |
| 283 | Crane truck | CRP |
| 284 | Snow mobile | CRP |
| 285 | Jeep Cherokee Sheriff | CRP |
| 286 | Fiat Tipo | CRP |
| 287 | Bulldozer | CRP |
| 291 | Blazer 4 x 4 | CRP |
| 292 | Toyota Hilux 4 x 4 | CRP |
| 293 | Jaguar XJ6 | CRP |
| 296 | Pick up El Camino | CRP |
| 297 | Dump truck | CRP |

### 220 series "Special Forces":

| # | Name | Price |
|---|---|---|
| 220-1 | 4 x 4 with machine gun | CRP |
| 220-2 | Missile launcher | CRP |
| 220-3 | Tank with cannon | CRP |
| 220-4 | Military ambulance | CRP |
| 220-5 | Military police | CRP |
| 220-6 | Tank rocket launcher | CRP |
| 220-7 | Military Jeep | CRP |
| 220-8 | Anti aircraft | CRP |

### 300 series:

| # | Name | Price |
|---|---|---|
| 310 | Scraper | CRP |
| 312 | Semi fighter plane transporter | CRP |
| 313 | Deluxe camping car | CRP |
| 314 | Dump truck | CRP |
| 316 | Tractor + Trailer | CRP |
| 318 | Jeep CJ + racing car | CRP |
| 319 | Fire Engine | CRP |
| 320 | Glider + GMC Jimmy | CRP |
| 321 | Semi boat carrier | CRP |
| 322 | Coast guard helicopter | CRP |
| 323 | Pick up animal trailer | CRP |
| 325 | Sedan + camping trailer | CRP |
| 326 | Mercedes stretch limousine | CRP |
| 327 | Oil tanker + trailer | CRP |
| 328 | Land Rover with lion cage trailer | CRP |
| 331 | Levelling scraper | CRP |
| 334 | Tractor + log trailer | CRP |
| 335 | Toyota Runner + moto trailer | CRP |
| 336 | Pick up + bicycles trailer | CRP |
| 338 | Blazer + sailboat on trailer | CRP |
| 339 | Cadillac stretch limousine | CRP |
| 340 | Semi-container | CRP |
| 350 | Cabin cruiser transporter | CRP |
| 355 | Semi oil tanker | CRP |
| 362 | 4 x 4 with radar trailer | CRP |
| 365 | Semi-sailboat carrier | CRP |
| 366 | Truck and trailer | CRP |
| 371 | Rescue helicopter | CRP |
| 373 | Bus | CRP |
| 375 | Custom tow truck + F1 | CRP |
| 376 | Fire engine + tanker | CRP |

### 600 series (1/87 scale):

| # | Name | Price |
|---|---|---|
| 601 | Semi + helicopter transporter | CRP |
| 604 | Kenworth truck | CRP |

| # | Name | Price |
|---|---|---|
| 605 | Oil tanker + trailer | CRP |
| 606 | Kenworth Oil tanker | CRP |
| 610 | Semi rocket transporter | CRP |
| 611 | Circus | CRP |
| 612 | Semi fire engine trailer | CRP |
| 613 | Semi speed boat transporter | CRP |
| 614 | Kenworth cattle transporter | CRP |
| 615 | Semi pro stock firebird | CRP |
| 616 | Semi bulldozer carrier | CRP |
| 617 | Semi with telescopic crane | CRP |
| 618 | Semi seaplane transporter | CRP |

### Hot Rod 2600 series:

| # | Name | Price |
|---|---|---|
| 2601 | Ford coupe 1932 | CRP |
| 2602 | Willys coupe 1941 | CRP |
| 2603 | Ford Sedan 1934 | CRP |
| 2604 | Chevy 57 | CRP |
| 2605 | Pick up Hot Rod | CRP |

### 3000 series:

| # | Name | Price |
|---|---|---|
| 3006 | Kenworth | CRP |
| 3007 | Dune Buggy | CRP |
| 3008 | Police car | CRP |
| 3012 | Tractor | CRP |
| 3017 | Mercedes 4 x 4 police | CRP |
| 3018 | Range Rover | CRP |
| 3019 | Road construction truck | CRP |
| 3025 | Breakdown truck | CRP |
| 3026 | Ford Mustang | CRP |
| 3027 | Camaro | CRP |
| 3028 | Racing truck | CRP |
| 3029 | Van Ford Model A | CRP |
| 3030.1 | Winnebago camping car | CRP |
| 3030.2 | Holiday Van | CRP |
| 3030.3 | Ambulance | CRP |
| 3030.4 | Fire | CRP |
| 3033 | Fire engine | CRP |
| 3035 | Kenworth Wrecker | CRP |
| 3036 | Kenworth Dump Truck | CRP |
| 3037 | Garbage Truck | CRP |
| 3046 | Autocar | CRP |
| 3049 | Tractor + tank trailer | CRP |
| 3051 | Tractor + hay trailer | CRP |
| 3053 | Range Rover + camping trailer | CRP |

| # | Name | Price |
|---|---|---|
| 3055 | Container | CRP |
| 3057 | Camaro + racer | CRP |
| 3060 | Sailboat + transporter | CRP |
| 3067 | GM semi horse trailer | CRP |
| 3071 | Car carrier | CRP |
| 3073 | Off shore racer semi transporter | CRP |
| 3075 | Dragster transporter | CRP |
| 3076 | Truck oil tanker | CRP |
| 3092 | Van Holidays + Trailer Hot Rods | CRP |
| 3093 | Racing Truck Transporter + 1 Racing Truck | CRP |
| 3094 | Kenworth helicopter transporter + Land Rover | CRP |
| 3095 | Kenworth car carrier with 5 cars | CRP |
| 3096 | Fire engine with extension ladder | CRP |
| 3097 | Semi bulldozer transporter | CRP |
| 3098 | Racing car transporter + 4 formula one cars | CRP |
| 3099 | Chevy + buggy | CRP |

### Road Kings & Ultra Custom 1/32 scale 3200 series:

| # | Name | Price |
|---|---|---|
| 3201 | 95 Mustang | CRP |
| 3202 | 95 Camaro convertible | CRP |
| 3203 | Chevy Sportside extended cab | CRP |
| 3204 | Chevy Sportside & camper top | CRP |
| 3221 | 95 Mustang | CRP |
| 3222 | 95 Camaro | CRP |
| 3223 | Custom Chevy Dually | CRP |
| 3224 | Custom Chevy Dually & camper top | CRP |

### 4500 series:

| # | Name | Price |
|---|---|---|
| 4501 | Front end loader | CRP |
| 4502 | Cement Mixer | CRP |
| 4503 | Heavy duty transporter | CRP |
| 4504 | Roller | CRP |
| 4505 | Bulldozer | CRP |
| 4506 | Wheeled excavator | CRP |
| 4511 | Telescopic crane | CRP |
| 4512 | Levelling scraper | CRP |
| 4513 | Crawler shovel | CRP |
| 4514 | Dump truck + Land Rover | CRP |
| 4515 | Caterpillar tracked crane | CRP |
| 4517 | Scraper | CRP |

*One of the 1/32 scale "Legends" series: #2402, the 1956 Ford Thunderbird.*

# Manoil

This New York-based company is perhaps best known for the die cast cars and military vehicles that it produced prior to World War II. The #706 Rocket Car, in particular, is a commonly found Manoil that is very popular with collectors. But Manoil also produced die cast toys following the war, most of which compared favorably with the American market leader at the time, Tootsietoy.

Manoil generally painted their die cast toys red, blue, yellow or green (although orange occasionally turns up), and often highlighted features like grilles and roofs in silver. Although not designated as such by the company, some of the Manoil cars do resemble specific makes. The #707 Sedan looks somewhat like a Chrysler, and the #716 through #720 cars were almost certainly based on Buicks of the day.

Brothers Jack and Maurice Manoil ran the company; after twenty-some-odd years of toy manufacture, Manoil went out of business in the mid-1950s.

The black rubber tires used on the post-war Manoils are typical of tires used on American die cast toys of the period.

As for packaging, the author has not seen any original Manoil toys with individual boxes. However, it is possible that some of the toys (such as the #716 through #720 automobiles) did come in their own boxes.

*This Manoil #708 Roadster (vertical radiator) sports the silver paint highlights that appeared on many of the post-war Manoil toys.*

| # | Name | Price | # | Name | Price | # | Name | Price |
|---|------|-------|---|------|-------|---|------|-------|
| 707 | Sedan | $70 | 712 | Pumper | $425 | 717 | Hard Top Convertible | $70 |
| 708 | Roadster with vertical radiator | 75 | 713 | Bus | 60 | 718 | Convertible | 80 |
| 708 | Roadster with horizontal radiator | 60 | 714 | Towing Truck | 45 | 719 | Sport Car | 80 |
| 709 | Fire Engine | 45 | 715 | Commercial Truck (with removable side panels) | 60 | 720 | Ranch Wagon | 65 |
| 710 | Oil Tanker | 40 | | | | | | |
| 711 | Aerial Ladder | 425 | 716 | Sedan | 70 | | | |

# Märklin

Göppingen, Germany, is the home of one of the most revered names in the history of toy making. For nearly 140 years, Märklin has been making playthings for children around the world. They are well-known for making some of the finest model trains in the world, as well as for making reproductions of their larger clockwork-powered tinplate toy trucks of the 1930s.

Die cast, though, is also a part of Märklin's history. Prior to World War II, the company put out a series of approximately 1/43 scale models; included were numerous Mercedes-Benz cars and trucks, as well as Auto Union race cars that dominated Grand Prix racing (with Mercedes-Benz) in the 1930s. There was even a model of the original Volkswagen "KdF Wagen," which would go on to become the Beetle.

These pre-war die casts are now quite rare; collectors often pay many hundreds of dollars for original examples. It is unclear whether any of these models were produced after the war; if so, the number was comparatively small.

After the war, Märklin introduced a new line of 1/43 scale cars and 1/50 scale trucks. Included were Mercedes, Porsche and VW models, and they were of very good quality when compared to the Dinkys and Solidos then on the market. They did not have windows or interiors, but they were accurate models. They came with black rubber tires on spun metal hubs, and a majority of the models had a tinplate baseplate that had some information, such as the model name and/or the number, etc. These early Märklins were numbered with a 5521 or 5524 number, which would be followed by a /, and then another number to indicate the model. By the mid-1950s, though, the series received its own number: 8000. (The models that were numbered both ways are indicated in the listing; note that such models had one type of number or the other, not both together.)

The 8000 series remained in production until the mid-1960s. In 1968, the new 1800 series appeared, and these accurate and detailed 1/43 scale models came with window glazing, opening doors and hoods, and other features. They came with either standard passenger-car-style wheels, or with "speed"-type units. The chassis were die cast, and although they had the model name and the Märklin name on them, they did not have the model number.

The 1800 series remained in production until 1977. Since then, there have been two "sets" of die cast models produced for the collector market. In the late 1980s, a set of

four Mercedes-Benz racing cars was produced, all of which were reproductions of old Märklin models. And the 1994/1995 Märklin catalog features three two-car sets; the models, according to Märklin, are made from "reworked" original tooling. All six are from the 1800 series; included are models like the #1818 Chevrolet Corvette.

The 8000 and 1800 series are included in the following listing. CRP (Current Retail Price) for the 1980s Mercedes-Benz race cars is unknown, while the CRP for a reproduction 1800 set would likely be in the $40-$50 range.

For more information on the Märklin range of products, please consult Dr. Edward Force's excellent book, *Classic Miniature Vehicles Made in Germany*. It is an invaluable reference tool for the collector. Details on the book may be found in Part Three, Additional Resources.

| # | Name | Price |
|---|---|---|
| **8000 series:** | | |
| 8000 | MAN "ARAL" Tanker (originally numbered 5521/27) | $200 |
| 8001 | Buick Special (originally numbered 5521/52) | 225 |
| 8002 | Lanz Tractor (originally numbered 5521/71) | 160 |
| 8003 | Mercedes-Benz 300 (originally numbered 5524/1) | 200 |
| 8004 | Porsche 356 (originally numbered 5524/2) | 140 |
| 8005 | Volkswagen Beetle (originally numbered 5524/3) | 150 |
| 8006 | Volkswagen Van (originally numbered 5524/5) | 150 |
| 8007 | Volkswagen Van "GASOLIN" (originally numbered 5524/5G) | 185 |
| 8008 | Volkswagen Van (two-tone color) (originally numbered 5524/5Z) | 150 |
| 8009 | Krupp Open Truck (originally numbered 5524/10) | 125 |
| 8010 | Mercedes-Benz W 196 Racing Car with racing number decal (originally numbered 5524/11) | 110 |
| 8011 | Mercedes-Benz W 196 Racing Car without racing number decal (originally numbered 5524/11A) | 110 |
| 8012 | Krupp Open Trailer (originally numbered 5524/12) | 50 |
| 8013 | Volkswagen Bus (originally numbered 5524/14E) | 150 |
| 8014 | Volkswagen Bus (two-tone color) (originally numbered 5524/14Z) | 150 |
| 8015 | Borgward Isabella (originally numbered 5524/15) | 135 |
| 8016 | BMW 501-502 Sedan (originally numbered 5524/16) | 145 |
| 8017 | Tire Van "PHOENIX" (originally numbered 5524/17) | 210 |
| 8018 | Ford Taunus 15M (originally numbered 5524/4) | 105 |
| 8019 | Mercedes-Benz 300SL Coupe | 140 |
| 8020 | Borgward Isabella (two-tone version of #8015) | 135 |

*This #8019 Mercedes-Benz 300SL is chipped, and would therefore sell for about half of the $140 near mint price.*

| # | Name | Price |
|---|---|---|
| 8021 | Volkswagen Karmann Ghia Coupe | $135 |
| 8022 | BMW 507 Coupe | 135 |
| 8023 | Magirus Fire Ladder Truck | 150 |
| 8024 | Porsche 356 Police Car | 170 |
| 8025 | Mercedes-Benz 190SL Roadster | 140 |
| 8026 | Tempo Open Truck | 110 |
| 8027 | Ford Taunus 17M (two-tone) | 125 |
| 8028 | Ford Taunus 17M (one color) | 125 |
| 8029 | Lanz Tractor (same basic casting as #8002) | 100 |
| 8030 | Volkswagen Ambulance (same basic casting as #8013 and #8014) | 165 |
| 8031 | Magirus Crane Truck | 125 |
| 8032 | Mercedes-Benz Tanker "ARAL" | 160 |
| 8033 | Volkswagen Van "UNION TRANSPORT" (same casting as #8006, #8007 and #8008) | 275 |
| 8033 | Volkswagen Van "SILLAN" (same casting as #8006, #8007 and #8008) | 275 |
| 8033 | Volkswagen Van "DER SPIEGEL" (same casting as #8006, #8007 and #8008) | 275 |
| 8034 | Krupp Open Truck | 110 |
| 8035 | Fuchs 301 Excavator | 90 |
| 8036 | Kaelble Quarry Dump Truck | 110 |

| # | Name | Price |
|---|---|---|
| 8037 | Krupp Open Trailer (same casting as #8012) | $40 |
| **1800 series:** | | |
| 1800 | Porsche 911 Targa | 50 |
| 1801 | BMW 2000 CS | 50 |
| 1802 | Chapparal 2F | 40 |
| 1803 | Ford OSI 20M | 40 |
| 1804 | BMW 2800 CS Coupe | 40 |
| 1805 | Volkswagen 1600 Variant | 50 |
| 1806 | Volkswagen 1600 Variant Police Car | 50 |
| 1807 | Volkswagen 1600 Variant Fire Chief Car | 50 |
| 1808 | Volkswagen 1600 Variant "ADAC" | 50 |
| 1809 | Volkswagen 1600 Variant Ambulance | 50 |
| 1810 | Porsche 910 | 50 |
| 1811 | NSU RO 80 | 40 |
| 1812 | BMW 1600 GT | 50 |
| 1813 | Mercedes-Benz C-111 | 35 |
| 1814 | BMW Glas 3000 Coupe | 50 |
| 1815 | Porsche 907 | 40 |
| 1816 | Matra M30 | 40 |
| 1817 | Mercedes-Benz 250 | 40 |
| 1818 | Chevrolet Corvette | 50 |
| 1819 | BMW 2002 TI | 40 |
| 1820 | BMW 2500 | 40 |
| 1821 | Audi 100LS | 40 |

| # | Name | Price |
|---|------|-------|
| 1829 | Mercedes-Benz 250 Taxi (same casting as #1817) . . . . . . . . . . . . . . . | $40 |
| 1830 | Mercedes-Benz Unimog . . . . . . . . . . | 40 |
| 1831 | Mercedes-Benz Unimog and Equipment (#s 1830, 1832 and 1833) . . . . . | 70 |
| 1832 | Equipment for Unimog . . . . . . . . . . | 15 |
| 1833 | Equipment for Unimog . . . . . . . . . . | 15 |
| 1834 | Audi 100 Coupe . . . . . . . . . . . . . | 40 |
| 1835 | Opel Manta . . . . . . . . . . . . . . . | 50 |
| 1837 | Volkswagen K-70 . . . . . . . . . . . . | 40 |
| 1838 | BMW 1600 GT Rally Car . . . . . . . . . | 40 |
| 1839 | Mercedes-Benz 350SL . . . . . . . . . . | 40 |

### Late 1980s Mercedes-Benz racing cars:

| # | Name | Price |
|---|------|-------|
| 4020 | Mercedes-Benz W25 . . . . . . . . . . . | CRP |
| 4021 | Mercedes-Benz W154 . . . . . . . . . . | CRP |
| 4022 | Mercedes-Benz W25B . . . . . . . . . . | CRP |
| 4023 | Mercedes-Benz W196 . . . . . . . . . . | CRP |

### 1800 series repros:

| # | Name | Price |
|---|------|-------|
| 1803 | RAK Auto Set (#1803 Ford OSI and #1822 Ford Capri) . . . . . . . . . . . . . | CRP |
| 1813 | RAK Auto Set (#1813 Mercedes-Benz C-111 and #1839 Mercedes-Benz 350SL) . . . . . . . . . . . . . . . | CRP |
| 1818 | RAK Auto Set (#1818 Chevrolet Corvette and #1835 Opel Manta) . . . . . . | CRP |

*A Märklin #8013 Volkswagen Bus, sporting typical Märklin spun-metal wheel hubs. This may be a repainted example, since the brown color has not been recorded.*

| # | Name | Price |
|---|------|-------|
| 1822 | Ford Capri 2300 . . . . . . . . . . . . | $40 |
| 1823 | Volkswagen 1600 Variant "POLIZEI" (same casting as #1805) . . . . . . . . . | 50 |
| 1824 | Eriba Caravan . . . . . . . . . . . . . . | 40 |

| # | Name | Price |
|---|------|-------|
| 1825 | Volkswagen 411 . . . . . . . . . . . . . | $50 |
| 1826 | VW-Porsche 914 . . . . . . . . . . . . | 40 |
| 1828 | Mercedes-Benz 250 Police Car (same casting as #1817) . . . . . . . . . | 40 |

# Marusan

Collectors of tinplate toys will recognize the Marusan name, since the Japanese company made a number of superb tin toy cars during the 1950s. These have become highly prized by tinplate collectors.

Marusan also made a small group of approximately 1/43 scale die cast commercial vehicles for what was apparently a short time. In 1960 or '61, a group of eight toys made their debut (there may have been more, but the author has no record of any others). The models were: #8501 Panhard Semi Truck; #8502 Morris J Mail Van; #8503 Daimler Ambulance; #8504 Ford Milk Truck; #8505 Avenue Bus; #8506 Euclid Dump Truck; #8507 Austin Van; and an un-numbered Toyota Truck.

All Marusans seen to date have no window glazing or interiors, and the wheel hubs appear to be spun metal, with black rubber tires. The baseplates are tinplate, and most, if not all, of the baseplates have the word "SAN." Marusan often used this three-letter abbreviation for its name. As for the color of the models, Marusan favored blue; however, the Daimler Ambulance was white, the Morris J Van was red and the Panhard truck has been reported in orange.

The models came in individual boxes, which bear the name of the manufacturer (Marusan Shoten Ltd.). The end flaps of the boxes were sealed with a tennis-racquet-shaped sticker. On the front of each box, there is a line drawing of the model contained inside, and above the drawing are the words "FIRST WITH THE DIECA MODELS." One assumes that "DIECA" referred to die cast.

The use of the word "first" is perhaps less than accurate, since the Marusan models were obviously copies of Dinky Toys that had been available for a number of years. The #8505 Avenue Bus, for example, so closely matches the Dinky #29f/280 Observation Coach that it can be mistaken for the English toy at first glance. (The Dinky Coach went out of production in 1960). The same is true of the #8502 Morris Van, which is a copy of the Dinky #260 Royal Mail Van. There are fundamental differences between the castings, however, indicating that the Dinky tooling was not used by Marusan.

Marusan die casts are quite rare today, and a near mint to mint, boxed example can sell for $200-$300.

# Matchbox

Few companies in any industry enjoy the instant name recognition that Matchbox does. These "pocket money" toys have been with us since 1953, and their history has been well-chronicled through the years. A brief recap, however, will set the stage for the listings which follow.

Matchbox started as the result of a partnership between two men. Leslie and Rodney Smith, who were not related, had been boyhood friends in England. Upon being discharged from the Royal Navy after World War II, they decided to launch a business together. In 1947 they formed Lesney Products, the name being the result of combining their first names.

They rented an old bar called "The Rifleman" in north London, and set up their die casting equipment to fulfill orders for die cast components for industry. They were soon joined by John Odell, better known as Jack, who had been a fellow employee of Rodney Smith's at Die Casting Machine Tools Ltd. (D.C.M.T.). Odell made the dies for Lesney's products, and soon became a full partner in the firm. (Odell would go on to found Lledo in the 1980s.)

The first die cast toy made by Lesney was the Aveling Barford Diesel Road Roller, which was introduced in 1948. This was joined by a number of other toys, including a tinplate wind-up elephant.

Jack Odell experimented with various smaller toy designs, including a tiny road roller that his daughter took to school in a matchbox. Her classmates all clamored for their own road rollers, and somewhere along the way Odell and Lesney came up with the idea of designing an entire line of toy vehicles that could be packaged in matchbox-size boxes.

The new "Matchbox" line made its debut in 1953, and it initially was comprised of smaller versions of Lesney's other, larger toys. (These were soon phased out as the Matchbox line took hold.) The box would soon became as recognizable as the name, with the early boxes bearing the legend "A Moko Lesney Product." Moko was the name of the company that marketed Matchbox toys, and it was owned by Richard Kohnstam. The marketing agreement lasted until

the late 1950s, when Lesney bought out Kohnstam's interest. (The buy-out had been brewing for several years, ever since Lesney discovered that Kohnstam had registered the Matchbox name to himself.)

The Matchbox toys sold very well, and Lesney Products grew and expanded. (Rodney Smith had left the company in the early '50s.) Each new model was given a number; once the series reached 75, the numbering of new models changed. When an existing model was phased out, its number would be taken by a new model. This worked well until 1981, at which point the "1-75" line was split into two separate lines, one for the United States and the other for "ROW" (rest of the world). This has created problems for collectors in sorting out just what was made when.

*A Matchbox #17 Austin FX3 Taxi. Produced from 1960 until 1963, this Matchbox later was fitted with silver plastic wheels to replace the gray plastic units shown here.*

## Major Packs and King-Size models

Beginning in the late 1950s, Lesney offered a line of larger Matchbox toys. These were called "Major Packs," and they included tractor trailer trucks and earth-moving equipment. And "Major" they were: they ranged from the four-inch long #M4A Ruston Bucyrus Power Shovel to the eleven-inch long #M9 Interstate Double Freighter.

The King-Size series made its debut in 1960, and it, too, featured larger commercial vehicle toys. There were also several cars in the King-Size line; eventually, the Major Packs series was phased out in 1966 as the King-Size series took precedence.

## Models of Yesteryear

In 1956, Lesney launched the "Models of Yesteryear" series. This line of older and antique models was the brain-child of Jack Odell, who was a fan of veteran vehicles. The series, which has always been aimed more at the adult collector, sold well, particularly in the United Kingdom. It is still in production today.

Throughout the 1960s, the Matchbox line enjoyed success after success as children around the world bought millions of the small toys. Then, in 1968, Mattel dropped a bomb on the toy car market with its introduction of Hot

The box for the Accessory Pack #5 Home Store is typical of Matchbox boxes of the period, with the distinctive blue and yellow colors.

This die cast shop, entitled "Home Stores," was Accessory Pack #5, and was produced starting in 1960.

Wheels. Overnight, the market changed completely. Lesney was now forced to play catch-up to the fast and flashy cars from California, and the company suffered severe financial difficulties before it came out with its "Superfast" line in 1969.

These "revamped" Matchbox models eventually enjoyed great success, and new models were added throughout the 1970s. The "1-75" numbering system was retained, although older models were naturally phased out eventually. (Models produced from 1968 to about 1971 can be found with both Superfast and the old "regular" wheels.)

In addition to being sold individually, Matchbox toys were also sold in sets. During the 1970s, Lesney even produced plastic kits. By the late 1970s, however, the company was in serious financial trouble. In 1982, Lesney was bought by the Universal Group, the new company being named Universal Matchbox. In order to cut costs, production was promptly transferred to the Far East. However, certain operations—such as research and the manufacture of the Models of Yesteryears—remained in England. (In 1987, Universal Matchbox also acquired the rights to the name Dinky, out of which grew the Dinky Collection.)

## Matchbox Today

In 1992, Universal Matchbox was purchased by Tyco Toys, Inc. That same year the adult "nostalgia" market was tapped into with the introduction of the Matchbox "Originals" line, which was made up of reproductions of original Matchbox toys from the 1950s. These are packaged in a blisterpack, with the toy sitting inside on top of a reproduction "Moko Lesney" box.

Several series of the "Originals" have been released, and they include models such as the #32 Jaguar XK140, the #11 ERF Petrol Tanker and the #52 Maserati 4CLT racing car. The Originals series cars sell for about $2 at retail.

Other series, such as the Indy 500 line and the Harley Davidson line, have been launched in recent years. Toys in these series are also available in retail outlets; the Indy 500 cars sell for about $5, while the Harley-Davidson toys go for $5-$15. Also worthy of mention is the "World Class" line that was launched in 1993, made up of "high-end" versions of current 1-75 models. These generally sell for $3-$5.

The Models of Yesteryear line was switched over, in 1993, to a direct-marketing-only system. A division known as Matchbox Collectibles was established to oversee marketing and distribution, and the system was first tested with the "A Taste of France" series, followed by "Great Beers of the World." This system has meant that M-of-Y collectors can purchase new products only through mail order (although there are reportedly a few retail outlets left that carry the product).

The 1-75 line continues to be the "core" line for Matchbox, and these toys can be found in outlets such as Toys R Us, Target, etc. The current 1-75's sell for $1 or less, which continues to make them competitive with modern Hot Wheels products.

Another very popular segment of the Matchbox collecting scene are the catalogs. Lesney (and then Universal) published out catalogs each year that were eagerly snapped up by consumers. Many of them survive in great numbers, so that even older catalogs can be purchased for a reasonable price.

## The Original Box

Perhaps more than any other group of collectors, enthusiasts of older Matchbox focus on toys in their original boxes. (Matchboxes released in the 1980s and '90s can be found in both boxes and blisterpacks.) Matchbox toys without their original boxes do sell, but many collectors insist on the original box being with the toy.

This means that "loose" Matchbox toys can be had for lower (some would say "bargain") prices. The exception, as always, is the model that is very rare, which will generally sell relatively quickly.

## The Clubs

There are a number of Matchbox collector's clubs that can provide help and information to the Matchbox enthusiast. Many of them also offer collector's shows. These organizations exist in countries around the world; in the United States, there are several to choose from. They are listed in Part Three, Additional Resources.

## Using This Listing

The following listing is for the most commonly found Matchbox models, in near mint to mint condition **with the original box or other packaging.** Certain color or casting variations are worth considerably more than the more common version. For example, the #11 ERF Petrol Tanker can sell for as low as $40 for one of the commonly found red versions. But the more rare green version (which had metal wheels) is valued at $300 and up,

depending on who is offering it for sale. At the same time, a variation may be a minor change such as a slightly different texture on a radiator grille. Where possible, unusual or rare variations such as this are noted. However, space does not allow for a comprehensive listing; the reader is therefore advised to consult one of the Matchbox books listed in Part Three, Additional Resources. In particular, Charlie Mack's series of books on the subject are excellent sources of further information.

*Note on the Models of Yesteryear listing:* There is a seemingly endless variety of variations with the Models of Yesteryear. To list all of these variations would require far more space than can be devoted here. Therefore, each major casting is listed with its number, and a value or range of values is given for the model. A range indicates the high and low ends of the value scale for that particular model. For further information on the Models of Yesteryear series, the reader is again advised to consult the books on Matchbox that are listed in Part Three, Additional Resources.

*#40 Leyland Royal Tiger Coach, available from 1961 until 1967.*

*At left is a #9 Merryweather Fire Engine; at right is a #55 Ford Fairlane Police Car. Both models feature the black plastic wheels that the 1-75 line was fitted with during the mid- to late-1960s.*

| # | Name | Price |
|---|------|-------|

## I-75 SERIES

### Regular Wheels:

| # | Name | Price |
|---|------|-------|
| I | Aveling Barford Road Roller (canopy nearly to front wheel) | |
| | dark green | $50 |
| | light green | 80 |
| I | Road Roller (2¼ inches; canopy over driver only) | 55 |
| I | Road Roller (2⅜ inches; canopy over driver only) | 50 |
| I | Road Roller (2⅝ inches; canopy over driver only) | 20 |
| I | Mercedes Truck | 15 |
| 2 | Dumper (1⅝ inches) | |
| | green metal wheels | 125 |
| | unpainted metal wheels | 50 |
| 2 | Dumper (1⅞ inches) | 50 |
| 2 | Muir Hill Dumper | |
| | "Laing" decals | 20 |
| | "Muir Hill" decals | 60 |
| 2 | Mercedes Trailer | 10 |
| 3 | Cement Mixer | 35 |
| 3 | Bedford Tipper Lorry (maroon or red rear) | 25 |
| 3 | Mercedes Ambulance | 15 |
| 4 | Massey-Harris Tractor | 50 |
| 4 | Triumph Motorcycle and Sidecar | 50 |
| 4 | Stake Truck | |
| | yellow/blue | 90 |
| | yellow/green | 15 |
| 5 | London Bus (2 inches) "Buy Matchbox Series" | 60 |
| 5 | London Bus (2¼ inches) | |
| | "Buy Matchbox Series" | 60 |
| | "Players Please" | 100 |
| | "Visco static" | 140 |
| 5 | London Bus (2⁹/₁₆ inches) | |
| | "Players Please" | 100 |
| | "Visco static" | 40 |

| # | Name | Price |
|---|------|-------|
| | "Drink Peardrax" | $115 |
| | "Baron of Beef" | 160 |
| 5 | London Bus (2¾ inches) | |
| | "Visco static" or "Longlife" | 15 |
| | "Baron of Beef" | 160 |
| 6 | Quarry Truck | 35 |
| 6 | Euclid Quarry Truck | 15 |
| 6 | Ford Pick-up | 15 |
| 7 | Horse Drawn milk float | 60 |
| 7 | Ford Anglia | 20 |
| 7 | Ford Refuse Truck | 10 |
| 8 | Caterpillar Tractor (1½ inches) | |
| | yellow | 60 |
| | orange | 75 |
| 8 | Caterpillar Tractor (1⅝ inches) | 50 |
| 8 | Caterpillar Tractor (1⅞ inches) | 50 |
| 8 | Caterpillar Tractor (2 inches) | 20 |
| 8 | Ford Mustang | |
| | orange | 135 |
| | white | 25 |
| 9 | Dennis Fire Engine | 50 |
| 9 | Merryweather Fire Engine | 35 |
| 9 | Boat and Trailer | 15 |
| 10 | Mechanical Horse and Trailer | 40 |
| 10 | Foden Sugar Container | 45 |
| 10 | Pipe Truck | 15 |
| 11 | ERF Petrol Tanker (2 inches) | |
| | red, yellow | 55 |
| | green | 350 |
| 11 | ERF Petrol Tanker (2½ inches) | 50 |
| 11 | Taylor Jumbo Crane | 15 |
| 11 | Mercedes Scaffolding Truck | 15 |
| 12 | Land Rover (1¾ inches) | 40 |
| 12 | Land Rover (2¼ inches) | 35 |
| 12 | Safari Land Rover | 15 |
| 13 | Bedford Breakdown Lorry | 50 |
| 13 | Thames Trader Breakdown Lorry | 40 |
| 13 | Dodge Breakdown Lorry | 15 |
| 14 | Daimler Ambulance | 40 |

| # | Name | Price |
|---|------|-------|
| 14 | Bedford Ambulance | $35 |
| 14 | ISO Grifo | 15 |
| 15 | Prime Mover | 35 |
| 15 | Tippax Refuse Lorry | 20 |
| 15 | Volkswagen 1500 | 20 |
| 16 | Atlantic Trailer | 35 |
| 16 | Scammell Snow Plow | 35 |
| 16 | Case Tractor | 15 |
| 17 | Removal Van | |
| | maroon red | 210 |
| | blue | 180 |
| | green | 50 |
| 17 | Austin FX3 Taxi | 60 |
| 17 | 'Hoveringham' Tipper | 20 |
| 17 | Horse Box | 15 |
| 18 | Caterpillar Bulldozer | 50 |
| 18 | Field Car | 15 |
| 19 | MG 'TD' Sports Car | 75 |
| 19 | MG 'A' Sports Car | 95 |
| 19 | Aston Martin Race Car | 40 |
| 19 | Lotus Sports Car | |
| | orange | 45 |
| | green | 25 |
| 20 | ERF Lorry | 45 |
| 20 | ERF Lorry "Ever Ready" | 55 |
| 20 | Chevrolet Impala Taxi | 20 |
| 21 | Long Distance Coach | 45 |
| 21 | Commer Milk Float | 40 |
| 21 | Foden Concrete Mixer | 15 |
| 22 | Vauxhall Cresta | 50 |
| 22 | Pontiac Gran Prix | 20 |
| 23 | Berkeley Cavalier Caravan | 50 |
| 23 | Bluebird Dauphine Caravan | 60 |
| 23 | Mobile Home | 15 |
| 24 | Weatherhill Hydraulic Excavator (small) | 45 |
| 24 | Rolls-Royce Silver Shadow | 15 |
| 25 | Bedford Van 'Dunlop' | 45 |
| 25 | Volkswagen 1200 | 50 |
| 25 | Petrol Tanker 'BP' | 25 |
| 25 | Petrol Tanker 'Aral' | 100 |
| 25 | Ford Cortina | 15 |
| 26 | ERF Cement Mixer | 50 |
| 26 | Foden Cement Mixer | 40 |
| 26 | GMC Tipper | 10 |
| 27 | Bedford Low Loader (3⅛ inches) | |
| | two-tone blue | 400 |
| | green/tan | 50 |
| 27 | Bedford Low Loader (3¾ inches) | 60 |
| 27 | Cadillac | |
| | light green | 320 |
| | other colors | 45 |
| 27 | Mercedes 230SL Convertible | 15 |
| 28 | Bedford Compressor | 35 |
| 28 | Ford Thames Compressor | 35 |
| 28 | Jaguar Mk10 | 20 |
| 28 | Mack Dump Truck | 15 |
| 29 | Bedford Milk Float | 40 |
| 29 | Austin Cambridge | 35 |
| 29 | Fire Pumper | 15 |
| 30 | Ford Prefect | |
| | gray or brown | 45 |
| | light blue | 125 |

*The #19 Lotus Racing Car also came in orange. The plastic driver is often missing on surviving examples.*

| # | Name | Price |
|---|------|-------|
| 30 | Magirus-Deutz six-wheeled crane | $50 |
| 30 | Eight-wheeled crane | 15 |
| 31 | Ford Station Wagon (2⅝ inches) | 45 |
| 31 | Ford Station Wagon (2¾ inches) | |
| | yellow | 115 |
| | green/pink | 50 |
| 31 | Lincoln Continental | 15 |
| 32 | Jaguar XK140 Coupe (2⅜ inches) | |
| | red | 110 |
| | white | 45 |
| 32 | Jaguar E Type (2⅝ inches) | 40 |
| 32 | Leyland Tanker 'BP' | 15 |
| 32 | Leyland Tanker 'Aral' | 60 |
| 33 | Ford Zodiac | |
| | dark blue | 500 |
| | other colors | 50 |
| 33 | Ford Zephyr | 25 |
| 33 | Lamborghini Miura | |
| | yellow | 15 |
| | gold | 100 |
| 34 | Volkswagen Van (2¼ inches) | 50 |
| 34 | Volkswagen Caravan (2⅝ inches) | 50 |
| 34 | Volkswagen Camper (2⅝ inches) | 20 |
| 35 | Marshall Horse Box | 45 |
| 35 | Snow-trac Tractor | 25 |
| 36 | Austin A50 | 40 |
| 36 | Lambretta Scooter and Sidecar | 65 |
| 36 | Opel Diplomat | 15 |
| 37 | Coca Cola Lorry 'Karrier Bantam' (without base) | |
| | uneven crates | 100 |
| | even crates | 70 |
| 37 | Coca Cola Lorry 'Karrier Bantam' (with base) | 75 |
| 37 | Dodge Cattle Truck | 15 |
| 38 | Karrier Refuse Lorry | |
| | tan | 150 |
| | gray, silver | 50 |
| 38 | Vauxhall Victor Estate Car | 30 |
| 38 | Honda Motorcycle on Trailer | 25 |
| 39 | Ford Zodiac convertible | |
| | brown interior | 140 |
| | green interior | 50 |
| 39 | Pontiac convertible | |
| | violet | 90 |
| | yellow | 35 |
| 39 | Ford Tractor | |
| | blue | 20 |
| | blue/yellow | 15 |
| | orange | 130 |
| 40 | Bedford Tipper Lorry | 40 |
| 40 | Leyland Royal Tiger Coach | 35 |
| 40 | Hay Trailer | 10 |
| 41 | Jaguar D Type (2³⁄₁₆ inches) | 45 |
| 41 | Jaguar D Type (2⁷⁄₁₆ inches) | 80 |
| 41 | Ford 'GT' | |
| | white | 15 |
| | yellow | 90 |
| 42 | Bedford Van 'Evening News' | 55 |
| 42 | Studebaker Station Wagon | 20 |
| 42 | Iron Fairy Crane | 15 |
| 43 | Hillman Minx | |
| | green | 210 |

| # | Name | Price |
|---|------|-------|
| | blue/gray | $50 |
| | turquoise/cream | 45 |
| 43 | Aveling Barford Tractor Shovel | 45 |
| 43 | Pony Trailer with ponies | 15 |
| 44 | Rolls-Royce Silver Cloud | 45 |
| 44 | Rolls-Royce Phantom V | 35 |
| 44 | GMC Refrigerator Lorry | 10 |
| 45 | Vauxhall Victor | 45 |
| 45 | Ford Corsair with Boat | 25 |
| 46 | Morris Minor | |
| | blue | 120 |
| | green | 70 |
| 46 | Pickfords Removals van | |
| | blue | 85 |
| | green | 55 |
| 46 | Mercedes 300SE | 15 |
| 47 | Trojan Van 'Brooke Bond Tea' | 45 |
| 47 | Commer 'Lyons Ice Cream' Mobile Shop | |
| | metallic blue | 110 |
| | blue | 45 |
| | cream | 60 |
| 47 | DAF Tipper Lorry | |
| | turquoise/yellow | 45 |
| | silver/yellow | 15 |

| # | Name | Price |
|---|------|-------|
| 48 | Motor Boat and Trailer | $45 |
| 48 | Speed Boat and Trailer | 40 |
| 48 | Dodge Dump Lorry | 10 |
| 49 | M3 Army Personnel Carrier | 35 |
| 49 | Unimog | 15 |
| 50 | Commer Pick-up Truck | |
| | tan | 45 |
| | red/gray | 90 |
| 50 | John Deere Tractor | 25 |
| 50 | Kennel Truck | 15 |
| 51 | Albion Chieftain cement lorry | 45 |
| 51 | John Deere Trailer | 25 |
| 51 | AEC Eight-wheel Tipper | 20 |
| 52 | Maserati 4CLT | 55 |
| 52 | BRM Racing Car | 25 |
| 53 | Aston Martin DB2 | |
| | green | 45 |
| | red | 150 |
| 53 | Mercedes Benz 220SE | 30 |
| 53 | Ford Zodiac MkIV | 15 |
| 54 | Saracen Personnel Carrier | 20 |
| 54 | Cadillac Ambulance | 15 |
| 55 | D.U.K.W. | 40 |

*#31 Lincoln Continental in the blisterpack packaging that Lesney used during the mid- to late-1960s.*

| # | Name | Price |
|---|------|-------|
| 55 | Ford Fairlane Police car | |
| | light blue | $50 |
| | dark blue | 160 |
| 55 | Ford Galaxie Police Car | 25 |
| 55 | Mercury Police Car | 15 |
| 56 | London Trolleybus | 50 |
| 56 | Fiat 1500 | |
| | green | 15 |
| | red | 115 |
| 57 | Wolseley 1500 | 45 |
| 57 | Chevrolet Impala | 30 |
| 57 | Land Rover—Kent Fire Brigade | 20 |
| 58 | BEA Coach | 50 |
| 58 | Drott Excavator | 50 |
| 58 | DAF Girder Lorry | 15 |
| 59 | Ford Thames van 'Singer' | |
| | light green | 50 |
| | dark green | 130 |
| 59 | Ford Fairlane Fire Chiefs car | 30 |
| 59 | Ford Galaxie Fire Chiefs car | 15 |
| 60 | Morris J2 Pick-up | 40 |
| 60 | Leyland site hut lorry | 15 |
| 61 | Ferret Scout car | 20 |
| 61 | Alvis Stalwart | 15 |
| 62 | AEC General Service Lorry | 40 |
| 62 | TV Service Van | |
| | "Rentaset" | 45 |
| | Radio Rentals | 70 |
| 62 | Mercury Cougar | 10 |
| 63 | Ford Army Ambulance | 45 |
| 63 | Airport Fire Crash Tender | 30 |
| 63 | Dodge Crane | 15 |
| 64 | Scammell Army Breakdown Truck | 50 |
| 64 | MG 1100 | 15 |
| 65 | Jaguar 3.4 litre | 45 |
| 65 | Combine Harvester | 15 |
| 66 | Citroën DS19 | 65 |
| 66 | Harley-Davidson Motorcycle and Sidecar | 95 |

| # | Name | Price |
|---|------|-------|
| 66 | Greyhound Coach | |
| | clear windows | $70 |
| | amber windows | 15 |
| 67 | Saladin Armoured Car | 25 |
| 67 | Volkswagen 1600TL | |
| | red | 15 |
| | purple | 140 |
| 68 | Austin Army Radio Truck | 40 |
| 68 | Mercedes Coach | |
| | orange/white | 15 |
| | green/white | 100 |
| 69 | Commer Van 'Nestles' | 50 |
| 69 | Hatra Tractor Shovel | 25 |
| 70 | Ford Thames Estate Car | 45 |
| 70 | Ford Grit Spreader | 20 |
| 71 | Austin 200 Gallon Army Water Tank | 50 |
| 71 | Jeep Pick-up Truck | 30 |
| 71 | Ford Breakdown Lorry | 15 |
| 72 | Fordson Tractor | 40 |
| 72 | Jeep | 15 |
| 73 | RAF Refuelling Tanker | 50 |
| 73 | Ferrari F1 Racing car | 30 |
| 73 | Mercury Estate car | 15 |
| 74 | Mobile Canteen | |
| | silver | 45 |
| | white, cream, pink | 250 |
| 74 | Daimler bus | 20 |
| 75 | Ford Thunderbird | 70 |
| 75 | Ferrari Berlinetta | 15 |

**Superfast Wheels:**

| # | Name | Price |
|---|------|-------|
| 1 | Mercedes Truck | 10 |
| 1 | Mod Rod | 15 |
| 1 | Dodge Challenger | 5 |
| 1 | Jaguar XJ6 | 5 |
| 2 | Mercedes Trailer | 10 |
| 2 | Jeep Hot Rod | 15 |
| 2 | Rescue Hovercraft | 10 |
| 2 | S-2 Jet | 5 |

| # | Name | Price |
|---|------|-------|
| 2 | Pontiac Fiero | $5 |
| 2 | Rover Sterling | 5 |
| 2 | BMW 850i | 3 |
| 3 | Mercedes Benz Binz Ambulance | 15 |
| 3 | Monteverdi Hai | 10 |
| 3 | Porsche Turbo | 10 |
| 3 | Hummer | 2 |
| 4 | Dodge Stake Truck | 15 |
| 4 | Gruesome Twosome | 7 |
| 4 | Pontiac Firebird | 7 |
| 4 | '57 Chevy | 5 |
| 4 | Austin FX4 Taxi | 3 |
| 5 | Lotus Europa | 10 |
| 5 | Seafire | 8 |
| 5 | US Mail Truck | 8 |
| 5 | 4 x 4 Off-Road Jeep | 7 |
| 5 | Peterbilt Tanker | 5 |
| 6 | Ford Pick-up | 10 |
| 6 | Mercedes 350 SL | 7 |
| 6 | Formula One Racer | 5 |
| 6 | Alfa Romeo SZ | 5 |
| 7 | Ford Refuse Truck | 8 |
| 7 | Hairy Hustler | 8 |
| 7 | Volkswagen Golf | 7 |
| 7 | Romping Rabbit | 8 |
| 7 | Ruff Rabbit | 8 |
| 7 | IMSA Mazda | 7 |
| 7 | Porsche 959 | 5 |
| 7 | Ford Thunderbird | 7 |
| 8 | Ford Mustang | 20 |
| 8 | Wildcat Dragster | 12 |
| 8 | De Tomaso Pantera | 10 |
| 8 | Rover 3500 | 5 |
| 8 | Greased Lightnin' | 7 |
| 8 | Vauxhall Astra GTE | 4 |
| 8 | Chevrolet Corvette | 5 |
| 9 | Cabin Cruiser and Trailer | 8 |
| 9 | AMX Javelin | 10 |
| 9 | Ford Escort RS 2000 | 12 |
| 9 | AMX Prostocker | 5 |
| 9 | Caterpillar D9 Bulldozer | 4 |
| 10 | Pipe Truck | 10 |
| 10 | Mustang Piston Popper | 10 |
| 10 | Plymouth Gran Fury Police Car | 4 |
| 10 | Buick Le Sabre | 3 |
| 10 | Chevy Van | 3 |
| 11 | Mercedes Scaffolding Truck | 10 |
| 11 | Flying Bug | 7 |
| 11 | Cobra Mustang | 7 |
| 11 | IMSA Mustang | 7 |
| 11 | Ferrari 308 GTB | 7 |
| 11 | Car Transporter | 5 |
| 11 | Lamborghini Countach | 3 |
| 12 | Land Rover Safari | 12 |
| 12 | Setra Coach | 15 |
| 12 | Big Bull | 7 |
| 12 | Citroën CX | 4 |
| 12 | Pontiac Firebird Racer | 5 |
| 12 | Modified Racer | 5 |
| 12 | Dodge Viper | 2 |
| 12 | Cattle Truck | 2 |
| 13 | Dodge Wreck Truck | 7 |

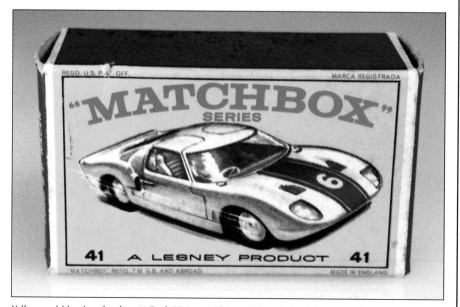

*Yellow and blue box for the #41 Ford GT Racer. This model made its debut in 1965.*

| # | Name | Price |
|---|------|-------|
| 13 | Baja Buggy | $15 |
| 13 | Snorkel Fire Engine | 7 |
| 13 | Snorkel Fire Engine (cut away cab) | 3 |
| 13 | Volvo Container | 3 |
| 14 | Iso Grifo | 10 |
| 14 | Mini Ha-Ha | 7 |
| 14 | Articulated tanker | 7 |
| 14 | 4 x 4 Jeep Laredo | 7 |
| 14 | BMW Cabriolet | 7 |
| 14 | Grand Prix Racing Car | 5 |
| 15 | Fork Lift Truck | 7 |
| 15 | Peugeot 205 Turbo 16 | 3 |
| 15 | Corvette Grand Sport | 3 |
| 16 | Badger Truck | 8 |
| 16 | Pontiac Trans-Am | 5 |
| 16 | Pontiac Trans Am T roof | 5 |
| 16 | Land Rover Ninety | 4 |
| 17 | Horse box | 12 |
| 17 | Leyland Atlantean Londoner Bus many liveries; prices range from 10-100 | |
| 17 | Leyland Titan Londoner Bus many liveries; prices range from 5-30 | |
| 18 | Field Car | 10 |
| 18 | Hondarora | 8 |
| 18 | Fire Engine | 5 |
| 19 | Lotus Racing Car | 15 |
| 19 | Road Dragster | 8 |
| | with "Scorpion" labels | 40 |
| | with "Wynns" labels | 40 |
| 19 | Cement Truck | 8 |
| 19 | Peterbilt Cement Truck | 3 |
| 20 | Lamborghini Marzal | 12 |
| 20 | Police Patrol many liveries; prices range from 3-40 | |
| 20 | Volvo Container Truck (many liveries) | 7 |
| 20 | Volkswagen Transporter | 3 |
| 21 | Foden Concrete Truck | 15 |
| 21 | Road Roller | 10 |
| 21 | Renault 5TL | 7 |
| 21 | Breakdown Van | 7 |
| 21 | Corvette Pace Car | 3 |
| 21 | Nissan Prairie | 3 |
| 22 | Pontiac GP Sports Coupe | 15 |
| 22 | Freeman Inter-City Commuter | 10 |
| 22 | Blazer Buster | 5 |
| 22 | BIG FOOT | 7 |
| 22 | Jaguar XK120 | 7 |
| 22 | Saab 9000 Turbo | 3 |
| 22 | Pontiac Stock Car | 2 |
| 23 | Volkswagen Camper | 15 |
| 23 | Atlas Dump Truck | 8 |
| 23 | Peterbilt Quarry Truck | 3 |
| 23 | GT350 Wildcat Dragster | 7 |
| 23 | Honda ATC 250 | 8 |
| 24 | Rolls-Royce Silver Shadow | 15 |
| 24 | Team Matchbox | |
| | red | 8 |
| | green | 30 |
| 24 | Diesel Shunter | 3 |
| 24 | Datsun 280 ZX | 10 |
| 24 | Datsun 280 ZX 2 x 2 | 3 |

| # | Name | Price |
|---|------|-------|
| 24 | Nissan 300 ZX Turbo | $5 |
| 24 | Lincoln Town Car Limousine | 5 |
| 24 | Airport Fire Tender | 5 |
| 24 | Rhino Rod | 2 |
| 25 | Ford Cortina GT | |
| | light brown | 50 |
| | blue | 15 |
| 25 | Mod Tractor | 10 |
| 25 | Flat Car/Container | 8 |
| 25 | Toyota Celica GT | 10 |
| 25 | Yellow Fever | 8 |
| 25 | Audi Quattro | 5 |
| 25 | Ambulance | 3 |

The #51 Citröen SM, which came out in 1973 as part of the Matchbox Superfast series. Made until 1978, it featured the standard Superfast wheels.

| # | Name | Price |
|---|------|-------|
| 25 | Peugeot 205 Turbo 16 | 3 |
| 25 | Model A Ford | 3 |
| 26 | GMC Tipper Truck | 8 |
| 26 | Big Banger | 8 |
| 26 | Brown Sugar | 12 |
| 26 | Site Dumper | 5 |
| 26 | Volvo Cable Truck | 3 |
| 26 | Cosmic Blues | 8 |
| 26 | Volvo Tilt Truck | 5 |
| 26 | Jaguar XJ220 | 5 |
| 27 | Mercedes-Benz 230SL | 15 |
| 27 | Lamborghini Countach | 7 |
| 27 | Swing Wing | 7 |
| 27 | Jeep Cherokee | 5 |
| 27 | Mercedes-Benz Tractor | 3 |
| 27 | Alligator | 2 |
| 28 | Chrysler Daytona Turbo Z | 3 |
| 28 | 1987 Corvette | 3 |
| 28 | BMW 323i Cabriolet | 2 |
| 28 | Mack Dump Truck | 8 |
| 28 | Stoat | 8 |
| 28 | Lincoln Continental Mark V | 5 |
| 28 | Formula 5000 Racing Car | 5 |
| 28 | Mustang Mach III | 3 |
| 29 | Fire Pumper Truck | 10 |
| 29 | Racing Mini | 15 |

| # | Name | Price |
|---|------|-------|
| 29 | Tractor Shovel many colors and liveries | $5-40 |
| 30 | Eight-wheel crane | 8 |
| 30 | Beach Buggy | 8 |
| 30 | Swamp Rat | 5 |
| 30 | Leyland Articulated Truck | 8 |
| 30 | Mercedes-Benz 280GE Truck | 5 |
| 31 | Lincoln Continental | 10 |
| 31 | Volks-dragon | 12 |
| 31 | Caravan | 5 |
| 31 | Mazda RX-7 | 12 |
| 31 | Lady Bug | 8 |
| 31 | Rolls-Royce Silver Cloud II | 5 |
| 31 | BMW 5-Series | 3 |
| 32 | Leyland Petrol Tanker | |
| | green/white "BP" | 15 |
| | blue/white "Aral" | 75 |
| 32 | Maserati Bora | 5 |
| 32 | Field Gun | 5 |
| 32 | Atlas Excavator | 5 |
| 33 | Lamborghini Miura | 25 |
| 33 | Datsun 126X | 8 |
| 33 | Honda CB 750 Police Motorcycle | 7 |
| 33 | Renault 11 | 7 |
| 33 | Mercury Sable Wagon | 8 |
| 33 | Mercedes Benz 500SL | 3 |
| 34 | Formula One Racing Car | 8 |
| 34 | Vantastic | 5 |
| 34 | Chevy Prostocker | 7 |
| 34 | Ford RS 200 | 5 |
| 34 | Dodge Challenger | 3 |
| 35 | Merryweather Fire Engine | 10 |
| 35 | Fandango | 8 |
| 35 | Volvo Zoo Truck | 3 |
| 35 | Mini Pick-up Camper | 5 |
| 35 | Ford Bronco II | 5 |
| 35 | Pontiac Grand Prix | 5 |
| 36 | Opel Diplomat | 12 |
| 36 | Hot Rod "Draguar" | 12 |
| 36 | Formula 5000 | 8 |

| # | Name | Price |
|---|---|---|
| 36 | Refuse Truck | $5 |
| 37 | Cattle Truck | |
| | orange/silver | 110 |
| | other colors | 12 |
| 37 | Soopa Coopa | |
| | orange "Jaffa-Mobile" | 75 |
| | purple/blue | 10 |

| # | Name | Price |
|---|---|---|
| 40 | Rocket Transporter | $5 |
| 41 | Ford GT Racing Car | 15 |
| 41 | Siva Spyder | 7 |
| 41 | Ambulance | 10 |
| 41 | Kenworth Conventional Aerodyne | 7 |
| 41 | Racing Porsche 935 | 5 |
| 41 | Vauxhall Cavalier GSi 2000 | 5 |

| # | Name | Price |
|---|---|---|
| 45 | BMW 3.0 CSL | $5 |
| 45 | Kenworth Cabover Aerodyne | 5 |
| 45 | Ford Cargo Skip Truck | 3 |
| 46 | Mercedes 300SE coupe | |
| | gold | 8 |
| | silver | 35 |
| 46 | Stretcha Fetcha | 10 |
| 46 | Ford Tractor and Harrow | 5 |
| 46 | Sauber Group 'C' Racer | 5 |
| 47 | DAF Tipper Container Truck | 15 |
| 47 | Beach Hopper | 8 |
| 47 | Pannier Tank Locomotive | 5 |
| 47 | Jaguar SS100 | 5 |
| 47 | School bus | 8 |
| 48 | Dodge Dumper Truck | 12 |
| 48 | Pie-eyed Piper | 10 |
| 48 | Sambron Jacklift | 5 |
| 48 | White Lightning | 8 |
| 48 | Unimog | 5 |
| 48 | Vauxhall Astra GTE | 5 |
| 48 | Pontiac Firebird Racer | 3 |
| 49 | Unimog | 15 |
| 49 | Chop Suey | 15 |
| 49 | Crane Truck | 5 |
| 49 | Sand Digger | 7 |
| 49 | Peugeot Quasar | 5 |
| 49 | Lamborghini Diablo | 5 |
| 50 | Kennel Truck | 12 |
| 50 | Articulated Truck | 8 |
| 50 | Harley Davidson Motorcycle | 8 |
| 50 | Chevy Blazer 4 x 4 | 5 |
| 50 | Dodge Dakota | 5 |
| 50 | Auxiliary Power Truck | 5 |
| 51 | Eight-wheel Tipper | 15 |
| 51 | Citroën SM | 12 |
| 51 | Combine Harvester | 3 |
| 51 | Pontiac Firebird | 5 |
| 51 | Ford LTD Police | 5 |
| 52 | Dodge Charger Mk III | 8 |
| 52 | Police Launch | 5 |
| 52 | BMW MI | 5 |
| 52 | Isuzu Amigo | 3 |
| 52 | Escort Cosworth | 2 |
| 53 | Ford Zodiac MkIV | |
| | metallic green | 15 |
| | light green | 30 |
| 53 | Tanzara | 8 |
| 53 | CJ6 Jeep | 7 |
| 53 | Flareside Pick-up | 7 |
| 53 | Dump Truck | 2 |
| 54 | Cadillac Ambulance | 15 |
| 54 | Ford Capri | 8 |
| 54 | Personnel Carrier | 5 |
| 54 | Mobile Home | 7 |
| 54 | NASA Tracking Vehicle | 5 |
| 54 | Airport Foam Monitor Vehicle | 5 |
| 54 | Chevrolet Lumina | 7 |
| 54 | Mazda RX7 | 3 |
| 55 | Mercury Police Car | 7 |
| 55 | Mercury Police Car (station wagon) | 12 |
| 55 | Hellraiser | 8 |
| 55 | Ford Cortina | 8 |

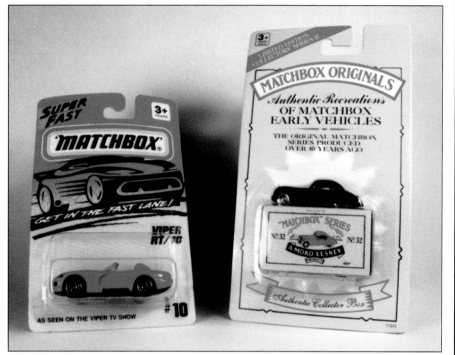

A couple of current Matchbox products. At left is a #10 Dodge Viper from the 1-75 line; at right is the #32 Jaguar XK140, which came out in 1993 as part of series 2 of the "Matchbox Originals" series.

| # | Name | Price |
|---|---|---|
| 37 | Skip Truck | 8 |
| 37 | Matra Rancho | 5 |
| 37 | Jeep 4 x 4 | 8 |
| 37 | Ford Escort XR3i Cabriolet | 5 |
| 37 | Nissan 300 ZX | 7 |
| 38 | Honda Motorcycle and trailer | 15 |
| 38 | Stingeroo | 15 |
| 38 | Jeep | 10 |
| 38 | Camper | 5 |
| 38 | Ford Model A Van many liveries and versions; | |
| | price varies widely | |
| 38 | Ford Courier | 8 |
| 38 | Corvette Stingray III | 5 |
| 39 | Ford Tractor | 15 |
| 39 | Clipper | 8 |
| 39 | Rolls-Royce Silver Shadow II | 7 |
| 39 | BMW 323i Cabriolet | 5 |
| 39 | Mack CH600 | 2 |
| 39 | Mercedes-Benz 600 SEL | 3 |
| 39 | Ford Thunderbird Stock Car | 8 |
| 40 | Hay Trailer | |
| | tan with black racks | 75 |
| | other colors | 15 |
| 40 | Vauxhall Guildsman I | 8 |
| 40 | Horse Box | 7 |

| # | Name | Price |
|---|---|---|
| 41 | Sunburner | 3 |
| 41 | Ferrari 456 GT | 3 |
| 42 | Iron Fairy Crane | 25 |
| 42 | Tyre Fryer | |
| | blue | 8 |
| | orange "Jaffa Mobile" | 75 |
| 42 | Mercedes Container Truck various | |
| | liveries | 8-30 |
| 42 | 1957 Thunderbird | 5 |
| 42 | Mobile Crane | 3 |
| 43 | Pony Trailer | 8 |
| 43 | Dragon Wheels | 8 |
| 43 | Steam Locomotive | 5 |
| 43 | Peterbilt Conventional | 8 |
| 43 | AMG Mercedes-Benz 500SBC | 5 |
| 43 | '57 Chevy | 3 |
| 44 | GMC Refrigerator Truck | 15 |
| 44 | Boss Mustang | 12 |
| 44 | Passenger Coach | 5 |
| 44 | Citroën 15CV | 5 |
| 44 | Datsun Fairlady 280ZX Police Car | 8 |
| 44 | Skoda 130 LR | 5 |
| 44 | Ford Model T van many liveries and versions; | |
| | price varies widely | |
| 45 | Ford Group 6 | 7 |

| # | Name | Price |
|---|------|-------|
| 55 | Ford Sierra XR4i | $5 |
| 55 | Flareside Pick-up | 3 |
| 56 | BMC 1800 Pininfarina | 10 |
| 56 | Hi-Tailer | 5 |
| 56 | Mercedes 450 SEL | 7 |
| 56 | Mercedes 450 SEL Taxi | 7 |
| 56 | Mercedes 450 SEL Police Car | 5 |
| 56 | Volkswagen Golf GTI | 5 |
| 56 | 4 x 4 Off-Road Jeep | 3 |
| 56 | Ford LTD Taxi | 2 |
| 56 | Camaro Z-28 | 3 |
| 57 | Land Rover Fire Truck | 25 |
| 57 | Trailer Caravan | 10 |
| 57 | Wild Life Truck | 8 |
| 57 | 4 x 4 Mini Pick-up | 8 |
| 57 | Carmichael Commando Rescue Vehicle | 5 |
| 58 | DAF Girder Truck | 8 |
| 58 | Woosh-N-Push | 10 |
| 58 | Faun Dump Truck | 7 |
| 58 | Ruff Trek | 5 |
| 58 | Mercedes Benz 300E | 3 |
| 59 | Ford Galaxie Fire Chief Car | 12 |
| 59 | Mercury Fire Chief Car | 8 |
| 59 | Planet Scout | 10 |
| 59 | Porsche 928 | 7 |
| 59 | Porsche 944 Turbo | 5 |
| 60 | Leyland Site Hut Truck | 12 |
| 60 | Lotus Super Seven | 10 |
| 60 | Holden Pick-up | 5 |
| 60 | Toyota Supra | 5 |
| 60 | New Ford Transit many liveries and versions; price varies widely | |
| 61 | Blue Shark | |
| | "Scorpion" label" | 20 |
| | "69" label | 20 |
| | "86" label | 10 |
| | metallic blue | 5 |
| 61 | Wreck truck | 7 |
| 61 | Peterbilt Wreck Truck | 5 |
| 61 | '87 T-Bird Turbo Coupe | 5 |
| 61 | Fork Lift | 2 |
| 62 | Mercury Cougar | 10 |
| 62 | Mercury Cougar Rat Rod Dragster | 8 |
| 62 | Renault 17TL | 10 |
| 62 | Chevrolet Corvette | 7 |
| 62 | Chevrolet Corvette T-Roof | 5 |
| 62 | Volvo 760 | 3 |
| 62 | Volvo Container Truck | 5 |
| 63 | Dodge Crane Truck | 15 |
| 63 | Freeway Gas Tanker many liveries and versions; price varies widely | |
| 63 | Dodge Challenger | 12 |
| 63 | 4 x 4 Open Back Truck | 7 |
| 63 | Volkswagen Golf GTI | 3 |
| 63 | Aston Martin DB7 | 3 |
| 64 | MG 1100 | 12 |
| 64 | Slingshot Dragster | |
| | orange | 100 |
| | metallic green | 25 |
| | pink, green | 10 |
| | blue | 5 |
| 64 | Fire Chief Car | 5 |

| # | Name | Price |
|---|------|-------|
| 64 | Caterpillar D8H Bulldozer | $5 |
| 64 | 1988 Dodge Caravan | 7 |
| 64 | Oldsmobile Aerotech | 2 |
| 65 | Saab Sonnet III | 8 |
| 65 | Airport Coach | 7 |
| 65 | Kenworth Tyrone Malone | 7 |
| 65 | Indy Racer | 5 |
| 65 | Plane Transporter Vehicle | 5 |
| 65 | Cadillac Allante | 5 |
| 66 | Greyhound Coach | 12 |
| 66 | Mazda RX500 | 7 |
| 66 | Ford Transit Pick-up | 10 |
| 66 | Kenworth Tyrone Malone "Superboss" | 7 |
| 66 | Rolls-Royce Silver Spirit | 5 |
| 67 | Volkswagen 1600TL | 10 |
| 67 | Hot Rocker | 12 |
| 67 | Datsun 260Z | 8 |
| 67 | IMSA Mustang | 5 |
| 67 | Ikarus Coach | 5 |
| 68 | Porsche 910 | |
| | white | 25 |
| | other colors | 7 |
| 68 | Cosmobile | |
| | blue/black | 35 |
| | other colors | 10 |
| 68 | Chevy Van many liveries; price ranges from 7-25 | |
| 68 | 4x4 Chevy Van many liveries; price ranges from 5-18 | |
| 68 | Camaro IROC Z28 | 7 |
| 68 | Road Roller | 2 |
| 69 | Rolls-Royce Silver Shadow Coupe | 12 |
| 69 | Turbofury | 8 |
| 69 | Armored Security Truck | 7 |
| 69 | Willys Street Rod | 8 |
| 69 | 1983 Corvette | 7 |
| 69 | Volvo 480 ES | 3 |

| # | Name | Price |
|---|------|-------|
| 69 | Snow Plough | $5 |
| 70 | Grit Spreading Truck | 15 |
| 70 | Dodge Dragster | 10 |
| 70 | Self-propelled Gun | 8 |
| 70 | Ferrari 308 GTB | 5 |
| 70 | Ferrari F40 | 3 |
| 71 | Ford Heavy Wreck Truck | 12 |
| 71 | Jumbo Jet Motorcycle | 15 |
| 71 | Cattle Truck | 7 |
| 71 | 1962 Corvette | 7 |
| 71 | Scania T142 various liveries | 3 |
| 71 | GMC Wrecker | 5 |
| 72 | Standard Jeep | 15 |
| 72 | SRN6 Hovercraft | 7 |
| 72 | Bomag Road Roller | 7 |
| 72 | Dodge Commando Delivery Truck many liveries; price ranges from 3-20 | |
| 72 | Sand Racer | 15 |
| 72 | Ford Supervan II | 7 |
| 72 | Sprint Racer | 5 |
| 72 | '62 Corvette | 5 |
| 73 | 1968 Mercury | 10 |
| 73 | Weasel | 7 |
| 73 | Model A Ford | 7 |
| 73 | TV News Truck | 5 |
| 74 | Daimler Bus | |
| | red "Inn on the Park" | 90 |
| | red "The Baron of Beef" | 90 |
| | pink "Esso Extra Patrol" | 25 |
| | red "Esso Extra Patrol" | 15 |
| 74 | Tow Joe Breakdown Truck | |
| | yellow with red jibs "Hitchhiker" | 90 |
| | other colors | 10 |
| 74 | Cougar Villager | 8 |
| 74 | Fiat Abarth | 5 |
| 74 | Mustang GT | 8 |

*The Models of Yesteryear Y13 1911 Daimler. This model was released starting in 1966, and it was to approximately 1/45 scale.*

| # | Name | Price |
|---|------|-------|
| 74 | Toyota MR2 | $5 |
| 74 | Utility Truck | 5 |
| 75 | Ferrari Berlinetta | |
| | red | 25 |
| | metallic green | 60 |
| 75 | Alfa Carabo many liveries; price ranges | |
| | from 5-40 | |
| 75 | Ferrari Testarossa | 7 |

### Major Packs:

| # | Name | Price |
|---|------|-------|
| M-1A | Caterpillar Earthmover | 50 |
| M-1B | BP Petrol Tanker | 30 |
| M-2A | Bedford Artic. Truck "Walls" | 70 |
| M-2B | Bedford Tractor with York Trailer | 65 |
| M3 | Centurion Tank on Transporter | 50 |
| M-4A | Ruston Bucyrus Power Shovel | 60 |
| M-4B | Freuhof Hopper Train | 50 |
| M-5 | Massey Ferguson Combine Harvester | 60 |
| M-6A | Pickford's Transporter | 60 |
| M-6B | BP Racing Transporter | 40 |
| M-7 | Jennings Cattle Truck | 55 |
| M-8A | Mobilgas Petrol Tanker | 85 |
| M-8B | Car Transporter | 45 |
| M-9 | Interstate Double Freighter | 75 |
| M-10 | Dinkum Rear Dumper | 40 |

### King-Size models:

| # | Name | Price |
|---|------|-------|
| K-1A | Weatherhill Hydraulic Shovel | 40 |
| K-1B | Hoveringham Tipper Truck | 35 |
| K-2A | Muir Hill Dumper | 40 |
| K-2B | K.W. Dump Truck | 25 |
| K-2C | Scammell Heavy Wreck Truck | 30 |
| K-3A | Caterpillar Bulldozer | 30 |
| K-3B | Hatra Tractor Shovel | 25 |
| K-4A | International Tractor | 30 |
| K-4B | GMC Tractor & Freuhof Hopper Train | 40 |
| K-4C | Leyland Tipper | 25 |
| K-5A | Foden Tipper Truck | 30 |

| # | Name | Price |
|---|------|-------|
| K-5B | Racing Car Transporter | $35 |
| K-6A | Allis-Chalmers Earth Scraper | 30 |
| K-6B | Mercedes-Benz Ambulance | 25 |
| K-7A | Curtiss-Wright Rear Dumper | 25 |
| K-7B | Refuse Truck | 15 |
| K-8A | Prime Mover & Caterpillar Tractor | 70 |
| K-8B | Guy Warrior Car Transporter | 40 |
| K-9A | Diesel Road Roller | 20 |
| K-9B | Claas Combine Harvester | 25 |
| K-10A | Aveling Barford Tractor Shovel | 30 |
| K-10B | Pipe Truck | 25 |
| K-11A | Fordson Tractor & Farm Trailer | 35 |
| K-11B | DAF Car Transporter | 25 |
| K-12A | Heavy Breakdown Wreck Truck | 40 |
| K-12B | Scammell Crane Truck | 15 |
| K-13 | Readymix Concrete Truck | 30 |
| K-14 | Taylor Jumbo Crane | 20 |
| K-15A | Merryweather Fire Engine | 25 |
| K-15B | The Londoner Double-Deck Bus | |
| | various liveries | 15 |
| K-16 | Dodge Tractor with Twin Tipper | 45 |
| K-17 | Low Loader with Bulldozer | 40 |
| K-18 | Articulated Horse Box | 30 |
| K-19 | Scammell Tipper Truck | 25 |
| K-20 | Tractor Transporter | 45 |
| K-21 | Mercury Cougar | 25 |
| K-22 | Dodge Charger | 25 |
| K-23 | Mercury Police Commuter | 25 |
| K-24 | Lamborghini Miura | 25 |

## "ORIGINALS" SERIES (1993-PRESENT):

### Series 1

| # | Name | Price |
|---|------|-------|
| 1 | Diesel Road Roller | CRP |
| 4 | Massey-Harris Tractor | CRP |
| 5 | London Bus | CRP |

| # | Name | Price |
|---|------|-------|
| 7 | Horse-Drawn Milk Float | CRP |
| 9 | Dennis Fire Escape | CRP |

### Series 2

| # | Name | Price |
|---|------|-------|
| 6 | Quarry Truck | CRP |
| 13 | Bedford Wreck Truck | CRP |
| 19 | MG TD Midget | CRP |
| 26 | ERF Cement Mixer | CRP |
| 32 | Jaguar XK140 | CRP |

### Series 3

| # | Name | Price |
|---|------|-------|
| 11 | ERF Petrol Tanker | CRP |
| 12 | Land Rover | CRP |
| 17 | Bedford Removal Van | CRP |
| 18 | Caterpillar Bulldozer | CRP |
| 52 | Maserati 4CLT | CRP |

### Models of Yesteryear:

| # | Name | Price |
|---|------|-------|
| Y1 | Allchin Traction Engine | $125-300 |
| Y1 | 1991 Model T Ford | 20-250 |
| Y1 | 1936 SS100 Jaguar | 10-250 |
| Y2 | 1911 B Type London Bus | 125-225 |
| Y2 | 1911 Renault Two-Seater | 20-100 |
| Y2 | 1914 Prince Henry Vauxhall | 15-160 |
| Y2 | 1930 4.5 Litre Bentley | 10-25 |
| Y3 | 1907 "E" Class Tramcar | 110-400 |
| Y3 | 1910 Benz Limousine | 30-300 |
| Y3 | 1934 Riley MPH | 15-225 |
| Y3 | 1912 Ford Model T Tanker | 10-75 |
| Y4 | Sentinel Steam Wagon | 125-150 |
| Y4 | Shand Mason Fire Engine | 210-275 |
| Y4 | 1909 Opel Car | 25-60 |
| Y4 | 1930 Duesenberg J Town Car | 15-300 |
| Y5 | 1929 Le Mans Bentley | 125-275 |
| Y5 | 1929 4.5 Liter Bentley | 40-75 |
| Y5 | 1907 Peugeot | 15-225 |
| Y5 | 1927 Talbot Van | 10-45 |
| Y5 | Leyland Titan Bus | 15-50 |
| Y6 | 1916 AEC "Y" Type Lorry | 175-300 |
| Y6 | 1926 Type 35 Bugatti | 60-400 |
| Y6 | 1913 Cadillac | 30-185 |
| Y6 | 1920 Rolls-Royce Fire Engine | 15-150 |
| Y6 | 1932 Mercedes L5 Lorry | 10 |
| Y7 | Four Ton Leyland Van | 150-190 |
| Y7 | 1913 Mercer Runabout | 45-60 |
| Y7 | 1912 Rolls-Royce | 15-175 |
| Y7 | 1930 Ford Model A Breakdown Truck | 15-40 |
| Y8 | 1926 Morris Cowley | 125-150 |
| Y8 | 1914 Sunbeam Motorcycle and | |
| | Sidecar | 60-80 |
| Y8 | 1914 Stutz | 15-60 |
| Y8 | 1945 MG TC | 10-75 |
| Y8 | Yorkshire Steam Wagon | 10-20 |
| Y9 | 1924 Fowler Showmans Engine | 125-175 |
| Y9 | 1912 Simplex | 10-45 |
| Y9 | 1920 3-Ton Leyland Lorry | 25-45 |
| Y9 | 1936 Leyland Cub Fire Engine | 60-75 |
| Y10 | 1908 Grand Prix Mercedes | 135-175 |
| Y10 | 1928 Mercedes-Benz 36-220 | 30-65 |
| Y10 | 1906 Rolls-Royce Silver Ghost | 10-30 |
| Y10 | 1957 Maserati 250F | 10-20 |
| Y10 | 1931 Diddler Trolley Bus | 20-35 |

*Part of Matchbox Collectibles' "Great Beers of the World" series: the #YGB09 Mack Truck in "Moosehead" livery. The Great Beers series was introduced in 1993.*

| # | Name | Price | # | Name | Price | # | Name | Price |
|---|------|-------|---|------|-------|---|------|-------|
| Y11 | 1920 Aveling & Porter Steam Roller | $135-210 | Y21 | 1955 BMW 507 | $15 | | **A TASTE OF FRANCE SERIES (1993-94):** | |
| Y11 | 1912 Packard Landaulet | 25-45 | Y21 | 1926 Ford Model TT Van | 15 | | **Citroën H vans** | |
| Y11 | 1938 Lagonda Drophead Coupe | 10-75 | Y22 | Ford Model A Van | 10-30 | YTF1 | Avian Mineral Water | $15 |
| Y11 | 1932 Bugatti Type 51 | 10-25 | Y23 | 1922 AEC Omnibus | 15 | YTF2 | Martell Cognac | 15 |
| Y12 | 1899 Horse Drawn Bus | 110-125 | Y23 | Mack Bulldog Tanker | 20 | YTF3 | Yoplait Yoghurt | 15 |
| Y12 | 1909 Thomas Flyabout | 15-30 | Y24 | 1928 Bugatti T44 | 10-50 | YTF4 | Marcillat Brie | 15 |
| Y12 | 1912 Ford Model T Van | 10-300 | Y25 | 1910 Renault AG Van | 10-50 | YTF5 | Taittinger Champagne | 15 |
| Y12 | 1829 Stephenson's Rocket | 10-25 | Y26 | Crossley Delivery Truck | 10-20 | YTF6 | Pommery Mustard | 15 |
| Y12 | 1937 GMC Van | 10-25 | Y27 | 1922 Foden Steam Lorry | 10-30 | | | |
| Y13 | 1862 Santa Fe Locomotive | 110-150 | Y28 | 1907 Unic Taxi | 10-20 | | **Great Beers of the World series (1993-94):** | |
| Y13 | 1911 Daimler | 25-50 | Y29 | 1919 Walker Electric Van | 10 | YGB01 | Ford A Van "Castlemain" | 15 |
| Y13 | 1918 Crossley | 15-100 | Y30 | 1920 Mack Truck | 10 | YGB02 | Ford TT Van "Becks" | 15 |
| Y13 | 1918 Crossley Lorry | 15-25 | Y31 | 1931 Morris Courier Van | 15 | YGB03 | Atkinson Steam Lorry "Swan" | 15 |
| Y14 | 1903 Duke of Connaught Locomotive | 125-150 | Y32 | Yorkshire Steam Wagon | 15 | YGB04 | Morris Van "Fuller's" | 15 |
| Y14 | 1911 Maxwell Roadster | 15-90 | Y33 | 1920 Mack AC Truck | 10 | YGB05 | Ford AA Van "Carlsberg" | 15 |
| Y14 | 1931 Stutz Bearcat | 10-25 | Y34 | 1933 Cadillac V-16 | 15 | YGB06 | Mercedes Truck "Holstein" | 15 |
| Y14 | 1936 E.R.A. Type R1-B | 10-15 | Y35 | 1930 Ford Pick-up Truck | 15 | YGB07 | Renault Van "Kronenbourg" | 15 |
| Y15 | 1907 Rolls-Royce Silver Ghost | 30-60 | Y36 | 1936 Rolls-Royce Phantom I | 15 | YGB08 | GMC Van "Steinlager" | 15 |
| Y15 | 1930 Packard Victoria | 15-60 | Y37 | 1931 Garrett Steam Wagon | 15-40 | YGB09 | Mack Truck "Moosehead" | 15 |
| Y15 | 1920 Preston Type Tramcar | 10-15 | Y38 | 1920 Rolls-Royce Armored Car | 25 | YGB10 | Talbot Van "South Pacific" | 15 |
| Y16 | 1904 Spyker | 25-50 | Y39 | 1820 Passenger Coach | 40 | YGB11 | Foden Steam Wagon "Whitbread" | 15 |
| Y16 | 1928 Mercedes-Benz SS Coupe | 15-60 | Y40 | 1931 Mercedes-Benz 770 | 10 | YGB12 | Yorkshire Steam Wagon "Lowenbrau" | 15 |
| Y16 | 1960 Ferrari Dino 246-V12 | 15-25 | Y41 | 1932 Mercedes L5 Lorry | 10 | | | |
| Y16 | 1923 Scania-Vabis Post Bus | 15 | Y42 | 1939 Albion 10 Ton CX27 | 15 | | **Heritage Horse-Drawn Vehicles (1994):** | |
| Y16 | Scammell 100 Ton Truck and Trailer with Locomotive | 125 | Y43 | 1905 Busch Steam Fire Engine | 40 | YSH1 | Gypsy Caravan | 45 |
| Y17 | 1938 Hispano Suiza | 15-25 | Y44 | 1910 Renault T45 Bus | 15 | YSH2 | London Omnibus | 45 |
| Y18 | 1937 Cord 812 | 10-20 | Y45 | 1930 Bugatti Royale | 25 | YSH3 | Wells Fargo Stagecoach | 45 |
| Y18 | 1918 Atkinson D-Type Steam Wagon | 15-20 | Y46 | 1868 Merryweather Horse-Drawn Fire Engine | 40 | | | |
| Y19 | 1936 Auburn Speedster | 15-20 | Y47 | 1929 Morris Cowley Van | 15 | | **Fire series (1994-95):** | |
| Y19 | Fowler B6 Showman's Engine | 45 | Y61 | 1933 Cadillac Fire Engine | 15 | | 1920 Mack Fire Engine | 30 |
| Y19 | 1929 Morris Cowley Van | 15 | Y62 | 1932 Ford AA Truck | 15 | | 1932 Ford AA Fire Engine | 30 |
| Y20 | 1937 Mercedes-Benz 540K | 20 | Y63 | 1939 Bedford KD Truck | 40 | | 1952 Land Rover with Trailer | 30 |
| Y21 | 1930 Ford Model A Woody Wagon | 15-50 | Y64 | 1938 Lincoln Zephyr | 15 | | 1939 Bedford Tanker Truck | 30 |
| Y21 | Aveling and Porter Road Roller | 40 | Y65 | 1928 Austin 7 (set) | 50 | | 1932 Mercedes-Benz Turntable Ladder Truck | 30 |
| | | | Y66 | Queen Elizabeth's Coronation Coach | 25 | | 1933 Cadillac Pumper | 30 |
| | | | | | | | 1930 Ahrens-Fox Quad | 90 |

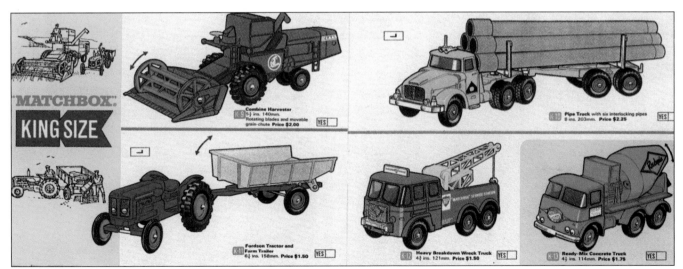

*A spread from the 1969 "USA Edition" Matchbox catalog, showing several of the King-Size models available at that time. Interestingly, the retail price for each item is shown; that Pipe Truck would have required at least several weeks allowance!*

# Maxwell

As is the case with other die cast manufacturers in India, the Maxwell Co. of Calcutta has followed a winding road in terms of what it has manufactured, and when. There is disagreement as to when the company started making die cast toys; and whether any are still made is unknown.

It is thought by some that Maxwell "Mini Auto Toys" were made in India during the 1970s. Certainly, the catalog shown in this section would seem to validate this assumption, featuring as it does models that are based on 1960s vehicles. The timing of 1960s vehicles made in the 1970s would follow here, since Maxwell manufactured their models from tooling purchased from other manufacturers. For example, the Maxwell #574 Riley MPH was originally a Matchbox Models of Yesteryear product, and the #503 Greyhound Luxury Coach and the #506 Mercedes 1100 were ex-Matchbox 1-75 models. (The Mercedes 1100, incidentally, was actually an MG 1100.) Corgi also sold or gave tooling to Maxwell at some point, since the #512 Volvo P1800 and the "Ambassador" models were all ex-Corgi. Companies like Lesney and Corgi passed on tooling only after they had gotten all the use they could out of it.

Another indicator of 1970s production is that the catalog was printed by the "letterpress" method; although this printing process is still used today, it was far more prevalent twenty to thirty years ago.

However, another Calcutta-based company known as Morgan Milton Pvt. Ltd., (better known simply as Milton) apparently changed its name sometime in the late 1970s or early 1980s, to Milton of Calcutta. Later, this firm supposedly became Maxwell. Whether this is the same Maxwell is unknown at present.

In any event, Maxwell models were not up to the standard set by British and European manufacturers. The casting of the models tended to be rough, and the quality of the paint finish was generally poor. However, it must be said that some of the models, while looking rather tired, were actually fairly accurate depictions of the real vehicles. The #537 Gold Spot Van shown here is an excellent example. As crude as the model is, it is a rather realistic representation of the "Hindusthan" trucks and buses that could be seen on the roads of India. These vehicles were not exactly aerodynamically advanced, but they were locally designed and built, and Maxwell undoubtedly wanted to capitalize on that recognition factor.

Another relatively accurate model was the Ambassador, which was actually based on a Morris Cowley, the full-size version of which has been very popular in India for many years.

Although Maxwell models were intended for the domestic market in India, the boxes and baseplates are in English. This was due to the fact that, although there are several languages spoken in India, English is the unifying language spoken by a majority of the population.

In terms of scale, Maxwell was all over the map. The #517 Double Decker Bus was around 1/120, being an ex-Matchbox, whereas many of the passenger cars were 1/43 scale. In between were 1/50 scale trucks and buses, and even some 1/60-1/85 scale models.

The following listing is based on the information supplied in the Maxwell catalog; errors in spelling and grammar have been left uncorrected. Values are for near mint to mint examples with original boxes.

The "Hindusthan" trucks and buses that were prevalent in India were represented by this #537 Gold Spot Van. The sign and bottle display were made of plastic, and the model had those horrendous "speed"-type wheels.

Maxwell #510 Ambassador Mark II with original box. Although some Maxwells have been seen with more realistic wheels, this style of wheel did much to hurt the appearance of the models.

**maxwell MINI**

LINCON POLICE CAR
Model No. 513

AMBASSADOR TAXI
Model No 522

FIAT TAXI
Model No. 523

LINCOLN FIRE CAR
Model No. 514

BURMAH – SHELL

PETROL TANKER BURMAH SHELL
Model No. 568

*A page from the Maxwell catalog. Note both correct and incorrect spellings of "Lincoln" on the same page. The foreword to the catalog rather optimistically states "Partly because of their bright colour and partly because of their minute details look so real that they can be called authentic works of art."*

| # | Name | Price |
|---|------|-------|
| 501 | Tank | $5 |
| 502 | Road Roller | 5 |
| 503 | Greyhound Luxury Coach | 15 |
| 504 | Racing Car | 10 |
| 505 | Lincoln Continental | 15 |
| 506 | Mercedes 1100 (actually an MG 1100) | 15 |
| 507 | Premier President (Fiat 1100) | 20 |
| 508 | Jeep with Engine | 10 |
| 509 | Vauxhall Guildsman | 10 |
| 510 | Ambassador Mark II | 20 |
| 511 | Racing Mini | 20 |
| 512 | Volvo P1800 | 20 |
| 513 | Lincoln Police Car | 10 |
| 514 | Lincoln Fire Car | 10 |
| 515 | Lincoln Ambulance Car | 10 |
| 517 | Double Decker Bus | 15 |
| 518 | Jeep with Bonnet | 10 |
| 519 | Jeep Ambulance | 10 |
| 520 | Ambassador Fire | 15 |
| 521 | Ambassador State Patrol | 15 |
| 522 | Ambassador Yellow Cab | 20 |
| 523 | Fiat Taxi | 20 |
| 524 | Mini Bus | 15 |
| 525 | Inter City Commuter | 15 |
| 526 | Pick up Van | 15 |
| 527 | School Bus | 15 |
| 528 | Setra Bus | 15 |
| 530 | Indian Airlines Passenger Coach | 20 |
| 531 | Jeep Fire Service | 5 |
| 532 | B.O.A.C. Passenger Coach | 20 |
| 533 | Ambulance | 15 |
| 534 | Pipe Carrier | 5 |

| # | Name | Price |
|---|------|-------|
| 535 | Freight Carrier | $10 |
| 536 | Circus Van | 15 |
| 537 | Gold spot Van | 15 |
| 538 | Brake Van Service | 15 |
| 540 | Fruit Carrier | 15 |
| 543 | Mini Jeep | 10 |
| 544 | Racing Motor Cycle | 10 |
| 547 | Coca-Cola Van | 25 |
| 548 | Animal Carrier | 15 |
| 549 | Tractor | 10 |
| 550 | Jeep | 15 |
| 551 | Jeep Ambulance | 15 |
| 552 | Racing Car | 5 |
| 553 | Volks Wagon | 10 |
| 554 | Jeep Carrier | 5 |
| 555 | Two Seater | 5 |
| 556 | Ambassador Taxi | 20 |
| 558 | Impala Plain | 25 |
| 559 | Impala Highway Patrol | 20 |
| 560 | Impala Fire | 20 |
| 561 | Impala Police | 20 |
| 562 | Impala Taxi | 25 |
| 563 | Petrol Tanker H.P. | 20 |
| 564 | Petrol Tanker I.B.P. | 20 |
| 565 | Petrol Tanker Indian Oil | 20 |
| 566 | Petrol Tanker Esso | 25 |
| 567 | Petrol Tanker Caltex | 20 |
| 568 | Petrol Tanker Burmah Shell | 25 |
| 569 | Ford Tractor 3600 | 10 |
| 570 | Tractor H.M.T. Zetor | 10 |
| 571 | Jeep Armoured Car | 5 |
| 572 | Escort 335 | 10 |

| # | Name | Price |
|---|------|-------|
| 574 | Vintage Car 1934 Riley M.P.H. | $15 |
| 575 | Earth Dumper | 10 |
| 577 | Campa Cola Van | 15 |
| 678 | Thums Up Van | 15 |
| 579 | Hindusthan Mini Tractor | 10 |
| 581 | Small Petrol Tanker H.P. | 10 |
| 582 | Small Petrol Tanker I.B.P. | 10 |
| 583 | Small Petrol Tanker Indian Oil | 10 |
| 584 | Small Petrol Tanker Esso | 15 |
| 585 | Small Petrol Tanker Caltex | 10 |
| 586 | Small Petrol Tanker Burmah Shell | 10 |
| 587 | Field Gun & Plastic Base | 5 |
| 588 | Field Gun | 5 |
| 589 | 007 James Bond Car | 20 |
| 590 | Ford Door Opening | 20 |
| 591 | Medium Petrol Tanker H.P. | 15 |
| 592 | Medium Petrol Tanker I.B.P. | 15 |
| 593 | Medium Petrol Tanker Indian Oil | 15 |
| 594 | Medium Petrol Tanker Esso | 20 |
| 595 | Medium Petrol Tanker Caltex | 15 |
| 596 | Medium Petrol Tanker Burmah Shell | 15 |
| 597 | Medium Petrol Tanker Bharat Petroleum | 15 |
| 598 | Medium Petrol Tanker Assam Oil | 15 |
| 599 | Eicher Tractor | 10 |
| 601 | SWRAJ Tractor | 10 |
| 603 | Big Petrol Tanker Bharat Petroleum | 15 |
| 604 | Big Petrol Tanker Assam Oil | 15 |
| 605 | Big Jeep Highway Patrol | 15 |
| 606 | Big Jeep Fire | 15 |
| 607 | Big Jeep Police | 15 |
| 608 | Big Jeep Armoured Car | 15 |

# Mebetoys

**M**any collectors think of Mebetoys as "overgrown Hot Wheels." This is understandable, since a number of this Italian company's models do indeed bear more than a passing resemblance to 1960s and '70s Hot Wheels products. The reason is that Mattel, the owner of Hot Wheels, purchased Mebetoys in 1969 or 1970, and names like "Silhouette," "Boss Mustang 302" and "Twin Mill" appeared in the Mebetoys line-up almost immediately.

These were 1/43 scale models, however, unlike the smaller Hot Wheels cars, and they were numbered in the 6600s. (Mebetoys made this series until 1972 or '73.) The 6600s joined the existing Mebetoys product line, which was comprised of distinctive models in their own right, with no connection to Hot Wheels.

Since 1966, Mebetoys had produced the "A" series of 1/43 scale models. Alfa Romeo and Fiat were well-represented in the series, which is natural for an Italian manufacturer; but the line also included Mercedes-Benz and Porsche entries. Even Rolls-Royce was represented with a Silver Shadow.

Most of the "A" series models were quite accurate, and the line enjoyed good success until well into the 1980s, adding new models each year. Like many other manufacturers, Mebetoys succumbed to the "speed"-wheels fad of the 1970s, fitting them to the "A" series models from about 1973 onward.

Mebetoys had an association with another Italian company called Formaplast, which resulted in Mebetoys re-releasing a series of 1/43 scale trucks and farm vehicles. A number of these models (if not all) were originally marketed by Formaplast. Recognized 1/43 scale expert Paolo

Rampini says that these re-issues came out in 1977. This series, with numbers in the 2500s, was not on the market for long.

Another short-lived Mebetoys product was the "Jolly" series—which consisted of one car, a Lotus-Climax Formula One racer. It came in various colors and was approximately 1/66 scale, but it was apparently never joined by any other models. It sells today for about $15.

Mebetoys has produced other models in various scales, but both the 1/43 scale "A" series and the 6600 series are the most widely collected.

*This A33 Porsche 912 was introduced in 1969. The model featured spring suspension, like many of the Mebetoys models of the period.*

*Mebetoys A27 Ferrari P4. Both the front and rear hoods open on this model, and it originally came with number stickers.*

| # | Name | Price | # | Name | Price | # | Name | Price |
|---|------|-------|---|------|-------|---|------|-------|
| **"A" series:** | | | A53 | Ford Escort | $30 | A112 | Fiat 126 Personal | $30 |
| A1 | Fiat 850 | $40 | A54 | Fiat 127 | 30 | A113 | BMW 320 Rally | 20 |
| A2 | Fiat 1500 C | 40 | A55 | Ford Escort Mexico | 25 | A114 | Volkswagen Golf "ADAC" | 30 |
| A3 | Alfa Romeo Giulia | 40 | A56 | Ferrari 312 PB | 40 | A115 | Volkswagen Golf Polizei | 30 |
| A4 | Alfa Romeo 2600 | 50 | A57 | Alfasud | 25 | A117 | Alfasud with Boat | 20 |
| A5 | Autobianchi Primula | 40 | A58 | Autobianchi A112 Abarth | 30 | A118 | Audi 100 GLS | 20 |
| A6 | Lancia Flavia | 40 | A59 | Fiat 128 | 25 | A119 | Fiat Ritmo 65 | 20 |
| A7 | Alfa Romeo Giulia TI Carabinieri | 40 | A60 | Fiat 128 Rally | 30 | A120 | BMW 730 | 20 |
| A7 | Fiat 128 Carabinieri | 40 | A61 | Innocenti Mini Minor with skis | 40 | A121 | Ford Granada | 20 |
| A8 | Alfa Romeo Giulia TI | 40 | A62 | Fiat 126 | 30 | A122 | Willys Desert Jeep | 20 |
| A8 | Fiat 128 Polizia | 30 | A63 | BMW 2000 CS Alpina | 40 | A123 | Matra Simca Ranch | 20 |
| A9 | Fiat 1100R | 40 | A64 | Porsche 912 with skis | 40 | A124 | Opel Manta | 20 |
| A10 | Maserati Mistral | 50 | A65 | Alfa Romeo Duetto | 40 | A125 | Fiat Panda | 20 |
| A11 | Lancia Fulvia Coupe | 40 | A66 | Innocenti Primula "AGIP" | 40 | A126 | Volkswagen Golf Rally | 20 |
| A12 | Porsche 912 | 60 | A67 | Land Rover Army | 40 | A127 | Ford Fiesta | 20 |
| A13 | Opel Kadett Coupe | 40 | A68 | Fiat 127 Rally | 25 | A128 | Simca 1308GT Special | 20 |
| A14 | Fiat Dino Coupe | 40 | A69 | Renault TL | 25 | A129 | Talbot Horizon | 20 |
| A15 | Fiat 1500 C "Vigili Urbani" | 40 | A70 | Volkswagen 1303 | 30 | A130 | Volvo 343 | 25 |
| A15 | Fiat 128 "Vigili Urbani" | 30 | A71 | Innocenti Mini Minor Hippy | 40 | A131 | Fiat 131 Abarth | 20 |
| A16 | Fiat 124 | 40 | A72 | Maserati Bora | 50 | A132 | Volkswagen Golf with Boat | 20 |
| A17 | BMW 2000 CS | 40 | A73 | Lancia Fulvia Coupe "MARLBORO" | 30 | A133 | Peugeot 305 | 15 |
| A18 | Alfa Romeo Duetto | 60 | A74 | Land Rover Fire Van | 40 | A134 | Citroën Visa | 15 |
| A19 | Mercedes-Benz 250 Coupe | 45 | A75 | Fiat 124 | 30 | A135 | Alfa Romeo Giulietta Carabinieri | 15 |
| A20 | Lamborghini Miura 400 S | 50 | A76 | Alfa Romeo Alfetta | 25 | A136 | Alfa Romeo Giulietta Polizia | 15 |
| A21 | Fiat 1500 C Firecar | 40 | A77 | Fiat 128 Sports Coupe | 30 | A137 | Audi 100 Raid | 15 |
| A21 | Fiat 128 Firecar | 30 | A78 | Porsche 911S Rally | 40 | A138 | Alfa Romeo Giulietta Special | 15 |
| A22 | Chevrolet Corvette Pinin Farina | 50 | A79 | Willys Jeep Army | 25 | A139 | Fiat Ritmo Special | 15 |
| A23 | Chaparral 2F | 50 | A80 | Willys Jeep | 25 | A140 | Audi 100 GLS Polizei | 25 |
| A24 | Ford Mark II | 40 | A81 | Willys Fire Jeep | 30 | A141 | Audi 100 GLS ADAC | 25 |
| A25 | Porsche Carrera 10 | 50 | A82 | Alfa Romeo Alfetta Carabinieri | 25 | A142 | Talbot Horizon Special | 15 |
| A26 | Rolls-Royce Silver Shadow | 60 | A83 | Alfa Romeo Alfetta Police Car | 30 | A143 | Opel Monza Special | 15 |
| A27 | Ferrari P4 | 50 | A84 | Citroën Dyane | 20 | A145 | Ford Granada | 15 |
| A28 | Innocenti Mini Minor | 40 | A85 | Fiat 131 | 20 | A146 | BMW 730 Stunt Car | 15 |
| A29 | Toyota 2000 GT | 40 | A86 | Innocenti Mini 90 | 25 | A149 | Willys Jeep Rally Service Car | 15 |
| A30 | Iso Rivolta S4 | 40 | A87 | Volkswagen Golf | 20 | A150 | Fiat Ritmo with Boat | 15 |
| A31 | Innocenti Mini Cooper Rally Montecarlo | 40 | A88 | Volkswagen 1303 Jeans | 25 | A152 | Fiat 131 Abarth Rally | 20 |
| A32 | Lancia Fulvia HF Rally | 40 | A89 | Willys Police Jeep "PUBBLICA SICUREZZA" | 20 | A156 | Opel Kadett Rally | 15 |
| A33 | Porsche 912 Rally Montecarlo | 55 | A90 | Alfasud Rally Bandama | 20 | A157 | Renault Rally | 15 |
| A34 | Opel Kadett Rally Montecarlo | 40 | A91 | Lancia Fulvia HF Rally Alitalia | 20 | A159 | Fiat Ritmo Racing | 15 |
| A35 | Yogi and Boo Boo's Car | 50 | A92 | Alfa Romeo Alfetta Fire Chief | 25 | A160 | Alfa Romeo Giulietta Rally | 15 |
| A36 | Fiat 500 F | 40 | A93 | Porsche 924 (FW/SE/WN) | 30 | A161 | Porsche 924 Esso Racing | 15 |
| A37 | NSU RO 80 Wankel | 40 | A94 | Renault 5 TL Rally | 20 | A162 | Volvo 343 Esso Racing | 15 |
| A38 | Matra Vignale 530 | 40 | A95 | Willys Carabinieri Jeep | 20 | A164 | Ford Granada Stunt Car | 15 |
| A39 | Lotus Europa | 50 | A96 | Willys United Nations Jeep | 20 | A165 | Lancia Delta Rally | 15 |
| A40 | Land Rover Trans American | 40 | A97 | Alfasud TI Rally | 20 | A166 | Fiat Panda Abarth Rally | 15 |
| A41 | Fiat 124 Safari | 40 | A98 | Fiat 131 Rally | 20 | A167 | Lancia Delta Racing | 15 |
| A42 | Land Rover Ambulance | 40 | A99 | Citroën Dyane Holiday | 20 | A168 | Porsche 924 Rally | 20 |
| A42 | Land Rover Army Ambulance | 50 | A100 | Ferrari 512 | 40 | A169 | Opel Kadett with Surfboards | 15 |
| A43 | Fiat 124 Taxi | 40 | A101 | Porsche 917 | 40 | A170 | Volvo 343 Rally | 15 |
| A43 | Fiat 128 Taxi | 30 | A102 | De Tomaso Pantera | 30 | A171 | Willys Jeep Renegade | 15 |
| A44 | Bertone Runabout | 40 | A103 | BMW 320 | 25 | A172 | Lancia Delta with Surfboard | 15 |
| A45 | Alfa Romeo Iguana | 40 | A105 | Alfasud Sprint | 25 | A173 | Peugeot 305 with Skis | 15 |
| A46 | Alfa Romeo Junior Zagato | 40 | A106 | Ford Fiesta | 20 | A174 | Citroën Visa Raid | 15 |
| A47 | Lamborghini Urraco | 40 | A107 | Simca 1308 | 20 | **2500 series:** | | |
| A48 | Autobianchi A112 | 30 | A108 | Innocenti Mini DeTomaso | 20 | 2501 | Fiat 880 Tractor | 20 |
| A49 | Lancia Stratos HF Bertone | 40 | A109 | Citroën Dyane Cross | 20 | 2502 | Same Buffalo 130 Tractor | 20 |
| A50 | Ferrari 365 GTC | 50 | A110 | Fiat 131 Abarth Alitalia | 20 | 2503 | Lamborghini 1056 Tractor | 25 |
| A51 | Porsche 912 London-Sydney | 40 | A111 | Alfa Romeo Giulietta | 20 | 2504 | Fiat Tractor and Tank Trailer | 25 |
| A52 | Fiat Dino with Boat | 40 | | | | 2505 | Fiat Tractor and Manure Spreader | 25 |

| # | Name | Price |
|---|------|------:|
| 2506 | Fiat Tractor and Open Trailer | $25 |
| 2507 | Fiat Tractor and Hay Loader | 25 |
| 2510 | Fiat Bergomi 170 Refuse Wagon | 20 |
| 2511 | Mercedes Open Truck | 25 |
| 2512 | Fiat 170 Container Truck | 25 |
| 2513 | Fiat Cella 170 | 25 |
| 2514 | Fiat 170 Semi Trailer Truck | 35 |
| 2515 | O.M. 190 Open Semi Trailer Truck | 50 |
| 2516 | O.M. 190 Semi Trailer Truck | 50 |
| 2517 | O.M. 190 Lumber Semi | 50 |
| 2518 | Mercedes Open Truck and Trailer | 35 |
| 2519 | Fiat 170 Container Semi | 30 |

| # | Name | Price |
|---|------|------:|
| **6600 series:** | | |
| 6601 | Ferrari Can-Am | $50 |
| 6602 | Chevrolet Astro II | 35 |
| 6603 | Trantula Dragster | 35 |
| 6604 | Torpedo Dragster | 35 |
| 6605 | Lamborghini Miura | 40 |
| 6606 | Chaparral 2F | 50 |
| 6607 | Ford GT Mark II | 50 |
| 6608 | Fiat Abarth 695 SS | 40 |
| 6611 | Ford Mustang Boss 302 | 60 |
| 6612 | Alfa Romeo 33/3 | 35 |
| 6613 | Porsche Carrera 10 | 45 |
| 6614 | Ferrari P4 | 50 |

| # | Name | Price |
|---|------|------:|
| 6615 | Twin Mill | $35 |
| 6616 | Silhouette | 35 |
| 6617 | Toyota 2000 GT | 35 |
| 6618 | Lotus Europa | 35 |
| 6621 | Ferrari 512 S Pinin Farina | 50 |
| 6622 | Mercedes-Benz C-111 | 35 |
| 6623 | Porsche 917 | 35 |
| 6624 | Abarth 3000 | 35 |
| 6625 | Mantis | 35 |
| 6626 | McLaren Can-Am | 40 |
| 6627 | DeTomaso Pantera | 35 |
| 6628 | Chaparral 2J | 50 |
| 6629 | Lola T-212 Can-Am | 40 |

# Mercury

Mercury, founded in 1932 in Turin, Italy, is considered by many to be the greatest of the Italian die cast manufacturers. It began producing die cast toys (models) in 1945, and the early products were fairly simple and crude. They do, however, possess a period charm that appeals greatly to collectors today.

The 1940s to early 1950s models included Lancias and Fiats, naturally enough, but there were other marques represented as well. Most notable were the Cadillac 60 (based on the 1948-49 Cadillac model) and a Studebaker Commander. The models of this period were generally of two scales: 1/40 and the smaller 1/80 line. The 1/40 scale models were simple affairs; some had tinplate baseplates and a few even came with clockwork motors. The 1/80 line items were numbered in the '40s (except for a Tank and a

Gun, numbered 231 and 232, respectively), and the toys had stamped-steel wheels. It appears that the series was made until sometime in the early '50s. (The trucks in this series were actually a bit smaller than 1/80 scale.)

Mercurys made in the 1940s and '50s are now relatively scarce, particularly in excellent (or better) original condition. The 1/40 scale models, in particular, are highly sought after, and some examples sell for several hundred dollars.

## Numbering Chaos

Mercury's numbering system can be confusing, due to the company reusing old numbers. The 1940s and early '50s 1/40 scale products were numbered from 1 through 95, although there were large sections of numbers that had no models. In 1954, Mercury switched over to 1/48 scale, and

*A Mercury #29 Alfa Romeo Cangura with original box. This model was introduced in the mid-1960s. The four leaf clover decal is original.*

the first such model was numbered 13, the Fiat 1100/103. In 1956, the company began reusing numbers, a move that it repeated during the 1970s. Therefore, for example, there are three #10s: a Fiat 500/C that came out about 1950; an Innocenti 950 Roadster, which debuted in 1961; and a Fiat 128 that came out in the mid-1970s.

The 1/48 scale lasted until around 1962, when the company changed over to the more standard 1/43 scale. Mercury models had been steadily improving: The second half of the 1950s and early 1960s saw the gradual addition of features like window glazing, interiors and suspension. All of these improvements were undoubtedly in response to the success being enjoyed by British rival Corgi.

The 1960s saw intense competition not only from Corgi, but from Meccano's Dinky Toys and even at home from fellow Italian manufacturer, Politoys. Mercury responded with many excellent models; they even took a whack at the Matchbox-size market by launching a 1/66 scale series called "Speedy" during the 1960s. (They would repeat the exercise in the late 1970s with the "Micro" line.)

As can be seen in the listing, Mercury made a variety of model types including farm vehicles and earth-moving equipment. Mercury is also well-known for their line of toy airplanes.

The #39 Ferrari 250 LeMans was also introduced during the mid-1960s. Like many Mercurys, it featured opening hoods and doors.

There is disagreement as to exactly when Mercury ceased production of die cast toys and models. It was probably in 1979 or 1980, around the time that Meccano (manufacturers of Dinky Toys) closed its doors for good in England.

Since 1993, a firm called "Scottoy," based in Genova, Italy, has made and marketed "re-creations" of some of the original Mercurys of the 1950s. Included in their line is a Fiat 600, an Alfa Romeo Giulietta, and a number of other models. They also reportedly have made some new models; both these and the re-creations are intended to look as basic as the original Mercurys.

The author has not seen these models; however, photos of them have appeared in the hobby press, and they do indeed resemble the early Mercurys.

The following listing encompasses the original Mercury categories just examined. All values are for near mint to mint examples with original boxes, where applicable.

For further information on Mercury models, the reader is encouraged to consult *Classic Miniature Vehicles Made in Italy*, by Dr. Edward Force, and *The Golden Book of Model Cars*, by Paolo Rampini. Both books are excellent sources of information on die cast models; see Part Three, Additional Resources.

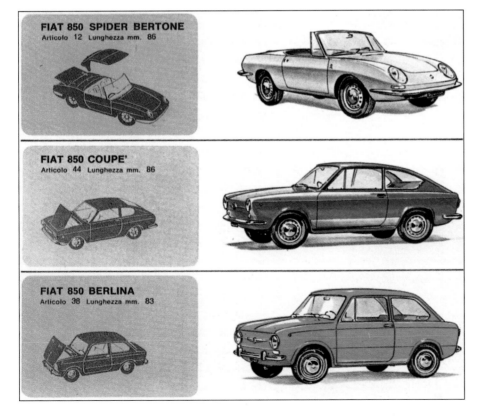

FIAT 850 SPIDER BERTONE
Articolo 12 Lunghezza mm. 86

FIAT 850 COUPE'
Articolo 44 Lunghezza mm. 86

FIAT 850 BERLINA
Articolo 38 Lunghezza mm. 83

*This page from a circa 1968 catalog shows several Fiat models offered by Mercury at the time. The model number for each can be seen after the word "Articolo."*

| # | Name | Price |
|---|------|-------|
| | **Early 1/40 scale models (through early 1950s):** | |
| 1 | Aero Coupe | $350 |
| 2 | Farina Coupe | 350 |
| 3 | Lancia Aprilia | 350 |
| 4 | Americana | 350 |
| 5 | Lincoln Continental Convertible | 350 |
| 6 | Studebaker Commander | 300 |
| 7 | Caravan Trailer | 150 |
| 8 | Willys Jeep S.W. | 400 |
| 9 | Cadillac 60 Special | 300 |
| 10 | Fiat 500/C | 250 |
| 11 | Fiat 1400 | 250 |
| 12 | Lancia Aurelia | 250 |
| 20 | Limousine | 250 |
| 21 | Roadster | 250 |
| 22 | Dump Truck | 150 |
| 23 | Crane Truck | 150 |
| 24 | Tanker | 150 |
| 31 | Maserati Racing Car | 175 |
| 32 | Autounion Racing Car | 200 |
| 33 | Mercedes W 154 Racing Car | 175 |
| 34 | Maserati G.P. | 125 |
| 35 | Alfa Romeo Alfetta G.P. | 125 |
| 36 | Ferrari 1500 G.P. | 175 |
| 37 | Cisitalia 1100 G.P. | 125 |
| 38 | Cisitalia 1500 G.P. | 125 |
| 39 | S.V.A. Racing Car | 125 |
| 40 | Mercedes W 163 G.P. | 125 |
| 62 | Americana | 125 |
| 64 | Tractor | 100 |
| 90 | Americana | 150 |
| 94A | Ciclope Flat Truck | 100 |
| 94B | Ciclope Dump Truck | 100 |
| 94C | Ciclope Ladder Truck | 100 |
| 94D | Ciclope Crane Truck | 100 |
| 95 | Vulcano Trailer | 50 |
| 307B | Trailer for Tractor | 40 |
| | **Early 1/80 scale models (through early 1950s):** | |
| 41A | Aero | 50 |
| 41B | Farina Coupe | 50 |
| 41C | Lancia Aprilia | 50 |
| 41D | Americana | 50 |
| 41E | Studebaker Commander | 65 |
| 42A | Maserati Racing Car | 50 |
| 42B | Autounion Racing Car | 50 |
| 42C | Mercedes-Benz W154 Racing Car | 50 |
| 43A | Open Truck | 40 |
| 43B | Tank Truck various liveries ("ESSO," "SHELL," etc.) | 50 |
| 44A | Maserati Racing Car | 50 |
| 44B | Alfa Romeo Alfetta Racing Car | 40 |
| 44C | Ferrari 125 Racing Car | 50 |
| 44D | Cisitalia 1100 Racing Car | 40 |
| 44E | Cisitalia 1500 Racing Car | 40 |
| 44F | SVA Racing Car | 40 |
| 44G | Mercedes-Benz 1500 Racing Car | 50 |
| 47A | Covered Truck | 40 |
| 47B | Crane Truck | 40 |
| 47C | Bus | 40 |
| 48A | Cadillac 60 Special | 60 |

| # | Name | Price |
|---|------|-------|
| 48B | Fiat 500/C | $40 |
| 48C | Fiat 1400 | 40 |
| 48D | Lancia Aurelia | 40 |
| 49A | Semi-Trailer Truck | 40 |
| 49B | Semi-Trailer Tanker various liveries ("MOBIL," "STANDARD," etc.) | 50 |
| 49C | Flat Semi-Trailer Truck | 40 |
| 231 | Tank | 30 |
| 232 | Gun | 30 |
| | **Models of the 1950s and '60s:** | |
| 1 | Fiat Nuova 500 | 100 |
| 2 | Fiat 1800 | 80 |
| 3 | Alfa Romeo Giulietta Sprint | 175 |
| 4 | Ford Continental Mark II | 200 |
| 5 | Lancia Appia III | 100 |
| 6 | Autobianchi Bianchina | 80 |
| 7 | Fiat 1500 Roadster | 80 |
| 8 | Lancia Flaminia | 80 |
| 9 | Fiat 1300 | 70 |
| 9A | Fiat 1500 | 70 |
| 10 | Innocenti 950 Roadster | 70 |
| 11 | Autobianchi Bianchina S.W. | 70 |
| 13 | Fiat 1100 103 | 125 |
| 14 | Lancia Appia I | 125 |
| 15 | Volkswagen 1200 | 100 |
| 15A | Volkswagen 1200 PTT | 300 |
| 16 | Alfa Romeo 1900 Super | 100 |
| 17 | Alfa Romeo Giulietta | 100 |
| 18 | Fiat 600 | 75 |
| 19 | Fiat 600 Multipla | 75 |
| 20 | Alfa Romeo Giulietta TI | 75 |
| 21 | Ferrari 750 Sport | 100 |
| 22 | Mercedes-Benz W 196 R | 65 |
| 25 | Saurer Bus PTT | 150 |
| 25A | Saurer Bus | 150 |
| 26 | Lancia D 24 Carrera | 55 |
| 27 | Studebaker Golden Hawk | 125 |
| 28 | Cadillac Eldorado Convertible | 125 |
| 29 | Rolls-Royce Silver Cloud | 150 |
| 30 | Bentley S Series | 150 |
| 31 | Lancia Flavia | 70 |
| 35 | Fiat 1300 Polizia | 90 |
| 52 | Maserati 250 Formula I | 110 |
| 53 | Ferrari 55 Supersqualo Formula I | 150 |
| 54 | Lancia-Ferrari D50 Formula I | 100 |
| 55 | Mercedes RW 196 Formula I | 100 |
| 56 | Mercedes RW 196 | 100 |
| 88 | Saurer Van various liveries | 350 |
| 89A | Saurer Dump Truck | 125 |
| 89B | Saurer Flat Truck | 125 |
| 95 | Fiat 682 N Car Transporter | 200 |
| 96 | Viberti BC5 Tanker various liveries ("PETROLEA," "MOBIL," etc.) | 225 |
| 96A | Viberti BC5 Military Tanker | 225 |
| 97 | Fiat 682N Tipping Truck | 150 |
| 97 | Fiat 682N Covered Truck | 150 |
| 97A | Fiat 682N Military Truck | 150 |
| 99 | Fiat 682N Car Transporter | 175 |
| 100 | Trailer for 99 | 60 |
| 212 | Vespa 125 Scooter | 100 |
| 213 | Lambretta 125C Scooter | 100 |
| 214 | Ariete Field Gun | 40 |

| # | Name | Price |
|---|------|-------|
| 215 | Ape Motor-Tricycle | $125 |
| 216 | Lambretta 125 FC Motor-Tricycle | 150 |
| 217 | Lambretta 125 LC Scooter | 100 |
| 221 | Fiorentini Excavator | 55 |
| | **Farm and earth-moving vehicles (1/43-1/120 scale; late 1950s through early 1960s):** | |
| 501 | Michigan 375 Tractor Shovel | 40 |
| 502 | Michigan 380 Tractor Plow | 40 |
| 503 | Michigan 310 Scraper | 40 |
| 504 | Caterpillar 12 Road Grader | 40 |
| 505 | Euclid R 40 Dump Truck | 40 |
| 506 | Caterpillar 12 Road Grader | 40 |
| 507 | Lima Excavator | 60 |
| 508 | Autocar AP 40 Dump Truck | 40 |
| 508A | Autocar AP 25 Dump Truck | 40 |
| 509 | Lorain Crane Truck | 60 |
| 510 | Massey Ferguson Set | 90 |
| 511 | Farm Trailer | 30 |
| 512 | Hay Baler | 30 |
| 513 | Euclid Road Scraper | 40 |
| 514 | Drott Tractor Shovel | 40 |
| 514A | International Bulldozer | 40 |
| 515 | Blaw-Knox Cement Mixer | 60 |
| 517 | Allis Chalmers Bulldozer | 40 |
| 518 | Austin Western Road Roller | 50 |
| 519 | Euclid C6 Bulldozer | 40 |
| 520 | Euclid L30 Mechanical Shovel | 40 |
| 521 | Truck "GRADALL" | 60 |
| 521A | Truck "Warney & Swasey" | 60 |
| 522 | Austin Western Road Grader | 60 |
| 523 | Landini Tractor | 60 |
| | **Speedy series (1/66 scale; 1960s):** | |
| 801 | Porsche Carrera 6 | 20 |
| 802 | Chaparral 2F | 20 |
| 803 | Ferrari 330 P4 | 25 |
| 804 | Ford GT40 | 20 |
| 805 | Lamborghini Marzal | 25 |
| 806 | Ferrari 250 LeMans | 25 |
| 807 | OSI Silver Fox | 20 |
| 808 | Alfa Romeo 33 | 20 |
| 809 | Alfa Romeo Montreal | 20 |
| 810 | Dino Pinin Farina | 20 |
| 811 | Lamborghini Miura | 25 |
| 812 | Matra | 20 |
| 813 | Ford Mustang | 25 |
| 814 | Lola T-70 GT | 20 |
| 815 | Ferrari P5 | 25 |
| 816 | Sigma Grand Prix | 20 |
| 817 | Lotus Europa | 20 |
| 818 | Mercedes-Benz C-111 | 20 |
| 850 | Covered Wagon | 15 |
| 851 | Stagecoach | 15 |
| 870 | Fiat 238 Van | 20 |
| 872 | Fiat 238 School Bus | 20 |
| 873 | Fiat 238 High-Roof Van | 20 |
| 1201 | Grand Prix Car Jarama | 10 |
| 1202 | Grand Prix Car Monte Carlo | 10 |
| 1203 | Grand Prix Car Zeltweg | 10 |
| 1204 | Grand Prix Car Hockenheim | 10 |
| 1205 | Grand Prix Car Zandvoort | 10 |

| # | Name | Price |
|---|------|-------|
| **Miscellaneous smaller models (approximately 1/100 scale; circa 1970):** | | |
| 1701 | Fiat 850 Coupe | $20 |
| 1702 | Fiat Dino 2400 Coupe | 20 |
| 1703 | Fiat 124 Coupe 1600 | 20 |
| **Micro series (1/66 scale; late 1970s):** | | |
| 801 | Fiat Campagnola | 25 |
| 802 | Fiat 697 Tanker | 25 |
| 803 | Fiat 697 Open Truck | 20 |
| 804 | Caravan Trailer | 10 |
| 806 | Fiat 127 | 20 |
| 807 | Fiat 131 Abarth | 20 |
| 809 | Fiat 697 Cement Truck | 20 |
| 810 | Fiat 780 Tractor | 20 |
| 811 | Lancia Stratos | 20 |
| 812 | Porsche 935 Turbo | 25 |
| 813 | BMW 3. CSL | 20 |
| 816 | Alfa Romeo Giulietta 1300 | 20 |
| 901 | Fiat Campagnola and Caravan | 25 |
| 902 | Fiat 127 and Caravan | 25 |
| 903 | Alfa Romeo Giulietta 1300 and Caravan | 25 |
| 904 | Fiat 131 Abarth and Caravan | 25 |
| 905 | Fiat 697 Covered Truck and Trailer | 20 |
| 906 | Fiat 780 Tractor and Trailer | 20 |
| 907 | Fiat 697 Open Truck and Trailer | 20 |
| **Last series (early 1960s through late 1970s):** | | |
| 1 | Fiat 131 | 15 |
| 2 | Fiat 131 Rally | 15 |
| 3 | Alfa Romeo Giulia TI Carabinieri | 75 |
| 3 | Fiat 131 Polizia | 20 |
| 4 | Alfa Romeo Giulia TI | 60 |
| 4 | Alfa Romeo Giulia TI Rally | 60 |
| 4 | Fiat 131 Fire Chief | 20 |
| 5 | Fiat 131 Carabinieri | 25 |
| 6 | BMW 320 | 30 |
| 7 | Fiat 131 S. W. Ambulance | 25 |
| 8 | Fiat 128 Polizia | 40 |
| 9 | Fiat 128 Fire Chief | 40 |
| 10 | Fiat 128 Carabinieri | 40 |
| 11 | Fiat 131 Taxi | 30 |
| 12 | Fiat 850 Bertone Hardtop | 40 |
| 12A | Fiat 850 Bertone Roadster | 40 |
| 12B | Fiat 850 Bertone Coupe | 40 |
| 12D | Fiat 131 with skis | 25 |
| 14 | Fiat Abarth 595 SS | 45 |
| 17 | Fiat 500 L | 40 |
| 20 | Innocenti Mini 90 | 20 |
| 21 | Ranger Ferves | 40 |
| 22 | Fiat 128 Four-Door Sedan | 40 |
| 23 | Fiat 2300 S Coupe | 75 |
| 23A | Innocenti Mini 90 Rally | 20 |
| 24 | Maserati 3500GT Coupe | 75 |
| 24A | Innocenti Mini 90 with skis | 20 |
| 25 | Fiat 125 | 30 |
| 26 | Fiat 130 Saloon | 60 |
| 27 | Lancia Fulvia Coupe | 60 |
| 27A | Lancia Fulvia Coupe Safari | 75 |
| 28 | Ferrari P2 | 75 |
| 28A | Fiat Campagnola | 25 |
| 29 | Alfa Romeo Canguro | 50 |

| # | Name | Price |
|---|------|-------|
| 29A | Alfa Romeo Canguro Rally | $50 |
| 29B | Fiat Campagnola Polizia | 25 |
| 30 | Chaparral 2F | 35 |
| 30A | Fiat Campagnola Fire Car | 25 |
| 31 | Fiat Campagnola Carabinieri | 25 |
| 32 | Lancia Flavia Coupe | 75 |
| 32A | Lancia Flavia Coupe with skis | 75 |
| 32B | Fiat Campagnola Ambulance | 25 |
| 33 | Lancia Fulvia | 50 |
| 33A | Fiat Campagnola Safari | 20 |
| 34 | Maserati 3500 GT Racing | 75 |
| 34A | Fiat Campagnola with Snowplow | 55 |
| 36 | Mercedes 230SL Roadster | 60 |
| 37 | Mercedes 230SL Coupe | 60 |
| 37A | Mercedes 230SL Hardtop | 60 |
| 38 | Fiat 850 | 55 |
| 39 | Ferrari 250 LeMans | 75 |
| 40 | Alfa Romeo Giulia GT Coupe | 60 |
| 40A | Alfa Romeo Giulia GT Coupe Rally | 60 |
| 40B | Alfa Romeo Giulia GTA | 60 |
| 41 | Abarth 1000 Coupe | 45 |
| 42 | Fiat Abarth 1000 OT | 45 |
| 44 | Fiat 850 Coupe | 45 |
| 45 | Ferrari Dino 206 | 70 |
| 46 | Fiat 124 | 40 |
| 46A | Fiat 124 Rally | 40 |
| 48 | Ferrari Dino Coupe Pinin Farina | 70 |
| 50 | Mercedes-Benz 230 SL Safari | 60 |
| 50A | Fiat Ritmo | 40 |
| 51 | Lancia Fulvia Coupe HF | 60 |
| 51 | Lancia Fulvia Coupe HF Montecarlo | 60 |
| 52 | Lancia Beta Coupe Rally | 30 |
| 53 | Alfa Romeo 33 Pinin Farina | 55 |
| 53 | Lancia Alfetta GT Rally | 30 |
| 54 | Lancia Beta Coupe Davos with skis | 25 |
| 55 | Alfa Romeo Alfetta GT with skis | 35 |
| 56 | BMW 320 Rally | 30 |
| 57 | Ferrari 330 P Monza | 70 |
| 58 | Ferrari 330 P Sebring | 70 |
| 58A | Alfa Romeo Alfetta GT Carabinieri | 50 |
| 59 | Ferrari 330 P Silverstone | 70 |
| 59A | BMW 320 Polizei | 40 |
| 60 | Ferrari 330 P Nurburgring | 70 |
| 60 | Alfa Romeo Alfetta GT with Boat | 45 |
| 61 | Porsche Carrera 6 | 50 |
| 61A | Fiat 131, S.W. "Servizio Corse" | 30 |
| 63 | Fiat Dino Coupe Bertone | 50 |
| 63A | Fiat 131, S.W. Carabinieri | 35 |
| 64 | Alfa Romeo 33 Prototipo | 60 |
| 65 | Ferrari 330 P4 | 75 |
| 66 | Ferrari 12 Pinin Farina | 75 |
| 68 | Bertone Panther | 40 |
| 69 | Fiat Jack's Demon Dragster | 40 |
| 70 | Fiat Balilla Coppa d'oro Roadster | 60 |
| 80 | Fiat Campagnola | 40 |
| 81 | Fiat Campagnola Mexico | 40 |
| 82 | Fiat Campagnola Ambulance | 40 |
| 83 | Fiat Campagnola Carabinieri | 40 |
| 84 | Fiat Campagnola Fire | 40 |
| 100 | Fiat 697 Tanker various liveries | 35 |
| 101 | Fiat 697 Cement Truck | 35 |
| 102 | Fiat 697 Open Truck | 35 |
| 103 | Fiat 697 Dump Truck | 35 |

| # | Name | Price |
|---|------|-------|
| 104 | O.M. 90P 4 x 4 Dump Truck | $35 |
| 105 | O.M. 90P 4 x 4 Bucket Truck | 35 |
| 106 | O.M. 90P 4 x 4 Open Truck | 35 |
| 107 | O.M. 90P 4 x 4 Truck with Digger | 35 |
| 201 | Fiat Campagnola Wrecker | 25 |
| 202 | Fiat Campagnola African Safari | 25 |
| 203 | Lancia Beta Coupe Alitalia Safari | 25 |
| 204 | Fiat 131 S.W. with skis | 25 |
| 205 | Fiat 131 S.W. with Luggage Rack | 25 |
| 206 | Fiat Campagnola African Tour Car | 25 |
| 207 | Rembrandt Caravan | 15 |
| 208 | Fiat 131 with Boat | 20 |
| 209 | Fiat 131 with Roof Rack | 20 |
| 210 | Fiat 131 S.W. Polizia | 25 |
| 211 | Alfa Romeo Alfetta GT Kenya Safari | 40 |
| 212 | Fiat 131 S. W. with Boat | 25 |
| 213 | Fiat Campagnola with A.A. Gun | 20 |
| 214 | Fiat Campagnola with Lance-Rockets | 20 |
| 215 | Fiat Campagnola with Radio | 20 |
| 216 | Fiat Campagnola with Searchlight | 20 |
| 217 | BMW 320 Racing | 35 |
| 218 | BMW 320 with Luggage Rack | 30 |
| 219 | BMW 320 with Boat | 30 |
| 301 | Ferrari Sigma G.P. Pinin Farina | 50 |
| 302 | Fiat 124 Coupe | 40 |
| 302A | Fiat 124 Coupe Rally Elba | 40 |
| 302B | Fiat 124 Coupe Rally Montecarlo | 40 |
| 302C | Fiat 124 Coupe Coupe des Alpes | 40 |
| 302D | Fiat 124 Coupe Rally Fiori | 40 |
| 302E | Fiat 124 Coupe Tulpen Rally | 40 |
| 302F | Fiat 124 Coupe "Liege-Sofia-Liege" | 40 |
| 302G | Fiat 124 Coupe Acropolis Rally | 40 |
| 302H | Fiat 124 Coupe 1600 | 40 |
| 302I | Fiat 124 Coupe 1600 Rally | 40 |
| 302J | Fiat 124 Coupe 1600 Rally Elba | 40 |
| 303 | Alfa Romeo Carabo | 50 |
| 303A | Lancia Beta Coupe | 25 |
| 304 | Alfa Romeo Montreal | 50 |
| 304A | Fiat 131 S.W. | 25 |
| 305 | Bizzarrini Manta | 50 |
| 305A | Fiat Campagnola | 25 |
| 306 | Ferrari 312P Sebring | 60 |
| 306A | Ferrari 312P Monza | 60 |
| 306B | Alfa Romeo Alfetta GT | 40 |
| 307 | Mercedes-Benz C-111 | 45 |
| 308 | Porsche 917 Gulf | 50 |
| 308A | Porsche 917 Shell | 50 |
| 308B | Porsche 917 LeMans | 50 |
| 308C | Porsche 917 Nurburgring | 50 |
| 308D | Porsche 917 Austria | 50 |
| 308E | Porsche 917 Monza | 50 |
| 309 | Porsche 908/03 Gulf | 45 |
| 309A | Porsche 908/03 Shell | 45 |
| 310 | Chaparral 2 J | 35 |
| 311 | Fiat 127 | 35 |
| 313 | Fiat 132 | 30 |
| 313A | Fiat 132 GLS | 35 |
| 314 | Fiat 128 2-Door Sedan Rally | 40 |
| 315 | Fiat 128SL Coupe | 50 |
| 316 | Fiat 128SL Coupe Rally | 40 |
| 316A | Fiat 128SL Coupe Rally Elba | 40 |
| 317 | Fiat 132 Rally | 40 |
| 318 | Fiat 127 Rally Elba | 40 |

| # | Name | Price |
|---|------|-------|
| 318A | Fiat 127 Rally | $40 |
| 320 | Fiat 132 GLS Polizia | 40 |
| 401 | Fiat 131 and Caravan | 35 |
| 402 | Fiat 131 and Caravan | 35 |
| 403 | Fiat Campagnola African Tour and Caravan | 35 |
| 404 | Alfa Romeo Alfetta GT and Caravan | 45 |
| 405 | Fiat 131 S.W. with Skis and Caravan | 35 |
| 406 | Fiat 131 S.W. and Caravan | 35 |
| 407 | Fiat 131 S.W. and Caravan | 35 |
| 408 | Fiat 131 with Skis and Caravan | 35 |
| 409 | Lancia Beta Coupe with Skis and Caravan | 35 |
| 410 | Fiat Campagnola with A.A. Gun and Trailer | 30 |
| 411 | Fiat Campagnola with Searchlight and Trailer | 30 |
| 412 | Fiat Campagnola with Radio and Trailer | 30 |

| # | Name | Price |
|---|------|-------|
| 413 | Fiat Campagnola Army Ambulance and Trailer | $30 |
| 414 | Fiat Campagnola Fire and Trailer | 35 |
| 415 | Alfa Romeo Alfetta GT and Trailer | 40 |
| 416 | BMW 320 and Trailer | 40 |
| 418 | Fiat 131 S.W. and Trailer | 40 |
| 419 | Alfa Romeo Alfetta GT and Trailer | 40 |
| 420 | BMW 320 and Caravan | 40 |
| 422 | BMW 320 and Trailer | 40 |
| 423 | Fiat Campagnola and Trailer | 25 |
| 424 | Alfa Romeo Alfetta GT and Caravan | 40 |
| 426 | BMW 320 and Caravan | 40 |
| 430 | BMW 320 and Trailer | 40 |
| 431 | Fiat 131 S.W. and Trailer | 25 |
| 432 | Fiat 131 and Trailer | 25 |

| # | Name | Price |
|---|------|-------|
| 501 | Fiat 697 Dump Truck | $40 |
| 502 | Fiat 697 Container Truck | 40 |
| 503 | Fiat 242 Camper | 40 |
| 506 | Fiat 242 Crane Truck | 40 |
| 531 | Fiat 697 Container Semi | 40 |
| 532 | Fiat 697 Tanker Semi | 40 |
| 533 | Fiat 242 Camper and Trailer | 40 |
| 551 | Motobi Minicross | 30 |
| 552 | Fantic TX 10 Diablo Cross | 30 |
| 553 | Piaqoio Vespa Elestart Scooter | 60 |
| 554 | Honda DAX 70 | 30 |
| 651 | Ferrari Modulo Pinin Farina | 50 |
| 652 | Lancia Fulvia Stratos | 40 |
| 751 | Fred Flintstone's Car | 100 |

# Metosul

The die cast model line known as Metosul was introduced in 1965. This Portugese company must have had a former (or aspiring) police officer in its employ, as an inordinate number of the models were of police cars. Taxis were also a popular subject for Metosul. Like other European manufacturers, Metosul made their car models 1/43 scale, while their trucks and buses were 1/50.

A number of countries were represented in the Metosul line-up. France (with Renault, Peugeot and Citroën) perhaps led the way, but Germany was right behind (with Mercedes-Benz and Volkswagen). The Mercedes trucks were particularly interesting, as was the Volvo P 1800 and a very well done Camping Caravan.

While the proportions of certain Metosul models were questionable (the Mercedes sedans, for example) others were of very high quality. The models came with interior fittings, window glazing and suspension. Paint finish varied,

but was generally of good quality. The wheels on many of the cars were of a convex spun metal disc, while the trucks had a larger wheel that was the same color as the body.

The variance in quality of these models doubtless had to do with the fact that many of them were re-issues of models originally produced by other companies. The #12 Rolls-Royce Silver Ghost, for example, was an ex-Models of Yesteryear item, and the afore-mentioned #19 Notin Caravan was originally manufactured by C.I.J.

The current status of Metosul is unclear. A 1988 Metosul catalog issued by English publisher Malvern House Publications shows a number of Metosul models. The catalog states that "Metosul diecast models are made in Portugal by Henriques & Irmao LDA." Whether these were new production models or merely leftover stocks being sold off is unknown. It is not known whether or not Metosuls are still being produced.

| # | Name | Price |
|---|------|-------|
| 1 | Renault Floride | $20 |
| 2 | Citroën DS 19 | 40 |
| 3 | Alfa Romeo Giulietta Roadster | 30 |
| 3 | Alfa Romeo Giulietta Roadster Policia | 30 |
| 3 | Alfa Romeo Giulietta Roadster GNR | 30 |
| 3 | Alfa Romeo Giulietta Roadster GNR BT | 30 |
| 4 | Volkswagen 1200 | 60 |
| 4 | Volkswagen 1200 Army | 60 |
| 4 | Volkswagen 1200 | 30 |
| 5 | Volkswagen 1200 Policia | 60 |
| 5 | Volkswagen 1200 Policia | 30 |
| 6 | Volkswagen 1200 GNR BT | 60 |
| 6 | Volkswagen 1200 GNR BT | 30 |
| 7 | Morris Mini Minor | 30 |
| 8 | Volkswagen 1200 GNR | 60 |

| # | Name | Price |
|---|------|-------|
| 8 | Volkswagen 1200 GNR | $30 |
| 9 | Mercedes-Benz 190 D | 50 |
| 9 | Mercedes-Benz 190 D Taxi | 50 |
| 9 | Mercedes-Benz 190 D Policia | 50 |
| 9 | Mercedes-Benz 200 | 25 |
| 10 | Mercedes-Benz 200 Taxi | 25 |
| 11 | Volvo P 1800 Coupe | 25 |
| 12 | Rolls-Royce Silver Ghost | 15 |
| 13 | Mercedes-Benz 200 Aluguer | 25 |
| 14 | Renault R16 | 20 |
| 14 | Renault R16 GNR | 20 |
| 15 | Renault R16 Taxi | 20 |
| 16 | Renault R16 Aluguer | 20 |
| 17 | Volvo P 1800 Coupe Policia | 20 |
| 18 | Volvo P 1800 Coupe GNR BT | 20 |

| # | Name | Price |
|---|------|-------|
| 19 | Notin Rulote Camping Caravan | $25 |
| 20 | Citroën DS 19 Taxi | 30 |
| 21 | Citroën DS 19 Aluguer | 30 |
| 22 | Citroën DS 19 Policia | 30 |
| 23 | Leyland Atlantean Bus "CARRIS" | 30 |
| 24 | Peugeot 204 | 20 |
| 25 | Mercedes-Benz 200 Policia | 20 |
| 26 | Mercedes-Benz 1113 Dump Truck | 30 |
| 27 | Mercedes-Benz 200 Army | 30 |
| 28 | Mercedes-Benz 1113 Tanker "SACOR" | 35 |
| 29 | Mercedes-Benz 1113 Tanker "SONAP" | 35 |
| 30 | Mercedes-Benz 200 Polizei | 20 |
| 31 | Peugeot 204 Taxi | 25 |
| 32 | Peugeot 204 Aluguer | 25 |
| 33 | Leyland Atlantean Bus "STCP" | 30 |

| # | Name | Price |
|---|------|-------|
| 34 | Leyland Atlantean Bus "SMC" | $30 |
| 35 | Leyland Atlantean Bus "TRANSUL" | 30 |
| 36 | Leyland Atlantean Bus "GAZCIDLA" | 30 |
| 37 | Mercedes-Benz 1113 EGT Truck | 30 |
| 38 | Mercedes-Benz 1113 Army Truck | 30 |
| 39 | Mercedes-Benz 1113 GNR Truck | 30 |
| 40 | Mercedes-Benz 1113 Policia Truck | 30 |
| 41 | Mercedes-Benz 1113 JAE Truck | 30 |
| 42 | Volkswagen Transporter | 15 |
| 43 | Citroën DS 19 and Caravan | 60 |
| 44 | Leyland Atlantean Bus "STCP" | 20 |

| # | Name | Price |
|---|------|-------|
| 45 | Leyland Atlantean Bus "CARRIS" | $20 |
| 46 | Mercedes-Benz 1113 Tanker "GALP" | 20 |
| 48 | Citroën DS19 Bombeiros | 30 |
| 49 | Peugeot 304 Estate | 25 |
| 50 | Mercedes-Benz 1113 Correios | 30 |
| 51 | Mercedes-Benz 200 Emergencia | 25 |
| 52 | Mercedes-Benz 200 Bombeiros | 25 |
| 53 | Mercedes-Benz 1113 Bombeiros | 30 |
| 54 | Mercedes-Benz 1113 Tanker Bombeiros | 35 |
| 55 | Peugeot 304 Estate Policia | 25 |
| 56 | Volkswagon 1200 Polis | 30 |

| # | Name | Price |
|---|------|-------|
| 57 | Volkswagon 1200 Bombeiros | $30 |
| 58 | Peugeot 304 Estate J.A.E. Municipal | 25 |
| 59 | Peugeot 304 Estate Police | 25 |
| 60 | Peugeot 304 Estate Bombeiros | 30 |
| 61 | Citroën DS19 GNR | 30 |
| 108 | Mini Cooper | 30 |
| 110 | Mercedes-Benz 200 Taxi Amsterdam | 25 |
| 117 | Volvo P1800 Polis | 25 |
| 120 | Citroën DS19 Taxi Portugal | 30 |

# Micro Models

These Australian die casts were introduced around 1953 in Melbourne, Australia. Although names like Ford and Jaguar were included, it is the Holden models that this brand is known for. Since Holden cars and trucks could be seen on Australian roads every day, these models were manufactured for the home market. To the author's knowledge, they were never exported to the United States.

Although basic (none of them had window glazing, and most had no interior fittings), they were nonetheless accurate models. Their simplicity makes them very appealing to collectors today.

Production of Micro Models ceased in the late 1950s, but the molds were just getting started. Around 1974, they resurfaced in Australia, and were used to produce a re-issue series known as "Matai," which were decently cast and painted. The Matais also had chrome-plated baseplates.

Just after the Matai series, the molds apparently arrived in Christchurch, New Zealand. They were then used to make another re-issue series entitled "Torro." This series was made up of just a handful of the models produced by Matai. How long the Torro versions were produced is unknown.

It doesn't end there. Since 1994, another Christchurch-based company named "Micro Models Ltd." has been marketing Micro Models. The company states in its advertising that the models are ". . . made from the original 1950s tools." Like the originals, they have no window glazing or interiors (although the Jaguar and the MGA convertibles do have seats and steering wheels).

The numbering of the original Micro Models is somewhat confusing, with some models having a "G" prefix, and others having "GB." Also, some models share the same number (such as the G37 Ford Zephyr and the G37 Ford Dump Truck). The last six models have four-digit numbers. Why this is so is unknown.

All of the known Matai, Torro and Micro Models Ltd. re-issues are listed after the listing of the original Micro Models. CRP (Current Retail Price) of the current Micro Models Ltd. models is $30-$40.

| # | Name | Price |
|---|------|-------|
| GB3 | Jaguar XK 120 Roadster (blue, red, green) | $110 |
| GB5 | Bedford Dump Truck (green/red, yellow/green, yellow/red) | 75 |
| GB8 | International Van "MICROMODELS" (green/red) | 150 |
| GB8 | International Van "PETERS ICE cream" (cream/blue) | 150 |
| GB9 | Holden FX Sedan (gray, red) | 160 |
| GB9 | Holden FX Police Car (black) | 125 |
| GB9 | Holden FX Taxi (red/yellow) | 150 |
| GB10 | Humber Super Snipe (green, blue, black, red) | 100 |
| GB10 | Humber Super Snipe Police Car (black) | 80 |
| GB11 | Commer Truck (yellow) | 75 |
| GB12 | Talbot Lago Racing Car (green) | 100 |

| # | Name | Price |
|---|------|-------|
| GB13 | Morris Fire Engine (red) | $80 |
| GB14 | Elevator | 60 |
| GB15 | Standard Vanguard S.W. (gray, red, blue, green) | 100 |
| GB16 | International "COCA-COLA" Truck (red/yellow) | 200 |
| GB17 | Holden FJ New Look Sedan (green, red) | 100 |
| GB17 | Holden FJ New Look Police Car (green) | 75 |
| GB17 | Holden FJ New Look Taxi (black/white, black/orange) | 100 |
| GB18 | Commer Articulated Truck (red, yellow) | 90 |
| GB19 | Trailer (red yellow) | 40 |
| GB20 | International Ambulance (gray, cream) | 125 |
| GB20 | International Army Ambulance (olive) | 160 |

| # | Name | Price |
|---|------|-------|
| GB21 | Holden FJ Van (red/blue, red, green, blue) | $110 |
| GB21 | Holden FJ Van Taxi (red) | 110 |
| GB21 | Holden FJ Van "ROYAL MAIL P. MG." (red) | 150 |
| GB21 | Holden FJ Van "ROYAL MAIL NEW ZEALAND P.O." (red) | 150 |
| GB22 | Commer Tanker "SHELL" (red/yellow/black) | 100 |
| GB22 | Commer Tanker "AMPOL" (red/cream/black) | 170 |
| GB23 | International Breakdown (green) | 90 |
| GB25 | Volkswagen 1200 (cream, blue, green, red, gray) | 130 |
| G26 | Ferguson Tractor (red) | 80 |

| # | Name | Price |
|---|------|-------|
| G26 | Ferguson Tractor with Shovel (red/yellow/black) | $100 |
| G27 | Commer Artic. Tanker "SHELL" (red/yellow/black) | 150 |
| G27 | Commer Artic. Tanker "MOBILGAS" (red/white/black) | 150 |
| G27 | Commer Artic. Tanker "PETERS ICE cream" (cream) | 150 |
| G27 | Commer Artic. Tanker Milk (cream) | 150 |
| G28 | Ford V8 Covered Truck (red/green, red/yellow) | 110 |
| G29 | Ford V8 Army Truck (olive) | 110 |
| G31 | Vauxhall Velox (black, green, red, blue) | 75 |
| G31 | Bedford Bus "MICRO BUS LINES" (red/silver, green/silver) | 150 |
| G32 | Holden FX Pickup (red, green) | 90 |
| G32 | M.G.A Roadster (green, red, blue, cream) | 100 |
| G33 | Holden FE Sedan (blue/cream, blue/dark blue, gray/red) | 150 |
| G33 | Holden FE Police Car | 120 |
| G33 | Holden FE Taxi (red/silver) | 150 |
| G34 | Bedford Open Truck (green/red, yellow/green, red/yellow) | 55 |
| G34 | Ford Customline (red/cream, light yellow/red) | 160 |
| G35 | Ford Mainline Pickup (red, blue, cream) | 120 |
| G36 | Trailer (red, green) | 40 |

| # | Name | Price |
|---|------|-------|
| G36 | Volkswagen Bus (red) | $175 |
| G37 | Ford Zephyr Saloon (red, blue, black) | 100 |
| G37 | Ford V8 Dump Truck (red/yellow, red/green) | 110 |
| G38 | Holden FE Pickup (red/gray, red/cream) | 140 |
| G39 | Holden FC Station Wagon (blue/dark blue, green/blue, green/gray) | 130 |
| G40 | Chrysler Royal (red/silver, green/silver) | 175 |
| G41 | Vauxhall Cresta (light green, blue, red) | 110 |
| 4322 | Massey Harris Tractor (red) | 100 |
| 4340 | Massey Harris Tractor with Shovel (red/yellow) | 100 |
| 4341 | Commer Articulated Low Loader (red/yellow/black) | 130 |
| 4342 | Commer Articulated Logging Truck (yellow/black) | 140 |
| 4350 | Ford V8 Canopy Truck (red/yellow) | 100 |
| 4355 | Caterpillar Bulldozer (yellow) | 175 |

**Matai models (1970s):**

| # | Name | Price |
|---|------|-------|
| GB8 | International Van | 40 |
| GB13 | Morris Fire Engine | 40 |
| GB15 | Standard Vanguard S.W. | 50 |
| GB16 | International Brewery Truck | 40 |
| GB23 | International Breakdown | 40 |
| GB25 | Volkswagen 1200 | 75 |
| G32 | M.G.A Roadster | 50 |
| G33 | Holden FE Sedan | 50 |
| G34 | Ford Customline | 50 |

| # | Name | Price |
|---|------|-------|
| G35 | Ford Mainline Pickup | $40 |
| G38 | Holden FE Pickup | 40 |
| G39 | Holden FC Station Wagon | 50 |
| G40 | Chrysler Royal | 70 |
| G41 | Vauxhall Cresta | 50 |

**Torro models (1970s):**

| # | Name | Price |
|---|------|-------|
| GB8 | International Van | 40 |
| GB13 | Morris Fire Engine | 40 |
| GB16 | International Brewery Truck | 40 |
| GB23 | International Breakdown | 40 |
| GB25 | Volkswagen 1200 | 75 |
| G32 | M.G.A Roadster | 50 |
| G40 | Chrysler Royal | 70 |
| G41 | Vauxhall Cresta | 50 |

**Micro Models Ltd. (current):**

| # | Name | Price |
|---|------|-------|
| MM001 | International Delivery Van "MICRO MODELS" | CRP |
| No # | International Bottle Truck | CRP |
| MM402 | FJ Holden Special Sedan | CRP |
| MM403 | Fe Ute "PUBLIC WORKS" | CRP |
| MM404 | FJ Holden Panel Van | CRP |
| MM405 | FX Holden Sedan Police | CRP |
| MM406 | VW Bus | CRP |
| MM407 | Jaguar XK120 | CRP |
| MM409 | Ford Zephyr Police | CRP |
| MM502 | MGA | CRP |
| MM506 | Fe Sedan Police | CRP |

# Micropet

These Japanese die cast models were produced in Japan in the early 1960s. The series was comprised mostly of Japanese marques, but there were a few American models as well (including a Ford Falcon, which for some reason was a popular model with Japanese manufacturers in the 1960s).

Micropets, like the Asahi models of the time, rarely turn up in the United States. It is likely that the models were not imported here.

The following listing is comprised of known models. Due to the great rarity of these items, there can be a wide variation of price when one does come up for sale. A model listed at $100 may sell for two or three times that amount.

| # | Name | Price |
|---|------|-------|
| 1 | Subaru 360 (blue, copper) | $100 |
| 2 | Datsun Bluebird (red, gray) | 100 |
| 2 | Datsun Bluebird (chrome-plated) | 125 |
| 5 | Nissan Cedric (blue, pink, copper/gray) | 100 |
| 5 | Nissan Cedric (chrome-plated) | 125 |
| 6 | Prince Skyline (copper/gray, blue/gray) | 100 |
| 6 | Prince Skyline (chrome-plated) | 125 |
| 7 | Mazda Coupe R 360 (white/red, orange/gray) | 100 |
| 7 | Mazda Coupe R 360 (chrome-plated) | 1258 |
|   | Toyota Corona S.W. (green/gray, orange/cream) | 100 |

| # | Name | Price |
|---|------|-------|
| 8 | Toyota Corona S.W. (chrome-plated) | $125 |
| 9 | Chevrolet Impala Sedan (blue/white) | 125 |
| 9 | Chevrolet Impala Sedan (chrome-plated) | 125 |
| 10 | Chevrolet Impala Police Car (white/black) | 125 |
| 11 | Prince Skyway S.W. (pink/gray, red/yellow/white) | 100 |
| 12 | Ford Falcon Sedan (red/black, green/green) | 125 |
| 14 | Prince Bus (pink/white/blue, red/white/red) | 150 |

| # | Name | Price |
|---|------|-------|
| 14 | Prince Bus (chrome-plated) | $150 |
| 15 | Hillman Minx (red, blue/white, blue/cream) | 100 |
| 16 | Ford Falcon Police Car (black/white) | 125 |
| 17 | Datsun Bluebird S.W. (blue/white, yellow/brown) | 100 |
| 17 | Datsun Bluebird S.W. (chrome-plated) | 125 |
| 18 | Nissan Light Truck (brown/green, blue/gray) | 100 |
| 19 | Isuzu Bellel 2000 Saloon (green/white) | 100 |

# Midgetoy

The name "Midgetoy" is well-known among collectors of American die cast toys. For nearly 40 years, these simple cars, trucks, military vehicles and aircraft were produced in Rockford, Illinois, and shipped to five-and-dimes across the country. Midgetoys were inexpensive toys, and by the mid-1950s they were the second largest selling die cast toys, behind those of Tootsietoy.

One reason they were cheap to make and to buy was the lack of a baseplate. Fortunately, Midgetoy always put their name on the interior surface of the toys, along with "ROCK-FORD ILL" and (usually) a "U.S.A." inscription.

A full history and company profile of Midgetoy can be found in the section entitled "The Year Was 1946," in Part One of this book.

In the 1940s and '50s, some Midgetoys were packaged individually (or in groups of two or more) on blistercards. The plastic of the blister itself was generally of a softer material than today's blisterpacks; during the 1960s, the company switched to a more brittle material that is similar to today's product. Midgetoys also marketed its toys in counter display boxes, from which a customer could choose which toy he or she wanted. As a result, the only "original" boxes that exist are the counter display units, and they are rare.

Midgetoy also offered their toys in sets for many years, particularly in the 1960s and '70s. (In fact, the company's first product, the 4-in-1 Truck Set, established the tradition of marketing the toys in groups.) Some sets were quite elaborate; the Speedway Set, for example, offered the "Flat Racer," the Indy Car, the MG and various other vehicles, all packaged in a tray-like cardboard box which was made up like a raceway.

And don't be surprised to find a Midgetoy in a military livery. Many Midgetoys were painted in both civilian and military versions; and many of the military versions were available in military sets with names like "Attack Force" and "Army Convoy." (There were several King Size toys that were available only in a military version, and these are listed separately.)

Midgetoy also produced a line of die cast aircraft, sold both individually and in sets. And a line of die cast trains was also produced by the company.

The following listing includes individual Midgetoys without blistercards or other packaging, since this is how most Midgetoys turn up. For a set, or for several toys packaged together in a blisterpack, a premium of 25% over the total value of the toys themselves is a good rule of thumb when deciding what to pay.

*The Midgetoy MGs. At left is the "Midget" version (also sold with the "Junior" series); at right is the "Mini" version.*

*The "heavy iron" of the Midgetoy product line. These Tractor Trailer Trucks shared the same cab; there was also an Auto Transporter that came with two "Mini" cars.*

*At left is a "three pack," used during the 1950s and '60s (note the 49 cent price for three Junior cars); on the right is one of many "theme" packs used by Midgetoy. This pack contains two of the "Mini" cars.*

| Name | Price |
|---|---|
| **Midget series (2¹/₂–2³/₄ inches in length):** | |
| MG Sports Car | $15 |
| Hot Rod | 10 |
| Corvette Convertible | 15 |
| Battle Bug (amphibious vehicle) | 25 |
| Fire Truck | 10 |
| Cannon | 10 |
| **Junior series (average 3¹/₂ inches in length):** | |
| "Spaceship" Car | 15 |
| Futuristic Auto | 10 |
| Cadillac Convertible | 20 |
| Fire Truck | 15 |
| Hot Rod | 10 |
| Jeep | 10 |
| Indy Car | 15 |
| Volkswagen Beetle (2⁷/₈ inches) | 20 |
| Bonneville "Flat" Racer | 10 |
| Greyhound Bus | 20 |

| Name | Price |
|---|---|
| 1949 Ford Pick-up Truck | $10 |
| 1971 Ford Pick-up Truck | 10 |
| Ford Ranchero Pick-up Truck | 10 |
| **King Size series (average 4¹/₂ inches in length):** | |
| Ford Pick-up | 15 |
| Fire Truck | 15 |
| Convertible | 20 |
| Oil Truck | 15 |
| Four door Sedan | 20 |
| Coupe | 20 |
| Bus | 20 |
| Station Wagon (windows on sides) | 20 |
| Ambulance (Station Wagon with solid side panels) | 15 |
| **Military King Size:** | |
| Tank | 15 |
| Personnel Carrier | 15 |
| Half-Track Truck | 15 |

| Name | Price |
|---|---|
| **Jumbo series (average 6 inches in length):** | |
| Oil Truck | $20 |
| Convertible | 20 |
| Bus | 20 |
| Fire Truck | 20 |
| Tank | 20 |
| Pick-up Truck | 20 |
| **Tractor Trailers:** | |
| Auto Transporter (with two "Mini" cars) | 40 |
| Oil Tanker | 30 |
| Moving Van | 25 |
| Fire Truck | 25 |
| **Mini series (average 2 inches in length):** | |
| MG Sports Car | 10 |
| Jaguar | 5 |
| Chevrolet Corvette Coupe | 10 |
| Chevrolet Corvette Convertible | 10 |
| Dodge Charger | 5 |
| Indy Car (front engine) | 10 |
| Indy Car (rear engine) | 5 |
| Dragster | 5 |
| Jeep | 5 |
| Station Wagon Ambulance | 10 |
| Station Wagon Fire Chief | 5 |
| Hot Rod | 5 |
| Fire Truck | 5 |
| **Miscellaneous:** | |
| 4-in-1 Truck Set (late 1940s) | 40 |
| House Trailer (2³/₈ inches) | 10 |
| U-Haul Trailer | 5 |
| Boat Trailer (with plastic boat) | 10 |
| Flat Race Car Trailer | 10 |
| Rear "Cap" for Pick-up Trucks | 10 |
| Gasoline Pumps (metal) | 25 |

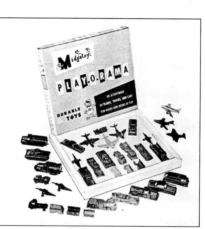

**No. 9350 MIDGETOY PLAY-O-RAMA**

IDEAL FOR THE MOTOR-MINDED YOUNGSTERS!

A complete assortment of all time favorites to give boys and girls hours and hours of fun.

This set LOOKS BIG — And it IS BIG!

It will keep the youngsters amused for hours at a time. Suitable for indoor or outdoor play. This can truly be your best traffic stopper.

Beautifully finished in Midgetoys traditionally fine manner.

**DURABLE ALL METAL DIE-CAST CONSTRUCTION!**

Packed 1 dozen boxes per shipper.
Shipping weight 33 lbs.

*This illustration is taken from a late 1940s Midgetoy catalog. The #9350 set contained a number of different Midgetoys, including the original 4-in-1 Truck Set at bottom left.*

*Three of the Juniors in their original 49-cent blisterpacks, which Midgetoy began using in 1967. At left is the Bonneville "Flat" Racer; center is the Fire Truck; and at right is the Hot Rod.*

# Milton

After Nicky Toys, Milton Morgan of Calcutta is probably the best known of the die cast manufacturers in India. During the 1970s, Milton produced numerous die cast models under the name "Mini Auto Cars." The line was a hodgepodge of sizes, since Milton used tooling that had been acquired from Dinky, Corgi and other manufacturers.

This sort of arrangement worked well for both parties. Once a company like Corgi decided it had gotten all of the sales it could out of a particular model, it no longer had any use for the tooling. It could then be sold to a manufacturer like Milton, who would be only too glad to not have to cut new dies, the cost of which was (and is) prohibitive. (Today, such tooling would be carefully preserved for the inevitable "anniversary" re-issue of the model.)

As might be expected, Milton's products bear a resemblance to the original versions made by the major firms, but closer inspection reveals that they were of an inferior standard. The wheels were initially black rubber tires on spun aluminum hubs, which looked acceptable. But the company then switched to a cheap plastic one-piece unit. The quality of the paintwork ranged from fair to lousy; however, most of the models featured window glazing and interiors (the 1/43 models also had suspension). And, as they were models of well-known marques, they represent part of the history of die cast toys and models.

At some point during the late 1970s or early 1980s, Milton Morgan apparently changed its name and eventually wound up merging with (or simply taking over) the company known as Maxwell. To confuse things even more, they also did business for a short period under the name "Miltan."

The following listing is comprised of those models produced during the first half of the 1970s. Models are 1/43 scale except where noted. (Milton Morgan models came in individual boxes.)

Milton #305 Chevrolet Impala "State Patrol" car with original box. Note the sloppily applied silver trim paint.

| # | Name | Price |
|---|------|-------|
| 201 | Volkswagen 1200 (1/90 scale) | $20 |
| 202 | Mercedes-Benz 220 Coupe (1/90 scale) | 15 |
| 203 | Pontiac Firebird (1/90 scale) | 20 |
| 204 | BMW 507 (1/90 scale) | 15 |
| 205 | Austin-Healey (1/90 scale) | 15 |
| 301 | Flat Truck (1/70 scale) | 10 |
| 302 | Open Truck (1/70 scale) | 10 |
| 303 | Chevrolet Impala | 30 |
| 304 | Plymouth Suburban | 30 |
| 305 | Chevrolet Impala State Patrol | 30 |
| 306 | Chevrolet Impala Taxi | 30 |
| 307 | Plymouth Suburban Ambulance | 30 |
| 308 | Chevrolet Impala Police Car | 30 |
| 309 | Chevrolet Impala Fire Chief | 30 |
| 310 | Studebaker Golden Hawk | 40 |
| 311 | Lumber Truck (1/70 scale) | 10 |
| 312 | Army Ambulance (1/70 scale) | 10 |
| 313 | Royal Mail Van (1/70 scale) | 15 |
| 314 | Articulated Tank Truck "CALTEX" (1/50 scale) | 40 |

| # | Name | Price |
|---|------|-------|
| 314 | Articulated Tank Truck "MOBILGAS" (1/50 scale) | $40 |
| 314 | Articulated Tank Truck "BURMAH-SHELL" (1/50 scale) | 40 |
| 314 | Articulated Tank Truck "ESSO" (1/50 scale) | 40 |
| 314 | Articulated Tank Truck "INDIAN OIL" (1/50 scale) | 40 |
| 315 | Articulated Refrigeration Truck (1/50 scale) | 35 |
| 316 | Luxury Coach (1/50 scale) | 50 |
| 317 | Articulated Lumber Transporter (1/50 scale) | 35 |
| 319 | Commer Van "MILTON" | 40 |
| 320 | Commer Ambulance | 40 |
| 321 | Commer Army Ambulance | 40 |
| 322 | Commer School Bus | 40 |
| 323 | Commer Pick-up | 40 |
| 324 | Commer Open Truck | 40 |
| 325 | Commer Milk Van | 40 |

| # | Name | Price |
|---|------|-------|
| 327 | Jaguar 3.8 Saloon | $40 |
| 329 | Ford Mustang | 35 |
| 330 | Foden Tank Truck "CALTEX" (1/50 scale) | 55 |
| 331 | Foden Tank Truck "BURMAH-SHELL" (1/50 scale) | 55 |
| 332 | Commer Fruit Carrier | 40 |
| 333 | Morris Mini Minor | 50 |
| 334 | Commer "COCA-COLA" Truck | 55 |
| 335 | Tractor and Trailer | 40 |
| 336 | Ford Model T | 25 |
| 337 | D.D. Bus "INSIST ON MILTON MINI CARS" (1/50 scale) | 50 |
| 338 | Tipping Truck (1/50 scale) | 20 |
| 341 | Racing Car | 20 |
| 342 | Roadster | 20 |
| 344 | Ladder Truck (1/70 scale) | 10 |
| 349 | Mini Bus | 25 |

# Morestone

Morestone is a name that is intertwined with a number of others in die cast toy history. In the late 1940s, Morris & Stone, a British toy distributor, launched their "Morestone" series of die cast toys. Some of the toys were manufactured by outside vendors, including Modern Products, and the toys varied in scale from 1/38 to about 1/70 (although the smaller Fire Escape was much smaller, at about 2 1/2 inches in length). Early toys included items such as a Horse-Drawn Snack Bar, and an Air Compressor with wheels and a tow bar. And, during the mid-'50s, Morestone put out a series of four Foden trucks in approximately 1/50 scale that are now highly sought by collectors (see photos).

Morris & Stone opened its own die casting facility in 1954; they reportedly continued to use other manufacturers

to make their toys, as well. They also continued to market the toys of Modern Products. In 1956, Morestone debuted its "Esso Petrol Pump Series," which was made up of 1/70 and 1/80 scale cars and trucks, sold in "Esso" gas pump-style boxes. They were one-piece castings with a baseplate, and excellent to near mint examples can be hard to find today since the paint quality was poor on some of the toys. The name of this series was changed in 1959 to "Budgie Miniatures," joined that year by the larger Budgie series of 1/43 to 1/60 scale cars and trucks. In 1961, Morris & Stone was purchased by S. Guiterman & Co. Ltd. Guiterman gave the Morestone division a new name: Budgie Models Ltd.

For further information on the development of the Budgie series, please see the Budgie section in this book.

The four Morestone 8-wheel Foden trucks. From left to right: Open Lorry, Petrol Tanker, Flat Lorry and Flat Lorry with chains. As was typical of Morestone products, the models have no window glazing or interiors.

The four Fodens shared the same style box. Shown here is a side panel for the Flat Lorry with Chains (called the #3 "14 Ton Milk Delivery Wagon" by Morestone).

*Underside detail of the Flat Lorry; for some reason, the axles have orange paint on them. This may indicate that Morestone sprayed the entire baseplate/ axle/wheel hub assembly at the same time.*

By the time the name changed to Budgie Miniatures, the Esso Petrol Pump series had reached twenty models. Along with the general Morestone die cast toys, those first twenty Esso Petrol Pumps are listed here. At the time of the change, a number of the Esso Petrol Pump models were discontinued, and therefore never appeared as Budgie Miniatures. Included in this category are models such as the #6 Cooper-Bristol Racing Car and the #4 AA Bedford Van.

Morestone toys came in a variety of boxes, each featuring artwork of the toy. At some point the box for the Esso Petrol Pump series changed from the gas pump style to a more standard format. These newer boxes showed artwork of the vehicle, and said either "Mobile Vehicle Series" or "Modern Vehicle Series." (These newer boxes seem to have been used at the same time that the series was being packaged in Budgie "bubble packs.") As with any older toy, boxes for Morestone toys are scarce.

| Name | Price |
|---|---|
| **Trucks of the World International series (1958):** | |
| Scammell Articulated Tank Truck | $65 |
| International Articulated Refrigeration Lorry | 65 |
| Klückner Side Tipping Truck | 100 |
| **Esso Petrol Pump Series:** | |
| 1 AA Motorcycle and Sidecar | 35 |
| 2 RAC Motorcycle and Sidecar | 35 |
| 3 AA Land Rover | 25 |
| 4 AA Bedford Van | 25 |
| 5 Wolseley 6/80 Police Car | 20 |
| 6 Cooper-Bristol Racing Car | 20 |
| 7 Mercedes-Benz Racing Car | 20 |
| 8 Volkswagen 1200 Sedan | 30 |
| 9 Maudslay Horse Box | 30 |
| 10 Karrier GPO Telephones Van | 30 |
| 11 Morris Commercial Van | 20 |
| 12 Volkswagen Microbus | 30 |
| 13 Austin FX3 Taxi | 40 |
| 14 Packard Convertible | 30 |
| 15 Austin A95 Westminster Countryman | 20 |
| 16 Austin-Healey 100 | 35 |
| 17 Ford Thames 5 cwt. Van | 50 |
| 18 Foden Dumper | 20 |
| 19 Rover 105R | 20 |
| 20 Plymouth Belvedere Convertible | 30 |

| Name | Price |
|---|---|
| **Other Morestone products:** | |
| Racing Car | $50 |
| Stage Coach with 4 horses | 90 |
| Fire Escape (large) | 90 |
| Fire Escape (smaller) | 60 |
| Fire Engine (clockwork motor with bell) | 100 |
| 0-6-0 Tank Locomotive | 40 |
| Horse Drawn Snack Bar | 110 |
| Horse Drawn Hansom Cab | 55 |
| Horse Drawn Covered Wagon with 4 Horses | 75 |
| Wells Fargo Stage Coach with 2 Galloping Horses | 90 |
| Wells Fargo Stage Coach (4 horses) | 90 |
| Stage Coach with 2 horses | 90 |
| Horse Drawn Covered Wagon with Six Horses | 90 |
| Road Sweeper | 125 |
| Compressor | 60 |
| State Landau with 6 horses | 45 |
| Prime Mover with Trailer | 45 |
| Sleigh with Father Xmas | 90 |
| RAC Motorcycle and Sidecar | 125 |
| AA Motorcycle and Sidecar | 125 |
| RAC Motorcycle and Sidecar | 125 |
| AA Motorcycle and Sidecar | 125 |
| Solo Motorcycle | 70 |
| Horse Drawn Gipsy Caravan | 150 |

| Name | Price |
|---|---|
| Bedford Dormobile | $175 |
| Leyland Double Deck Bus | 125 |
| Aveling-Barford Road Roller | 50 |
| Wolseley 6/80 Police Car | 75 |
| Foden 8-wheel Petrol Tanker | 125 |
| Foden 8-wheel Open Lorry | 125 |
| Foden Flat Lorry with chains | 125 |
| Foden 8-wheel Flat Lorry | 125 |
| Bedford Car Transporter | 125 |
| Daimler Ambulance | 110 |
| AA Land Rover (4 1/4 inches) | 150 |
| AA Land Rover (3 inches) | 110 |
| Military Police Land Rover | 200 |
| Breakdown Service Land Rover | 110 |
| Foden Dumper | 45 |
| **"Noddy" character toys:** | |
| Noddy and His Car (about 4 inches) | 100 |
| Noddy and His Car (about 2 inches) | 60 |
| Big Ears on Bicycle (about 2 1/2 inches) | 100 |
| Big Ears on Bicycle (about 1 3/4 inches) | 70 |
| Clown on Bicycle (about 2 1/2 inches) | 90 |
| Noddy on Bicycle with Trailer | 75 |
| Noddy's Garage Set | 150 |

# Motor City U.S.A.

**T**his North Hollywood, California-based company produces 1/43 scale white metal models of 1940s through 1960s automobiles. The models are hand-built to a high standard, and are very highly detailed and accurate.

In addition to the regular Motor City models (designated with an "MC" prefix in the listing), the company manufactures and sells the "Design Studio" line, which are also 1/43 scale hand-built units. The same applies to the Design Studio "Rods & Customs" series, which is comprised of custom cars and hot rods of the 1950s.

Motor City generally builds 100 to 200 of each model, and sells them direct to customers who place orders with the firm. The models can also be occasionally found at shows and through other dealers.

The following listing indicates the value of each model to be CRP (Current Retail Price). This ranges from a low of $175 to a high of about $250.

*Motor City U.S.A.'s #MC36 1952 Hudson Hornet Hollywood. It is part of the "Distinctive Hudson Series."*

*This #MC41 1959 Nash Metropolitan Convertible was not listed on Motor City's September 1995 product list, so it may have been discontinued.*

| # | Name | Price |
|---|------|-------|

# MOTOR CITY MODELS

### The Distinctive Hudson Series:
| MC17 | 1949 Hudson Commodore Four Door Sedan | CRP |
| MC17T | 1949 Hudson Commodore Four Door Sedan (two-tone) | CRP |
| MC36 | 1952 Hudson Hornet Hollywood Hardtop | CRP |
| MC37 | 1952 Hudson Hornet Convertible | CRP |
| MC37U | 1952 Hudson Hornet Convertible (top up) | CRP |
| MC38 | 1952 Hudson Hornet Coupe | CRP |

### The Distinctive Cadillac Series:
| MC19 | 1949 Cadillac 62 Sedanet | CRP |
| MC20 | 1949 Cadillac 62 Coupe de Ville | CRP |
| MC21 | 1949 Cadillac Convertible (top up or down) | CRP |

### The 1949 Buick Series:
| MC26 | 1949 Buick Riviera Hardtop | CRP |
| MC27 | 1949 Buick Roadmaster Convertible | CRP |

### The Beautiful 1955 Cadillac Series:
| MC28 | 1955 Cadillac Series 75 Limousine | CRP |
| MC29 | 1955 Cadillac 62 Convertible | CRP |
| MC30 | 1955 Cadillac 62 Coupe de Ville | CRP |

### The Deluxe 1956 Chevrolet Series:
| MC31 | 1956 Chevrolet Bel Air Convertible (top down) | CRP |
| MC31U | 1956 Chevrolet Bel Air Convertible (top up) | CRP |
| MC32 | 1956 Chevrolet Bel Air Hardtop | CRP |
| MC33 | 1956 Chevrolet Bel Air Four Door Hardtop | CRP |

### The Elegant Buick Skylark Series:
| MC40 | 1954 Buick Skylark Convertible | CRP |

### The 1955 Pontiac Series:
| MC42 | 1955 Pontiac Star Chief Convertible | CRP |
| MC42U | 1955 Pontiac Star Chief Convertible (top up) | CRP |
| MC43 | 1955 Pontiac Custom Catalina Hardtop | CRP |
| MC48 | 1955 Pontiac Safari Station Wagon | CRP |

### The Marvelous 1956 Chrysler Series:
| MC44 | 1956 Chrysler New Yorker St. Regis Hardtop | CRP |
| MC45 | 1956 Chrysler New Yorker Convertible | CRP |

### The 1950 Pontiac Series:
| MC46 | 1950 Pontiac Convertible (top down) | CRP |
| MC47 | 1950 Pontiac Catalina Hardtop | CRP |

### The 1951 Ford Series:
| MC51 | 1951 Ford Victoria Hardtop | CRP |
| MC52 | 1951 Ford Convertible (top down) | CRP |

### The Packard Series:
| MC49 | 1954 Packard Caribbean Convertible | CRP |
| MC53 | 1949 Packard Convertible (top down) | CRP |
| MC53U | 1949 Packard Convertible (top up) | CRP |

### The DeSoto Series:
| MC59 | 1949 DeSoto Custom Convertible (top up or down) | CRP |

### The 1948 Chevrolet Series:
| MC60 | 1948 Chevrolet Fleetline Aero Sedan | CRP |
| MC61 | 1948 Chevrolet Fleetmaster Convertible | CRP |
| MC61U | 1948 Chevrolet Fleetmaster Convertible (top up) | CRP |
| MC62 | 1948 Chevrolet Indy Pace Car | CRP |

### The 1947 Ford Series:
| MC56 | 1947 Ford Sportsman (Woody) Convertible (top down) | CRP |
| MC56U | 1947 Ford Sportsman (Woody) Convertible (top up) | CRP |

### The 1955 Lincoln Series:
| MC64 | 1955 Lincoln Capri Convertible (top down) | CRP |
| MC64U | 1955 Lincoln Capri Convertible (top up) | CRP |
| MC65 | 1955 Lincoln Capri Convertible Hardtop | CRP |

### The 1955 Chrysler Series:
| MC66 | 1955 Chrysler Imperial Hardtop Coupe | CRP |

### The Oldsmobile Series:
| MC67 | 1956 Oldsmobile Starfire Convertible | CRP |
| MC69 | 1950 Oldsmobile 88 Convertible | CRP |

### The Special Vehicle Series:
| MC9AMB | 1953 Chevrolet Ambulance, Body by National | CRP |

### Limited Editions:
| MC4G | 1955 Chevrolet Bel Air Hardtop | CRP |
| MC9AMS | 1953 Chevrolet Ambulance, Body by National | CRP |
| MC23 | 1950 Ford Yellow Cab | CRP |
| MC50 | 1967 Corvette Convertible | CRP |

### The Deluxe 1953 Chevy Series:
| MC7 | 1953 Chevrolet Bel Air Hardtop | CRP |
| MC8 | 1953 Chevrolet Bel Air Convertible (top down) | CRP |

### 
| MC8U | 1953 Chevrolet Bel Air Convertible (top up) | CRP |
| MC9 | 1953 Chevrolet Sedan Delivery "Smitty's Muffler" | CRP |

### The Deluxe 1950 Ford Series:
| MC10 | 1950 Ford Custom Convertible (top down) | CRP |
| MC10C | 1950 Ford Custom Convertible | CRP |
| MC10U | 1950 Ford Custom Convertible (top up) | CRP |
| MC10A | 1950 Ford Custom Four Door Sedan | CRP |
| MC11 | 1950 Ford Club Coupe | CRP |
| MC12 | 1950 Ford Tudor Sedan | CRP |
| MC13 | 1950 Ford "Woody" Station Wagon | CRP |
| MC14 | 1950 Ford Crestliner | CRP |

### The Deluxe 1955 Ford Series:
| MC15 | 1955 Ford Sunliner Convertible | CRP |
| MC15U | 1955 Ford Sunliner Convertible (top up) | CRP |
| MC16 | 1955 Ford Crown Victoria | CRP |

### DESIGN STUDIO MODELS:
| DS-09 | 1940 Ford Convertible (top down) | CRP |
| DS-09U | 1940 Ford Convertible (top up) | CRP |
| DS-09C | 1940 Ford Coupe | CRP |
| DS-10 | 1955 Mercury Sunvalley | CRP |
| DS-10C | 1955 Mercury Convertible (top down) | CRP |
| DS-10H | 1955 Mercury Monterey Hardtop | CRP |
| DS-11 | 1950 Nash Rambler Convertible | CRP |
| DS-12 | 1949 Nash Ambassador Four Door | CRP |
| DS-14 | 1957 Chevrolet Nomad Station Wagon | CRP |
| DS-15 | 1951 Lincoln Cosmopolitan Convertible (top down) | CRP |
| DS-17 | 1954 Buick Century Hardtop | CRP |
| DS-19 | 1951 Chevrolet Bel Air Hardtop | CRP |
| DS-54 | 1958 Oldsmobile 98 Convertible (top down) | CRP |
| DS-55 | 1958 Oldsmobile 98 Hardtop | CRP |
| W-36 | 1941 Buick Century Sedanet | CRP |

### DESIGN STUDIO RODS & CUSTOMS MODELS:
| DS-200 | 1940 Mercury Custom Coupe | CRP |
| DS-201 | 1949 Mercury Custom Tudor | CRP |
| DS-202 | 1940 Ford Custom Convertible | CRP |
| DS-203 | 1940 Ford Street Rod Coupe | CRP |
| DS-204 | 1940 Ford Street Rod Coupe | CRP |
| DS-205 | 1934 Ford Three Window Coupe | CRP |
| DS-206 | 1940 Ford Custom Top Down Convertible | CRP |
| DS-207 | 1940 Mercury "Modern Custom" Coupe | CRP |

# Nacoral

This company got its start in the mid-1960s, making die cast models of a variety of different marques. The models were called "Inter-Cars," and they came in clear plastic display boxes. The cars were 1/43 scale, with the trucks being 1/50 scale. The model was screwed to a plastic base inside the box. Included in the Inter-Cars line were models of Porsches, Land Rovers and American makes like Chevrolet and Ford.

The models were fair to good in the accuracy department, but they suffered from ill-fitting opening parts such as hoods and doors. Adding to the problem on many of the models were chrome-painted bumpers and grilles that were too large; they also often didn't fit correctly. Nacorals came with interiors and window glazing, and many of them also featured suspension.

Nacoral had dealings with the Belgian company Sablon; nine of Nacoral's models were re-issues of Sablon products. Sablon had originally manufactured these models starting in 1968 as part of a promotion for the Belgian chocolate candy manufacturer, "Jacques." Sometime around 1970, after production had ceased, Sablon passed the tooling on to Nacoral. The models are numbered 1 through 9 in the listing.

Values listed are for near mint or better examples in their original display boxes.

*Nacoral Inter-Cars #101 Chevrolet Corvette. The "Mobil" and Shell stickers are original; stickers were placed on many of the Nacoral sports/exotic cars.*

*The #201 Volvo FB 89 Covered Truck by Nacoral. The rear cover is plastic.*

| # | Name | Price | # | Name | Price | # | Name | Price |
|---|------|-------|---|------|-------|---|------|-------|
| 1 | Porsche 911 Targa Roadster | $30 | 100 | Mercedes-Benz 280 | $25 | 109 | Lamborghini Espada | $25 |
| 1 | Porsche 911 Targa Hardtop | 30 | 101 | Chevrolet Corvette | 35 | 110 | Lamborghini Marzal | 25 |
| 2 | Mercedes-Benz 250SE | 25 | 102 | Ford Mustang Fastback | 35 | 111 | Mercedes-Benz C III | 25 |
| 3 | Renault 16 | 25 | 102 | Ford Mustang Fastback Rally | 30 | 112 | Morris Mini 1000 Rally | 25 |
| 4 | BMW 2000 CS | 25 | 103 | Chevrolet Camaro | 30 | 113 | Ferrari Dino Pinin Farina | 35 |
| 5 | BMW 1600 | 25 | 104 | AMX Coupe | 30 | 114 | Land Rover Guardia Civil | 25 |
| 6 | Lamborghini Marzal | 25 | 105 | Ford Thunderbird | 30 | 115 | Land Rover Safari | 25 |
| 7 | N.S.U. Ro80 | 25 | 106 | De Tomaso Mangusta | 25 | 116 | Land Rover Zoo | 25 |
| 8 | BMW 1600 GT | 25 | 107 | Ferrari P4 | 35 | 117 | Land Rover Wrecker | 25 |
| 9 | BMW-Glas 3000 GT | 25 | 108 | Matra 630 Le Mans | 25 | 118 | Land Rover Fire | 25 |

| # | Name | Price | # | Name | Price | # | Name | Price |
|---|---|---|---|---|---|---|---|---|
| 119 | Rolls-Royce Silver Cloud III | $25 | 211 | Mercedes 1919 S Tanker "ESSO" | $35 | 506 | Scania Vabis 140 Army Truck | $30 |
| 120 | Fiat 127 | 25 | 212 | Trailer for 211 | 35 | 507 | Jeep with Cannon | * |
| 121 | Volvo 144 | 25 | 213 | Scania Vabis 140 Tanker "SHELL" | 35 | | Ferrari Formula I (1/66) | 15 |
| 122 | Volvo 145 Station Wagon | 25 | 214 | Trailer for 213 | 15 | | B.R.M. Formula I (1/66) | 10 |
| 123 | Saab 99 | 25 | 215 | Scania Vabis 140 Milk Tanker | 35 | | Lotus 49 B Formula I (1/66) | 10 |
| 124 | Volvo 244 DL | 25 | 216 | Trailer for 215 | 15 | | Honda Formula I (1/66) | 10 |
| 125 | Volvo 245 DL Station Wagon | 25 | 301 | Alfa Romeo 33 Pinin Farina | 20 | | Brabham-Repco Formula I (1/66) | 10 |
| 126 | Matra Simca Bagheera | 25 | 302 | Sigma Grand Prix | 30 | 2003M | Morris 1100 | 25 |
| 127 | Mercedes-Benz 350 SL Coupe | 25 | 303 | Fiat 508 Balilla Coppa d'oro | 20 | 2005M | Seat 600 Rally | 25 |
| 128 | Ford Fiesta | 25 | 304 | Alfa Romeo Carabo Bertone | 20 | 2007M | Citroën 2 CV Van | 25 |
| 201 | Volvo FB 89 Covered Truck | 30 | 305 | Panther Bertone | 20 | 2009M | Renault R 16 | 25 |
| 202 | Trailer for 201 | 15 | 306 | Dragster Fiat 508 | 20 | 2010M | Porsche 912 | 25 |
| 203 | Scania Vabis 140 Covered Truck | 30 | 307 | Alfa Romeo Montreal | 20 | 2011M | Maserati Mistral | 25 |
| 204 | Trailer for 203 | 15 | 308 | Bizzarrini Manta | 20 | 2012M | Mercedes-Benz 250 SE | 25 |
| 205 | Scania Vabis 140 Tanker "TOTAL" | 35 | 309 | Alfa Romeo Pinin Farina | 20 | 2013M | Porsche Carrera 6 | 25 |
| 206 | Trailer for 205 | 15 | 500 | Patton Tank | 30 | 2014M | Ford GT 40 | 25 |
| 207 | Mercedes 1919 S Covered Truck | 30 | 501 | Sherman Tank | 30 | 2021M | Ferrari Dino Pinin Farina | 35 |
| 208 | Trailer for 207 | 15 | 502 | Army Jeep | 25 | | | |
| 209 | Volvo FB 89 Tanker "ESSO" | 35 | 503 | Cannon | 15 | | *  May not have been issued | |
| 210 | Trailer for 209 | 15 | 505 | Land Rover Ambulance | * | | | |

# Nicky Toys

**I**t is no coincidence that "Nicky" sounds like "Dinky." Nor is it by chance that both names have five letters. In 1968, when Meccano gave the tooling for a number of Dinky Toys to the firm S. Kumar & Co. of Calcutta, India, the parties involved wanted to capitalize on the world-wide recognition that Dinky Toys enjoyed. Unable to use the actual Dinky name, they settled for something close.

Kumar used the name Atamco Private Ltd. for the Nicky series of toys; in fact, Atamco appeared on some of the boxes the toys came in. Since the dies that Meccano gave to Kumar were by then quite worn, the quality of the toys was sub-standard. The same was true of the paint finish, and the majority of the wheels used on these toys were simply horrendous. The fact that the models featured window glazing and interiors didn't help much.

The baseplates on some of the Nicky Toys have the Dinky name removed, while on others the name is quite visible. Apparently Kumar did not see removal of the name as being a high priority.

In their definitive book *Dinky Toys & Modelled Miniatures*, Mike and Sue Richardson point out that the choice of models in the Nicky line was puzzling, since cars such as Jaguars and Plymouths were not seen in India.

It appears that Nicky Toys were made until 1970 or '71, after which point they disappeared. The boxes varied; some were made specifically for Nicky Toys, while others were left-over stock from Meccano that Kumar merely altered by hand with a pen to read "Nicky." *Note:* It is not certain that the #949 Wayne School Bus was ever produced as a Nicky Toy. Also, although Meccano listed the #146 Daimler as being part of the Nicky line, it was actually Dinky #195, the Jaguar 3.4, that was used.

| # | Name | Price | # | Name | Price | # | Name | Price |
|---|---|---|---|---|---|---|---|---|
| 113 | MGB | $40 | 170 | Lincoln Continental | $40 | 405 | Universal Jeep | $40 |
| 115 | Plymouth Fury Convertible | 40 | 186 | Mercedes-Benz 220 SE | 40 | 405 | Universal Army Jeep | 40 |
| 115 | Plymouth Fury Hardtop | 40 | 186 | Mercedes-Benz 220 SE Taxi | 50 | 626 | Military Ambulance | 40 |
| 120 | Jaguar E-Type | 40 | 194 | Bentley S Coupe | 40 | 660/908 | Mighty Antar Tank Transporter | 75 |
| 134 | Triumph Vitesse | 40 | 238 | Jaguar D Type | 40 | 693 | Howitzer | 20 |
| 142 | Jaguar Mk X | 40 | 239 | Vanwall | 40 | 949 | Wayne School Bus | * |
| 144 | Volkswagen 1500 | 50 | 295 | Standard 20 Mini Bus (Atlas Kenebrake) | 40 | 962 | Dumper Truck (civilian and military versions) | 60 |
| 144 | Volkswagen 1500 Police | 50 | 295 | Standard 20 Mini Bus (Atlas Kenebrake) Ambulance | 40 | | | |
| 146 | Daimler (Jaguar 3.4) | 40 | | | | | *  May not have been issued by Nicky Toys | |
| 146 | Daimler (Jaguar 3.4) Police | 40 | | | | | | |

# Norev

Norev had its beginnings in the French industrial city of Lyon in 1946. Joseph Veron, the founder, merely turned around his last name to make the company name, and Norev began producing a variety of toys. The Norev line included toy watches and a tinplate toy garage with two cars and two trucks.

Norev introduced a series of 1/43 scale plastic models in 1953, and soon after built a new factory in the town of Villeurbanne. (In 1961, Emil Veron, who was part of the same family as Norev's founder, would launch the Majorette company in Villeurbanne.) From 1953 until the early 1970s, Norev turned out an enormous variety of plastic models.

*This Volvo Milk Tanker was #523 in the Maxi-Jet series. Much of the tanker assembly is plastic, while the cab and chassis are die cast.*

*The #886 Volvo 264. This example was made in Portugal by Cinerius (Minibri) in the late 1980s.*

French makes figured prominently, of course, but British names like Rolls-Royce and Austin were also to be included, as were Mercedes-Benz and Volkswagen.

The Norev products were well-made and very accurate. But with the demise of French Dinky in the early 1970s, Norev seized the opportunity to fill the gap in the market for cheaper die cast models. The initial result was the "Cometal" series in 1971, which was what might be termed a "hybrid" series: the bodies were plastic but the baseplates were die cast metal.

It would be the "Jet-Car" series, though, that would prove to be the big seller, starting in the early 1970s. This 1/43 scale series included French marques such as Peugeot and Renault, as well as Volvos, BMWs and Fords. The Jet-Cars were very good quality castings, and those made up until the late 1970s had a number of opening parts. Unfortunately, these parts were gradually phased out, while at the same time lower-quality "speed"-type wheels crept into the line.

Meanwhile, Norev also produced, from 1975 until 1985, a smaller (approximately 1/72 scale) die cast vehicle series entitled "Mini-Jet," to compete with Matchbox and Majorette.

Norev continued producing its models into the 1980s, and in 1986 entered into a manufacturing agreement with Cinerius of Portugal (makers of the Vitesse line of die cast models). These models still bore the Norev name, but the baseplates state that they were made in Portugal.

In the late 1980s, Norev released a "new" line of models aimed at the adult collector market. They were plastic re-issues of old Norev models, but the tooling had been re-worked to produce models that were more detailed than the originals. And other old Norev tooling eventually found its way into the hands of the Louis Surber company, who re-issued a number of the old Norevs (which originally had been plastic) in die cast form as part of the Eligor series. See the section on Eligor for more information.

Another new venture for Norev was the "Ligne Noire" series. This line premiered around 1992 and was comprised of 1/43 scale plastic models of very unusual French cars. They were very highly detailed models, but were perhaps too expensive for their intended market. No new releases have been seen since 1994. In fact, it is believed that Norev has gone out of business.

The following listing is comprised of Norev's die cast models made through the years. The majority of the models were part of the Jet-Car series, but the models numbered in the 500s were part of the "Maxi-Jet" series of 1/43 scale trucks (Maxi-Jets had die cast chassis and cabs, but plastic rear sections). This listing represents the basic castings only; for more information on the myriad of variations that appeared on these models, the reader is advised to consult Dr. Edward Force's *Classic Miniature Vehicles Made in France*, details of which may be found in Part Three, Additional Resources.

| # | Name | Price |
|---|------|-------|
| **Mini-Jet (1/72 scale) series:** | | |
| 400 | Citroën BX | $5 |
| 401 | Ligier JS2 | 5 |
| 402 | Matra Bagheera | 5 |
| 404 | Citroën GS | 5 |
| 405 | Peugeot 504 | 5 |
| 406 | Citroën CX | 5 |
| 407 | Renault 12 | 5 |
| 408 | Citroën Dyane | 5 |
| 409 | Renault 4L | 5 |
| 410 | Mercedes-Benz Ambulance | 5 |
| 411 | Maserati Boomerang | 5 |
| 412 | Bertone Trapeze | 5 |
| 413 | Renault 30TS | 5 |
| 414 | Peugeot 604 | 5 |
| 415 | Simca 1308GT | 5 |
| 415 | Talbot 1500SX | 5 |
| 416 | BMW 633 CSI | 5 |
| 417 | Fiat 1315 | 5 |
| 418 | Porsche Turbo | 5 |
| 419 | Renault 14 | 5 |
| 420 | Peugeot 305SR | 5 |
| 421 | Simca | 5 |
| 421 | Talbot Horizon | 5 |
| 422 | Renault 18GTS | 5 |
| 423 | Volvo 264 | 5 |
| 424 | Ford Mustang | 5 |
| 425 | Mercedes-Benz 280SE | 5 |
| 428 | Citroën Visa | 5 |
| 429 | Volkswagen Golf | 5 |
| 430 | Alfa Romeo 6 | 5 |
| 431 | Peugeot 505 | 5 |
| 432 | Fiat Ritmo | 5 |
| 433 | Volvo F89 Crane Truck | 5 |
| 434 | Volvo F89 Fire Engine | 5 |
| 435 | Volvo F89 Tanker | 5 |
| 436 | Volvo F89 Covered Truck | 5 |
| 437 | Renault Fuego | 5 |
| 438 | Ford Escort | 5 |
| 439 | Talbot Solara | 5 |
| 440 | Volvo F89 Milk Tanker | 5 |
| 441 | Volvo F89 Propane Tanker | 5 |
| 442 | Volvo F89 Ladder Truck | 5 |
| 443 | Volvo F89 Container Truck | 5 |
| 445 | Renault Cherry Picker | 5 |
| 446 | Renault Cement Truck | 5 |
| 447 | Renault Bucket Truck | 5 |
| 448 | Renault Dump Truck | 5 |
| 449 | Renault Container Truck | 5 |
| 450 | Renault 9 | 5 |
| 451 | Citroën BX | 5 |
| 452 | Renault Garbage Truck | 5 |
| 460 | Chevrolet Camper Pick-up | 5 |
| 461 | Chevrolet Fire Van | 5 |
| 462 | Chevrolet Covered Truck | 5 |
| 463 | Chevrolet Camper with Surfboard | 5 |

| # | Name | Price |
|---|------|-------|
| 464 | Chevrolet Wrecker | $5 |
| 465 | Chevrolet Pick-up | 5 |
| 466 | Chevrolet Airport Truck | 5 |
| 467 | Chevrolet Cattle Truck | 5 |
| 468 | Chevrolet Pick-up with Motorcycle | 5 |
| **Maxi-Jet series:** | | |
| 508 | Saviem Breakdown Truck | 15 |
| 509 | Daf Breakdown Truck | 15 |
| 510 | Volvo Breakdown Truck | 15 |
| 515 | Saviem Drinks Truck | 15 |
| 516 | Daf Drinks Truck | 15 |
| 517 | Volvo Drinks Truck | 15 |
| 518 | Saviem Mobile Shop | 15 |
| 519 | Daf Mobile Shop | 15 |
| 520 | Volvo Mobile Shop | 15 |
| 521 | Saviem Milk Tanker | 15 |
| 522 | Daf Milk Tanker | 15 |
| 523 | Volvo Milk Tanker | 15 |
| 524 | Saviem Fire Engine | 15 |
| 525 | Daf Fire Engine | 15 |
| 526 | Volvo Fire Engine | 15 |
| 527 | Saviem/Renault Cattle Truck | 15 |
| 528 | Daf Cattle Truck | 15 |
| 529 | Volvo Cattle Truck | 15 |
| 530 | Saviem Elevator Truck | 15 |
| 531 | Daf Elevator Truck | 15 |
| 532 | Volvo Elevator Truck | 15 |
| 533 | Caravan | 15 |
| 534 | Saviem Circus Truck | 15 |
| 535 | Daf Circus Truck | 15 |
| 536 | Volvo Circus Truck | 15 |
| 537 | Saviem Box Van "Norev" | 15 |
| 538 | Daf Box Van "Norev" | 15 |
| 539 | Volvo Box Van "Norev" | 15 |
| **Jet-Car series:** | | |
| 601 | Matra F1 | 20 |
| 603 | DKW Junior | 30 |
| 604 | Volkswagen 1500 | 30 |
| 606 | Simca 1500 | 30 |
| 607 | Fiat 1500 | 30 |
| 609 | Citroën 2CV Van | 25 |
| 610 | Renault 4L | 30 |
| 612 | Citroën 2CV AZ Luxe | 30 |
| 613 | Volkswagen 1300 | 30 |
| 701 | Peugeot 404 Coupe | 35 |
| 702 | Fiat 2300S Coupe | 25 |
| 703 | Simca 1000 Coupe | 25 |
| 704 | Ford Taunus 12M | 25 |
| 705 | Ford Cortina | 25 |
| 706 | Fiat 124 | 25 |
| 707 | Simca 1100 S | 25 |
| 707 | Talbot 1100 S | 10 |
| 708 | Volkswagen 1600 | 35 |
| 708 | Renault 5TL various liveries | 10 |
| 709 | Mercedes C111 | 15 |

| # | Name | Price |
|---|------|-------|
| 710 | Ligier JS3 | $15 |
| 711 | Renault 5TL | 15 |
| 711 | Renault 4F6 Van various liveries | 10 |
| 712 | Porsche 917 | 15 |
| 712 | Alpine Renault A310 | 10 |
| 713 | Lancia Stratos | 10 |
| 714 | Citroën GS Camargue Bertone | 10 |
| 718 | Ligier JS2 | 10 |
| 722 | Citroën 2C V6 | 10 |
| 736 | Fiat X1/9 | 5 |
| 743 | Citroën 2C V6 various liveries | 10 |
| 757 | Peugeot 604 | 10 |
| 761 | Renault 14TL various liveries | 5 |
| 762 | Renault 20 | 5 |
| 764 | Porsche 924 | 5 |
| 773 | Ford Fiesta | 5 |
| 778 | Volkswagen Golf | 10 |
| 779 | Peugeot 305SR various liveries | 10 |
| 780 | Talbot Horizon | 10 |
| 781 | Renault 18TL | 10 |
| 782 | Citroën Visa various liveries | 10 |
| 792 | Ford Escort XR3 | 10 |
| 794 | Citroën BX various liveries | 10 |
| 798 | Renault 9 | 10 |
| 801 | Peugeot 204 Coupe | 35 |
| 801 | Citroën Visa "Rallye" | 5 |
| 802 | Renault 20TL various liveries | 5 |
| 803 | Opel Rekord 1700 | 30 |
| 803 | Peugeot 505 various liveries | 5 |
| 804 | Peugeot 304 | 25 |
| 804 | Renault Fuego various liveries | 5 |
| 805 | Renault 12 | 25 |
| 805 | Renault 12 "Police" | 10 |
| 806 | Citroën DS21 | 25 |
| 806 | Ligier JS3 | 10 |
| 807 | Citroën SM Coupe | 25 |
| 807 | Talbot 1100 S | 10 |
| 808 | Chrysler 180 | 25 |
| 809 | Alpine Renault A220 | 15 |
| 810 | Citroën GS | 20 |
| 811 | Opel 1900GT Coupe | 20 |
| 812 | Alpine A310 | 20 |
| 813 | Lola T294 | 25 |
| 815 | Alfa Romeo 33 | 20 |
| 815 | Renault 18TL | 20 |
| 816 | Alfa Romeo Montreal | 20 |
| 818 | Ligier JS2 | 15 |
| 820 | Maserati Ghibli | 15 |
| 821 | Mercedes-Benz 350SL Coupe | 15 |
| 822 | Renault 15TS | 10 |
| 823 | Renault 17TS Coupe | 10 |
| 824 | Ferrari 246 GTS | 15 |
| 825 | Matra Simca Bagheera | 10 |
| 826 | Peugeot 104 | 10 |
| 828 | Pedalorev | 20 |
| 829 | De Tomaso Pantera GT4 | 15 |

*Norev #807, the Citroën SM. This 1/43 scale car was made during the 1970s.*

| # | Name | Price |
|---|------|-------|
| 830 | Norevbug | $20 |
| 831 | Helicorev | 20 |
| 832 | Matra Simca 670B (short wheelbase) | 15 |
| 833 | Matra Simca 670B (long wheelbase) | 15 |
| 833 | Citroën CX Taxi | 10 |
| 834 | Chevron B23 | 10 |
| 835 | Ferrari 312P | 15 |
| 836 | Fiat X1/9 | 10 |
| 838 | Citroën SM Presidential Cabriolet | 15 |
| 839 | Porsche Carrera 911 RSR various liveries | 15 |
| 840 | Alpine A440 | 10 |
| 841 | Renault 16TX | 10 |
| 842 | Peugeot 504 | 10 |
| 842 | Renault 18T Police | 10 |
| 843 | Renault 18T | 10 |
| 843 | Citroën 2C V6 | 10 |
| 845 | Citroën CX2200 various liveries | 10 |

| # | Name | Price |
|---|------|-------|
| 846 | Renault 17TS | $10 |
| 847 | Fiat X1/9 Abarth | 15 |
| 849 | Peugeot 504 "Police" | 10 |
| 850 | Renault 5TL | 15 |
| 851 | Matra Bagheera with Skis | 10 |
| 852 | Renault 16TX Taxi | 10 |
| 852 | Citroën CX2200 Taxi | 15 |
| 853 | Renault 5TL "Elf" | 10 |
| 853 | Mercedes-Benz 280 Taxi | 10 |
| 853 | Volvo 264 Taxi | 10 |
| 854 | BMW Turbo various liveries | 15 |
| 855 | Alpine A310 "Elf" | 10 |
| 856 | Renault 30TS | 10 |
| 857 | Peugeot 604 various liveries | 15 |
| 858 | Alpine A442 Turbo "Elf" | 10 |
| 859 | Peugeot 504 "Safari" | 10 |
| 860 | Talbot 1510SX | 5 |

| # | Name | Price |
|---|------|-------|
| 861 | Renault 14TL | $10 |
| 862 | Renault 20TL various liveries | 10 |
| 863 | Lancia Stratos "Monte Carlo Rally" | 10 |
| 864 | Porsche 924 various liveries | 10 |
| 865 | Renault 4F6 Van various liveries | 10 |
| 868 | BMW 633 Coupe | 10 |
| 869 | BMW 633 Prototype | 5 |
| 870 | De Tomaso Pantera | 10 |
| 871 | Alpine A310 "Gendarmerie" | 10 |
| 872 | Renault 18 Estate Car "Police" | 10 |
| 873 | Ford Fiesta | 5 |
| 874 | Mercedes-Benz "Binz" ambulance various liveries | 10 |
| 875 | Renault 5 "SOS Medicins" | 10 |
| 876 | Simca 1308 "Europe 1" | 10 |
| 876 | Ferrari 246 GTS "Apple" | 10 |
| 878 | Volkswagen Golf | 10 |
| 879 | Peugeot 305 SR | 10 |
| 880 | Talbot Horizon | 10 |
| 881 | Renault 18TL various liveries | 10 |
| 882 | Citroën Visa Super | 10 |
| 883 | Volkswagen Golf Police | 10 |
| 884 | Volkswagen Golf "ADAC" | 10 |
| 885 | Porsche 924 Police | 10 |
| 886 | Volvo 264 GL various liveries | 10 |
| 887 | Ford Mustang various liveries | 10 |
| 888 | Alfa Romeo 6 various liveries | 10 |
| 889 | Peugeot 505 various liveries | 10 |
| 890 | Mercedes 280 SE | 10 |
| 891 | Renault Fuego Coupe | 10 |
| 892 | Ford Escort various liveries | 10 |
| 893 | Talbot Solara | 10 |
| 895 | Citroën BX | 10 |
| 896 | Volvo 264 Estate various liveries | 10 |
| 897 | Renault 18TL Estate various liveries | 10 |
| 898 | Renault 9 | 10 |
| 899 | Volkswagen Golf GTI | 10 |

# NZG

**N**ZG is a German model manufacturer located in the town of Nürnberg. Since 1968, NZG has produced a line of die cast construction and earth moving vehicle models, as well as buses, farm equipment, and trucks of various descriptions. They also make a number of 1/43 scale Porsche and 1/35 scale Mercedes-Benz passenger car models.

The scale of NZG's models ranges from 1/24 to around 1/87, and they have always been well-made and accurately detailed products. NZG is unusual in that the company tends to keep a model in its product line for many years. It is therefore possible to find a twenty-year old example of a particular model next to an example of the same model made last year. The values in this listing reflect this, with many models being listed as CRP (Current Retail Price), which can vary from $20 to over $100, depending upon the size and complexity of the item.

NZG has always numbered its models in sequential order, which makes dating them easier. The values given for model numbers 101 through 139 (made from 1968 through about 1974) indicate what those obsolete models can sell for on the secondary market. The lowest numbers still in production are in the 140s and 150s.

| # | Name | Price |
|---|------|-------|
| 101 | Weserhütte Trencher | $100 |
| 102 | Fuchs 50 R Trencher | 100 |
| 103 | Caterpillar Bulldozer | 125 |
| 104 | Atlas AB 1702 Trencher | 100 |
| 105 | JCB Excavator Loader | 125 |
| 106 | Massey Ferguson Excavator | 100 |
| 107 | Schaff HR 25 Excavator | 100 |
| 108 | Caterpillar 941 Track Loader with Cab | 75 |
| 109 | JCB 3C II Tractor Loader | 100 |
| 110 | Whitlock 50 R Excavator | 125 |
| 111 | Menck SR 85 Scrapedozer | 135 |
| 112 | Caterpillar 920 Wheel Loader | 75 |
| 113 | Demag H 41 Excavator | 100 |
| 114 | Kramer 411 Excavator | 100 |
| 115 | Caterpillar 955 Loader Ripper | 125 |
| 116 | Caterpillar 955 Loader | 100 |
| 117 | Magirus Deutz Dump Truck | 125 |
| 118 | Broyt X4 Excavator | 90 |
| 119 | Caterpillar D4D Dozer | 75 |
| 120 | Caterpillar D4D Dozer-Ripper | 60 |
| 121 | Caterpillar D4 Tractor-Ripper | 75 |
| 122 | Caterpillar 621 Wheel Scraper | 60 |
| 123 | Demag HC 100 Crane Truck | 75 |
| 124 | Caterpillar B 25 Fork Lift | 35 |
| 125 | Volvo BM-LM 841 Wheel Loader | 75 |
| 126 | Caterpillar 627 Tractor Scraper | 75 |
| 127 | Caterpillar 627 Push-Pull Scraper | 75 |
| 128 | Duomat Double Roller | 60 |
| 129 | Massey-Ferguson Bulldozer | 60 |
| 130 | Ford Excavator Loader | 60 |
| 132 | Caterpillar Rear Dump Hauler | 60 |
| 133 | Fiat Fork Lift | 100 |
| 134 | Caterpillar 988 Wheel Loader | 60 |
| 135 | Caterpillar 825 Compacter | 60 |
| 136 | Grove TM 800 Crane Truck | 60 |
| 139 | Bucyrus Erie Excavator | 60 |
| 140 | Caterpillar 983 Track Loader | CRP |
| 141 | JCB 807 Excavator | CRP |
| 142 | JCB 418 Articulated Loader | CRP |
| 143 | Caterpillar 225 Excavator | CRP |
| 144 | Wagner Electric Truck and Trailer | CRP |
| 145 | Atlas AB 2002 Excavator | CRP |
| 146 | Mercedes-Benz Covered Truck and Trailer | CRP |
| 147 | Clark Lima 2505 Track Backhoe | CRP |
| 148 | Akerman H 25 C Excavator | CRP |
| 149 | Grove TM 800 Crane | CRP |
| 150 | Caterpillar 12 G Motor Grader | CRP |
| 151 | Bomag BW 90 SL Roller | CRP |
| 152 | Grove 120 Crane Truck | CRP |
| 153 | Mercedes-Benz Covered Truck | CRP |
| 154 | Case 2870 Traction King | CRP |
| 155 | Broyt X 4 Excavator | CRP |
| 156 | Case David Brown 1412 Tractor | CRP |
| 157 | Ingersoll Rand SP 60 Roller | CRP |
| 159 | Case 1412 Tractor | CRP |
| 160 | Caterpillar 245 Excavator | CRP |
| 161 | Ford 550 Tractor Loader Backhoe | CRP |
| 162 | 0 & K MH4 Excavator | CRP |

| # | Name | Price |
|---|------|-------|
| 163 | Terex 33-07 Dump Truck | CRP |
| 164 | Terex 82-50 Crawler | CRP |
| 165 | Fuchs 712 Mobile Excavator | CRP |
| 166 | DJB D300 Dumper | CRP |
| 167 | Caterpillar 988B Loader | CRP |
| 168 | Magirus M2000 Tour Bus | CRP |
| 169 | Mercedes 2223 Cement Pump | CRP |
| 170 | Mercedes-Benz Schwing Cement Pump | CRP |
| 172 | Mercedes-Benz 20T Container Truck | CRP |
| 173 | O&K V25 Fork Lift | CRP |
| 174 | Faun HM 1035 Excavator | CRP |
| 175 | JCB 520 Telescopic Lift | CRP |
| 176 | Case 850B Bulldozer | CRP |
| 177 | Caterpillar 245 Excavator | CRP |
| 178 | Coles 36/40 Telescopic Crane | CRP |
| 179 | Broyt X21 Wheel Excavator | CRP |
| 180 | Broyt X21 Track Excavator | CRP |
| 182 | Caterpillar V80D Fork Lift | CRP |
| 183 | Caterpillar 3208 Diesel Engine | CRP |
| 185 | Fuchs X118M Mobile Crane | CRP |
| 186 | Mercedes-Benz Covered Truck | CRP |
| 187 | Mercedes-Benz Container Truck | CRP |
| 188 | RH40 Excavator | CRP |
| 189 | Ingersoll-Rand P175 Compressor | CRP |
| 190 | Caterpillar 215 Excavator | CRP |
| 191 | Kramer Shovel Loader | CRP |
| 192 | Faun-Frisch F1400-C Loader | CRP |
| 193 | O&K TH40 Telescopic Crane | CRP |
| 194 | O&K SH 400 Belt Loader | CRP |
| 195 | Atlas AR41B Loader | CRP |
| 196 | Case 1845 All-Purpose Loader | CRP |
| 197 | Zettelmeyer ZD300 Dozer | CRP |
| 198 | Demag HC 170 Telescopic Crane | CRP |
| 200 | Mercedes-Benz 280 SE | CRP |
| 202 | Demag SC 10DS Compressor | CRP |
| 203 | Ingersoll-Rand DA 50 Roller | CRP |
| 204 | Bucyrus 155 RH Shovel | CRP |
| 205 | Caterpillar D4E Bulldozer | CRP |
| 208 | Case 850B Loader | CRP |
| 209 | Hyster 50 Fork Lift | CRP |

| # | Name | Price |
|---|------|-------|
| 210 | Caterpillar Generator Set | CRP |
| 213 | Ingersoll-Rand 450 Drill | CRP |
| 214 | Case W20B Wheel Loader | CRP |
| 216 | JCB 3CX All-Purpose Loader | CRP |
| 218 | Mercedes-Benz 03500 Oldtimer Bus | CRP |
| 219 | Ford 1981 Covered Truck | CRP |
| 220 | Caterpillar 528 Log Skidder | CRP |
| 221 | Bomag BW 141 AD Roller | CRP |
| 222 | Caterpillar 769C Dump Truck | CRP |
| 223 | Caterpillar 953 Track Loader | CRP |
| 224 | Hamm DV8 Vibrating Roller | CRP |
| 225 | Caterpillar M Series B Fork Lift | CRP |
| 226 | Mercedes-Benz 380/500 SEC | CRP |
| 227 | Ford Cargo Truck and Trailer | CRP |
| 229 | Ingersoll-Rand T4W Drillmaster | CRP |
| 230 | Broyt X50 Shovel Loader | CRP |
| 231 | Demag DF 120C Paver | CRP |
| 232 | O&K G130 Grader | CRP |
| 233 | Caterpillar D8L Dozer Ripper | CRP |
| 234 | Mercedes-Benz Container Truck and Trailer | CRP |
| 235 | Zeppelin 908 Wheel Loader | CRP |
| 236 | Gehl 4610 Loader | CRP |
| 237 | Caterpillar 966D Wheel Loader | CRP |
| 238 | Eder R835-LC Excavator | CRP |
| 239 | Eder M835 Wheel Excavator | CRP |
| 240 | Demag HC 130 Crane | CRP |
| 241 | Demag H185 Shovel | CRP |
| 242 | Schaff SKL 840 Wheel Loader | CRP |
| 245 | Blaw-Knox Paver | CRP |
| 246 | O&K RH 30C Excavator | CRP |
| 247 | Eder Excavator with Krupp Hammer | CRP |
| 248 | Bomag BW 90S Roller | CRP |
| 249 | Mercedes-Benz 709 Covered Truck | CRP |
| 250 | Mercedes-Benz 709 Box Van | CRP |
| 251 | JBC 430 Front Loader | CRP |
| 252 | Mercedes-Benz Covered Truck and Trailer | CRP |
| 253 | Mercedes-Benz Refrigeration Truck | CRP |
| 254 | Mercedes-Benz 190E 2.3 Litre | CRP |

*This Caterpillar Fork Lift, #124 in the NZG product line, started in production in 1973 (this is a more recent example). Even at 1/87 scale, the fork goes up and down and the fork assembly tilts back realistically.*

| # | Name | Price | # | Name | Price | # | Name | Price |
|---|------|-------|---|------|-------|---|------|-------|
| 255 | Mercedes-Benz 0405 Bus | CRP | 286 | JCB 820 Crawler Excavator | CRP | 319 | JLG Boomlift | CRP |
| 256 | Grove MZ JG Manlift | CRP | 287 | O&K MH2 Mobile Shovel | CRP | 320 | Atlas Wheel Loader | CRP |
| 257 | Zeppelin 206R Track Excavator | CRP | 288 | O&K RH2 Track Shovel | CRP | 321 | Kahl Fork Lift Wagon | CRP |
| 258 | Zeppelin 206M Wheel Excavator | CRP | 289 | Mercedes-Benz LN1 Truck | CRP | 322 | Porsche 944 | CRP |
| 259 | Caterpillar 224 Wheel Excavator | CRP | 290 | Blaw-Knox PF 500 Paver | CRP | 323 | Porsche 944 Cabriolet | CRP |
| 260 | Caterpillar 615 Scraper | CRP | 291 | Kramer Allrad 314 Shovel | CRP | 324 | Schaeff Excavator | CRP |
| 261 | Porsche 911 Carrera | CRP | 293 | Scania CN 112 City Bus | CRP | 327 | Porsche 911 Speedster | CRP |
| 262 | Porsche 928S | CRP | 294 | New Holland L555 Lift | CRP | 328 | Wagner Fork Lift | CRP |
| 263 | Porsche 944 | CRP | 295 | Ingersoll-Rand P175 Compressor | CRP | 332 | O&K F156 Grader | CRP |
| 264 | Porsche 944 Turbo | CRP | 296 | Steinbock Boss NH 16 Fork Lift | CRP | 333 | O&K MH5 Excavator | CRP |
| 265 | Porsche 911 Cabriolet | CRP | 297 | Porsche 959 | CRP | 334 | O&K RH6 Excavator | CRP |
| 266 | Porsche 911 Turbo | CRP | 298 | Caterpillar DN9 Bulldozer Ripper | CRP | 335 | Mercedes-Benz Tipping Truck | CRP |
| 267 | Porsche 911 Targa | CRP | 299 | Caterpillar 450 Pavement Profiler | CRP | 336 | Mercedes-Benz Covered Truck and |  |
| 268 | New Holland 940 Baler | CRP | 300 | Kramer Tremo Pick-up Truck | CRP |  | Trailer | CRP |
| 269 | New Holland TF 42 Thresher | CRP | 301 | O&K 23.2 Dumper | CRP | 337 | BT Fork Lift Wagon | CRP |
| 270 | Atlas Copco XAS 85 Compressor | CRP | 303 | Porsche 911 Turbo Targa | CRP | 338 | Volvo BM10 Bus | CRP |
| 271 | Bomag BW75 ADL Roller | CRP | 304 | Porsche 911 Turbo Cabriolet | CRP | 339 | Mercedes-Benz Articulated Truck | CRP |
| 272 | Zettelmeyer ZL 5001 Loader | CRP | 309 | Caterpillar V50D Fork Lift | CRP | 341 | Atlas Copco XAS90 Compressor | CRP |
| 273 | Demag H55 Hydraulic Shovel | CRP | 310 | Fiat Transporter | CRP | 343 | Hamm Walze Roller | CRP |
| 276 | Sperry New Holland L555 Loader | CRP | 311 | Volvo B10M Flexible Bus | CRP | 345 | Rosenbauer Fire Engine | CRP |
| 277 | JCB 3X Excavator Loader | CRP | 312 | Steinbock Fork Lift Wagon | CRP | 346 | Schaeff Wheel Loader | CRP |
| 278 | O&K L4 Wheel Loader | CRP | 313 | Mercedes-Benz Container Truck | CRP | 347 | Zeppelin Wheel Loader | CRP |
| 280 | Neoplan Skyliner Doubledeck Bus | CRP | 314 | Mercedes-Benz Covered Truck and |  | 348 | Porsche 911 Carrera | CRP |
| 281 | Mercedes-Benz 280 SE | CRP |  | Trailer | CRP | 349 | Porsche 911 Carrera Targa | CRP |
| 282 | Mercedes-Benz 380 SEC | CRP | 315 | Mercedes-Benz Dump Truck | CRP | 350 | Porsche 911 Carrera Cabriolet | CRP |
| 283 | Krupp 30 GMT Crane | CRP | 316 | BT Fork Lift | CRP | 351 | Mustang Loader 940 | CRP |
| 284 | Mercedes-Benz 380/500 SL | CRP | 317 | Mercedes-Benz Tanker | CRP | 353 | Peugeot J5 Van | CRP |
| 285 | Caterpillar 416 Backhoe Loader | CRP | 318 | Link-Belt Crane Truck | CRP | 356 | Demag H55 Excavator | CRP |

# Old Cars

**O**ld Cars is a manufacturer of 1/43 to 1/50 scale truck and earth moving models. The company is located north of Turin, in Italy, and their name is sometimes spelled as one word: Oldcars. However, their 1995 catalog has it as two words.

Old Cars was founded in 1975. They entered the die cast market in 1978 with a group of five "veteran" or vintage models, and soon moved into making models of Italian trucks and commercial vehicles. They continue to offer these models, along with several Ferrari models of late 1950s vintage. In 1993, Old Cars released its 1/43 scale model of a late 1950s Fiat Formula One Racing Transporter, as used by the Ferrari team. Although it has a fair amount of plastic, it has proven to be very popular with collectors.

The following listing includes the five veteran models, which are no longer made, and current Old Cars models. CRP (Current Retail Price) for the smaller Old Cars models, such as the Vans and Jeeps, is generally $20-$25. The buses sell for $50-$60, while the larger tractor trailer trucks can cost $75 or more.

*Introduced around 1980, this OM N100 Covered Truck featured a tilt back and cardboard cover for the load. The chassis reads "N. 4," perhaps indicating that it shared the chassis with the number 4 Fiat Covered Truck.*

| # | Name | Price |
|---|------|-------|
| **Original veteran models (1978):** | | |
| 101 | 1931 Bugatti | $20 |
| 102 | 1907 Ford | 25 |
| 103 | 1909 Opel Doktorwagen | 20 |
| 104 | 1905 Fiat Berlina | 20 |
| 105 | 1905 Fiat Cabriolet | 20 |
| **Current models:** | | |
| 1200 | Scania 143M Race Transporter "Benetton" | CRP |
| 1400 | Scania 143M Tractor Trailer | CRP |
| 1451 | Scania 143M Tractor Trailer "GOODYEAR" | CRP |
| 1600 | Iveco Eurotech MP Tractor Trailer | CRP |
| 1601 | Iveco Eurotech MP Tractor Trailer "Ford" | CRP |
| 1602 | Iveco Eurotech MP Tractor Trailer "Pegaso" | CRP |
| 1700 | Iveco Eurostar LD Tractor Trailer | CRP |
| 1701 | Iveco Eurostar LD Tractor Trailer "Buitoni" | CRP |
| 2301 | Fiat Daily VVFF Van | CRP |
| 2310 | Fiat Daily "Alfacorse" Van | CRP |
| 2410 | Fiat Daily Ambulance Van | CRP |
| 2421 | Fiat Daily "Ferrari" | CRP |
| 2450 | Fiat Daily Military Ambulance | CRP |
| 2600 | Iveco Daily Van "POLIZIA" | CRP |
| 2900 | Scuolabus Van | CRP |
| 3000 | Fiat Daily "SOMMOZZATORI" Van | CRP |
| 3125 | Fiat Daily Van "Agip" | CRP |
| 4500 | Fiat Daily 4x4 Van | CRP |
| 4600 | Fiat Daily 4x4 Carro Covered Pick-up | CRP |
| 5000 | Turbodaily Carro 4x2 Pick-up | CRP |

| # | Name | Price |
|---|------|-------|
| 5001 | Iveco Turbodaily 4x2 Covered Pick-up | CRP |
| 5100 | Turbodaily Carro 4x2 Pick-up | CRP |
| 5200 | Turbodaily Furgone 4x2 Van | CRP |
| 5201 | Iveco Turbodaily 4x2 | CRP |
| 5300 | Turbodaily Furgone 4x4 Van | CRP |
| 5400 | Iveco Turbodaily Minibus | CRP |
| 5500 | Iveco Turbodaily Van "Ferrari" | CRP |
| 6501 | Iveco Daily Van "CARABINIERI" | CRP |
| 6721 | Fiat 370 S Granturismo Bus | CRP |
| 6800 | Fiat 370 S Bus | CRP |
| 6802 | Fiat 370S Military Bus | CRP |
| 6803 | Fiat 370S Bus "CARABINIERI" | CRP |
| 6804 | Fiat 370S Bus "POLIZIA" | CRP |
| 6805 | Fiat 370S Vigili del Fuoco Bus | CRP |
| 6900 | Domino Orlandi Bus | CRP |
| 6901 | Domino Orlandi Bus "Ferrari" | CRP |
| 6902 | Domino Orlandi "Alfacorse" Bus | CRP |
| 7000 | Iveco Turbocity Bus | CRP |
| 7200 | Padane MX Bus | CRP |
| 7300 | Euroclass Orlandi Bus | CRP |
| 7700 | Iveco Turbostar Tractor Trailer "Ferrari" | CRP |
| 15000 | Ferrari Superfast 410 1956 | CRP |
| 15001 | Ferrari Superfast 410 1956 | CRP |
| 15100 | Ferrari 250 GT 1961 | CRP |
| 15101 | Ferrari 250 GT 1961 | CRP |
| 15102 | Ferrari 250 GT 1961 | CRP |
| 15300 | Ferrari 250 GT LWB 1958 | CRP |
| 15301 | Ferrari 250 GT LWB 1958 | CRP |
| 15302 | Ferrari 250 GT LWB 1958 | CRP |
| 15400 | Ferrari 250 GT SWB California 1961 | CRP |
| 15401 | Ferrari 250 GT SWB California 1961 | CRP |
| 15402 | Ferrari 250 GT SWB California 1961 | CRP |
| 15500 | Ferrari 250 GT SWB California 1960 | CRP |

| # | Name | Price |
|---|------|-------|
| 15501 | Ferrari 250 GT SWB California 1960 | CRP |
| 15502 | Ferrari 250 GT SWB California 1960 | CRP |
| 15600 | Ferrari Ingrid Bergman 1954 | CRP |
| 15601 | Ferrari Ingrid Bergman 1954 | CRP |
| 15602 | Ferrari Ingrid Bergman 1954 | CRP |
| 25000 | Fiat Fork Lift | CRP |
| 25100 | Fiat Fork Lift | CRP |
| 25200 | Fiat Fork Lift | CRP |
| 26001 | Trailer | CRP |
| 30200 | Fiat Campagnola Tow Truck "ACI" | CRP |
| 30300 | Fiat Campagnola Jeep "POLIZIA" | CRP |
| 30400 | Fiat Campagnola "CARABINIERI" | CRP |
| 31102 | Fiat Campagnola Military Jeep | CRP |
| 31500 | Fiat Campagnola VVFF Jeep | CRP |
| 56000 | Fiat 642RN2 Race Transporter "Ferrari" | CRP |
| 60100 | Fiat Allis FL 20 Front Loader | CRP |
| 60300 | Rossi 1600B Front Loader | CRP |
| 60500 | Fiat Allis FR 20B Log Lifter | CRP |
| 60600 | Fiat Allis FL 20 Front Loader | CRP |
| 60800 | Fiat Allis FR 20B Front Loader | CRP |
| 60900 | Fiat Allis FR 20B Front Loader | CRP |
| 61000 | Fiat Allis FE 45 Excavator | CRP |
| 70210 | Iveco 360 HP Articulated Dumper | CRP |
| 70400 | Iveco Low Loader | CRP |
| 70527 | Iveco Tractor Trailer "CAMPARI" | CRP |
| 75021 | Iveco Turbostar Tractor Trailer | CRP |
| 75030 | Iveco Turbostar 480 HP Tractor Trailer | CRP |
| 85021 | Moxy Dump Truck | CRP |
| 85022 | Komatsu Dump Truck | CRP |

# Onyx

**O**nyx is a line of 1/43 and 1/24 scale Formula One and IndyCar die cast models made by Minibri Ltd., in Portugal. Minibri is part of the Vitesse Group of companies which includes Cinerius Ltd., makers of Vitesse models.

Onyx Formula One models made their debut in 1/43 scale in 1988, with the first two models appropriately being the McLarens of Alain Prost and Ayrton Senna. These drivers had dominated the 1988 Formula One racing season, with Senna beating Prost to the World Championship. Ferrari, Williams and Lotus models soon followed as new models were introduced each year to reflect that year's group of Formula One cars. Names like Piquet, Mansell and Schumacher appeared in the line.

*This 1993 K-Mart Lola as driven by Nigel Mansell was numbered 160B.*

In 1990 or 1991, the first 1/43 scale IndyCar models appeared, with names like Andretti, Sullivan and Rahal appearing on models of Penskes, Lolas and Marches. In 1992, Onyx expanded into the 1/24 scale category, with IndyCars and Formula One cars appearing in that size.

Onyx models have always been of very good quality with accurate paint finish and detailing. They have rubber tires and plastic baseplates. They are currently available packaged in a square plastic display box with a mirror finish along the back side, to enable the other side of the model to be seen (see photo). Until 1991, however, Onyx models came in a cardboard display box that featured spon-

sor artwork specific to each car. These models are considered by some to be the most collectible. In 1991 the boxes were changed to an all-black design before changing over to the current square display box in 1993.

The following listing is a cross-section of Onyx models that have been available since the beginning of production; it is not an exhaustive list. The CRP (Current Retail Price) for Onyx models is generally $15-$20 for the 1/43 models, and $25-$28 for the 1/24. Certain models, such as those of the late Ayrton Senna, can command a premium over that amount.

| # | Name | Price |
|---|------|-------|
| **Formula One 1/43 models:** | | |
| 001 | McLaren Honda (Prost 1988) | CRP |
| 002 | McLaren Honda (Senna 1988) | CRP |
| 021 | McLaren Honda MP4/5 (Senna 1989) | CRP |
| 022 | McLaren Honda MP4/5 (Prost 1989) | CRP |
| 075 | Ferrari 641 (Prost 1990) | CRP |
| 077 | McLaren Honda (Senna 1990) | CRP |
| 117 | McLaren Honda MP4/6 (Senna 1991) | CRP |
| 118 | McLaren Honda MP4/6 (Berger 1991) | CRP |
| 119 | Williams Renault FW14 (Mansell 1991) | CRP |
| 120 | Williams Renault FW14 (Patrese 1991) | CRP |
| 121 | Ferrari 643 (Prost 1991) | CRP |
| 121 | Ferrari 643 (Morbidelli 1991) | CRP |
| 122 | Ferrari 643 (Alesi 1991) | CRP |
| 123 | Benetton Ford B191 (Schumacher 1991) | CRP |
| 124 | Benetton Ford B191 (Piquet 1991) | CRP |
| 125 | Tyrell Honda 020 (Nakajima 1991) | CRP |
| 126 | Tyrell Honda 020 (Modena 1991) | CRP |
| 127 | Jordan Ford 191 (Gachot 1991) | CRP |
| 127 | Jordan Ford 191 (Moreno 1991) | CRP |
| 128 | Jordan Ford 191 (De Cesaris 1991) | CRP |
| 129 | Lotus Judd 102B (Hakkinen 1991) | CRP |
| 130 | Lotus Judd 102B (Herbert 1991) | CRP |
| 131 | Larrousse Ford 091 (Bernard 1991) | CRP |
| 132 | Larrousse Ford 091 (Suzuki 1991) | CRP |
| 133 | Jordan Yamaha 192 (Modena 1992) | CRP |
| 134 | Jordan Yamaha 192 (Gugelmin 1992) | CRP |
| 135 | Ligier JS37 (Boutsen 1992) | CRP |
| 136 | Ligier JS (Comas 1992) | CRP |
| 137 | Ferrari F92A (Alesi 1992) | CRP |
| 138 | Ferrari F92A (Capelli 1992) | CRP |
| 139 | Williams Renault FW14B (Mansell 1992) | CRP |
| 140 | Williams Renault FW14B (Patrese 1992) | CRP |
| 141 | Tyrell 020B (Grouillard 1992) | CRP |
| 142 | Tyrell 020B (De Cesaris 1992) | CRP |
| 143 | Benetton Ford B192 (Schumacher 1992) | CRP |
| 144 | Benetton Ford B192 (Brundle 1992) | CRP |
| 145 | Arrows FA13 (Alboreto 1992) | CRP |
| 146 | Arrows FA13 (Suzuki 1992) | CRP |
| 147 | Lotus Ford 107 (Hakkinen 1992) | CRP |
| 148 | Lotus Ford 107 (Herbert 1992) | CRP |
| 162 | Benetton Ford B193A (Schumacher 1993) | CRP |
| 163 | Benetton Ford B193A (Patrese 1993) | CRP |

| # | Name | Price |
|---|------|-------|
| 164 | Tyrell Yamaha 020C (Katayama 1993) | CRP |
| 165 | Tyrell Yamaha 020C (De Cesaris 1993) | CRP |
| 166 | Lotus Ford 107B (Zanardi 1993) | CRP |
| 167 | Lotus Ford 107B (Herbert 1993) | CRP |
| 168 | Ferrari F93A (Alesi 1993) | CRP |
| 169 | Ferrari F93A (Berger 1993) | CRP |
| 170 | Sauber Mercedes C12 (Wendlinger 1993) | CRP |
| 171 | Sauber Mercedes C12 (Lehto 1993) | CRP |
| 172 | Williams Renault FW15B (Prost 1993) | CRP |
| 173 | Williams Renault FW15B (Hill 1993) | CRP |
| 185 | Benetton B193B (Schumacher 1994 test car) | CRP |
| 187 | Williams Renault FW15C (Senna 1994 test car) | CRP |
| 188 | Williams Renault FW15C (Hill 1994 test car) | CRP |
| 189 | Ferrari 412 (Alesi 1994) | CRP |
| 189 | Ferrari 412 (Larini 1994) | CRP |
| 190 | Ferrari 412 (Berger 1994) | CRP |
| 191 | Lotus Mugen 107C (Lamy 1994) | CRP |
| 192 | Lotus Mugen 107C (Herbert 1994) | CRP |
| 193 | Sauber C13 (Wendlinger 1994) | CRP |
| 193 | Sauber C13 (De Cesaris 1994) | CRP |
| 194 | Sauber C13 (Frentzen 1994) | CRP |
| 195 | Jordan 194 (Barrichello 1994) | CRP |

| # | Name | Price |
|---|------|-------|
| 196 | Jordan 194 (Irvine 1994) | CRP |
| 196 | Jordan 194 (De Cesaris 1994) | CRP |
| 198 | Pacific Ilmor PR01 (Belmondo 1994) | CRP |
| 199 | Pacific Ilmor PR01 (Gachot 1994) | CRP |
| 200 | Ligier Renault JS39 (Bernard 1994) | CRP |
| 201 | Ligier Renault JS39 (Panis 1994) | CRP |
| 202 | Williams Renault FW16 (Senna 1994) | CRP |
| 202 | Williams Renault FW16 (Coulthard 1994) | CRP |
| 202 | Williams Renault FW16 (Mansell 1994) | CRP |
| 203 | Williams Renault FW16 (Hill 1994) | CRP |
| 204 | Benetton Ford B194 (Schumacher 1994) | CRP |
| 205 | Benetton Ford B194 (Lehto 1994) | CRP |
| 205 | Benetton Ford B194 (Verstappen 1994) | CRP |
| 206 | Tyrell Yamaha 022 (Katayama 1994) | CRP |
| 207 | Tyrell Yamaha 022 (Blundell 1994) | CRP |
| 208 | Williams Renault FW16 (Hill 1994 Australia) | CRP |
| 209 | Benetton Ford B194 (Schumacher 1994 Australia) | CRP |
| 210 | Benetton Ford B194 (Herbert 1994 Australia) | CRP |
| 211 | Ferrari 412 (Alesi 1994 Germany) | CRP |
| 212 | Ferrari 412 (Berger 1994 Germany) | CRP |

*This Onyx #168 Ferrari F93A, as driven by Jean Alesi in 1993, is mounted on Onyx's square display base. The mirror at the rear reflects the other side of the model.*

| # | Name | Price |
|---|------|-------|
| **IndyCar 1/43 models:** | | |
| 051 | Penske (Fittipaldi 1990) | CRP |
| 052 | Penske (Mears 1990) | CRP |
| 054 | Fosters March Porsche (Fabi 1990) | CRP |
| 056 | K-Mart Lola (Mario Andretti 1990) | CRP |
| 057 | Penske (Sullivan 1990) | CRP |
| 070 | Dominos Pizza Lola (Luyendyk 1990) | CRP |
| 094 | Valvoline Lola (Unser, Jr. 1992) | CRP |
| 096 | Pennzoil Lola (J. Andretti 1992) | CRP |
| 098 | K-Mart Lola (Michael Andretti 1992) | CRP |
| 102 | K-Mart Lola (Mario Andretti 1992) | CRP |
| 151 | Glidden Lola (Unser, Sr. 1992) | CRP |
| 152 | Mackenzie Lola (Goodyear 1992) | CRP |
| 153 | Copenhagen Lola (Foyt 1992) | CRP |

| # | Name | Price |
|---|------|-------|
| 154 | Budweiser Lola (Pruett 1992) | CRP |
| 155 | Quaker State Lola (Guerrero 1992) | CRP |
| 156 | Target Scotch Lola (Luyendyk 1992) | CRP |
| 157 | Amway Lola (Brayton 1992) | CRP |
| 158 | Miller Lola (Rahal 1992) | CRP |
| 160B | K-Mart Lola (Mansell 1993) | CRP |
| **Formula One 1/24 models:** | | |
| 5000 | Williams Renault FW14 (Mansell 1992) | CRP |
| 5001 | Williams Renault FW14 (Patrese 1992) | CRP |
| 5002 | Ligier Renault JS37 (Boutsen 1992) | CRP |
| 5003 | Ligier Renault JS37 (Comas 1992) | CRP |
| 5004 | Ferrari F92A (Alesi 1992) | CRP |
| 5005 | Ferrari F92A (Capelli 1992) | CRP |

| # | Name | Price |
|---|------|-------|
| 5006 | Benetton Ford B193 (Schumacher 1993) | CRP |
| 5007 | Benetton Ford B193 (Patrese 1993) | CRP |
| 5008 | Williams Renault FW15 (Prost 1993) | CRP |
| 5009 | Williams Renault FW15 (Hill 1993) | CRP |
| 5016 | Williams Renault FW16 (Senna 1994) | CRP |
| 5016 | Williams Renault FW16 (Mansell 1994) | CRP |
| 5017 | Williams Renault FW16 (Hill 1994) | CRP |
| 5018 | Benetton Ford B194 (Schumacher 1994) | CRP |
| **IndyCar 1/24 models:** | | |
| 5010 | K-Mart Lola (Mansell 1993) | CRP |
| 5011 | K-Mart Lola (Mario Andretti 1993) | CRP |
| 5012 | Mackenzie Lola (Goodyear 1993) | CRP |

# Paul's Model Art

**T**his German company is best-known for its "Minichamps" line of 1/43 scale die cast models. Although located in Germany, the company has its manufacturing done in China. Among its other product lines are a couple of 1/24 scale series: "Classic Line" and "First Class Collection." The company also puts out numerous 1/43 racing models, predominantly under the "Minichamps Formula" and "Minichamps Racing" banners. It also produces models in what might be termed "sub-categories," such as the models offered in "The Michael Schumacher Collection."

When Paul's Model Art entered the die cast arena in the early 1990s, the accuracy and quality of their product forced other manufacturers to improve their quality and value in order to compete. PMA models have excellent paint finishes and accurate details such as hood ornaments and door handles. The models generally come packaged in a cardboard sleeve containing a plastic display box, to which the model is mounted with a screw.

CRP (Current Retail Price) for Paul's Model Art 1/43 scale models generally range from $20-$35, while the larger 1/24's sell for $35 to over $100, depending upon complexity and whether the model is a "limited edition."

| | Name | Price |
|---|------|-------|
| **Minichamps Classic:** | | |
| 2220 | Jaguar XJ220 | CRP |
| 2221 | Jaguar XJ220 | CRP |
| 2222 | Jaguar XJ220 | CRP |
| 3203 | Mercedes W 124 Limousine | CRP |
| 3208 | Mercedes W 124 Limousine | CRP |
| 3209 | Mercedes W 124 Limousine | CRP |
| 3230 | Mercedes 400 E V8 Limousine | CRP |
| 3231 | Mercedes 400 E V8 Limousine | CRP |
| 3240 | Mercedes 500 E V8 Limousine | CRP |
| 3241 | Mercedes 500 E V8 Limousine | CRP |
| 3302 | Mercedes T-Modell | CRP |
| 3303 | Mercedes T-Modell | CRP |
| 3304 | Mercedes T-Modell | CRP |
| 3308 | Mercedes T-Modell | CRP |
| 3309 | Mercedes T-Modell | CRP |
| 3310 | Mercedes T-Modell | CRP |
| 3403 | Mercedes W 124 Coupe | CRP |
| 3408 | Mercedes W 124 Coupe | CRP |
| 3414 | Mercedes W 124 Coupe | CRP |
| 3514 | Mercedes 300 CE-24 Cabriolet | CRP |

| | Name | Price |
|---|------|-------|
| 3550 | Mercedes 300 CE-24 Cabriolet | CRP |
| 3551 | Mercedes 300 CE-24 Cabriolet | CRP |
| 3800 | Mercedes 250 D Taxi | CRP |

| | Name | Price |
|---|------|-------|
| 3820 | Mercedes 250 D Taxi | CRP |
| 3900 | Mercedes 250 D Polizei | CRP |
| 3920 | Mercedes 250 D Polizei | CRP |

*The Paul's Model Art Karmann-Ghia Coupe, from the Minichamps Classic series, has proven to be quite popular in the United States. This example is #5001, painted light blue, a color which has been discontinued (along with #5000 black and #5002 red).*

| # | Name | Price | # | Name | Price | # | Name | Price |
|---|------|-------|---|------|-------|---|------|-------|
| 4000 | Opel Omega EVO 3000 | CRP | 23700 | BMW 700 Limousine | CRP | 33420 | Mercedes 450 SLC | CRP |
| 4001 | Opel Omega EVO 3000 | CRP | 23701 | BMW 700 Limousine | CRP | 33421 | Mercedes 450 SLC | CRP |
| 4002 | Opel Omega EVO 3000 | CRP | 23702 | BMW 700 Limousine | CRP | 33422 | Mercedes 450 SLC | CRP |
| 5003 | Karmann-Ghia Coupe | CRP | 32100 | Mercedes W202 | CRP | 33430 | Mercedes 350 SL Cabriolet | CRP |
| 5004 | Karmann-Ghia Coupe | CRP | 32101 | Mercedes W202 | CRP | 33430 | McLaren F1 | CRP |
| 5005 | Karmann-Ghia Coupe | CRP | 32102 | Mercedes W202 | CRP | 33431 | McLaren F1 | CRP |
| 5030 | Karmann-Ghia Cabriolet | CRP | 32105 | Mercedes C-Class | CRP | 33432 | McLaren F1 | CRP |
| 5031 | Karmann-Ghia Cabriolet | CRP | 32200 | Mercedes W123 Limousine | CRP | 33431 | Mercedes 350 SL Cabriolet | CRP |
| 5032 | Karmann-Ghia Cabriolet | CRP | 32201 | Mercedes W123 Limousine | CRP | 33432 | Mercedes 350 SL Cabriolet | CRP |
| 5060 | Karmann-Ghia Cabriolet (softtop) | CRP | 32202 | Mercedes W123 Limousine | CRP | 43000 | Opel Kadett A Limousine | CRP |
| 5061 | Karmann-Ghia Cabriolet (softtop) | CRP | 32210 | Mercedes W123 Kombi 200T | CRP | 43001 | Opel Kadett A Limousine | CRP |
| 5062 | Karmann-Ghia Cabriolet (softtop) | CRP | 32211 | Mercedes W123 Kombi 230TE | CRP | 43002 | Opel Kadett A Limousine | CRP |
| 22100 | BMW 1600/2 Limousine | CRP | 32212 | Mercedes W123 Kombi 280TE | CRP | 43010 | Opel Kadett A Caravan | CRP |
| 22101 | BMW 1600/2 Limousine | CRP | 32220 | Mercedes W123 Coupe | CRP | 43011 | Opel Kadett A Caravan | CRP |
| 22102 | BMW 1600/2 Limousine | CRP | 32221 | Mercedes W123 Coupe | CRP | 43012 | Opel Kadett A Caravan | CRP |
| 22130 | BMW 1602 Cabriolet | CRP | 32222 | Mercedes W123 Coupe | CRP | 43020 | Opel Kadett A Coupe | CRP |
| 22131 | BMW 1602 Cabriolet | CRP | 32230 | Mercedes 280 SL Cabriolet | CRP | 43021 | Opel Kadett A Coupe | CRP |
| 22132 | BMW 1602 Cabriolet | CRP | 32231 | Mercedes 280 SL Cabriolet | CRP | 43022 | Opel Kadett A Coupe | CRP |
| 22170 | BMW 1600 Touring | CRP | 32232 | Mercedes 280 SL Cabriolet | CRP | 43200 | Opel Rekord P1 Limousine | CRP |
| 22171 | BMW 1600 Touring | CRP | 32240 | Mercedes 280 SL Softtop | CRP | 43201 | Opel Rekord P1 Limousine | CRP |
| 22172 | BMW 1600 Touring | CRP | 32241 | Mercedes 280 SL Softtop | CRP | 43202 | Opel Rekord P1 Limousine | CRP |
| 22300 | BMW M3 Coupe | CRP | 32242 | Mercedes 280 SL Softtop | CRP | 43300 | Opel Kapitän | CRP |
| 22301 | BMW M3 Coupe | CRP | 32250 | Mercedes 280 SL Pagode | CRP | 43301 | Opel Kapitän | CRP |
| 22302 | BMW M3 Coupe | CRP | 32251 | Mercedes 280 SL Pagode | CRP | 43302 | Opel Kapitän | CRP |
| 22305 | BMW M3 Coupe | CRP | 32252 | Mercedes 280 SL Pagode | CRP | 43400 | Opel Manta A | CRP |
| 22400 | BMW 501/502 Limousine | CRP | 32320 | Mercedes 300 S Coupe | CRP | 43401 | Opel Manta A | CRP |
| 22401 | BMW 501/502 Limousine | CRP | 32321 | Mercedes 300 S Coupe | CRP | 43402 | Opel Manta A | CRP |
| 22402 | BMW 501/502 Limousine | CRP | 32322 | Mercedes 300 S Coupe | CRP | 52130 | VW Hebmüller Cabriolet | CRP |
| 22507 | BMW 507 Cabriolet | CRP | 32330 | Mercedes 300 S | CRP | 52131 | VW Hebmüller Cabriolet | CRP |
| 22508 | BMW 507 Cabriolet | CRP | 32331 | Mercedes 300 S | CRP | 53132 | VW Hebmüller Cabriolet | CRP |
| 22509 | BMW 507 Cabriolet | CRP | 32332 | Mercedes 300 S | CRP | 52140 | VW Hebmüller Softtop | CRP |
| 22520 | BMW 507 Cabriolet (softtop) | CRP | 32340 | Mercedes 300 S Softtop | CRP | 52141 | VW Hebmüller Softtop | CRP |
| 22521 | BMW 507 Cabriolet (softtop) | CRP | 32341 | Mercedes 300 S Softtop | CRP | 52142 | VW Hebmüller Softtop | CRP |
| 22522 | BMW 507 Cabriolet (softtop) | CRP | 32342 | Mercedes 300 S Softtop | CRP | 52300 | VW Samba Bus | CRP |
| 22530 | BMW 507 Hardtop | CRP | 32600 | Mercedes 600 SEC | CRP | 52301 | VW Samba Bus | CRP |
| 22531 | BMW 507 Hardtop | CRP | 32601 | Mercedes 600 SEC | CRP | 52302 | VW Samba Bus | CRP |
| 22532 | BMW 507 Hardtop | CRP | 32602 | Mercedes 600 SEC | CRP | 62020 | Porsche 911 Coupe | CRP |
| 23000 | BMW E1 | CRP | 33000 | Mercedes 220 Limousine | CRP | 62021 | Porsche 911 Coupe | CRP |
| 23001 | BMW E1 | CRP | 33001 | Mercedes 220 Limousine | CRP | 62022 | Porsche 911 Coupe | CRP |
| 23002 | BMW E1 | CRP | 33002 | Mercedes 220 Limousine | CRP | 62120 | Porsche 911 Carrera 2/4 | CRP |
| 23430 | BMW 502 Cabriolet | CRP | 33230 | Mercedes 220 S Cabriolet | CRP | 62121 | Porsche 911 Carrera 2/4 | CRP |
| 23431 | BMW 502 Cabriolet | CRP | 33231 | Mercedes 220 S Cabriolet | CRP | 62122 | Porsche 911 Carrera 2/4 | CRP |
| 23432 | BMW 502 Cabriolet | CRP | 33232 | Mercedes 220 S Cabriolet | CRP | 62320 | Porsche 356 C Coupe | CRP |
| | | | | | | 62321 | Porsche 356 C Coupe | CRP |
| | | | | | | 62322 | Porsche 356 C Coupe | CRP |
| | | | | | | 63001 | Porsche 993 | CRP |
| | | | | | | 63007 | Porsche 993 | CRP |
| | | | | | | 63008 | Porsche 993 | CRP |
| | | | | | | 63030 | Porsche 993 Cabriolet | CRP |
| | | | | | | 63031 | Porsche 993 Cabriolet | CRP |
| | | | | | | 63032 | Porsche 993 Cabriolet | CRP |
| | | | | | | 63130 | Porsche Boxster | CRP |
| | | | | | | 63131 | Porsche Boxster | CRP |
| | | | | | | 63132 | Porsche Boxster | CRP |
| | | | | | | 72000 | Ferrari 250 GTO | CRP |
| | | | | | | 72250 | Ferrari 250 GTO | CRP |
| | | | | | | 72400 | Ferrari 456 GT 2+2 | CRP |
| | | | | | | 72401 | Ferrari 456 GT 2+2 | CRP |
| | | | | | | 72402 | Ferrari 456 GT 2+2 | CRP |
| | | | | | | 72500 | Ferrari 512 TR | CRP |
| | | | | | | 72501 | Ferrari 512 TR | CRP |
| | | | | | | 72502 | Ferrari 512 TR | CRP |

*A Jaguar XJ220, which is #102220 in the Paul's Model Art Minichamps Classic series. The detail on this 1/43 scale piece is very accurate, including the silver wheel hubs.*

| # | Name | Price |
|---|------|-------|
| 82000 | Ford Mondeo Limousine | CRP |
| 82001 | Ford Mondeo Limousine | CRP |
| 82002 | Ford Mondeo Limousine | CRP |
| 82070 | Ford Mondeo Limousine | CRP |
| 82071 | Ford Mondeo Limousine | CRP |
| 82072 | Ford Mondeo Limousine | CRP |
| 82100 | Ford Escort RS Cosworth | CRP |
| 82101 | Ford Escort RS Cosworth | CRP |
| 82102 | Ford Escort RS Cosworth | CRP |
| 102110 | Bugatti EB 110 | CRP |
| 102111 | Bugatti EB 110 | CRP |
| 102112 | Bugatti EB 110 | CRP |
| 102115 | Bugatti EB 110 | CRP |
| 102220 | Jaguar XJ 220 | CRP |
| 102221 | Jaguar XJ 220 | CRP |
| 102222 | Jaguar XJ 220 | CRP |
| 103000 | Lamborghini Miura | CRP |
| 103011 | Lamborghini Miura | CRP |
| 103012 | Lamborghini Miura | CRP |

## Minichamps Formula:

| # | Name | Price |
|---|------|-------|
| 30004 | Benetton Ford B193B (Schumacher 1993) | CRP |
| 30006 | Benetton Ford B193B (Patreses 1993) | CRP |
| 40001 | Williams Renault (Hill 1994) | CRP |
| 40002 | Williams Renault (Senna 1994) | CRP |
| 40003 | Tyrell Yamaha (Katayama 1994) | CRP |
| 40004 | Tyrell Yamaha (Katayama 1994) | CRP |
| 40027 | Ferrari 412 (Alesi 1994) | CRP |
| 40028 | Ferrari 412 (Berger 1994) | CRP |
| 40029 | Sauber Mercedes C13 (Wendlinger 1994) | CRP |
| 40030 | Sauber Mercedes C13 (Frentzen 1994) | CRP |
| 40206 | Benetton Ford B194 (Verstappen 1994) | CRP |
| 44305 | Benetton Ford B194 (Schumacher 1994) | CRP |
| 44307 | McLaren Peugeot (Hakkinen 1994) | CRP |
| 44308 | McLaren Peugeot (Brundle 1994) | CRP |
| 920005 | Williams Renault (Mansell 1992) | CRP |
| 920006 | Williams Renault (Patrese 1992) | CRP |
| 920019 | Benetton Ford (Schumacher 1992) | CRP |
| 920020 | Benetton Ford (Brundle 1992) | CRP |
| 920027 | Ferrari F92A (Alesi 1992) | CRP |
| 920028 | Ferrari F92A (Capelli 1992) | CRP |
| 930001 | Williams Renault (Hill 1993) | CRP |
| 930002 | Williams Renault (Prost 1993) | CRP |
| 930006 | Benetton Ford B193B (Patrese 1993) | CRP |
| 930007 | McLaren (Andretti 1993) | CRP |
| 930008 | McLaren (Senna 1993) | CRP |
| 930009 | Sauber C12 (Wendlinger 1993) | CRP |
| 930010 | Sauber C12 (Lehto 1993) | CRP |
| 930027 | Ferrari F93A (Alesi 1993) | CRP |
| 930028 | Ferrari F93A (Berger 1993) | CRP |
| C1000 | Audi V8 | CRP |
| I1000 | Audi V8 | CRP |
| T1000 | Audi V8 | CRP |
| B2000 | BMW M3 | CRP |
| R2000 | BMW M3 | CRP |
| W2000 | BMW M3 | CRP |
| B3000 | Mercedes 190 2.5 EVO 1 | CRP |

| # | Name | Price |
|---|------|-------|
| G3000 | Mercedes 190 2.5 EVO 1 | CRP |
| R3000 | Mercedes 190 2.5 EVO 1 | CRP |
| B3100 | Mercedes 190 2.5 EVO 2 | CRP |
| G3100 | Mercedes 190 2.5 EVO 2 | CRP |
| R3100 | Mercedes 190 2.5 EVO 2 | CRP |

## Minichamps Racing:

| # | Name | Price |
|---|------|-------|
| 3040 | Mercedes Evo 1 | CRP |
| 12004 | BMW M3 | CRP |
| 13103 | Mercedes-Benz Evo 2 | CRP |
| 13104 | Mercedes-Benz Evo 2 | CRP |
| 13105 | Mercedes-Benz Evo 2 | CRP |
| 14020 | Opel Omega | CRP |
| 14030 | Opel Omega | CRP |
| 21101 | Audi V8 | CRP |
| 21102 | Audi V8 | CRP |
| 21110 | Audi V8 | CRP |
| 21111 | Audi V8 | CRP |
| 22003 | BMW M3 | CRP |
| 22004 | BMW M3 | CRP |
| 22013 | BMW M3 | CRP |
| 22020 | BMW M3 | CRP |
| 22030 | BMW M3 | CRP |
| 22040 | BMW M3 | CRP |
| 22061 | BMW M3 | CRP |
| 22090 | BMW M3 | CRP |
| 22096 | BMW M3 | CRP |
| 23101 | Mercedes Evo 2 | CRP |
| 23102 | Mercedes Evo 2 | CRP |
| 23120 | Mercedes Evo 2 | CRP |
| 23121 | Mercedes Evo 2 | CRP |
| 23130 | Mercedes Evo 2 | CRP |
| 23131 | Mercedes Evo 2 | CRP |
| 23140 | Mercedes Evo 2 | CRP |
| 23141 | Mercedes Evo 2 | CRP |
| 31121 | Audi V8 | CRP |
| 31120 | Audi V8 | CRP |
| 32040 | BMW M3 | CRP |
| 32380 | BMW M3 GTR | CRP |
| 32381 | BMW M3 GTR | CRP |
| 33101 | Mercedes Evo 2 | CRP |
| 33102 | Mercedes Evo 2 | CRP |
| 33111 | Mercedes Evo 2 | CRP |
| 33130 | Mercedes Evo 2 | CRP |
| 33131 | Mercedes Evo 2 | CRP |
| 33140 | Mercedes Evo 2 | CRP |
| 33141 | Mercedes Evo 2 | CRP |
| 33150 | Mercedes Evo 2 | CRP |
| 38200 | Ford Escort Cosworth | CRP |
| 38204 | Ford Escort ADAC Cup | CRP |
| 38205 | Ford Escort ADAC Cup | CRP |
| 38217 | Ford Escort ADAC Cup | CRP |
| 38218 | Ford Escort ADAC Cup | CRP |
| 40130 | Alfa Romeo 155 | CRP |
| 40201 | Alfa Romeo 155 | CRP |
| 40202 | Alfa Romeo 155 | CRP |
| 40211 | Alfa Romeo 155 | CRP |
| 40212 | Alfa Romeo 155 | CRP |
| 40218 | Alfa Romeo 155 | CRP |
| 43303 | AMG Mercedes C 180 | CRP |
| 43304 | AMG Mercedes C 180 | CRP |
| 43307 | AMG Mercedes C 180 | CRP |
| 43308 | AMG Mercedes C 180 | CRP |

| # | Name | Price |
|---|------|-------|
| 43314 | AMG Mercedes C 180 | CRP |
| 43315 | AMG Mercedes C 180 | CRP |
| 93010 | Mercedes-Benz Evo 1 | CRP |
| 926001 | Porsche | CRP |
| 926006 | Porsche | CRP |
| 926015 | Porsche | CRP |
| 926016 | Porsche | CRP |
| 926022 | Porsche | CRP |
| 926024 | Porsche | CRP |
| 930100 | Alfa Romeo 155 | CRP |
| 930120 | Alfa Romeo 155 | CRP |
| 930121 | Alfa Romeo 155 | CRP |
| 930122 | Alfa Romeo 155 | CRP |
| 930123 | Alfa Romeo 155 | CRP |
| 932020 | BMW M3 | CRP |
| 932030 | BMW M3 | CRP |
| 932040 | BMW M3 | CRP |
| 933100 | Mercedes W202 | CRP |
| 933101 | Mercedes Evo 2 | CRP |
| 933102 | Mercedes Evo 2 | CRP |
| 933110 | Mercedes Evo 2 | CRP |
| 933111 | Mercedes Evo 2 | CRP |
| 933130 | Mercedes Evo 2 | CRP |
| 933131 | Mercedes Evo 2 | CRP |
| 933140 | Mercedes Evo 2 | CRP |
| 933141 | Mercedes Evo 2 | CRP |
| 933150 | Mercedes Evo 2 | CRP |
| 933160 | Mercedes Evo 2 | CRP |
| 934000 | Opel | CRP |
| 934012 | Opel Omega Evo 500 | CRP |
| 934101 | Opel | CRP |
| 936001 | Porsche | CRP |
| 936008 | Porsche | CRP |
| 936009 | Porsche | CRP |
| 936010 | Porsche | CRP |
| 936015 | Porsche | CRP |
| 936027 | Porsche | CRP |
| 938200 | Ford Escort Cosworth Rally | CRP |

## Classic Line (1/24 scale):

| # | Name | Price |
|---|------|-------|
| 245000 | Karmann-Ghia Coupe | CRP |
| 245001 | Karmann-Ghia Coupe | CRP |
| 245003 | Karmann-Ghia Coupe | CRP |
| 245010 | Karmann-Ghia Cabriolet | CRP |
| 245011 | Karmann-Ghia Cabriolet | CRP |
| 245013 | Karmann-Ghia Cabriolet | CRP |

## Cycle Line (1/24 scale):

| # | Name | Price |
|---|------|-------|
| RS1101 | BMW 1100RS | CRP |
| RS1102 | BMW 1100RS | CRP |
| RS1103 | BMW 1100RS | CRP |
| RS1104 | BMW 1100RS | CRP |
| RS1105 | BMW 1100RS | CRP |
| RS1106 | BMW 1100RS | CRP |
| R32001 | BMW R 32 | CRP |
| R32101 | BMW R 32 | CRP |

## First Class Collection (1/24 scale):

| # | Name | Price |
|---|------|-------|
| 90 | Mercedes 770K | CRP |
| 100 | Mercedes 770K. | CRP |
| 200 | Mercedes SSKL | CRP |
| 300 | Mercedes 300 SLR | CRP |
| 310 | Mercedes 300 SLR Coupe | CRP |

# Pilen

**B**eginning in the late 1960s, Pilen of Spain manufactured a diverse line of die cast models. A series of 1/43 scale Formula One race cars appears to have been the company's earliest product, followed by 1/43 models of passenger and rally cars. The company is also known as "Auto-Pilen."

Pilen models were of very good quality with accurate detailing. They featured window glazing and interiors, and the opening doors and hoods usually fit very well. The models had rubber tires with die cast hubs and die cast baseplates. Many Pilens (if not all) came in a plastic display box that was a two-piece snap-together affair which protected the model very well; the model was screwed to the base (see photo).

Pilen expanded into the smaller scale market in the late 1970s, with a line of 1/63 scale models. The castings were quite accurate for their size, but the company unfortunately put "speed"-type wheels on them, which spoiled their appearance in terms of authenticity.

In 1974, Pilen entered into an agreement with Meccano France to manufacture a number of existing French Dinky models, to be marketed under the Dinky name. These were made from 1974 until around 1978, at which point Pilen began manufacturing some of its own models, also sold as Dinkys. This was done until around 1981. These two lines of products often had their baseplates and boxes marked "Made in Spain," and the models are known to collectors as "Spanish Dinky." They are listed at the end of the following Pilen listing.

Some of the "Spanish Dinky" models also appeared in the regular Pilen line. Whether these were produced before, during, or after the Spanish Dinky models is unknown.

*Pilen #535 Matra Bagheera Rally on top of original box. The see-through plastic dome allowed easy visibilty for the customer.*

It is also unclear whether Pilen is still in business. In early 1995, a number of ex-Pilen models appeared marketed under the name "Oto." These included a Mini Cooper, a Citroën SM, a Ferrari P5, and a number of others. The retail price of these re-issues was reportedly around $12.

The following listing is for models in near mint or better condition in the original packaging. *Note:* Like many manufacturers, Pilen frequently discontinued products, and then used the old number for a new product. As a result, two or more models wound up having the same number.

| # | Name | Price | # | Name | Price | # | Name | Price |
|---|------|-------|---|------|-------|---|------|-------|
| 1 | Eagle Formula I | $30 | 250 | Volkswagen Scirocco (Push & Go) | $20 | 289 | Citroën 2 CV Pop Cross | $15 |
| 2 | B.R.M. H 16 Formula I | 30 | 251 | Matra Bagheera (Push & Go) | 20 | 290 | Fiat 127 Rally | 15 |
| 3 | Cooper-Maserati Formula I | 30 | 252 | Lotus Elite (Push & Go) | 20 | 291 | Mini Cooper Rally | 20 |
| 4 | Ferrari 312 Formula I | 40 | 253 | Alfa Romeo Alfetta GT Coupe (Push & Go) | 20 | 292 | Renault 17 Rally | 15 |
| 5 | Honda V 12 Formula I | 30 | | | | 293 | Renault 5 Policia | 15 |
| 6 | Lola Climax Formula I | 30 | 271 | Ligier JS 11 Formula I | 15 | 294 | Renault 12 Bomberos Fire Car | 15 |
| 7 | B.R.M. Formula I | 30 | 272 | Renault RS 10 Turbo Formula I | 15 | 295 | Renault 12 Policia Trafico | 15 |
| 8 | Lotus Climax Formula I | 30 | 276 | AMC Javelin Starsky and Hutch | 25 | 296 | Mercedes-Benz 250 Coupe Urgencias | 20 |
| 9 | Ferrari 156 Formula I | 40 | 277 | Opel ASC Rally | 20 | 296 | Citroën SM Urgencias | 20 |
| 10 | Brabham Formula I | 30 | 278 | Fiat 850 Bertone Roadster "Playero" | 20 | 297-1 | Mercedes-Benz 250 Coupe Taxi | 20 |
| 200 | Peugeot 304 | 20 | 279 | Citroën 2 CV Safari | 20 | 297-2 | Renault 12 Taxi | 15 |
| 201 | Simca 1200 | 20 | 280 | AMC Javelin Daytona | 20 | 298 | Oldsmobile Toronado Policia | 20 |
| 202 | Renault 4 L | 20 | 281 | Maserati Chibli Rally | 20 | 299 | Chevrolet Corvette (chrome-plated) | 30 |
| 203 | Renault R 16 | 20 | 282 | Indra Rally | 20 | 299 | Peugeot 504 | 15 |
| 204 | Renault 6 | 20 | 283 | Renault 5 Rally | 15 | 300 | Chevrolet Corvette | 30 |
| 205 | Volkswagen Scirocco | 20 | 284 | De Tomaso Mangusta Rally | 20 | 301 | Chevrolet Monza GT Coupe | 20 |
| 206 | Matra Bagheera | 20 | 285 | Renault 12 Rally | 15 | 301 | Monteverdi Hai Rally | 15 |
| 207 | Volvo 66 DL | 20 | 286 | Opel Manta Rally | 15 | 302 | Chevrolet Monza GT Roadster | 20 |
| 208 | Citroën Dyane | 20 | 287 | Fiat 600 Rally | 15 | 303 | Porsche Carrera 6 | 25 |
| 209 | Peugeot 204 | 20 | 288 | Fiat 1600 Coupe Rally | 15 | 304 | Porsche Carrera 6 (chrome-plated) | 25 |

| # | Name | Price |
|---|------|-------|
| 305 | Mercedes-Benz 250 Coupe | $20 |
| 306 | Mercedes-Benz 250 Coupe (chrome-plated) | 20 |
| 307 | Oldsmobile Toronado | 25 |
| 308 | Oldsmobile Toronado (chrome-plated) | 25 |
| 309 | Ferrari P5 | 20 |
| 309 | Citroën DS 23 | 15 |
| 310 | Ferrari P5 (chrome-plated) | 20 |
| 311 | Ford Mark II | 20 |
| 312 | Ford Mark II (chrome-plated) | 20 |
| 313 | De Tomaso Mangusta | 20 |
| 314 | De Tomaso Mangusta (chrome-plated) | 20 |
| 315 | Chevrolet Astro | 20 |
| 316 | Chevrolet Astro (chrome-plated) | 20 |
| 317 | Fiat 850 Roadster | 20 |
| 318 | Fiat 850 Roadster (chrome-plated) | 20 |
| 319 | Mini Cooper | 20 |
| 320 | Mini Cooper (chrome-plated) | 20 |
| 321 | Mercedes-Benz C-111 | 15 |
| 322 | Mercedes-Benz C-111 (chrome-plated) | 15 |
| 323 | AMC Javelin | 20 |
| 324 | AMC Javelin (chrome-plated) | 20 |
| 325 | Ferrari 512 | 20 |
| 326 | Ferrari 512 (chrome-plated) | 20 |
| 327 | Modulo Pinin Farina | 20 |
| 328 | Modulo Pinin Farina (chrome-plated) | 20 |
| 329 | Fiat 1600 Coupe | 20 |
| 330 | Fiat 1600 Coupe (chrome-plated) | 20 |
| 331 | Porsche 917 | 20 |
| 332 | Porsche 917 (chrome-plated) | 20 |
| 333 | Fiat 127 | 20 |
| 335 | Fiat 600 | 20 |
| 337 | Vauxhall S.R.V. | 15 |
| 339 | Citroën SM | 15 |
| 341 | Renault 17 TS | 15 |
| 343 | Indra | 20 |
| 345 | Opel Manta Coupe | 20 |
| 347 | Monteverdi Hai | 20 |
| 349 | Renault 5 | 15 |
| 351 | Citroën 2CV | 15 |
| 353 | Ferrari P5 | 20 |
| 355 | Citroën CX | 15 |
| 357 | Citroën Dyane | 15 |
| 358 | Renault R 16 TL | 15 |
| 359 | Range Rover Safari | 15 |
| 361 | Range Rover Ambulance | 15 |
| 362 | Range Rover Fire Car | 15 |
| 377 | Mercedes-Benz Van | 15 |
| 501 | Beach Buggy | 15 |
| 502 | Beach Buggy (chrome-plated) | 15 |
| 503 | Renault 12 | 20 |
| 504 | Renault 12 (chrome-plated) | 20 |
| 505 | Adams Probe 16 | 20 |
| 506 | Adams Probe 16 (chrome-plated) | 20 |
| 507 | Chibli Maserati | 20 |
| 508 | Chibli Maserati (chrome-plated) | 20 |
| 509 | Lancia Stratos | 20 |
| 510 | Lancia Stratos (chrome-plated) | 20 |
| 511 | Citroën 2CV | 20 |
| 511 | Volkswagen Scirocco | 20 |

*Pilen #343 Indra. Note that the opening doors fit quite well; they are mounted on strong springs that snap the doors closed. Even the small rear trunk opens.*

| # | Name | Price |
|---|------|-------|
| 513 | Peugeot 504 | $15 |
| 513 | Chevrolet Corvette | 20 |
| 515 | Citroën DS 23 | 20 |
| 515 | Matra Simca Bagheera | 15 |
| 517 | Opel Ascona | 15 |
| 519 | Citroën CX | 15 |
| 519 | Volvo 66 DL | 15 |
| 521 | Fiat 131 E | 15 |
| 523 | Fiat 1200 Coupe | 20 |
| 525 | Renault 14 | 15 |
| 527 | Renault 16 TX | 15 |
| 527 | Ford Fiesta | 15 |
| 529 | Citroën Dyane | 15 |
| 529 | Chrysler 150 | 15 |
| 529 | Talbot 150 | 15 |
| 531 | Chevrolet Monza GT Rally | 15 |
| 533 | Volkswagen Scirocco Rally | 15 |
| 535 | Matra Bagheera Rally | 15 |
| 537 | Volvo 66 DB Rally | 15 |
| 539 | Fiat 1200 Coupe Rally | 15 |
| 541 | Renault 14 Rally | 15 |
| 543 | Ford Fiesta Iberia | 15 |
| 545 | Ford Fiesta Policia | 15 |
| 547 | Chrysler 150 Rally | 15 |
| 547 | Talbot 150 Rally | 15 |
| 549 | Range Rover | 15 |
| 551 | Volkswagen Scirocco Urgencias | 15 |
| 553 | Chrysler 150 Policia | 15 |
| 553 | Talbot 150 Policia | 15 |
| 553 | Talbot 150 Fire Car | 15 |
| 700 | Tiger I Tank | 20 |
| 701 | Tiger I Tank | 20 |

**1/63 scale models:**

| # | Name | Price |
|---|------|-------|
| 800 | Fiat 131 Familiar | 10 |
| 801 | Fiat 131 Familiar Ambulance | 10 |
| 802 | Porsche 917 | 10 |
| 803 | Porsche 917 "Martini" | 10 |
| 804 | Chrysler 150 | 10 |

| # | Name | Price |
|---|------|-------|
| 804 | Talbot 150 | $10 |
| 805 | Chrysler 150 Policia | 10 |
| 806 | Ford Fiesta | 10 |
| 807 | Ford Fiesta Rally | 10 |
| 807 | Renault 4F | 10 |
| 808 | Fiat 131 Safari | 10 |
| 809 | Fiat 131 G.C. Trafico | 10 |
| 809 | Peugeot 504 | 10 |
| 810 | Chrysler 150 Taxi | 10 |
| 810 | Fiat Ritmo | 10 |
| 811 | Chrysler 150 Rally | 10 |
| 811 | Ford Fiesta | 10 |
| 812 | Ford Fiesta Iberia | 10 |
| 813 | Ford Fiesta Policia | 10 |
| 814 | Fiat 131 Fire Car | 10 |
| 814 | Range Rover | 10 |
| 815 | Renault 4 Van | 10 |
| 815 | Range Rover Bombero | 10 |
| 816 | Renault 4 Telephone Van | 10 |
| 816 | Range Rover "Safari" | 10 |
| 817 | Fiat 132 | 10 |
| 817 | Ford Torino | 10 |
| 818 | Fiat 132 Rally | 10 |
| 818 | Ford Torino Policia | 10 |
| 819 | Renault 4 TV Van | 10 |
| 819 | Ford Torino Starsky and Hutch | 10 |

**French Dinkys made by Pilen:**

| # | Name | Price |
|---|------|-------|
| 500 | Citroën 2CV saloon | 50 |
| 510 | Peugeot 204 saloon | 40 |
| 518 | Renault R4 saloon | 40 |
| 520 | Simca 1000 Rally | 40 |
| 530 | Citroën DS23 saloon | 45 |
| 537 | Renault R16 saloon | 40 |
| 538 | Renault R16TX saloon | 50 |
| 1407 | Simca 1100 saloon | 40 |
| 1413 | Citroën Dyane saloon | 40 |
| 1415 | Peugeot 504 saloon | 50 |
| 1416 | Renault 6 saloon | 40 |

*This Fiat 600 Rally was #287 in the Pilen line.*

| # | Name | Price |
|---|------|-------|
| 1424 | Renault 12 saloon | $40 |
| 1424G | Renault 12 Gordini saloon | 75 |
| 1428 | Peugeot 304 saloon | 50 |
| 1450 | Simca 1100 saloon Police car | 40 |
| 1452 | Peugeot 504 saloon | 40 |
| 1453 | Renault 6 saloon | 45 |

**Pilen models marketed under Dinky name:**

| # | Name | Price |
|---|------|-------|
| 1451 | Renault 17TS coupe | 40 |
| 1454 | Simca Matra Bagheera coupe | 40 |
| 1455 | Citroën CX Pallas saloon | 45 |
| 1539 | VW Scirocco coupe | 40 |
| 1540 | Renault 14 saloon | 30 |
| 1541 | Ford Fiesta saloon | 30 |
| 1542 | Chrysler 1308GT (Alpine) saloon | 30 |
| 1543 | Opel Ascona two-door saloon | 30 |

# Politoys/Polistil

Politoys is an Italian company that has been producing die cast models since 1965 (although they had been producing plastic models for several years prior to that). The first models were 1/43 scale and were given numbers in the 500's.

The 500 series was followed by series beginning with numbers prefixed by E and by M; both of these debuted in the early 1970s. More "prefixed" series were to follow, with the 1/43 scale AE, EL and CE's being introduced as the 1970s went on. While the body castings of the models in these series were often fairly accurate, Politoys (whose name was changed to Polistil during the early '70s), chose to outfit the majority of them with the "speed"-type wheels that became popular in the late '60s and early '70s. (Most of the models in the M series, however, retained the more accurate standard wheel.)

Other series included the "CA" Tanks, which were 1/43 scale tanks that were introduced in the mid-1970s; and a group of four "orphan" cars to which Polistil gave the prefix "OC." They were put out in the late '70s; two were "veteran" Alfa Romeos and two were Rolls-Royces.

Politoys also made smaller scale die casts; the "Penny" series was introduced in 1966 or '67. It consisted of 1/66 scale cars, trucks and Formula One race cars. The passenger car models were rather crude in appearance, although they did have window glazing and interiors. The Formula One race cars were fairly well detailed

and accurate for the time. The Pennys were discontinued in the early 1970s, to be replaced by a new series of 1/66 scale vehicles that were truly toys, being equipped with the speed type wheels (including the heavy equipment vehicles). These models had a J or Y prefix to the numbers (J is used in the following listing).

In the late 1980s, Polistil was acquired by Tonka. Larger die casts in 1/16 and 1/18 scale were produced, including models of supercars such as the Ferrari F40 and the Porsche 959. Tonka, now owned by Hasbro, no longer owns Polistil;

*The #508 Innocenti Morris IM3 by Politoys. This was one of the original 500 series models by Politoys, and as such featured the spun metal hubs typical of the series during the 1960s.*

new Polistil models still appear on the market, so the company is presumably still in business.

The following listing includes the most widely collected Polistil series. For further information, the reader is advised to consult Dr. Edward Force's Classic *Miniature Vehicles*

*Made in Italy* or Paolo Rampini's *The Golden Book of Model Cars*. Both books contain a wealth of information on this and other brands; please see Part Three, Additional Resources for information on these books.

| # | Name | Price |
|---|------|-------|
| 500 | Alfa Romeo Giulia GT | $25 |
| 501 | Maserati 3500 GT | 30 |
| 502 | Fiat Siata Coupe | 25 |
| 503 | Mercedes-Benz 230 SL Coupe | 25 |
| 504 | Ferrari 250 GT Berlinetta | 35 |
| 505 | Autobianchi Bianchina | 30 |
| 506 | Alfa Romeo Giulia SS | 25 |
| 507 | Ford Cortina | 25 |
| 508 | Innocenti Morris IM3 | 25 |
| 509 | Lancia Flavia Zagato 1800 | 40 |
| 510 | Opel Cadet | 25 |
| 511 | Fiat 600 | 25 |
| 512 | Fiat 500 Station Wagon | 25 |
| 513 | Fiat 850 | 25 |
| 514 | Alfa Romeo 2600 Bertone | 30 |
| 515 | Iso Rivolta Coupe | 30 |
| 516 | Alfa Romeo Giulia Zagato | 30 |
| 517 | Fiat 850 Coupe | 25 |
| 518 | Rolls-Royce Silver Cloud Coupe | 30 |
| 519 | Ford Taunus 20M TS | 25 |
| 520 | Lancia Fulvia Coupe | 30 |
| 521 | Opel Diplomat | 25 |
| 522 | Autobianchi Primula | 30 |
| 523 | Alfa Romeo Giulia TI | 30 |
| 524 | Simca 1500 | 25 |
| 525 | Ferrari 250 LM Pinin Farina | 35 |
| 526 | Fiat 1100 | 25 |
| 527 | Porsche 912 | 30 |
| 528 | Fiat 1500 GT Ghia Coupe | 25 |
| 529 | Alfa Romeo Giulia Canguro | 30 |
| 530 | Alfa Romeo 2600 Zagato | 30 |
| 531 | Alfa Romeo Giulia Carabinieri | 40 |
| 532 | Alfa Romeo 1931 Zagato Hardtop | 35 |
| 532 | Alfa Romeo 1931 Zagato Roadster | 35 |
| 533 | Fiat Osi Coupe | 25 |
| 534 | Lola Ford GT | 35 |
| 535 | Porsche 904 | 40 |
| 536 | Ferrari Dino Pinin Farina | 40 |
| 537 | Alfa Romeo 2600 Coupe Bertone Polizia | 40 |
| 538 | Volkswagen 1600 | 30 |
| 539 | Lamborghini 350 GT | 35 |
| 540 | Ferrari 275 GTB | 40 |
| 541 | Maserati Quattroporte | 30 |
| 542 | Volkswagen 1600 Station Wagon | 30 |
| 543 | N.S.U. 110 | 30 |
| 544 | Isuzu 117 Sports Ghia | 25 |
| 545 | Citroën DS 21 | 25 |
| 546 | BMW 2000 CS | 30 |
| 548 | Autobianchi Primula Coupe | 30 |
| 549 | Ford Mustang Bertone | 35 |
| 550 | Ghia V 280 | 25 |
| 551 | Chevrolet Corvair Bertone | 30 |
| 552 | Lamborghini Miura P 400 | 35 |
| 553 | Iso Grifo Bertone | 30 |
| 554 | Donald Duck's Car | 30 |
| 555 | Fiat 124 Roadster | 30 |

| # | Name | Price |
|---|------|-------|
| 556 | Corvette Rondine Pinin Farina | $30 |
| 557 | Lamborghini 4000 GT | 30 |
| 558 | Lamborghini Islero | 30 |
| 559 | Uncle Scrooge's Car | 30 |
| 560 | Chaparral 2 F | 40 |
| 561 | Aston Martin DBS | 30 |
| 562 | Ferrari 330 GTC | 35 |
| 563 | Lotus Europa | 30 |
| 564 | Panther Bertone | 30 |
| 565 | Lola Aston Martin | 30 |
| 566 | Ferrari P5 | 35 |
| 567 | Oldsmobile Toronado | 50 |
| 568 | Lamborghini Marzal | 35 |
| 571 | Matra 30 Sport | 25 |
| 573 | Jensen Vignale Coupe | 30 |
| 574 | Ferrari P 4 | 40 |
| 577 | Alfa Romeo Giulia | 30 |
| 578 | Fiat 125 | 25 |
| 579 | Renault 16 | 25 |
| 580 | B.R.E. Samurai | 25 |
| 583 | Alfa Romeo 33 | 30 |
| 586 | Ford GT J | 30 |
| 587 | Lamborghini Espada | 35 |
| 588 | Jaguar Pirana Bertone | 30 |
| 589 | Ferrari Dino Berlinetta | 30 |
| 591 | Maserati Ghibli Ghia | 35 |
| 593 | Rolls-Royce Silver Shadow Convertible | 50 |
| 594 | Abarth 3000 | 30 |
| 595 | Matra 630 Sport | 30 |
| 598 | Alpine Renault Le Mans | 30 |
| 600 | Mickey Mouse's Car | 50 |
| 602 | Drago Dragster | 25 |
| AE14 | Alfa Romeo Giulia Ambulance | 15 |
| AE15 | Giulia Carabinieri | 15 |
| AE16 | Alfa Romeo Giulia Fire Car | 15 |
| AE19 | Alfa Romeo Giulia Police Car | 15 |
| AE41 | Lancia Beta Alitalia | 15 |
| AE42 | Porsche Carrera RS Polizei | 20 |
| AE44 | Peugeot 104 Taxi | 15 |
| AE45 | Alfa Romeo Alfetta Carabinieri | 15 |
| AE49 | Alfasud TI Rally | 15 |
| AE53 | Renault R12 Tour de France | 15 |
| CA101 | T 62 Tank | 40 |
| CA102 | Chieftain Tank | 40 |
| CA103 | Konigstiger Tank | 40 |
| CA104 | Centurion Tank | 40 |
| CA105 | Leopard Tank | 40 |
| CA106 | M 60 Tank | 40 |
| CE32 | Suzuki Jimmy with Luggage Rack | 10 |
| CE33 | Land Rover with Luggage Rack | 10 |
| CE34 | Range Rover with Boat | 10 |
| CE35 | Fiat Campagnola with Luggage Rack | 10 |
| CE36 | Toyota with Skis | 10 |
| CE38 | UAZ with Skis | 10 |
| CE39 | Jeep CJ with Bicycles | 10 |
| CE40 | Citroën Mehari with Luggage Rack | 10 |

| # | Name | Price |
|---|------|-------|
| CE41 | Volkswagen Pescaccia with Luggage Rack | $15 |
| CE46 | BMW 2002 Polizei | 15 |
| CE56 | Saab 99 Rally | 10 |
| CE70A | Fiat Campagnola Carabinieri | 20 |
| CE70B | Fiat Campagnola Polizia | 20 |
| CE76A | Fiat 131 Polizia | 20 |
| CE76B | Fiat 131 Carabinieri | 20 |
| CE79A | Range Rover Firecar | 20 |
| CE79B | Range Rover Ambulance | 20 |
| CE104 | JPS Lotus | 10 |
| CE105 | Renault RS | 10 |
| CE106 | Brabham BT45C | 10 |
| CE107 | Ferrari 312T2 | 15 |
| CE108 | March 761 | 10 |
| CE109 | March 761 | 10 |
| CE110 | Tyrell 008 | 10 |
| CE111 | Ferrari 312T3 | 15 |
| CE112 | Copersucar | 10 |
| CE113 | International Tractor | 10 |
| CE114 | Fendt Tractor | 10 |
| CE115 | Ford 8700 Tractor | 10 |
| CE116 | Same Tiger Tractor | 10 |
| CE117 | Ferrari 312T4 | 15 |
| CE118 | Ligier JS11 | 10 |
| CE119 | Lotus 80 | 10 |
| CE120 | Brabham Alfa BT48 | 10 |
| CE121 | Alfa Romeo 179 | 10 |
| CE122 | Ferrari 312T5 | 10 |
| CE123 | Williams FW07 | 10 |
| CE150 | Ghia | 10 |
| CE156 | Lamborghini Marzal | 15 |
| CE188 | Pirana Bertone | 10 |
| CE215 | Ford Mirage | 10 |
| CE233 | Lola Can Am | 10 |
| CE234 | BRM P154 Can Am | 10 |
| CE235 | Lola 222 Can Am | 10 |
| E14 | Alfa Romeo Giulia Ambulance | 10 |
| E15 | Ford Mirage | 10 |
| E16 | Mercedes-Benz C-111 | 20 |
| E17 | Porsche 914 | 20 |
| E18 | Porsche 917 | 20 |
| E19 | Alfa Romeo Giulia Police | 10 |
| E20 | Honda N 360 | 10 |
| E21 | Opel CD Coupe | 10 |
| E22 | Ferrari 512 S | 25 |
| E23 | Fiat 500 L | 10 |
| E24 | Fiat 850 Van | 25 |
| E25 | Osi Bisiluro | 25 |
| E26 | Autobianchi A112 | 10 |
| E27 | Citroën Mehari | 10 |
| E28 | AMC Phaze II 343 | 10 |
| E29 | GAZ 69 AM | 10 |
| E30 | Citroën GS | 10 |
| E31 | Ford GT 70 | 25 |
| E32 | McLaren M8F Can Am | 25 |
| E33 | Lola Can Am | 10 |

| # | Name | Price |
|---|------|-------|
| E34 | B.R.M. P154 Can Am | $10 |
| E35 | Lola T222 Can Am | 10 |
| E36 | Alfa Romeo Alfasud | 10 |
| E37 | Renault 5 | 10 |
| E38 | Honda Z Coupe Z | 10 |
| E39 | Porsche-Audi Can Am | 25 |
| E40 | Fiat 126 | 10 |
| E41 | Lancia Beta | 10 |
| E42 | Porsche Carrera RS | 20 |
| E43 | Volkswagen 1303 Convertible | 20 |
| E44 | Peugeot 104 | 10 |
| EL15 | Ford Mirage | 10 |
| EL23 | Fiat 500 L | 10 |
| EL27 | Citroën Mehari | 10 |
| EL33 | Lola T 260 Can Am | 10 |

| # | Name | Price |
|---|------|-------|
| EL66 | Land Rover | $10 |
| EL67 | UAZ 469 B | 10 |
| EL70 | Fiat Campagnola | 10 |
| EL72 | Toyota Land Cruiser | 10 |
| EL73 | Volkswagen Pescaccia | 15 |
| EL74 | Jeep CJ | 10 |
| EL75 | Mercedes-Benz 280 SE | 10 |
| EL76 | Fiat 131 | 10 |
| EL77 | Opel Rekord | 10 |
| EL78 | Audi 100 LS | 10 |
| EL79 | Range Rover | 10 |
| EL568 | Lamborghini Marzal | 20 |
| HE26 | Autobianchi A 122 with Bicycles | 15 |
| HE30 | Citroën GS with Boat | 15 |
| HE36 | Alfa Romeo Alfasud with Skis | 15 |

| # | Name | Price |
|---|------|-------|
| OC3 | Alfa Romeo 1750 (top up) | $20 |
| OC4 | Alfa Romeo 1750 Roadster (top down) | 20 |
| OC6 | Rolls Royce Corniche Convertible | 25 |

**Penny 1/66 scale models:**

| # | Name | Price |
|---|------|-------|
| 1 | B.R.M. V8 Formula I | 15 |
| 2 | Lola Climax Formula I | 15 |
| 3 | Lotus Climax | 15 |
| 4 | Ferrari 156 Formula I | 15 |
| 5 | Brabham Formula I | 15 |
| 6 | Cooper Maserati Formula I | 15 |
| 7 | Eagle Formula I | 15 |
| 8 | B.R.M. H16 Formula I | 15 |
| 9 | Ferrari 312 Formula I | 15 |
| 10 | Honda V12 Formula I | 15 |
| 11 | Brabham-Repco Formula I | 15 |
| 12 | McLaren Ford Formula I | 15 |
| 13 | McLaren Formula I | 15 |
| 14 | Eagle Weslake Formula I | 15 |
| 15 | Lotus B.R.M. H16 Formula I | 15 |
| 21 | Ferrari 250 GT Lusso | 25 |
| 22 | Alfa Romeo Giulia TZ I Canguro | 20 |
| 24 | Porsche 912 | 20 |
| 25 | Alfa Romeo 2600 Sprint Bertone | 20 |
| 26 | Alfa Romeo Giulia SS | 20 |
| 27 | Lancia Flavia Zagato Coupe | 20 |
| 28 | Alfa Romeo Giulia GT Junior | 20 |
| 29 | Maserati 3500 GT | 20 |
| 30 | Fiat 850 Coupe | 20 |
| 32 | Iso Rivolta | 20 |
| 33 | Ferrari Dino Pinin Farina | 40 |
| 34 | Mercedes-Benz 230 SL | 20 |
| 35 | Alfa Romeo 2600 Sprint Police | 20 |
| 46 | Alfa Romeo Giulia GT Junior Police | 25 |
| 53 | Iso Rivolta and Boat Trailer | 20 |
| 54 | Romeo Minibus "SCUDERIA CORSE" | 20 |
| 110 | Romeo Minibus | 20 |
| 110 | Romeo F12 Minibus | 20 |
| 111 | Romeo Police Van | 20 |
| 111 | Romeo F12 Police Van | 20 |
| 112 | Romeo Ambulance | 20 |
| 112 | Romeo F12 Ambulance | 20 |
| 113 | Lancia Esadelta Open Truck | 30 |
| 113 | Lancia Esadelta Covered Truck | 30 |
| 114 | Lancia Esadelta Covered Truck with Plow | 30 |
| 115 | Lancia Esadelta Covered Truck and Trailer | 30 |
| 116 | Lancia Esadelta Crane Truck | 30 |
| 117 | Lancia Esadelta Fire Truck | 30 |
| 118 | Lancia Esadelta Covered Truck with Snowplow | 30 |
| 119 | Lancia Esadelta Car Transporter | 30 |
| 120 | Lancia Esadelta Car Transporter and 4 Cars | 75 |
| 121 | Lancia Esadelta Tanker "AGIP" | 30 |
| 122 | Aveling-Bedford Tractor Shovel | 15 |
| 200 | Ferrari P4 | 20 |
| 200 | Lamborghini Marzal | 20 |
| 200 | Ferrari Dino 206 Competizione | 20 |
| 200 | Osi Bisiluro | 20 |
| 201 | Alfa Romeo Giulia TI | 20 |
| 201 | Maserati Mistral | 20 |
| 201 | Ferrari Dino 206 Speciale Pinin Farina | 20 |
| 201 | Fiat 124 | 20 |

*This number 532 Alfa Romeo Zagato Roadster featured opening hood and doors, as well as an adjustable windshield.*

| # | Name | Price |
|---|------|-------|
| EL34 | B.R.M. P 154 Can Am | 10 |
| EL35 | Lola T 222 Can Am | 10 |
| EL39 | Porsche-Audi Can Am | 15 |
| EL43 | Volkswagen 1303 Convertible | 15 |
| EL45 | Alfa Romeo Alfetta | 10 |
| EL46 | BMW 2002 | 15 |
| EL47 | Fiat 126 | 10 |
| EL48 | Fiat 127 | 10 |
| EL49 | Alfa Romeo Alfasud TI | 10 |
| EL50 | Mini Cooper | 20 |
| EL51 | Peugeot 504 | 10 |
| EL52 | Citroën Dyane | 10 |
| EL53 | Renault 12 TS | 10 |
| EL54 | Volkswagen Scirocco | 15 |
| EL55 | Volkswagen 1300 L | 15 |
| EL56 | Saab 99 | 10 |
| EL57 | Volvo 164 E | 10 |
| EL58 | Ferrari Dino 308 | 20 |
| EL59 | Volkswagen Polo | 10 |
| EL60 | Ford Escort | 10 |
| EL61 | Jaguar XJ 12L | 15 |
| EL62 | AMC Gremlin | 20 |
| EL63 | Alfa Romeo Alfetta GT | 10 |
| EL64 | Datsun Fairlady 240Z | 15 |
| EL65 | Suzuki Jimmy | 10 |

| # | Name | Price |
|---|------|-------|
| HE37 | Renault 5T with Bicycles | 15 |
| HE40 | Fiat 126 with Luggage Rack | 15 |
| HE41 | Lancia Beta With Luggage Rack | 15 |
| M1 | Lancia Esagamma Car Transporter and 4 Cars | 100 |
| M2 | Lancia Esagamma Car Transporter | 45 |
| M10 | Howmet TX Turbine | 25 |
| M11 | Alfa Romeo 33 Berlinetta | 25 |
| M12 | Abarth 2000 Pinin Farina | 25 |
| M13 | Ferrari 512S Pinin Farina | 35 |
| M14 | Alfa Romeo Iguana | 25 |
| M15 | Serenissima 4800 | 25 |
| M16 | Matra Simca 660 | 25 |
| M17 | Ferrari Modulo | 35 |
| M18 | Chaparral 2J | 30 |
| M19 | De Tomaso Pantera | 30 |
| M20 | Porsche 917 LeMans | 30 |
| M21 | Chevron B16 | 25 |
| M22 | Lamborghini Urraco | 35 |
| M23 | Lancia Stratos Bertone | 25 |
| M24 | Alfa Romeo 33 LeMans | 25 |
| M25 | Lamborghini Jarama | 35 |
| M26 | March 717 Can Am | 25 |
| M27 | Ford Mustang Mach IV | 35 |
| OC2 | Rolls Royce Silver Cloud Coupe | 25 |

| # | Name | Price | # | Name | Price | # | Name | Price |
|---|------|-------|---|------|-------|---|------|-------|
| **The J or Y 1/66 scale models:** | | | J21 | Road Roller | $10 | J57 | Horse Trailer | $5 |
| J10 | Porsche 917 | $5 | J22 | Vulcano Dump Truck | 10 | J80 | Leone Tractor and Tank Trailer | 10 |
| J11 | Matra Sport | 5 | J23 | Perlini Dump Truck | 10 | J81 | Centauro Tractor and Open Trailer | 10 |
| J12 | Alpine Renault | 5 | J24 | Perlini Cement Mixer | 10 | J82 | Centauro Tractor and Seeder | 10 |
| J13 | Alfa Romeo Carabo | 5 | J25 | Tractor Shovel | 10 | J84 | FS Truck and Horse Trailer | 10 |
| J14 | Ford GT J | 5 | J26 | FS Truck | 10 | J85 | FS Truck and Dumping Trailer | 10 |
| J15 | Lola Aston Martin | 5 | J27 | Farm Tractor | 10 | J86 | Kaeble Truck and Flat Trailer | 15 |
| J16 | Alfa Romeo 33 | 5 | J28 | Dune Buggy | 10 | J88 | Centauro Tractor and Log Trailer | 10 |
| J17 | Ferrari 312 | 10 | J29 | Kaeble Dump Truck | 10 | J119 | Lancia Esadelta Car Transporter | 10 |
| J18 | Abarth 2000 | 5 | J33 | Tractor Shovel | 10 | J120 | Lancia Esadelta Car Transporter and 4 Cars | 30 |
| J19 | Abarth 2000 Pinin Farina | 5 | J34 | Centauro Tractor | 10 | J121 | Lancia Esadelta Tank Truck "AGIP" | 10 |
| J20 | Leone Tractor | 10 | J52 | Flat Trailer | 5 | | | |

# Prämeta

**P**rämeta die cast cars are a small but very much sought after group of toys. They were made by Kölner Automodelle Werke Prämeta in Cologne, Germany, during the early 1950s, and they varied in scale from 1/30 to 1/40.

There were four models in the series, although the company had made a Volkswagen prior to the four main models. It differed from the others in that it did not share all of their mechanical features. (It was also probably made before World War II.) The four principal models in the line were a Buick 405 Sedan (1/40 scale), a Mercedes-Benz 300 (1/37 scale), a Jaguar XK 120 (1/30 scale) and an Opel Kapitan (1/33 scale).

Considering the era in which they were produced, the Prämeta cars were very realistic and attractive. They came painted in various colors such as red, green or blue; they also were available in a chrome-plated finish. The windows were solid, being painted green on the plated cars and silver on the painted versions. The white tires are often yellowed from age on examples found today.

But it was the operating features that made these toys so memorable. They were powered by clockwork motors that could be wound with a distinctive key made in the shape of a policeman. The speed of the car could be controlled by means of a lever that protruded from the rear of the car, underneath the bumper. (It could even be set to go in reverse.) Each car was also equipped with a steering mechanism controlled by a lever that protruded from beneath the front bumper.

All in all, they were well-made, impressive toys. The Prämeta company also made available versions of the Mercedes, Buick and Opel with nearly half the body cut away to showcase the workings of the motor and steering mechanisms.

Prämeta cars came in individual boxes that were very well-illustrated in color, showing the model inside along with the logo of the full-size manufacturer. Near mint or better examples of Prämetas in their original boxes generally sell for $200-$300.

*The Prämeta Mercedes-Benz in red. The lever protruding from under the front bumper controlled the steering; it was attached to a bar mounted behind the grille. This bar protruded through holes in the bodywork, behind the headlights.*

# Pressomeccanica

The name of the company that produced Pressomeccanica toys was actually "Pressofusione Meccanica," although it is also referred to as "P.M." The company was located in Milan, Italy, and appears to have made die cast toy cars and trucks during the late 1940s. Judging by their scarcity today, they probably were made for only a few years.

Three basic castings were used to create a variety of different vehicles in the Pressomeccanica line; the models were approximately 1/40. The three were a Lancia Ardea Van, a Streamlined Race Car and an O.M. Taurus Truck. The Lancia Van came in several versions that had decals reading "Radio Roma," "Accessori Auto," etc. Some versions came with either a loudspeaker or roof board. The Lancia Van also came in Ambulance and Fire Van versions.

The Streamlined Race Car is undoubtedly the rarest of the Pressomeccanica toys. It had a streamlined shape typical of late 1930s racing machines.

The O.M. Taurus Truck came in numerous configurations, among which were a Tow Truck, a Fire Engine and a Street Sweeper. There was even a Tanker truck with attached tanker trailer; this came in both "Benzina" and water tanker versions. (There was a casting change made to this truck at some point; versions exist that have the headlights cast in as part of the front fenders, while others have the headlights mounted separately, between the fender and grille.)

It is not known whether Pressomeccanica toys came in individual boxes. They did, however, come packaged as part of a play set, containing things like a gas pump and street signs. By themselves, near mint to mint condition original Pressomeccanica models can sell for $75-$125 (the Ardea Vans and the one-piece O.M. Trucks). A price of $175-$200 for the more elaborate models (the Tanker with Trailer, for example) is not unusual. The Streamlined Race Car is so rare that there is no history of an established selling price.

# Quartzo

This Portugese line of 1/43 scale die cast race cars is made by Minibri Ltd. The Vitesse Group of companies owns Minibri, which also manufactures the Onyx series of models. Cinerius Ltd., makers of the Vitesse line of die casts, is also part of the Vitesse Group.

The Quartzo line made its debut in 1992 with a group of vintage NASCAR models. Since then it has expanded into current NASCAR entries as well as older Formula One and sports race cars. Like many manufacturers, Quartzo maximizes the usefulness of its castings by offering each in numerous liveries. Quartzo models currently come in a square plastic display box, with the model held to the base with a screw.

Although the Vitesse Group companies have traditionally done their manufacturing in Portugal, the baseplate of a recent Quartzo release stated that it had been made in China. Perhaps manufacture has been transferred to the Far East.

CRP (Current Retail Price) of Quartzo models is $20-$25.

| # | Name | Price | # | Name | Price | # | Name | Price |
|---|------|-------|---|------|-------|---|------|-------|
| 1001 | Chevy Impala (Baker 1959) | CRP | 2005 | Chevy Lumina "Raybestos" | CRP | 2023 | Ford Thunderbird "Quaker State" | CRP |
| 1002 | Chevy Impala (Pearson 1959) | CRP | 2006 | Pontiac Grand Prix "Mello Yello" | CRP | 2024 | Chevy Lumina "Western Auto" | CRP |
| 1003 | Ford Fairlane (Turner 1956) | CRP | 2007 | Pontiac Grand Prix "Pennzoil" | CRP | 3001 | Porsche 935K3 (LeMans 1979) | CRP |
| 1004 | Ford Fairlane (Roberts 1956) | CRP | 2008 | Ford Thunderbird "Maxwell House" | CRP | 3002 | Porsche 935K3 (LeMans 1980) | CRP |
| 1005 | Chevy Impala (Welborn 1959) | CRP | 2009 | Chevy Lumina "Purolator" | CRP | 3003 | Porsche 935K3 (LeMans 1982) | CRP |
| 1006 | Ford Fairlane (Weatherly 1956) | CRP | 2010 | Ford Thunderbird "Valvoline" | CRP | 3004 | Porsche 935K3 (LeMans 1981) | CRP |
| 1007 | Chevy Impala (White 1959) | CRP | 2011 | Ford Thunderbird "Budweiser" | CRP | 3005 | Porsche 935K3 (LeMans 1980) | CRP |
| 1008 | Ford Fairlane (Wood 1956) | CRP | 2012 | Pontiac Grand Prix "Miller" | CRP | 3006 | Porsche 935K3 (LeMans 1980) | CRP |
| 1009 | Ford Fairlane (Castles 1956) | CRP | 2013 | Ford Thunderbird "Hooters" | CRP | 4001 | Lotus 49 (Clark 1967) | CRP |
| 1015 | Chevy Impala (Thompson 1959) | CRP | 2014 | Pontiac Grand Prix "Dirt Devil" | CRP | 4002 | Lotus 49 (Clark 1968) | CRP |
| 1016 | Chevy Impala (Lund 1959) | CRP | 2015 | Chevy Lumina "Kodak" | CRP | 4003 | Lotus 49 (Siffert 1968) | CRP |
| 1017 | Ford Fairlane (Larson 1956) | CRP | 2016 | Chevy Lumina "Dupont Paints" | CRP | 4004 | Lotus 49 (Hill 1968) | CRP |
| 1018 | Chevy Impala Convertible (Frank 1959) | CRP | 2017 | Ford Thunderbird "Skoal Classic" | CRP | 4005 | Lotus 49B (Hill 1968) | CRP |
| | | | 2018 | Ford Thunderbird "Citgo" | CRP | 4006 | Matra MS80 (Beltoise 1969) | CRP |
| 2001 | Chevy Lumina "Goodwrench" | CRP | 2019 | Chevy Lumina "Valvoline" | CRP | 4007 | Matra MS80 (Stewart 1969) | CRP |
| 2002 | Chevy Lumina "Interstate Batteries" | CRP | 2020 | Chevy Lumina "Kodiak" | CRP | 4008 | Lotus 72 (Rindt 1970) | CRP |
| 2003 | Pontiac Grand Prix "STP" | CRP | 2021 | Ford Thunderbird "Motorcraft" | CRP | 4009 | Lotus 72D (Fittipaldi 1972) | CRP |
| 2004 | Ford Thunderbird "Havoline" | CRP | 2022 | Chevy Lumina "Tide" | CRP | 4010 | Lotus 72D (Charlton 1972) | CRP |

# Quiralu

This line of predominantly 1/43 scale die cast models was originally produced in France from 1957 until 1959. Although the Quiralu company had been in existence since 1933, it would be the die cast models that would give it lasting fame among collectors.

Quiralu initially produced these simple models without window glazing or interiors. As time went on, however, they added glazing to certain models; this was undoubtedly in response to what Corgi was offering at the same time in England. As might be expected, there were a number of French marques in the line, but Jaguar and Mercedes-Benz also were represented. There were also a couple of "bubble cars" included.

For all their simplicity and period charm, Quiralus were fairly realistic models for their time. They came with white rubber tires mounted on spun aluminum wheel hubs (except the larger trucks, which came with black tires).

In 1991 or '92, the French company Louis Surber SA started using the original Quiralu tooling that it had purchased to produce re-issues of the original Quiralus. The re-issues are quite simple, like the originals. Some have window glazing, and some don't. They also sport the same type of spun-aluminum wheel hubs. The baseplates of the re-issues are unpainted aluminum, whereas the originals had

An original Quiralu Mercedes-Benz 300SL with its original box. Although it did not come with windows, Louis Surber SA's re-issue of the model does have window glazing.

tinplate bases painted black. The re-issues come packaged in a simple cardboard box that has artwork of the car contained inside.

To date, nearly all of the original Quiralus have been re-issued by Surber. These re-issues sell at retail for $25-$35.

The following values are for near mint to mint condition **original** Quiralus with their original box.

| Name | Price | Name | Price | Name | Price |
|---|---|---|---|---|---|
| Mercedes-Benz 300SL Coupe | $100 | Simca Marly Station Wagon | $80 | Peugeot D4 A Army Ambulance | $300 |
| Jaguar XK140 | 100 | Simca Regence | 90 | Peugeot D4 A Van | 250 |
| Messerschmitt KR 200 | 125 | Simca Trianon | 90 | various liveries | 250 |
| Peugeot 403 | 90 | Simca Versailles | 90 | Berliet GBO Covered Truck | 300 |
| Porsche 356 | 160 | Vespa 400 | 100 | Berliet GBO Covered Trailer | 150 |
| Renault Etoile Filante Record Car | 120 | Velam Isetta | 100 | Berliet GBO Dump Truck | 350 |
| Rolls-Royce Silver Cloud | 175 | Simca Marly Ambulance | 100 | | |

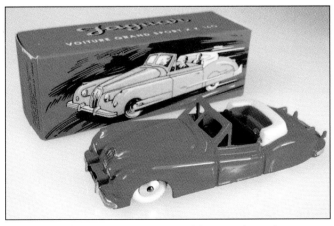

This Jaguar XK 140 is the Surber re-issue of the original Quiralu.

Baseplate of the Surber Jaguar re-issue. Note that the aluminum is unpainted.

# Racing Champions

NASCAR and IndyCar racing are very popular sports in the United States, and a number of die cast manufacturers cater to this segment of the market. Racing Champions, Inc. is one of the major players.

Based in Glen Ellyn, Illinois, Racing Champions entered the market in 1993 with a line of NASCAR toys. They can also be called models, because the accuracy of most of the products is quite good. Sponsor logos are tampo printed, and the models come with rubber tires.

A number of different racing series are covered in the product line, including the World of Outlaws, NASCAR Winston Cup and SuperTruck, CART IndyCar, and IROC. Names like Andretti, Waltrip and Gordon feature prominently on these models.

Following is an outline of the categories of model offered by

Racing Champions. Each type of model generally is available in many different liveries.

The smaller (1/64 scale) models come on blister cards, while the 1/43 scale and 1/24 scale products are available in display boxes. The CRP (Current Retail Price) for Racing Champions models ranges from a low of $2 for some of the 1/64 scale single race cars, to $15-$20 for the 1/24 scale items.

*This #8300 Channellock Ford (driven by Sammy Swindell) was part of the 1/24 scale 1995 SuperTruck series, packaged in a window display box.*

*Racing Champions #5100 IndyCar in 1/64 scale, as driven by Adrian Fernandez. This version came on a blister card.*

| # | Name | Price | # | Name | Price | # | Name | Price |
|---|------|-------|---|------|-------|---|------|-------|
| 900 | NASCAR Stock Car Bank (1/24 scale) | . . CRP | 4300 | NASCAR Stock Car (1/43 scale) | . . . . . CRP | 8200 | NASCAR SuperTruck (1/64 scale) | . . . . . CRP |
| 1153 | NASCAR Stock Car (1/64 scale) | . . . . . CRP | 5100 | IndyCar (1/64 scale) | . . . . . . . . . . CRP | 8300 | NASCAR SuperTruck (1/24 scale) | . . . . . CRP |
| 1800 | NASCAR Stock Car (1/64 scale) | . . . . . CRP | 5300 | IndyCar (1/43 scale) | . . . . . . . . . . CRP | 8700 | NASCAR Team Transporter | |
| 3102 | NASCAR Racing Team Transporter with stock car (1/87 scale) | . . . . . . . . . . CRP | 5400 | IndyCar (1/24 scale) | . . . . . . . . . . CRP | | (1/87 scale) | . . . . . . . . . . . . . CRP |
| 3400 | NASCAR Racing Team Transporter (1/64 scale) | . . . . . . . . . . . . . CRP | 6400 | NASCAR Team Transporter (1/64 scale) | . . . . . . . . . . . . . CRP | 9035 | World of Outlaws Sprint Car (1/24 scale) | . . . . . . . . . . . . . CRP |
| 3500 | World of Outlaws Sprint Car (1/64 scale) | . . . . . . . . . . . . . CRP | 7053 | NASCAR Stock Car (1/43 scale) | . . . . . CRP | 9050 | NASCAR Stock Car (1/24 scale) | . . . . . CRP |
| | | | 7400 | NASCAR Racing Team Transporter (1/43 scale) | . . . . . . . . . . . . . CRP | | | |

# Ralstoy

Ralston, Nebraska, was the home of the die cast toys known as Ralstoys. The original name of the company was Ralston Toy & Novelty Co., and it was founded in the late 1930s.

The die cast toys made after World War II were typical of American die cast toys of the period: they were rugged, simple castings with rubber tires. Most had no baseplate. In many cases, the make of car or truck assigned to Ralstoys is merely a guess, since many of the toys were approximations of full-size vehicles.

Dates of manufacture are unclear; it seems that Ralstoys were made through the 1950s and into the 1960s. In recent years, simple die cast trucks featuring numerous logos have been marketed by the company. The following listing is by no means exhaustive.

*This Oldsmobile Sedan (some call it a Cadillac) was probably made during the late 1940s. It had a chrome-plated finish.*

| Name | Price |
|------|-------|
| Anti-aircraft Unit | $40 |
| Cannon | 30 |
| Fire Engine | 150 |
| Ford High-Side Tractor Trailer | 75 |
| Ford Low Loader Tractor Trailer | 75 |
| Ford Gasoline Tanker Tractor Trailer | 85 |
| Ford Lumber Tractor Trailer | 75 |
| Ford Flatbed Tractor Trailer | 75 |
| Ford Van Tractor Trailer | 75 |
| Kenworth Tanker Tractor Trailer | 75 |
| Moving Van Tractor Trailer | 55 |
| Freight Van Tractor Trailer | 55 |
| Flatbed Tractor Trailer | 55 |
| Transporter with Tank | 100 |
| Tank | 40 |
| Oldsmobile Sedan | 150 |

*Ralstoy made a number of tractor trailers using this Ford-type cab unit. This one was called a low loader.*

# RAMI

These French die cast models of vintage automobiles were manufactured by a company called J.M.K. beginning in 1958. J.M.K. was located in the Haute-Saone region of France, and the RAMI series was undoubtedly launched to compete with Lesney's Matchbox Models of Yesteryear, which had been on the market since 1956. RAMI was an acronym for "Les Rétrospectives Automobiles Miniature."

The models were based on actual cars housed in the Musée Francais de l'Automobile, located near Lyon. Although RAMI models were good general representations of the actual cars, they were somewhat simplistic compared to the competition. There was no window glazing, and the wheels and tires were made from a flexible plastic, as were other parts such as steering wheels. But there were some interesting subjects included among the models, and they were nice looking products. The baseplates showed the model name and the manufacturer, as well as a Made in France inscription.

Thirty-eight models made up the RAMI line, and production ended around 1969. RAMI used a simple numbering system, starting with 1. The only numbering change seems to have been that of number 2: the De Dion-Bouton was replaced in the late 1960s by a Motobloc Tonneau of 1902 vintage.

RAMI boxes were generally of two types. The first was an orange and white cardboard affair, with the same artwork of a Panhard on all boxes. (The actual model contained inside was indicated elsewhere on the box.) The second type of packaging was a clear, lift-off-lid plastic box with plastic base.

The following listing provides values for near mint or better examples with their original boxes.

*RAMI number 21, the 1902 Georges Richard Tonneau. The plastic wheels and tires were typical of almost all RAMI models. This example came packaged in the plastic lift-off-lid type of box.*

*A two-page spread from a late 1960s RAMI catalog. The number 4 Citroën is actually a photo of the full-size car, taken on the grounds of the Musée Francais de l'Automobile. J.M.K. frequently showed actual automobiles in the RAMI catalogs.*

| # | Name | Price | # | Name | Price | # | Name | Price |
|---|------|-------|---|------|-------|---|------|-------|
| 1 | Renault Taxi de la Marne 1907 | $25 | 13 | Packard Landaulet 1912 | $35 | 26 | Delahaye 1904 | $25 |
| 2 | De Dion-Bouton vis-a-vis 1900 | 25 | 14 | Peugeot Coupe 1898 | 25 | 27 | Audibert & Lavirotte 1898 | 25 |
| 2 | Tonneau Motobloc 1902 | 50 | 15 | Ford T Roadster | 35 | 28 | Léon Bollée 1911 | 25 |
| 3 | Lion-Peugeot 1907 | 25 | 16 | Ford T Torpedo 1908 | 35 | 29 | S P A 1912 | 35 |
| 4 | Citroën 5 CV 1924 | 25 | 17 | Panhard & Levassor La Marquise 1908 | 25 | 30 | Amédée Bollée La Mancelle 1878 | 25 |
| 5 | De Dion-Bouton Cab 1900 | 25 | 18 | Panhard & Levassor Tonneau Ballon 1899 | 25 | 31 | Luc Court 1901 | 25 |
| 6 | Bugatti 35C 1928 | 35 | 19 | Hautier 1898 | 25 | 32 | Brazier 1908 | 25 |
| 7 | Citroën B2 | 35 | 20 | Delaunay Belleville 1904 | 25 | 33 | Berliet 1910 | 25 |
| 8 | Sizaire & Naudin 1906 | 25 | 21 | Georges Richard Tonneau 1902 | 25 | 34 | Mieusset 1903 | 25 |
| 9 | Rochet Schneider | 25 | 22 | Scotte 1892 | 25 | 35 | De Dion-Bouton 1902 | 25 |
| 10 | Hispano Suiza 1934 | 35 | 23 | Renault Tonneau 1900 | 25 | 36 | Lacroix de Laville 1898 | 35 |
| 11 | Gobron Brillié Double Phaeton 1899 | 25 | 24 | Lorraine Diétrich 1911 | 25 | 37 | Delage Torpedo 1932 | 35 |
| 12 | Gauthier Wehrlé 1897 | 25 | 25 | Panhard & Levassor Tonneau 1895 | 25 | 38 | Mercedes SSK 1927 | 35 |

# Renwal

The name Renwal is very familiar to collectors of plastic toys and models; it is less so to die cast enthusiasts. Renwal was a leading producer of plastic toys during the late 1940s and '50s, and these are very popular pieces today.

But Renwal made a contribution to the die cast world in 1955, when the New York-based company decided to attempt to compete with the likes of Hubley and Tootsietoy with a line of die cast toys. Included would be metal versions of their three-inch and four-inch cars and trucks, as well as larger (six to nine inches) cars and trucks. (The metal series also featured several airplanes.)

Unfortunately for Renwal, the product did not match the hype. The metal toys suffered from sloppy paint finishes, rough spots in the castings, and generally poor quality. Sales were undoubtedly not what the company had hoped for, and the toys were only on the market during 1955. This accounts for their scarcity today.

Most of the metal Renwals came with rubber tires, and the larger vehicles (six inches and longer) came with a metal baseplate. The four-inch metal vehicles came with a friction motor, as did the larger "True Scale Replicas" cars. Interestingly, a number of the three-inch metal vehicles were manufactured using the tooling for the plastic versions. As a result, aside from the occasional minor casting change, identical vehicles can be found in both metal and plastic.

The following listing provides values for the three- and four-inch vehicles by themselves, since they were apparently sold only in bulk, with no individual box. (The exception was the #8801 "Turnpike Set," which was a boxed set of five of the three-inch metal vehicles. It is quite rare today, and would likely sell for $200-$300 if put up for sale.) The values for the larger vehicles are for near mint examples with original boxes.

*A page from the 1955 Renwal catalog, showing a die cast metal series that apparently never made it to store shelves. Several of these six-inch long "Sport and Foreign Cars" were later produced by Renwal in a plastic version, however.*

*Renwal's number 8010 Delivery Truck. Aside from the chipping, note the sloppy fashion in which the red paint was applied.*

| # | Name | Price |
|---|------|-------|
| **True Scale Replica series** | | |
| **(8 inch to 9 1/2 inch):** | | |
| 8001 | Ferrari Racer | $150 |
| 8002 | Maserati Racer | 150 |
| 8003 | Pontiac Convertible | 125 |
| 8004 | Plymouth Convertible | 125 |
| 8005 | Chevrolet Sedan | 125 |
| 8006 | Ford Sedan | 125 |
| **5 1/2-inch to 7-inch series:** | | |
| 8007 | Sedan | 75 |
| 8008 | Gasoline Truck | 75 |
| 8009 | Racer | 90 |
| 8010 | Delivery Truck | 75 |

| # | Name | Price |
|---|------|-------|
| 8011 | Pick-up Truck | $75 |
| 8012 | Hot Rod | 75 |
| 8013 | Jeep | 75 |
| 8014 | Fire Truck | 75 |
| 8015 | Convertible | 75 |
| **4-inch series:** | | |
| | Convertible | 100 |
| | Gasoline Truck | 75 |
| | Coupe | 75 |
| | City Bus | 75 |
| **3-inch series:** | | |
| 143 | Sedan | 30 |
| 144 | Coupe | 30 |

| # | Name | Price |
|---|------|-------|
| 145 | Fire Truck | $25 |
| 146 | Hook & Ladder | 25 |
| 147 | Convertible | 25 |
| 148 | Gasoline Truck | 25 |
| 149 | Pick-Up Truck | 25 |
| 150 | Racer | 50 |
| 8020 | Futuristic Two-Door Coupe | 25 |
| 8021 | Gasoline Truck | 25 |
| 8022 | Ladder Fire Truck | 25 |
| 8023 | Ford Sunliner Convertible | 40 |
| 8028 | Ford Victoria Hardtop | 40 |
| 8039 | Pick-Up Truck | 25 |
| 8040 | Pumper Fire Truck | 25 |
| 8041 | Speed King Racer | 50 |

*This three-inch metal Gasoline Truck (#148) is essentially identical to Renwal's plastic version.*

# Revell

Revell-Monogram, Inc., long-time manufacturer of plastic model kits, entered the die cast market in 1989 or 1990. Although they produce models in 1/24 scale (and even a couple in 1/12 scale), it is their 1/18 scale products for which they are best known.

Revell 1/18 models are of similiar quality to those of competitors like Maisto and Bburago, and they are priced to compete with those brands. They generally are packaged in cardboard and plastic display boxes, and can be found in many of the larger chain stores.

Revell has also been putting out a higher-end 1/20 scale series in recent years called "Creative Masters Collection." These are models with greater detail and more features than the standard Revell line, and they generally sell for $100-$150. Subjects have included a 1967 Chevrolet Corvette Convertible, a '65 Shelby Mustang GT-350, a Ford GT-40, a '65 Shelby 427 Cobra and a Dodge Viper.

*This 1/20 scale Dodge Viper is part of Revell's "Creative Masters Collection," which features greater detailing and more features than the standard line.*

Following is a listing of models shown in Revell's 1994 and 1995 die cast catalogs. CRP (Current Retail Price) for the 1/18 scale items is $15-$25, while the 1/24 scale models sell for $10-$15 (although the 1/24 "Big Trucks" may sell for more). CRP for the 1/12 models is in the $100-$125 range.

| # | Name | Price |
|---|------|-------|
| **1/12 scale:** | | |
| 8851 | 1954 Mercedes-Benz 300 SLR | CRP |
| 8853 | 1962 Ferrari 250 GTO (red) | CRP |
| 8854 | 1962 Ferrari 250 GTO (yellow) | CRP |
| **1/12 scale Motorcycles:** | | |
| 8869 | BMW R1100RS (yellow) | CRP |
| 8870 | BMW R1100RS (white) | CRP |
| 8871 | BMW R1100RS (blue) | CRP |
| 8872 | BMW R1100RS (red) | CRP |
| 8873 | MV Agusta (red) | CRP |
| 8874 | MV Agusta (street racer) | CRP |
| **1/18 scale:** | | |
| 8649 | 1956 Ford Thunderbird (black) | CRP |
| 8691 | 1969 Corvette Convertible (blue) | CRP |

| # | Name | Price |
|---|------|-------|
| 8753 | 1965 Mustang Convertible (blue) | CRP |
| 8755 | 1969 Corvette Convertible (red) | CRP |
| 8757 | 1965 Ford Mustang Convertible Top Up (red) | CRP |
| 8817 | 1956 Ford Thunderbird (pink) | CRP |
| 8826 | 1969 Corvette Convertible (yellow) | CRP |
| 8829 | 1969 Corvette Convertible (green) | CRP |
| 8830 | Audi Avus Quattro (aluminum finish) | CRP |
| 8831 | 1965 Ford Mustang Hardtop (black) | CRP |
| 8832 | 1965 Ford Mustang Indy Pace Car | CRP |
| 8833 | 1955 Ford Thunderbird (red) | CRP |
| 8835 | Audi Avus Quattro (white) | CRP |
| 8837 | 1955 BMW Isetta 250 (blue) | CRP |
| **1/24 scale:** | | |
| 8613 | 1963 Corvette Sting Ray (black) | CRP |

| # | Name | Price |
|---|------|-------|
| 8617 | Shelby Cobra 427 (red) | CRP |
| 8618 | Corvette ZR-1 Coupe (blue) | CRP |
| 8619 | 1963 Corvette Roadster (blue) | CRP |
| 8623 | Shelby Cobra 427 (blue) | CRP |
| 8693 | Chevy S-10 Pickup Truck (black) | CRP |
| 8834 | Chevy S-10 Pickup Truck | CRP |
| **1/24 scale Big Trucks:** | | |
| 8890 | Peterbilt 359 (white) | CRP |
| 8891 | Peterbilt 359 (black) | CRP |
| 8892 | Peterbilt 359 Classic (blue) | CRP |
| 8893 | Peterbilt 359 Road Train (tab) | CRP |
| 8895 | Peterbilt Iron 359 (metal finish) | CRP |
| 8896 | Box Trailer | CRP |

# Rextoys

**R**extoys is a Swiss manufacturer of 1/43 scale models, located in Lausanne. They traditionally have specialized in pre-war American automobiles.

The models are unusual due to the fact that they are made entirely of metal. Plastic is not used for features normally associated with that material: headlights, hood ornaments, etc. The company gets everything it can out of each casting, releasing each in a variety of versions and liveries.

The following listing is from a 1980s (or perhaps early 1990s) Rextoys catalog, and it is broken down by basic body type. CRP (Current Retail Price) of Rextoy models is $30-$40.

*Rextoys #3, the 1938-1940 Cadillac V16 Formal Sedan.*

| # | Name | Price |
|---|------|-------|
| **Cadillac V16 1938-1940:** | | |
| 1 | S.S. Pie XII open front sedan | CRP |
| 2 | Open front sedan | CRP |
| 3 | Formal sedan | CRP |
| 4 | Touring sedan | CRP |
| 4/1 | Touring sedan, US Army | CRP |
| 4/2 | Touring sedan, US Air Force | CRP |
| 4/3 | Touring sedan, US Navy | CRP |
| 5 | Sport Coupe | CRP |
| 6 | Convertible coupe | CRP |
| 7 | Convertible coupe, Cicciolina | CRP |
| 12 | Four-door convertible sedan | CRP |
| 12R | Four-door convertible sedan, President Roosevelt | CRP |

| # | Name | Price |
|---|------|-------|
| **Chrysler Airflow 1935:** | | |
| 21 | Touring sedan | CRP |
| 24 | Fire brigade touring sedan | CRP |
| 26 | Police patrol touring sedan | CRP |
| 27 | Yellow cab touring sedan | CRP |
| **Rolls-Royce Phantom IV 1953-1954:** | | |
| 31 | Limousine H.M. the King of Spain | CRP |
| 32 | Convertible sedan H.M. the King of Spain | CRP |
| 33 | Limousine H.R.H. Princess Margaret | CRP |
| 34 | Limousine Duke of Gloucester | CRP |
| 35 | Limousine Shah of Kuwait | CRP |

| # | Name | Price |
|---|------|-------|
| 36 | Limousine H.M. the Queen of England | CRP |
| 37 | Limousine H.R.H. Princess Elisabeth | CRP |
| **Ford 1935 Type 48:** | | |
| 42 | Fordor touring sedan | CRP |
| 43 | Convertible coupe | CRP |
| 45 | Sean delivery | CRP |
| 46 | Sport coupe | CRP |
| 47 | Station wagon | CRP |
| 48 | Sedan, US Army | CRP |
| 49 | Fire brigade | CRP |
| 50 | Taxi | CRP |
| 51 | Police USA | CRP |

# Rio

This Italian company entered the die cast market in 1962 with a line of 1/43 scale vintage or "veteran" models. They were of very good quality, representing mostly Italian makes. As time went on, they expanded into French and German cars. The United States also was represented with a Lincoln Continental and a Duesenberg.

Rio continued to manufacture its models throughout the 1960s and '70s, eventually expanding the product line to include cars from the 1950s and '60s. (Early models had focused on the 1900s through the 1930s.) Rio continues to market its models today; interestingly, they still manufacture the same models as they did thirty years ago. A collector can therefore display a #17 1909 Mercedes-Benz made in 1966 with another made in 1994. There have been minor changes made to some models over the years, but the line has largely remained intact.

Since all Rio models are currently available, the following listing gives values as CRP (Current Retail Price), which is generally $20-$25. An older version of any model (with earlier type packaging, for example) could sell for a bit more.

*Two-page spread from a late 1960s Rio catalog, showing models 1 through 8.*

| # | Name | Price | # | Name | Price | # | Name | Price |
|---|------|-------|---|------|-------|---|------|-------|
| 1 | Itala 1 Targa Florio 1906 | CRP | 21 | Mercedes-Benz 770 open cabriolet 1938 | CRP | 40 | Rolls-Royce Phantom II open 1932 | CRP |
| 2 | Itala Raid Pechino-Parigi 1907 | CRP | | | | 41 | Lancia Dilambda 1929 | CRP |
| 3 | Fiat 501 Sport 1919-26 | CRP | 22 | Mercedes-Benz 770 closed cabriolet 1938 | CRP | 42 | Lancia Dilambda torpedo 1929 | CRP |
| 4 | Fiat 501 Torpedo 1919-26 | CRP | | | | 43 | Lincoln Continental closed 1941 | CRP |
| 5 | Alfa Romeo P3 1932 | CRP | 23 | Fiat 60 CV 1905 | CRP | 44 | Lincoln Continental open 1941 | CRP |
| 6 | Fiat 0 1912 | CRP | 24 | Fiat 60 CV open 1905 | CRP | 45 | Duesenberg "sj" torpedo phaeton closed 1934 | CRP |
| 7 | Fiat 0 Spider 1912 | CRP | 25 | Fiat 24 CV double phaeton 1906 | CRP | | | |
| 8 | Isotta Fraschini 8a 1924 | CRP | 26 | Fiat 12 CV open 1902 | CRP | 46 | Duesenberg "sj" torpedo phaeton open 1934 | CRP |
| 9 | Isotta Fraschini 8a open 1924 | CRP | 27 | Fiat 24 CV limousine 1905 | CRP | | | |
| 10 | Bianchi Landaulet 1909 | CRP | 28 | Bianchi 20/30 CV landaulet 1905 | CRP | 47 | Thomas Flyer Rallye New York-Paris 1908 | CRP |
| 11 | Bianchi Landaulet open 1909 | CRP | 29 | Mercedes-Benz Simplex 1902 | CRP | | | |
| 12 | Fiat Spider open 1912 | CRP | 30 | De Dion-Bouton "Victoria" 1894 | CRP | 48 | Bugatti T50 1932 | CRP |
| 13 | Fiat 508 "Balilla" 1932-37 | CRP | 31 | Fiat 8 CV 1901 | CRP | 49 | Fiat V 12 "Dorsay de ville" 1921 | CRP |
| 14 | Fiat 2 1910-20 | CRP | 32 | Fiat 16/24CV 1903 | CRP | 50 | Lincoln sport phaeton closed 1928 | CRP |
| 15 | Isotta Fraschini 8a Spider 1924 | CRP | 33 | Mercedes-Benz limousine 1908 | CRP | 51 | Lincoln sport phaeton open 1928 | CRP |
| 16 | Chalmers-Detroit 1909 | CRP | 34 | Renault X 1907 | CRP | 52 | Renault 40 CV torpedo 1923 | CRP |
| 17 | Mercedes-Benz Touriste 1909 | CRP | 35 | Renault AG 1910 fiacre | CRP | 53 | Renault 40 CV sport 1923 | CRP |
| 18 | Bianchi Coupe de ville 15/20 CV 1906 | CRP | 36 | Bugatti 41 Royale closed 1927 | CRP | 54 | Bugatti 41 Royale 1927 | CRP |
| 19 | Alfa Romeo 6c 1750 1932 | CRP | 37 | Bugatti 41 Royale open 1927 | CRP | 55 | Alfa Ricotti 1914 | CRP |
| 20 | Fiat 18 BL Autobus 1915 | CRP | 38 | Fiat 18/24CV 1908 | CRP | 56 | General "Grand Prix" 1902 | CRP |
| | | | 39 | Rolls-Royce Phantom II closed 1932 | CRP | 57 | Fiat 519 S closed 1923 | CRP |

| # | Name | Price |
|---|------|-------|
| 58 | Fiat 519 S open 1923 | CRP |
| 59 | Fiat 519 S limousine 1923 | CRP |
| 60 | Jenatzy "Jamais Contente" 1899 | CRP |
| 61 | Hispano-Suiza V 12 1932 | CRP |
| 62 | Leyat 1923 | CRP |
| 63 | Delahaye 135 M 1935 | CRP |
| 64 | Mercedes-Benz 770 Reich Führer Adolf Hitler 1942 | CRP |
| 65 | Hispano-Suiza V 12 limousine 1932 | CRP |
| 66 | Bugatti 41 Royale 1927-33 | CRP |
| 67 | Isotta Fraschini 8a Cabriolet de Ville closed 1929 | CRP |
| 68 | Isotta Fraschini 8a Cabriolet de Ville open 1929 | CRP |
| 69 | Ford 999 1902 | CRP |
| 70 | Alfa Romeo P3 B "Targa Florio" 1934 | CRP |
| 71 | Alfa Romeo P3 B "double-wheels" 1935 | CRP |
| 72 | Rolls-Royce Twenty closed 1923 | CRP |
| 73 | Rolls-Royce Twenty open 1923 | CRP |
| 74 | Bugatti 41 Royale 1929 | CRP |
| 75 | Fiat 60CV limousine 1905 | CRP |
| 76 | Cadillac V 16 closed cabriolet 1931 | CRP |
| 77 | Cadillac V 16 open cabriolet 1931 | CRP |
| 78 | Bugatti 57 SC Atlantic 1938 | CRP |
| 79 | Mercedes-Benz SSKL 1931 | CRP |
| 80 | Mercedes-Benz SSK 1927 | CRP |
| 81 | Alfa Ricotti torpedo 1915 | CRP |
| 82 | Lincoln Continental limousine 1941 | CRP |
| 83 | Hispano-Suiza V 12 closed cabriolet 1936 | CRP |
| 84 | Hispano-Suiza V 12 open cabriolet 1936 | CRP |
| 85 | Mercedes-Benz 770 pullman-limousine 1938 | CRP |
| 86 | Duesenberg "sj" spider "fish-tail" 1933 | CRP |
| 87 | Fiat 18 BL omnibus 1915 | CRP |
| 88 | Volkswagen Beetle 1948 | CRP |
| 89 | Isotta Fraschini 8a torpedo "Castagna" 1930 | CRP |
| 90 | Mercedes-Benz 300 W189 "Adenauer" 1951 | CRP |
| 91 | Volkswagen Beetle 1953 | CRP |
| 92 | Volkswagen Beetle open cabriolet 1950 | CRP |
| 93 | Volkswagen Beetle closed cabriolet 1950 | CRP |
| 94 | Bugatti 41 Royale closed torpedo 1927 | CRP |
| 95 | Bugatti 41 Royale open torpedo 1927 | CRP |
| 96 | Bugatti 41 Royale Weymann 1929 | CRP |
| 97 | Citroën DS 19 limousine 1956 | CRP |
| 98 | Citroën DS 19 cabriolet 1961 | CRP |
| 99 | Citroën ID 19 break 1958 | CRP |
| 100 | Mercedes-Benz 300d limousine 1960 "Pope Giovanni XXIII" | CRP |
| 100/P | Mercedes-Benz 300d limousine 1960 "Pope Giovanni XXIII" with figure | CRP |
| 101 | Mercedes-Benz 300d closed cabriolet 1958 | CRP |
| 102 | Mercedes-Benz 300d open Cabriolet 195X | CRP |
| 103 | Volkswagen KdF standard limousine 1939 | CRP |
| 104 | Volkswagen KdF standard limousine open sunroof 1939 | CRP |
| 105 | Volkswagen KdF standard cabriolet 1939 | CRP |
| 106 | Volkswagen KdF Wehrmacht gray 1939 | CRP |
| 107 | Volkswagen Beetle export limousine open sunroof 1950 | CRP |
| 108 | Volkswagen Beetle millionth anniversary 1955 | CRP |
| 109 | Citroën DS 19 I Rallye Montecarlo 1959 | CRP |
| 110 | Citroën DS 19 Pallas 1965 | CRP |
| 111 | Citroën ID 19 break "Pompiers" 1960 | CRP |
| 112 | Citroën DS 19 "Gendarmerie" 1966 | CRP |
| 113 | Citroën DS 19 "6-cylindres" 1960 | CRP |
| 114 | Citroën DS 19 "General De Gaulle" 1962 | CRP |
| 115 | Citroën DS 19 "Salon de l'auto de Paris" 1955 | CRP |
| 116 | Citroën ID 19 break "Ambulance" 1960 | CRP |
| 117 | Citroën ID 19 break "Ambulance Pompiers" 1962 | CRP |
| 118 | Alfa Romeo "Giulietta" berlina 1955 | CRP |
| 119 | Alfa Romeo "Giulietta" T.I. 1955 | CRP |
| 120 | Mercedes-Benz 300 L "Adenauer-Kennedy" 1963 | CRP |
| 121 | Mercedes-Benz 300 L closed cabriolet 1960 | CRP |
| 122 | Mercedes-Benz 300 L open cabriolet 1960 | CRP |
| R1 | Ferrari 365 GTB Daytona 1967 | CRP |
| R2 | Ferrari 365 GTB Daytona spider 1969 | CRP |
| R3 | Ferrari 365 GTB Le Mans "Thomson" 1973 | CRP |
| R4 | Ford Thunderbird 1956 | CRP |
| R5 | Ford Thunderbird hard top 1956 | CRP |
| R6 | Mercedes-Benz 190 SL open roadster 1955 | CRP |
| R7 | Mercedes-Benz 190 SL closed roadster 1955 | CRP |
| R8 | Lamborghini Miura S 1968 | CRP |
| R9 | Lamborghini Miura Roadster 1968 | CRP |
| A1 | Fiat 18 BL Autocarro Militare 1914 | CRP |
| A2 | Fiat 18 BL Autocarro centinato 1914 | CRP |
| A3 | Fiat 18 BL Autocarro civile 1914 | CRP |
| A4 | Fiat 18 BL Autocarro civile 1914 | CRP |
| SL001 | Mercedes-Benz SSKL I M.M. 1931 | CRP |
| SL002 | Alfa Romeo P3 I Coppa Ciano 193 | CRP |
| SL003 | Silver Lorry "for Christmas" | CRP |
| SL004 | Volkswagen "Red Cross" first aid 1954 | CRP |
| SL005 | Volkswagen "Feuerwehr" 1955 | CRP |
| SL006 | Volkswagen "Polizei" 1953 | CRP |
| SL007 | Alfa Romeo tipo B 1935 Scuderia Ferrari | CRP |
| SL008 | Citroën DS 19 "Taxi de Paris" 1963 | CRP |
| SL009 | Bugatti 57 SC Atlantic (red body) 1938 | CRP |
| SL010 | Bugatti 57 SC Atlantic (black body) 1938 | CRP |

*Rio #92 Volkswagen Beetle of 1949-1950.*

*This 1902 Ford 999 (model #69) is typical of Rio's veteran cars.*

# Road Champs

Road Champs, Inc. is an American manufacturer of inexpensive die cast toys. Based in New Jersey, Road Champs has its products manufactured in China. Several different series are offered, including a 1/64 scale line entitled "Deluxe," made up of vehicles such as an Elgin Street Sweeper, a Winnebago Motor Home, and a Panel Delivery Van in various liveries. These generally sell for $2-$3.

The 1/43 scale State Police Cars line consists of numerous regional versions of a Chevrolet Caprice police car. These sell for approximately $3. And Road Champs also produces 1/43 scale Chevrolet and Ford Trucks, which also sell for approximately $3.

# Sablon

This Belgian manufacturer got is start in 1968 by entering into an agreement with "Jacques," another firm in Belgium that was well known for its line of chocolate candy. Jacques agreed to buy Sablon's first six months worth of product to use in the advertising of its chocolate products. Sablon tooled up and produced a total of nine models (although three also came in "Police" versions).

How successful the Jacques promotion was is unknown, but Sablon made the models for just a couple of years. They were fairly accurate models, featuring window glazing and interiors, and nearly all of them had opening doors and hoods. Unfortunately, the wheels and tires had a tendency to react chemically with one another, with the result that the wheels on Sablons that turn up today are a mess. This tends to ruin the model's appearance.

Versions with both Sablon and Jacques baseplates were

made, and the models came in either a Sablon or Jacques box. Sablon appears to have been rather casual about the numbering of its models; the numbers referred to in this listing were taken from original Sablon boxes, which may or may not have been 100% accurate. Around 1970, after production had ceased, the tooling for nine of these models found its way into the hands of Nacoral, the Spanish model maker. Nacoral marketed these models as part of its own line; see the Nacoral section for further information.

Sablon went on to make a line of inexpensive Mercedes-Benz trucks that had plastic rear loads and wheel hubs. These were made in the early 1970s; how long production continued is unknown.

The values in this listing are for near mint examples (for the cars, this is with either damaged or undamaged tires) in their original boxes.

| # | Name | Price | # | Name | Price | # | Name | Price |
|---|------|-------|---|------|-------|---|------|-------|
| 1 | Porsche 911 Targa Convertible | $40 | 9 | Porsche 911 Targa Hardtop | $40 | 153 | Mercedes-Benz Van | $30 |
| 2 | Mercedes-Benz 250 SE | 30 | 10 | BMW-Glas 3000 V8 | 30 | 154 | Mercedes-Benz Tank Truck | 30 |
| 3 | Renault 16 | 30 | 11 | Porsche 911 Targa "Polizei" | 30 | 155 | Mercedes-Benz Breakdown Truck | 30 |
| 4 | BMW 2000 CS | 30 | 12 | Mercedes-Benz 250 SE "Polizei" | 30 | 156 | Mercedes-Benz Cattle Truck | 30 |
| 5 | BMW 1600 | 30 | 13 | Renault 16 "Police" | 30 | 157 | Mercedes-Benz Covered Truck | 30 |
| 6 | Lamborghini Marzal | 30 | 14 | Mercedes-Benz 200 | 75 | 158 | Mercedes-Benz Flat Dumper | 30 |
| 7 | NSU RO 80 | 30 | 151 | Mercedes-Benz Truck | 30 | | | |
| 8 | BMW 1600 GT | 30 | 152 | Mercedes-Benz Dumper | 30 | | | |

# Sabra

The Sabra line of die cast models is of particular interest to American collectors, since all but one of them were models of American cars. They were made in Israel in the late 1960s and early 1970s by a company that had already had some ups and downs in the die cast market.

After production ceased on their "Gamda" line of die cast models, Habonim, a company located in northern Israel, entered into a partnership with another Israeli firm, Koor. Gamda would manufacture a line of models under the name "Gamda-Koor" for the American toy distributor Cragstan. The new line would be called "Detroit Seniors" for models exported to the United States, and "Sabra," for those exported to other countries. Production began in 1969 or 1970.

The models were designed to compete with established names like Corgi and Solido, so they featured window glazing, interiors and high-quality paint finishes. Many of them also had opening parts, such as doors or trunks lids. Tires were rubber, mounted on spun-aluminum hubs. The baseplates were plastic, covered with chrome plating. They were accurate models for their time, and are popular with collectors today.

Sabras and Detroit Seniors came packaged in a rectangular plastic box attached to a cardboard backing. The box had a hinged door on the end, and Gamda-Koor marketed the whole thing as a "stackable pocket garage." Unfortunately, the fit of the model in the box was so tight that the cars were frequently damaged from being taken out and put back in; the roofs of many

models were particularly susceptible. Early models also came with a small plastic gas pump, an Israeli coin and a leaflet explaining how six coins could be redeemed for a collection of Israeli coins. Later models came without the coin and leaflet.

Despite their quality and the fact that the line was growing steadily, Gamda-Koor ceased production of the models in the early 1970s. Koor Industries is still in business in Israel, producing products as diverse as insectisides and barber chairs.

The following listing gives values for models in near mint or better condition with the original packaging. Gamda-Koor generally gave a four-digit number to basic models, then gave variations (such as Police or Army liveries) an additional one-digit number after a slash, such as 8103/1.

*Sabra/Detroit Seniors #8107 Pontiac GTO.*

*Like many Sabra/Detroit Senior models, this #8114 Plymouth Barracuda came with opening doors.*

| # | Name | Price |
|---|------|-------|
| 8100 | Chevrolet Chevelle Station Wagon (white, red) . . . . . . . . . . . . . . | $30 |
| 8100/1 | Chevrolet Chevelle Station Wagon "United Nations" (white) . . . . . . . . . . . | 30 |
| 8100/2 | Chevrolet Chevelle Station Wagon "Police" (white) . . . . . . . . . . . . . | 30 |
| 8100/3 | Chevrolet Chevelle Army Station Wagon (tan) . . . . . . . . . . . . . . . | 30 |
| 8100/4 | Chevrolet Chevelle Station Wagon "Israeli Post" (red) . . . . . . . . . . . | 40 |
| 8101 | Chevrolet Chevelle Station Wagon Ambulance (white) . . . . . . . . . . | 30 |
| 8101/1 | Chevrolet Chevelle Station Wagon Israeli Ambulance (white) . . . . . . . . | 40 |
| 8101/2 | Chevrolet Chevelle Station Wagon Army Ambulance (tan) . . . . . . . . . . | 30 |
| 8102 | Chevrolet Chevelle Station Wagon Fire Chief (red) . . . . . . . . . . . | 30 |
| 8102/1 | Chevrolet Chevelle Station Wagon Israeli Fire Chief (red) . . . . . . . . . | 40 |
| 8103 | Chevrolet Impala Coupe (red) . . . . . . . | 30 |
| 8103/1 | Chevrolet Impala Fire Chief (red/white) . . | 30 |
| 8104 | Ford GT (red/silver) . . . . . . . . . . . | 30 |
| 8105 | Chevrolet Corvette Stingray (blue/black) . . | 40 |
| 8105 | Chevrolet Corvette Stingray (hot rod version) . . . . . . . . . . . . . . . | 30 |
| 8106 | Ford Mustang (red) . . . . . . . . . . . | 40 |
| 8106/1 | Ford Mustang (psychedelic) (red) . . . . . | 30 |
| 8107 | Pontiac GTO (red) . . . . . . . . . . . | 30 |
| 8107/1 | Pontiac GTO Israeli Tourist Board (gray) . . . . . . . . . . . . . . . | 40 |

| # | Name | Price |
|---|------|-------|
| 8108 | Buick Riviera (gold) . . . . . . . . . . . | $35 |
| 8108 | Buick Riviera President of Israel (blue) . . | 40 |
| 8109 | Oldsmobile Toronado (silver) . . . . . . . | 30 |
| 8110 | Cadillac Eldorado (blue) . . . . . . . . . | 35 |
| 8110/1 | Cadillac Eldorado President of Israel (blue) . . . . . . . . . . . . . . . | 40 |
| 8111 | Chrysler Imperial Cabriolet (green) . . . . | 30 |
| 8112 | Dodge Charger (white) . . . . . . . . . | 30 |
| 8112/1 | Dodge Charger (hippies) (white, bronze) . . . . . . . . . . . . . . . | 30 |
| 8112/2 | Dodge Charger "UN" (white) . . . . . . . | 35 |
| 8113 | Chevrolet Corvair Monza (green) . . . . . | 30 |
| 8114 | Plymouth Barracuda (yellow, orange) . . . | 30 |
| 8114/1 | Plymouth Barracuda Military Staff Car (tan) . . . . . . . . . . . . . . . | 30 |
| 8115 | Chevrolet Impala 4-door (red) . . . . . . | 30 |
| 8115/1 | Chevrolet Impala Israeli Police (blue/white) . . . . . . . . . . . . | 40 |
| 8115 | Chevrolet Impala Police (blue) . . . . . . | 30 |
| 8116 | Chevrolet Impala Taxi (yellow) . . . . . . | 30 |

| # | Name | Price |
|---|------|-------|
| 8116/1 | Chevrolet Impala Israeli Taxi (yellow) . . | $40 |
| 8117 | Volkswagen (red, black) . . . . . . . . . | 30 |
| 8117/1 | Volkswagen (hippies) (red) . . . . . . . . | 30 |
| 8117/2 | Volkswagen "Polizei" (green/white) . . . . . | 30 |
| 8117/3 | Volkswagen "Deutsche Bundespost" (yellow) . . . . . . . . . . . . . . | 30 |
| 8117/4 | Volkswagen "Swiss PTT" (yellow) . . . . . | 30 |
| 8118 | Ford Thunderbird (bronze) . . . . . . . . | 30 |
| 8119 | Pontiac Firebird (silver/black) . . . . . . | 30 |
| 8120 | Chevrolet Camaro SS (blue/fawn) . . . . | 30 |
| 8121 | Ford Torino (blue) . . . . . . . . . . . | 30 |
| 8122 | Chevrolet Pick-up . . . . . . . . . . . | 30 |
| 8122 | Chevrolet Police Pick-up . . . . . . . . . | 30 |
| 8122 | Chevrolet Army Pick-up . . . . . . . . . | 30 |
| 8122 | Chevrolet Wrecker . . . . . . . . . . . | 30 |
| 8122 | Chevrolet Police Wrecker . . . . . . . . . | 30 |
| 8122 | Chevrolet Army Wrecker . . . . . . . . . | 30 |
| 8123 | Cadillac de Ville Cabriolet (purple, brown) . . . . . . . . . . . . . . | 40 |

*At left is the #8100 Chevelle Station Wagon; at right is the #8102 Chevelle Station Wagon in "Fire Chief" livery. Gamda-Koor frequently produced several different liveries of a basic casting.*

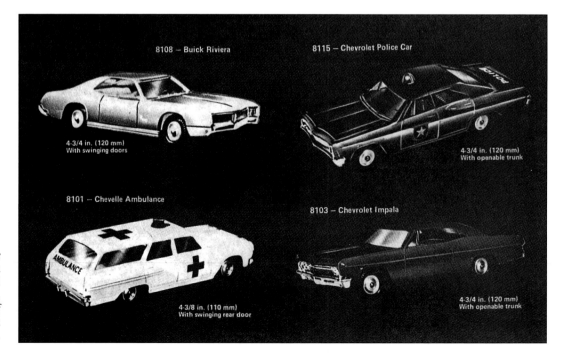

*Two-page spread from a circa 1971 Sabra catalog, showing four of the models in the series.*

# Safir

This French company entered the die cast arena in the early 1960s with a line of 1/43 scale veteran car models. These were followed by a series of sports/endurance racing cars, and also by commercial and military trucks.

Safir models were generally well made with good detailing. Like other manufacturers, Safir frequently produced multiple liveries of a single casting in order to reduce cost. So, the Porsche 917 or the Ferrari 512, to name two examples, could be found in various colors with various racing numbers. Of particular interest to collectors of racing cars

was a group of four 1/43 scale Formula One cars that Safir made just prior to going out of business in the late 1970s. These four models were very accurate; the group was comprised of two Tyrell six-wheelers, a Ferrari and a Ligier.

Safir also made a 1/66 scale Formula One car series called "Champion." These were models of cars raced during the 1968 Grand Prix season, and were introduced probably during 1969. The company also marketed plastic models of various types (many of which had cast baseplates or chassis), but those are beyond the scope of this book.

| # | Name | Price |
|---|------|-------|
| 1 | Peugeot Vis-a-vis (1892) | $15 |
| 2 | Peugeot Victoria (1898) | 15 |
| 3 | Peugeot Victoria (1899) | 15 |
| 4 | Peugeot 4 hp Paris-Marseille (1896) | 15 |
| 5 | Decauville Vis-a-vis (1901) | 15 |
| 6 | Delahaye Vis-a-vis (1901) | 15 |
| 7 | Renault Paris-Vienna (1902) | 15 |
| 8 | Ford Model T (1911) | 15 |
| 9 | Citroën Landaulet Taxi (1924) | 25 |
| 10 | Renault Coupe (1900) | 15 |
| 11 | Citroën Fire Car (1924) | 25 |
| 12 | Citroën Ambulance (1924) | 25 |
| 13 | Citroën Mail Car (1924) | 25 |
| 14 | Fiat 8 HP top up (1901) | 15 |
| 14 | Fiat 8 HP top down (1901) | 15 |
| 15 | Mercedes-Benz 9 HP top up (1901) | 15 |
| 16 | Renault (1901) | 15 |
| 17 | Panhard 8 HP top down (1898) | 15 |
| 17 | Panhard 8 HP top up (1898) | 15 |
| 18 | Peugeot Coupe (1900) | 15 |
| 19 | Peugeot Vis-a-vis (1892) | 15 |
| 20 | Mercedes-Benz 9HP top down (1901) | 15 |
| 21 | Citroën Taxi (1924) | 25 |
| 22 | Citroën Taxi (1924) | 25 |
| 23 | Citroën Taxi (1924) | 25 |
| 24 | Renault 35 HP top up (1906) | 15 |
| 25 | Renault 35 HP top down (1906) | 15 |
| 26 | Unic Taxi top down (1908) | 15 |
| 27 | Unic Taxi top up (1908) | 15 |
| 101 | Gregoire Limousine (1910) | 40 |

**Sports and Formula One racing cars:**

| # | Name | Price |
|---|------|-------|
| 30 | Lola T70 | 20 |
| 31 | Lola T70 | 20 |

| # | Name | Price |
|---|------|-------|
| 32 | Lola T70 | $20 |
| 33 | Lola T70 | 20 |
| 34 | Lola T70 | 20 |
| 35 | Lola T70 | 20 |
| 40 | Porsche 917 | 30 |
| 41 | Porsche 917 | 30 |
| 42 | Porsche 917 | 30 |
| 43 | Porsche 917 | 30 |
| 44 | Porsche 917 | 30 |
| 45 | Porsche 917 | 30 |
| 50 | Porsche 917 Long Tail | 30 |
| 51 | Porsche 917 Long Tail | 30 |
| 52 | Porsche 917 Long Tail | 30 |
| 53 | Porsche 917 | 30 |
| 54 | Porsche 917 | 30 |
| 55 | Porsche 917 | 30 |
| 60 | Ferrari 512 M | 30 |
| 61 | Ferrari 512 M | 30 |
| 62 | Ferrari 512 M | 30 |
| 63 | Ferrari 512 M | 30 |
| 64 | Ferrari 512 M | 30 |
| 65 | Ferrari 512 M | 30 |
| 70 | Porsche 917 | 30 |
| 71 | Porsche 917 | 30 |
| 72 | Porsche 917 | 30 |
| 73 | Porsche 917 | 30 |
| 74 | Porsche 917 Long Tail | 30 |
| 75 | Porsche 917 Long Tail | 30 |
| 80 | Ferrari 312 T Formula I | 25 |
| 81 | Ligier JS 5 Formula I | 25 |
| 82 | Tyrell P34 | 25 |
| 83 | Tyrell P34 | 25 |

| Name | Price |
|------|-------|
| Willys Jeep—various models such as US Army, Police Patrol, Searchlight, etc. | $15 |
| Dodge 6x6 Truck—various models, such as Radar, Rocket-Launcher, etc. | 15 |
| Berliet Fire Truck | 20 |
| Berliet Garbage Truck | 20 |
| Berliet Stake Truck "FRANCIADE" | 20 |
| Berliet Covered Truck "CALBERSON" | 20 |
| Berliet Truck "LES CARRIERES REUNIS" | 20 |
| Berliet Stradair Beverage Truck "KANTERBRAU" | 20 |
| Berliet Stradair Truck "CIRQUE JEAN RICHARD" | 20 |
| Berliet Stradair Breakdown Truck | 20 |
| Berliet Stradair Fire Truck | 20 |
| Berliet Stradair Refuse Wagon | 20 |
| Mercedes-Benz 1313 Tanker | 15 |
| various liveries ("ESSO," "SHELL," etc.) | 15 |
| Mercedes-Benz 1313 Truck "AUX PROFESSIONNELS REUNIS" | 15 |
| Mercedes-Benz 1313 Cement Mixer | 15 |
| Mercedes-Benz 1313 Tow Truck | 15 |
| Mercedes-Benz 1313 Ambulance | 15 |
| Mercedes-Benz 1313 Dump Truck | 15 |
| Trailer various liveries ("Esso," "Total," etc.) | 15 |

**Champion Formula One series (1969):**

| Name | Price |
|------|-------|
| Lotus 56 Indianapolis | 20 |
| Matra MS11 Formula I | 15 |
| McLaren M7A Formula I | 15 |
| Lotus-Ford Formula I | 15 |
| Lotus 49B Formula I | 15 |
| Honda V12 Formula I | 15 |
| Ferrari V12 Formula I | 20 |

# Schabak

Schabak is located in the center of German toy making: Nürnberg. They began producing 1/43 scale die cast models of German cars in the early 1980s, and currently offer numerous Volkswagens, Mercedes and Audis. The product line also now includes 1/35 and 1/24 scale models.

Schabak models have good detail, and the CRP (Current Retail Price) is $15-$20 for the 1/43 models, and $35-$40 for the 1/24's.

| # | Name | Price |
|---|------|-------|
| **1/24 scale:** | | |
| 1400 | VW 1992 Golf VR6 | CRP |
| 1415 | Audi Cabriolet 1991 | CRP |
| 1420 | Audi 100 | CRP |
| 1500 | Ford Scorpio | CRP |
| 1501 | Ford Granada right-hand drive | CRP |
| 1502 | Ford Scorpio German Police | CRP |
| 1503 | Ford Scorpio stretched model | CRP |
| 1504 | Ford Scorpio stretched model right-hand drive | CRP |
| 1510 | Ford 1987 Sierra stretched model | CRP |
| 1511 | Ford 1987 Sierra right-hand drive | CRP |
| 1512 | Ford Sierra Cosworth | CRP |
| 1513 | Ford Sierra Cosworth right-hand drive | CRP |
| 1514 | Ford 1987 Sierra German Police | CRP |
| 1515 | Ford Sierra Cosworth FINA Racing | CRP |
| 1520 | Ford 1989 Fiesta XR 2i | CRP |
| 1521 | Ford 1989 Fiesta XR 2i right-hand drive | CRP |
| 1525 | Ford 1990 Escort Ghia | CRP |
| 1526 | Ford 1990 Escort Ghia right-hand drive | CRP |
| 1527 | Ford 1990 Orion Ghia | CRP |
| 1528 | Ford 1990 Orion Ghia right-hand drive | CRP |
| 1600 | BMW Z1 | CRP |
| 1605 | BMW Cabriolet 1993 | CRP |
| 1610 | BMW 535i | CRP |
| 1611 | BMW 535 Taxi | CRP |
| 1620 | BMW 750iL | CRP |
| 1630 | BMW 850i | CRP |
| 1700 | Mercedes 500 SEL | CRP |
| 1800 | Porsche Carrera Cabriolet | CRP |
| **1/35 scale:** | | |
| 1300 | Ford 1986 Van | CRP |
| 1301 | Ford 1986 Van with windows | CRP |
| 1302 | Ford 1986 Van Rescue | CRP |
| 1303 | Ford 1986 Van "Ryder" | CRP |
| 1304 | Ford 1986 Van German Mail | CRP |
| **1/43 scale:** | | |
| 1000 | VW 1991 Polo | CRP |
| 1001 | VW 1991 Polo Coupe | CRP |
| 1001 | VW Jetta 1979 | CRP |
| 1002 | VW 1984 Golf | CRP |
| 1002 | VW 1984 Golf "PTT" | CRP |
| 1003 | VW 1984 Golf ADAC | CRP |
| 1003 | VW 1994 | CRP |
| 1004 | VW 1984 Golf "Golf Tuning" | CRP |
| 1005 | VW 1992 Golf (A3) | CRP |
| 1006 | VW 1993 Golf Cabriolet | CRP |
| 1007 | VW 1992 Golf VR6 | CRP |
| 1008 | VW 1986 Golf GTI | CRP |
| 1009 | VW 1993 Golf station wagon | CRP |
| 1010 | VW 1984 Jetta | CRP |
| 1011 | VW 1984 Jetta Police | CRP |
| 1011 | VW 1992 VW Vento | CRP |
| 1012 | VW 1984 Jetta "Jetta Tuning" | CRP |
| 1012 | VW 1992 Vento VR6 | CRP |
| 1014 | VW 1986 Passat Variant Police | CRP |
| 1015 | VW 1988 Passat | CRP |
| 1016 | VW 1986 Passant-Variant | CRP |
| 1017 | VW 1988 Passat German Police | CRP |
| 1018 | VW 1989 Corrado | CRP |
| 1019 | VW 1986 Passat Variant Taxi | CRP |
| 1020 | Audi 1984 Avant station wagon | CRP |
| 1021 | Audi 1984 Avant quattro | CRP |
| 1022 | Audi 1984 Avant ONS | CRP |
| 1023 | Audi V8 DTM race car | CRP |
| 1024 | Audi 1988 V8 | CRP |
| 1030 | Audi 1985 90 quattro | CRP |
| 1031 | Audi 1985 90 quattro tuning "Quattro" | CRP |
| 1031 | Audi 1992 80 B3 | CRP |
| 1033 | Audi 1992 80 Avant station wagon | CRP |
| 1035 | Audi 1987 80 quattro | CRP |
| 1036 | Audi 1987 80 quattro German Bavarian Police | CRP |
| 1037 | Audi 1988 90 quattro | CRP |
| 1038 | Audi 1988 90 quattro Rally | CRP |
| 1039 | Audi 1987 80 quattro German Police | CRP |
| 1040 | VW 1986 Caravelle Bus | CRP |
| 1041 | VW 1986 Caravelle rescue | CRP |
| 1042 | VW 1986 Transporter 4 wheel drive | CRP |
| 1043 | VW 1986 Transporter Fir Van "Notruf 112" | CRP |
| 1044 | VW 1993 VW Passat | CRP |
| 1045 | VW 1986 Caravelle Lufthansa crew bus | CRP |
| 1046 | VW 1986 Caravelle Condor crew bus | CRP |
| 1047 | VW 1986 Caravelle Task Force Police | CRP |
| 1048 | VW 1986 Caravelle Police | CRP |
| 1049 | VW 1993 Passat Variant station wagon | CRP |
| 1050 | Audi 1991 Coupe | CRP |
| 1051 | Audi 1991 Cabriolet | CRP |
| 1052 | Audi 1991 100 | CRP |
| 1055 | Audi 1991 100 Avant | CRP |
| 1060 | VW 1990 Caravelle | CRP |
| 1061 | VW 1990 Caravelle Lufthansa crew bus | CRP |
| 1062 | VW 1990 Caravelle Police | CRP |
| 1065 | VW 1990 Transporter | CRP |
| 1070 | VW 1990 Pick-Up | CRP |
| 1080 | Ford 1987 Sierra | CRP |
| 1081 | Ford 1987 Sierra German Police | CRP |
| 1085 | Ford 1989 Fiesta XR 2i | CRP |
| 1086 | Ford 1989 Fiesta XR 2i right-hand drive | CRP |
| 1090 | Ford 1990 Escort Ghia | CRP |
| 1091 | Ford 1990 Escort Ghia right-hand drive | CRP |
| 1092 | Ford 1990 Orion Ghia | CRP |
| 1093 | Ford 1990 Orion Ghia right-hand drive | CRP |
| 1094 | Ford 1990 Escort Cabriolet | CRP |
| 1095 | Ford 1990 Escort Cabriolet right-hand drive | CRP |
| 1096 | Ford 1990 Escort station wagon | CRP |
| 1097 | Ford 1990 Escort station wagon right-hand drive | CRP |
| 1110 | Porsche 1991 Carrera Cabriolet | CRP |
| 1150 | BMW 535i | CRP |
| 1151 | BMW 535i German Taxi | CRP |
| 1152 | BMW 535i German Bavarian Police | CRP |
| 1153 | BMW 535i German Police | CRP |
| 1154 | BMW 535i Fire Chief | CRP |
| 1155 | BMW 535i Fire Chief Nord | CRP |
| 1156 | BMW 535i German Doctor car | CRP |
| 1157 | BMW 535i Service car | CRP |
| 1158 | BMW M5 | CRP |
| 1160 | BMW Z1 Cabriolet | CRP |
| 1165 | BMW 3er Cabriolet | CRP |
| 1170 | BMW 7er | CRP |
| 1180 | BMW 850i | CRP |
| 1250 | Mercedes 1989 SL Roadster | CRP |
| 1260 | Mercedes 1991 600 SEL | CRP |
| 1261 | Mercedes 1991 600 SEL | CRP |
| 1270 | Mercedes 1993 600 SEC | CRP |

# Schuco

**H**einrich Müller, a German toy designer and pattern maker, joined forces with another German businessman, Heinrich Schreyer, in 1912. Together they formed Schreyer and Co. in Nuremberg, and began producing a line of tinplate mechanical toys. After World War I ended, Müller bought out Schreyer and changed the name of the firm to Schuco. Over the course of the next 60 years, Schuco became one of the most innovative and successful toy companies in the world.

They entered the die cast market in 1951 with the introduction of "Micro Racers," a line of clockwork-powered cars (roughly 1/40 scale) that proved to be big sellers throughout the world. These cars had four-digit numbers beginning with 10, such as 1040, 1041, etc. The Micro Racers were joined in 1958 by the "Piccolo" series. These tiny (1/90 scale) cars and trucks were truly toys, many of them being only an approximate representation of the real vehicle. But others were quite accurate for their size, and all of them are very popular with collectors today. They were made until the mid-1960s.

The Piccolos were followed, in 1969, by the debut of a 1/66 scale series (with numbers in the 800s and 900s), as well as a 1/43 scale series (with numbers in the 600s) that came out in the early 1970s.

Schuco toys and models were very well made, with great attention to accuracy (many had opening or working parts). But the competition was too much for the legendary firm, and in 1977 the doors were closed for good. The tooling for many Schuco products survived, however, and other com-

*Schuco Piccolo #715 Volkswagen Karmann-Ghia. The wheels and the silver painted windows were typical of the Piccolo line.*

panies have kept the name alive. The most prominent of these is Gama, Schuco's old rival, which bought the rights to the Schuco name (along with a great deal of original tooling) in 1980. Since 1994, Gama has marketed the Schuco line of die cast models.

REI, a Brazilian company, bought a number of Schuco dies in the 1970s, and has been re-issuing some of the 1/43 and 1/66 scale models for many years. These models have "Made in Brasil" on the baseplates. And, a former employee of Schuco, Werner Nutz, used some original Schuco tooling to begin what would eventually become a line of re-issued Micro Racers. These re-issues are now put out by Lilliput Motor Company of Nevada.

The following listing gives market values for original Schucos only (that is, those products made until 1976), in near mint or better condition with the original packaging. Current re-issues (such as the Micro Racers put out by Lilliput, which generally sell for about $50) are not included in this listing.

*This MAN Doubledeck Bus, #776 in the Schuco Piccolo series, is one of the more sought after entries in the line.*

| # | Name | Price |
|---|------|-------|
| 1035 | Go Kart | $175 |
| 1036 | Ford Hot Rod | 175 |
| 1036 | Mercer 35-J | 100 |
| 1037 | Porsche Formula 2 | 140 |
| 1038 | Mercedes-Benz 220S | 175 |
| 1039 | Volkswagen 1200 Police car | 200 |
| 1039 | Volkswagen 1200 Fire car | 200 |
| 1040 | Ferrari Formula I | 150 |
| 1040 | Ferrari Formula I rear engine | 100 |
| 1041 | Midget Racer | 150 |
| 1042 | Midget Racer | 150 |
| 1043 | Mercedes-Benz Formula Racer | 150 |
| 1043 | Mercedes-Benz SSK | 125 |
| 1043 | Mercedes-Benz 1935 Racer | 125 |
| 1044 | Mercedes-Benz 190SL Coupe | 200 |
| 1044 | Porsche Carrera | 125 |
| 1045 | Ford Fairlane | 175 |
| 1045 | Chaparral 2F | 90 |
| 1046 | Volkswagen 1200 | 175 |
| 1047 | Porsche 356 Coup | 200 |
| 1047 | Jaguar E Type | 175 |
| 1048 | BMW 503 Convertible | 200 |
| 1048 | Opel GT Coupe | 100 |
| 1049 | Ford FK 100 Pick-up | 175 |

**Piccolo series:**

| # | Name | Price |
|---|------|-------|
| 701 | Ferrari Formula 2 | 75 |
| 702 | Mercedes-Benz Formula I | 75 |
| 703 | Mercedes-Benz W196 | 75 |
| 704 | Mercedes-Benz 1936 W25 Racer | 75 |
| 705 | Midget Racer | 75 |
| 706 | Maserati Grand Prix | 75 |
| 707 | BMW 507 Convertible | 75 |
| 708 | Porsche Roadster | 75 |
| 709 | Austin Healey 100 | 75 |
| 709 | Mercedes-Benz 300SL | 75 |
| 710 | Firebird II | 75 |
| 711 | FX Atmos | 75 |
| 712 | Volkswagen 1200 | 75 |
| 713 | Mercedes-Benz 190SL | 75 |
| 714 | M.G.A. Coupe | 75 |
| 715 | Volkswagen Karmann-Ghia | 75 |
| 716 | NSU-Fiat 1100 | 75 |
| 717 | Mercedes-Benz 220S | 75 |
| 718 | Volvo PV 544 | 75 |
| 719 | Citroën DS19 | 75 |
| 720 | Volkswagen 1200 Police car | 75 |
| 720 | Volkswagen 1200 Fire car | 75 |
| 722 | Travel Trailer | 75 |
| 723 | Volkswagen Karmann-Ghia and Trailer | 125 |
| 724 | Mercedes-Benz 220S | 75 |
| 725 | Ford Hot Rod | 75 |
| 740 | Mercedes-Benz Bus | 75 |
| 741 | Mercedes-Benz Delivery Van | 75 |
| 742 | Mercedes-Benz Low Loader | 90 |
| 743 | Mercedes-Benz Refrigerator Van | 90 |
| 744 | Mercedes-Benz Tank Truck | 90 |
| 745 | Magirus Ladder Truck | 90 |
| 746 | Krupp Open Truck | 90 |
| 747 | Magirus Wrecker | 90 |
| 748 | Krupp Dumper | 90 |
| 749 | Krupp Flat Truck | 90 |

| # | Name | Price |
|---|------|-------|
| 750 | Krupp Quarry Dumper | $90 |
| 751 | Krupp Lumber Truck | 90 |
| 752 | Deutz Farm Tractor | 75 |
| 753 | Deutz Caterpillar Tractor | 75 |
| 754 | Deutz Bulldozer | 75 |
| 755 | Mercedes-Benz Searchlight Truck | 75 |
| 756 | Mercedes-Benz Fire Van | 75 |
| 757 | Tipping Trailer | 75 |
| 758 | Faun Street Sweeper | 75 |
| 759 | Conveyor Belt | 75 |
| 760 | Demag Power Shovel | 75 |
| 761 | Krupp Car Transporter | 100 |
| 762 | Liebherr Tower Crane | 75 |
| 763 | Krupp Tanker | 75 |
| 764 | Boat and Trailer | 75 |
| 765 | Fork Lift Truck | 75 |
| 766 | Volkswagen Karmann-Ghia and Boat Trailer | 100 |
| 767 | Krupp Bucket Truck | 75 |
| 768 | Hopper Trailer | 75 |
| 769 | Krupp Crane Truck | 75 |
| 770 | Krupp Cheery Picker | 75 |
| 771 | Dingler Road Roller | 75 |
| 772 | Krupp Cement Mixer | 75 |
| 773 | Henschel Covered Semi | 90 |
| 774 | Faun Quarry Dumper | 75 |
| 775 | Coles Crane Truck and Trailer | 100 |
| 776 | MAN Doubledeck Bus | 100 |
| 777 | Linhoff Road Paver | 100 |
| 778 | Krupp Cement Carrier | 90 |
| 799 | Coles Hydraulic Crane | 75 |
| 800 | Road Building Set (#754, #774 and #777) | 200 |
| 801 | Coles Mobile Crane and Trailer | 150 |

**1/66 scale series:**

| # | Name | Price |
|---|------|-------|
| 805 | Mercedes-Benz 200 | 20 |
| 805 | Mercedes-Benz 200 Police car | 20 |
| 807 | Ford Taunus 20M | 20 |
| 808 | BMW 1600 | 20 |
| 809 | BMW 2002 | 20 |
| 810 | Ford Escort 1300 GT | 20 |

| # | Name | Price |
|---|------|-------|
| 811 | Opel Commodore GS | $20 |
| 812 | Volkswagen 411 | 20 |
| 813 | Porsche 911 S | 25 |
| 814 | Opel GT 1900 | 20 |
| 815 | BMW 2800 CS | 20 |
| 816 | Ford Capri 1700 | 25 |
| 817 | Audi 100 LS | 20 |
| 818 | Volkswagen 1300 | 30 |
| 819 | Opel Admiral 2800E | 20 |
| 820 | Mercedes-Benz 250CE | 20 |
| 821 | Audi 100 Coupe | 20 |
| 822 | Opel Commodore GS Rally | 20 |
| 823 | Mercedes-Benz 200 Taxi | 20 |
| 824 | Volkswagen 411 Fire Chief | 20 |
| 825 | Porsche 911 S Police | 25 |
| 826 | VW Porsche 914 | 25 |
| 827 | VW Porsche 914/6 | 25 |
| 828 | Mercedes-Benz C-111 | 20 |
| 829 | BMW 2500 | 20 |
| 830 | BMW 2800 | 20 |
| 831 | Volkswagen K70 | 20 |
| 832 | Volkswagen I | 25 |
| 833 | Volkswagen I ADAC | 25 |
| 834 | Ford Capri 1700 GT Rally | 20 |
| 835 | Porsche 911 S Racing Car | 25 |
| 836 | VW Porsche 914/6 Racing car | 20 |
| 837 | Ford Taunus GT Coupe | 20 |
| 838 | Ford Taunus GXL Coupe | 20 |
| 839 | Opel Manta SR | 20 |
| 840 | Ferrari Formula I | 25 |
| 841 | BMW Formula 2 | 20 |
| 842 | Matra-Ford Formula I | 20 |
| 843 | Porsche 917 | 25 |
| 844 | Mercedes-Benz 350 SL Convertible | 25 |
| 845 | BMW 2000 Ti | 20 |
| 846 | Opel Ascona Voyage | 20 |
| 847 | Brabham Ford Formula I | 20 |
| 848 | Opel GTJ | 20 |
| 849 | Opel Manta SR | 20 |
| 850 | Renault R 16 | 20 |
| 851 | Ford Escort Rally | 20 |
| 852 | Audi 100 GL | 20 |

*Original box for the #712 Volkswagen 1200 (Schuco Piccolo).*

| # | Name | Price | # | Name | Price | # | Name | Price |
|---|------|-------|---|------|-------|---|------|-------|
| 853 | Renault R 17 | $20 | 900 | Mercedes-Benz Bus | $30 | **1/43 scale 600 series:** | | |
| 854 | Porsche Martini 917 | 25 | 901 | Büssing Open Truck | 30 | 610 | Audi 80 LS | $40 |
| 855 | Audi 80 LS | 20 | 901 | Büssing Open Truck "HEINEKEN BIER" | 60 | 611 | Audi 80 GL | 40 |
| 856 | Opel Rekord II | 20 | 902 | Büssing Dump Truck | 30 | 612 | Mercedes 350 SE | 40 |
| 857 | Opel Commodore | 20 | 903 | Büssing Flat Truck | 30 | 613 | BMW Turbo | 40 |
| 858 | Ford Consul | 20 | 904 | Büssing Quarry Dumper | 30 | 614 | Volkswagen Passat LS | 40 |
| 859 | Ford Granada | 20 | 905 | Büssing Covered Semi Truck | 35 | 615 | Volkswagen Passat TS | 40 |
| 860 | Renault R 16 TS | 20 | 906 | Büssing Cement Carrier | 35 | 616 | Mercedes 350 SE Polizei | 40 |
| 861 | Renault R 17 TS | 20 | 907 | Demag Power Shovel | 25 | 617 | BMW 520 | 40 |
| 862 | Audi 80 GL | 20 | 908 | Faun Quarry Dumper | 30 | 618 | Mercedes 450 SE | 40 |
| 863 | Tyrell Ford Formula I | 20 | 909 | Magirus Deutz 232D Dumper | 30 | 619 | Volkswagen Passat LS Variant | 40 |
| 864 | BMW M1 Turbo | 25 | 910 | Volkswagen Bus | 30 | 620 | Volkswagen Scirocco | 50 |
| 866 | Mercedes-Benz 350SE | 20 | 910 | Volkswagen Bus "BURO ACTUEL" | 50 | 621 | Volkswagen Golf | 40 |
| 867 | Volkswagen Passat LS | 20 | 911 | Volkswagen Van | 30 | 622 | Audi 50 | 40 |
| 868 | Mercedes-Benz 450 SE Polizei | 20 | 911 | Volkswagen Van "MERKELBACH" | 50 | 623 | Volkswagen Polo | 40 |
| 869 | VW Porsche 914 Race Control Car | 20 | 911 | Volkswagen Van "DIE WELT" | 50 | 624 | Volkswagen Golf Rally | 40 |
| 870 | Lotus-Ford 72 Formula I | 20 | 911 | Volkswagen Van "MIELE" | 50 | 625 | BMW 525 | 40 |
| 871 | Renault R5 TL | 20 | 911 | Volkswagen Van "RHEINISCHE POST" | 50 | 626 | BMW 316 | 40 |
| 872 | Volkswagen Passat TS | 20 | 911 | Volkswagen Van "KREISSPARKASSE" | 50 | 627 | BMW 320 | 40 |
| 873 | Mercedes-Benz 450 SE | 20 | 911 | Volkswagen Van "MAIN POST" | 50 | 628 | Porsche 924 | 40 |
| 874 | Ford Capri II | 25 | 912 | Ford Transit Van | 25 | 629 | BMW 630 CS | 40 |
| 875 | BMW 3.0 CSL | 20 | 912 | Ford Transit Van "BADISCHE ZEITUNG" | 35 | 630 | Volkswagen Passat Variant ADAC | 30 |
| 876 | Audi 80 Fire Chief | 20 | 912 | Ford Transit Van "SPARKASSE" | 35 | 631 | Volkswagen Passat Variant Fire Car | 30 |
| 877 | Ford Capri RS | 25 | 912 | Ford Transit Van "DER ABEND" | 35 | 632 | Volkswagen Scirocco Racing Service Car | 30 |
| 878 | Matra Simca Bagheera | 20 | 912 | Ford Transit Van "BAUKNECHT" | 35 | 633 | Mercedes 350 SE Taxi | 40 |
| 879 | Volkswagen Scirocco TS | 25 | 912 | Ford Transit Van "NACHRICHTEN" | 35 | 634 | Audi 80 Polizei | 40 |
| 880 | Volkswagen Golf LS | 20 | 912 | Ford Transit Van "SECURITAS" | 35 | 635 | BMW 520 Polizei | 40 |
| 881 | Ford Escort | 20 | 913 | Ford Transit Bus | 25 | 636 | BMW 320 Rally | 30 |
| 882 | Volkswagen Golf Mail Car | 20 | 914 | Volkswagen Ambulance | 35 | 637 | BMW 520 Doctor's Car | 40 |
| 883 | Volkswagen Polo L | 20 | 915 | Volkswagen Mail Van | 30 | 638 | Volkswagen Golf Mail Car | 40 |
| 884 | Mercedes-Benz 200/123 | 20 | 916 | Mercedes-Benz 0303 Bus | 40 | 639 | Audi 100 | 40 |
| 888 | Ford Escort Rally | 20 | 916 | Mercedes-Benz 0303 PTT Bus | 60 | 640 | Mercedes 350 SE Medical Emergency Car | 40 |
| 889 | Volkswagen Polizei Bus | 30 | 917 | Magirus Deutz 232 D Quarry Dumper | 25 | | | |
| 890 | Ford Transit Fire Van | 30 | 919 | Volkswagen LT 35 Pickup | 50 | | | |

# Siku

During the 1950s and '60s, many manufacturers of die cast toys and models gradually made a transition to producing plastic products. While this may have made sense from a cost savings point of view, it often meant a decline in the quality of the product.

There are a handful of manufacturers, though, that went in the opposite direction. German manufacturer Siku is one of them. The company was founded in 1921 by Richard Sieper, who opened a foundry in the town of Lüdenscheid, Germany. In the 1930s the company name was changed to Richard Sieper and Sohne. The company made a variety of metal products until 1949, when it launched a line of toys. In 1950 the company's name was changed again, this time to Siku, which was a combination of the first two letters of the words Sieper and kunstsoffe (which means plastic). Siku introduced a line of 1/60 scale plastic toy vehicles in 1955.

This series eventually grew into more than 200 models, and these were produced until 1967.

In 1963, Siku introduced a new line of die cast metal vehicles, also to 1/60 scale. Like the plastic series, the numbers of the die cast products were given a "V" prefix, which stood for "Verkehr" (which means "traffic"). These die casts were numbered starting at 201 and, initially, a number of the existing plastic models were merely done in metal. New models, though, were soon introduced. The series was comprised of mostly European marques, but there were a number of American subjects included, as well.

Although aimed at the children's market, many of them were fairly accurate models. They featured window glazing and interiors, and many had suspension. They also often had working features such as cranes and dump beds and so offered a good deal of play value.

The 1/60 scale was used until 1973, when the line changed over to 1/55. Another change made that year was the dropping of the "V" prefix for the model numbers.

Siku has continued making die cast toys to the present day. Current product lines include 1/32 scale farm vehicles and the extensive 1/55 scale Super series. And, the company entered the adult collector market in 1992 with the introduction of its 1/43 scale series, comprised of more highly detailed models.

Cataloging all of the output of the Siku company would in itself require a book, particularly since the company has released countless promotional products in recent years. The following

listing therefore outlines the die cast line-up until the mid-1970s. Following this is a listing of the company's more recent products. CRP (Current Retail Price) for the 1/43 scale models is $20-$25; the Super series items range from a couple of dollars for the small cars and trucks up to $40 or more for the larger commercial and fire vehicles.

*Siku #V292 Mercedes-Benz Ambulance, introduced in the late 1960s. In addition to the opening doors front and rear, this model came with a stretcher that slides into a slot in the rear of the vehicle.*

| # | Name | Price |
|---|------|-------|
| **1/60 scale (introduced 1963; 1/55 after 1973):** | | |
| V201 | Fiat 1800 | $25 |
| V202 | BMW 1500 | 25 |
| V203 | Ford Taunus 12 M | 25 |
| V204 | Opel Kadett | 25 |
| V206 | Ford Taunus 17 M Station Wagon | 25 |
| V209 | Cadillac Fleetwood 75 | 35 |
| V211 | Volkswagen Minibus | 35 |
| V212 | Volkswagen Police Loudspeaker Bus | 25 |
| V218 | Porsche T Tractor | 25 |
| V220 | Tempo Matador Bus | 25 |
| V221 | Mercedes-Benz 300 SL Coupe | 25 |
| V222 | Ford F 500 Truck | 25 |
| V223 | Opel Rekord 1700 | 25 |
| V224 | DKW. F12 | 25 |
| V225 | 4-Wheel Trailer | 15 |
| V226 | Opel Caravan 1500 | 25 |
| V228 | Military Jeep and Trailer | 25 |
| V229 | Mercedes-Benz 230 SL Roadster | 25 |
| V230 | Volkswagen 1200 | 35 |
| V231 | Volkswagen 1200 Postal Car | 25 |
| V232 | Ford Taunus 17 M | 25 |
| V233 | Binz Ambulance | 25 |
| V234 | Porsche 901 | 30 |
| V234 | Porsche 911 Targa | 35 |
| V235 | Porsche 901 Polizei | 25 |
| V235 | Ford Capri Polizei | 25 |
| V237 | Ford Fire Van | 25 |
| V238 | Fiat 40 CA Tractor with Shovel | 25 |
| V239 | Fiat 40 CA Tractor with Leveller | 25 |
| V241 | Road Roller | 15 |
| V242 | Harrow | 25 |
| V244 | Fiat 1800 Taxi | 25 |

| # | Name | Price |
|---|------|-------|
| V244 | Mercedes-Benz 250SE Taxi | $25 |
| V244 | Mercedes-Benz 250 Taxi | 25 |
| V245 | Oldsmobile 98 Holiday Hardtop | 35 |
| V246 | Ford Taunus 12 M and Trailer | 25 |
| V246 | Ford Taunus 15 M and Trailer | 25 |
| V247 | Volkswagen 1500 Variant | 25 |
| V248 | Volkswagen 1500 Karmann Ghia | 35 |
| V249 | Faun K Quarry Dumper | 25 |
| V250 | Mercedes-Benz 190 Polizei | 25 |
| V250 | Mercedes-Benz 250 Polizei | 25 |
| V251 | Ford Transit Pickup | 25 |
| V252 | Opel Kapitan | 25 |
| V253 | Mercedes-Benz 600 Pullmann | 25 |
| V254 | Porsche T Tractor and Trailer | 25 |
| V255 | Buick Wildcat Coupe | 25 |
| V256 | Mercedes-Benz 250 | 25 |
| V257 | Ford F 500 Tow Truck | 25 |
| V257 | Hanomag Henschel Tow Truck | 25 |
| V258 | Liebherr AK 50 B Mobile Crane | 25 |
| V259 | 2-Wheel Trailer | 15 |
| V260 | Klaus Truck with Shovel | 25 |
| V261 | Mercedes Metz DL 30 H Fire Truck | 30 |
| V262 | Pontiac Bonneville Convertible | 35 |
| V263 | Lumber Trailer | 15 |
| V264 | Tempo Matador Minibus with Canoe | 25 |
| V264 | Ford Transit Minibus with Canoe | 25 |
| V265 | Cadillac Fleetwood | 25 |
| V266 | BMW 2000 CS | 25 |
| V267 | Oldsmobile Toronado | 30 |
| V268-1 | Ford Transit Minibus | 25 |
| V268-2 | Ford Transit Van "BOHLE" | 40 |
| V268-3 | Ford Transit Van "VAN GRIEKEN MELCH" | 40 |
| V268-3 | Ford Transit Van "W. ZEEMANN MARKEN" | 40 |

| # | Name | Price |
|---|------|-------|
| V269 | Ferrari 275 GTB | $35 |
| V270 | L 2000 Excavator | 15 |
| V271 | Opel Rekord Coupe | 25 |
| V272 | Opel Rekord Caravan with Skis | 25 |
| V273 | Ford Taunus 15 M | 25 |
| V274 | Magirus Garbage Truck | 25 |
| V275 | Magirus Car Transporter | 25 |
| V276 | Ford OSI 20N TS | 25 |
| V277 | Pontiac GTO Convertible | 35 |
| V278 | Trailer for Tractor | 15 |
| V279 | Opel Kapitan and Travel Trailer | 35 |
| V279 | Ford Taunus 20M and Travel Trailer | 35 |
| V279 | Oldsmobile Toronado and Travel Trailer | 25 |
| V280 | Euclid Scraper | 25 |
| V281 | Magirus Deutz H250 D22 Dump Truck | 25 |
| V282 | Chevrolet Corvette Sting Ray | 30 |
| V283 | Ford Taunus 20 | 25 |
| V284 | Ford Taunus 17M Station Wagon | 25 |
| V285 | Porsche Carrera 6 | 25 |
| V286 | Opel Olympia | 25 |
| V287 | Hanomag Robust 900 Tractor | 15 |
| V288 | Hanomag Henschel Artic. Tanker "ARAL" | 30 |
| V289 | Magirus Low Loader | 25 |
| V290 | Citroën DS 21 | 25 |
| V291 | Magirus Cement Mixer | 25 |
| V292 | Mercedes-Benz Ambulance | 25 |
| V293 | Mercedes-Benz Crane Truck | 25 |
| V294 | Jaguar E Coupe | 30 |
| V295 | Maserati Mistral | 30 |
| V296 | Ford GT 40 | 30 |
| V297 | Oldsmobile Toronado with Boat on Trailer | 35 |
| V298 | Lincoln Continental Mark III | 35 |
| V299 | Europ S 12 Road Roller | 15 |

| # | Name | Price |
|---|------|-------|
| V300 | Volkswagen 411 | $30 |
| V301 | Fiat 850 Coupe | 25 |
| V302 | Mercedes-Benz 280SL | 25 |
| V303 | Hanomag Tractor and Lumber Trailer | 25 |
| V304 | Opel GT 1900 Coupe | 25 |
| V305 | Mercedes-Benz Mail Van | 25 |
| V306 | Binz Ambulance | 25 |
| V307 | Hanomag Henschel with Prefabricated Box | 35 |
| V308 | Audi 100 LS | 20 |
| V309 | Mercedes-Benz 250 | 25 |
| V310 | Ford Capri 1700 GT | 25 |
| V311 | Volkswagen 1300 | 25 |
| V312 | VW-Porsche 914/6 | 25 |
| V313 | Ford Taunus Station Wagon "ADAC" | 25 |
| V314 | Ford F500 Pick-up and Trailer | 25 |
| V315 | Ford F500 Pick-up and Trailer | 25 |
| V316 | Toyota 2000 GT | 25 |
| V317 | Lamborghini Espada | 25 |
| V318 | Hanomag Henschel Container Truck | 25 |
| V319 | Mercedes-Benz LP 608 ADAC Truck | 25 |
| V320 | Volkswagen Mail Bus | 25 |
| V320 | Volkswagen Mail Bus | 20 |
| V321 | Alfa Romeo Montreal | 25 |
| V322 | Citroën SM | 25 |
| V323 | Ford Taunus Transit Covered Pick-up | 25 |
| V324 | Ford Transit Polizei Bus | 25 |
| V325 | Menck Excavator | 25 |
| V326 | Michigan 180 Bulldozer | 25 |
| V328 | Pontiac GTO "THE JUDGE" | 35 |
| V329 | Hanomag Tractor and Trailer | 30 |
| V330 | Ford Mustang Mach 1 | 25 |
| V331 | MAN Tanker "ARAL" | 35 |
| V332 | Metz Airport Fire Truck | 25 |
| V333 | Lamborghini Espada and Trailer | 35 |
| V334 | Ford Transit School Bus | 20 |
| V335 | Mercedes-Benz LP 608D Recovery Truck | 35 |
| V336 | Mercedes-Benz LP 608D Silo Carrier | 35 |
| V337 | Faun Snow Plow | 20 |
| V338 | Hanomag Henschel Covered Truck | 15 |
| V339 | Mercedes-Benz Fire Van | 25 |
| V341 | BMW 2000 CS Polizei | 25 |
| V342 | Ford Taunus 17M Fire Car | 25 |
| V343 | Hanomag Henschel ADAC Artic. Truck S | 30 |
| V343 | Hanomag Henschel ANWB Artic. Truck | 50 |
| 344 | Lamborghini Fire Car | 25 |
| 345 | Volkswagen Bus with Radar | 25 |
| 346 | Volkswagen Porsche 914/6 "ADAC-RENNPOLIZEI" | 25 |
| 347 | Magirus Tipping Truck | 25 |
| 348 | MAN Container Truck | 25 |
| 349 | MAN Stake Truck with Crane | 25 |
| 350 | Hanomag Henschel Recovery Truck | 30 |
| 351 | Maserati Boomerang | 20 |
| 352 | Magirus Transporter and Tractors | 60 |
| 353 | Audi 100 LS "ARZT" | 25 |
| 354 | Hanomag Henschel Covered Truck and Trailer | 30 |
| 355 | Hanomag Henschel with Prefabricated Box | 35 |
| 356 | Volkswagen Ambulance | 25 |

| # | Name | Price |
|---|------|-------|
| 357 | Mercedes-Benz Fire Van | $20 |
| 360 | Hanomag Henschel "HEIZOL" Truck | 30 |
| 361 | Mercedes-Benz Unimog "D.B.P." Truck | 35 |
| 362 | Magirus Bucket Truck | 35 |

## CURRENT PRODUCTION

### 1/43 scale models:

| # | Name | Price |
|---|------|-------|
| 2612 | VW 1303 Cabriolet (blue) | CRP |
| 2613 | VW 1303 Cabriolet (white) | CRP |
| 3426 | Mercedes-Benz 500SEL (blue) | CRP |
| 3427 | Mercedes-Benz 500SEL (silver) | CRP |

### Super series:

| # | Name | Price |
|---|------|-------|
| 801 | Excavator | CRP |
| 802 | Front Loader | CRP |
| 803 | Scraper | CRP |
| 804 | Police Van | CRP |
| 805 | Ambulance | CRP |
| 806 | Bus | CRP |
| 808 | Tipper Truck | CRP |
| 811 | Refuse Truck | CRP |
| 813 | Cement Mixer | CRP |
| 814 | Dump Truck | CRP |
| 815 | Livestock Transporter | CRP |
| 817 | Space Shuttle | CRP |
| 820 | VW Delivery Van | CRP |
| 821 | Unimog Snow Plow | CRP |
| 822 | Tipper Truck | CRP |
| 823 | Bulldozer | CRP |
| 824 | School Bus | CRP |
| 825 | VW Bus | CRP |
| 826 | Airport Fire Engine | CRP |
| 828 | Recycling Transporter | CRP |
| 833 | Police Van | CRP |
| 834 | Fire Rescue Bus | CRP |
| 835 | Rescue Van | CRP |
| 836 | Morgan Plus 8 | CRP |
| 837 | Porsche 911 Cabriolet | CRP |
| 838 | Peugeot 205 Convertible | CRP |
| 839 | VW Beetle Cabriolet | CRP |
| 840 | Iveco Pick-up | CRP |
| 841 | Audi 80 Convertible | CRP |
| 1010 | VW Golf | CRP |
| 1011 | Mercedes-Benz 500 SL Cabriolet | CRP |
| 1012 | Mercedes-Benz 500 SL Hardtop | CRP |
| 1013 | Skip Truck | CRP |
| 1014 | Wrecker Truck | CRP |
| 1015 | Fire Engine | CRP |
| 1016 | Container Truck | CRP |
| 1017 | Mercedes Racing Truck | CRP |
| 1018 | Iveco Racing Truck | CRP |
| 1019 | Simon Snorkel | CRP |
| 1022 | Iveco Dormobile | CRP |
| 1023 | Unimog with Crane | CRP |
| 1024 | Combine | CRP |
| 1039 | Golf/Rabbit Convertible | CRP |
| 1044 | Mercedes-Benz 280 GE | CRP |
| 1051 | Camaro Z28 | CRP |
| 1058 | Jeep CJ7 | CRP |
| 1059 | Porsche 911 Turbo | CRP |
| 1060 | Ferrari GTO | CRP |
| 1063 | Mercedes-Benz 300 E | CRP |

| # | Name | Price |
|---|------|-------|
| 1064 | Mercedes-Benz 300 TE | CRP |
| 1068 | Porsche 959 | CRP |
| 1069 | Jaguar XJ6 | CRP |
| 1072 | Suzuki SJ413 | CRP |
| 1073 | Mercedes-Benz 300 SL | CRP |
| 1075 | Ferrari F40 | CRP |
| 1076 | VW Passat Variant | CRP |
| 1078 | VW Beetle | CRP |
| 1310 | Taxi | CRP |
| 1311 | Police Car | CRP |
| 1312 | Car Club Patrol Car | CRP |
| 1313 | ADAC Pick-up Service | CRP |
| 1314 | Radio-TV Control Car | CRP |
| 1316 | Motorway Patrol Car | CRP |
| 1321 | Police Car with Loudspeaker | CRP |
| 1331 | VW Minibus | CRP |
| 1339 | Emergency Doctor | CRP |
| 1343 | Fire Rescue Tender | CRP |
| 1344 | Fire Command Car | CRP |
| 1346 | Police Command Car | CRP |
| 1349 | Fire Command Car | CRP |
| 1713 | Renault Tractor | CRP |
| 1714 | MF Tractor | CRP |
| 1716 | Unimog | CRP |
| 1717 | Linde Forklift Truck | CRP |
| 1923 | Car with Fire Rescue Boat | CRP |
| 1924 | Wheel Loader | CRP |
| 1925 | Renault Front End Loader | CRP |
| 1928 | Binz Ambulance | CRP |
| 2010 | Jeep with Horse Box | CRP |
| 2011 | Binz Rescue Van | CRP |
| 2014 | Roller | CRP |
| 2015 | Red Cross Recovery Van | CRP |
| 2221 | ADAC Breakdown Service | CRP |
| 2226 | Renault Tractor with Tanker | CRP |
| 2227 | MF Tractor with Hay Trailer | CRP |
| 2229 | Massey Ferguson with Tandem Trailer | CRP |
| 2518 | Car with Caravan | CRP |
| 2520 | Breakdown Truck with Car | CRP |
| 2522 | Unimog with Forklift Truck | CRP |
| 2528 | Piste Bully | CRP |
| 2532 | Car and Caravan | CRP |
| 2582 | Mercedes Racing Truck | CRP |
| 2610 | Road Maintenance Lorry | CRP |
| 2615 | Unimog Excavator | CRP |
| 2824 | Road Sweeper | CRP |
| 2826 | Skip Lorry | CRP |
| 2827 | Winter Service | CRP |
| 2828 | Zettelmeyer Wheel Loader | CRP |
| 2880 | Binz Ambulance | CRP |
| 2919 | Tipper Truck | CRP |
| 2920 | Recycling Transporter | CRP |
| 2924 | Faun Fire Engine | CRP |
| 2925 | Fire Engine | CRP |
| 2926 | Refuse Truck | CRP |
| 2927 | Fire Brigade Team Bus | CRP |
| 3112 | Car Transporter | CRP |
| 3121 | Bus | CRP |
| 3122 | Forklift Truck | CRP |
| 3123 | Wheel Loader with Accessories | CRP |
| 3124 | Wheel Loader with Digger | SIRU |
| 3125 | Roll-off Skip Loader | CRP |

| # | Name | Price | | # | Name | Price | | # | Name | Price |
|---|------|-------|---|---|------|-------|---|---|------|-------|
| 3126 | Breakdown Service | CRP | | 1951 | Plow | CRP | | 2864 | Steyr Tractor | CRP |
| 3127 | Mobile Crane | CRP | | 1952 | Amazone Seed Drill | CRP | | 2865 | Deutz Fun-Trac | CRP |
| 3419 | Car Transporter | CRP | | 1953 | Deutz Rotary Mower | CRP | | 2866 | Tipping Trailer | CRP |
| 3424 | Container Truck | CRP | | 1955 | Crop Sprayer | CRP | | 2951 | Tractor with Tipping Hopper | CRP |
| 3425 | Garage Transporter | CRP | | 1956 | Reversible Plow | CRP | | 2956 | Deutz Tractor with Twin Rear Wheels | CRP |
| 3510 | Hydraulic Excavator | CRP | | 1957 | Harrow | CRP | | 3153 | Unimog | CRP |
| 3511 | Shell Tanker | CRP | | 2252 | Vacuum Tanker | CRP | | 3155 | Forester Trailer | CRP |
| 3512 | Fire Equipment Truck | CRP | | 2254 | Deutz Hay Rake | CRP | | 3450 | Tractor with Front Loader | CRP |
| 3513 | Airport Fire Engine | CRP | | 2257 | Live-Stock Trailer | CRP | | 3451 | Tractor with Snow Plow | CRP |
| 3514 | Crane Grabber | CRP | | 2551 | Trailer | CRP | | 3453 | Massey Ferguson Front End Loader | CRP |
| 3719 | Low Loader with Helicopter | CRP | | 2552 | Trailer | CRP | | 3454 | Automatic Hay Loader | CRP |
| 3720 | Snorkel Fire Engine | CRP | | 2553 | Manure Spreader | CRP | | 3550 | Deutz Forestry Tractor | CRP |
| 3721 | Lorry with Trailer | CRP | | 2555 | Elevator with 2 Hay Bales | CRP | | 3750 | Massey Ferguson Tractor with Trailer | CRP |
| 3812 | Truck with Garage | CRP | | 2556 | Round Baler | CRP | | 3751 | Deutz Tractor with Trailer | CRP |
| 3813 | Recycling Lorry | CRP | | 2559 | Horse Box | CRP | | 3752 | Fendt Tractor with Vacuum Tanker | CRP |
| 3814 | Bus | CRP | | 2850 | Tractor | CRP | | 3755 | Renault Tractor with Rear Digger | CRP |
| 3880 | Water Canon | CRP | | 2851 | Tractor | CRP | | 3854 | Claas Jaguar Combine | CRP |
| 3912 | Lorry with Trailer and Bulldozer | CRP | | 2853 | MF Tractor with Transporter Box | CRP | | 4051 | Combine Harvester | CRP |
| 4016 | Low Loader with Space Shuttle | CRP | | 2855 | Ford Tractor | CRP | | 4052 | Combine Maize | CRP |
| 4017 | Transporter Set with 5 Cars | CRP | | 2856 | Renault Tractor | CRP | | 4053 | Forester | CRP |
| 4110 | Hydraulic Crane Truck | CRP | | 2859 | Beet Trailer | CRP | | | | |
| 4111 | Lorry with Trailer and Excavator | CRP | | 2860 | Round Bale Trailer | CRP | | **Gift Sets:** | | |
| 4112 | Tower Construction Crane | CRP | | 2861 | Fiat Tractor | CRP | | 6315 | ADAC Gift Set | CRP |
| | | | | 2862 | Baler | CRP | | 6316 | Building Gift Set | CRP |
| **Farmer series (1/32 scale):** | | | | 2863 | Deutz Tractor | CRP | | 6317 | Fire Fighter Gift Set | CRP |
| 1950 | Disc Harrow | CRP | | | | | | 6350 | Farmer Gift Set | CRP |

# Solido

Solido is one of the few companies in die cast toy history that can truly be called legendary. When the discussion turns to the classic brands, the French company is mentioned in the same breath as Meccano Dinky, Tootsietoy, Matchbox and Corgi.

It certainly is one of the oldest firms, having been founded in 1932 by Ferdinand de Vazeilles. Its early products fell into one of three series: the Major, the Junior and the Baby. After World War II, the company resumed die cast production of the Junior series (which was approximately 1/40 scale), as well as some items in the Baby line (the Babys being around 1/50 scale). Many of the these vehicles came with a clockwork motor; the winding hole was on the left side of the vehicle.

The early 1950s saw the addition of the smaller (1/66 scale) Mosquito models, but it would be in 1957 that Solido would enter the highly competitive world of 1/43. The 100 series of model cars introduced that year are among the most popular products ever offered by Solido. The 100s featured window glazing and excellent detail in order to compete with what was coming out of the Corgi and Dinky factories.

*This Solido #178 Matra 650 Sports Racer was introduced in 1970; it stayed in production until 1974. It featured an opening rear engine cover.*

A series of military models, numbered in the 200s, was introduced in the early 1960s, along with a 300 series of commercial vehicles.

Like many manufacturers, Solido changed and rearranged the numbers of its products as time went on. When the 100 series reached #199 in the early 1970s, a new number series was introduced, beginning with 10. When Solido was purchased in 1980 by another French company, Majorette, the new owners introduced a revised numbering system. The new series were given four-digit numbers, a practice which Solido has continued to the present day.

Through the years, Solido worked with a number of other manufacturers. As a result, Solido products were produced, for example, in Spain by Dalia (see the section on Dalia for details). Solido also made a line of models that were marketed as Dinky Toys in 1980 and '81; these models had been part of Solido's lower-cost "Cougar" series. For the Dinky arrangement they were marked Dinky on the baseplates, and came in boxes that also said Dinky.

In May 1993, Solido and Majorette were purchased by Ideal Loisirs Group. Solido continues to produce die cast models and toys in a variety of scales. The 1/43 scale "Yesterday," "Age d'or" and "Racing" series are among its most popular, along with the 1/18 "Prestige" line. Solido has also tapped into the re-issue market with its "Nostalgia" and "Yesterday" models, which are re-issues of Solido models from the 1950s, '60s and '70s. (Prior to the early 1990s, the various types of 1/43 models were marketed simply as the "L'Age d'or" line, before being split into the aforementioned collections.)

To catalog the enormous number of products that Solido has made during the past 50 years would take far more space than is available in this volume. Therefore, the following listing is comprised of the most collected groups of models, including the 100 and 300 series; the Baby, Junior and Mosquito lines from the 1940s and '50s; and the models currently being manufactured by Solido. Per the usual format, the values given here are for models in near mint or better condition, in original packaging.

More detailed information on the history and products of Solido may be found in Dr. Edward Force's excellent book *Solido Toys*. Please see Part Three, Additional Resources, for details on this valuable reference work.

*Solido #130 Aston Martin DB5 Vantage, introduced in 1964.*

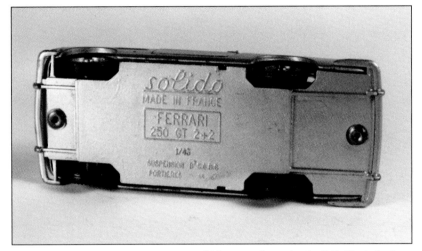

*Baseplate of the #123 Ferrari 250 GT 2 + 2, which was made starting in 1962. The lack of detailing was not unusual for die casts of this era. Later in the 1960s, Solido began to include the date of issue on the baseplates.*

*Solido #136 Bugatti Royale, made by Solido from 1964 until the late 1970s. Its long production run makes it one of the easier to find 100-series models today.*

| # | Name | Price |
|---|------|-------|
| **Baby series:** | | |
| 124 | Ford Vedette | $90 |
| 129 | Ford Vedette Coupe | 90 |
| 132 | Streamlined Coupe | 90 |
| 133 | Peugeot 203 Convertible | 125 |
| 134 | Bus | 100 |
| 135 | Berline Saloon | 135 |
| 135 | Peugeot 203 | 100 |
| 136 | Simca Aronde | 90 |
| 137 | Nash Ambassador Sedan | 100 |
| 138 | Camion Tanker | 75 |
| 139 | Ford Zephyr | 100 |
| 140 | Kaiser Henry J | 140 |
| 141 | Van | 75 |
| 141 | Ambulance | 75 |
| **Junior series:** | | |
| 76 | Studebaker Coupe | 100 |
| 77 | Limousine | 100 |
| 78 | Bus | 100 |
| 79 | Tatra | 100 |
| 80 | Alfa Romeo Convertible | 100 |
| 81 | Delahaye Convertible | 100 |
| 82 | Ferrari 166 Barquette | 125 |
| 83 | Chevrolet Berline | 100 |
| 84 | Studebaker Coupe | 100 |
| 85 | Beauce Tractor | 75 |
| 86 | Cattle Trailer | 50 |
| 86 | Trailer | 50 |
| 86 | Plow | 50 |
| 86 | Mower | 50 |
| 86 | Harrow | 50 |
| 86 | Roller | 50 |
| 86 | 3 Row-Harrow | 50 |
| 87 | Flandre Bulldozer | 60 |
| 88 | Oldsmobile Sedan | 100 |
| 89 | Nash Ambassador | 100 |
| 90 | Cadillac Fleetwood | 100 |
| 91 | Renault Fregate | 100 |
| 92 | Ladder Fire Truck | 100 |
| 93 | Dump Truck | 75 |
| 94 | Six Wheel Trailer | 50 |
| 95 | Fire Truck | 100 |
| 96 | Fire Truck | 100 |
| 97 | Wrecker | 100 |
| 98 | Lambretta Scooter | 125 |
| 99 | Lambretta Motor-Tricycle | 160 |
| 100 | Lambretta Ice Cream Motor-Tricycle | 175 |
| 101 | Terrot Scooter | 100 |
| 102 | Elevator with Crane | 75 |
| 103 | Elevator with Fork | 75 |
| 104 | Railway Mechanical Horse and Cycle | 75 |
| 105 | Elevator with Platform | 75 |
| 106 | Elevator with Tipper | 75 |
| 107 | Railway Mechanical Horse and 2 Trailers | 75 |
| 113 | Ford Comete | 125 |
| 114 | Packard Convertible | 125 |
| 115 | Studebaker Commander Hardtop | 175 |
| 116 | Ford Vedette | 100 |
| 188 | Chausson Trolleybus | 200 |
| 189 | Chausson AP2 Bus | 200 |

| # | Name | Price |
|---|------|-------|
| 190 | Chausson AP2 Bus with Roof Rack | $200 |
| 191 | Mercury Monterey Convertible | 200 |
| 192 | Simca Versailles | 100 |
| 193 | Peugeot 403 | 100 |
| 194 | Mercedes-Benz 300 Saloon | 125 |
| 195 | Ford Thunderbird Convertible | 150 |
| 195 | Ford Thunderbird Hardtop | 150 |
| 196 | Ford Fairlane Station Wagon | 125 |
| 197 | Ford Fairlane Pickup | 100 |
| 198 | Ford Fairlane Covered Pickup | 100 |
| 199 | Citroën DS 19 | 125 |
| 207 | Simca Beaulieu | 100 |
| 208 | Notin Caravan | 75 |
| 209 | Trailer with Boat | 60 |
| 210 | Rolls-Royce Silver Cloud | 150 |
| **Mosquito series (1/66 scale):** | | |
| 151 | Citroën 11 CV | 60 |
| 152 | Maserati Coupe | 50 |
| 153 | Renault Fregate | 50 |
| 154 | Hotchkiss Anjou | 50 |
| 155 | Peugeot 203 | 50 |
| 156 | Renault Pick-up | 50 |
| 157 | Ford Vedette | 50 |
| 158 | Renault Tanker | 50 |
| 159 | Simca Sport Convertible | 60 |
| 160 | Tatraplan | 50 |
| 161 | Ford Comete | 60 |
| 162 | Latil Bus | 50 |
| **100 series:** | | |
| 100 | Jaguar D LeMans | 75 |
| 101 | Porsche Spyder | 90 |
| 102 | Maserati 250 Formula I | 75 |
| 103 | Ferrari 500 TRC | 90 |
| 104 | Vanwall Formula I | 75 |
| 105 | Mercedes-Benz 190SL Convertible | 75 |
| 106 | Alfa Romeo Giulietta 1300 | 75 |
| 107 | Aston Martin 3L DBR I | 75 |
| 108 | Peugeot 403 Convertible | 60 |
| 109 | Renault Floride Convertible | 60 |

| # | Name | Price |
|---|------|-------|
| 110 | Simca Oceane Convertible | $75 |
| 111 | Aston Martin DB4 | 75 |
| 112 | DB Panhard LeMans | 60 |
| 113 | Fiat Abarth Record | 75 |
| 113B | Ford Thunderbird Convertible | 120 |
| 114 | Citroën Ami 6 | 60 |
| 115 | Rolls-Royce Silver Cloud | 110 |
| 116 | Cooper 1500 | 60 |
| 117 | Porsche Formula 2 | 75 |
| 118 | Lotus Formula I | 60 |
| 119 | Chausson Bus | 175 |
| 120 | Chausson Trolleybus | 175 |
| 121 | Lancia Flaminia Coupe | 60 |
| 122 | Ferrari Formula I | 75 |
| 123 | Ferrari 250 GT 2+2 | 85 |
| 124 | Abarth 1000 | 60 |
| 125 | Alfa Romeo 2600 Coupe | 60 |
| 126 | Mercedes-Benz 220SE Coupe | 60 |
| 127 | NSU Prinz IV | 60 |
| 128 | Ford Thunderbird Hardtop | 120 |
| 129 | Ferrari 2.5 Liter | 75 |
| 130 | Aston Martin DB5 Vantage | 75 |
| 131 | B.R.M. V8 Formula I | 60 |
| 132 | Mercedes SS 1928 | 45 |
| 133 | Fiat 2300 S Ghia Convertible | 65 |
| 134 | Porsche GT LeMans | 75 |
| 135 | Lola Climax V8 Formula I | 60 |
| 136 | Bugatti Royale | 40 |
| 137 | Mercedes SS 1928 (top down) | 40 |
| 138 | Harvey Special Indy Car | 75 |
| 139 | Maserati Mistral | 60 |
| 140 | Panhard Levassor Landaulet 1925 | 35 |
| 141 | Citroen Ami 6 Station Wagon | 60 |
| 142 | Alpine Formula 3 | 45 |
| 143 | Panhard 24 BT | 50 |
| 144 | Voisin Carene 1934 | 50 |
| 145 | Hispano-Suiza H6B 1926 | 40 |
| 146 | Ford GT 40 LeMans | 60 |
| 147 | Ford Mustang | 125 |
| 147B | Ford Mustang Rally | 125 |

*The rear engine cover on this #41 Alfa Romeo 33TT 12 lifts up toward the front of the car to reveal the engine. (Damage to the number decals is common on this model, due to their being applied directly over the engine hood seam.) Although the tires are plastic, the wheel detail is excellent on this 1970s Solido.*

| # | Name | Price |
|---|------|-------|
| 148 | Alfa Romeo Giulia TZ | $65 |
| 149 | Renault 40 Landaulet 1926 | 35 |
| 150 | Oldsmobile Toronado | 110 |
| 151 | Porsche Carrera 6 | 60 |
| 152 | Ferrari 330 P3 | 60 |
| 153 | Chaparral 2D | 60 |
| 154 | Fiat 525 N with Pope 1929 | 40 |
| 155 | Ferrari Superfast 500 | * |
| 156 | Duesenberg J 1931 | 40 |
| 157 | BMW 2000 CS | 60 |
| 157B | BMW 2000 CS Rally | 60 |
| 158 | Alfa Romeo and Travel Trailer | 100 |
| 159 | Citroën Ami 6 and Boat Trailer | 10 |
| 160 | Ford Thunderbird and Travel Trailer | * |
| 161 | Lamborghini Miura | 65 |
| 164 | Simca 1100 | 50 |
| 164B | Simca 1100 Police car | * |
| 165 | Ferrari 365 GTB4 | 75 |
| 166 | De Tomaso Mangusta | 60 |
| 167 | Ferrari Formula I | 60 |
| 168 | Alpine Renault 3 Liter | 45 |
| 169 | Chaparral 2 F | 65 |
| 170 | Ford Mark IV | 50 |
| 171 | Opel GT | 50 |
| 172 | Alfa Romeo Carabo Bertone | 40 |
| 173 | Matra V8 Formula I | 40 |
| 174 | Porsche 908 LeMans | 50 |
| 175 | Lola T70 MK 3B | 45 |
| 176 | McLaren M8B Can Am | 50 |
| 177 | Ferrari 312P | 60 |
| 178 | Matra 650 | 45 |
| 179 | Porsche 914/6 | 40 |
| 180 | Mercedes-Benz C-111 | 40 |
| 181 | Alpine Renault | 40 |
| 182 | Ferrari 512 S | 50 |
| 183 | Alfa Romeo Zagato Junior | 40 |
| 184 | Citroën SM | 40 |
| 185 | Maserati Indy | 50 |
| 186 | Porsche 917 | 50 |
| 186M | Porsche 917 "Martini" | 50 |
| 187 | Alfa Romeo 33/3 | 50 |
| 188 | Opel Manta | 40 |
| 188R | Opel Manta Rally | 45 |
| 189 | Bertone Buggy | 35 |
| 190 | Ford Capri 2900 | 40 |
| 192 | Alpine Renault A310 | 40 |
| 192B | Alpine Renault A310 Police car | 40 |
| 193 | Citroën GS | 35 |
| 194 | Ferrari 312 PB | 40 |
| 195 | Ligier JS 3 | 35 |
| 196 | Renault 17 TS | 35 |
| 197 | Ferrari 512M Sunoco | 40 |
| 197B | Ferrari 512M Piper | 40 |
| 198 | Porsche 917 | 45 |
| 199 | March 707 Can Am | 40 |

* never produced

**300 series (1/50 scale):**

| # | Name | Price |
|---|------|-------|
| 300 | Berliet TBO 200 Titan | 100 |
| 301 | Unic Sahara Tank Truck various liveries | 100 |

| # | Name | Price |
|---|------|-------|
| 302 | Willeme Horizon Open Semi | $100 |
| 303 | Berliet Dump Truck | 75 |
| 304 | Bernard T12 Refrigerator Truck | 75 |
| 305 | Berliet T12 with Prefab House | 125 |
| 305B | Berliet T12 with Renault 4 Van | 90 |
| 306 | Berliet Stradair Dump Truck | 65 |
| 307 | Berliet Stradair Van | 60 |
| 308 | Willeme Tanker "ELF" | 75 |
| 316 | Saviem SM 300 Open Semi with Crane | 75 |
| 317 | Berliet TR 300 Tanker | 75 |
| 318 | Saviem SM 300 "ELF" Tanker | 50 |
| 319 | Saviem SM 300 "ESSO" Tanker | 50 |
| 320 | Saviem SM 300 "SHELL" Tanker | 50 |
| 321 | Saviem Car Transporter and Trailer | 50 |
| 330 | Citroën C 35 Circus Van | 40 |
| 331 | Mercedes Circus Truck | 40 |
| 332 | Saviem Flat Truck with Cages | 40 |
| 333 | Daf Circus Box Office | 40 |
| 334 | Richier Circus Crane Truck | 40 |
| 335 | Daf Animal Transporter Semi | 40 |
| 336 | Daf Stakeside Circus Semi | 40 |
| 337 | Daf Circus Caravan Semi | 40 |
| 338 | Stakeside Circus Trailer | 40 |
| 350 | Berliet Fire Engine | 40 |
| 351 | Berliet Airport Fire Truck | 30 |
| 352 | Berliet Ladder Fire Engine | 30 |
| 353 | Richier Crane Truck | 30 |
| 354 | Berliet Forest Fire Truck and Trailer | 30 |
| 355 | Peugeot J7 Bus | 40 |
| 355B | Peugeot J7 School Bus | 40 |
| 356 | Volvo BM Dumper | 30 |
| 357 | Unic Sahara Dump Truck | 30 |
| 358 | Mercedes Truck | 30 |
| 359 | Simca Unic Snow Plow Truck | 30 |
| 360 | Guinard Fire Pump Trailer | 10 |
| 361 | Mercedes Ladder Fire Engine | 30 |
| 362 | Hotchkiss Fire Engine | 30 |
| 363 | Magirus Covered Semi | 30 |
| 364 | Mercedes 2624 Bucket Truck | 30 |
| 365 | International Harvester Shovel | 50 |
| 366 | Saviem SG4 Tow Truck various liveries | 30 |
| 367 | Volvo Loader | 30 |
| 368 | Citroën C 35 Fire Ambulance | 30 |
| 369 | Daf 2800 Tanker Truck various liveries | 30 |
| 370 | Saviem H875 Semi | 30 |
| 371 | Citroën Ambulance and Boat Trailer | 30 |
| 372 | Peugeot J7 Police Bus | 30 |
| 373 | Mercedes 1217 Cattle Truck | 30 |
| 374 | Unic Iveco Dump Truck | 30 |
| 375 | Berliet GAK Fire Van | 30 |
| 376 | Mercedes Bulk Carrier Semi | 30 |
| 377 | Mercedes Snorkel Fire Truck | * |
| 378 | Mercedes Truck with Shovel | 30 |
| 379 | Mercedes 1217 Refuse Truck | 30 |
| 380 | Peugeot J7 Fire Ambulance | 30 |
| 382 | Mercedes Refrigerator Truck | * |
| 383 | Mercedes Moving Van | * |
| 384 | Mercedes Covered Truck | 30 |
| 385 | Saviem Horse Van Semi | 40 |
| 386 | Mercedes Propane Tanker | 40 |
| 388 | Saviem Stakeside Semi | 30 |

| # | Name | Price |
|---|------|-------|
| 389 | Stakeside Trailer | $15 |
| 390 | Daf Semi | * |
| 391 | Dodge 6x6 Fire Truck and Trailer | 30 |

* never produced

## CURRENT PRODUCTION

**1/12 scale:**

| # | Name | Price |
|---|------|-------|
| 1201 | 1958 Chevrolet Corvette | CRP |

**Actua series (1/18 scale):**

| # | Name | Price |
|---|------|-------|
| 8001 | Bugatti Royale 1930 | CRP |
| 8006 | Rolls-Royce Silver Cloud II 1961 | CRP |
| 8009 | Ford Roadster 1934 | CRP |
| 8503 | Citroën ZX Rally | CRP |
| 8504 | Renault Safrane 1992 | CRP |

**Prestige series (1/18 scale):**

| # | Name | Price |
|---|------|-------|
| 8011 | Cadillac Eldorado 1955 | CRP |
| 8014 | VW Beetle Cabriolet 1949 | CRP |
| 8016 | VW Beetle Berline 1949 | CRP |
| 8022 | Mini Cooper S 1964 | CRP |
| 8023 | Mini Cooper S Rally 1967 | CRP |
| 8026 | Ford Pick-up Fire 1936 | CRP |
| 8027 | Ford Tanker 1936 | CRP |
| 8028 | Citroën 2CV 1966 | CRP |
| 8029 | Citroën 2CV Open 1966 | CRP |
| 8030 | Citroën 2CV Open 1971 | CRP |
| 8031 | VW Combi 1966 | CRP |
| 8032 | VW Combi Van 1966 | CRP |
| 8033 | Citroën DS19 Berline 1963 | CRP |
| 8034 | Citroën DS19 Rally 1963 | CRP |
| 8035 | Citroën DS19 Presidentielle 1963 | CRP |
| 8036 | Citroën 2CV Rally 1966 | CRP |
| 8306 | VW Beetle Berline 1958 | CRP |

**Signature series:**

| # | Name | Price |
|---|------|-------|
| 9801 | Cadillac Eldorado 1955 "James Dean" (1/18) | CRP |
| 9802 | Ford Roadster 1934 "Humphrey Bogart" | CRP |
| 9803 | Rolls-Royce 1961 "Orson Welles" (1/18) | CRP |
| 9804 | Cadillac Eldorado 1955 "Marilyn Monroe" (1/18) | CRP |
| 9901 | Buick Super 1950 "James Dean" (1/43) | CRP |
| 9902 | Packard Sedan 1937 "Humphrey Bogart" (1/43) | CRP |
| 9903 | Rolls-Royce 1939 "Orson Welles" (1/43) | CRP |
| 9904 | Cadillac Eldorado 1950 "Marilyn Monroe" (1/43) | CRP |

**Age d'or series (1/43):**

| # | Name | Price |
|---|------|-------|
| 4002 | Jaguar SS 100 | CRP |
| 4032 | Citroën 15 CV | CRP |
| 4036 | Bugatti Royale 1930 | CRP |
| 4051 | Delage Coupe de Ville 1938 | CRP |
| 4077 | Rolls-Royce Cabriolet 1939 | CRP |
| 4085 | Cadillac 452A 1931 | CRP |
| 4086 | Mercedes-Benz 540 K Cabriolet 1938 | CRP |
| 4088 | Bugatti Atalante 1939 | CRP |

| # | Name | Price |
|---|------|-------|
| 4149 | Renault 40 CV Landaulet 1926 | CRP |
| 4160 | Alfa Romeo 2500 Sport 1939 | CRP |
| 4162 | Hispano-Suiza Torpedo 1926 | CRP |
| 4163 | Ford V8 Taxi 1936 | CRP |
| 4433 | Ford V8 Pick-up 1936 "Kodak" | CRP |
| 4434 | Ford V8 Fire Tanker 1936 | CRP |
| 4435 | Ford V8 Coal Truck 1936 | CRP |
| 4436 | Ford V8 Pick-up 1936 "Miko" | CRP |

**Sixties series (1/43):**

| # | Name | Price |
|---|------|-------|
| 4500 | Cadillac Eldorado Biarritz 1957 | CRP |
| 4502 | Mercedes-Benz 300SL 1954 | CRP |
| 4506 | Ferrari 250 GTO 1963 | CRP |
| 4508 | Chevrolet 1950 | CRP |
| 4512 | Buick Super 1950 | CRP |
| 4524 | Tucker 1948 | CRP |
| 4533 | AC Cobra 427 1965 | CRP |
| 4534 | VW Combi 1966 | CRP |
| 4535 | VW Combi Fire Brigade 1966 | CRP |
| 4536 | Citroën 15CV Taxi 1952 | CRP |
| 4537 | Renault 4CV 1954 | CRP |
| 4538 | Renault 4CV Open 1954 | CRP |
| 4539 | Triumph Spitfire Mark 1 1962 | CRP |
| 4540 | Ford Mustang 1964-1/2 | CRP |
| 4541 | Renault Dauphine Berline 1961 | CRP |
| 4542 | Renault Dauphine Open 1961 | CRP |

**Yesterday series (1/43):**

| # | Name | Price |
|---|------|-------|
| 1801 | Maserati Indy 1970 | CRP |
| 1802 | Ferrari BB 1976 | CRP |
| 1803 | Alpine A 110 1970 | CRP |
| 1805 | Opel GT 1900 1968 | CRP |
| 1806 | Jaguar XJ12 1978 | CRP |
| 1807 | Citroën SM 1970 | CRP |
| 1808 | Porsche Carrera 1973 | CRP |
| 1810 | Ferrari 365 GTB4 | CRP |
| 1812 | BMW M1 1979 | CRP |
| 1813 | Chevrolet Corvette 1968 | CRP |
| 1814 | Alpine A310 1972 | CRP |
| 1816 | Alfa Romeo Carabo 1968 | CRP |
| 1817 | Range Rover 1978 | CRP |
| 1818 | Peugeot 504 Coupe 1978 | CRP |
| 1819 | Citroën 2CV Open 1979 | CRP |
| 1820 | Citroën 2CV 1979 | CRP |

**Today series (1/43):**

| # | Name | Price |
|---|------|-------|
| 1508 | Peugeot 205 GTI 1984 | CRP |
| 1511 | Rolls-Royce Corniche 1987 | CRP |
| 1514 | Chevrolet Corvette Cabriolet 1984 | CRP |
| 1516 | Peugeot 605 1989 | CRP |
| 1517 | Mercedes-Benz SL Cabriolet 1989 | CRP |
| 1520 | Renault Clio 16S 1991 | CRP |
| 1521 | BMW Serie 3 1990 | CRP |
| 1522 | Renault Espace 1991 | CRP |
| 1523 | Citroën ZX Aura 1991 | CRP |
| 1527 | Lamborghini Diablo 1990 | CRP |
| 1528 | Renault Twingo 1992 | CRP |
| 1529 | BMW Serie 3 Cabriolet 1993 | CRP |
| 1530 | Renault Twingo 1992 | CRP |
| 1531 | Renault Clio 1993 "Williams" | CRP |
| 1532 | Renault Twingo 1993 Open | CRP |
| 1533 | Renault 19 Cabriolet 1995 | CRP |

**Racing series (1/43):**

| # | Name | Price |
|---|------|-------|
| 1903 | Citroën 15CV Monte Carlo 1952 | CRP |
| 1904 | Alpine A110 Monte Carlo 1973 | CRP |
| 1908 | Renault 5 Maxi Turbo 1985 | CRP |
| 1909 | AC Cobra 427 1965 | CRP |
| 1910 | Chevrolet Corvette 1968 | CRP |
| 1913 | Fiat 131 Racing | CRP |
| 1914 | Land Rover 1980 | CRP |
| 1915 | Toyota Celica 1977 | CRP |
| 1916 | Audi Quattro 1983 | CRP |
| 1917 | Peugeot 504 Safari 1975 | CRP |
| 1918 | Renault Clio Rally 1993 | CRP |
| 1919 | Renault 4CV Rally 1954 | CRP |
| 1920 | Porsche Carrera 1973 | CRP |
| 1921 | Triumph Spitfire MK 1 1962 | CRP |
| 1922 | Ford Mustang 1965 | CRP |
| 1923 | Lancia Rally 1983 | CRP |
| 1924 | Peugeot 504 Coupe Rally 1978 | CRP |
| 1925 | Porsche 935 1979 | CRP |
| 1926 | Renault Dauphine 1962 | CRP |
| 1927 | Range Rover Rally 1984 | CRP |

**Nostalgia series (1/43):**

| # | Name | Price |
|---|------|-------|
| 1101 | Ferrari 500 TRC 1956 | CRP |
| 1102 | Cooper F2 1959 | CRP |
| 1103 | Lola Climax V8 F1 1962 | CRP |
| 1104 | Maserati 250 1956 | CRP |
| 1105 | Lotus F1 1960 | CRP |
| 1106 | Porsche Spyder 1955 | CRP |
| 1107 | Panhard DB 1959 | CRP |
| 1108 | Ferrari 2.5L 1962 | CRP |

**Toner Gam series:**

| # | Name | Price |
|---|------|-------|
| 2101 | Saviem First Aid Van | CRP |
| 2106 | Multi Purpose Tender | CRP |
| 2217 | Jeep with Hose Reel | CRP |
| 2228 | Dodge WC 54 | CRP |
| 2130 | Express + Trailer | CRP |
| 2133 | Mercedes-Benz Ambulance | CRP |
| 2135 | Peugeot J9 Ambulance | CRP |

| # | Name | Price |
|---|------|-------|
| 2137 | Renault Trafic | CRP |
| 2138 | Renault Trafic Ambulance | CRP |
| 2139 | Dodge WC 56 Echelle | CRP |
| 2140 | Dodge WC 51 Citerne | CRP |
| 2141 | Renault Trafic Bus | CRP |
| 3106 | Mack Fire Truck | CRP |
| 3111 | Mercedes-Benz Ladder Truck | CRP |
| 3112 | Berliet Hydraulic Platform | CRP |
| 3116 | GMC Tanker | CRP |
| 3118 | Iveco Tanker | CRP |
| 3119 | Sides 2000 Pumper Truck | CRP |
| 3124 | Volvo Excavator | CRP |
| 3125 | Acmat Forest Fire Tender | CRP |
| 3127 | Dodge WC 56 + Zodiac | CRP |
| 3128 | Dodge WV 51 + Trailer | CRP |
| 3129 | Renault Trafic + Zodiac | CRP |
| 3130 | Peugeot J9 Express + Trailer | CRP |
| 3511 | Mack R600 Fire Truck | CRP |
| 3512 | Mercedes-Benz Fire Brigade Tanker | CRP |
| 3513 | Mack R600 Fire Brigade Tanker | CRP |
| 3514 | Mack R600 Fire Truck | CRP |
| 3515 | Renault Field Casualty Vehicle | CRP |
| 3516 | Mercedes-Benz Training Simulator | CRP |
| 3601 | Kässbohrer Track Rammer | CRP |
| 4401 | Paris Bus | CRP |
| 4402 | London Bus | CRP |

**Military series:**

| # | Name | Price |
|---|------|-------|
| 6101 | GMC Truck with Protective Cover | CRP |
| 6102 | Citroën Traction Gaz FFI | CRP |
| 6103 | Dodge WC 51 4x4 | CRP |
| 6104 | Combat Car M20 | CRP |
| 6105 | Jeep US + Trailer | CRP |
| 6106 | GMC + Accessories | CRP |
| 6201 | Sherman M4 A3 Tank | CRP |
| 6202 | Destroyer M10 Tank | CRP |
| 6203 | Half-Track Radio US M3 | CRP |
| 6204 | Tigre Tank | CRP |
| 6205 | Renault R35 Tank | CRP |
| 6206 | Jagdpanther | CRP |

*This Porsche Spyder is #1106 in Solido's current "Nostalgia" 1/43 scale line. It is a re-issue of #101 Porsche, originally produced from 1957 until the mid-1960s. Both box and baseplate say "REEDITION."*

# Spot-On

The Tri-ang Spot-On line of die cast toys was launched by the British company, Lines Bros., in 1959. Having produced the Tri-ang Minic line of tinplate (and then plastic) toy cars and trucks since 1935, Lines Bros. were now looking to compete with Meccano's Dinky and Mettoy's Corgi products. They advertised their new Spot-On models as all being of the same scale; therefore, they would all look in scale with each other on a model train layout or display shelf. The models were manufactured at the Lines Bros. factory in Belfast, Northern Ireland.

Lines Bros. also made them just a bit larger than the competition, at 1/42 scale. This included the commercial vehicles, which made them particularly heavy and imposing. Spot-Ons also featured opening doors, window glazing and interiors; some models also came with working steering and battery-operated head and tail lights. Lines Bros. also marketed a line of buildings, road signs, road surfaces and figures of people—all meant to be used with the Spot-On vehicles. And, the company introduced a line of themed gift sets entitled "Tommy Spot." These generally included vehicles and figures, such as those contained in the "Cops and Robbers with Tommy Spot" set. The boxes that these sets came in were meant to be cut apart in order to make a play scene for the toys, which may help explain why there are so many Spot-Ons without boxes today.

Spot-On's larger size and extra features contributed to a higher retail price than the competition. This, along with the fact that Lines Bros. had a difficult time penetrating the established Dinky and Corgi retail market, meant that Spot-Ons were hard to find from the start.

Lines Bros. bought the legendary Meccano company in 1963 or '64, acquiring the Dinky Toys line in the process. The Spot-On line was gradually phased out as Lines Bros. focused its energies on developing the Dinky line. Production of Spot-Ons ended around 1967, although some of the tooling was shipped to New Zealand, where certain models were made for a time.

Its lack of success at the time notwithstanding, the Spot-On series is quite popular with collectors today. In one sense, things haven't changed much since Spot-Ons generally sell for more than Corgi and Dinky models made during the same period. Spot-Ons were for the most part very accurate models, although the wheel hubs were generally of the nondescript spun-metal variety (tires were rubber).

*Spot-On photos courtesy of Andrew Ralston.*

*Spot-On #217 Jaguar E Type. This model was introduced in 1963.*

*The first Spot-On, #100SL Ford Zodiac with original box. This is the version fitted with electric lights; the chassis contains a plastic battery and bulb carrier. Lighted Spot-Ons were more costly than their non-lighted counterparts. The Zodiac was deleted from the Spot-On series in 1963.*

Because of the relatively low percentage of Spot-On boxes that have survived (due to the previously-mentioned cutting apart of boxes), the following listing gives values for near mint to mint condition models **by themselves**. A model with its original box would likely sell for 25-50% more than the values listed here. *Note:* There were a handful of plastic Spot-Ons made near the end of production, all having numbers in the 500s. These are not included here.

| #      | Name                                          | Price |
|--------|-----------------------------------------------|-------|
| 100    | Ford Zodiac                                   | $125  |
| 100SL  | Ford Zodiac with lights                       | 140   |
| 101    | Armstrong Siddeley 236                        | 140   |
| 102    | Bentley Sports Saloon                         | 190   |
| 103    | Rolls-Royce Silver Wraith                     | 280   |
| 104    | MGA Sports Car                                | 200   |
| 105    | Austin Healey 100/6 Sports Car                | 200   |
| 106A/1 | Austin Prime mover and flat float with sides  | 290   |
| 106A/1C| Austin Prime Mover and flat float with sides and crate load | 375 |
| 106A/OC| Austin Prime Mover with MGA Sports Car in Crate "BMC" | 400 |
| 107    | Jaguar XK-SS                                  | 200   |
| 108    | Triumph TR3A                                  | 200   |
| 109/2  | ERF 68G with flat float                       | 230   |
| 109/2P | ERF 68G with flat float and wood planks       | 300   |
| 109/3  | ERF 68G flat float with sides                 | 250   |
| 109/3B | ERF 68G flat float with sides and barrel load | 300   |
| 110/2  | AEC Mammoth Major 8 with flat float           | 300   |
| 110/2B | AEC Mammoth Major 8 with flat float and brick load "London Brick Co." | 300 |
| 110/3  | AEC Mammoth Major 8 with flat float and sides "British Road Services" | 325 |
| 110/3D | AEC Mammoth Major 8 flat float with sides and oil drum load | 300 |
| 110/4  | AEC Mammoth Major 8 Shell BP Tanker           | 800   |
| 111A/1 | Ford Thames Trader with sides "British Railways" | 300 |
| 111A/1S| Ford Thames Trader with sides and sack load   | 300   |
| 111A/OT| Ford Thames Trader with log load              | 300   |
| 111A/OG| Ford Thames Trader with garage load           | 400   |
| 112    | Jensen 541                                    | 200   |
| 113    | Aston Martin DB3                              | 200   |
| 114    | Jaguar 3.4 Mk I                               | 175   |
| 115    | Bristol 406                                   | 175   |
| 116    | Caterpillar D9 Bulldozer                      | 700   |
| 117    | Jones Mobile Crane                            | 325   |
| 118    | BMW Isetta Bubble Car                         | 135   |
| 119    | Meadows Friskysport                           | 100   |
| 120    | Fiat Multipla                                 | 125   |
| 122    | United Dairies Milk Float                     | 150   |
| 131    | Goggomobil Super                              | 110   |

| #      | Name                                          | Price |
|--------|-----------------------------------------------|-------|
| 135    | Sailing Dinghy and Trailer                    | $50   |
| 136    | Sailing Dinghy                                | 35    |
| 137    | Massey Harris Tractor                         | 625   |
| 145    | AEC Routemaster Bus                           | 700   |
| 154    | Austin A40                                    | 135   |
| 155    | Austin FX4 Taxi Cab                           | 135   |
| 156    | Mulliner Luxury Coach                         | 425   |
| 157    | Rover 3-Litre                                 | 190   |
| 157SL  | Rover 3-Litre, with lights                    | 225   |
| 158A/2 | Bedford 10-ton tanker Shell BP                | 800   |
| 161    | Long wheelbase Land Rover                     | 135   |
| 165    | Vauxhall Cresta PA                            | 200   |
| 166    | Renault Floride Convertible                   | 135   |
| 183    | Humber Super Snipe Estate                     | 210   |
| 184    | Austin A60 with roof rack and skis            | 135   |
| 185    | Fiat 500                                      | 150   |
| 191/1  | Sunbeam Alpine Convertible                    | 190   |
| 191/2  | Sunbeam Alpine Hard top                       | 190   |
| 193    | NSU Prinz                                     | 140   |
| 195    | Volkswagen 1200 Rally                         | 135   |
| 207    | Wadham Ambulance                              | 550   |
| 210/1  | Morris Mini Van "Royal Mail"                  | 175   |
| 210/2  | Morris Mini Van "Post Office Telephones"      | 175   |
| 211    | Austin Seven Mini                             | 175   |
| 213    | Ford Anglia                                   | 135   |
| 215    | Daimler Dart SP250                            | 200   |
| 216    | Volvo 122S                                    | 175   |
| 217    | Jaguar E Type                                 | 200   |
| 218    | Jaguar Mk 10                                  | 175   |
| 219    | Austin Healey Sprite                          | 175   |
| 229    | Lambretta Scooter                             | 175   |
| 256    | Jaguar 3.4 Mk I Police Car (white, black)     | 250   |
| 258    | Land Rover RAC                                | 225   |
| 259    | Ford Consul Classic                           | 150   |

| #      | Name                                          | Price |
|--------|-----------------------------------------------|-------|
| 260    | Royal Rolls-Royce Phantom V                   | $450  |
| 261    | Volvo P1800                                    | 135   |
| 262    | Morris 1100                                    | 125   |
| 263    | Bentley Supercharged 4.5 Liter                 | 135   |
| 264    | Tourist Caravan                                | 80    |
| 265    | Bedford "Tonibell" Ice Cream Van               | 175   |
| 266    | Bullnose Morris Cowley                          | 95    |
| 267    | MG 1100                                         | 125   |
| 270    | Ford Zephyr 6                                   | 160   |
| 271    | Express Dairies Milk Float                      | 160   |
| 273    | Commer Security Van                             | 240   |
| 274    | Morris 1100 with canoe                          | 110   |
| 276    | Jaguar S Type                                   | 225   |
| 278    | Mercedes-Benz 230SL                             | 125   |
| 279    | 1935 MG PB Midget                               | 100   |
| 280    | Vauxhall Cresta PB                              | 125   |
| 281    | MG Midget Mk II                                 | 175   |
| 286    | Austin 1800                                     | 110   |
| 287    | Hillman Minx                                    | 110   |
| 289    | Morris Minor 1000                               | 200   |
| 306    | Humber Super Snipe with luggage rack           | 200   |
| 307    | Volkswagen Beetle 1200                          | 300   |
| 308    | Land Rover and Trailer                          | 175   |
| 309    | Police "Z" Car                                  | 175   |
| 315    | Commer Window Cleaner's Van                     | 200   |
| 316    | Fire Dept. Land Rover                           | 175   |
| 401    | Volkswagen Variant with skis                    | 550   |
| 402    | Crash Service Land Rover                        | 125   |
| 403    | Hillman Minx and dinghy                         | 125   |
| 404    | Morris Mini Van                                 | 400   |
| 405    | Vauxhall Cresta PB "BEA"                        | 125   |
| 407    | Mercedes-Benz 230SL                             | 130   |
| 410    | Austin 1800, with row boat                      | 135   |
| 415    | RAF Land Rover                                  | 160   |
| 417    | Bedford Military Field Kitchen                  | 150   |
| 419    | Land Rover and Missile Carrier                  | 300   |

*At left is a #289 Morris Minor 1000, at right a #267 MG 1100.*

# Tekno

This most famous of Scandinavian toy companies traces its roots back to the late 1920s, when a man named Siegumfeldt began making tinplate toys in Denmark. The business took hold with the introduction, in the 1930s, of a line of tinplate toy trucks. When the war started, production was suspended, picking up again after the cessation of hostilities and continuing until the mid-1950s.

Although Tekno had apparently made some die cast airplane toys prior to the war, the firm began production in earnest around 1946, when it introduced a line of die cast road vehicle toys. A group of Ford V8 trucks, a "Triangel" series of emergency vehicles, and several Dodge trucks were among the early products. Actually, the toys were manufactured by a company called H. Lange; it was only after Tekno reached an agreement with Lange in the late 1940s that the name Tekno appeared on the toys and their boxes.

The toys were well-made, and some of them were also fairly accurate models of full-size vehicles. Many of them had die cast cab and chassis units, onto which were fitted tinplate rear loads such as a dump bed or box trailer. They came with rubber tires, and the cast wheel hubs often had "Dodge," or "V8" on them. Interestingly, some of the early 700 series Dodge and Buick trucks (made in the late '40s) had their wheel hubs switched: Buicks turn up with hubs that say Dodge, and vice-versa.

These early products were made in a number of different liveries, a practice that Tekno would employ with great success in years to come. The ever-expanding truck series was joined by die cast cars in 1955, when the #719 Morris Oxford made its debut. This was the first in a long line of Tekno die cast cars, a line that would grow and flourish through the 1950s and '60s.

The 700, 800 and 900 series included German, American, British and Swedish makes, and production continued on these excellent toys (models) until the early 1970s. In the late 1960s, Tekno reached an agreement with the Spanish Dalia company to produce a number of Tekno models in Spain. Included were the #930 Monza GT (a model that was also put out, using the Tekno tooling, by other manufacturers such as Joal) and the #829

*Tekno #731 Buick Ambulance. Oddly, the early 700 series trucks (made during the late 1940s) often turn up with "switched" wheel hubs: the Buicks say Dodge, and vice-versa. This example has the correct hubs.*

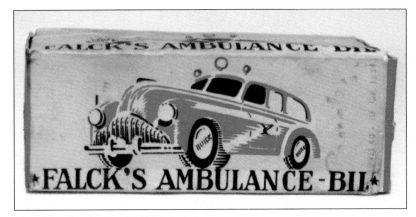

*The original box for the #731 Buick Ambulance.*

*At left is a Tekno #422 Ford V8 Cement Mixer, next to a #482 Ford V8 Generator Truck. The Generator Truck, which also came with "HOLGER DANSKE" decals as well as with no decals, is quite rare today.*

*One of the "Mini Dodge" trucks of the 1950s, the #772 Covered Truck.*

*Tekno #428 Ford Taxa (Taxi) with original box. This model came out in the late 1940s.*

Lincoln Continental. The boxes for the Dalia versions say "Dalia-Tekno" and Made in Spain, while the baseplates of the models read Tekno.

It is unclear exactly how Tekno's fortunes declined, but here is what is known at present. In 1969, Tekno's founder died, leaving his family to carry on the business. By now the firm was owned by Kirk, which had bought the Lange/Tekno operation around 1960. Lange's agreement with Tekno ended in 1969, and Kirk decided to produce the Tekno 900 sports car series and the Ford D800 trucks under its own name. The baseplates were changed to read Kirk instead of Tekno, and the models were marketed under the name "Model Products."

This arrangement did not last long, as Kirk went under in 1970 or '71. Around the same time, both Tekno and H. Lange were purchased by a company named Algrema. Unfortunately, Algrema subsequently went out of business, and after a series of difficulties, the Tekno name was sold in 1973 to a company in Holland. Tekno Holland models, as they're known, have been made since about 1975.

The following listing outlines the Danish Teknos made through 1972. It includes major castings used through the years, some of which were produced in many different liveries. In addition, Tekno often marketed a product with different liveries for their home and export markets so that, for example, a fire engine can be found with either "FALCK" or "FIRE DEPT" decals. Tekno apparently also changed numbers at various times, which makes sorting out which item had which number, and when, somewhat confusing.

Per the usual format, this listing is for near mint or better examples with their original boxes.

*The #816 Lloyd Alexander LP 600 also came in a station wagon version.*

| # | Name | Price |
|---|------|-------|
| 404 | Volkswagen Pick-up Ladder Truck | $150 |
| 404 | VW Pick-up with Crane "FALCK ZONEN" | 275 |
| 405 | Volkswagen Van many liveries | 150-400 |
| 406 | Volkswagen Pick-up many liveries | 150-250 |
| 407 | Volkswagen Bus various liveries | 175 |
| 408 | Volkswagen Pick-up Fire Truck | 150 |
| 409 | Volkswagen Army Bus | 150 |
| 409 | Fire Trailer | 50 |
| 410 | Volkswagen Bus | 150 |
| 410 | Volkswagen Pick-up | 150 |
| 411 | Volkswagen Ambulance | 150 |
| 412 | Volkswagen Bus | 200 |
| 413 | Volkswagen Van many liveries | 125-225 |
| 415 | Ford Taunus Transit Van many liveries | 100-250 |
| 415 | Ford Taunus Transit Ambulance | 150 |
| 416 | Volkswagen Pick-up various liveries | 150 |
| 417 | Volkswagen Bus | 125 |
| 418 | Volkswagen Van | 200 |
| 419 | Ford Taunus 1000 Van many liveries | 125 |
| 419 | Ford Taunus 1000 Ambulance | 150 |
| 419 | Ford Taunus 1000 Mail Van | 125 |
| 420 | Ford Taunus 1000 Bus various liveries | 125 |
| 420 | Scania Super Truck | 100 |
| 421 | Ford Taunus 1000 Pick-up various liveries | 125 |
| 422 | Ford V8 Cement Mixer Lorry | 175 |
| 423 | Ford V8 Refuse Truck | 200 |
| 424 | Packard Ambulance | 200 |
| 424 | Ford V8 Milk Truck | 200 |
| 425 | Packard Mail Car | 225 |
| 425 | Volvo Covered Truck various liveries | 100-150 |
| 426 | Ford V8 Tanker | 175 |
| 427 | Police Truck | 150 |
| 427 | Police Truck "BLACK MARIA" | 275 |
| 428 | Ford TAXA | 150-250 |
| 429 | Mercury Police Car | 150 |
| 431 | Volvo Car Carrier | 100 |
| 431 | Scania Car Carrier | 150 |
| 432 | Volvo Truck various liveries | 100-225 |
| 433 | Volvo Flat Truck with Chains | 225 |
| 434 | Volvo Tank Truck various liveries | 125-200 |
| 435 | Volvo Tractor Trailer various liveries | 300-750 |
| 436 | Volvo Tow Truck various liveries | 100-175 |
| 437 | Trailer | 50 |
| 438 | Volvo Covered Truck various liveries | 100-250 |
| 439 | Volvo Timber Truck | 125 |
| 440 | Mercury Sedan | 200 |
| 442 | Vespa Scooter | 150 |
| 443 | Vespa Scooter with Sidecar | 200 |
| 444 | Vespa Scooter with Container Sidecar | 200 |
| 445 | Scania Vabis Fire Truck various liveries | 100-150 |
| 446 | Scania Vabis Truck various liveries | 125-200 |
| 447 | Scania Vabis Tanker various liveries | 125-200 |
| 448 | Scania Vabis Truck various liveries | 200-300 |
| 449 | Scania Vabis Timber Truck | 150 |
| 449 | Scania Vabis Concrete Truck | $175 |
| 450 | Streamlined Tractor (truck cab) | 100 |
| 450 | Scania Vabis Covered Truck various liveries | 100-275 |
| 451 | Streamlined Tractor (truck cab with clockwork motor) | 100 |
| 451 | Scania Vabis Six Wheel Covered Truck various liveries | 100-200 |
| 452 | Covered Trailer various liveries | 50 |
| 453 | Tractor with Box Trailer | 125 |
| 453 | Scania Vabis Cement Mixer various liveries | 100 |
| 454 | Tractor with Box Trailer "INTERNATIONAL TRANSPORT" | 150 |
| 455 | Tractor with Flat Trailer | 125 |
| 455 | Volvo Express Truck various liveries | 100-150 |
| 456 | Volvo Express Covered Truck various liveries | 100-300 |
| 457 | Volvo Express Van various liveries | 150-300 |
| 458 | Volvo Express Tractor Trailer | 200 |
| 459 | Volvo Express Fire Truck | 150 |
| 460 | Ferguson Tractor | 50 |
| 461 | Milk Crates | 25 |
| 462 | Plow | 25 |
| 463 | Harrow | 25 |
| 464 | Trailer | 25 |
| 465 | International Harvester Tractor | 75 |
| 466 | McCormick Tractor | 75 |
| 470 | Ferguson Tractor Set | 150 |
| 480 | Ford V8 Truck | 200 |
| 481 | Ford V8 Tow Truck | 200 |
| 481 | Scania Tractor Trailer Tanker various liveries | 125 |
| 482 | Ford V8 Generator Truck | 400 |
| 482 | Ford V8 Generator Truck "ZONEN" | 400 |
| 482 | Ford V8 Generator Truck "HOLGER DANSKE" | 450 |
| 482 | Mercury Fire Car "ZONEN" | 200 |
| 483 | Mercury Loudspeaker Car | 250 |
| 483 | Mercury Loudspeaker Car "ZONEN" | 250 |
| 483 | Scania Timber Truck | $100 |
| 485 | Triangel Fire Engine "FIRE DEPT" | 250 |
| 485 | Triangel Fire Engine "ZONEN" | 175 |
| 486 | Triangel Fire Van "FIRE DEPT" | 250 |
| 486 | Triangel Fire Van "ZONEN" | 175 |
| 486 | Triangel Fire Van "FALCK" | 250 |
| 487 | Motor Pump Trailer | 100 |
| 491 | Miraco Coupe | 100 |
| 491 | Gyro Coupe | 100 |

**700 series:**

| # | Name | Price |
|---|------|-------|
| 719 | Morris Oxford Series II | 100 |
| 719 | Morris Oxford Series II with Red Cross decals | 175 |
| 720 | Opel Rekord | 100 |
| 720 | Opel Rekord "A&M" (promotional version) | 200 |
| 723 | Mercedes-Benz 180 | 150 |
| 723 | Mercedes-Benz 180 Taxi | 150 |
| 723 | Mercedes-Benz 180 Taxa | 150 |
| 723 | Mercedes-Benz 180 "Ring Bilen" | 175 |
| 724 | Trailer | 40 |
| 724 | Opel Kadett | 100 |
| 725 | Mercedes-Benz 220 SE Fire Chief | 100 |
| 726 | Mercedes-Benz 220 SE | 150 |
| 726 | Mercedes-Benz 220 SE Taxi | 150 |
| 726 | Mercedes-Benz 220 SE Taxa | 150 |
| 726 | Mercedes-Benz 220 SE "SKOLSKJULTS" | 150 |
| 727 | DKW Junior Deluxe | 100 |
| 730 | Mercedes-Benz 220 Ambulance various liveries | 150 |
| 731 | Buick Ambulance "FALCK" | 150 |
| 731 | Mercedes-Benz 220 Ambulance | 150 |
| 732 | Buick Ambulance | 150 |
| 732 | Buick Ambulance "ZONEN" | 150 |
| 732 | Buick Ambulance "FALCK" | 150 |
| 732 | Mercedes-Benz 220 Ambulance various liveries | 150-300 |
| 733 | Buick Ambulance various liveries | 150-300 |
| 734 | Chevrolet Truck | 150 |
| 735 | Chevrolet Truck various liveries | 175 |

*The #719 Morris Oxford was the first of the 700 series cars to be released, in late 1955. It had window glazing, which means Tekno beat Corgi to market with this feature. This example is shown with its original box.*

| # | Name | Price |
|---|------|-------|
| 736 | Chevrolet Truck various liveries | $150 |
| 737 | Trailer | 40 |
| 738 | Chevrolet Truck various liveries | 150-250 |
| 739 | Chevrolet Covered Truck various liveries | 150-225 |
| 740 | Chevrolet Milk Truck various liveries | 150-250 |
| 741 | Chevrolet Timber Truck | 125 |
| 742 | Trailer | 35 |
| 743 | Chevrolet Truck | 150 |
| 746 | Chevrolet Truck with Bricks | 125 |
| 748 | Chevrolet Sand & Gravel Truck | 150 |
| 750 | Chevrolet Truck | 125 |
| 760 | Forklift Truck | 100 |
| 761 | Motorcycle | 100 |
| 762 | Motorcycle with Sidecar | 100 |
| 763 | Motorcycle with Container Sidecar Mail | 100 |
| 764 | Motorcycle with Container Sidecar various liveries | 150 |
| 770 | Dodge Mini Truck | 60 |
| 771 | Dodge Mini Flat Truck | 60 |
| 772 | Dodge Mini Covered Truck | 60 |
| 773 | Dodge Mini Stake Truck | 60 |
| 774 | Dodge Mini Coal Truck | 60 |
| 776 | Dodge Mini Semi Trailer | 60 |
| 777 | Dodge Mini Cement Truck | 60 |
| 778 | Dodge Mini Tank Truck various liveries | 90 |
| 779 | Dodge Mini Dump Truck | 60 |
| 780 | Dodge Mini Tow Truck | 60 |
| 781 | Tanker Trailer various liveries | 35 |

**800 series:**

| # | Name | Price |
|---|------|-------|
| 801 | Jaguar XK120 | 175 |
| 802 | Alfa Romeo 2500 | 175 |
| 803 | Porsche 356 | 200 |
| 804 | MG Midget TD | 175 |
| 805 | Volkswagen 1200 | 250 |
| 806 | Opel Rekord | 200 |
| 807 | Austin Healey 100 | 175 |
| 808 | Triumph TR2 | 175 |
| 809 | Ford Thunderbird Convertible | 175 |
| 810 | Volvo Amazon various liveries, including Police | 150 |
| 811 | Renault 4CV | 175 |
| 812 | Cooper Norton Race Car | 75 |
| 813 | Ferrari 750 Monza | 90 |
| 814 | Willys Jeep various liveries | 75-125 |
| 814 | Gun | 35 |
| 814 | Trailer various liveries | 35 |
| 814 | Willys Army Jeep, Gun and Trailer | 150 |
| 815 | Travel Trailer | 75 |
| 815 | Sprite Musketeer Travel Trailer | 50 |
| 816 | Lloyd Alexander LP 600 | 200 |
| 817 | Lloyd Alexander LS 600 Station Wagon | 200 |
| 818 | Lloyd Alexander LKS 600 Van | 200 |
| 819 | Volkswagen 1200 various liveries | 100-175 |
| 820 | Ford Thunderbird | 175 |
| 821 | Saab 93 | 150 |
| 822 | Volvo PV 544 | 150 |
| 823 | Ford Taunus 17M | 100 |
| 824 | MGA Coupe | 125 |

| # | Name | Price |
|---|------|-------|
| 825 | Volvo P1800 Coupe | $100 |
| 826 | Ford Taunus 17M | 100 |
| 827 | Saab 96 | 125 |
| 828 | Volkswagen 1500 | 75 |
| 829 | Lincoln Continental | 100 |
| 830 | Volvo Amazon Station Wagon | 175 |
| 831 | Morris 1100 | 50 |
| 832 | MG 1100 | 50 |
| 833 | Ford Mustang Convertible | 75 |
| 834 | Ford Mustang Hardtop | 75 |
| 834 | Ford Mustang Rally | 60 |
| 834 | Ford Mustang Police | 90 |
| 835 | Volvo 144 various liveries | 50 |
| 836 | NSU RO 80 | 75 |
| 837 | Saab 99 | 60 |
| 838 | Volvo 164 | 60 |
| 850 | Volvo Bus various liveries | 125-225 |
| 851 | Scania CR 76 Bus various liveries | 100 |
| 852 | Mercedes Mini Bus | 150 |
| 853 | Trailer for #852 | 90 |
| 854 | Volvo Bus Bank | 150-250 |
| 860 | Akerman Excavator | 60 |
| 861 | Scania Vabis Semi Trailer various liveries | 100 |
| 861 | Volvo Semi Trailer various liveries | 100 |
| 862 | Volvo Tipping Truck | 75 |
| 862 | Scania Vabis Tipping Truck | 75 |
| 863 | Scania Vabis with Crane | 90 |
| 864 | Lift Truck | 60 |
| 870 | Scania Vabis Missile Truck | 100 |
| 910 | Mercedes-Benz LP 322 Truck | 75 |
| 910 | Mercedes-Benz LP 322 Truck with Five Pigs | 90 |
| 911 | Mercedes-Benz LP 322 Truck with Gas Cylinders | 90 |
| 912 | Mercedes-Benz LP 322 Garbage Truck | 90 |
| 913 | Mercedes-Benz LP 322 Truck "TUBORGS" | 125 |
| 914 | Ford D800 Tipper | 50 |

| # | Name | Price |
|---|------|-------|
| 915 | Ford D800 Truck | $50 |
| 916 | Ford D800 Covered Truck | 50 |
| 917 | Ford D800 Timber Truck | 50 |
| 918 | Ford D800 Brewery Truck | 50 |
| 918 | Ford D800 Brewery Truck "TUBORGS" | 50 |
| 919 | Ford D800 Covered Truck "IRMA KAFFE" | 150 |
| 920 | Ford D800 Tow Truck | 50 |
| 922 | Ford D800 Covered Truck various liveries | 150 |
| 924 | Mercedes-Benz 300SL Convertible | 75 |
| 925 | Mercedes-Benz 300SL Hardtop | 75 |
| 926 | Jaguar E | 75 |
| 927 | Jaguar E | 75 |
| 928 | Mercedes-Benz 230SL | 75 |
| 928 | Mercedes-Benz 250SL | 75 |
| 928 | Mercedes-Benz 280SL | 75 |
| 929 | Mercedes-Benz 230SL | 75 |
| 929 | Mercedes-Benz 250SL | 75 |
| 929 | Mercedes-Benz 280SL | 75 |
| 930 | Corvair Monza GT | 50 |
| 931 | Corvair Monza GT Convertible | 50 |
| 932 | Mercedes-Benz 250SL various liveries | 75 |
| 932 | Mercedes-Benz 280SL various liveries | 75 |
| 933 | Oldsmobile Toronado | 75 |
| 948 | Dodge Missile Launcher | 75 |
| 949 | Dodge Missile Launcher | 75 |
| 950 | Dodge Troop Carrier | 75 |
| 950 | Mercedes-Benz O302 Bus | 75 |
| 951 | Dodge Covered Truck | 75 |
| 951 | Dodge Covered Army Truck | 75 |
| 952 | Dodge Ambulance | 75 |
| 953 | Dodge Truck with Machine Gun | 75 |
| 954 | Dodge Radar Truck | 75 |
| 955 | Dodge Army Truck with Searchlight | 75 |
| 956 | Dodge Truck with Searchlight | 90 |
| 957 | Dodge Fire Truck | 90 |
| 958 | Dodge Van various liveries | 200 |

*Like many of Tekno's products, this #810 Volvo Amazon was quite an accurate model. It also came in several different police versions.*

# Tomica

Japanese Tomica die cast toys first appeared on the market in the early 1970s, manufactured by the well-known Tomy company. They were introduced to the American market in the mid-1970s, but failed to give the established Matchbox and Hot Wheels lines serious competition. Many of the Tomicas were modeled after Japanese cars, which undoubtedly contributed to their lack of popularity. As the 1970s progressed, though, Tomica introduced American, German and Italian cars to go with the Toyotas, Datsuns and Hinos.

The main series of Tomicas (ranging in scale from 1/60 to over 1/100) sold in the United States as "Pocket Cars," and were packaged in a blue blister card that resembled a denim pocket.

Many of them were fairly accurate castings; however, Tomica jumped on the "speed" or "whizz" wheel bandwagon of the 1970s, and these wheels detract from the appearance of the vehicle. On the plus side, the cars featured interiors and opening parts. Sometime during the early 1980s the Pocket Cars were taken off the American market. Tomicas are still apparently being made, but are not being imported into the United States.

Of greater interest to collectors of scale models was the "Dandy" series of 1/43 scale models that Tomica produced

*This Fiat Abarth 131 Rally car was #F20 in the Tomica Dandy series. It is left-hand drive and came in a cardboard box with a cellophane window.*

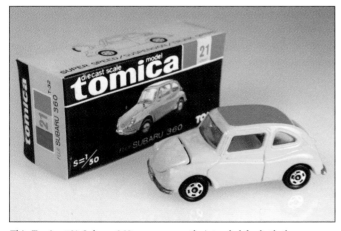

*This Tomica #21 Subaru 360 was apparently intended for both the Japanese and British markets, as the car is right-hand drive, and the box is in both English and Japanese.*

*Tomica #33 Toyota Celica with original box. Like the Subaru 360, this is a right-hand drive model.*

starting in the early 1970s. Until the late 1970s, the Dandy line was made up only of Japanese makes. But a 1978 Tomica catalog in the Japanese language shows a selection of 1/43 to 1/49 scale models, with names like Porsche, Cadillac and Volkswagen. There was even a Citroën 1200 kg Van included in the line. The Dandys were very good scale models, with most of them having realistic wheel hubs and opening parts that fit better than those on the Pocket Car models. Whether the Dandys are still manufactured is unknown.

The numbering system used by Tomica has been very confusing, making a coherent listing very difficult to compile. Generally, the Pocket Cars sell today for as little as $2-$3 up to around $15. The Dandys are also relatively affordable, selling for $10-$45 apiece.

*Page from a 1978 Tomica Japanese language catalog, depicting some of the 1/43 scale models. Note the unusual Citroën 1200 kg Van, #DF14.*

# Tootsietoys

**F**or generations of Americans, it is hard to imagine a time when Tootsietoys did not exist. Such is the depth of penetration of these toys into the conciousness of a nation. For more than eight decades these toy cars, trucks, boats and airplanes have been purchased by children and adults alike. The founders of the company that made Tootsietoys invented the die cast toy, for all intents and purposes. And, it all started with a typesetting machine.

Brothers Charles and Samuel Dowst were visiting the World's Columbian Exposition in 1893 when they were shown a machine that could set type in metal forms. The Mergenthaler Linotype Co. would go on to revolutionize the worlds of publishing and commercial art, but the Dowst

brothers had other ideas. They adapted the typesetting technology to produce a line of small novelties for the laundry trade. As publishers of the *National Laundry Journal*, they were aware of the importance of promoting one's business, which they helped laundry owners to do by selling them the metal novelty items. A miniature flat iron was among the novelties offered.

By the turn of the century, the Dowst Manufacturing Company, as it was now called, was established in Chicago, manufacturing metal prizes for sale to candy manufacturers. Dowst would eventually supply the metal prizes found in boxes of Cracker Jacks. In 1926, Dowst merged with the Cosmo Manufacturing Company, which had also been mak-

*The Tootsietoy three-inch 1950 Plymouth Deluxe. The solid wheel wells are typical of many three- and four-inch Toosietoys of the late 1940s and '50s.*

*This four-inch 1956 Chevrolet Cameo Carrier was introduced in 1959.*

ing metal candy prizes. Cosmo had been founded in 1892 by Nathan Shure, and the two companies together continued manufacturing metal products. In fact, Dowst continued making them until the 1950s.

In the 1930s, Dowst introduced a hugely popular line of toy cars and trucks. Included were Graham and Lasalle cars and Mack trucks, among others. These toys are today avidly sought by Tootsietoy collectors. In 1936, Dowst introduced its "Tootsietoy Midgets" line of small (two inches long on average) die cast cars and trucks (and airplanes).

Following the end of World War II, the Dowst company began manufacturing the Tootsietoy line again. A few of the pre-war toys were brought back for a time, such as the six-inch Jumbo vehicles, the six-inch 1937 Reo Tanker Truck, and a number of the three-inch vehicles. Pre-war versions can generally be differentiated from post-war in that the pre-wars came with white rubber tires, while post-war units came with black rubber tires.

New models were introduced regularly during the 1940s and '50s in a variety of sizes. Three-, four- and six-inch toys were popular, as were the tractor trailer trucks and military vehicles. Tootsietoys also came in boxed sets that had a theme, such as the Interchangeable Truck Set or the Playtime sets.

It was during this time that Tootsietoys became the number one selling die cast toy in the country, at least in part because they were meant to be simple and inexpensive. They varied in terms of accuracy; they were, after all, marketed as toys. They had no window glazing and generally no interiors or baseplates. But, in terms of general body shape, some were fairly accurate models of the full-size vehicle. Two of the most accurate Tootsietoys ever produced were the seven-inch models done in the later 1950s. The #895 Pontiac Safari Wagon and #995 Mercedes-Benz 300SL were well-detailed models, sold in individual boxes. They featured interiors, and the doors of the Mercedes (gull-wing type) and the rear gate of the Pontiac opened. These two models are now quite rare and sought after, and their current values reflect this.

During the 1960s the Dowst Manufacturing Company bought part of the Strombeck-Becker Company, and then changed its name a few years later to Strombecker Corporation. They debuted a number of new product lines in the 1960s, including the "Classic" series of 1/50 scale models that were made for the company by the British firm Die Casting Machine Tools Ltd. (D.C.M.T.). These models were quite realistic; they were also sold in the United Kingdom as the "Lone Star Roadmaster" series. The "Midget"

*The 1954 Oldsmobile 98 Holiday, introduced in 1955 as part of the four-inch line. This car also came with solid wheel wells.*

*The six-inch 1948 Cadillac. The Cadillac crest is just visible above the grille.*

*1954 Experimental Coupe; part of the six-inches series (although it actually measured 5¾ inches).*

*This six-inch 1946 International Oil Truck in SINCLAIR livery also came in a STANDARD oil livery.*

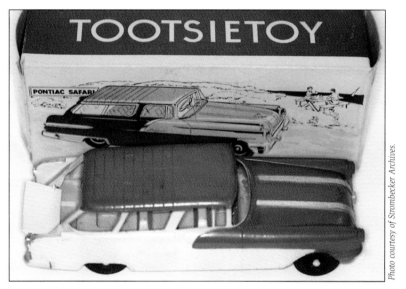

*This seven-inch Pontiac Safari Wagon (shown here with the original box) was numbered 895, and was produced for just a few years in the 1950s. It featured a working tailgate.*

Photo courtesy of Strombecker Archives.

*The 1947 Diamond T Fire Ladder Truck was thought by some to have not been produced. But this example was found by a Virginia collector during the 1980s. It was supposed to come in the #5211 Fire Department Set. The box art for the set shows this Diamond T Truck, but it was generally the Mack Fire Ladder Truck that was included in the set. This example appears to be 100% original.*

series of two-inch cars and trucks, and the "Super Tootsietoy" series, which were trucks and race cars that averaged eight inches in length, also made their debuts during the 1960s.

Since the 1960s, the Chicago-based Strombecker (now led by President and CEO Daniel Shure, the great grandson of Nathan Shure) has continued to manufacture Tootsietoys, and they are still aimed squarely at the children's market. As such, they make much use of plastic as well as cast metal. Current product include the "Hard Body" line, which includes everything from Sprint Race Cars to Farm vehicles to 1/24 scale pick-up trucks; and the "Jam Pac" line of two-inch die cast cars, which is the continuation of the Midget series launched in the 1960s. The die cast toys are now made in China.

Flashy, bright colors and graphics dominate these toy lines in order to appeal to the children's market. Other lines marketed under the Tootsietoy name include western cap guns and outfits.

The following listing is comprised of the most collected lines of Tootsietoys. Like many manufacturers, Dowst (and then Strombecker) offered its products packaged in several ways. Many toys were shipped in boxes or bins that were placed on a retailer's counter; the customer would pick out one to buy. Some toys came on blister cards, while others came in individual boxes (such as the large Tractor Trailer trucks, some of the six-inch car and truck trailer sets and the seven-inch Pontiac and Mercedes-Benz models).

Since Tootsietoys were sold as toys, original packaging has survived in far lesser numbers than packages for scale models, for example. For this reason, **this listing is for near mint to mint condition examples without the original packaging.** A Tootsietoy with the original box or still in the original blister pack will sell for more than the values listed here; the increase can be as much as 25%-50% over the value of the toy by itself.

An asterisk (*) in place of an item's value indicates that, although the item appeared in Tootsietoy catalogs, it may not have been produced and an example has yet to be found. A realistic market price therefore cannot be determined.

For further information on Tootsietoys (including data on color variations, casting changes, etc.), the reader is advised to consult *Greenberg's Guide to Tootsietoys 1945-1969* by Raymond Klein; and *Tootsietoys, World's First Diecast Models* by James Weiland and Edward Force. Both books contain a great deal of useful information on this classic brand of toys. See Part Three, Additional Resources for more details.

| Name | Price |
|---|---|
| **Three-inch vehicles:** | |
| 1937 GMC Tank Truck | $25 |
| 1937 International Wagon | 30 |
| 1938 Federal Truck | 25 |
| 1939 Coupe | 25 |
| 1939 Four-Door Sedan | 25 |
| 1940 Convertible | 25 |
| Fire Hose Truck | 30 |
| Fire Ladder Truck | 30 |
| Fire Pumper and Hose Truck | 30 |
| Single-Seat Convertible | 25 |
| 1947 Studebaker Champion | 50 |
| 1948 Willys Jeepster | 25 |
| 1949 American LaFrance Fire Engine | 25 |
| 1949 Bus | 30 |
| 1949 Chevrolet Panel Truck | 25 |
| 1949 Ford Convertible | 25 |
| 1949 Ford Custom Sedan | 25 |
| 1949 Ford Pick-up Truck | 25 |
| 1950 Chevrolet Fleetline Deluxe | 25 |
| 1950 Plymouth Deluxe | 25 |
| 1952 Ford Sedan | 25 |
| 1954 Ford Ranch Wagon | 20 |
| 1954 Jaguar | 20 |
| 1954 MG | 20 |
| 1954 Nash Metropolitan | 50 |
| 1954 Volkswagen | 20 |
| 1955 Chevrolet Bel Air | 20 |
| 1955 Ford Custom | 20 |
| 1955 Ford Tanker | 20 |
| 1955 Ford Thunderbird | 20 |
| 1956 Triumph TR3 | 20 |
| 1957 Ford Fairlane 500 Convertible | 20 |
| 1957 Ford Pick-up Truck | 15 |
| 1957 Formula D Jaguar | 20 |
| 1957 Plymouth Belvedere | 20 |
| 1960 Ford Falcon | 15 |
| 1960 Ford Ranch Wagon | 20 |
| 1960 Studebaker Convertible | 20 |
| Civilian Jeep | 15 |
| Hot Rod Model B | 15 |
| Indianapolis Race Car | 15 |

| Name | Price |
|---|---|
| **Four-inch vehicles:** | |
| 1937 International Wagon | $50 |
| 1938 Buick Experimental Convertible | 40 |
| 1941 Buick Special | 40 |
| 1941 Chrysler Convertible | 40 |
| Civilian Jeep | 25 |
| Midget Racer | 25 |
| Pull Toy Wagon | 60 |
| 1949 Mercury Fire Chief Car | 45 |
| 1949 Mercury Sedan | 35 |
| 1949 Oldsmobile Convertible | 35 |
| 1950 Pontiac Chieftain | 40 |
| 1950 Pontiac Fire Chief Chieftain | 45 |
| 1952 Mercury Sedan | 30 |
| 1953 Chevrolet Corvette | 30 |
| 1954 Ford Ranch Wagon | 35 |
| 1954 Oldsmobile 98 Holiday | 45 |
| 1955 Ford Thunderbird | 40 |
| 1959 Pontiac Star Chief | 25 |
| 1960 Chrysler Convertible | 25 |
| 1960 Rambler Wagon | 35 |
| 1969 Ford LTD Hardtop | 25 |
| 1937 Mack Hook and Ladder Fire Truck | 75 |
| 1937 Mack Hose Truck | 75 |
| 1937 Mack Pumper Truck | 75 |
| 1938 Federal Truck | 50 |
| 1941 International Ambulance | 50 |
| 1941 International Panel Truck | 45 |
| 1947 Pick-up Truck | 45 |
| 1949 Chevrolet Ambulance | 40 |
| 1949 Chevrolet Panel Truck | 35 |
| 1949 Ford Stake Truck | 30 |
| 1949 Ford Tank Truck | 25 |
| 1950 Dodge Pick-up Truck | 30 |
| 1956 Chevrolet Cameo Carrier | 25 |

| Name | Price |
|---|---|
| **Four-inch trailers:** | |
| Horse Trailer | 25 |
| Refreshment Stand Trailer | 55 |
| Stake Trailer | 40 |
| Trailer with Race Car | 30 |
| U-Haul Trailer | 15 |
| U-Haul Trailer | 15 |

| Name | Price |
|---|---|
| ATV Trailer | $5 |
| Boat Trailer | 5 |
| Cycle Trailer | 5 |
| Generator Trailer (2³/₄ inches) | 5 |
| Motorcycle Trailer | 5 |
| Small Trailer with Cabin Cruiser | 15 |
| Small U-Haul Trailer (3 inches) | 5 |
| Snowmobile Trailer | 5 |
| Twin Scooter Trailer | 15 |

| Name | Price |
|---|---|
| **Six-inch cars:** | |
| Jumbo Convertible | 50 |
| Jumbo Coupe | 50 |
| Jumbo Sedan | 45 |
| Civilian Jeep | 30 |
| 1932 Hot Rod | 30 |
| 1940 Ford Convertible | 40 |
| 1942 Rocket Roadster | 40 |
| 1947 Buick Estate Wagon | 65 |
| 1947 Kaiser | 50 |
| 1948 Cadillac | 35 |
| 1949 Buick Roadster | 45 |
| 1950 Chrysler Windsor Convertible | 125 |
| 1951 Buick Experimental Sportster Convertible | 60 |
| 1952 Lincoln Capri | 50 |
| 1953 Chrysler New Yorker | 50 |
| 1954 Buick Century Wagon | 50 |
| 1954 Cadillac 62 Sedan | 50 |
| 1954 Experimental Coupe | 50 |
| 1954 MG Classic | 30 |
| 1954 Volkswagen | 30 |
| 1955 Chrysler Regent | * |
| 1955 Packard Patrician | 50 |
| 1956 Austin-Healey | 40 |
| 1956 Jaguar XK140 | 30 |
| 1956 Jeep CJ5 | 40 |
| 1956 Jeep CJ5 with Snowplow | 55 |
| 1956 Jeep CJ5 (windshield in down position) | 30 |
| 1956 Mercedes-Benz 190 SL | 30 |
| 1956 Porsche Spyder | 30 |
| 1959 Ford Country Sedan | 30 |
| 1959 Oldsmobile Convertible | 35 |
| 1962 Ford Station Wagon | 25 |

| Name | Price |
|---|---|
| **Six-inch Trucks and Commercial Vehicles:** | |
| Jumbo Bus | 60 |
| Jumbo Pick-up Truck | 50 |
| Jumbo Tow Truck | 50 |
| 1937 Reo Tank Truck | 55 |
| 1946 International Oil Truck | 60 |

*Photo courtesy of Strombecker Archives.*

*This Mack Tanker Truck (shown with original box) was produced during the mid- to late-1950s.*

| Name | Price |
|---|---|
| 1948 Diamond T Bottle Truck | $60 |
| 1947 Diamond T Dump Truck | 50 |
| 1947 Diamond T Stake Truck | 40 |
| 1947 Diamond T Tow Truck | 45 |
| 1947 Diamond T Truck | 45 |
| 1947 GMC Bus | 55 |
| 1947 Mack Dump Truck | 40 |
| 1947 Mack Fire Truck | 75 |
| 1947 Mack Tow Truck | 45 |
| 1947 Mack Truck | 50 |
| 1949 Ford Tank Truck | 50 |
| 1955 Greyhound Bus | 60 |
| 1955 Mack Cement Truck | 50 |
| 1956 Dodge Panel Truck | 50 |
| 1956 Ford Stake Truck | 50 |
| 1959 Metro Van | 175 |
| 1960 Chevrolet El Camino | 30 |
| 1960 Chevrolet El Camino with Camper Top and Boat | 50 |
| 1962 Ford Econoline Pick-up Truck | 40 |
| 1962 Ford Fuel Truck | 40 |

### Six-inch Car and Truck with Trailer sets:

| Name | Price |
|---|---|
| 1932 Ford Hot Rod with Race Car and Trailer | 70 |
| 1954 MG with Chris Craft Boat | 75 |
| 1954 MG with U-Haul Trailer | 70 |
| 1954 Cadillac and Trailer with Boat | 75 |
| 1954 Cadillac and U-Haul Trailer | 70 |
| 1955 Packard with Boat and Trailer | 75 |
| 1955 Packard with U-Haul Trailer | 70 |
| 1956 Jeep with Horse Trailer | 50 |
| 1959 Ford Wagon with Camping Trailer | 65 |
| 1959 Ford Wagon with Race Car and Trailer | 70 |
| 1959 Ford Wagon and Trailer with Boat | 60 |
| 1959 Oldsmobile with U-Haul Trailer | 55 |
| 1959 Oldsmobile Convertible with Horse Trailer | 60 |
| 1959 Oldsmobile Convertible with Boat and Trailer | 65 |
| 1960 Chevrolet El Camino with Boat and Trailer | 70 |
| 1960 Chevrolet El Camino with Race Car and Trailer | 70 |
| 1960 Chevrolet El Camino with Refreshment Stand | 95 |
| 1962 Ford Wagon with Race Car and Trailer | 65 |
| 1962 Ford Wagon with Boat and Trailer | 65 |
| 1962 Ford Station Wagon with U-Haul Trailer | 50 |
| 1962 Ford Econoline Pick-up Truck and Trailer | 65 |

### Six-inch trailers:

| Name | Price |
|---|---|
| Trailer with Chris-Craft Boat | $30 |
| Travel Trailer | 35 |

### Seven-inch special cars:

| | Name | Price |
|---|---|---|
| 895 | Pontiac Safari Wagon | 250 |
| 995 | Mercedes-Benz 300SL | 250 |

### Tractor Trailer Trucks:

| Name | Price |
|---|---|
| 1947 Diamond T Fire Ladder Truck | * |
| 1947 Diamond T Machinery Hauler | 60 |
| 1947 Diamond T Shipping Van | 50 |
| 1947 Diamond T Transport Truck | 60 |
| 1947 Diamond T Utility Truck | 50 |
| 1947 Mack Fire Ladder Truck | 75 |
| 1947 Mack Log Trailer Truck | 75 |
| 1947 Mack Machinery Truck | 75 |
| 1947 Mack Pipe Truck | 75 |
| 1947 Mack Stake Truck | 125 |
| 1947 Mack Tanker Truck | 75 |
| 1947 Mack Utility Truck | 60 |
| 1947 Mack Van Truck | 75 |
| 1955 International Machinery Truck | 75 |
| 1955 International Tanker Truck | 65 |
| 1955 International Transport Truck | 90 |
| 1955 International Utility Truck | 60 |
| 1955 International Van Truck | 75 |
| 1955 Mack Auto Transport Truck | 75 |
| 1955 Mack Boat Transporter | 75 |
| 1955 Mack Fire Ladder Truck | 75 |
| 1955 Mack Log Truck | 60 |
| 1955 Mack Machinery Truck | 75 |
| 1955 Mack Tanker Truck "MOBIL" | 75 |
| 1955 Mack Pipe Truck | 75 |
| 1955 Mack Utility Truck | 50 |
| 1955 Mack Van Truck | 75 |
| 1958 International Boat Transporter | 60 |
| 1958 International Machinery Truck | 75 |
| 1958 International Moving Van | 75 |
| 1958 International Utility Truck | 45 |
| 1958 International Vehicle Transporter | 75 |
| 1959 Chevrolet Auto Transporter | 125 |
| 1959 Chevrolet Boat Transporter | 100 |
| 1959 Chevrolet Hook and Ladder Fire Truck | 125 |
| 1959 Chevrolet Log Truck | 100 |

| Name | Price |
|---|---|
| 1959 Chevrolet Moving Van | $100 |
| 1959 Chevrolet Oil Tanker "MOBIL" | 100 |

### Classic Series (1/50 scale):

| Name | Price |
|---|---|
| Cadillac 62 Sedan | 50 |
| Chevrolet Corvair | 50 |
| Dodge Polara | 50 |
| Ford Galaxie (Sunliner) Convertible | 50 |
| Rambler Station Wagon | 50 |

### Classic Antique Series (1/50 scale):

| | Name | Price |
|---|---|---|
| 3101 | Ford Model 1912 | 15 |
| 3102 | Ford Model A 1929 | 15 |
| 3107 | Cadillac 1906 | 15 |
| 3108 | Stutz Bearcat 1919 | 15 |
| 3109 | Stanley Steamer 1907 | 15 |
| 3111 | Mack Truck 1922 | 15 |

### Pocket Series (HO scale):

| | Name | Price |
|---|---|---|
| 2325 | 1960 Rambler Station Wagon with U-Haul Trailer | 30 |
| 2425 | Ford Sunliner Convertible with Boat and Trailer | 40 |
| 2440 | Ford Sunliner Convertible with Midget Racer and Trailer | 40 |
| 2460 | 1960 Rambler Station Wagon and Ford Sunliner Convertible | 40 |
| 2465 | Metro Van various liveries | 25 |
| 2470 | 1960 Ford Dump Truck | 15 |
| 2485 | 1960 Ford Two Truck | 15 |
| 2490 | School Bus "TOWNSHIP SCHOOL BUS" | 25 |

### Farm and Construction toys:

| Name | Price |
|---|---|
| Caterpillar Bulldozer (4¹/₂ inches) | 60 |
| Caterpillar Scraper (5¹/₂ inches) | 50 |
| Ford Farm Tractor (4³/₄ inches) | 50 |
| Ford Farm Tractor with Disc Harrow (7¹/₂ inches) | 75 |
| Ford Farm Tractor with Fertilizer Spreader (10 inches) | 75 |
| Ford Farm Tractor with Wagon (14 inches) | 100 |
| Ford Tractor with Scoop (7 inches) | 75 |
| Harrow Plow | 25 |

*May not have been produced*

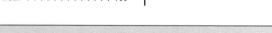

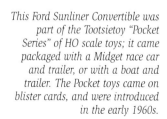

*This Ford Sunliner Convertible was part of the Tootsietoy "Pocket Series" of HO scale toys; it came packaged with a Midget race car and trailer, or with a boat and trailer. The Pocket toys came on blister cards, and were introduced in the early 1960s.*

# Underwood Engineering

The Underwood Engineering Co., Ltd. was the manufacturer of the Fun Ho! series of die cast toys, and was located on Mamaku Street in Inglewood, New Zealand. Although they had made a group of cast aluminum toy cars and commercial vehicles during the 1950s, it would be the small (approximately 1/87 scale) Fun Ho! models for which the company would be remembered. The series was launched in the early 1960s.

Underwood actually stated in their product literature that the series was "Midget" scale, whatever that means. (The Fun Ho! flyer, shown here, states that the models were 1/80 scale from #10 onward.) The models came in cardboard boxes that resembled miniature "Mobil" gas pumps. The cars and smaller trucks came in a box that measured about 2 1/2 inches in height, while the bigger models (such as the tractor trailers) came in a box that was about 3 1/2 inches in height. The boxes said "MOBIL MIDGET MODELS," along with the name and address of the Underwood company.

The Mobil Oil Company was involved with the series from the start, although the nature of their participation is unclear. Sometime around 1968, the Mobil name was removed from the product line, which was then sold as the Midget Scale Model Series.

The models themselves were of good quality, with a number of them being very good replicas of the full-size vehicles (particularly considering their small size and the time in which they were made). They seem to have gone out of production in the early to mid-1970s. Whether they were exported to the United States is unknown, although their scarcity would suggest that they were not.

The following listing provides values for models in near mint or better condition in their original boxes.

*Original flyer for the Fun Ho! Mobil die cast series, circa 1966 or '67. Shown are the first 40 models; note the #27 Mobil Tanker, which was apparently kept in the series even after Mobil had ceased its association with the product.*

| # | Name | Price | # | Name | Price | # | Name | Price |
|---|------|-------|---|------|-------|---|------|-------|
| 1 | MF 35 Tractor | $10 | 18 | Austin Articulated Truck | $15 | 35 | Ambulance | $15 |
| 2 | Holden Car | 15 | 19 | Land Rover | 15 | 36 | Police Van | 15 |
| 3 | Austin Truck | 15 | 20 | Thames Freighter Van | 15 | 37 | Aveling Road Roller | 15 |
| 4 | Mobile Tanker | 15 | 21 | Fire Engine | 15 | 38 | Car Trailer | 10 |
| 5 | Volkswagen Combi Bus | 20 | 22 | Bedford Articulated Truck | 15 | 39 | Farm Trailer | 10 |
| 6 | Mercedes-Benz Racer | 15 | 23 | Jaguar Mark 10 | 15 | 40 | Articulated Milk Tanker | 15 |
| 7 | BOAC Bus | 15 | 24 | Chevrolet Bel Air | 20 | 41 | Ford Zephyr Mk IV | 15 |
| 8 | Austin Tip Truck | 15 | 25 | MG Sports Car | 15 | 42 | Caterpillar Tractor | 10 |
| 9 | Volkswagen Beetle | 20 | 26 | Thames Freighter Pick-up Truck | 15 | 43 | Jaguar E Type | 15 |
| 10 | Ford Falcon | 15 | 27 | Mobil Articulated Tanker | 20 | 44 | Front End Loader | 10 |
| 11 | Morris Mini Minor | 15 | 28 | Morris Pick-up Truck | 15 | 45 | Mercedes-Benz | 15 |
| 12 | Vauxhall Velox | 15 | 29 | Bedford Truck | 15 | 46 | Bulldozer | 10 |
| 13 | Morris 1100 | 15 | 30 | Car Trailer | 10 | 47 | Fork Lift | 10 |
| 14 | Cortina Estate Car | 15 | 31 | White Heavy Duty Tip Truck | 15 | 48 | Ford Truck | 10 |
| 15 | Hillman Imp | 15 | 32 | Austin 1100 | 15 | 49 | Ford Sand Dump Truck | 10 |
| 16 | Fordson Super Major Tractor | 10 | 33 | Rolls-Royce Phantom V | 15 | 50 | Ford Dump Truck | 10 |
| 17 | Austin Mini | 15 | 34 | Holden Saloon | 15 | 51 | Ford Articulated Truck | 10 |

| # | Name | Price | # | Name | Price | # | Name | Price |
|---|------|-------|---|------|-------|---|------|-------|
| 52 | Trailer | $10 | 59 | Willys Jeep with Gun | $10 | 66 | Army Road Grader | $10 |
| 53 | Tow Truck | 10 | 60 | Road Grader | 10 | 67 | Ford Articulated Army Truck | 10 |
| 54 | Tractor Shovel | 10 | 61 | Holden Van | 15 | 68 | Army Dump Truck | 10 |
| 55 | Tractor Scraper | 10 | 62 | Holden Army Ambulance | 15 | 69 | Army Scraper | 10 |
| 56 | Bus | 15 | 63 | Willys Army Jeep | 10 | 70 | Army Excavator | 10 |
| 57 | Utility Runabout | 15 | 64 | Army Caterpillar | 10 | 71 | Army Tanker | 10 |
| 58 | Willys Jeep | 10 | 65 | Army Road Roller | 10 | 72 | Army Excavator with Tracks | 10 |

# Vilmer

For about ten years (from 1956 until about 1966), this Danish company did its best to give rival Tekno a run for its money. Vilmer's models were similiar to those of Tekno, with trucks dominating the product line, particularly those of the Chevrolet and Dodge makes.

Vilmer also made a small group of 1/43 scale model cars, which are very scarce and sought after today. They were quite accurate, and they had window glazing. The Vilmer trucks, which ranged from 1/43 to roughly 1/60 scale, featured window glazing as well (except for the smaller Dodge units). Many of them also had interiors.

After production ceased for Vilmer, some of the tooling for the Mercedes trucks reportedly wound up in the hands of the Portugese manufacturer Metosul. And Vilmer didn't make things easy for collectors, changing its numbering system around as it did. The numbers in this listing are believed to be correct, but are subject to change or correction.

Vilmer products were probably not imported into the United States in any significant numbers, although some of the smaller Dodge trucks do occasionally turn up at American shows. Vilmers came in individual boxes, so the following listing provides values for near mint or better condition examples with those original boxes.

*The BEV Electric Baggage Cart was one of Vilmer's more unusual subjects.*

*The Mercedes-Benz 1113 Refuse Wagon was numbered 855 by Vilmer. It featured an opening engine hood, and it also came without the "FODERBUS" graphics.*

*Vilmer's small Dodge Stake Truck, which is thought to have been number 340 in the product line.*

| # | Name | Price |
|---|------|-------|
| **Cars and Scooters:** | | |
| 475 | Renault 4CV | $150 |
| 585 | Volvo PV444 | 250 |
| #? | Opel Rekord | 150 |
| 586 | Opel Rekord Station Wagon | 150 |
| #? | Mercedes 220 | 200 |
| #? | Mercedes W196R | 175 |
| #? | Lambretta Scooter | 100 |
| #? | Lambretta Scooter with Sidecar | 150 |
| #? | Lambretta Scooter with Container Sidecar | 150 |
| **Trucks:** | | |
| 50 | Volvo Truck | 75 |
| 51 | Volvo Milk Truck | 75 |
| 52 | Volvo Covered Truck | 75 |
| 53 | Volvo Red Cross Truck | 75 |
| 54 | Volvo Covered Military Truck | 75 |
| 55 | Volvo Refuse Truck | 75 |
| 56 | Volvo Truck with Shovel | 75 |
| 57 | Volvo Fire Truck | 75 |
| 60 | Volvo Tow Truck | 75 |
| 62 | Volvo Stake Truck | 75 |
| 339 | BEV Electric Baggage Cart | 100 |
| 340 | Dodge Stake Truck | 60 |
| 341 | Dodge Flatbed | 60 |
| 342 | Dodge Cattle Truck | 60 |
| 345 | Dodge Wooden Barrel Truck | 90 |
| 346 | Dodge Tow Truck | 60 |
| 347 | Dodge Flatbed with Tailboard | 60 |
| 348 | Dodge Dropside Truck | 60 |
| 350 | Dodge Cement Truck | 60 |
| #? | Dodge Truck "CARLSBERG" Truck | 90 |
| 454 | Chevrolet Military Tanker | 60 |
| 455 | Chevrolet Three Rocket Truck | 60 |

| # | Name | Price |
|---|------|-------|
| 456 | Chevrolet Military Tow Truck | $60 |
| 457 | Chevrolet Four Cannon Truck | 60 |
| 457 | Chevrolet Two Cannon Truck | 60 |
| 458 | Chevrolet Military Spotlight Truck | 60 |
| 459 | Chevrolet Radar Truck | 60 |
| 460 | Chevrolet Ten Rocket Launcher | 60 |
| 461 | Chevrolet Single Cannon Truck | 60 |
| 462 | Chevrolet Single Rocket Truck | 60 |
| 463 | Dodge Military Dropside Truck | 60 |
| 463 | Chevrolet Military Dropside Truck | 60 |
| 464 | Chevrolet Military Tarp-covered Truck | 60 |
| 464 | Dodge Military Tarp-covered Truck | 60 |
| 465 | Chevrolet Red Cross Covered Truck | 60 |
| 467 | Chevrolet Dropside Milk Truck | 100 |
| 468 | Chevrolet Covered Truck | 75 |
| 469 | Chevrolet Tow Truck | 75 |
| 469 | Dodge Tow Truck | 75 |
| 470 | Chevrolet Spotlight Truck | 75 |
| 471 | Chevrolet Open Truck | 60 |
| 472 | Chevrolet Fuel Tanker "ESSO" | 90 |
| 472 | Chevrolet Gas Tanker "SHELL" | 90 |
| 474 | Chevrolet Dump Truck | 60 |
| 476 | Chevrolet Cement Truck | 75 |
| 477 | Chevrolet Cement Mixer with chute | 75 |
| 578 | Ferguson Tractor | 75 |
| 580 | Austin Champ | 100 |
| #? | Austin Champ Military with gun | 100 |
| 620 | Bedford Stake Truck | 75 |
| 621 | Bedford Cattle Truck and Trailer | 100 |
| 624 | Bedford Flat Milk Truck | 100 |
| 625 | Bedford Flat Milk Truck with Trailer | 125 |
| 654 | Bedford Military Gas Tanker | 100 |
| 656 | Bedford Military Tow Truck | 100 |
| 657 | Bedford Military Four cannon Truck | 75 |

| # | Name | Price |
|---|------|-------|
| 658 | Bedford Military Searchlight Truck | $75 |
| 659 | Bedford Military Radar Truck | 75 |
| 660 | Bedford Ten Rocket Launcher | 75 |
| 661 | Bedford Single Cannon Truck | 75 |
| 662 | Bedford Single Missile Truck | 75 |
| 663 | Bedford Military Dropside Truck | 75 |
| 664 | Bedford Military Covered Truck | 75 |
| 665 | Bedford Red Cross Covered Truck | 90 |
| 668 | Bedford Covered Truck | 90 |
| 669 | Bedford Tow Truck | 90 |
| 670 | Bedford Spotlight Truck | 90 |
| 671 | Bedford Open Truck | 90 |
| 672 | Bedford Gas Tanker "ESSO" | 125 |
| 672 | Bedford Gas tanker "SHELL" | 125 |
| 677 | Bedford Cement Mixer with chute | 90 |
| 710 | Mercedes-Benz Dump Truck | 75 |
| 720 | Ford Thames Bucket Truck | 75 |
| 725 | Ford Thames Truck with Magnet | 75 |
| 725 | Ford Thames Crane Truck | 75 |
| 730 | Ford Thames Cable Truck | 75 |
| 850 | Mercedes-Benz Tipping Truck | 75 |
| 851 | Mercedes-Benz Milk Truck | 75 |
| 852 | Mercedes-Benz Tarp-covered Truck | 75 |
| 853 | Mercedes Benz Red Cross Covered Truck | 75 |
| 854 | Mercedes-Benz Covered Military Truck | 75 |
| 855 | Mercedes-Benz Refuse Truck ("FODERBUS" or plain) | 75 |
| 856 | Mercedes-Benz Dump Truck with Front Shovel | 75 |
| 857 | Mercedes-Benz Fire Ladder Truck | 90 |
| 860 | Mercedes-Benz Tow Truck | 75 |
| 862 | Mercedes-Benz Stake Truck | 75 |

# Vitesse

This Portugese line of 1/43 scale models was introduced to the market in 1982 or 1983, with the debut of the first model in the series: a Lancia 037 Rally Car. This model is still a part of the Vitesse line.

Vitesse makes good use of its castings. The Lancia is a good example: It has been produced in a multitude of liveries through the years. Even passenger cars are produced not only in various colors, but as convertibles (top up and top down), hardtops, racing versions, etc.

Vitesse models are manufactured by Cinerius Ltd., which is a part of the Vitesse Group of companies. (The Vitesse Group also encompasses Minibri, makers of the Onyx and Quartzo die cast model lines.) The Vitesse products are of very good quality, with good detail and accuracy. Like nearly all 1/43 models today, they come with win-

*This Volkswagen 1500 is no longer made by Vitesse. Its departure from the product line (around 1992) may have had to do with the poor quality of the casting, which is evident in this photo. It was number 620.*

dow glazing, interiors and suspension. The packaging is also standard 1/43: a cardboard window box, inside of which goes the plastic case that holds the model.

German, American, British, Italian and French makes have always been part of the Vitesse range. In 1993, they released their model of the 1959 Nash Metropolitan, which has become one of their most popular products.

The following listing is comprised of early Vitesse models (numbered 100 through 375), and current offerings (numbered 001 through 044). Where one basic model

has been made in multiple liveries, the numbers concerned have been grouped; i.e., the 170-174 Austin Healey 3000. Likewise, the multitude of "limited editions" that Vitesse produces are not listed since they are liveries of the basic castings.

CRP (Current Retail Price) for Vitesse models is around $25. For models that are no longer made, the CRP still applies as values have not as yet risen significantly above this amount.

*This 1956 Citroën DS 19, introduced into the Vitesse line-up in the early 1990s, is an excellent quality model. (It is number 011).*

| # | Name | Price |
|---|------|-------|
| 100-104 | Lancia 037 Rally Car | CRP |
| 110-114 | Chevrolet Corvette 1960 | CRP |
| 120-123 | BMW 328 1938 | CRP |
| 130-132 | Opel Manta 400 | CRP |
| 140-142 | Ferrari 250 Spyder 1960 | CRP |
| 150-154 | Chevrolet Corvette 1961-62 | CRP |
| 160-168 | Mercedes-Benz 170 V 1939-49 | CRP |
| 170-174 | Austin Healey 3000 | CRP |
| 180 | Ford RS 200 Rally | CRP |
| 190-200 | Porsche 956 1982-83 | CRP |
| 210-218 | Saurer S4C 1952 | CRP |
| 220-231 | Saurer Type C 1943-76 | CRP |
| 240-242 | Triumph TR3A 1957 | CRP |
| 243-245 | Triumph TR2 | CRP |
| 250-254 | Jaguar Mk VII-VIII | CRP |
| 260-264 | Renault Dauphine 1956 | CRP |
| 270 | MG Metro 6R4 Rally | CRP |
| 280-286 | Cadillac Eldorado and Type 62 | CRP |
| 290-298 | Mercedes-Benz 170 Van 1939 | CRP |
| 300-302 | Peugeot 205 Turbo | CRP |
| 310-322 | Porsche 956 1984-85 | CRP |
| 330-333 | Porsche 911 1964-69 | CRP |
| 340-341 | Porsche 959 Gruppe B | CRP |
| 350-352 | Mercedes-Benz 170 Station Wagon 1949 | CRP |
| 360-362 | Lancia Delta S4 Rally | CRP |
| 370-373 | Chrysler Windsor Six Sedan 1946-48 | CRP |
| 374 | DeSoto Deluxe Sedan Taxi | CRP |

| # | Name | Price |
|---|------|-------|
| **Current models:** | | |
| 001 | Volkswagen Deluxe 1949 | CRP |
| 002 | Volkswagen 1200 Deluxe 1959 | CRP |
| 003 | Volkswagen Karmann 1949 Cabriolet | CRP |
| 004 | Volkswagen Bulli 1955 "VW SERVICE" | CRP |
| 005 | Volkswagen Kombi 1955 | CRP |
| 006 | Messerschmitt KR200 1960 | CRP |
| 007 | Messerschmitt "Tiger" TG500 1958 | CRP |
| 008 | Fiat 500 1957 | CRP |
| 009 | Citroën 2CV 1957 open | CRP |
| 011 | Citroën DS19 1956 | CRP |
| 012 | Austin Seven Deluxe 1959 | CRP |
| 013 | Morris Cooper S 1963 | CRP |
| 014 | Triumph TR3A 1959 Convertible | CRP |
| 015 | Austin Healey 3000 1963 | CRP |
| 016 | Porsche 911 1964 | CRP |
| 017 | Ferrari Dino 246GT 1968 | CRP |
| 018 | Ferrari 308GTB 1977 | CRP |
| 019 | Chrysler Windsor Six Sedan 1947 | CRP |
| 020 | Chrysler Town & Country Convertible 1947 | CRP |
| 021 | Cadillac 2-Door Sedan 1950 | CRP |
| 022 | Ford Fairlane Sunliner Convertible 1956 | CRP |
| 023 | Buick Special Convertible 1958 | CRP |
| 024 | Cadillac Convertible 1959 | CRP |
| 025 | Cadillac Convertible 1959 "Just Married" | CRP |
| 026 | Chevrolet Impala Convertible 1959 | CRP |
| 027 | Peugeot 106XSi | CRP |

| # | Name | Price |
|---|------|-------|
| 029 | Porsche Carrera 4 1992 | CRP |
| 030 | Lancia Super Delta "MARTINI" 1992 | CRP |
| 030B | Lancia Super Delta "REPSOL" 1993 | CRP |
| 031 | Steyr-Puch 650T 1960 | CRP |
| 032 | Nash Metropolitan Convertible 1959 | CRP |
| 033 | Mercedes-Benz 600 Pullman 1965 | CRP |
| 034A | Lancia 037 Rally "MARTINI" 1982 | CRP |
| 034B | Lancia 037 Rally "MARTINI" 1982 | CRP |
| 034C | Lancia 037 Rally 1982 Stradale | CRP |
| 035 | Renault Twingo 1993 | CRP |
| 036 | Chevrolet Corvette Convertible 1969 | CRP |
| 037 | Citroën 2CV Sahara 4x4 1960 | CRP |
| 038 | Buick Roadmaster 1958 | CRP |
| 039A | Peugeot 905 EVO I 1993 | CRP |
| 039B | Peugeot 905 EVO I 1993 | CRP |
| 039C | Peugeot 905 EVO I 1993 | CRP |
| 039D | Peugeot 905 EVO I 1993 | CRP |
| 040 | Renault Laguna V6 TXE 1994 | CRP |
| 041A | Renault Safrane V6 RXE 1993 | CRP |
| 041B | Renault Safrane V6 "BACCARA" 1993 | CRP |
| 041C | Renault Safrane "BITURBO" 1994 | CRP |
| 042 | Fiat Abarth 595SS 1964 | CRP |
| 043 | Citroën 2CV "CHARLESTON" 1981 | CRP |
| 044 | Chevrolet Corvette LeMans 1968-69 | CRP |
| 045 | Renault 4L 1961-62 | CRP |
| 046 | Fiat 124 Spyder 1966 | CRP |
| 046B | Fiat 124 Spyder Abarth 1970 | CRP |
| 047 | Mercedes-Benz 220SE 1959 | CRP |
| 050 | Volkswagen Kubelwagen 1939 | CRP |
| 051 | Volkswagen Lieferwagen 1945 | CRP |
| 052 | Cadillac Fleetwood Limo 1959 | CRP |

# Western Models Ltd.

Western Models Ltd. is a manufacturer of hand-built white metal models. The company is located in Somerset, England, and was founded in the mid-1970s. The products are diverse, ranging from 1920s luxury cars and land speed record and racing cars to modern exotics. Some Western Models products are marketed as Small Wheels models.

Western and Small Wheels models are mostly 1/43 scale, although there have been 1/24 scale cars included. They come either as kits or fully assembled. The following listing is not exhaustive; it is comprised of the models in production during the early 1980s, along with the company's current offerings as shown in company catalogs. CRP (Current Retail Price) for the standard assembled models is $100-$125.

*Western WMS31, the 1938 Packard Darrin Convertible (top up).*

| # | Name | Price |
|---|------|-------|
| **1982 PRODUCTION** | | |
| **Western Classics:** | | |
| WMS1 | 1938 Mercedes-Benz 540K | CRP |
| WMS3 | 1951 Jaguar XK120 Fixed Head | CRP |
| WMS7 | 1938 Bugatti 57SC Atlantic | CRP |
| WMS8 | 1933 Rolls-Royce Phantom II | CRP |
| WMS10 | 1937 Cord Beverly Custom Sedan | CRP |
| WMS11 | 1938 Jaguar SS100 | CRP |
| WMS12 | 1953 MG TF Midget | CRP |
| WMS13 | 1931 Daimler Double Six/50 | CRP |
| WMS16 | 1935 Bugatti 46 Gangloff | CRP |
| WMS18 | 1951 Morgan Plus 4 | CRP |
| WMS20 | 1933 Hispano-Suiza 68 V12 | CRP |
| WMS21 | 1938 Talbot-Lago 4 Litre | CRP |
| WMS22 | 1932 Bucciali TAV16 | CRP |
| WMS24 | 1935 Duesenberg SJ Special | CRP |
| WMS26 | 1929 Mercedes-Benz SSK Corsica | CRP |
| WMS27 | 1926 Rolls-Royce Phantom I | CRP |
| WMS28 | 1933 Cadillac V16 Convertible | CRP |
| WMS29 | 1931 Bugatti 41 Royale Esders | CRP |
| WMS31 | 1938 Packard Darrin Convertible | CRP |
| WMS32 | 1930 Bentley 6.5 Barnato | CRP |
| WMS33 | 1938 Alfa Romeo 8C 2900B | CRP |
| WMS34 | 1936 Bentley 4.25 Mulliner | CRP |
| WMS35 | 1934 Jaguar SS1 | CRP |
| WMS36 | 1927 Rolls-Royce Phantom I | CRP |
| WMS37 | 1933 Chrysler Imperial Le Baron | CRP |
| **Record Cars:** | | |
| WMS9 | 1933 Campbell Bluebird | CRP |
| WMS15 | 1929 Segrave Golden Arrow | CRP |
| WMS19 | 1978 Mercedes-Benz C-111/3 | CRP |
| WMS23 | 1927 Segrave Sunbeam 1000 HP | CRP |
| WMS25 | 1939 Cobb Napier Railton | CRP |
| WMS30 | 1938 Eyston Thunderbolt | CRP |
| **Racing Cars:** | | |
| WRK2 | 1958 Lister Jaguar | CRP |
| WRK3 | 1958 Jaguar XK120 "Montlhery" | CRP |
| WRK4 | 1976 Elf Tyrell Project 34/2 | CRP |
| WRK17 | 1962 Ferrari 330P Testa Rossa | CRP |
| WRK25 | 1979 Ferrari 312 T4 | CRP |
| WRK26 | 1980 Leyland Williams FW07B | CRP |
| WRK27 | 1980 Essex Lotus 81 | CRP |
| WRK28 | 1955 LeMans Jaguar D-Type | CRP |
| WRK28X | 1956 Cunningham D-Type | CRP |
| WRK29 | 1955 LeMans Aston Martin DB3S | CRP |
| WRK30 | 1981 Marlboro MP4 | CRP |
| **Prestige Cars:** | | |
| WP100 | 1976 Aston Martin Lagonda | CRP |
| WP102 | 1976 Lincoln Continental Mk IV | CRP |
| WP103 | 1981 Jaguar XJS HE | CRP |
| WP104 | 1979 Lotus Esprit S2 | CRP |
| WP104X | 1980 Lotus Esprit Essex Turbo | CRP |
| WP105 | 1981 Rolls-Royce Silver Spirit | CRP |
| WP106 | 1981 Bentley Mulsanne | CRP |
| **1/24 scale models:** | | |
| WF1 | 1978 JPS Lotus 79 (kit only) | CRP |
| WF2 | 1979 Brabham BT48 (kit only) | CRP |
| WF3 | 1979 Williams FW07 (kit only) | CRP |
| WF4 | 1957 Maserati 250F | CRP |
| WF5 | Mercedes-Benz W125 | CRP |
| **1994 PRODUCTION:** | | |
| K1 | Chrysler 300F | CRP |
| K2 | Cadillac Limo | CRP |
| K3 | Chevrolet C10 | CRP |
| K3F | Chevrolet C10 Fire | CRP |

*This Plymouth Belvedere, WMS5Lx, also came in a top-up version (WMS51). Both are very accurate models.*

*Western perfectly captured the lines of the classic '70s muscle car, the Pontiac Firebird Trans Am, with WP118.*

| # | Name | Price |
|---|------|-------|
| WMS55T | Checker Cab | CRP |
| WMS56 | Buick Electra | CRP |
| WMS57 | Rolls-Royce Dawn | CRP |
| WMS60 | Desoto Adventurer | CRP |
| WMS61 | Cadillac Eldorado | CRP |
| WMS62 | Alfa Romeo | CRP |
| WMS63 | Chrysler Saratoga | CRP |
| WMS64 | Dodge Custom Royal | CRP |
| WMS64x | Dodge Custom Royal | CRP |
| WMS65 | Plymouth Plaza | CRP |
| WMS65P | Plymouth Police | CRP |
| WMS67 | Buick Sedanet | CRP |
| WP100 | Aston Martin Lagonda | CRP |
| WP107 | Ferrari Dino | CRP |
| WP107x | Ferrari Dino | CRP |
| WP108 | Corvette | CRP |
| WP109 | Aston Martin V8 | CRP |
| WP109x | Aston Martin Vantage | CRP |
| WP109Z | Aston Martin Volante | CRP |
| WP110 | Ferrari 308 | CRP |
| WP110x | Ferrari 308 | CRP |
| WP111 | Lincoln Continental | CRP |
| WP112 | Camaro IROC Z | CRP |
| WP113 | Testarossa | CRP |
| WP115 | Jaguar XJS | CRP |
| WP116 | Rolls-Royce Spirit | CRP |
| WP117 | Bentley | CRP |
| WP118 | Pontiac Trans Am | CRP |
| WP119 | Aston Martin Virage | CRP |
| WP120 | Jaguar XJRS | CRP |
| WP121 | Ferrari 348 TB | CRP |
| WP121x | Ferrari 348 TS | CRP |
| WP123 | Aston Martin Volante | CRP |
| WP124 | Aston Martin Vantage | CRP |
| WP125 | Dodge Viper | CRP |
| WRK17 | Ferrari 330P | CRP |
| WRK28 | Jaguar D-Type | CRP |
| WRK28x | Jaguar D-Type | CRP |
| WRK29 | Aston Martin DB3S | CRP |
| WRK31 | Maserati 450S | CRP |
| WRK33 | Aston Martin DBR1 | CRP |
| WRK40x | Ferrari 375 | CRP |
| WRK42 | Jaguar XK120 | CRP |
| WRK43 | Alfa Romeo 158 | CRP |
| WRK44 | Talbot Lago | CRP |
| WRK45 | Lister Jaguar | CRP |

| # | Name | Price |
|---|------|-------|
| K3P | GMC Police | CRP |
| K5 | Rover | CRP |
| K6 | Jaguar XJ6 | CRP |
| SW1 | Jaguar XK140 | CRP |
| SW2 | Ferrari 275GTB | CRP |
| SW3 | Roll-Royce Silver Cloud | CRP |
| SW4 | Jaguar Mk2 | CRP |
| SW5 | Bentley Continental R | CRP |
| SW10 | Ford Mustang | CRP |
| SW11 | Jaguar E-Type | CRP |
| SW12 | Desoto | CRP |
| SW12T | Desoto Taxi | CRP |
| SW13 | Corvette | CRP |
| SW14 | Chrysler Windsor | CRP |
| SW15 | Hudson | CRP |
| SW15P | Hudson Police | CRP |
| SW16 | Lamborghini | CRP |
| SW17 | Ford Custom | CRP |
| SW17F | Ford Fire | CRP |
| SW17T | Ford Taxi | CRP |
| SW18P | Desoto Police | CRP |
| SW19 | E-Type Roadster | CRP |
| WMS9 | Bluebird | CRP |
| WMS15 | Golden Arrow | CRP |
| WMS22 | Bucciali | CRP |
| WMS23 | Sunbeam | CRP |
| WMS24 | Duesenberg | CRP |
| WMS25 | Railton | CRP |
| WMS28 | Cadillac V16 | CRP |

| # | Name | Price |
|---|------|-------|
| WMS28x | Cadillac V16 (open) | CRP |
| WMS29 | Bugatti Royale | CRP |
| WMS30 | Thunderbolt | CRP |
| WMS31 | Packard Darrin | CRP |
| WMS32 | Bentley Barnato | CRP |
| WMS33 | Alfa Romeo | CRP |
| WMS34 | Bentley 41/4 | CRP |
| WMS35 | Jaguar SS1 | CRP |
| WMS37 | Chrysler Imperial | CRP |
| WMS38 | Gardner MG | CRP |
| WMS39 | Bugatti 57 | CRP |
| WMS40x | Daimler DE36 | CRP |
| WMS41Z | Jaguar Mk V | CRP |
| WMS42 | Bluebird | CRP |
| WMS43 | Jaguar SS1 Tourer | CRP |
| WMS44 | Chevrolet Belair | CRP |
| WMS45 | Jaguar XK120 | CRP |
| WMS46 | Ford Galaxie | CRP |
| WMS47 | Speed of the Wind | CRP |
| WMS48 | Rolls-Royce Silver Cloud | CRP |
| WMS49 | Bentley S3 | CRP |
| WMS50 | Plymouth Fury | CRP |
| WMS51 | Plymouth Belvedere | CRP |
| WMS51x | Plymouth Belvedere (open) | CRP |
| WMS52 | Bluebird | CRP |
| WMS53 | Ranchero Pick-up | CRP |
| WMS53x | Ranchero Pick-up | CRP |
| WMS54 | Alfa Coupe | CRP |
| WMS55P | Checker Police | CRP |

*The WP125 Dodge Viper was released by Western Models in 1994.*

# Winross

This American company has been manufacturing 1/64 scale die cast model trucks since the late 1960s. The name Winross was reportedly based on the name of a town in Scotland: Kinross; why a "W" was substituted for the "K" is a mystery. The company was founded by Roger Austin in upstate New York. As an architect, Austin joined his professional interest in transportation and highway planning with his love of toy vehicles. He had tooling made for a White 3000 truck cab, and the business took off from there.

At first, Winross trucks were sold in retail outlets, but eventually the promotional side of the business grew to the point that the company turned its attention to promotionals exclusively. These were produced (usually in very small quantities) for customers looking for a way to promote their business. Winross would silk-screen the company's artwork/logo on the sides of the truck, and the customer would generally buy the whole run.

The trucks have always been well detailed, and are therefore more models than toys. Some of the late 1960s-early 1970s models are now highly sought after by collectors, particularly trucks that were made in smaller numbers.

Winross continues to produce truck models which can

*This White 9000 truck was made by Winross for the 1981 Classic Automobile meet in Hershey, Pennsylvania. The truck was originally given only to those who exhibited a registered, full-size classic car at the meet.*

be purchased directly from the company. They can also be found at toy and model shows. Basic models have included the White Van Tractor Trailer, the White Tanker Tractor Trailer, the White 1500 Van and the White 3000 Van, among others. New Winross releases generally sell for anywhere from $35 to $75. Certain models have been seen in the $100 and up price range. Older models can go for several hundred dollars, depending on demand.

For further information, the reader is advised to contact the Winross Collectors Club of America, Inc. Details may be found in Part Three, Additional Resources.

*This White 9000 Tractor Trailer in Howard Johnson's livery likely was produced in the early 1970s.*

# Yat Ming

**Y**at Ming is a Hong Kong-based company that manufactures a line of die cast toys and models. The line is called "Road Tough." Included are inexpensive 1/64 toy cars with "speed"-type wheels, and 1/18 scale models of some classic automobiles.

These 1/18 models have opening doors, working steering and decent detail. They generally are accurate replicas of the full-size cars, with some exceptions (such as the VW Beetle shown here).

The Road Tough products can be found in major chain stores. CRP (Current Retail Price) for the 1/18 scale models is around $20.

*Although features like the wheels and interior are accurate on this 1/18 scale 1967 VW Beetle, Yat Ming modeled the headlights incorrectly. The opening hoods and doors have large gaps, which further detract from the model's appearance.*

# Ziss

The company known as Ziss-Modell was located in the town of Lintorf, just outside Düsseldorf, Germany. Their best known products were the "veteran" die cast models produced from 1963 until about 1972. These 1/43 scale cars and trucks were well-detailed for their time, particularly in the area of the radiator grilles. The only negative aspect of their appearance tended to be the spoked plastic wheel hubs, which were rather cheap looking.

The firm was owned by a man named Wittek, and his company also produced a number of other models in 1/43 to 1/50 scale. These included construction and commercial vehicles.

Although production originally ceased in the 1970s, a number of the veteran car models were offered in a late 1980s edition of the German "Danhausen" mail order model catalog. Whether these were newly produced models or merely left-over stock is unknown.

The Ziss veteran cars came in blue and white cardboard boxes that featured color artwork of the specific model contained inside. The following listing gives values for near mint examples in the original boxes.

| # | Name | Price |
|---|------|-------|
| 14 | 1905 Mercedes Grand Prix | $20 |
| 15 | 1908 Ford Model T | * |
| 16 | 1907 Ford Model T Roadster | 20 |
| 17 | 1908 Ford Model T Torpedo | 20 |
| 20 | 1909 Opel Doktorwagen | 20 |
| 21 | 1901 Mercedes Simplex | 20 |
| 22 | 1908 Opel Town Coupe | 20 |
| 23 | 1910 Benz Limousine | 20 |
| 27 | 1904 NAG Phaeton | 20 |
| 30 | 1906 Adler Limousine | 20 |
| 31 | 1905 Mercedes Roadster | 20 |
| 38 | 1904 NAG Tourer | 20 |
| 39 | 1906 Adler Phaeton | 20 |
| 40 | 1905 Mercedes Town Car | 20 |
| 43 | 1909 Opel Torpedo | 20 |
| 44 | 1909 Ford Ranch Car | 20 |
| 50 | 1910 Benz Landaulet | 20 |
| 52 | 1924 Hanomag Roadster | 20 |
| 53 | 1924 Hanomag Coupe | 20 |
| 57 | 1928 BMW Dixi | 20 |
| 60 | 1913 Audi Alpensieger | 20 |
| 62 | 1916 Chevrolet Phaeton | 20 |

| # | Name | Price |
|---|------|-------|
| 65 | 1914 NSU Phaeton | $20 |
| 66 | 1932 Fiat Balilla | 20 |
| 289 | Krupp Hydraulic Hammer | 40 |
| 290 | Fiat Bulldozer | 40 |
| 291 | O & K Fork Lift | 40 |
| 292 | Clark Fork Lift | 40 |
| 293 | Hyster 40 Fork Lift | 40 |
| 294 | Fiat 550 Farm Tractor | 50 |
| 294 | Fiat 600 Farm Tractor | 50 |
| 295 | O & K RH 6 Excavator | 40 |
| 295 | P & K RH 6 Excavator | 40 |
| 296 | O & K MH6 Excavator | 40 |
| 297 | Deutz Farm Tractor | 50 |
| 298 | Hanomag Matador Open Truck | 40 |
| 299 | Wickuler Three Musketeers Jeep | 60 |
| 300 | Army Jeep | 40 |
| 301 | Mercedes Benz 600 | 60 |
| 302 | 1926 Henschel Open Truck | 50 |
| 303 | 1926 Henschel "ARAL" Tank Truck | 50 |
| 304 | 1925 MAN Open Truck | 50 |
| 305 | 1925 MAN "B.P." Tank Truck | 50 |
| 306 | 1925 MAN Bus | 60 |

| # | Name | Price |
|---|------|-------|
| 310 | 1971 Opel Rekord Sedan | $50 |
| 311 | 1971 Opel Commodore Coupe | 50 |
| 312 | 1975 Opel Manta | 50 |
| 400 | Ford Transit Bus | 50 |
| 400 | Ford Transit Ambulance | 50 |
| 401 | Ford Transit Van | 50 |
| 401 | Ford Transit Mail Van | 60 |
| 401 | Ford Transit "ARAL" Van | 60 |
| 401 | Ford Transit "B.P." Van | 60 |
| 401 | Ford Transit "MINI AUTO CLUB" Van | 60 |
| 410 | Hanomag Dump Truck | 50 |
| 411 | Hanomag Open Semi Trailer Truck | 50 |
| 412 | Hanomag Open Truck | 50 |
| 413 | Hanomag Container Semi Trailer Truck | 50 |
| 414 | Hanomag "ARAL" Tank Truck | 50 |
| 414 | Hanomag "ESSO" Tank Truck | 50 |
| 415 | Hanomag Cement Truck | 50 |
| 430 | Mercedes Benz 1313 Dump Truck | 50 |
| 431 | H & Q Caterpillar Tractor | 50 |

* May not have been produced

# PART THREE

## Additional Resources

# Books, Periodicals and Clubs

$A$ hobby or activity that is passionately pursued naturally gives rise to the exchange of information. This can take many forms, but two of the most common (and effective) ways of learning are by reading and joining.

Books and magazines on the hobby have been around for a long time, but the volume and availability has increased dramatically in the last five years. Books like Cecil Gibson's *History of British Dinky Toys* laid the groundwork, in the 1960s, for modern classics such as the *Great Book of Corgi*, by Marcel Van Cleemput. Sometimes, the very lack of information available on a particular model or manufacturer will cause someone to do the research and get something into print, even if they have to go the "self-publish" route. Charles A. Jones' informative *Hubley Die-Cast Toys 1936-1976* is an excellent example.

Joining a collector's club can be of great benefit for two reasons: you get to both give and receive. A club can provide the collector with news, product updates, tips on where to find toys or models, and so on. As part of the club, the collector can share his or her expertise and knowledge with others of like interest, a process that can bring just as much enjoyment as finding out where to get that elusive piece you've long had your eye on.

Some clubs have regular meetings and various other events during the year, while others consist only of a newsletter that is regularly sent to members. So the collector can be as involved or uninvolved as he or she chooses.

The reader would be well-advised to remember that all of the books, magazines and newsletters listed here are listed as additional sources of information on die cast toys and models. Some are slick, colorful, expensive items published by large publishing companies. Others are simple, "home-grown" affairs put out by someone working at their kitchen table.

Similarly, some collector's clubs are small, independent groups of casual collectors, while others are more formal organizations connected to a manufacturer or manufacturers. The clubs and publications listed here are included because, in the author's opinion, each of them has something to offer that can benefit the reader. However, the inclusion of a publication or club in this listing in no way implies the author's endorsement of said publication or club, nor can the author be held responsible for any damage or losses incurred as a result of consulting these publications or clubs.

## BOOKS

### British manufacturers:

*British Diecast Model Toys,* by John Ramsay
Published 1983 by Swapmeet Toys and Models Ltd., Suffolk, England
Updated periodically; 6th edition published 1996

*Budgie Models,* by Robert Newson
Published 1988 by Leisure-Time Publications Ltd., England

*Corgi Toys,* by Dr. Edward Force
Published 1991 by Schiffer Publishing Ltd., West Chester, PA

*Dinky Toys,* by Dr. Edward Force
Published 1988 by Schiffer Publishing Ltd., West Chester, PA

*Dinky Toys & Modelled Miniatures,* by Mike and Sue Richardson
Volume four of The Hornby Companion Series
Published 1981 by New Cavendish Books, London, England
Revised 1986 and 1989

*Great Book of Corgi,* by Marcel Van Cleemput
Published 1989 by New Cavendish Books, London, England

*History of British Dinky Toys,* by Cecil Gibson
Published 1966 by Model Aeronautical Press, Ltd., Watford, England
(Out of print)

*Lesney's Matchbox Toys: Regular Wheel Years, 1947-1969,* by Charlie Mack
Published 1992 by Schiffer Publishing Ltd., West Chester, PA

*Lesney's Matchbox Toys: The Superfast Years, 1969-1982,* by Charlie Mack
Published 1993 by Schiffer Publishing Ltd., West Chester, PA

*Lledo 1996 Collectors Guide,* by Ray Dowding and Peter Lloyd
Published by RDP Publications, Halesowen, England
Updated yearly

*Matchbox and Lledo Toys,* by Dr. Edward Force
Published 1988 by Schiffer Publishing Ltd., West Chester, PA

*Matchbox Toys,* by Bruce and Diane Stoneback
Published 1993 by Chartwell Books, Secaucus, NJ

*Matchbox Toys, 1948-1993,* by Dana Johnson
Published 1994 by Collector Books, Paducah, KY

*Matchbox Toys: The Tyco Years, 1993-1994,* by Charlie Mack
Published 1995 by Schiffer Publishing Ltd., West Chester, PA

*Universal's Matchbox Toys: The Universal Years, 1982-1992,* by Charlie Mack
Published 1993 by Schiffer Publishing Ltd., West Chester, PA

## American manufacturers:

*The Complete Book of Hot Wheels,* by Bob Parker
Published 1995 by Schiffer Publishing Ltd., West Chester, PA

*Greenberg's Guide to Tootsietoys 1945-1969,* by Raymond R. Klein
Published 1993 by Greenberg Book Division, Kalmbach Publishing Company,
Waukesha, WI

*Hubley Die-Cast Toys 1936-1976,* by Charles A. Jones
Published 1994 by Charles A. Jones

*Johnny Lightning Collector's Guide,* by Carter Pennington
Published 1993 by Carter Pennington, Hastings, NY

*McElwee's Collector's Guide #7—Big Ertl,* by Neil McElwee
Published by Neil McElwee, Pittsburgh, PA

*Tomart's Price Guide to Hot Wheels,* by Michael Thomas Strauss
Published 1993 by Tomart Publications, Dayton, OH

*Tootsietoys, World's First Diecast Models,* by James Weiland and Edward Force
Published 1980 by Motorbooks International, Osceola, WI

### European manufacturers:

*Classic Miniature Vehicles Made in France,* by Dr. Edward Force
Published 1991 by Schiffer Publishing Ltd., West Chester, PA

*Classic Miniature Vehicles Made in Germany,* by Dr. Edward Force
Published 1990 by Schiffer Publishing Ltd., West Chester, PA

*Classic Miniature Vehicles Made in Italy,* by Dr. Edward Force
Published 1992 by Schiffer Publishing Ltd., West Chester, PA

*Solido Toys,* by Dr. Edward Force
Published 1993 by Schiffer Publishing Ltd., West Chester, PA

### General books:

*The Golden Book of Model Cars 1900-1975,* by Paolo Rampini
Published 1995 by Paolo Rampini, Milan, Italy

*Collecting Toy Cars & Trucks,* by Richard O'Brien
Published 1994 by Books Americana, Inc.

# BOOK DEALERS

Some of the books listed can be found in general interest bookstores, while others are available only from specialist book dealers. The following dealers specialize in books on toys and models.

**Blystone's**
2132 Delaware Ave.
Pittsburgh, PA 15218
Phone: (412) 371-3511
Fax: (412) 244-8028

**F. Russack Books**
20 Beach Plain Rd.
Danville, NH 03819
Phone and fax: (603) 642-7718

# MAGAZINES

### American:

*Antique Toy World*
Antique Toy World Publications
P.O. Box 34509
Chicago, IL 60634
Phone: (312) 725-0633
Published monthly; covers older (pre-1970) toys, with some coverage of die cast.

*Car Toys*
Challenge Publications, Inc.
7950 Deering Ave.
Canoga Park, CA  91304
Phone: (818) 887-0550
Published bi-monthly; covers a variety of automotive-related toys and models.

*Collecting Toys*
Kalmbach Publishing Co.
21027 Crossroads Circle
Waukesha, WI  21027
Phone: (414) 796-8776
Published monthly; covers old and new toys such as action figures, die cast, tin toys, space toys, etc.

*Hot Wheels Newsletter*
26 Madera Ave.
San Carlos, CA  94070
Phone: (415) 591-6482
Published quarterly.

*Toy Shop*
Krause Publications
700 E. State St.
Iola, WI  54990
Phone: (715) 445-2214
Published bi-weekly; display and classified ads for many types of old and new toys.

*Toy Trader*
Antique Trader Publications
922 Churchill St., Suite 1
Waupaca, WI  54981
Phone: (715) 258-7525
Published monthly; covers many types of old and new toys, including die cast.

*U.S. Toy Collector*
Gordon Rice
P.O. Box 4244
Missoula, MT  59806-4244
Phone: (406) 549-3175
Published monthly; covers toy vehicles including die cast.

## British:

*Model Collector*
Link House
Dingwall Avenue
Croydon  CR9 2TA
ENGLAND
Phone: 0181 686 2599
Published monthly; covers old and new vehicle models and toys, with emphasis on die cast.

*Model Auto Review*
Malvern House Publications
P.O. Box SM2
Leeds  LS25 5XA
ENGLAND
Phone: 0113 268 6685
Published ten times per year; covers old and new vehicle models and toys, with emphasis on die cast.

*Classic Toys*
Classic Toys Ltd.
P.O. Box 47
Coventry  CV5 9YY
ENGLAND
Phone: 0120 369 1212
Published bi-monthly; covers a variety of old and new toys, including die cast.

# COLLECTOR'S CLUBS

Note: when writing to a club to request information, it is advisable to include a self-addressed, stamped envelope.

**Die Cast Car Collectors Club**
Contact: Jay Olins
P.O. Box 2480
Huntington Beach, CA  92647
Phone: (213) 500-4355
For collectors of Danbury Mint and Franklin Mint models.
Dues: $12.50 per year, which includes subscription to club's monthly newsletter.

**Dinky Toy Club of America**
Contact: Jerry Fralick
P.O. Box 11
Highland, MD  20777
Phone: (301) 854-2217
For Dinky collectors and enthusiasts.
Dues: $20 per year, which includes subscription to DTCA's quarterly Newsletter.

**Johnny Lightning Club**
P.O. Box 248
Cassopolis, MI  49031-0248
Phone: (800) MANTIS-8
For collectors of Johnny Lightning cars.
Dues: $14.95 per year, which includes five issues of club magazine, "NewsFlash."

**Matchbox Collectors Club**
Contact: Everett Marshall
P.O. Box 977
Newfield, NJ  08344
Phone: (609) 697-2800

**Matchbox International Collectors Association (MICA)**
M.I.C.A. North America
c/o Rita Schneider
P.O. Box 28072
Waterloo, Ontario  N2L 6J8
CANADA
Phone: (519) 885-0529
or

**M.I.C.A. UK & Europe**
c/o Maureen Quayle
13A Lower Bridge Street
Chester  CH1 1RS
ENGLAND
Phone: 0124 434 6297
Founded in 1985; club publishes a bi-monthly magazine.

**Matchbox USA**
Contact: Charlie Mack
62 Saw Mill Road
Durham, CT  06422
Phone: (203) 349-1655

**North American Diecast Toy Collectors Association**
Contact: Dana Johnson
P.O. Box 1824
Bend, OR  97709-1824
For collectors of newer (1980s and 1990s) die cast toys and models.
Dues: $15 per year, which includes subscription to club newsletter.

**Toy Car Collectors Club**
Contact: Peter Foss
33290 West 14 Mile Road, #454
West Bloomfield, MI  48322
Phone: (810) 682-0272
For collectors of "all toy vehicles."
Dues: $15 per year, which includes subscription to quarterly magazine,
Toy Car, and a copy of the Model Car Directory.

**Winross Collector's Club of America, Inc.**
P.O. Box 444
Mount Joy, PA  17552-0444

# Shows and Auctions

**A**long with reading and absorbing as much information as possible on die cast toys and models, "getting out in the trenches" is a great way to see who's selling what, and for how much. A collector can also build his or her collection by getting out to shows and auctions as often as possible.

There are regular die cast oriented events held all over the United States, and they vary in terms of size and the quality of the items for sale. Before traveling to an event, it is a good idea to contact the organizers and ask some questions:

- How many dealers will be at the show?
- What is the emphasis of the show in terms of older versus newer items? Is it antique only, or are there dealers offering new products?
- How long has the show been in existence?
- Are there hotels and motels near the show for those traveling long distances?
- Will there be food available for purchase, or are there restaurants nearby?
- Getting directions to the show, if you're not familiar with the area, is also a good idea.

Attending a toy or model show can make you feel like a kid in a candy store. There is the anticipation of finding unknown treasures, and the excitement of seeing all of those people and toys in one place. There are two schools of thought on approaching a show. The first says: If you come across a truly desirable item (rare, or with a low price, etc.), buy it on the spot. Because if you don't, the next person will, and it won't be there when you return.

The other way of thinking says: There are a lot of dealers and a lot of toys (or models) here. Sure, you may find a rare item, but don't jump the gun before you have a chance to really see the whole show.

Both approaches work, and neither one works. That simply means that it's a judgment call. You win some and you lose some, as the saying goes. The key is to enjoy yourself and the hobby.

If possible, it's a good idea to arrive early at a show. In fact, many shows offer "floor rights," or "early bird rights," for which you must pay an additional fee (sometimes $30-$50). This allows you to get in before the general public and see what the dealers are pulling out of their boxes. Is it worth it? Again, it's a judgment call; if you can afford it; and if you really want to be in on the early action, then it may be worth your while.

These same thoughts generally apply to auctions (although everybody has a chance to view the items being auctioned, before the event, at no charge). Auctions can also be a great place to find what you're looking for. Depending on the location, the day of the week, and the amount of publicity the organizers have done, bargains can be found. But prices can just as easily escalate to ridiculous levels if there are two or more people who want the same thing. Realizing that there are always items out there, waiting to be discovered, can help a smart collector avoid the "bidding war" syndrome.

In terms of payment, it is easiest to pay with cash at shows, although some dealers accept credit cards or checks. Method of payment is less of a concern at auctions, where any number of payment types are used.

The following is a list of some of the shows and auctions that take place in the United States. It is by no means exhaustive, since to list every event would require a book in itself (not to mention the fact that these events are subject to change). These events and auction houses are listed here because they offer something for the die cast collector (although many different kinds of collectibles are represented at these events, as well).

# TOY AND MODEL SHOWS:

### Allentown Antique Toy Show
Allentown, PA
Takes place in November
Telephone: (610) 821-8259

### Antique Toy & Doll World Show (Chicago)
Kane County Fairgrounds, St. Charles, IL
Takes place three times a year
Contact: Antique Toy World Shows, Inc. at (708) 526-1645

### Antique Toy Circus Maximus
Kalamazoo, MI
Takes place twice a year
Contact: Bruce Beimers at (616) 361-9887

### Atlantique City
Atlantic City, NJ
Takes place twice a year
Telephone: (800) 526-2724

### Baltimore Die-Cast & Antique Toy Show
Baltimore, MD
Takes place in September; sponsored by the Dinky Toy Club of America
Contact: Jerry Fralick at (301) 854-2217

### Big-D Super Collectibles Show
Dallas, TX
Takes place in July and November
Contact: Don Maris at (817) 261-8745

### Carlisle Toy Shows
Carlisle, PA
Take place several times a year
Telephone: (717) 243-7855

### Collectibles Extravaganza
Boston, MA
Takes place in December
Contact: Gary Sohmers at (508) 569-0856

### Dearborn Antique Toy Show
Dearborn, MI
Takes place several times a year
Telephone: (810) 399-3491

### Glendale All-American Collector's Show
Glendale, CA
Takes place several times a year
Telephone: (310) 455-2894

### Humdinger Toy Show
San Jose, CA
Takes place in February
Telephone: (209) 787-2208

**Indianapolis Antique Toy Show**
Indianapolis, IN
Takes place several times a year
Contact: Barb and Don DeSalle at (800) 392-TOYS

**Macungie Antique Toy Show**
Macungie, PA
Takes place in August
Contact: Dave Bausch at (610) 432-3355

**Macungie DeSalle Shows**
Allentown, PA
Take place the day before the Saturday Macungie show in August
Contact: Barb and Don DeSalle at (800) 392-TOYS

**Philadelphia International**
Philadelphia, PA
Takes place twice a year
Contact: Bob Bostoff, 331 Cochran Place, Valley Stream, NY 11581

**Rochester Antique Toy Show (R.A.T.S)**
Rochester, NY
Takes place twice a year
Contact: Bob Smith at (716) 377-8394

**San Francisco International Toy Show**
San Mateo, CA
Takes place several times a year
Telephone: (916) 888-0291

**Toledo Collector's Shows**
Toledo, OH
Take place several times a year
Contact: John Carlisle, Old Toyland Shows, Bewley Bldg. Rm. 409
Lockport, NY 14094-2914

**Toy Car Collector's Club Meet**
Novi, MI
Takes place in August
Contact: Peter Foss at (810) 682-0272

**Washington Antique Collectible Toy Show**
Falls Church, VA
Takes place several times a year
Telephone: (703) 524-2061

## U.S. TOY AND MODEL AUCTION HOUSES:

**Bill Bertoia Auctions**
Vineland, NJ
Organizers of regular auctions in the Philadelphia, PA area
Telephone: (609) 692-1881

**Phillips New York**
New York, NY
Organizers of regular auctions in New York
Telephone: (800) 825-2781

**Lloyd Ralston Toys**
Fairfield, CT
Organizers of regular auctions in Norwalk, CT
Telephone: (203) 845-0033

**Skinner**
Boston, MA
Organizers of regular auctions in the Boston area
Telephone: (617) 350-5400

# BRITISH AUCTION HOUSES:

### Christie's South Kensington
85 Old Brompton Rd., London  SW7 3LD  ENGLAND
Telephone: 0171-581 7611

### Vectis Model Auctions
35 Castle St., East Cowes, Isle of Wight  PO32 6RD  ENGLAND
Telephone: 0198-328 2005

The following businesses hold regular phone and mail auctions of antique and collectible toys. These are events in which a bidder can bid via telephone (or fax) or by letter, on a variety of items. Die cast toys and models are often included in auctions conducted by these businesses. A catalog of items for sale in an upcoming auction can be purchased in advance; many phone/mail auction houses offer a "subscription" to these catalogs.

### Global Toy Merchants
Medinah, IL
Telephone: (708) 893-8312

### Smith House
Eliot, ME
Telephone: (207) 439-4614

# BIBLIOGRAPHY

## Books

Donovan, Charles F. *Renwal World's Finest Toys Volume 2.* Ohatchee, AL: Charles F. Donovan, 1996.

Fawdry, Marguerite. *British Tin Toys.* London: New Cavendish Books, 1990.

Force, Dr. Edward. *Classic Miniature Vehicles Made in France.* West Chester, PA: Schiffer Publishing Ltd., 1991.

Force, Dr. Edward. *Classic Miniature Vehicles Made in Germany.* West Chester, PA: Schiffer Publishing Ltd., 1990.

Force, Dr. Edward. *Classic Miniature Vehicles Made in Italy.* West Chester, PA: Schiffer Publishing Ltd., 1992.

Force, Dr. Edward. *Solido Toys.* West Chester, PA: Schiffer Publishing Ltd., 1993.

Gibson, Cecil. *History of British Dinky Toys.* Watford, England: Model Aeronautical Press, Ltd., 1966.

Jones, Charles A. *Hubley Die-Cast Toys 1936-1976.* Nashville, GA: Charles A. Jones, 1994.

Klein, Raymond R. *Greenberg's Guide to Tootsietoys 1945-1969.* Waukesha, WI: Kalmbach Publishing Co., 1993.

Mack, Charlie. *Lesney's Matchbox Toys: Regular Wheel Years, 1947-1969.* West Chester, PA: Schiffer Publishing Ltd., 1992.

O'Brien, Richard. *Collecting Toy Cars & Trucks.* Florence, AL: Books Americana, Inc., 1994.

Pennington, Carter. *Johnny Lightning Collector's Guide.* Hastings, NY: Carter Pennington, 1993.

Rampini, Paolo. *The Golden Book of Model Cars 1900-1975.* Milan: Paolo Rampini, 1995.

Ramsay, John. *British Diecast Model Toys.* Suffolk, England: Swapmeet Toys and Models Ltd., 1993.

Richardson, Mike and Sue. *Dinky Toys & Modelled Miniatures.* London: New Cavendish Books, 1989.

Stoneback, Bruce and Diane. *Matchbox Toys.* Secaucus, NJ: Chartwell Books, 1993.

Strauss, Michael Thomas. *Tomart's Price Guide to Hot Wheels.* Dayton: Tomart Publications, 1993.

## Periodicals & Catalogs

*Antique Toy World.* Chicago: Antique Toy World Publications, monthly.

*Classic Toys.* Coventry, England: Classic Toys Ltd., bi-monthly.

*Collecting Toys.* Waukesha, WI: Kalmbach Publishing Co., bi-monthly.

*Die Cast & Tin Toy Report.* Williamsburg, VA: Shoreline Publishing, monthly.

*Model Auto Review.* Leeds, England: Malvern House Publications, bi-monthly.

*Model Cars.* Watford, England: Model Aeronautical Press, Ltd., monthly.

*Model Collector.* Croydon, England: Link House, monthly.

*Toy Trader.* Waupaca, WI: Antique Trader Publications, monthly.

*U.S. Toy Collector.* Missoula, MT: Gordon Rice, monthly.

Original manufacturers catalogs and product literature, 1940s through 1990s.

# Index